RICHARDSON

THE BIG

BOOK

10,000 GENERAL KNOWLEDGE QUESTIONS

DAVID MCGAUGHEY & JACK WALEY-COHEN

Published by Richardson Publishing Limited.
www.richardsonpublishing.com

10 9 8 7 6 5 4 3 2

Typeset by Clarity Media Ltd.

Cover design by Junior London Ltd.

ISBN 978-1-913602-27-7

Printed and bound by CPI Group (UK) Ltd, Croydon CR0 4YY.

A catalogue record for this book is available from the British Library.

If you would like to comment on any aspect of this book, please contact us at:
E-mail: puzzles@richardsonpublishing.com

𝕏 Follow us on Twitter @puzzlesandgames
⌾ instagram.com/richardsonpuzzlesandgames
f facebook.com/richardsonpuzzlesandgames

FSC
www.fsc.org
MIX
Paper | Supporting responsible forestry
FSC® C171272

INTRODUCTION

We hope this book will offer something for every quizzer. We've tried to capture our decades-long experience of writing and hosting quizzes (and taking part in quizzes as well!). We've written questions for BBC TV shows, primary school buzzer quizzes, pub quizzes, online apps, corporate events and everything in between; we've hosted quizzes for people who think they don't like quizzes, for the world's best quizzers, for celebrities, for journalists, for family groups, for work colleagues, for locals at the pub and pretty much any other type of group you could think of.

The only short answer to "What is a good quiz question?" or "What makes an enjoyable quiz?" is "It depends".

So, we've divided the book into six sections, which will hopefully allow you to use it however it suits you: dip in and out; cherry-pick rounds or questions for your own events; use oven-ready balanced quizzes; or even read it cover-to-cover.

The chapters are:

- **The Daily Quiz**: 365+ five-question mini-quizzes for a quick daily brain booster
- **Family-Friendly**: 29 quizzes of four standard subject rounds of ten questions that work for young and old
- **Ready-Made**: 50 quizzes of four format-themed rounds of ten questions, or sometimes ten, ten, five and fifteen questions
- **Subject Rounds**: 200 rounds of ten questions on classic quiz subjects
- **Specialist Subjects**: 150 ten-question quizzes on a vast range of topics
- **Something Else**: 150 ten-question quizzes, but a little bit more niche or left-field...

We've done our best to make the quizzes fair, balanced and, above all, accurate. We've tried to note where there's a possibility an answer may date, though sometimes facts change in the most surprising ways. The book was compiled in 2022, so if a piece of information has recently changed, bear that in mind.

We are based in the UK, and naturally there is a slight bias towards some questions being UK-specific, but we have tried to make the majority fun and accessible to all quizzers, wherever you are based.

Not all rounds will be at the same level of difficulty, but hopefully, throughout, there'll be gettable questions and more challenging questions alongside each other, so that you never feel that you're out of your depth or that, conversely, things are too facile. Difficulty levels are mixed throughout, so if something is too difficult then stick with it: you'll find plenty that you do know soon enough!

The answers appear at the bottom of each page to minimise page turning and ferreting around in the back of the book, so no peeking.

Our general rules for quizzing include: be generous with yourself and others; don't worry about spelling if the answer given is clearly the right piece of knowledge; it's OK to just put the surname unless specifically asked for the first name as well; don't take it too seriously.

We hope you enjoy the book!

David McGaughey & Jack Waley-Cohen

CONTENTS

CONTENTS

THE DAILY QUIZ

This chapter offers you one quiz for every day of the year (and a couple more for good luck).

Since 2008, we've been publishing a "Friday Quiz" every week to provide a little light relief to thousands of office workers and families across the UK and beyond. For some, the Friday Quiz has become a crucial pre-weekend tradition complete with its own rituals: we've seen evidence of spreadsheets with years' worth of scores, weekly Zoom calls, and carefully managed WhatsApp groups.

If you want to subscribe to the Friday Quiz, you'll find it at: qqq.vc/Friday

This chapter is in the spirit of the Friday Quiz. Each quiz is made up of just five questions, but covers a range of subjects, and always ends with a multi-answer question which you can ponder long into the afternoon, either alone or with friends or colleagues.

NOTE: because of their "list" format, the multi-answer Q5s have answers which are sometimes more subject to change than others, but we wanted to include this type of question nevertheless, because we've found on the Friday Quiz that people really enjoy being stretched by them. We've added "time stamps" to several questions where appropriate.

Of course, we're not saying you're only allowed to do one of these quizzes a day but give it a try. Maybe keep a running score.

QUIZ 1 — 1st January

1 To which American President did Marilyn Monroe sing 'Happy Birthday' in May 1962?

2 What H is the name of the crustacean which lives in empty seashells?

3 Which mausoleum was built by Shah Jahan in Agra, India?

4 Which 60s band from Liverpool, managed by Brian Epstein, was the first to reach Number 1 in the UK charts with their first three singles?

5 Name any five chemical elements with names beginning with the letter S.

QUIZ 2 — 2nd January

1 What is the main colour of the middle stripe on the flag of Spain?

2 Which British motorway will take you from London to Oxford?

3 In which sporting competition do the winners travel backwards, while the losers travel forwards?

4 If you were in Italy and asked for "mela" from a shop, what would you be hoping to receive?

5 Name any five of the US States that have a unique first letter, i.e. start with a letter that no other state begins with.

QUIZ 3 — 3rd January

1 What colour was the boat in which 'The Owl and the Pussy-Cat' went to sea, in the poem by Edward Lear?

2 What word can be a vehicle, a group of offspring, rubbish and an absorbent indoor material?

3 How many letters are there in the modern Greek alphabet?

4 True or False? The final goal in the 1930 FIFA World Cup final was scored by a man called Hector Castro, who lost his right forearm in a tragic sawing accident when he was 13.

5 Which five cities in the United Kingdom have a single letter postcode (apart from London)?

QUIZ 4 — 4th January

1 Which of the tropics passes through Mexico?

2 Which American who grew up in Australia won an Oscar playing a Scotsman in a film shot in Ireland?

3 In Scrabble, how many points would you score with the word QUIZ placed on a double word score?

4 Which store was founded in Southampton in 1969 by Richard Block and David Quayle?

5 Name five official James Bond films with one word titles. [up to 2022]

QUIZ 1
1 John F Kennedy
2 Hermit crab
3 Taj Mahal
4 Gerry and the Pacemakers ('How Do You Do It', 'I Like It', 'You'll Never Walk Alone')
5 Sodium, Silicon, Sulphur, Scandium, Selenium, Strontium, Silver, Samarium, Seaborgium

QUIZ 2
1 Yellow
2 M40
3 Tug of War
4 Apple
5 Delaware, Florida, Georgia, Hawaii, Louisiana, Pennsylvania, Rhode Island, Utah

QUIZ 3
1 Pea green
2 Litter
3 24
4 True
5 Birmingham, Glasgow, Liverpool, Manchester, Sheffield

QUIZ 4
1 Tropic of Cancer
2 Mel Gibson (in 'Braveheart')
3 44
4 B&Q
5 Goldfinger, Thunderball, Moonraker, Octopussy, Goldeneye, Skyfall, Spectre

QUIZ 5 — 5ᵗʰ January

1 In which American city are the headquarters of Starbucks and Amazon?

2 What make of car was the time machine in 'Back to the Future'?

3 Which musical instrument weighs approximately 36 kg, is about 6 ft tall, and is almost always played by a seated musician?

4 In which film does Eddie Murphy play the character of conman Billy Ray Valentine?

5 Which five African countries have a coastline on the Mediterranean Sea?

QUIZ 6 — 6ᵗʰ January

1 If the temperature is 0° Celsius, what is it in Fahrenheit?

2 What would be the most direct route from the M20 motorway to the A16 motorway?

3 Where does Yogi Bear live and work?

4 A term for the sounding of a ram's horn on the Jewish Day of Atonement – not, as some think, the Latin word for rejoicing – is the original etymology of which word, much heard in the UK in 1977 and 2022?

5 Name any five of the six historic counties in Northern Ireland.

QUIZ 7 — 7ᵗʰ January

1 How is the animal sometimes called the caribou more commonly known in the UK?

2 Who, in Greek mythology, was the first woman, whose story seeks to explain why there is evil in the world?

3 What green space in London can be accessed by Sheen Gate, Ham Gate, and Roehampton Gate amongst others?

4 What were the first names of the two Wright brothers, who are credited with building the world's first successful aeroplane?

5 Name any five of the thirteen countries in the world that have tigers in the wild.

QUIZ 8 — 8ᵗʰ January

1 Which word for a period of isolation derives from the Italian word for a forty day period?

2 In chess, which is the only piece that always moves to a white square if it starts its move from a black square, and vice versa?

3 According to UK law, is a Jaffa Cake a cake or a biscuit?

4 Which legendary singer died on the same day (in 1998) as the final episode of 'Seinfeld' was broadcast in the US?

5 Name five of the six longest bones in the human body.

QUIZ 5
1 Seattle
2 DeLorean
3 Harp (If you put the double bass, it doesn't weigh anywhere near 36 kg)
4 Trading Places
5 Egypt, Libya, Tunisia, Morocco, Algeria

QUIZ 6
1 32°F
2 Channel Tunnel
3 Jellystone Park
4 Jubilee
5 Antrim, Armagh, Derry/Londonderry, Down, Fermanagh, Tyrone

QUIZ 7
1 Reindeer
2 Pandora (she let all the evil out of the box)
3 Richmond Park
4 Orville and Wilbur
5 India, Malaysia, Bangladesh, Russia, Indonesia, Nepal, Thailand, Myanmar/Burma, Bhutan, China, Cambodia, Laos, Vietnam (according to WWF website)

QUIZ 8
1 Quarantine
2 Knight
3 Cake
4 Frank Sinatra
5 Femur/Thighbone, Tibia/Shinbone, Fibula/lower leg, Humerus/Upper Arm, Ulna/Inner Lower Arm, Radius/outer lower arm

QUIZ 9 — 9th January

1 Which spirit has a name meaning "little water" in Russian?

2 What is the surname of Craig and Charlie, the brothers in The Proclaimers?

3 Which book by Stephen Hawking was first published in 1988?

4 What name is given to the symbol representing "and" that appears above the number 7 on a standard UK keyboard?

5 In the 2001 movie, name five of the actors who played 'Ocean's Eleven'?

QUIZ 10 — 10th January

1 What symbol does the British Standards Institute use to indicate a product that has been assessed as exceeding a particular quality standard?

2 What word can be an intermediate floor between main floors of a building, and the name of a 1998 album by Massive Attack?

3 Which notorious poison smells of bitter almonds, and is found in tiny amounts in mangoes?

4 The musical 'The Producers' opens at a show called 'Funny Boy' which is a musical version of which Shakespeare tragedy?

5 Name any five of the nine original British "Public Schools" as defined in the 1868 Public Schools Act.

QUIZ 11 — 11th January

1 What is the name of the town where the Flintstones live?

2 The Olympic Mountains are in which American state?

3 In which South coast English town is 'Fawlty Towers' set?

4 Who was the inspiration for Eric Clapton's 'Layla' and 'Something' by The Beatles (which was written by George Harrison)?

5 Name any five animals swallowed by the 'Old Lady Who Swallowed a Fly' (apart from the fly).

QUIZ 12 — 12th January

1 What type of shoe takes its name from an Italian word for a small dagger?

2 Which is the only property on a London Monopoly board which is south of the river Thames?

3 Which country is bordered by the Gulf of Finland, the Baltic Sea, Latvia and Russia?

4 What is the surname of the Chief Inspector, played by Philip Jackson, who regularly appears in the Hercule Poirot books and TV series?

5 Name any five of the Seven Deadly Sins.

QUIZ 9
1 Vodka
2 Reid
3 A Brief History of Time
4 Ampersand
5 George Clooney, Brad Pitt, Matt Damon, Don Cheadle, Elliott Gould, Casey Affleck, Scott Caan, Bernie Mac, Eddie Jemison, Carl Reiner, Shaobo Qin

QUIZ 10
1 Kitemark / Kite (accept CE mark as well)
2 Mezzanine
3 Cyanide
4 Hamlet
5 Charterhouse, Eton, Harrow, Merchant Taylors', Rugby, Shrewsbury, St. Paul's, Westminster, Winchester

QUIZ 11
1 Bedrock
2 Washington
3 Torquay
4 Pattie Boyd
5 Spider, bird, cat, dog, goat, cow, horse

QUIZ 12
1 Stiletto
2 Old Kent Road
3 Estonia
4 Japp
5 Lust, Gluttony, Greed, Sloth, Wrath, Envy, Pride (accept synonyms for these words)

QUIZ 13 — 13th January

1 When do nocturnal animals sleep?

2 Only two countries in the world have three alphabetically consecutive letters in their normal English name. One of them is TUValu (TUV). What is the other?

3 Which English football club was promoted to the top division in 1992 and was Premier League champion in 1995?

4 In 'Slumdog Millionaire', Jamal's last 'Who Wants To Be A Millionaire' question was on which classic of French literature?

5 Name any five elements that have a chemical symbol beginning with a different letter from the normal English name of the element. [ten to choose from]

QUIZ 14 — 14th January

1 How many times bigger than a normal bottle is a Magnum of champagne?

2 Which country has a six-letter name in English, with half of the letters being 'e'?

3 Which TV comedy had episodes including 'Cash and Curry', 'He Ain't Heavy, He's My Uncle' and 'A Slow Bus To Chingford'?

4 Which singer, who had a global Number 1 single and album in 2007, released an album in 2019 called 'My Name is Michael Holbrook'?

5 Name any five of the original 'ThunderCats' who appeared in the first series of the 80s cartoon.

QUIZ 15 — 15th January

1 What does HGV stand for (if describing a large truck)?

2 What animal is on the logo of the Worldwide Fund for Nature?

3 The great West Indian cricketers Frank Worrell, Everton Weekes and Clyde Walcott were known as The Three ... whats?

4 Who launched the National Viewers' and Listeners' Association in 1965?

5 Name five of the first six Presidents of France's Fifth Republic, which began in 1958. [full Presidents, not counting interim Presidents]

QUIZ 16 — 16th January

1 Which British frontman got in trouble with Taylor Swift fans in January 2022 for falsely suggesting she didn't write her own songs?

2 What goes between the chocolate and the shortbread in traditional Millionaire Shortbread?

3 What was the maiden name of Sophia Brunel, mother of Isambard?

4 In the American soap opera 'Days Of Our Lives', who played Dr Drake Ramoray?

5 Seven London boroughs begin with the letter H. Name five of them.

QUIZ 13
1 During the day
2 Afghanistan (FGH)
3 Blackburn Rovers
4 The Three Musketeers
5 Antimony (Sb), Gold (Au), Iron (Fe), Lead (Pb), Mercury (Hg), Potassium (K), Silver (Ag), Sodium (Na), Tin (Sn), Tungsten (W)

QUIZ 14
1 Two
2 Greece
3 Only Fools and Horses
4 Mika (his birth name is Michael Holbrook Penniman Jr)
5 Lion-O, Jaga, Tygra, Panthro, Cheetara, Wilykit, Wilykat, Snarf

QUIZ 15
1 Heavy Goods Vehicle
2 Giant Panda
3 Ws
4 Mary Whitehouse
5 Charles de Gaulle, Georges Pompidou, Valery Giscard d'Estaing, François Mitterrand, Jacques Chirac, Nicolas Sarkozy

QUIZ 16
1 Damon Albarn
2 Caramel
3 Kingdom
4 Joey Tribbiani (in 'Friends' – played in turn by Matt LeBlanc)
5 Hammersmith and Fulham, Hackney, Hounslow, Havering, Haringey, Harrow, Hillingdon

QUIZ 17 — 17th January

1 What is the currency of Finland?

2 In 'The Lord of the Rings', what type of creatures are Haldir, Galadriel and Legolas?

3 What make of car is an anagram of a standard gear stick position in a car?

4 What links, among others: Milan, New York, Japan, my shirt, my car, and my cat?

5 Name the five 20th Century US Presidents with the longest surnames.

QUIZ 18 — 18th January

1 What name is shared by a sweet, a fashion label, a sport, and a car?

2 What was the first name of David Bowie's first wife, as sung about by Mick Jagger?

3 Which puzzle game was included in the package for the original Nintendo Game Boy?

4 What was the name of the character played by David Hasselhoff in 'Baywatch'? [first and surname, please]

5 Name five of the original six main members of the 'Monty Python' team.

QUIZ 19 — 19th January

1 The Seychelles are in which ocean?

2 What is the surname of the family that Paddington Bear lives with?

3 What is the most northerly place to which you can get a direct train from London?

4 What was the surname of Vincente, Judy Garland's second husband?

5 Name five of the six founding members of the European Economic Community (now the EU).

QUIZ 20 — 20th January

1 What shape is the base of the Great Pyramid of Giza in Egypt?

2 What is the next prime number above 80?

3 Which title character in a Disney film from 1941 has no lines of dialogue in the film?

4 The Silverstone motor racing circuit is actually in two counties. One half is in Northamptonshire: in which county is the other half?

5 Name five of the movies to have won the Best Picture Oscar for a year in the 1990s. [so, not counting the movie released in 1989 which won the Oscar at the ceremony in early 1990. That was 'Driving Miss Daisy']

QUIZ 17
1 Euro
2 Elves
3 Renault (Neutral)
4 Things that Right Said Fred was "too sexy" for – from the 1991 song 'I'm Too Sexy'
5 Dwight D Eisenhower, Theodore Roosevelt, Franklin D Roosevelt, Calvin Coolidge, William McKinley

QUIZ 18
1 Polo
2 Angie
3 Tetris
4 Mitch Buchannon
5 Michael Palin, Terry Jones, Eric Idle, John Cleese, Graham Chapman, Terry Gilliam

QUIZ 19
1 Indian
2 Brown
3 Inverness
4 Minnelli
5 France, Belgium, Netherlands, Luxembourg, West Germany, Italy

QUIZ 20
1 Square
2 83
3 Dumbo (not Bambi, who does speak, in 1942)
4 Buckinghamshire
5 Dances With Wolves, Silence of the Lambs, Unforgiven, Schindler's List, Forrest Gump, Braveheart, The English Patient, Titanic, Shakespeare in Love, American Beauty

QUIZ 21 — 21st January

1 Which act of deception, more commonly used in entertainment, gets its name from the Latin meaning "speaking from the belly"?

2 How many moons does the planet Mars have?

3 What year links the death of Winston Churchill, the Beatles receiving their MBEs and Major Edward White being the first American to walk in space?

4 What are the first three words of the Don McLean song 'Vincent'?

5 Name five US States that have twelve or more letters in their name.

QUIZ 22 — 22nd January

1 The two largest islands in the Mediterranean are part of which country?

2 Which city is served by an airport with the IATA code LGA?

3 Which phrase, first uttered by promoter Horace Lee Logan in 1956, was made famous by Al Dvorin to indicate that "The King" would not be performing an encore?

4 What is the better known name of the notorious Mexican criminal Joaquín Guzmán, who was recaptured in 2016 having escaped from prison?

5 Name five of the six original characters adopted by the members of the Village People.

QUIZ 23 — 23rd January

1 In 'Peter Pan', what does Wendy manage to reattach for Peter Pan?

2 Luxembourg's Head of State has what title?

3 What is the football team that has both lost and drawn the most matches, in total, in the English Premier League? [up to 2022, and unlikely to change]

4 In 2003, which British broadsheet newspaper was the first to introduce a tabloid-sized edition?

5 What are the first names of the four acting Baldwin brothers?

QUIZ 24 — 24th January

1 Who, in the Bible, is St Peter's brother?

2 Which area of London shares its name with a famous car manufacturer which built its first car in 1903?

3 What is a Scottish rugby club, a bingo operator and a type of apple?

4 Which girls' doll, still available today, was created by Pedigree Soft Toys Ltd and launched in September 1963?

5 Name any five of the female tennis players who have won ten or more Grand Slam Singles titles. [up to 2022]

QUIZ 21
1 Ventriloquism
2 Two (Demos and Phobos)
3 1965
4 Starry, Starry Night
5 North Carolina, South Carolina, Massachusetts, New Hampshire, West Virginia, Pennsylvania. Also, Rhode Island's full name is Rhode Island and Providence Plantations

QUIZ 22
1 Italy
2 New York (La Guardia)
3 Elvis has left the building
4 El Chapo
5 Native American, Cowboy, Construction Worker, Cop, Biker/ Leather Man, Soldier

QUIZ 23
1 His shadow
2 Grand Duke
3 Everton
4 The Independent
5 Alec, Daniel, William/ Billy and Stephen

QUIZ 24
1 Andrew
2 Vauxhall
3 Gala
4 Sindy
5 Margaret Court (24), Serena Williams (23), Steffi Graf (22), Helen Wills Moody (19), Chris Evert (18), Martina Navrátilová (18), Billie Jean King (12).
(Allow Suzanne Lenglen, who won eight Grand Slams and four "World Championship" titles which are seen by some as "Grand Slams" in that era)

QUIZ 25 — 25th January

1 Who lived at 263 Prinsengracht in Amsterdam, which is now a museum?

2 Eamon de Valera and Erskine Childers were Presidents of which country?

3 Which animal takes its name from the Greek for "river-horse"?

4 True or False? In his 2009 autobiography, tennis legend Andre Agassi revealed that he did not eat any fruit or vegetables for over nine months in 1986.

5 Name any five first names mentioned in the title of Roald Dahl novels.

QUIZ 26 — 26th January

1 Which branch of maths derives its name from the Ancient Greek for "earth measure"?

2 Complete the baby-holding trio: Tom Selleck, Steve Guttenberg and ... who?

3 What is the currency of Denmark?

4 Which notoriously weak footballing nation describes itself as 'The Most Serene Republic' and claims to be the oldest republic in the world?

5 Name any five national capital cities which have just four letters in their name. [normal English spelling, UN member states. 12 to choose from]

QUIZ 27 — 27th January

1 The leader of an orchestra plays which instrument?

2 At Starbucks, which size of drink comes above Tall and Grande?

3 Omaha is the largest city in which US state, whose name is also the title of a Bruce Springsteen album?

4 Whose only world title fight victory was against Oliver McCall for the WBC Heavyweight Title on 2nd September 1995?

5 Russia, Canada, China and the USA are the four biggest independent countries in the world in terms of area. Name any five of the next six.

QUIZ 28 — 28th January

1 Which arts centre in London shares its name with a term for a fortified outpost or gateway?

2 Who was the Democrat challenger defeated by George W Bush when he won his first US presidential election?

3 After which explorer is Venice's main international airport named?

4 What links "revenge" and the Spanish soup gazpacho?

5 Name the four teenagers who travelled with Scooby-Doo.

QUIZ 25
1 Anne Frank (and her family)
2 Ireland
3 Hippopotamus
4 False
5 James, Charlie, Danny, George, Matilda, Henry ('The Wonderful Story of Henry Sugar' - not strictly a novel, but allowed), Oswald ('My Uncle Oswald' - a novel for adults). We'll even allow Esio, in 'Esio Trot' and Billy as in the short book 'Billy and the Minpins'

QUIZ 26
1 Geometry
2 Ted Danson
3 Krone
4 San Marino
5 Apia (Samoa), Baku (Azerbaijan), Bern (Switzerland), Dili (Timor-Leste), Kyiv (Ukraine), Lima (Peru), Lomé (Togo), Malé (Maldives), Oslo (Norway), Riga (Latvia), Rome (Italy), Suva (Fiji).

QUIZ 27
1 Violin
2 Venti
3 Nebraska
4 Frank Bruno
5 Brazil, Australia, India, Argentina, Kazakhstan, Algeria

QUIZ 28
1 Barbican
2 Al Gore
3 Marco Polo
4 It is a dish best served cold
5 Fred "Freddie" Jones; Daphne Blake; Velma Dinkley; Norville "Shaggy" Rogers

QUIZ 29 — 29th January

1 What colour is the neutral wire in a modern British plug?

2 On 'Blind Date', as presented by Cilla Black, what was the first name of the man who did the voiceover summaries of each contestant?

3 Who said in 2007: "I have a lot of good moments, but the one I prefer is when I kicked the hooligan"?

4 Who replaced the injured Marvin Berry on guitar at the Enchantment Under The Sea Dance at Hill Valley High School in 1955?

5 Name any five independent countries whose normal English name ends in the letter R.

QUIZ 30 — 30th January

1 Which is larger out of Malta and the Isle of Wight? [in terms of area]

2 Which singer sang at the opening ceremony to the 1994 men's FIFA World Cup?

3 Who was Henry VIII's father?

4 Which city in England comes last in alphabetical order?

5 Michael Jackson had seven solo UK Number 1 singles. Name five of them. [solo means he is the named artist i.e. not The Jacksons, but would not discount duets]

QUIZ 31 — 31st January

1 What is the meat of calves called?

2 Which is the only English county that has two completely separate coastlines?

3 In early 2022, Heather Small was the first person eliminated from Series 3 of which UK TV show?

4 What five words are engraved on the brass letter box of 10 Downing Street?

5 Which four US Presidents have their heads carved into Mount Rushmore?

QUIZ 32 — 1st February

1 In the film and book, what does Oliver Twist ask for more of, specifically?

2 What term did Winston Churchill use in a 1946 speech to describe the division of Europe?

3 What is the English name of the bard of Asterix's village, whose singing is famously unbearable?

4 What links Aldwych, British Museum, Lord's, and Brompton Road, amongst others?

5 Name any five of the inhabited Channel Islands.

QUIZ 29
1 Blue
2 (Our) Graham
3 Eric Cantona
4 Marty McFly (in 'Back to the Future')
5 Ecuador, El Salvador, Madagascar, Niger, Qatar, East Timor, Myanmar

QUIZ 30
1 Isle of Wight (380 sq km vs 316 sq km)
2 Diana Ross
3 Henry VII/Henry Tudor
4 York
5 One Day In Your Life, Billie Jean, I Just Can't Stop Loving You [with Siedah Garrett], Black Or White, You Are Not Alone, Earth Song, Blood on the Dancefloor

QUIZ 31
1 Veal
2 Devon (Cornwall has one continuous coastline)
3 The Masked Singer
4 First Lord of the Treasury
5 George Washington, Thomas Jefferson, Theodore Roosevelt, Abraham Lincoln

QUIZ 32
1 Gruel
2 Iron Curtain
3 Cacofonix
4 Closed tube stations
5 Jersey, Guernsey, Alderney, Sark, Herm, Brecqhou, Lihou, Jethou

QUIZ 33 — 2nd February

1 What name is given in France to the day before Ash Wednesday?

2 A gopher is native to which continent?

3 With what, according to a famous movie quote, does Luca Brasi sleep?

4 In the Shakespeare play, what is the name of Hamlet's father?

5 Name any five independent countries with a coast on the Red Sea.

QUIZ 34 — 3rd February

1 What colour is wine made from Cabernet Sauvignon?

2 Give any year in the life of Jane Austen.

3 On December 11th 1972, Eugene Cernan spoke the last words from which place?

4 In the film 'Being John Malkovich', who plays the role of John Malkovich?

5 Nine countries have so far hosted both the Summer and Winter Olympics. Name five of them.

QUIZ 35 — 4th February

1 Which UK band had Greatest Hits Collections in which their name was preceded by the words 'Complete', 'Utter', 'Total' and 'Divine'?

2 In 1959, which US state became the 50th to join the Union?

3 Which public figure's first novel was published in 1976 under the title 'Not A Penny More, Not A Penny Less'?

4 What American chat show presenter has a production company called Harpo Productions?

5 Name the last five leaders of the Conservative Party in the 20th century.

QUIZ 36 — 5th February

1 Which chain of cinemas was created in 1930 in the UK by Oskar Deutsch?

2 Who, in the book and film, is the woodcarver who made Pinocchio?

3 What was the professional name of the British wrestler whose actual name was Shirley Crabtree (a name shared with a Tennessee Williams character)?

4 In which American state is the historic cowboy town of Dodge City?

5 Name the five members of the Jackson Five other than Michael.

QUIZ 33
1 Mardi Gras
2 North America
3 "Luca Brasi sleeps with the fishes" (in 'The Godfather')
4 Hamlet
5 Egypt, Israel, Jordan, Sudan, Eritrea, Saudi Arabia, Yemen, Somalia, Djibouti

QUIZ 34
1 Red
2 1775-1817
3 The Moon (commander of Apollo XVII)
4 John Malkovich
5 France, United States, Canada, Germany, Japan, Italy, South Korea, Russia, China

QUIZ 35
1 Madness
2 Hawaii
3 Jeffrey Archer
4 Oprah Winfrey
5 Alec Douglas-Home, Edward Heath, Margaret Thatcher, John Major, William Hague

QUIZ 36
1 Odeon
2 Geppetto
3 Big Daddy
4 Kansas
5 Jackie; Tito; Jermaine; Marlon; Randy (Randy didn't join until 1972).

QUIZ 37 — 6th February

1 An atom is formed from protons, electrons and ... what?

2 How many half-dozens are there in a gross?

3 In the standard British version of Cluedo, what is the only combination of murder weapon, murder room, and murderer where all three begin with the same letter (only considering surnames for the murder suspects)?

4 Which prolific author died in 2000 aged 98, three years after the death of Princess Diana, her step-granddaughter?

5 Name these five Tom Cruise films from the brief synopsis given: (a) Tom Cruise plays a talented young barman who finds love in Jamaica; (b) Tom Cruise plays a talented young naval aviator who finds love at the Miramar flight academy; (c) Tom Cruise plays a talented young driver who finds love on the NASCAR circuit; (d) Tom Cruise plays a talented young pool player who finds love in a pool hall; (e) Tom Cruise plays a talented young football player who finds love in small-town Pennsylvania.

QUIZ 38 — 7th February

1 Which TV show was presented for most of its run between 1972 and 1992 by Geoffrey Hayes?

2 What does the C stand for in the name of the motoring organisation RAC?

3 What is the name of a small elevator used to transport food between different floors of a building?

4 What nickname was given to Douglas Jardine's "fast leg theory" cricket tactic used in 1932–33 in Australia?

5 Name the four children who go through the wardrobe, in CS Lewis' 'The Lion, The Witch and the Wardrobe'.

QUIZ 39 — 8th February

1 What name is shared by a type of potato, a fictional spider, and the wife of George III?

2 Which English actor, once described as "the loudest man alive" has a name that is an anagram of SENSIBLE BARD?

3 Who became Governor of New South Wales in 1805, 18 years after a famous mutiny on the ship he captained?

4 Which game can be played under the Regency Rules which state that "the Nash Convention allows superseding after parallel moves, and all Terraces ... are wild, unless of course you are in Spoon"?

5 Name five of the seven least populous independent countries in Europe, excluding the Vatican City.

QUIZ 40 — 9th February

1 The sitcom 'Joey' was a spin-off of which other show?

2 Which piece of athletics equipment weighs 800g for men and 600g for women?

3 A gerontocracy would be rule by which section of the population?

4 Who said in 2001: "Only some ghastly dehumanised moron would get rid of the Routemaster [bus]"?

5 Name any five US Presidents since World War II who did not serve as President for eight years. [not including Joe Biden]

QUIZ 37
1 Neutrons
2 24
3 Miss Scarlett, in the Study, with the Spanner.
4 Barbara Cartland
5 (a) Cocktail; (b) Top Gun; (c) Days of Thunder; (d) The Color of Money; (e) All the Right Moves

QUIZ 38
1 Rainbow
2 Club (Royal Automobile Club)
3 Dumb waiter
4 Bodyline
5 Lucy, Edmund, Peter, Susan

QUIZ 39
1 Charlotte
2 Brian Blessed
3 Captain William Bligh
4 Mornington Crescent (from 'I'm Sorry I Haven't a Clue')
5 San Marino, Monaco, Liechtenstein Andorra, Iceland, Malta, Luxembourg

QUIZ 40
1 Friends
2 The javelin
3 Old people
4 Ken Livingstone (who got rid of the Routemaster buses)
5 Donald Trump, George HW Bush, Jimmy Carter, Gerald Ford, Richard Nixon, Lyndon B Johnson, John F Kennedy

QUIZ 41 — 10th February

1 Which form of transport runs between Fishguard and Rosslare?

2 How many different British drivers were Formula 1 champions during the 1990s?

3 Complete the famous quote from the American lawyer Johnnie Cochran: "If the gloves don't fit, you must ..."?

4 On which TV show in 2001 did Darius Campbell Danesh first come to prominence singing a memorable version of '...Baby One More Time'?

5 Name the five countries in Africa with the largest population.

QUIZ 42 — 11th February

1 Which country's name is an anagram of the word SERIAL?

2 What does the abbreviation WASP stand for?

3 Whose leadership challenge to Margaret Thatcher in November 1990 prompted her resignation as Prime Minister?

4 What breed of dog is Snoopy?

5 After Brazil, what are the next five most populous countries in South America?

QUIZ 43 — 12th February

1 In British schooling terminology, what does SEN stand for?

2 Former Conservative minister Nicholas Soames is which other notable politician's grandson?

3 What did PJ and Duncan want us to watch them wrecking repeatedly in their breakthrough hit 'Let's get Ready to Rhumble'? Watch us wreck the WHAT?

4 In the London version of Monopoly, in a four-player game, how much money would you receive in total on your birthday (according to Chance or Community Chest)?

5 Name any five English cities whose name ends with the letter R. [not counting Rochester, which is no longer officially a city]

QUIZ 44 — 13th February

1 What number Apollo Mission took Neil Armstrong and Buzz Aldrin to the moon?

2 In a 1986 UK Number 1 hit, Falco asked which classical composer to rock him?

3 What internet browser had more than 90% market share in the mid-90s but was discontinued in 2008?

4 Which comedian and actor, born in 1961, shares his surname with a borough in the north of London?

5 Name any five independent countries whose normal English name begins with the letter E.

QUIZ 41
1 Ferry (Wales to Ireland)
2 Two (Nigel Mansell, Damon Hill)
3 Acquit (in the OJ Simpson trial)
4 Popstars (Darius, who died in 2022, also finished 3rd on 'Pop Idol' in 2002)
5 Nigeria, Ethiopia, Egypt, Democratic Republic of the Congo, South Africa

QUIZ 42
1 Israel
2 White Anglo-Saxon Protestant
3 Michael Heseltine
4 Beagle
5 Colombia, Argentina, Peru, Venezuela, Chile. Ecuador is next

QUIZ 43
1 Special Educational Needs
2 Winston Churchill
3 The Mike – ......(Psych)
4 £30 (£10 from each other player)
5 Chester, Chichester, Colchester, Doncaster, Exeter, Gloucester, Lancaster, Leicester, Manchester, Westminster, Winchester, Worcester

QUIZ 44
1 11
2 (Wolfgang) Amadeus (Mozart)
3 Netscape
4 Harry Enfield
5 East Timor (aka Timor-Leste), Ecuador, Egypt, El Salvador, Equatorial Guinea, Eritrea, Estonia, Ethiopia, Eswatini

QUIZ 45 — 14th February

1 How high, in feet, should a tennis net be at the centre?

2 Maris and Lilith are the former wives of which sitcom brothers?

3 Paternal describes someone who is fatherly. What is the equivalent word for someone who is like an uncle?

4 The first lines of which popular children's song translate into English from the original French as "skylark, nice skylark, skylark, I shall pluck you'"?

5 William Shakespeare wrote plays about seven real English kings since 1066. Name any five of the kings. [name and regnal number required]

QUIZ 46 — 15th February

1 In the book of Beatrix Potter, what kind of animal is Mrs Tiggy-Winkle?

2 Who was the cook on the fictional Hispaniola?

3 Which Englishman was the world Table Tennis champion in 1928, six years before winning the first of his three Wimbledon Tennis Championships?

4 How is the bell-tower in the Campo dei Miracoli in Tuscany better known?

5 Name five feature films directed by Alfred Hitchcock which have precisely four words in their title. [don't put 'North by Northwest', which is three words]

QUIZ 47 — 16th February

1 What is the currency used in Egypt?

2 If a Scottish person described themselves as "peely-wally" what would they be?

3 Which city in Saudi Arabia is the burial place of the Prophet Muhammad?

4 What kind of cheese is the English town of Melton Mowbray famous for?

5 China and India both have populations of over one billion people. Name any five of the next eight biggest countries by population.

QUIZ 48 — 17th February

1 In New Zealand, in what month of the year do the clocks go back?

2 Which strikingly coiffured Scotsman was the men's 2022 PDC World Darts champion? [referring to the Championship which ended at the start of 2022]

3 What specific product was advertised for many years with the line "How do you eat yours?"?

4 Which gangster dated singer Blousey Brown, managed boxer Leroy Smith, and was involved in an attempted hit on crime lord Dandy Dan?

5 Name the five independent countries whose common name in English has one syllable.

QUIZ 45
1 3 feet
2 The Crane Brothers (Frasier)
3 Avuncular
4 Alouette, Gentille Alouette
5 John, Richard II, Henry IV, Henry V Henry VI, Richard III, Henry VIII

QUIZ 46
1 Hedgehog
2 Long John Silver (in 'Treasure Island')
3 Fred Perry
4 The Leaning Tower of Pisa
5 Juno and the Paycock, Mr and Mrs Smith, Shadow of a Doubt, Strangers on a Train, Dial M for Murder, To Catch a Thief, The Trouble with Harry

QUIZ 47
1 (Egyptian) Pounds
2 Feeling sick/off-colour
3 Medina
4 Stilton
5 USA, Indonesia, Brazil, Pakistan, Bangladesh, Nigeria, Russia, Japan

QUIZ 48
1 March
2 Peter "Snakebite" Wright
3 Cadbury's Creme Egg
4 Bugsy Malone
5 France, Spain, Greece, Chad, Laos

QUIZ 49 — 18th February

1 According to the regulations of each game, which is the smallest: a squash ball, a golf ball or a table tennis ball?

2 Which product was advertised by John Barnes with the words "after 90 minutes of sheer hell"?

3 What town in Northamptonshire is sometimes known as Little Scotland for its large community of Scottish migrant workers (almost 20% Scottish born)?

4 What surname links a 'Pop Idol' winner, a snooker player, and a one-time professional wrestler?

5 Name five of the eight women who have been married to one of the four Beatles - either maiden name or married name is allowed. [up to 2022]

QUIZ 50 — 19th February

1 On which day does the action of both 'Die Hard' and 'Die Hard II' take place?

2 Which is the only one of the 150 longest rivers in the world that flows out into the Mediterranean?

3 Police cars often contain ANPR devices - what does ANPR stand for?

4 Which song begins with the line "I follow the Moskva down to Gorky Park"?

5 Name five British boxers to have won an Olympic gold medal since 2000. [up to and including Tokyo Olympics]

QUIZ 51 — 20th February

1 In the human body, the bone called the tibia is part of which limb?

2 Who was leader, in Britain, of the National Union of Mineworkers from 1981 to 2000?

3 What links Walker, Jefferson, Wilson, Earl, Rudolph, and Milhous amongst others?

4 Which chocolate sweets were first produced in 1941 in a collaboration between Forrest Mars (of Mars bar fame) and Bruce Murrie (son of the President of Hershey's)?

5 Name five movies directed by Steven Spielberg with one-word titles. [up to end of 2021]

QUIZ 52 — 21st February

1 In which city is the Museo del Prado?

2 According to the lyrics of a popular song, which mountain "rises like Olympus over the Serengeti"?

3 The monk, based in Jarrow, whose 'Ecclesiastical History of the English People' is considered the foundation of English history, was the Venerable ... who?

4 Which Himalayan kingdom's only international airport is Paro International Airport, considered by many to be the toughest international airport landing in the world?

5 Name five US states whose names derive specifically from European royalty. [worth thinking a little laterally in some cases]

QUIZ 49

1 Table tennis ball (38.2mm): a golf ball is 42.7mm, a squash ball 40mm
2 Lucozade (Sport)
3 Corby
4 McManus (Michelle, Alan, Mick)
5 Cynthia Powell (Lennon), Maureen Cox (Starr), Linda Eastman (McCartney), Pattie Boyd (Harrison), Yoko Ono (Lennon), Barbara Bach (Starr), Heather Mills (McCartney), Olivia Trinidad Aras (Harrison), Nancy Shevell (McCartney)

QUIZ 50

1 Christmas Eve/24th December
2 Nile
3 Automatic Number Plate Recognition
4 Wind of Change (by The Scorpions)
5 Audley Harrison, James DeGale, Luke Campbell, Nicola Adams (twice), Anthony Joshua, Galal Yafai, Lauren Price

QUIZ 51

1 Leg
2 Arthur Scargill
3 Middle names of US Presidents
4 M&M's
5 Firelight, Duel, Jaws, 1941, Always, Hook, Amistad, Munich, Lincoln (it's also rumoured he was de facto co-director on 'Poltergeist', so we'll allow that)

QUIZ 52

1 Madrid
2 Kilimanjaro
3 Bede
4 Bhutan
5 Louisiana (after Louis XIV), Virginia, West Virginia (both after Elizabeth I), Maryland (after wife of Charles I), North Carolina, South Carolina (after Charles I), Georgia (after George II), New York (after Duke of York, later James II)

QUIZ 53 — 22nd February

1 Who was the original presenter of 'Newsround' on BBC TV?

2 Which period of the Mesozoic era fell between the Triassic and Cretaceous?

3 Who was the third "Amigo" alongside Steve Martin and Martin Short in the 1986 film?

4 In French, what irritation is known as "Le Pourriel" or "Le Pollupostage"?

5 In Northern and Southern Ireland combined, there are, officially, 12 cities - six in the North, six in the Republic. Excluding Dublin and Belfast, name five of them.

QUIZ 54 — 23rd February

1 What perilous activity takes its name from the Greek for "high walking"?

2 Who was the first member of the English/British royal family to get a divorce?

3 A size zero in US measurements is equivalent to which size of ladies' clothes in the UK?

4 What is the name of the little boy in Raymond Briggs' 'The Snowman', as revealed by the label on the present given to him by Father Christmas?

5 Name five novels by Charles Dickens which contain the name of a character in the title - it doesn't have to be the full name.

QUIZ 55 — 24th February

1 Jacob Zuma is a former President of which country?

2 What is the name of the Society of London Theatre's annual awards (named after a famous British actor)?

3 Which country's flag has been officially changed 26 times since it was introduced in the 18th century?

4 Which 1954 film ends with the line "I now pronounce you men and wives"?

5 Name the four independent countries in the world with a unique last letter - their name ends in a letter that no other country ends with in the standard English spelling.

QUIZ 56 — 25th February

1 Solomon Grundy was born on Monday. On which day of the week did he die?

2 In June 2022, Labour's Simon Lightwood won which constituency from the Conservatives in a by-election?

3 Which cartoon featured minor characters like Gus Gravel, actor Gary Granite and quarry owner Sylvester Slate?

4 What was Sony's format of video tape that was overtaken by the VHS system?

5 Name the five countries in the Commonwealth with the largest populations.

QUIZ 53
1 John Craven
2 Jurassic
3 Chevy Chase
4 Spam
5 Cork, Galway, Limerick, Waterford, Kilkenny, Derry/Londonderry, Newry, Lisburn, Armagh, Bangor

QUIZ 54
1 Acrobatics
2 Henry VIII
3 Four
4 James
5 The Pickwick Papers, Oliver Twist, Nicholas Nickleby, Barnaby Rudge, Martin Chuzzlewit, Dombey and Son, David Copperfield, Little Dorrit, The Mystery of Edwin Drood

QUIZ 55
1 South Africa
2 Oliviers (The Laurence Olivier Awards)
3 USA (new stars added each time a new state (or multiple states) joins the Union)
4 Seven Brides for Seven Brothers
5 Luxembourg, Bangladesh, Denmark, Iraq

QUIZ 56
1 Saturday
2 Wakefield
3 The Flintstones
4 Betamax
5 India, Pakistan, Bangladesh, Nigeria, UK.

QUIZ 57 — 26th February

1 Grappa is a spirit which originates in which country?

2 What product is the company Victorinox renowned for making?

3 In North America, what is both the most northerly and largest of the Great Lakes?

4 Which actress, star of 'The Misfits' and 'How to Marry a Millionaire', graced the front cover of the first ever edition of 'Playboy'?

5 Name any five England test match cricket captains since the Second World War with the first name Michael. [up to end of 2021]

QUIZ 58 — 27th February

1 Innsbruck is a city in which country?

2 What is the maximum number of Michelin Stars that a restaurant can have at any one time?

3 Give any year in the life of the artist Johannes Vermeer.

4 As in the names of Santa's reindeer, what do the German words "Donner" and "Blitzen" mean?

5 Name the five countries that border Kenya.

QUIZ 59 — 28th February

1 Which company developed the internet browser Chrome?

2 Which famous family lives at 742 Evergreen Terrace, although from time to time the house number has been different?

3 Which Native American married John Rolfe in 1614?

4 With which other former British tennis player does Tim Henman share the same birthday, albeit a year earlier, as well as the same first name of their respective wives?

5 Give the first names of five spouses of British Prime Ministers between 1991 and 2021.

QUIZ 60 — 29th February

An extra quiz for leap years!

1 Which British king died in May 1972?

2 Which country does Kingfisher beer come from?

3 How many other countries does Liechtenstein border?

4 What was the capital city of Japan before Tokyo, its name being an anagram of Tokyo?

5 Name the four Shakespeare plays that contain the word "and" somewhere in their title. There may be some lateral thinking required for one of them.

QUIZ 57
1 Italy
2 Swiss Army Knife / Penknife
3 Lake Superior (naturally)
4 Marilyn Monroe
5 Michael Vaughan, Michael Atherton, Mike Gatting, Mike Brearley, Mike Denness, MJK Smith (Mike Smith), Michael Colin Cowdrey (Colin Cowdrey)

QUIZ 58
1 Austria
2 Three Stars
3 1632-1675
4 Thunder and Lightning
5 Uganda, Tanzania, Somalia, Ethiopia, Sudan

QUIZ 59
1 Google
2 The Simpsons
3 Pocahontas
4 Greg Rusedski (wives called Lucy)
5 Carrie, Phillip, Samantha, Sarah, Cherie, Norma

QUIZ 60
1 Edward VIII
2 India
3 Two
4 Kyoto
5 Romeo and Juliet, Troilus and Cressida, Anthony and Cleopatra, Titus Andronicus

QUIZ 61 — 1st March

1 What physical quantity is measured in joules?

2 In which decade was Barack Obama born?

3 In UK elections, what is the title of the person who oversees the processes of the election and announces the results?

4 Which foodstuff originally and traditionally could only be made within 30 miles of Wells Cathedral?

5 Name the five US states that have a shoreline on the Gulf of Mexico.

QUIZ 62 — 2nd March

1 What name was traditionally given to the flag flown by pirates, variants of which include the skull and crossbones?

2 Stella Rimington became, in 1992, the first female Director General of which organisation?

3 Which long-standing, successful British band took its name from the Department of Health and Security unemployment benefit form at the time?

4 What did my true love give to me for the first time on the eighth day of Christmas?

5 Name any five of the nine UN member states whose normal English name begins with the letter L.

QUIZ 63 — 3rd March

1 In which US State would you find the cities of Yonkers, Albany and Buffalo?

2 Kadima and Likud are political parties in which country?

3 How many letters of the alphabet are not used in the names of any of the months of the year?

4 What is a keema naan stuffed with?

5 Name five of the six US Space Shuttles.

QUIZ 64 — 4th March

1 What name is shared by a chain of hotels and a brand of circular salty crackers?

2 What is Captain Von Trapp's first name in 'The Sound of Music'?

3 What carol is based on a poem by Miss Cecil Humphreys and is the traditional opener to a carol service?

4 Which classic sci-fi TV series was first shown on TV the day after the assassination of John F Kennedy in 1963?

5 Name five of the ten provinces of Canada. [not including the three territories - Yukon, Northwest Territories, Nunavut]

QUIZ 61
1 Energy
2 1960s (1961)
3 Returning Officer
4 Cheddar Cheese
5 Texas, Louisiana, Alabama, Mississippi, Florida

QUIZ 62
1 Jolly Roger
2 MI5/Security Service
3 UB40 (it stood for Unemployment Benefit, Form 40)
4 Eight Maids-a-milking
5 Laos, Latvia, Lebanon, Lesotho, Liberia, Libya, Liechtenstein, Lithuania, Luxembourg

QUIZ 63
1 New York
2 Israel
3 Five (K, Q, W, X, Z)
4 Minced meat
5 Enterprise, Columbia, Challenger, Discovery, Endeavour, Atlantis (Enterprise was used for test flights but never space flight)

QUIZ 64
1 Ritz
2 Georg
3 Once in Royal David's City
4 Doctor Who (not 'Star Trek', which was first shown in the US in 1966, and the UK in 1969).
5 Ontario, Quebec, British Columbia, Saskatchewan, Manitoba, Prince Edward Island, Newfoundland and Labrador, Nova Scotia, Alberta, New Brunswick

QUIZ 65 — 5th March

1 In the PG Wodehouse stories, who is Bertie Wooster's famous valet?

2 The French word for Friday is named after which Roman goddess?

3 Which word could be a band who had a hit with 'Wires' or a generic term for a sportsperson?

4 Name a country and capital city which together have, in the normal English spelling, the fewest letters in total (e.g. France and Paris have (six + five) 11 letters)? There are three to choose from.

5 London contains four UNESCO World Heritage Sites. Name them. [If you are roughly right, give yourself the points]

QUIZ 66 — 6th March

1 In a rainbow, which colour lies in between green and indigo?

2 Which Academy Award-winning western told the story of Civil War veteran John J Dunbar and his encounters with a Sioux tribe?

3 Lada cars are from which country?

4 What O is a sportswear manufacturer founded by Jim Jannard, based in California, which specialises in sunglasses and other eyewear?

5 Name five of the first ten actors to have twice won the Academy Award for Best Actor in a Leading Role. [do not include anyone if they have won their second Oscar after 2022]

QUIZ 67 — 7th March

1 By what animal name is the bright star Sirius also known?

2 The Genco Pura Olive Oil Company was the front company for which fictional gangster's operations?

3 What is the name of a book by Malcolm Gladwell, an album by the Roots and an ITV gameshow which debuted in 2012?

4 What is the popular name of two twin landmarks, one in Central Park, New York, one by the Thames in London, which were originally located in Heliopolis, Egypt?

5 Name any five of the ten independent countries in the world with the longest coastlines, according to best estimates. [do not write Greenland, which is not independent]

QUIZ 68 — 8th March

1 What is the British equivalent of the American Secretary of State?

2 The Gobi desert covers large areas of China and which other country?

3 What is the name of Jerome K. Jerome's humorous account of his river journey with two friends?

4 Which European capital city was formerly called Christiania?

5 Name the four occasions in the year when you are legally allowed to set off fireworks after 11pm in the UK.

QUIZ 65
1 Jeeves
2 Venus (Vendredi)
3 Athlete
4 Peru & Lima, Fiji & Suva, Togo & Lomé
5 Tower of London, Westminster Abbey + Palace of Westminster, Royal Botanic Gardens at Kew, Greenwich (Observatory)

QUIZ 66
1 Blue
2 Dances With Wolves
3 Russia
4 Oakley
5 Spencer Tracy, Fredric March, Gary Cooper, Marlon Brando, Dustin Hoffman, Tom Hanks, Jack Nicholson, Daniel Day Lewis, Sean Penn, Anthony Hopkins

QUIZ 67
1 The Dog Star
2 Vito Corleone (or indeed Michael Corleone) in 'The Godfather'
3 The Tipping Point
4 Cleopatra's Needle
5 Canada, Indonesia, Russia, Philippines, Japan, Australia, Norway, USA, New Zealand, China

QUIZ 68
1 Foreign Secretary
2 Mongolia
3 Three Men In A Boat
4 Oslo
5 November 5th/Bonfire Night, New Year, Chinese New Year, Diwali

QUIZ 69 — 9th March

1 What was the first name of the British explorer Captain Cook?

2 Which Shakespeare play was the inspiration for the Cole Porter musical 'Kiss Me, Kate'?

3 What product was so named because it "Browns, Seasons and Thickens in One"?

4 Which prolific children's author, whose books have sold over 500 million copies, wrote the rather extraordinarily-titled 'Mr Pink-Whistle Interferes' in 1950?

5 Name any five of the six official languages of the United Nations.

QUIZ 70 — 10th March

1 Kalamata olives get their name from a place in which European country?

2 Which band has released singles with dramatic titles including 'Invincible', 'Resistance', Uprising', 'Survival', 'Hysteria' and 'Madness'?

3 On 13 July 1955 Ruth Ellis was the last woman in Britain to be what?

4 What was the actual first name of the artist Caravaggio - the same as another famous Italian artist who had died seven years before he was born?

5 Name any four of the five Bee Gees songs featured on the 'Saturday Night Fever' soundtrack.

QUIZ 71 — 11th March

1 In the TV comedy series, what was the first name of Blackadder?

2 What was the name of the ship in which Charles Darwin visited the Galápagos Islands?

3 Which artist created a work entitled 'For the Love of God' which was a skull adorned with £15m of diamonds?

4 In October 1999, which Hollywood leading man was discovered by police playing bongos naked in his own house, and charged with breaching the peace?

5 Name the five US States that have exactly six letters in their name.

QUIZ 72 — 12th March

1 According to his self-portrait, what colour was the hair of the famous artist Vincent Van Gogh?

2 The original version of Elton John's 'Candle in the Wind' was about which actress?

3 What shape is a "Give Way" road sign in the UK?

4 What city links a hymn for which the music was written by Sir Hubert Parry with an award-winning play by Jez Butterworth?

5 What are the six categories and their colours on the original classic Genus edition of Trivial Pursuit? [need both parts to be right]

QUIZ 69
1 James
2 The Taming of the Shrew
3 Bisto
4 Enid Blyton
5 Arabic, Chinese (Mandarin), English, French, Russian, Spanish

QUIZ 70
1 Greece
2 Muse
3 Executed/hanged
4 Michelangelo
5 Night Fever, Stayin' Alive, More Than A Woman, How Deep Is Your Love?, You Should Be Dancing

QUIZ 71
1 Edmund
2 Beagle
3 Damien Hirst
4 Matthew McConaughey
5 Alaska, Hawaii, Oregon, Kansas, Nevada

QUIZ 72
1 Orange/Red/Ginger
2 Marilyn Monroe
3 Triangle (inverted)
4 Jerusalem
5 Geography - Blue; Entertainment - Pink; History - Yellow; Art & Literature - Brown; Science & Nature - Green; Sports & Leisure - Orange

QUIZ 73 — 13th March

1 What has been advertised with the slogan "He who drinks Australian, thinks Australian"?

2 The architect Oscar Niemeyer, who died in 2012, is best known for his work in designing which capital city?

3 What colour are the seats in the House of Lords?

4 Who in 2022 became both the youngest and oldest woman to have a self-written UK Number 1 hit single?

5 Name any five EU member states ruled by monarchs or hereditary heads of state.

QUIZ 74 — 14th March

1 Tipo, Uno, Punta and Panda are cars which have been made by which company?

2 Richard Burton and Elizabeth Taylor played which two historical lovers in an epic 1963 film?

3 As far as can be known, what nationality is Jack from 'Jack and the Beanstalk'?

4 A library in Sydney put up a sign in January 2013 saying it was moving all the books of which sportsman to the Fiction section?

5 In economics, BRICS is an acronym referring to which five countries with advanced economic growth?

QUIZ 75 — 15th March

1 Smash musical 'We Will Rock You' is based on the music of which band?

2 Who sung the theme tune for the TV show 'Minder', although he didn't actually write the theme tune (even though he may have wanted to)?

3 Which G was the small but memorable role played by Stephen Hibbert in 'Pulp Fiction'?

4 Which novel, significantly, sold its 3,141,592nd copy in February 2013?

5 Name five of the seven countries with the most UNESCO World Heritage sites in the world.

QUIZ 76 — 16th March

1 At the end of 'The Ugly Duckling', the ugly duckling turns into what?

2 In yards, how long is a cricket wicket? [when the game is played by adults]

3 .aq is the top-level domain for which sparsely populated area of the world?

4 For which League One football club were the two goalscorers in a 2–1 win over Notts County in February 2013 Peter Hartley and James Poole?

5 Name five films Daniel Day-Lewis has been in since 2000. [up to 2022, as he claims he has retired]

QUIZ 73
1 Fosters
2 Brasília
3 Red
4 Kate Bush ('Wuthering Heights' and 'Running Up That Hill')
5 There are 6 - Belgium, Denmark, Luxembourg, the Netherlands, Spain, Sweden (Norway, UK, Monaco, Andorra and Liechtenstein are not EU member states)

QUIZ 74
1 FIAT
2 Antony and Cleopatra
3 English ("fi fy fo fum, I smell the blood of an Englishman")
4 Lance Armstrong
5 Brazil, Russia, India, China, South Africa

QUIZ 75
1 Queen
2 Dennis Waterman (the theme tune was written by his second wife Patricia)
3 (The) Gimp
4 Life of Pi
5 Italy, Spain, China, France, Germany, Mexico, India

QUIZ 76
1 A swan
2 22 yards
3 Antarctica
4 Hartlepool United (Hartley and Poole for Hartlepool)
5 Phantom Thread, Lincoln, Nine, There Will Be Blood, The Ballad of Jack and Rose, Gangs of New York

QUIZ 77 — 17th March

1 What first name links the comedians Kane, Howard and Brand?

2 Which civil rights leader was the subject of an Oscar-winning 1982 film directed by Richard Attenborough?

3 What J is the capital city of the state of Mississippi, as well as being the surname of a US President?

4 What number was the nickname of the former England rugby international Billy Twelvetrees, given to him originally by Irish club rugby colleagues?

5 Name the last five editors of the now-defunct News of the World newspaper.

QUIZ 78 — 18th March

1 Of which European country is Lake Garda the largest lake?

2 What does a cartographer create?

3 By what score did England's cricket team lose the 2021-22 men's Ashes series to Australia?

4 What does the LL and J of the name of rapper and actor LL Cool J stand for?

5 There are four characteristics commonly used as the basic descriptor of diamonds, all conveniently beginning with the letter C. What are these so-called 4 Cs? [cost is not one of them]

QUIZ 79 — 19th March

1 In which continent do you find ostriches in the wild?

2 What is Fungus, according to the book by Raymond Briggs?

3 What form of entertainment got its name from the fact that, when episodic weekday dramas were broadcast on radio in the 1930s, they were sponsored by the likes of Procter & Gamble and Lever Brothers?

4 Where, according to a famous poem, "did Kubla Khan a stately pleasure-dome decree"?

5 Name five of the eleven independent countries with the most land borders with other countries. [do not consider overseas territories and crown dependencies]

QUIZ 80 — 20th March

1 Which N went off with a "trumpety-trump, trump, trump, trump"?

2 In the Christian calendar, what is the Sunday before Easter called?

3 Which 2009 movie is about the quest to acquire the precious mineral unobtanium?

4 Which inventor, who holds over 1,000 patents in his name, was one of the founders of the company General Electric back in 1892?

5 Name five of the fourteen chemical elements whose chemical symbol is just one letter. [please give name of element, rather than just letter]

QUIZ 77
1 Russell
2 Mahatma Gandhi
3 Jackson (not Johnson or Jefferson)
4 36 (12 3s)
5 Piers Morgan, Phil Hall, Rebekah Wade/Brooks, Andy Coulson, Phil Myler

QUIZ 78
1 Italy
2 Maps
3 4-0
4 Ladies Love Cool James
5 Cut, Colour, Clarity, Carat

QUIZ 79
1 Africa
2 Bogeyman
3 Soap opera
4 In Xanadu
5 China, Russia, Brazil, DR Congo, Germany, Sudan, France, Austria, Turkey/Türkiye, Tanzania, Zambia (also allow Serbia which has seven plus Kosovo, which is not fully recognised at the time of writing)

QUIZ 80
1 Nelly the Elephant
2 Palm Sunday
3 Avatar
4 Thomas Edison
5 Hydrogen - H, Boron - B, Carbon - C, Nitrogen - N, Oxygen - O, Fluorine - F, Phosphorus - P, Sulphur - S, Potassium - K, Vanadium - V, Yttrium - Y, Iodine - I, Tungsten - W, Uranium - U

QUIZ 81 — 21st March

1 Which African country is entirely surrounded by South Africa?

2 Which of the 'Friends' gets married to Mike Hannigan?

3 Which word in use in English comes from the German for "rumbling ghost"?

4 Pubs called The Royal Oak refer to an incident in the life of which British monarch?

5 Name the first five films in the Disney Animated Canon, all released between 1937 and 1942.

QUIZ 82 — 22nd March

1 What is the name of the little girl who accompanies the BFG on his travels in the Roald Dahl novel?

2 Michael Eavis was the founder of which music festival in Somerset?

3 Which legendary movie mogul designed and flew a huge aeroplane called the Spruce Goose?

4 How did Luis Urzúa, Florencio Ávalos, Yonni Barrios, Mario Gómez and Mario Sepúlveda, amongst others, hit the headlines in Autumn 2010?

5 Name any five singles by Blur which have achieved Top 5 positions on the UK singles chart.

QUIZ 83 — 23rd March

1 Species of which saltwater fish include the bigeye, blackfin, bullet and albacore?

2 Which French fashion designer, who created Demi Moore's dress in 'Indecent Proposal', died in January 2022?

3 Aphra Behn, who lived in the 17th century, is thought to be the first English woman to make a living doing what?

4 Which building, designed by Terry Farrell and opened in 1994, stands by the River Thames, though many people round the world saw it on fire in late 2012?

5 Name any five Labour Home Secretaries between 1997 and 2010.

QUIZ 84 — 24th March

1 If someone is born on Halloween, what sign of the Zodiac are they?

2 Michael Douglas won a Golden Globe for playing which musician in the 2013 film 'Behind the Candelabra'?

3 In the Gospels, what name links two men, one a beggar in a parable of Jesus, the other a friend of Jesus from the town of Bethany whose sisters are Mary and Martha (who something miraculous happens to)?

4 What two-word name was commonly given to the Strategic Defence Initiative announced by Ronald Reagan on March 23 1983?

5 In terms of area, what are the five biggest islands in the Mediterranean?

QUIZ 81

1 Lesotho
2 Phoebe Buffay
3 Poltergeist
4 Charles II
5 Snow White and the Seven Dwarves, Pinocchio, Fantasia, Dumbo, Bambi (We will allow 'The Reluctant Dragon', from 1941, even though it is not part of the Canon, as it has animated sections)

QUIZ 82

1 Sophie
2 Glastonbury
3 Howard Hughes
4 They were Chilean Miners (trapped from August to October 2010 before being rescued)
5 Girls And Boys, Country House, The Universal, Charmless Man, Beetlebum, Song 2, On Your Own, Tender, Out Of Time

QUIZ 83

1 Tuna
2 Thierry Mugler
3 Writing (amongst her works is 'Oroonoko' one of the first novels written in English)
4 SIS Building/MI6 Building, blown up in the James Bond film 'Skyfall'
5 Jack Straw, David Blunkett, Charles Clarke, John Reid, Jacqui Smith, Alan Johnson

QUIZ 84

1 Scorpio
2 Liberace
3 Lazarus
4 Star Wars
5 Sicily, Sardinia, Cyprus, Corsica, Crete

QUIZ 85 — 25th March

1 In the 'Chronicles of Narnia', what kind of animal is Aslan?

2 Which South Atlantic islands have their capital at Stanley?

3 Whose final film role was as the ageing gunfighter JB Books in the 1976 movie 'The Shootist'?

4 The best selling album of 1995 in the UK included songs such as 'Danny Boy', 'Daydream Believer' and 'Up on the Roof'. It was a debut, self-titled album. What was its name?

5 Name five places in Wales which hold city status in the UK.

QUIZ 86 — 26th March

1 The Quantock Hills are in which English county?

2 Who produced, wrote and starred in the film 'Philomena'?

3 Which Shakespeare play has a plot which revolves around a pound of flesh?

4 Which animal features in the title of Booker Prize-winning novels by Penelope Lively and Aravind Adiga, and in the plot of the 2002 Booker Prize winner?

5 Name five official English cities which have, precisely, nine-letter names. [don't put Newcastle (upon-Tyne), or Rochester, which does not have official city status]

QUIZ 87 — 27th March

1 Which P is the comic strip in which you would meet Charlie Brown, Peppermint Patty and Woodstock?

2 Which music legend's compositions include 'Ecce Cor Meum', 'Standing Stone' and 'Liverpool Oratorio'?

3 What was the pen name of the British vet Alf Wight, whose semi-autobiographical novels were turned into a popular TV series?

4 In order to appease British national sentiment in World War I, what, significantly, did the British royal family do on 17 July 1917?

5 Name five of the ten highest grossing films of the 1970s worldwide.

QUIZ 88 — 28th March

1 The Avon, Stour, Teme and Usk are tributaries of which river?

2 The founder of which English condiment company said he made his fortune from what people left on the side of their plate?

3 What is the sweet Italian loaf (whose name means, roughly "large loaf") traditionally associated with Christmas and New Year?

4 Which famous film director has only directed six feature films, the first two called 'THX 1138' and 'American Graffiti', the next four all having official titles which begin with the same two words?

5 Name five of the eight places in Scotland which hold city status in the UK.

QUIZ 85
1 Lion
2 The Falkland Islands
3 John Wayne
4 Robson and Jerome
5 Bangor, Cardiff, Newport, St Davids (and the Cathedral Close), Swansea, St Asaph, Wrexham (Bangor, Caerdydd, Casnewydd, Tyddewi, Abertawe, Llanelwy, Wrecsam)

QUIZ 86
1 Somerset
2 Steve Coogan
3 The Merchant of Venice
4 Tiger (Moon Tiger/The White Tiger/Life of Pi)
5 Cambridge, Doncaster, Lancaster, Leicester, Lichfield, Liverpool, Salisbury, Sheffield, Wakefield, Worcester

QUIZ 87
1 Peanuts
2 Paul McCartney
3 James Herriot
4 They changed their name from Saxe-Coburg-Gotha to Windsor
5 Star Wars, Jaws, The Exorcist, Grease, Close Encounters of the Third Kind, Superman, Smokey and the Bandit, The Godfather, Saturday Night Fever, Rocky

QUIZ 88
1 Severn
2 Colman's (mustard)
3 Panettone
4 George Lucas - he directed the first 'Star Wars: A New Hope' and the three prequels, but not 'The Empire Strikes Back' or 'The Return of the Jedi'
5 Aberdeen, Dundee, Dunfermline, Edinburgh, Glasgow, Inverness, Perth, Stirling

QUIZ 89 — 29th March

1 What is the first name of Barney Rubble's wife in 'The Flintstones'?

2 Which country was known as Hibernia by the Romans?

3 Which car rental service shares its name with a famous battle in America in 1836?

4 In a 1987 sci-fi action movie, what happens to Police Officer Alex Murphy after he is brutally murdered?

5 The Euro 2000 football tournament was jointly staged by the Netherlands and Belgium. Name any five of the eight cities which hosted games. [no knowledge of sport really required for this - just think of the cities of the Netherlands and Belgium]

QUIZ 90 — 30th March

1 In which British city is Waverley train station?

2 What are the mineral formations that drip from the ceilings of caves called?

3 What poker hand contains three cards of one number (or rank) and two of another?

4 Which Hollywood star (whose middle name is Tiffany) played Danny Zuko in the original 1973 London production of 'Grease'?

5 Name five of the seven US Vice Presidents of the 20th century who went on to become President.

QUIZ 91 — 31st March

1 Which terrifying character was played in the 1968 film version of 'Chitty Chitty Bang Bang' by ballet dancer Sir Robert Helpmann?

2 Dogs are canine, cats are feline, but what animals are vulpine?

3 Boo Radley is one of the main characters in a novel by which American author?

4 Who was the first and so far only "Bundeskanzlerin"?

5 Name five of the eight US states with the lowest population.

QUIZ 92 — 1st April

1 Who wrote the children's book 'Green Eggs and Ham'?

2 Which brothers were responsible for the films 'Duck Soup' and 'A Night at the Opera'?

3 The first four words of which Blur hit single is the title of an F. Scott Fitzgerald novel?

4 In the last series of 'Friends', which diminutive actor performed a spectacular and suggestive dance routine to Sylvester's 'You Make Me Feel (Mighty Real)'?

5 Name any five independent countries (UN Member States) whose normal English name contains a double letter. [has to be a proper double letter, within the same word. Don't put Holland]

QUIZ 89
1 Betty
2 Ireland
3 Alamo
4 He becomes RoboCop
5 Amsterdam, Rotterdam, Eindhoven, Arnhem, Brussels, Bruges, Charleroi, Liege

QUIZ 90
1 Edinburgh
2 Stalactites
3 Full House
4 Richard Gere
5 Theodore Roosevelt, Calvin Coolidge, Harry S Truman, Richard Nixon, Lyndon B Johnson, Gerald Ford, George HW Bush

QUIZ 91
1 The Child Catcher
2 Foxes
3 Harper Lee (To Kill a Mockingbird)
4 Angela Merkel (it's the feminine form of Federal Chancellor)
5 Wyoming, Vermont, North Dakota, Alaska, South Dakota, Delaware, Montana, Rhode Island.

QUIZ 92
1 Dr Seuss
2 Marx Brothers
3 Tender (Tender is the Night)
4 Danny DeVito
5 Andorra, Cameroon, Greece, Guinea-Bissau, Marshall Islands, Morocco, Philippines, Russia, Saint Kitts and Nevis, Seychelles, Sierra Leone (Greenland and the Cook Islands not full countries)

QUIZ 93 — 2nd April

1 In which country is Guantanamo Bay?

2 What is the next line of this nursery rhyme that provided the name of a classic 1970s movie: "One flew east, one flew west ..."?

3 What is the second largest shark, often seen in UK waters, but harmless to humans?

4 Who, in a famous children's story, are Tootles, Nibs, Slightly, Curtly and The Twins?

5 Name any five independent countries in the world whose name, in their normal English spelling, has the letter Y at the end.

QUIZ 94 — 3rd April

1 In different examples of song and literature, Albie, Fafnir, Norbert, Puff and Smaug are what kind of creature?

2 Which continent has the most independent countries?

3 In relation to an opera, what is the libretto?

4 Which name appears in the title of the most Shakespeare plays?

5 Four US Presidents have had surnames beginning with the letter C. Name them.

QUIZ 95 — 4th April

1 Which male grooming brand is known as Axe in France?

2 Before going on to his own chat show and a stint on Radio Norwich, which sports commentator introduced the phrases "Eat my goal!" and "Liquid football" into the English language?

3 The region of Patagonia is shared by Chile and which other country?

4 In the original 'Grand Theft Auto' game, a 'Gouranga' bonus was obtained by running over a line of members of which religious sect?

5 Give the first names of the five First Ladies of the US between 1990 and 2020. [so not including Jill Biden]

QUIZ 96 — 5th April

1 The Red Sea lies between Asia and which other continent?

2 What is the name of the property at 3764 Elvis Presley Boulevard in Memphis, Tennessee?

3 Which political party was originally formed in September 1993 from a previous party called the Anti-Federalist League?

4 Bizarrely, in 1988, Michael Jackson was the first choice to play the title character in a suggested movie version of which British TV classic?

5 Name any five of the people who have served as Secretary-General of the United Nations. [up to 2022]

QUIZ 93
1 Cuba
2 One Flew Over the Cuckoo's Nest
3 Basking shark
4 The Lost Boys (in 'Peter Pan')
5 Germany, Hungary, Italy, Norway, Turkey (allow even though now officially "The Republic of Türkiye"), Uruguay, Vatican City

QUIZ 94
1 Dragon
2 Africa (has 54, Europe has 50, Asia has 48)
3 The text used/the words
4 Henry
5 Grover Cleveland, Calvin Coolidge, Jimmy Carter, Bill Clinton

QUIZ 95
1 Lynx
2 Alan Partridge, as played by Steve Coogan
3 Argentina
4 Hare Krishna
5 Melania (Trump), Michelle (Obama), Laura (Bush), Hillary (Clinton), Barbara (Bush)

QUIZ 96
1 Africa
2 Graceland
3 UK Independence Party
4 Doctor Who
5 Antonio Guterres, Ban ki-Moon, Kofi Annan, Boutros Boutros Ghali, Javier Perez de Cuellar, U Thant, Kurt Waldheim, Dag Hammarskjöld, Trygve Lie (Gladwyn Jebb was acting S-G for a few months too)

QUIZ 97 — 6ᵗʰ April

1 In terms of area, what is larger: the Isle of Man or the Isle of Wight?

2 Who has been played on screen by Albert Finney, Christian Slater, Timothy Spall, Richard Burton, Gary Oldman and Robert Hardy, amongst others?

3 From the 16th to 19th century, the Barbary Coast was a term used to refer to the north-western part of which continent?

4 InterCity 125 was once the brand name of British Rail's High Speed rail service. What did the 125 of its name refer to?

5 Name five national capitals of independent countries whose name, in the ordinary English spelling, begins with the letter K.

QUIZ 98 — 7ᵗʰ April

1 What word can be added to Droitwich, Dorton, Boston, Woodhall and Royal Leamington to make the names of towns in England?

2 In which state is Camp David, the country retreat of the US President?

3 Whose only opera was 'Fidelio', first performed in 1805?

4 Why does the small railway station at Castle Cary in Somerset become overrun with passengers in June of most years?

5 Name five of the seven independent states of mainland Central America i.e. between Mexico and Colombia.

QUIZ 99 — 8ᵗʰ April

1 What is the largest borough of New York City by area?

2 What, in the human body, can be true, false or floating?

3 Choppers, aged 48, died in April 2016 at Twycross Zoo in Leicestershire. Choppers was the last survivor of the original cast in a series of ads for which brand?

4 In which 2015 film does Daniel Craig deliver the line, "I'll tighten those restraints, scavenger scum"?

5 Name five sovereign states whose common English name begins with I.

QUIZ 100 — 9ᵗʰ April

1 Who was the last Conservative Prime Minister of the 20th century?

2 Which sleuth was played by Angela Lansbury in the TV series 'Murder, She Wrote'?

3 In Rastafarianism, what ancient city is a word used to describe decadent Western society?

4 Which former 'Countdown' presenter held the honorary position of Mayor of the Yorkshire village of Wetwang until his death in 2005?

5 The Madonna song 'Vogue' mentions 16 different Hollywood legends, 12 of them women (either their whole name, first or surname). Name five of the women she mentions.

QUIZ 97
1 Isle of Man (221 sq miles vs Isle of Wight 148 sq miles)
2 Winston Churchill
3 Africa
4 Its top speed (in miles per hour)
5 Kabul (Afghanistan), Kampala (Uganda), Kathmandu (Nepal), Khartoum (Sudan), Kyiv (Ukraine), Kingston (Jamaica), Kingstown (St Vincent and the Grenadines), Kinshasa (DR Congo), Kuala Lumpur (Malaysia), Kuwait City (Kuwait)

QUIZ 98
1 Spa
2 Maryland
3 Ludwig van Beethoven
4 It is the nearest station to the Glastonbury festival
5 Belize, Guatemala, El Salvador, Honduras, Nicaragua, Panama, Costa Rica

QUIZ 99
1 Queens
2 Rib
3 PG Tips (Choppers was a chimp)
4 Star Wars: The Force Awakens (as Stormtrooper JB-007)
5 Iceland, India, Indonesia, Iran, Iraq, Ireland, Israel, Italy, Ivory Coast (often known as Ivory Coast though officially Cote d'Ivoire)

QUIZ 100
1 John Major
2 Jessica Fletcher
3 Babylon
4 Richard Whiteley
5 Greta Garbo, Marilyn Monroe, Marlene Dietrich, Grace Kelly, Jean Harlow, Ginger Rogers, Rita Hayworth, Lauren Bacall, Katherine Hepburn, Lana Turner, Bette Davis

QUIZ 101 — 10th April

1 Which of the four Beatles was born first?

2 In the 2008 US presidential elections, who was John McCain's running mate?

3 What A is a chemical element whose name has one letter fewer in American English compared to British English? [sulphur/sulfur would be another example, but doesn't begin with A]

4 Which actor dies in the first Pierce Brosnan Bond film, the first 'Lord of the Rings' film, and the first series of 'Game of Thrones'?

5 Name any five feature films directed by Stanley Kubrick.

QUIZ 102 — 11th April

1 What F is the name commonly given to the shanty towns of Rio de Janeiro?

2 What is the standard number of working days people in the UK are called for jury service?

3 Apart from its final scene, in what year does 'Saving Private Ryan' take place?

4 Which show written by Roy Clarke, which ended in 2010, was the longest-running sitcom in British TV history?

5 Apart from the Antarctic and the Arctic (being the top two), name five of the next eight largest deserts in the world.

QUIZ 103 — 12th April

1 Who played the title character in the 2022 film 'Cyrano'?

2 For Venus, it is 224.65 days, for Mars it's 686.98 days. What?

3 The original logo for the Apple Computer Company (as it was then) depicted which scientist sitting under a tree?

4 What name, taken from the Greek for neck, is given to a thin strip of land connecting two larger land areas?

5 Name any five of the first eight full studio albums by Madonna, not including live albums, greatest hits collections or soundtrack albums.

QUIZ 104 — 13th April

1 Which cocktail is made of vodka, cream and coffee liqueur?

2 In 'Back to the Future', who is Marty McFly's arch enemy, played by Tom Wilson?

3 What word for an overwhelming sense of fear and anxiety comes from the name of the ancient Greek shepherd god?

4 In which year did Richard Nixon resign as US President?

5 Name five of the six counties of England which have a border with one of the other countries of the United Kingdom. [meaning the traditional, ceremonial counties, rather than the recently defined administrative regions]

QUIZ 101
1 Ringo Starr
2 Sarah Palin
3 Aluminium/aluminum
4 Sean Bean
5 Fear and Desire, Killer's Kiss, The Killing, Paths of Glory, Spartacus, Lolita, Dr Strangelove, 2001: A Space Odyssey, A Clockwork Orange, Barry Lyndon, The Shining, Full Metal Jacket, Eyes Wide Shut ('AI: Artificial Intelligence' he had the idea for but didn't direct)

QUIZ 102
1 Favela
2 10 working days (it may end up being more if a trial goes on longer)
3 1944
4 Last of the Summer Wine
5 Sahara, Arabian, Gobi, Kalahari, Patagonian, Great Victoria (accept Australian), Syrian, Great Basin

QUIZ 103
1 Peter Dinklage
2 Year
3 Isaac Newton
4 Isthmus
5 Madonna, Like a Virgin, True Blue, Like a Prayer, Erotica, Bedtime Stories, Ray of Light, Music

QUIZ 104
1 White Russian
2 Biff Tannen
3 Panic (from Pan)
4 1974
5 Cumbria, Northumberland (both Scotland) Gloucestershire, Herefordshire, Shropshire, Cheshire (all Wales)

QUIZ 105 — 14th April

1 The Boer War took place on which continent?

2 In 1997 who, at 16, became the youngest ever tennis World Number 1 - either male or female?

3 In 2012, the village of Dull, in Scotland, twinned with which small town in Oregon, USA (it begins with B!)?

4 Which aristocrat, who sponsored the original written rules of boxing, made the accusation that brought about the ruination and imprisonment of Oscar Wilde?

5 Apart from Charlie Bucket, name the four other children who have a golden ticket to visit Willy Wonka's chocolate factory in the film versions of the classic Roald Dahl book.

QUIZ 106 — 15th April

1 Which city in the UK comes first in alphabetical order?

2 Which former Olympic champion led London's successful bid to host the 2012 Olympic Games?

3 Dudeism is a modern religion with over 100,000 adherents which has its basis in which cult movie from 1998?

4 Which global fast food chain is known as Hungry Jack's in Australia (its international name already having been trademarked by someone else in Australia)?

5 Name five of the seven largest urban areas (i.e. cities) in Canada by population.

QUIZ 107 — 16th April

1 Which Disney movie features the characters Rafiki, Zazu and Scar?

2 The Puy de Sancy, at 1886m, is the tallest mountain in which European range?

3 Who directly followed Nelson Mandela as President of South Africa?

4 What 2013 movie takes its name from a military term for half past midnight?

5 Name five independent states of Africa whose name begins with M.

QUIZ 108 — 17th April

1 Erik ten Hag was appointed manager of which football club in April 2022?

2 Which man of magic, born Erich Weiss, died on Halloween 1926 after his appendix ruptured?

3 In the Sherlock Holmes stories, what is the first name of Dr Watson?

4 What movie closes with the following exchange of dialogue; "Fat Man, you shoot a great game of pool" "So do you, Fast Eddie"?

5 Name five of the first seven men to be World Number 1 in men's tennis this century, starting from 2000. [these are all the Number 1s before Roger Federer]

QUIZ 105
1 Africa
2 Martina Hingis
3 Boring
4 The Marquess of Queensberry (John Sholto Douglas)
5 Mike Teavee, Veruca Salt, Violet Beauregarde, Augustus Gloop

QUIZ 106
1 Aberdeen
2 Sebastian Coe
3 The Big Lebowski
4 Burger King
5 Toronto, Montreal, Vancouver, Calgary, Edmonton, Ottawa-Gatineau, Quebec City (accept just "Ottawa")

QUIZ 107
1 The Lion King
2 Massif Central (in France)
3 Thabo Mbeki
4 Zero Dark Thirty
5 Madagascar, Malawi, Mali, Mauritania, Mauritius, Morocco, Mozambique

QUIZ 108
1 Manchester United
2 Harry Houdini
3 John
4 The Hustler
5 Andre Agassi, Pete Sampras, Marat Safin, Gustavo Kuerten, Lleyton Hewitt, Juan Carlos Ferrero, Andy Roddick

QUIZ 109 — 18th April

1 Which film role links Gerard Butler, Leslie Nielsen, Gary Oldman and Christopher Lee, amongst others?

2 What is the first square after "Go" on a London Monopoly board?

3 Which African star was the only FIFA World Footballer of the Year never to have played in a World Cup? [the award ran from 1991 to 2009]

4 The Roman province called Africa was actually almost entirely contained within which small (north African) country?

5 Name five complete operettas written by Gilbert and Sullivan. [we want their main title, not their alternative title]

QUIZ 110 — 19th April

1 Which country was known as South-West Africa until 1990?

2 From which 1980s movie does the derogatory term "bunny boiler" originate?

3 Who was Prime Minister of Great Britain during the Suez Crisis?

4 Which Hollywood legend was the United States Ambassador to Czechoslovakia from 1989 to 1992?

5 Name five feature films directed by Baz Luhrmann. [up to 2022]

QUIZ 111 — 20th April

1 The pilgrimage town of Lourdes is in the foothills of which mountain range?

2 The character Forrest Gump is from the small town of Greenbow in which US state?

3 Who was the first American woman to marry a reigning monarch?

4 The 'Indiana Jones' film franchise began with a story idea for a film written in 1973 called 'The Adventures of Indiana Smith' by whom (he would be the first film's producer)?

5 Name five independent countries that share a border with Saudi Arabia.

QUIZ 112 — 21st April

1 What four words go at the start of the titles of a 1968 spaghetti western, a 1983 gangster epic and a violent 2003 action film?

2 What did Malcolm Little replace his surname with when he became a leading figure in the Civil Rights Movement in the 1960s?

3 Which band's 'Greatest Hits 1' became the first ever album to sell 7 million copies in the UK, in July 2022?

4 On which country did King Farouk of Egypt opportunistically declare war in 1945?

5 Name five of the twelve animals that represent years in the Chinese Zodiac - one of them is a fictional creature.

QUIZ 109
1 Dracula
2 Old Kent Road
3 George Weah
4 Tunisia
5 Thespis, Trial by Jury, The Sorcerer, HMS Pinafore, Pirates of Penzance, Patience, Iolanthe, Princess Ida, The Mikado, Ruddigore, The Yeomen of the Guard, The Gondoliers, Utopia Limited, The Grand Duke

QUIZ 110
1 Namibia
2 Fatal Attraction
3 Anthony Eden
4 Shirley Temple
5 Strictly Ballroom, William Shakespeare's Romeo and Juliet, Moulin Rouge, Australia, The Great Gatsby, Elvis

QUIZ 111
1 Pyrenees
2 Alabama
3 Grace Kelly (married Prince Rainier of Monaco)
4 George Lucas
5 Iraq, Jordan, Kuwait, Qatar, Bahrain, United Arab Emirates, Oman, Yemen

QUIZ 112
1 Once Upon a Time (... in the West, ... in America, ... in Mexico)
2 X
3 Queen
4 Germany
5 Rat, Ox, Tiger, Rabbit, Dragon, Snake, Horse, Goat, Monkey, Rooster, Dog, and Pig

QUIZ 113 — 22nd April

1 What colour lightsaber does Darth Vader use in the original 'Star Wars' films?

2 In which city was a Mutual Defence treaty of eight Communist states signed in May 1955?

3 What aniseed-flavoured aperitif was invented by monks living on Mount Athos in medieval times?

4 Which footballer played for a British club team which went unbeaten throughout the 2003-04 league season and another British club team which went unbeaten through the 2016-17 league season?

5 Name the UK Prime Ministers who have served more than one term since the start of the Second World War. [it does not have to be two full terms, just more than five years, whether in one or two separate periods]

QUIZ 114 — 23rd April

1 In which continent is the Kalahari desert?

2 A popular catchphrase from 'The Tonight Show Starring Johnny Carson' became an iconic line in which horror movie?

3 What is the name of the massive earthwork, thought to date from the 8th century, which runs on, or close to, the border between England and Wales?

4 The movie 'Saving Mr Banks' is about the creation of which classic film?

5 Name the five EU Member States that have a flag with vertical stripes of three different colours.

QUIZ 115 — 24th April

1 Munster and Leinster are provinces of which country?

2 Dia de los Muertos is a Mexican holiday which takes place on November 1st each year. What does 'Dia de los Muertos' mean?

3 In ancient times, Mesopotamia was the area between which two rivers in the Middle East?

4 Which is the only one of Disney's "Seven Dwarfs" whose name contains a repeated consonant?

5 Name any five Top 5 UK chart hits from Madness. [they had ten]

QUIZ 116 — 25th April

1 Before the Euro what was the currency in Greece?

2 Which actor might you remember from movies such as 'They Came to Burgle Carnegie Hall', 'The President's Neck is Missing' and 'The Greatest Story Ever Hula'ed', as well as the stage show 'Stop the Planet of the Apes, I Want to Get Off!'?

3 At the 1990 men's FIFA World Cup, Costa Rica managed to qualify from the group stages, ahead of which British team?

4 What links the character played by Gemma Arterton in 'Quantum of Solace' to the character played by Kate Hudson in 'Almost Famous'?

5 Name five cities in the UK with names of five letters or fewer. [can be England, Northern Ireland, Scotland or Wales]

QUIZ 113

1 Red
2 Warsaw
3 Ouzo
4 Kolo Touré (Arsenal and then Celtic)
5 Winston Churchill, Clement Attlee, Harold Macmillan, Harold Wilson, Margaret Thatcher, John Major, Tony Blair, David Cameron (Churchill, Attlee, Macmillan, Wilson and Major did not serve two full terms, but more than one)

QUIZ 114

1 Africa
2 The Shining (Here's Johnny!)
3 Offa's Dyke
4 Mary Poppins
5 Italy, France, Belgium, Ireland, Romania. [At time of publication, Moldova is an applicant for membership. Allow, if its application has been successful]

QUIZ 115

1 Republic of Ireland
2 Day of the Dead
3 Tigris and Euphrates
4 Happy
5 My Girl (3), Baggy Trousers (3), Embarrassment (4), Grey Day (4), It Must Be Love (4), House of Fun (1), Driving in my Car (4), Our House (5), Wings of a Dove (2), The Sun and the Rain (5). One Step Beyond was only a number 7.

QUIZ 116

1 Drachma
2 Troy McClure (from 'The Simpsons')
3 Scotland
4 Beatles songs (Strawberry Fields and Penny Lane)
5 Bath, Derby, Ely, Leeds, Ripon, Truro, Wells, York, Perth, Derry (aka Londonderry), Newry

QUIZ 117 — 26th April

1 What does the C stand for in CIA?

2 What name did Octavian take on becoming Emperor of Rome?

3 In the 1978 movie 'The Wiz', the African-American retelling of 'The Wizard of Oz', Diana Ross played Dorothy and Richard Pryor played the Wizard. Who played the Scarecrow?

4 The main character of which TV comedy was a slave called Lurcio?

5 Name the four US states whose name ends with the letter E.

QUIZ 118 — 27th April

1 What is the smallest independent nation bordering France, in terms of population?

2 Who killed the Scottish nobleman John "The Red" Comyn at a church in Dumfries on February 10th 1306?

3 Which member of a great double act used to send in sketches for his own show under the pseudonym Gerald Wiley?

4 Which video artist won the Turner Prize in 1999, 15 years before a work of his won an even more famous prize?

5 Four of the ceremonial counties of England end with the letter T. Name them.

QUIZ 119 — 28th April

1 Lauryn Hill was the lead singer of which hip-hop band?

2 The name of which independent Pacific state was preceded by "Western" until 1997?

3 Who was the first man to win three Oscars for Best Actor in a Leading Role?

4 Born in 1945, what is the name of the only woman to have been First Lady of two separate republics?

5 Name five of the first seven novels for adults written by Dan Brown.

QUIZ 120 — 29th April

1 On what continent is the Mojave Desert?

2 There is a city in south-eastern Turkey/Türkiye which shares its name with which superhero, who has been played by Adam West and George Clooney, amongst others?

3 What hit British movie from 2013 ends with a shoot-out on Cromer Pier?

4 Which brand of collectible stickers had to be modified after being sued by the makers of Cabbage Patch Kids for Trademark infringement in 1986?

5 Name five of the seven songs in the 20th century which spent ten weeks or more at top of the UK singles charts. The weeks don't have to be consecutive, but it does have to be the same version by the same artist.

QUIZ 117

1 Central (not Crime or Continental)
2 Augustus (Caesar)
3 Michael Jackson
4 Up Pompeii!
5 Delaware, Maine, New Hampshire, Tennessee

QUIZ 118

1 Monaco
2 Robert the Bruce
3 Ronnie Barker
4 Steve McQueen (went on to direct '12 Years a Slave' which won the Best Picture Oscar)
5 Dorset, Isle of Wight, Kent, Somerset

QUIZ 119

1 The Fugees
2 Samoa
3 Daniel Day-Lewis
4 Graça Machel (Mozambique and South Africa)
5 Digital Fortress, Deception Point, Angels and Demons, The Da Vinci Code, The Lost Symbol, Inferno, Origin (He wrote an illustrated children's book in 2020 called 'Wild Symphony')

QUIZ 120

1 North America
2 Batman
3 Alan Partridge: Alpha Papa
4 Garbage Pail Kids
5 I Believe (Frankie Laine), Everything I Do I Do it For You (Bryan Adams), Love is All Around (Wet Wet Wet), Bohemian Rhapsody (Queen), Rose Marie (Slim Whitman), Cara Mia (David Whitfield), I Will Always Love You (Whitney Houston)

QUIZ 121 — 30th April

1 Which actor links the roles of Khan Noonien Singh, Julian Assange, Sherlock Holmes and Smaug the Dragon?

2 In which country was media mogul Rupert Murdoch born?

3 Which leader of a failed rebellion in Britain was born in Rome in 1720 and died in Rome in 1788?

4 Despite being written by Irish playwrights, Oscar Wilde and Samuel Beckett respectively, what links the original written versions of the plays 'Salome' and 'Waiting for Godot'?

5 Besides Portugal, there are eight countries or territories where Portuguese is an official language. Name five of them. [despite its significant presence in Goa, India is not one of them; one of them is a territory not an independent country per se]

QUIZ 122 — 1st May

1 In an 1831 novel, which city's cathedral was home to the bellringer Quasimodo?

2 Dr Julius No, in the film 'Dr No', was, rather surprisingly, the first person to utter which timeless three-word phrase in a James Bond film?

3 Highclere Castle is a country house south of Newbury, with grounds designed by Lancelot "Capability" Brown. In what capacity did it start appearing on British television in 2010?

4 The Reverend and Right Honourable Lord Bannside died in September 2014. How was he better known?

5 Dustin Hoffman has been nominated for an acting Oscar seven times. Name five of the films for which he has been nominated.

QUIZ 123 — 2nd May

1 In German, if "Landschildkröte" is the word for a tortoise what does "Schildkröte" mean?

2 What is the nine-letter French word for a restaurant's wine specialist?

3 Which country became the 4th to successfully send a satellite into orbit around Mars in September 2014?

4 Which Jane Austen novel contains all five vowels in the title?

5 Name any five of the six colours on the flag of South Africa.

QUIZ 124 — 3rd May

1 In the famous advertising slogan, 'Beans Means ...' what brand?

2 Which TV character served in several military campaigns, including the Gordon Relief Expedition to the Sudan, the Boer War and the First World War, though is best known for his voluntary service in World War II and his advice for people to stay calm?

3 The Romans referred to the Mediterranean as "Mare Nostrum" - what does that mean?

4 The father of which Hollywood star, who has appeared in movies such as 'Natural Born Killers' and 'Zombieland', was himself a contract killer?

5 Name the five Conservative Chancellors of the Exchequer between 1979 and 1997.

QUIZ 121
1 Benedict Cumberbatch
2 Australia
3 Bonnie Prince Charlie (Charles Edward Stuart)
4 They were written in French (both authors would later translate them to English)
5 Angola, Brazil, Guinea-Bissau, Mozambique, Cape Verde, Sao Tome and Principe, Timor-Leste, Macau (Chinese territory)

QUIZ 122
1 Paris
2 Shaken not stirred
3 It is Downton Abbey
4 Ian Paisley
5 The Graduate, Midnight Cowboy, Lenny, Kramer vs Kramer (won), Tootsie, Rain Man (won), Wag the Dog

QUIZ 123
1 Turtle (so a tortoise is a "land turtle")
2 Sommelier
3 India (it was called Mangalyaan)
4 Persuasion
5 Black, Gold (yellow), Red, Green, Blue, White

QUIZ 124
1 Heinz
2 Lance-Corporal Jones (from 'Dad's Army')
3 Our sea
4 Woody Harrelson
5 Geoffrey Howe, Nigel Lawson, John Major, Norman Lamont, Kenneth Clarke

QUIZ 125 — 4ᵗʰ May

1 Who died first - Romeo or Juliet?

2 What regnal number for English or British monarchs links the years 1399-1413, 1461-1470, 1471-1483, 1820-1830 and 1830-1837?

3 What word, meaning "mother city" is a classic 1927 film directed by Fritz Lang as well as being a fictional city referred to as "The Big Apricot"?

4 Which TV show's last episode's last line, broadcast in July 1993 and spoken by Marcus Tandy, was "You can't trust anyone these days, can you?" (a thinly veiled reference to the BBC axing the show)?

5 Name five of the actors who played 'The Magnificent Seven' in the 1960 western.

QUIZ 126 — 5ᵗʰ May

1 Popeye the Sailor has tattoos of what on his forearms?

2 The Gatwick Express runs from which London railway station?

3 In the original Band Aid version of 'Do They Know It's Christmas', who sings their own stage name in the section they sing solo?

4 After the opening of a cafe in an upmarket New York store in November 2017, it was finally possible for the title of which classic 1961 film to be enacted?

5 Either as a solo artist or in collaboration, name the five David Bowie UK Number 1 singles.

QUIZ 127 — 6ᵗʰ May

1 Jordan Belfort is the title character of which Oscar-nominated 2014 movie?

2 What is the most common last letter of a US state name?

3 Which worldwide organisation has the motto 'Blood and Fire' displayed on the star in the middle of its flag?

4 In a 1976 movie, Sean Connery and Audrey Hepburn played which legendary couple in their later years?

5 Name the five countries to host the men's FIFA World Cup twice.

QUIZ 128 — 7ᵗʰ May

1 The book 'Watership Down' tells the tale of what type of intrepid animals?

2 The first issue of which music magazine was published in November 1978 with Blondie on the cover?

3 Which West African country has a name that reflects the fact that it was set up by previously enslaved people from the USA, and a capital named after an American President?

4 How many of Disney's Seven Dwarfs have a name that also happens to be an allowable word in Scrabble? [this is according to either the UK or US official Scrabble dictionary]

5 Name the top five US states in terms of area.

QUIZ 125
1 Romeo
2 IV (Fourth, Edward IV had two separate reigns)
3 Metropolis
4 Eldorado
5 Yul Brynner, Steve McQueen, Charles Bronson, Robert Vaughn, James Coburn, Brad Dexter, Horst Buchholz

QUIZ 126
1 Anchors
2 Victoria
3 Sting ("And the only water flowing is the bitter sting of tears")
4 Breakfast at Tiffany's
5 Space Oddity, Ashes to Ashes, Under Pressure (with Queen), Let's Dance, Dancing in the Street (with Mick Jagger)

QUIZ 127
1 The Wolf of Wall Street
2 A
3 Salvation Army
4 Robin Hood and Maid Marian (in 'Robin and Marian')
5 Italy (1934, 1990), France (1938, 1998), Mexico (1970, 1986), Brazil (1950, 2014), West Germany/Germany (1974/2006) (In 2026, USA will be added to list)

QUIZ 128
1 Rabbits
2 Smash Hits
3 Liberia (capital is Monrovia)
4 All seven
5 Alaska, Texas, California, Montana, New Mexico

QUIZ 129 — 8th May

1 In which month does the Edinburgh Festival mainly take place?

2 In which country would you find the majority of the Drakensberg mountain range?

3 What honour, in 1901, links Wilhelm Röntgen, Jacobus Henricus Van 't Hoff, Emil von Behring, Sally Prudhomme and Henry Dunant and Frédéric Passy?

4 In the film 'Apocalypse Now', what are Colonel Kurtz's final four words?

5 What are the first five independent countries in alphabetical order on the continent of South America? [ordinary English spelling]

QUIZ 130 — 9th May

1 In which century did India and Sri Lanka become independent?

2 Which of the three literary Brontë sisters lived longest?

3 The man who became Pope in 2013 named himself after which medieval saint?

4 Which actor, in 2014 and 2015, received an acting Oscar nomination for different movies which had the same first word in the title?

5 Name the five of the 12 Major Olympian Gods of Greek mythology whose names begin with the letter A. [so these are the Greek names, not Roman]

QUIZ 131 — 10th May

1 How is the German Shepherd dog also known in the UK?

2 What surname links acclaimed film directors called Lindsay, Paul Thomas and Wes?

3 What two-word phrase did Gwyneth Paltrow famously use to describe her split from Coldplay singer Chris Martin in a statement released in March 2014?

4 Which Oscar-winning film featured several important scenes set at the Colombes Olympic Stadium in Paris (but filmed at The Oval Sports Centre on Merseyside)?

5 Name five of the nine tennis players, including both men and women, who have won the most Grand Slam singles titles in history.

QUIZ 132 — 11th May

1 The epic book 'The Iliad' is set around which ancient city?

2 Which famous author's pen name was Boz?

3 In which film would you hear the songs 'Fat Sam's Grand Slam' and 'So You Wanna Be a Boxer'?

4 What is the regnal name of the man who became the King of Spain in 2014?

5 Name five actors, apart from Daniel Craig, who have been in at least three of the five Daniel Craig Bond films.

QUIZ 129
1 August
2 South Africa
3 They were the first winners of Nobel Prizes
4 The horror, the horror
5 Argentina, Bolivia, Brazil, Chile, Colombia

QUIZ 130
1 20th Century
2 Charlotte (the oldest, lived till she was 39, Emily to 30, Anne to 29)
3 St Francis of Assisi
4 Bradley Cooper (American Hustle and American Sniper)
5 Aphrodite, Apollo, Artemis, Ares, Athena

QUIZ 131
1 Alsatian
2 Anderson
3 Conscious Uncoupling
4 Chariots of Fire
5 Margaret Court, Serena Williams, Steffi Graf, Helen Wills Moody, Martina Navratilova, Chris Evert, Novak Djokovic, Roger Federer, Rafael Nadal

QUIZ 132
1 Troy
2 Charles Dickens
3 Bugsy Malone
4 Felipe VI
5 Judi Dench, Naomie Harris, Jeffrey Wright, Rory Kinnear, Ben Whishaw, Ralph Fiennes, Jesper Christensen, Michael G Wilson (in various cameos)

QUIZ 133 — 12th May

1 Who did Will Smith slap at the 2022 Oscars?

2 What middle initial links the writers of 'The Wasteland', 'Possession' and 'Prince Caspian'?

3 What C is both the name of a fictional Denver family and also that of Manchester United's training ground?

4 Derived from a famous line in Marlowe's 'Faustus', what M is a unit coined by author Isaac Asimov to mean the amount of beauty that it would take to launch one ship?

5 Name five of the six largest Canary Islands, in terms of area.

QUIZ 134 — 13th May

1 Which is greater - A) the width of Russia or B) The diameter of the moon?

2 The 2002 Oscar-nominated movie 'City of God' is named after a district of which city, in which it is set?

3 Who wrote the novels 'Jamaica Inn' and 'Rebecca'?

4 What term, usually associated with illicit alcohol in Prohibition Era America or with the illegal distribution of recordings of live music, is derived from the tendency of 19th century smugglers to hide contraband in their footwear?

5 Name five US state capitals that begin with a vowel.

QUIZ 135 — 14th May

1 What do you get when you add up the numbers on opposite sides of a six-sided dice?

2 In the play, who kills Hamlet?

3 Adam's Bridge is the name of a natural chain of underwater shoals, sandbanks and small islands which connects the 18 or so miles between which two Asian countries?

4 What name is shared by a 1979 Pink Floyd album and a feature on Facebook that in 2011 was rebranded as "Timeline"?

5 Name any four of the bells that feature in the song 'Oranges and Lemons'.

QUIZ 136 — 15th May

1 In Scotland, what is a haar?

2 Which English county's motto is 'Invicta'?

3 In 1986, a band with a name that is a city had a UK Number 1, and then were succeeded at Number 1 by a band whose name is the continent in which you'd find that city. Name the two songs involved.

4 Which D was the surname of the man hired by Massachusetts's Amherst College to organise their library in 1874?

5 Name five of the ten acts that spent the most total weeks on the UK singles chart in the 1990s.

QUIZ 133

1 Chris Rock
2 S (TS Eliot, AS Byatt, CS Lewis)
3 Carrington - as in 'Dynasty'
4 Millihelen
5 Tenerife, Fuerteventura, Gran Canaria, Lanzarote, La Palma, La Gomera

QUIZ 134

1 A - (Russia is 2,415.69 miles/3,887.67 km, the moon is 2,159 miles/3,474.8 km)
2 Rio de Janeiro
3 Daphne Du Maurier
4 Bootlegging
5 Albany, Annapolis, Atlanta, Augusta, Austin, Indianapolis, Oklahoma City, Olympia

QUIZ 135

1 Seven
2 Laertes (son of Polonius, brother of Ophelia)
3 India and Sri Lanka
4 The Wall
5 St Clements, St. Martin's, Old Bailey, Shoreditch, Stepney, Bow

QUIZ 136

1 Fog/sea mist
2 Kent
3 Take My Breath Away (Berlin) and The Final Countdown (Europe)
4 Dewey (Melvil Dewey, who developed the Dewey decimal system whilst working at Amherst)
5 Oasis, Madonna, Mariah Carey, Celine Dion, Boyzone, Janet Jackson, Michael Jackson, East 17, Whitney Houston, Bryan Adams

QUIZ 137 — 16th May

1 What do the letters P&L stand for when referring to a company's financial accounts?

2 What is the name given to the Royal House that ruled England from 1154 to 1399?

3 What award-winning movie has the alternative title 'The Unexpected Virtue of Ignorance'?

4 Why might an iatrophobe find it particularly difficult to be cured?

5 What are the only four UN Member States that are entirely south of the Tropic of Capricorn?

QUIZ 138 — 17th May

1 Which once ubiquitous internet browser was retired after 27 years of existence in 2022?

2 In which European City is the Atomium?

3 Which video game series has been set in the fictional Liberty City and Vice City?

4 Lascaux in France and Kakadu National Park in Australia are famous for what kind of ancient art?

5 Name five completed novels by the American detective novelist Raymond Chandler.

QUIZ 139 — 18th May

1 What is the first letter of the alphabet which is not the first letter of a US state?

2 According to most historical accounts and the famous opera by Rossini, which country was William Tell from?

3 There is a single blue plaque in the City of London. It says "Author lived here" and it is situated at Gough Square, at a house now named after its famous resident. Who is it?

4 What, on a train or aeroplane, is an antimacassar?

5 Name five of the eight countries which originally signed up, in 1955, to the Warsaw Pact. We need the names of the countries, in English, as they were then.

QUIZ 140 — 19th May

1 Traditionally, in what language are instructions on a musical score?

2 What Z is the secret identity of Don Diego de la Vega?

3 Which inventor, also associated with model trains, created the construction toy Meccano?

4 What five-letter word features in the title of a 1956 Elvis Presley hit, a Sherlock Holmes novel from 1902 and a Disney film from 1981?

5 Name five chemical elements whose name begins with the letter A.

QUIZ 137
1 Profit and Loss
2 Plantagenet
3 Birdman
4 It is a fear of doctors
5 Uruguay, New Zealand, Eswatini, Lesotho [South Africa nearly, but not quite]

QUIZ 138
1 Internet Explorer
2 Brussels
3 Grand Theft Auto
4 Cave Paintings
5 The Big Sleep, Farewell My Lovely, The High Window, The Lady in the Lake, The Little Sister, The Long Goodbye, Playback

QUIZ 139
1 B
2 Switzerland
3 Samuel Johnson
4 The small papery cloth on the headrests (to prevent soiling of the fabric: originally to protect them from macassar oil, used as a hair treatment in 19th century)
5 Albania (who later withdrew), Bulgaria, Czechoslovakia, East Germany, Hungary, Poland, Romania, Soviet Union

QUIZ 140
1 Italian
2 Zorro
3 Frank Hornby
4 Hound (Hound Dog, The Hound of the Baskervilles, The Fox and the Hound)
5 Aluminium, Argon, Antimony, Astatine, Arsenic, Americium, Actinium

QUIZ 141 — 20th May

1 The International Standards Organisation's four-page document, ISO 3103, clearly defines the proper way to make a cup of tea. It states the correct brewing time, proportion of milk, the material of the teacup and more. Does it state that milk should go in A) First or B) Last?

2 Whom did Angela Merkel succeed as Chancellor of Germany?

3 What TV show's first series, from 2010, was watched by an average of 2.8 million viewers and won by Edd Kimber?

4 What was the title of Thomas More's 1516 work about an idealised fictional island state?

5 Name five US states that have a border with Canada.

QUIZ 142 — 21st May

1 Which Chinese game is played with 144 tiles carrying various symbols and characters?

2 Which of the four Gospels of the New Testament gives the most prominent account of the Nativity (accounting for around 10% of the whole book's text)?

3 In which TV drama is the lead character known at different times as Jack Linden, Thomas Quince and Andrew Birch?

4 In what year did riots erupt across Great Britain following the shooting by the police of Mark Duggan?

5 Name five countries which border Austria.

QUIZ 143 — 22nd May

1 Who have had more UK Number 1 hit singles A) Take That or B) The Spice Girls?

2 Which former President of Egypt died in February 2020?

3 Where in the British Isles would you find the House of Keys?

4 On an episode of 'Friends', which former pop star presents the gameshow 'Pyramid' on which Joey Tribbiani competes?

5 Name five English cities that begin with the letter S.

QUIZ 144 — 23rd May

1 Which country has a larger population A) Czech Republic/Czechia or B) Slovakia?

2 What B, which originally meant the leading sheep in a flock, has come to mean something that indicates a trend, particularly in a political context?

3 Victoria Wood was married for many years to which TV magician?

4 How is 28th April known, in commemoration of a politician who posted his own name as a tweet on this day in 2011?

5 Including any that may still be alive, name five of the six US Presidents who have lived to be over 90.

QUIZ 141
1 First
2 Gerhard Schroder
3 The Great British Bake Off
4 Utopia
5 Washington, Idaho, Montana, North Dakota, Minnesota, Michigan, New York, Vermont, New Hampshire, Maine, Alaska

QUIZ 142
1 Mah jong
2 Luke (about three times more than Matthew, while Mark and John don't mention it at all)
3 The Night Manager (Jonathan Pine, as played by Tom Hiddleston)
4 2011
5 Germany, Czech Republic/Czechia, Slovakia, Hungary, Slovenia, Italy, Switzerland, Liechtenstein

QUIZ 143
1 A) Take That (12 up to 2022, compared to nine)
2 Hosni Mubarak
3 Isle of Man (it's the lower house of their Parliament)
4 Donny Osmond
5 Salford, Salisbury, Sheffield, Southampton, Sunderland, St Albans, Stoke-on-Trent, Southend-on-Sea

QUIZ 144
1 A) Czech Republic/Czechia
2 Bellwether
3 Geoffrey Durham aka The Great Soprendo
4 Ed Balls Day
5 John Adams, Herbert Hoover, Gerald Ford, Jimmy Carter, Ronald Reagan, George HW Bush

QUIZ 145 — 24th May

1 Is the duck-billed platypus A) a herbivore or B) a carnivore?

2 Which word is on the license plate of the taxi that Will gets from the airport in the title sequence of the original 'The Fresh Prince of Bel Air'?

3 How is Antonin Dvorak's 9th Symphony popularly known?

4 Which future superstar played drums in a band called The Breakfast Club in the early 1980s?

5 Name the five independent countries in the world, other than the UK or USA, whose common English name begins with the letter U. [we'll not allow United Mexican States or United Republic of Tanzania, as they are officially known, as that's not the common English name]

QUIZ 146 — 25th May

1 In which US city are the films 'Mystic River', 'Gone Baby Gone' and 'The Departed' set?

2 The BBFC is an organisation that rates films based on their suitability to specific audiences. What does the organisation PEGI classify in a similar way?

3 Which UK newspaper has a picture of a clock on the editorial page set at half past four?

4 Who played the part of holiday camp owner Joe Maplin in 'Hi-de-Hi!'?

5 Name five official James Bond films whose titles mention living, dying or killing.

QUIZ 147 — 26th May

1 What city in Northern England is home to the second most senior figure in the Church of England?

2 What, in French, is "framboise"?

3 General Sherman, a huge tree in California, is of what specific species?

4 Which hit play, first staged in 2011, was adapted from the 18th century Italian play 'Servant of Two Masters'?

5 As of 2022, what are the five largest EU member states, in terms of area? [At time of print, Ukraine is an applicant. This question does not include Ukraine.]

QUIZ 148 — 27th May

1 What was the name of the Octopus that successfully predicted several results in the 2010 FIFA World Cup?

2 The Kurgan, played by Clancy Brown, is a character in which movie?

3 Which acclaimed American show created by Matthew Weiner won the Primetime Emmy for Outstanding Drama Series every year from 2008 to 2011?

4 What word links a German company known for household appliances and a medieval painter known for fantastical, macabre imagery?

5 Apart from London, name five official cities in England with names beginning with L.

QUIZ 145
1 B - Carnivore
2 FRESH
3 From the New World/ New World Symphony
4 Madonna
5 Uganda, Ukraine, United Arab Emirates (UAE), Uruguay, Uzbekistan

QUIZ 146
1 Boston
2 Video games
3 The Times
4 Nobody (never seen on screen)
5 You Only Live Twice, Live and Let Die, A View to a Kill, The Living Daylights, Licence to Kill, Tomorrow Never Dies, Die Another Day, No Time to Die

QUIZ 147
1 York
2 Raspberry
3 Giant sequoia
4 One Man, Two Guvnors
5 France, Spain, Sweden, Germany, Finland

QUIZ 148
1 Paul
2 Highlander
3 Mad Men
4 Bosch (Hieronymus Bosch)
5 Leeds, Lichfield, Liverpool, Leicester, Lincoln, Lancaster

QUIZ 149 — 28th May

1 Strasbourg is on the border of France and which other country?

2 Kir Royal is a cocktail which contains champagne and what else?

3 Which film, released in the UK in 1985, featured detectives Rosewood and Taggart in supporting roles?

4 In Monty Python's 'The Meaning of Life', what food item causes the obese Mr Creosote to explode?

5 Name the first five captains to have lifted the men's FIFA World Cup this century. [so, not including 2022 or later]

QUIZ 150 — 29th May

1 What does a farrier make?

2 What hotel in New York is the place where Arthur C Clarke wrote '2001: A Space Odyssey', where Jack Kerouac wrote 'On the Road' and where Dylan Thomas was staying when he died?

3 What is the name of the strait formerly known as the Hellespont, which links the Sea of Marmara to the Aegean Sea?

4 What was the pseudonym used by research scientist Brooke Magnanti to publish her sensational diaries in the early 2000s?

5 Name five English cities that begin with the letter W.

QUIZ 151 — 30th May

1 An imprint of Penguin, what is the largest publisher of children's books in the UK?

2 Who was the notorious ruler of Wallachia, a region of Romania, from 1456 to 1462?

3 Which two-word phrase does Leonardo DiCaprio's title character say 51 times in the 2013 film 'The Great Gatsby'?

4 Who was President of the Democratic Republic of Vietnam from 1945 to 1969?

5 Name five of the first eight American winners of the Nobel Prize for Literature (allowing anyone who had American nationality). The last of the first eight was in 1976.

QUIZ 152 — 31st May

1 Which supervillain has been played by John Shea, Michael Rosenbaum, Gene Hackman and Jesse Eisenberg, amongst others?

2 Which east coast US city is served by Logan International Airport?

3 In the cartoon 'ThunderCats', what is the name of the weapon that contains the Eye of Thundera?

4 Not including the non-scoring outside area, how many segments are there on a dartboard?

5 Four of Henry VIII's wives died before him - one point for each.

QUIZ 149
1 Germany
2 Crème de cassis (blackcurrant liqueur)
3 Beverly Hills Cop
4 A wafer-thin mint
5 Cafu, Fabio Cannavaro, Iker Casillas, Phillip Lahm, Hugo Lloris

QUIZ 150
1 Horse shoes
2 Hotel Chelsea
3 Dardanelles
4 Belle de Jour
5 Worcester, Winchester, Wakefield, Wells, Wolverhampton, Westminster

QUIZ 151
1 Puffin
2 Vlad the Impaler/Vlad III/Vlad Dracula
3 Old sport
4 Ho Chi Minh
5 Sinclair Lewis, Eugene O'Neill, Pearl S Buck, TS Eliot, William Faulkner, Ernest Hemingway, John Steinbeck, Saul Bellow

QUIZ 152
1 Lex Luthor
2 Boston
3 Sword of Omens
4 82 (20 trebles, 20 doubles, two sets of 20 singles, 25, bull)
5 Catherine of Aragon, Anne Boleyn, Jane Seymour, Catherine Howard

QUIZ 153 — 1st June

1 What goes with "Harris" in the name of the largest island of the Outer Hebrides?

2 Who was the last Anglo-Saxon king of England?

3 What celebrity magazine was first published in the UK in 1988, though its Spanish equivalent was first published in 1944?

4 In Rudyard Kipling's 'The Jungle Book', which mongoose does battle with the cobras Nag and Nagaina?

5 Apart from London, name five counties the Thames borders or flows through.

QUIZ 154 — 2nd June

1 The Whispering Gallery is a famous part of which London cathedral?

2 What does "Las Vegas" mean in English?

3 Which French impressionist's most famous work is translated into English as 'The Luncheon on the Grass'?

4 'I Can't Sing' was a short-lived 2014 musical based on which TV show?

5 Apart from the UK (and not including Antarctica), name five independent countries the Greenwich Meridian passes through.

QUIZ 155 — 3rd June

1 Sandbanks is a small peninsula, known for its high property value, in which English county?

2 A Hindi word for "rule", how is the period in India between 1858 and 1947 commonly known?

3 The Frenchman Charles Perrault is best known for the 1697 work 'Histoires ou contes du temps passé', which is one of the earliest collections of what genre?

4 This famous section of commentary from 1991 accompanies a goal by whom? "Oh, I say! Brilliant! That is Schoolboy's Own stuff. Oh, I bet even he can't believe it. Is there anything left from this man to surprise us? That was one of the finest free-kicks this stadium has ever seen."

5 Originally chosen for the difficulty of hunting them on foot but now more associated with conservation efforts, what are the so-called "Big Five" African game animals?

QUIZ 156 — 4th June

1 In which English county would you find the Forest of Dean?

2 Which classic 70s sitcom popularised the words "naff" and "scrote" and introduced the word "nerk" into the English language?

3 What was the name of the collective of musicians and entertainers, including Billy Bragg, Paul Weller, Lenny Henry and Ben Elton, which tried to drum up support for the Labour Party in the run-up to the 1987 General Election?

4 Which Shakespeare character, who kills the title character, was "from his mother's womb/untimely ripped"?

5 Name five US states that touch any one of the Great Lakes.

QUIZ 153
1 Lewis
2 Harold
3 Hello!
4 Rikki-Tikki-Tavi
5 Gloucestershire, Wiltshire, Oxfordshire, Berkshire, Buckinghamshire, Surrey, Essex, Kent

QUIZ 154
1 St Paul's Cathedral
2 The Meadows
3 Édouard Manet (Le déjeuner sur l'herbe)
4 The X Factor
5 France, Spain, Algeria, Mali, Burkina Faso, Togo, Ghana

QUIZ 155
1 Dorset
2 The Raj
3 Fairy tales
4 Paul Gascoigne (vs Arsenal in 1991 FA Cup semi-final) (Commentary by Barry Davies)
5 Elephant, Lion, (Cape) Buffalo, Leopard, Rhinoceros

QUIZ 156
1 Gloucestershire
2 Porridge
3 Red Wedge
4 Macduff
5 Minnesota, Wisconsin, Illinois, Indiana, Michigan, Ohio, Pennsylvania, New York

QUIZ 157 — 5th June

1 Who wrote the epic nonsense poem 'The Hunting of the Snark'?

2 In which country was the Buena Vista Social Club which gave its name to a hit album and movie?

3 In the classic arcade game 'Pac-Man', what chase Pac-Man through the maze?

4 What name links the director of 'Rogue One: A Star Wars Story' with a Welsh scrum-half often cited as one of the greatest rugby union players of all time?

5 Name Wham!'s five UK Number 1 singles. This is up to the end of 2021.

QUIZ 158 — 6th June

1 What handheld video game device was first released in Japan on 21 April 1989 and in Europe on September 28, 1990?

2 Which disease was historically known as hydrophobia, due to one of the symptoms being an aversion to water?

3 What S is the surname of the villain in the 1895 novel 'Trilby', a manipulative, evil man who turns an innocent girl into a singing star?

4 If proper nouns were allowed in Scrabble, which country with a one-word name (in English) would score the most points? [not taking into account the squares the tiles would be placed on]

5 Name five independent countries the equator passes through.

QUIZ 159 — 7th June

1 Who is the arch-enemy of Yogi Bear?

2 Before Elizabeth II, how many previous monarchs of Great Britain (or of England before that) had reached the age of 90?

3 William Simmonite, Cyril Blamire and Norman Clegg were the original trio at the heart of which British sitcom?

4 Which popular hit song is written as an apology to the mother of the mother of the artist's child (who happens to be the singer Erykah Badu)?

5 Name five chemical elements whose name begins with the letter B.

QUIZ 160 — 8th June

1 What word is in the rap names of Tracy Marrow, O'Shea Jackson and Robert Van Winkle?

2 In urban planning, what colour goes before "field" to describe land previously used for industrial purposes?

3 What is the only country to border both the Caspian Sea and the Persian Gulf?

4 Which regional items of clothing have a name meaning "leather breaches"?

5 Name five countries which have land north of the Arctic Circle.

QUIZ 161 — 9th June

1 In which US city are the headquarters of Coca-Cola?

2 Which Irish county, nicknamed "The Rebel County", contains Ireland's second largest city and has one of the largest natural harbours in the world?

3 In the history of English and British monarchs, the longest uninterrupted stretch of the monarch having the same name was 116 years - what was the name?

4 What celestial object was discovered independently by two different people on 23rd July 1995 and then visible to the naked eye for 18 months?

5 Name five US state capitals that begin with the letter S.

QUIZ 162 — 10th June

1 The Aswan High Dam is on which river?

2 In which month does the Last Night of the Proms (almost always) take place?

3 What, in 1968, became the first rock album to win Album of the Year at the Grammys?

4 What was the famous three-word headline of The Sun newspaper on 11 January 1979, in reference to Prime Minister James Callaghan's denial of there being mounting problems in the UK?

5 In the Old Testament of the King James Bible, there are six books with names beginning with J. Name five of them.

QUIZ 163 — 11th June

1 In which decade did the Suez Crisis take place?

2 The first line to which 2000 film was, "What came first, the music or the misery"?

3 The Chinese musician Lang Lang is famous for playing which musical instrument?

4 Which author, who won the Nobel Prize for Literature in 1953, wrote 'Stemming the Tide', 'The World Crisis' and 'A History of the English-Speaking Peoples', among many other works?

5 Apart from the UK and the US, which countries are in the G7?

QUIZ 164 — 12th June

1 After whom was Madeira's International Airport renamed in 2017?

2 What stands on a hill near the small town of Birtley, overlooking the A1 and A167, on the site of the baths of a former colliery?

3 In September 2017, Bill Gates admitted he regretted not making which keyboard instruction simpler?

4 Goldie Wilson went from working in a cafe in the 1950s to being the first Black mayor of which small town decades later?

5 Name five independent countries which have a land border with South Africa.

QUIZ 161
1 Atlanta
2 Cork
3 George
4 Hale-Bopp Comet
5 Sacramento, Saint Paul, Salem, Santa Fe, Salt Lake City, Springfield

QUIZ 162
1 Nile
2 September
3 Sgt Pepper's Lonely Hearts Club Band
4 Crisis? What Crisis?
5 Joshua, Judges, Job, Jeremiah, Joel, Jonah

QUIZ 163
1 1950s
2 High Fidelity
3 Piano
4 Winston Churchill
5 Canada, Germany, France, Italy, Japan

QUIZ 164
1 Cristiano Ronaldo
2 The Angel of the North
3 Control-Alt-Delete (he said he should have made it a one key instruction)
4 Hill Valley (in 'Back to the Future')
5 Namibia, Botswana, Zimbabwe, Mozambique, Eswatini, Lesotho

QUIZ 165 — 13th June

1 Which long-running TV show was set in the village of Aidensfield?

2 What is the name of the oven used to fire the clay when doing pottery?

3 In the USA, what does the NRA stand for? [as in the abbreviation NRA, rather than what its values are ...]

4 What six-letter word features in the title of a 2009 romantic comedy starring Joseph Gordon Levitt, a long-running British sitcom created by Roy Clarke and a hit song from 1985 by Don Henley?

5 After Great Britain and Ireland, name five of the ten largest islands of the British Isles.

QUIZ 166 — 14th June

1 Who was Russell Brand's first wife?

2 Rabat is the capital of which country?

3 Who, in December 1991, helped Ian St John and Jimmy Greaves carry out the 5th Round Draw of what was then known as the Rumbelows Cup?

4 A lot of the events in which classic children's book (which became a Disney film) take place at Hill Hall, also known as Hell Hall, in Suffolk?

5 Name the five largest islands of the Caribbean, by area. [bear in mind an island is not, in every case, the name of a country]

QUIZ 167 — 15th June

1 Have more people A) climbed Everest or B) swam the English Channel?

2 Who was the first serving US President to survive being shot in an assassination attempt?

3 Which series of children's books began in the early 1970s when a young boy asked his father "What does a tickle look like?"?

4 Which couple did the moustachioed Reverend Sampson marry on 8th November 1988?

5 Name five acts which had five or more UK Number 1 singles in the 1960s. [from 1960 to 1969]

QUIZ 168 — 16th June

1 St George's Chapel lies within which English castle?

2 In 2017, Edward Enninful became the first male editor-in-chief of which magazine in the UK?

3 Who was offered but declined the position of Poet Laureate of the UK in 1984?

4 In 2017, which combat sport's federation rebranded in order to avoid being associated with an unfortunate acronym?

5 Name five men who were main judges of the main UK version of 'The X Factor' on ITV.

QUIZ 165
1 Heartbeat
2 Kiln
3 National Rifle Association
4 Summer (accept "of" as well!)
5 Lewis and Harris (one island), Skye, Shetland Mainland, Mull, Anglesey, Islay, Isle of Man, Orkney Mainland, Arran, Isle of Wight

QUIZ 166
1 Katy Perry
2 Morocco
3 Donald Trump
4 The Hundred and One Dalmatians
5 Cuba, Hispaniola (Haiti and Dominican Republic), Jamaica, Puerto Rico, Trinidad

QUIZ 167
1 A) Climbed Everest - Over 4000 vs over 2000
2 Ronald Reagan
3 Mr Men (it was Adam Hargreaves, who now actually writes the books, asking his father Roger - which then inspired the first book)
4 Scott and Charlene (in 'Neighbours')
5 Elvis Presley, The Beatles, Cliff Richard, The Rolling Stones, The Shadows

QUIZ 168
1 Windsor Castle
2 Vogue
3 Philip Larkin
4 Taekwondo (it had been WTF)
5 Simon Cowell, Louis Walsh, Brian Friedman, Gary Barlow, Nick Grimshaw, Robbie Williams, Louis Tomlinson

QUIZ 169 — 17th June

1 Which king's body was found under a car park in Leicester?

2 Exmoor National Park is in Devon and which other county?

3 The American Museum of Natural History noted a 20% increase in visitors during the holiday season immediately following the release of which film?

4 Who was the first non-European UN Secretary-General?

5 Name five winners of the Best Picture Oscar between 2000 and 2022 with one-word titles. [meaning, the Oscars awarded in 2000 and 2022, not for films in that year]

QUIZ 170 — 18th June

1 Besides tango, the name of which other dance is in the NATO phonetic alphabet?

2 What specific fear links the folk character Chicken Licken and the 'Asterix' village chief Vitalstatistix?

3 What kind of animal is a "Norwegian Blue", as made famous by John Cleese and Michael Palin?

4 Which seven-word phrase was first coined in English by Edward Bulwer Lytton in 1839, in a historical play about Cardinal Richelieu where the main character is unable to respond to enemy plots with force but must do so by other means?

5 Name five of the ten most common surnames in Germany.

QUIZ 171 — 19th June

1 In which century was Abraham Lincoln born?

2 London Underground announced in July 2017 that its staff would stop using which three-word phrase in order to be more gender-neutral?

3 Which character in the original series of 'Porridge' was played by an actor who had the same surname?

4 What number shirt did England cricketer Joe Root start wearing in Test cricket in 2019 (the same number he already wore in white ball cricket)?

5 In terms of votes cast, name five of the ten largest cities of the United Kingdom that voted for Britain to leave the EU in the 2016 Referendum.

QUIZ 172 — 20th June

1 Which bridge is to the immediate east of London Bridge on the Thames?

2 The 13th century leader of the barons, Simon de Montfort, was Earl of ... where?

3 What was the first Disney feature film to feature a character breaking wind on screen?

4 Which Frenchman is the only person to have had an acting role in a movie nominated for Best Picture and to appear on the winning side in a FIFA World Cup final?

5 Name five of the seven largest cities by population in South America.

QUIZ 169
1 Richard III
2 Somerset
3 Night at the Museum
4 U Thant
5 Gladiator, Chicago, Crash, Argo, Spotlight, Moonlight, Parasite, Nomadland, CODA

QUIZ 170
1 Foxtrot
2 That the sky will fall
3 Parrot
4 The pen is mightier than the sword
5 Müller, Schmidt, Schneider, Fischer, Weber, Meyer, Wagner, Becker, Schulz, Hoffman

QUIZ 171
1 19th (1809)
2 Ladies and Gentlemen
3 Mr Mackay (Fulton Mackay)
4 66 (as in Root 66)
5 Birmingham, Sheffield, Bradford, Wakefield, Coventry, Sunderland, Plymouth, Nottingham, Derby, Swansea

QUIZ 172
1 Tower Bridge
2 Leicester
3 The Lion King
4 Frank LeBoeuf (The Theory of Everything and France '98)
5 São Paulo, Lima, Bogotá, Rio de Janeiro, Santiago, Caracas, Buenos Aires (ahead of Brazilian cities Salvador, Brasília, Fortaleza)

QUIZ 173 — 21st June

1 What branch of the British Armed Forces is known as the "Senior Service"?

2 Which chemical element's symbol is taken from the element's Latin name Stibium?

3 Which river in Northern Italy did Julius Caesar famously cross in 49 BC, leading to a phrase which means "passing the point of no return"?

4 In 2009, Everton FC opened a new branch of their official store, in a shopping centre called Liverpool One. What did Everton call the new shop?

5 Name five of the eight members of Team GB at the 2016 Olympics who won an individual gold medal in the same event at the 2012 Olympics. [must be individuals in individual events]

QUIZ 174 — 22nd June

1 The hashtag #curlingiscoolfool started trending during the 2018 Winter Olympics, due to which unlikely fan expressing his enjoyment of the sport on twitter?

2 Which town is home to the National Library of Wales?

3 In legend, which ancient city was founded by its queen cutting an oxhide into fine strips and claiming all the land enclosed within?

4 On the sitcom 'Ellen', the character Ellen Morgan came out to her therapist. Who played that therapist, the same person to whom Ellen DeGeneres publicly came out in real life?

5 Name the five countries that have a land border with Myanmar.

QUIZ 175 — 23rd June

1 What fictional detective shares his surname with a type of puzzle which uses pictures to represent words?

2 In 1963 and again in 1967, which statesman vetoed the UK's entry to the Common Market?

3 What is the only country in the world in which all the ATMs have Latin as a language option?

4 'La Belle Sauvage', the first in a trilogy called 'The Book of Dust', was a 2017 book written by whom?

5 Name the five players who scored at least one goal (not including penalty shoot-outs) for England in Euro 2020.

QUIZ 176 — 24th June

1 In the Shakespeare play, what is the name of Othello's wife?

2 In the world of food, what would be measured on the Scoville Scale?

3 Which Anglo-American poet's nickname with his godchildren was "Old Possum"?

4 Which Austrian composer of 106 symphonies was a friend of Mozart and a tutor of Beethoven?

5 There are six independent states whose common English name contains the word "and" - name five of them. [this is not a trick question so nothing like Finl-and, we do mean the word "and", and this does not include 'The United Kingdom of Great Britain and Northern Ireland', as it's commonly known simply as the United Kingdom]

QUIZ 173
1 Royal Navy
2 Antimony (Sb)
3 Rubicon
4 Everton Two
5 Mo Farah, Jason Kenny, Laura Kenny (Trott), Alistair Brownlee, Jade Jones, Andy Murray, Charlotte Dujardin, Nicola Adams

QUIZ 174
1 Mr T
2 Aberystwyth
3 Carthage (it was Dido)
4 Oprah Winfrey
5 India, Bangladesh, China, Laos, Thailand

QUIZ 175
1 Rebus
2 Charles de Gaulle
3 Vatican City
4 Philip Pullman
5 Raheem Sterling, Harry Kane, Harry Maguire, Jordan Henderson, Luke Shaw (There was also an own goal)

QUIZ 176
1 Desdemona
2 Heat of peppers
3 TS Eliot (hence 'Old Possum's Book of Practical Cats', the basis for 'Cats')
4 Joseph Haydn
5 Antigua and Barbuda, Bosnia and Herzegovina, St Kitts and Nevis, St Vincent and the Grenadines, Trinidad and Tobago, Sao Tome and Principe

QUIZ 177 — 25th June

1 Huntsman cheese consists of alternating layers of Double Gloucester and which other cheese?

2 What film role links Nick Stahl, Jason Clarke, Christian Bale and Edward Furlong?

3 In which country is Syriza the name of a left-wing party?

4 Which film's climax involves a band waiting in vain for the soul singer Wilson Pickett to come to a small venue and perform with them?

5 Name any five English counties that do not contain an official city.

QUIZ 178 — 26th June

1 Which is the smallest big cat that can roar?

2 What word links a 70s rock band, a German novel and a Chicago theatre company?

3 What is significant about the part of the South Pacific Ocean referred to as Point Nemo?

4 Martha, who died on 1st September 1914 at Cincinnati Zoo, was the last ever of what species of pigeon?

5 What are the five largest Arab countries (defined as members of the 22-country Arab league) by population?

QUIZ 179 — 27th June

1 Is Jess in 'Postman Pat' male or female?

2 In November 2017, who offered to pay the fines of six Czech tourists arrested in Kazakhstan for wearing only mankinis?

3 Which town in Switzerland hosts the World Economic Forum (and has become synonymous with the global political elite)?

4 Who released the album '4:44' in 2017 which was seen as a response to his wife's album from the previous year?

5 Defining size in terms of total votes cast either way, name five of the seven largest cities of the United Kingdom that voted for Britain to remain in the EU in the 2016 Referendum.

QUIZ 180 — 28th June

1 What is the highest British military award for bravery?

2 The "Infinite Monkey Theorem" involves putting a monkey in front of a ... what?

3 Cyril Ramaphosa became President of which country in early 2018?

4 Whose bestselling book, published in September 2017, is called 'What Happened'?

5 In between Egypt and South Africa, there are seven independent countries on mainland Africa's east coast. Name five of them.

QUIZ 177
1 Stilton
2 John Connor (in the Terminator films)
3 Greece
4 The Commitments
5 Bedfordshire, Berkshire, Dorset, Isle of Wight, Northamptonshire, Northumberland, Rutland, Shropshire, Suffolk, Surrey, Warwickshire

QUIZ 178
1 Leopard
2 Steppenwolf
3 It is the furthest from land (2,688km from a small uninhabited part of the Pitcairn Islands. Nemo means nobody)
4 Passenger (pigeon)
5 Egypt, Algeria, Sudan, Iraq, Morocco

QUIZ 179
1 Male
2 Sacha Baron-Cohen
3 Davos
4 Jay-Z
5 London, Leeds, Glasgow, Edinburgh, Bristol, Liverpool, Manchester (then Cardiff, Belfast, Brighton)

QUIZ 180
1 Victoria Cross
2 Typewriter
3 South Africa
4 Hillary Clinton
5 Sudan, Eritrea, Djibouti, Somalia, Kenya, Tanzania, Mozambique

QUIZ 181 — 29th June

1 How many times does the word "really" appear in The Spice Girls' 'Wannabe' - A) 26 or B) 36?

2 For what purpose would you have to get a PADI certificate?

3 Which song by Wilson Pickett contains within its lyrics the name of the first American woman in space?

4 What work by Igor Stravinsky almost caused a riot when first performed in Paris in May 1913?

5 Name five UK cities that have so far hosted the Commonwealth Games (or the Empire Games as they were first called).

QUIZ 182 — 30th June

1 Is the speed of sound faster in A) air or B) water?

2 Which actor links 'The Big Lebowski', 'The Wedding Singer' and 'Reservoir Dogs'?

3 In which city is the University of East Anglia based?

4 Across 1969 and 1970, the Rolling Stones and the Beatles both released albums with the same two first words in their title. What were the two albums?

5 Name the five youngest ever US Presidents.

QUIZ 183 — 1st July

1 Which film is famous for the line, "I feel the need, the need for speed"?

2 Katrina and the Waves won Eurovision for the UK just one day after which man became Prime Minister?

3 Morgan Tsvangirai, who died in early 2018, was for many years the opposition leader in which country?

4 Who played rapper Ice Cube in the 2015 film 'Straight Outta Compton'?

5 Besides the six main characters, name five of the ten characters who made appearances in the most episodes of 'Friends'. [we'll accept first names without surnames, and not including babies]

QUIZ 184 — 2nd July

1 The Model T was a classic early car produced by which company?

2 What name is commonly given to Britain's oldest complete skeleton, discovered in Somerset 100 years ago, whom scientists have discovered most likely had blue eyes and dark skin?

3 In 1975, who became the first, and so far only, fictional character to receive an obituary in the New York Times?

4 Which song by Iggy Pop plays over the opening scene of 'Trainspotting' and the last scene of its sequel 'T2'?

5 Name Take That's five single-word UK Number 1 singles.

QUIZ 181

1 A) 26
2 To go scuba diving
3 Mustang Sally (all you gotta do is ride around Sally, Ride Sally Ride)
4 The Rite of Spring
5 London, Cardiff, Edinburgh, Manchester, Glasgow, Birmingham.

QUIZ 182

1 B) Air
2 Steve Buscemi
3 Norwich
4 'Let it Bleed' and 'Let it Be'
5 Theodore Roosevelt, John F Kennedy, Bill Clinton, Ulysses S Grant, Barack Obama

QUIZ 183

1 Top Gun
2 Tony Blair
3 Zimbabwe
4 His son, O'Shea Jackson Jr
5 Gunther, Jack (Geller), Judy (Geller), Janice (Litman Goralnik), Mike (Hannigan), Emily (Waltham), Carol (Willick), Susan (Bunch), Estelle (Leonard), Richard (Burke)

QUIZ 184

1 Ford
2 Cheddar Man
3 Hercule Poirot (on release of 'Curtain')
4 Lust for Life
5 Pray, Babe, Sure, Patience, Shine

QUIZ 185 — 3rd July

1 According to tradition, which way should a bottle of port be passed at a dinner party?

2 In Kent, Canterbury West station lies precisely in what direction from Canterbury East station?

3 Only one of the ten highest-grossing movies of the 1980s hasn't been given a sequel, prequel or been rebooted [as of 2022]. Which film?

4 A woman called Lana Peters, who died in Wisconsin in 2011, was the daughter of which 20th century dictator?

5 In the Peter Jackson 'The Lord of the Rings' films, the original Fellowship of the Ring consisted of nine members. Name five of the actors who played those nine members.

QUIZ 186 — 4th July

1 What is the Welsh word for "welcome"?

2 In 2017, Harry Styles made his film acting debut in which film?

3 London Black cab drivers often refer to the Royal Geographical Society as "Hot & Cold Corner" because of the statues of two explorers outside - one known for exploring cold places, the other for exploring hot places. Who are the two explorers?

4 On which late-night topical TV show did the likes of Sacha Baron Cohen, Ricky Gervais and Mackenzie Crook all get an early break?

5 Name five independent South American countries with an Atlantic coast.

QUIZ 187 — 5th July

1 Which cocktail is the national drink of Puerto Rico?

2 The Tupolev Tu-144, nicknamed the Charger, had a fairly brief commercial life, and was one of only two of its type. What was the other, which had a longer commercial life, from 1976 to 2003?

3 Who served ten days as White House Director of Communications in July 2017?

4 Which knight is the only man to have played in both the cricket World Cup and football World Cup qualifiers?

5 Name five of Kylie Minogue's seven UK Number 1 singles. [including duets, up to and including 2022]

QUIZ 188 — 6th July

1 Anacondas are snakes which are native to which continent - A) Asia or B) South America?

2 Whose science fiction novels include 'The Midwich Cuckoos', 'The Kraken Wakes' and 'Day of the Triffids'?

3 The comedian Vaughn Meader became popular in the early 1960s for his impression of which figure, winning a Grammy for "Album of the Year" in 1963 shortly before abruptly fading into obscurity and having his album pulled from stores?

4 What was the surname of two British writer brothers, one an animal enthusiast, the other a novelist best known for his 'Alexandria Quartet'?

5 TIME Magazine listed 100 Most Important People of the 20th Century in 1999. There were seven women who were born in Europe on that list. Name five of them.

QUIZ 185
1 To the left
2 North
3 E.T: the Extra-Terrestrial
4 Stalin (Svetlana Stalin - and her 3rd husband was an American called Peters)
5 Elijah Wood, Sean Astin, Sir Ian McKellen, Viggo Mortensen, Orlando Bloom, John Rhys-Davies, Sean Bean, Dominic Monaghan, Billy Boyd

QUIZ 186
1 Croeso
2 Dunkirk
3 Shackleton and Livingstone
4 The 11 O'Clock Show
5 Colombia, Venezuela, Guyana, Suriname, Brazil, Uruguay, Argentina, Chile (a tiny bit) - we will grudgingly accept France, of which French Guiana is an overseas department

QUIZ 187
1 Piña colada
2 Concorde (the Tupolev Tu-144 was the Russian supersonic aircraft)
3 Antonio Scaramucci (The Mooch)
4 Sir Viv Richards
5 I Should Be So Lucky, Especially for You, Hand On Your Heart, Tears on My Pillow, Spinning Around, Can't Get You Out of My Head, Slow

QUIZ 188
1 B) South America
2 John Wyndham
3 John F Kennedy
4 Durrell (Gerald who wrote 'My Family and Other Animals' and Lawrence)
5 Margaret Thatcher, Coco Chanel, Mary Leakey, Princess Diana, Anne Frank, Mother Teresa, Emmeline Pankhurst

QUIZ 189 — 7th July

1 Apart from the Sun, what is the closest star to Earth – A) Sirius A or B) Proxima Centauri?

2 Who was the first rapper to win an Oscar for Best Original Song?

3 Often seen in country houses and mentioned in Jane Austen, what kind of feature is a ha-ha?

4 What word links a village in Cornwall, a commonly eaten fish, and an action for which those about to carry it out should be saluted?

5 Name the first five feature films directed by Danny Boyle.

QUIZ 190 — 8th July

1 What does CNN stand for in the name of the American broadcaster?

2 What common legal word comes from the Medieval Latin for "He has declared upon oath"?

3 Which 19th Century novel has the subtitle 'The Modern Prometheus'?

4 Stanislav Petrov, a former Soviet military officer who died in September 2017, became known as "the man who saved the world" for doing what, or rather not doing what, on September 26 1983?

5 Name five of the ten cities in the UK with the smallest populations. [not including the City of London or Stanley in the Falklands]

QUIZ 191 — 9th July

1 Is Earth nearer to A) the Sun or B) Neptune?

2 Which comic opera begins with the line "If you want to know who we are, we are gentlemen of Japan"?

3 For which movie, in which he plays Fast Eddie Felson, did Paul Newman win his only Best Actor Oscar?

4 Sometimes known as "Track Town, USA", which city in Oregon hosted the 2022 World Athletics Championships?

5 The Tropic of Capricorn [the more southerly Tropic] passes through ten independent countries. Name five of them.

QUIZ 192 — 10th July

1 Roughly what percentage of the Earth's surface is covered by water – A) 71% or B) 81%?

2 When Wimbledon beat Liverpool in the 1988 FA Cup final, John Motson famously said "The Crazy Gang have beaten the ..." what?

3 Which game features pictures of Officer Mallory, Jake the Jailbird and Rich Uncle Pennybags?

4 Which rum cocktail's name comes from the Tahitian for "good"?

5 Name five independent countries with common English names ending with the letters "nia". [don't put Bosnia as that is not the country's name]

QUIZ 189
1 B) Proxima Centauri
2 Eminem (for 'Lose Yourself')
3 A ditch (sloped with a wall on one side)
4 Rock
5 Shallow Grave, Trainspotting, A Life Less Ordinary, The Beach, 28 Days Later

QUIZ 190
1 Cable News Network
2 Affidavit
3 Frankenstein
4 He ignored a warning that US missiles were coming (dismissing it, correctly, as a system malfunction)
5 Wells, Truro, St Davids and the Cathedral Close, St Asaph, Ripon, Newry, Lichfield, Ely, Chichester, Bangor (in Wales)

QUIZ 191
1 A) The Sun
2 The Mikado
3 The Color of Money, (not 'The Hustler')
4 Eugene
5 Namibia, Botswana, South Africa, Mozambique, Madagascar, Australia, Chile, Argentina, Paraguay, Brazil

QUIZ 192
1 A) 71%
2 Culture Club
3 Monopoly
4 Mai Tai
5 Albania, Armenia, Estonia, Lithuania, Mauritania, North Macedonia, Romania, Slovenia, Tanzania

QUIZ 193 — 11th July

1 Are the words on Love Hearts sweets written in capitals or lower case?

2 What is the Turkish word for "lion"?

3 Which film actor, who voices Marlin in 'Finding Nemo', has the real name Albert Einstein?

4 The M2 motorway is entirely within which English county?

5 Name the five oldest actors to have been chosen to play the lead character in 'Doctor Who'. We mean the main series "Doctor", and the key date for each is when they started in the role. [up to 2022]

QUIZ 194 — 12th July

1 Which film's tagline was 'There Can Be Only One'?

2 Dilma Rousseff was removed as President of which country in August 2016?

3 The book 'Shoeless Joe' by WP Kinsella inspired which sports film from 1989?

4 Who is the only singer of a Bond theme to appear in the opening credits of the film?

5 Name the first five Labour Prime Ministers of the UK.

QUIZ 195 — 13th July

1 Which was shown first in the UK - 'Neighbours' or 'Home and Away'?

2 Sal Paradise is the narrator of which influential novel?

3 James Corden's 'Carpool Karaoke' originated in a Comic Relief sketch with which star?

4 The winner of the Best Song Oscar for 1968 was sung by the son of the man who'd sung the winner of the Best Song Oscar in 1967. What was the surname of the two men?

5 Name five of the six independent countries which border Afghanistan.

QUIZ 196 — 14th July

1 What was the name of Joan Collins' novelist sister?

2 Kiefer Sutherland played a vampire in which 1987 film?

3 At Wimbledon, how many games are completed at the start of the match before the umpire first asks for "New Balls Please"?

4 There is one US state capital which is the name of an English city. What is it?

5 Name five Oasis Number 1 singles in the UK.

QUIZ 193
1 Capitals
2 Aslan
3 Albert Brooks
4 Kent
5 Peter Capaldi, William Hartnell, Jon Pertwee, Patrick Troughton, Sylvester McCoy

QUIZ 194
1 Highlander
2 Brazil
3 Field of Dreams
4 Sheena Easton - For Your Eyes Only
5 Ramsay MacDonald, Clement Attlee, Harold Wilson, James Callaghan, Tony Blair

QUIZ 195
1 Neighbours
2 On the Road
3 George Michael
4 Harrison (Rex (I Talk to the Animals) and Noel (The Windmills of Your Mind))
5 Pakistan, Iran, Turkmenistan, Tajikistan, Uzbekistan, China

QUIZ 196
1 Jackie Collins
2 The Lost Boys
3 7 games
4 Lincoln (Nebraska). Dover and Richmond, which are state capitals, are not UK cities
5 Some Might Say, Don't Look Back in Anger, Do You Know What I Mean?, All Around the World, Go Let it Out, The Hindu Times, Lyla, The Importance of Being Idle

QUIZ 197 — 15th July

1 What is the land speed record for travelling on the moon - A) 11.2 mph or B) 22.1 mph?

2 One of the reasons Steve Jobs chose to name his company Apple was so that it would appear in the phone book before the company he had previously worked for. What was that company?

3 Which venue has hosted the Royal Variety Performance most often?

4 In 2017, Sarah Clarke became the first woman to be appointed to which ceremonial position in its 669-year history?

5 Including presenters, name five of the ten people who appeared in the most episodes of the TV show 'Shooting Stars'. [basically anyone who was at any point a regular on the show. We will accept the name of character or actor in some cases]

QUIZ 198 — 16th July

1 Which, on average, weigh more - A) African Elephants or B) Indian Elephants?

2 In which TV series did Scott Bakula play the lead character, though a different actor in each episode would play his reflection?

3 On 8 August 1969, photographer Iain Macmillan took a renowned photograph on which London thoroughfare?

4 Who is the only person who both lit the Olympic flame and won a gold medal at the same Olympics? [lit the flame as in at the opening ceremony, not just carried the torch at some point]

5 Name five kings of England (for any length of time) in the 11th century AD.

QUIZ 199 — 17th July

1 Who's been played By Cary Elwes, Errol Flynn, Patrick Bergin, Russell Crowe and Kevin Costner?

2 Esch-sur-Alzette is the second largest city in which European country?

3 The first name of the wife of Winston Churchill is shared with a citrus fruit - what was it?

4 Which popular Scottish author added the initial M to his name when writing science fiction novels?

5 Name any five of the eight stadiums which hosted games during Euro 96, held in England.

QUIZ 200 — 18th July

1 Have there been more A) British Prime Ministers or B) US Presidents? (Prime Ministers going back to Sir Robert Walpole being the first de facto Prime Minister)

2 In which Tchaikovsky ballet does a Christmas present turn into a prince who defends Clara from the Mouse King?

3 In normal English typography, which two letters (which are next to each other in the alphabet) have a tittle?

4 What H is a type of felt hat popularised by King Edward VII after he visited Germany?

5 Name five current UK cities with names ending in the letter H. [English names]

QUIZ 197
1 A) 11.2 mph
2 Atari
3 London Palladium
4 Black Rod
5 Bob Mortimer, Vic Reeves/Jim Moir, Ulrika Jonsson, Matt Lucas/George Dawes, Mark Lamarr, Will Self, Johnny Vegas/Michael Pennington, Angelos Epithemiou/Dan Renton Skinner, Jack Dee, Rhys Thomas (he was Donald Cox the Sweaty Fox)

QUIZ 198
1 A) African Elephants (4-7500kg for males, against 3-6000kg)
2 Quantum Leap
3 Abbey Road
4 Cathy Freeman (2000 Olympics)
5 Aethelred (the Unready), Sweyn Forkbeard, Cnut, Edmund Ironside, Harold Harefoot, Harthacnut, Edward the Confessor, Harold, (Edgar the Atheling - allow), William the Conqueror, William Rufus, Henry I (allow, became king in 1100)

QUIZ 199
1 Robin Hood
2 Luxembourg
3 Clementine
4 Iain Banks
5 Wembley Stadium (London), Old Trafford (Manchester), Anfield (Liverpool), Villa Park (Birmingham), St James' Park (Newcastle), Hillsborough (Sheffield), Elland Road (Leeds), City Ground (Nottingham)

QUIZ 200
1 A) British Prime Ministers
2 The Nutcracker
3 i and j (lowercase)
4 Homburg
5 Armagh, Bath, Edinburgh, Norwich, Perth, Peterborough, Plymouth, Portsmouth, St Asaph

QUIZ 201 — 19th July

1 Which is longer - A) the biggest killer whale on record or B) the biggest whale shark?

2 What is the first word in the lyrics of the songs 'Back for Good', 'God Only Knows' and 'Angels'?

3 What name links a ship that is afloat but incapable of going to sea and a Marvel superhero?

4 Which 16th century English historical figure is officially recognised by the Catholic church as the patron saint of politicians?

5 Name five items of food the Very Hungry Caterpillar eats on his busiest day, Saturday.

QUIZ 202 — 20th July

1 How many kings of England have there been called Richard?

2 What is the mainland region of the Canadian province which also includes the island of Newfoundland?

3 What is the name of the 1938 novel by Evelyn Waugh which is a satire of sensationalist journalism?

4 What is a Brannock Device used to measure?

5 Name the seven acts that had the most UK Top 10 singles in the 1980s - 80s being from 1980 to 1989, and not counting one person in two different acts e.g. Morrissey and The Smiths combined.

QUIZ 203 — 21st July

1 Which letter in the NATO phonetic alphabet is represented by a sport?

2 What children's classic features a police force called the Owsla?

3 What language is used for almost all of the words in Handel's Messiah?

4 Which great American sportsman was the second husband of the second wife of the father of the wife of the son of the British poet laureate from 1968 to 1972?

5 Name five UK cities whose official names end with the letter N. [do not write Brighton for Brighton & Hove]

QUIZ 204 — 22nd July

1 The coyote is native to which continent?

2 The Queensferry Crossing is a bridge across which body of water?

3 What is the first word of the title of both a book by Robert Graves, adapted into a TV series in 1976, and an anthology of short stories by Isaac Asimov, turned into a film in 2004?

4 Estimated to have lived for around 400 years, a female of which animal is thought (as of 2021) to be the oldest vertebrate in existence?

5 Name five Blur studio albums. [up to 2022]

QUIZ 201

1 B) the biggest whale shark (12.6m to 9.8m)
2 I
3 Hulk
4 Thomas More
5 One piece of chocolate cake, one ice-cream cone, one pickle, one slice of Swiss cheese, one slice of salami, one lollipop, one piece of cherry pie, one sausage, one cupcake, and one slice of watermelon.

QUIZ 202

1 Three
2 Labrador (Newfoundland and Labrador)
3 Scoop
4 Feet, for shoe fittings
5 Madonna (22), Michael Jackson (16),Shakin' Stevens (15), Madness (14), Cliff Richard (14), UB40 (12), Duran Duran (12) (Queen (10), Status Quo (10), Spandau Ballet (10), Wham! (10), Pet Shop Boys (10), U2 (10) all had 10)

QUIZ 203

1 G (Golf)
2 Watership Down
3 English
4 Joe DiMaggio (Marilyn Monroe, Arthur Miller, Rebecca Miller, Daniel Day-Lewis, Cecil Day-Lewis)
5 Lincoln, London, Preston, Ripon, Southampton, Wolverhampton, Aberdeen, Lisburn

QUIZ 204

1 North America
2 Firth of Forth
3 I (I, Claudius and I, Robot)
4 (Greenland) Shark
5 Leisure, Modern Life is Rubbish, Parklife, The Great Escape, Blur, 13, Think Tank, The Magic Whip

QUIZ 205 — 23rd July

1 On which thoroughfare does the Tour de France always end?

2 Which word links a 1995 hit by McAlmont & Butler, a prog-rock band led by Jon Anderson, and a response only 32.1% of people in Britain gave to voting reform in 2011?

3 Goodluck Jonathan is the former President of which country?

4 Whose acclaimed second solo album, released in 1993, 16 years after her first solo album, had a name which implied it was her first solo album?

5 Name five managers who have led England's men's football team to a FIFA World Cup. [up to 2022]

QUIZ 206 — 24th July

1 England's highest mountain is in which National Park?

2 Which novel by John Williams sold only a few thousand copies when first published in 1965 but was the Waterstones Book of the Year almost 50 years later?

3 What breed of horses do you find at the Spanish Riding School in Vienna?

4 Mauritania was the last country in the world to officially abolish what, in 1981?

5 Give five of the names taken by Popes between 1903 and 2018. [i.e. one name counts once - so if there'd been a Pope Arthur II and Pope Arthur III, Arthur would only count once]

QUIZ 207 — 25th July

1 Ellis Island and Governors Island are in which city's harbour?

2 Who played Adenoid Hynkel in the 1940 satirical movie 'The Great Dictator'?

3 Which king was crowned in Westminster Abbey on Christmas Day 1066?

4 What is the nickname of the character Pete Mitchell, played by Tom Cruise in the 1986 film 'Top Gun'?

5 Name any five David Bowie studio albums with two-word titles. [full and proper titles]

QUIZ 208 — 26th July

1 What single letter is used on a musical score to indicate that the music should be played loudly?

2 What's the smallest number whose English name contains all five vowels exactly once each?

3 Which species of great ape lives exclusively in Asia?

4 Which influential figure qualified as a doctor of medicine at the University of Vienna in 1881, before dying in Hampstead, London in 1939?

5 Name the five largest cities in the USA (by population) whose name contains the word City.

QUIZ 205

1 The Champs-Élysées
2 Yes
3 Nigeria
4 Bjork - the 1993 album was called Debut, but she'd released an album called Bjork as a child in 1977 (she had been in the band The Sugarcubes in between)
5 Gareth Southgate, Roy Hodgson, Fabio Capello, Sven-Goran Eriksson, Glenn Hoddle, Bobby Robson, Ron Greenwood, Alf Ramsay, Walter Winterbottom

QUIZ 206

1 The Lake District (Scafell Pike)
2 Stoner
3 Lippizan/Lippizaner
4 Slavery
5 Benedict (XV and XVI), Pius (X, XI and XII), John (XXIII), Paul (VI), John Paul (I and II), Francis

QUIZ 207

1 New York City
2 Charlie Chaplin
3 William I
4 Maverick
5 David Bowie (we'll allow Space Oddity, as it was re-released under that title), Hunky Dory, Aladdin Sane, Pin Ups, Diamond Dogs, Young Americans, Let's Dance

QUIZ 208

1 f
2 Two hundred and six (vs one hundred and five which is the first to contain them all once, but not exactly once each)
3 Orangutan (there are in fact now thought to be two different species, Bornean orangutan and Sumatran orangutan)
4 Sigmund Freud
5 New York City, Oklahoma City, Kansas City, Jersey City, Salt Lake City

QUIZ 209 — 27th July

1 Which African country has a coastline on the Atlantic and the Indian Ocean?

2 In the 1994 film 'Speed', what is the minimum speed (in mph) for the bus to avoid blowing up?

3 Oakham and Uppingham are the only towns in which small English county?

4 In the late 1880s, the body of an unidentified young woman was pulled out of the Seine. This face of this so-called "unknown woman of the Seine" has been called the "most kissed face of all time" as her likeness was used by a toymaker and a physician as the model for what?

5 Name any five cast members who are credited with appearing in over 100 episodes of the sitcom 'Cheers'. [actors not characters]

QUIZ 210 — 28th July

1 The Scotsman Keir Hardie was the first leader of which political party?

2 What genus of tree was devastated throughout the late 20th century by a disease sometimes shortened to DED?

3 What word commonly used in politics comes from the gerund of the Latin verb meaning "to bring back"?

4 Which Asian country changed its timezone by half an hour in August 2015?

5 There are four chemical elements which have, in English, unique last letters. What are they?

QUIZ 211 — 29th July

1 Emmental cheese comes from which country?

2 The capital cities Bamako, Timbuktu and Niamey are all on which river?

3 What, in various media, are Crookshanks, Salem and Gobbolino?

4 Which British overseas territory in the Caribbean is named after its eel-like shape?

5 Name five UK Number 1 singles by The Police.

QUIZ 212 — 30th July

1 What title links different Top 10 hits by The Prodigy, The Stone Roses, Blue and Bob Marley?

2 Who became the MP for Islington North in 1983?

3 Which famous Italian saint was originally named Giovanni di Pietro di Bernardone, but was nicknamed "The Frenchman" by his father?

4 In which year of the 20th century did the Spanish Civil War end?

5 Name five chemical elements whose names end with an E.

QUIZ 209
1 South Africa
2 50 mph
3 Rutland
4 Resusci Anne (the CPR training doll)
5 Ted Danson, Rhea Perlman, George Wendt, John Ratzenberger, Kelsey Grammer, Woody Harrelson, Kirstie Alley, Shelley Long

QUIZ 210
1 Labour
2 Elm (Dutch Elm Disease)
3 Referendum
4 North Korea
5 Phosphorus, Cobalt, Nickel, Bismuth

QUIZ 211
1 Switzerland
2 Niger
3 Witches' cats (Harry Potter, Sabrina the Teenage Witch, Gobbolino the Witch's Cat)
4 Anguilla (eels belong to the order Anguilliformes)
5 Message in a Bottle, Walking on the Moon, Don't Stand So Close to Me, Every Little Thing She Does is Magic, Every Breath You Take

QUIZ 212
1 One Love
2 Jeremy Corbyn
3 St Francis of Assisi (he was nicknamed Francesco)
4 1939 (1936-1939)
5 Fluorine, Bromine, Astatine, Chlorine, Tennessine, Iodine, Manganese

QUIZ 213 — 31st July

1 What kind of food are gyoza and gnocchi?

2 Who was the first UK Poet Laureate not to die during their laureateship?

3 Which Nobel Prize winner received six A*s and 4 As in her GCSEs in 2015?

4 What German word, commonly used in English, literally means "children's garden"?

5 Name five of the actresses who make up the eight in 'Ocean's 8'.

QUIZ 214 — 1st August

1 The Caribbean Sea is part of which ocean?

2 Who did the American author Toni Morrison describe (in 1998) as "our first black President"?

3 Which Japanese company produced the world's first pocket calculator?

4 Who was the only known child of Prince Edward, Duke of Kent and Strathearn, who was the 4th son of King George III?

5 Name five independent countries with an English name that is four letters long, and made up of two vowels and two consonants.

QUIZ 215 — 2nd August

1 In which city would you find the Spanish Steps?

2 In the Nativity story in the Gospel of Luke, Mary visits her relative Elizabeth, who is herself pregnant - who is her child?

3 On the Blur album 'The Great Escape' the title of one song is an anagram of the band's lead singer's name. What is the song title?

4 What long-running TV show links the stars of movies 'Thor', 'Memento', 'Diana', 'Dawn of the Planet of the Apes', 'Red Hill', 'Confessions of a Shopaholic' and 'Brokeback Mountain'?

5 Name five capital cities in Europe with English names beginning with B. Capital cities of sovereign states.

QUIZ 216 — 3rd August

1 In German, it was Weihnachtsfrieden, in French, it was Trêve de Noël. How is this famous wartime event commonly known in English?

2 The Khyber Pass links which two countries?

3 Who played Mr Brown in 'Reservoir Dogs', Jimmy Dimmick in 'Pulp Fiction', an Answering Machine voice in 'Jackie Brown' and an employee of the LeQuint Dickey Mining Co. in 'Django Unchained'?

4 Which two bands shared a bill for the only time in history at the NME Pollwinners' Party at Wembley Arena in 1964?

5 Name five players who have beaten Serena Williams in the final of a Grand Slam singles tournament. [up to summer of 2022]

QUIZ 213
1 Dumplings
2 Andrew Motion
3 Malala Yousafzai
4 Kindergarten
5 Sandra Bullock, Cate Blanchett, Sarah Paulson, Rihanna, Mindy Kaling, Awkwafina, Helena Bonham-Carter, Anne Hathaway

QUIZ 214
1 Atlantic Ocean
2 Bill Clinton
3 Casio
4 Queen Victoria
5 Cuba, Fiji, Iran, Iraq, Laos, Mali, Oman, Peru, Togo

QUIZ 215
1 Rome
2 John the Baptist
3 Dan Abnormal (anagram of Damon Albarn)
4 Home and Away (Chris Hemsworth, Guy Pearce, Naomi Watts, Jason Clarke, Ryan Kwanten, Isla Fisher and Heath Ledger all appeared in it, amongst others)
5 Baku, Berlin, Belgrade, Bucharest, Budapest, Bern, Bratislava, Brussels

QUIZ 216
1 The Christmas Truce
2 Afghanistan and Pakistan
3 Quentin Tarantino
4 The Beatles and The Rolling Stones
5 Venus Williams, Maria Sharapova, Samantha Stosur, Angelique Kerber, Garbine Muguruza, Naomi Osaka, Simona Halep, Bianca Andreescu

QUIZ 217 — 4th August

1 The brand Toblerone comes from which country?

2 Which 2014 movie includes repeated use of the phrase "Sell me this pen"?

3 Who coined the word "Supermarionation" and then created several classic TV shows using that technique?

4 Which French author declined the Nobel Prize for Literature in 1964?

5 Apart from X, give five of the six letters that do not begin the official names of any cities of the UK.

QUIZ 218 — 5th August

1 In Greek Mythology, who was King of the Gods?

2 Who did the Greek shipping magnate, Aristotle Onassis, marry in 1968?

3 Holly Woodlawn, an actress born Haroldo Santiago Franceschi Rodriguez Danhakl, who died in December 2015, featured in which famous 1972 song?

4 Kamila Shamsie's 2017 novel 'Home Fire' is a retelling of which Greek tragedy by Sophocles?

5 Name five US states with names ending in S.

QUIZ 219 — 6th August

1 What is the only country which currently has an Emperor?

2 Which Kevin Costner film is famous for the line, "If you build it, he will come"?

3 Which Shakespeare play takes place in the Forest of Arden?

4 Which highly successful English singer-songwriter (who attended Harrow School) shares his name with a historical figure and minor character in Shakespeare's 'Richard III'?

5 Name five Asian cities that have hosted either the Summer or Winter Olympics.

QUIZ 220 — 7th August

1 A macchiato is a type of what drink?

2 What Treaty of 1957 formed the European Economic Community?

3 Salva Kiir Mayardit became the first President of which country in 2011?

4 In which month do maths enthusiasts celebrate, specifically, Pi Approximation Day?

5 The World Video Game Hall of Fame opened in 2015. Name five of the six original games to be inducted.

QUIZ 217
1 Switzerland
2 The Wolf of Wall Street
3 Gerry and Sylvia Anderson (accept either, or both)
4 Jean-Paul Sartre
5 F, J, Q, U, V, Z

QUIZ 218
1 Zeus
2 Jacqueline Kennedy
3 Walk on the Wild Side)- Lou Reed ("Holly came from Miami, F-L-A ...")
4 Antigone
5 Arkansas, Illinois, Kansas, Massachusetts, Texas

QUIZ 219
1 Japan
2 Field of Dreams
3 As You Like It
4 James Blunt (James Blunt's actual name is James Blount)
5 Tokyo, Seoul, Beijing (summer and winter), Sapporo, Nagano, Pyeongchang (which is a county not a city but we'll allow)

QUIZ 220
1 Coffee
2 The Treaty of Rome
3 South Sudan
4 July (22nd July since Pi approximately is 22/7 - Pi Day is 14th March - 3.14)
5 Doom, Pac-Man, Pong, Super Mario Bros, Tetris, World of Warcraft

QUIZ 221 — 8th August

1 Of which country is Zealand the largest island?

2 Who married his long-time girlfriend Kim at Dunblane Cathedral on 11 April 2015?

3 The state fruit of Idaho is also the first name of a famous literary character - what is it?

4 Who was the Kentuckian abolitionist appointed US Ambassador to Russia by Abraham Lincoln, whose name was later given to another famous Kentuckian, though he discarded it in 1964?

5 Can you name the five people who have hosted, or co-hosted the Oscar ceremony most often?

QUIZ 222 — 9th August

1 Who was Brad Pitt's first wife?

2 What F is a brass instrument which resembles the trumpet, taking the first part of its name from the German for "wing"?

3 Cadiz is the oldest continuously inhabited city in which country?

4 The seal of which city bears the Latin words "SIGILLUM CIVITATIS NOVI EBORACI"?

5 What four events - precisely - feature in both a heptathlon and a decathlon?

QUIZ 223 — 10th August

1 What is the 24th and last letter of the Ancient Greek Alphabet?

2 What goes between the fruit cake and the icing in a traditional Christmas cake?

3 In which movie did the retired marine R. Lee Ermey make a powerful impression playing Gunnery Sergeant Hartman?

4 Who sings backing vocals on 'Everglow', a track from Coldplay's album 'A Head Full of Dreams'?

5 What were the original Cinque Ports on the south-east coast of England?

QUIZ 224 — 11th August

1 Basel, Strasbourg and Cologne are all situated on which river?

2 Who played Emperor Commodus in the film 'Gladiator'?

3 What V is both the name of a huge reservoir in Ghana and of a famous Italian physicist known for the invention of the battery?

4 This is the first line of which film? "I always wondered why no-one did it before me. I mean, all those comic books, movies, TV shows ... you think that one eccentric loner would've made himself a costume."

5 Name five cricket teams that have won the men's 50-over World Cup. [up to and including 2019 competition]

QUIZ 221
1 Denmark
2 Andy Murray
3 Huckleberry
4 Cassius Marcellus Clay (the name of Muhammad Ali. Clay's father, also called Cassius Marcellus Clay had been given the name by his father in tribute to the politician)
5 Bob Hope (18), Billy Crystal (nine), Johnny Carson (five), Whoopi Goldberg and Jack Lemmon (four each)

QUIZ 222
1 Jennifer Aniston
2 Flugelhorn
3 Spain
4 New York City
5 High Jump, Long Jump, Javelin, Shot Put (not the hurdles. The men's is 110m, the women's 100m)

QUIZ 223
1 Omega
2 Marzipan
3 Full Metal Jacket
4 Gwyneth Paltrow (Chris Martin's ex-wife)
5 Dover, Sandwich, Hythe, New Romney (accept Rye), Hastings

QUIZ 224
1 Rhine
2 Joaquin Phoenix
3 Volta
4 Kick-Ass
5 West Indies (two), India (two), Australia (five), Pakistan (one), Sri Lanka (one), England (one)

QUIZ 225 — 12th August

1 Which National Park contains Wales's highest mountain?

2 Which eponymous movie character has the surname Rockatansky?

3 In English, how many signs of the Zodiac begin with the letter L?

4 In 2015, Danae Stratou, the wife of the (then) Greek finance minister, was claimed to be the inspiration for which classic song?

5 What are the top five languages in the world by number of native speakers?

QUIZ 226 — 13th August

1 What musical note is half of a crotchet?

2 Who received an honorary doctorate from the School of the Art Institute of Chicago in May 2015, a significant step up from the title of his debut album?

3 What links Eastleigh, Salisbury, Bexhill and Battle, South Thanet (twice), Bromley and Chislehurst and Buckingham?

4 How many countries does Belgium border?

5 In early 2019, a BBC show chose Seven Greatest Icons of the 20th century, one each from Arts, Sport, Activism, Entertainment, Science, Explorers and Leaders. Who were the seven finalists?

QUIZ 227 — 14th August

1 What island is separated from Southern England by the Solent?

2 What I is a word that appears in the title of plays by Tom Stoppard, Nikolai Gogol and JB Priestley?

3 What 1983 film's title is a reference to the lead actor saying 12 years earlier that he did not want to play the main character anymore?

4 Which two-word Latin aphorism, commonly used today, appears in the Roman poet Horace's 'Odes 1.11' and precedes the words "quam minimum credula postero" which roughly means "put little trust in tomorrow"?

5 The women's football World Cup was first held in 1991. Name five teams that have ever made the final. [up to 2019 competition]

QUIZ 228 — 15th August

1 If you travel due west from San Francisco, what country would you come to first?

2 Which artist supposedly sold only one painting, called 'The Red Vineyard', in his lifetime?

3 Which element was first discovered in Cornwall in 1791 and derives its name from deities of Greek mythology?

4 Whose last, posthumous, novel, 'The Shepherd's Crown' went on sale in August 2015?

5 Name five of the nine countries that contain part of the Amazon rainforest within their borders. [one of them is not an independent country, but you may include it]

QUIZ 225
1 Snowdonia
2 Mad Max
3 Two (Leo and Libra)
4 Common People (she did come from Greece, she did study sculpture at St Martin's College)
5 Mandarin (accept Chinese, but not Cantonese), Spanish, English, Hindi, Arabic

QUIZ 226
1 Quaver
2 Kanye West (first three albums were The College Dropout, Late Registration, then Graduation)
3 All constituencies Nigel Farage has contested unsuccessfully in parliamentary elections
4 Four (France, Netherlands, Germany, Luxembourg)
5 Pablo Picasso, Muhammad Ali, Martin Luther King Jr, David Bowie, Alan Turing, Ernest Shackleton, Nelson Mandela

QUIZ 227
1 Isle of Wight
2 Inspector (The Real Inspector Hound, The Government Inspector and An Inspector Calls)
3 Never Say Never Again
4 Carpe diem (seize the day)
5 USA, Norway, Germany, China, Sweden, Brazil, Japan, The Netherlands

QUIZ 228
1 Japan
2 Vincent van Gogh
3 Titanium
4 Terry Pratchett
5 Brazil, Peru, Colombia, Venezuela, Ecuador, Bolivia, Guyana, Suriname and French Guiana/France

QUIZ 229 — 16th August

1 What is the name for the first ever adhesive postage stamp, from 1840?

2 In 'Blackadder the Third', what is the name of Blackadder's Scottish cousin?

3 In which country was the pinotage red wine grape created?

4 What D is a word for rhythmically irregular poetry, of which the Scot William McGonagall is the most famous exponent?

5 In August 1995, Damon Albarn presented a one-off TV programme called 'Britpop Now' which included performances by some of the prominent artists of the era. Name five who performed on the show, not including Blur. [Oasis weren't one of them]

QUIZ 230 — 17th August

1 What nationality was Barack Obama's father?

2 Which decade saw the release of the most official James Bond films?

3 In which month of which year did Mother Teresa of Calcutta die?

4 What metallic element is also known as quicksilver?

5 Name the first five female celebrities to have won 'Strictly Come Dancing'. [main series, not specials, celebrities not dancers]

QUIZ 231 — 18th August

1 What kind of vehicle was a penny-farthing?

2 Which city has a red light district called the Reeperbahn?

3 Whose picture is on all the Chinese banknotes?

4 In the UK, the most senior of the three deputy speakers of the House of Commons is known as the Chairman of ... what?

5 Name five of the ten largest cities in India by population. [cities, not urban agglomerations, though there is not much difference in the result]

QUIZ 232 — 19th August

1 In which city would you find a Parliament building at Stormont?

2 Who wrote the children's book 'The Old Man of Lochnagar'?

3 In 1939 the Ministry of Information designed a poster to be issued in the event of a German invasion. Although it was never used, its five-word slogan has become something of a 21st century icon - what was it?

4 Which popular 1920s dance takes its name from the most famous transatlantic American aviator of the era?

5 What are the five highest grossing films, worldwide, of the 1990s?

QUIZ 229
1 Penny black
2 MacAdder
3 South Africa
4 Doggerel
5 Elastica, Boo Radleys, PJ Harvey, Menswear, Echobelly, Gene, Supergrass, Sleeper, Marion, Powder, Pulp

QUIZ 230
1 Kenyan
2 1960s - 6 films
3 September (5th) 1997 (a few days after Princess Diana)
4 Mercury
5 Natasha Kaplinsky, Jill Halfpenny, Alesha Dixon, Kara Tointon, Abbey Clancy

QUIZ 231
1 Bicycle
2 Hamburg
3 Mao Zedong (only since 1999, there used to be other Chinese figures on them)
4 Ways and Means
5 Mumbai, Delhi, Kolkata, Hyderabad, Ahmedabad, Chennai, Bengaluru, Pune, Surat, Jaipur

QUIZ 232
1 Belfast
2 King Charles III (Prince Charles at the time)
3 Keep Calm and Carry On
4 Lindy Hop (named after Charles Lindbergh)
5 Titanic, Jurassic Park, Star Wars Episode 1: The Phantom Menace, The Lion King, Independence Day

QUIZ 233 — 20th August

1 A milliner specialises in producing which type of clothing?

2 If you were engaged in the practice of Fartlek, what would you be doing?

3 Barbary macaques are the only monkeys that live freely in Europe - where, specifically, do they live?

4 What is the more common name for Hansen's disease, an infectious skin condition?

5 Name five of Britain's eight largest towns, which are not cities, by population. [clue - they're all within 150 miles of London]

QUIZ 234 — 21th August

1 What sort of animal is a sidewinder?

2 The Menai Strait separates mainland Britain from which island?

3 Former 'Fast Show' star Charlie Higson has written several books concerning the youthful adventures of which hero?

4 A tree planted in Los Angeles in 2004 to commemorate George Harrison was destroyed, a decade later, by an infestation of which insect?

5 Name the first five people to have led the UK Liberal Democrats, from 16 July 1988 onwards.

QUIZ 235 — 22nd August

1 What is the body shape of the Russian stringed instrument, the balalaika?

2 Which great metaphysical poet of the 16th and 17th century was also Dean of St Paul's Cathedral?

3 What name links a rap band who had a hit with 'Things I've Seen' with a BBC drama set in MI5 which ran from 2002 to 2011?

4 Which author created the characters Randall Flagg, Paul Sheldon, Paul Edgecomb, Jack Torrance, Carrie White and Pennywise the Dancing Clown?

5 Name five of Ricky Gervais's six stand-up tours since 2003. [up to start of 2022]

QUIZ 236 — 23rd August

1 In the play and film '12 Angry Men', what do those 12 angry men constitute?

2 The Notting Hill Carnival takes place, nearly every year, at the end of which month?

3 What kind of animal is the character of Ratty in 'Wind in the Willows'?

4 What 2014 movie features the song 'Everything is Awesome'?

5 Name five monarchs of Great Britain since 1700 who succeeded someone other than their own parent.

QUIZ 233
1 Hats
2 Running/training - it's a Swedish word used for a kind of unstructured interval training
3 Gibraltar
4 Leprosy
5 Reading, Dudley, Northampton, Luton, Walsall, Basildon, Bournemouth, Swindon

QUIZ 234
1 Snake
2 Anglesey
3 James Bond
4 Beetles (fittingly)
5 Paddy Ashdown, Charles Kennedy, Menzies Campbell, Vince Cable, Nick Clegg

QUIZ 235
1 Triangular
2 John Donne
3 Spooks
4 Stephen King
5 Animals, Politics, Fame, Science, Humanity, SuperNature

QUIZ 236
1 A jury
2 August
3 Water vole
4 The Lego Movie
5 George VI, Victoria, William IV (succeeded his brother), George III (George II his grandfather), George I, Anne, William III, who was king in 1700

QUIZ 237 — 24th August

1 The fashion brand Prada is from which country?

2 Which TV show takes its name from a scientific theory first advanced by the Belgian priest Georges Lemaitre in 1927?

3 Which European country has a currency that is denoted by the letters CHF?

4 In which movie does Norma Desmond say the famous line, "I am big, it's the pictures that got small!"?

5 What are the five largest islands of Japan called?

QUIZ 238 — 25th August

1 Which famous musical sees The Sharks pitted against The Jets?

2 What organisation was formally constituted by the London Declaration in 1949?

3 In film-making, what does CGI stand for?

4 What particular fear do the footballer Dennis Bergkamp and the 'A-Team' character BA Baracus have in common?

5 Since 1999, there has been a UK Children's Laureate, who has changed every two years. Name the first five.

QUIZ 239 — 26th August

1 What is the first name of the boy who owns the toys in the original 'Toy Story'?

2 In 1972, Dr Harrison Schmitt took a photo which is considered to be one of the most widely distributed photographs of all time. What was the subject of the photo?

3 Which large plant with yellow petals has the scientific name Helianthus?

4 A monument to the author EM Forster in Hertfordshire is inscribed with two words, which are the title of a BBC2 quiz show - what two words?

5 In the Roman Empire, in the 1st century BC, there was a First Triumvirate and then a Second Triumvirate, each made up of three extremely powerful men. Name four of the six members who made up the two triumvirates.

QUIZ 240 — 27th August

1 What is the currency of Malta?

2 Who did Andy Murray defeat in the final of Wimbledon 2013?

3 Trelawny Parish in Jamaica is the birthplace of Usain Bolt, as well as which other sprinter who ran a World Record and crossed the line first in the Olympics in 1988?

4 Which beloved character first appeared in a short story in The London Evening News on Christmas Eve 1925 called 'The Wrong Sort of Bees'?

5 Name five of the eight largest cities/ municipalities in Switzerland by population.

QUIZ 237
1 Italy
2 The Big Bang Theory
3 Switzerland
4 Sunset Boulevard
5 Honshu, Hokkaido, Shikoku, Kyushu, Okinawa

QUIZ 238
1 West Side Story
2 The Commonwealth
3 Computer-generated imagery
4 Fear of flying
5 Quentin Blake, Anne Fine, Michael Morpurgo, Jacqueline Wilson, Michael Rosen

QUIZ 239
1 Andy (Davis)
2 The Earth
3 Sunflower
4 Only Connect - the epigraph to his novel 'Howards End'
5 Julius Caesar, Pompey, Crassus, Octavian/ Augustus, Mark Antony, Lepidus

QUIZ 240
1 Euro
2 Novak Djokovic
3 Ben Johnson
4 Winnie-the-Pooh
5 Zurich, Geneva, Basel, Lausanne, Bern, Winterthur, Lucerne, St Gallen

QUIZ 241 — 28th August

1 What surname links the architect who designed the renowned West London tower block Trellick Tower with a film villain played by Gert Fröbe?

2 What is the name of the hill on which you'd find the Sacré-Coeur in Paris?

3 What term for an object which is expensive but not useful derives from a certain type of animal given as a gift by monarchs of Southeast Asia?

4 Which Hollywood action star has won the most Razzies for Worst Actor, as well as being nominated several more times?

5 Name five of the seven cities in the UK with names ending in Y. [not allowing "The City" (of London)]

QUIZ 242 — 29th August

1 They're known as candy apples in the USA, but what are they known as in the UK?

2 Who was Prime Minister of Russia from 2008 to 2012?

3 What is the longest common English word that can be formed using only letters that rhyme with "E"? [and we're saying Z as Zed, not that it makes any difference]

4 What is the name of both Ronald Reagan's last movie and a very successful Las Vegas band who took their name from an imaginary band in a New Order video?

5 Name five counties that border Leicestershire.

QUIZ 243 — 30th August

1 The Shannon is the longest river in which country?

2 Former World Heavyweight boxing champion Vitali Klitschko became mayor of which city in 2014?

3 Which Australian, then an unknown, played the part of Curly in an acclaimed 1998 production of 'Oklahoma!' at London's National Theatre?

4 In 2019, which well known barrister admitted clubbing a fox to death while dressed in kimono?

5 Name five actors who have ever played M or Q in official James Bond films.

QUIZ 244 — 31st August

1 Stephenson's Rocket is an early example of what means of transportation?

2 What word links an ice cream, a cricket bat, a bottle, a gun and a moustachioed detective?

3 The film festival set up by Robert Redford in 1978 is named after one of his most famous characters. What is it called?

4 In 'The Lord of the Rings' films, how is the hobbit played by Dominic Monaghan usually known?

5 Name the last five Democrats who have lost a US presidential election. [up to 2020 election]

QUIZ 241
1 Goldfinger (Erno and Auric)
2 Montmartre
3 White Elephant
4 Sylvester Stallone
5 Canterbury, Coventry, Derby, Ely, Salisbury, Newry, Derry/Londonderry

QUIZ 242
1 Toffee apples
2 Vladimir Putin - while Dmitry Medvedev was President
3 Detected [possible letters are BCDEGPTV]
4 The Killers
5 Nottinghamshire, Lincolnshire, Rutland, Northamptonshire, Warwickshire, Staffordshire, Derbyshire

QUIZ 243
1 Republic of Ireland
2 Kyiv
3 Hugh Jackman
4 Jolyon Maugham
5 Bernard Lee, Robert Brown, Judi Dench, Ralph Fiennes (M) Peter Burton, Desmond Llewellyn, John Cleese, Ben Whishaw (Peter Burton played Major Boothroyd in 'Dr No' who is Q. In non-official films, add John Huston, David Niven, Edward Fox (M), Geoffrey Bayldon, Alec McCowen (Q))

QUIZ 244
1 Locomotion/Train
2 Magnum
3 Sundance
4 Merry (Meriadoc Brandybuck)
5 Hillary Rodham Clinton, John Kerry, Al Gore, Michael Dukakis, Walter Mondale

QUIZ 245 — 1st September

1 Which large city has a name that means "January's river"?

2 Which British male subculture of the 1950s wore clothes which were partially inspired by those worn by young dandies in the Edwardian era?

3 Which foodstuff is awarded as the prize in the Flitch Trials, held every four years in the Essex town of Great Dunmow?

4 Peter Cook in 1960, Eric Idle in 1965, Clive Anderson in 1975, Hugh Laurie in 1981, Sue Perkins in 1991, David Mitchell in 1996 - all presidents of which famous student club?

5 Name the first five children's books by Julia Donaldson and Axel Scheffler that were made into Christmas animations by the BBC.

QUIZ 246 — 2nd September

1 Which came first - the premier of 'Dr No', the first James Bond film, or the first episode of 'Dr Who'?

2 What country in southern Africa was formerly known as Bechuanaland?

3 Which writer of another children's classic wrote 'Toad of Toad Hall', the dramatization of Kenneth Grahame's 'The Wind in the Willows'?

4 Which famous Lerner and Loewe musical takes its title from a line in the song 'London Bridge is Falling Down'?

5 Name the five top point scorers in NBA regular season history. [up to 2022]

QUIZ 247 — 3rd September

1 Michael D Higgins became President of which European country in 2011?

2 What name is shared by products from Ford, Samsung and Mars?

3 What, in terms of the Oscars, links Peter Finch in 1977 to Heath Ledger in 2009?

4 In May 2014, Mohammed Al-Fayed blamed the removal from Craven Cottage of what item for his former club Fulham's relegation from the Premier League?

5 Name five of the eight characters who have appeared in the most episodes of 'EastEnders'. Just first name required. [up to 2022]

QUIZ 248 — 4th September

1 In the film, is Bambi male or female?

2 Which musical legend had sons called Ziggy, Damian, Rohan and Steve?

3 What is the film known in Italian as 'Il buono, il brutto, il cattivo' called in English?

4 What surname links the winner of golf's Masters Tournament from 1977 and 1981 to the winner in 2012 and 2014?

5 Name the five US Presidents with four-letter surnames.

QUIZ 249 — 5th September

1 Easter Island, renowned for its massive stone heads, is in which ocean?

2 According to the opening credits of the TV cartoon 'SuperTed', who gave the title character his powers?

3 Which English football club famously won trophies in 1951, 1961, 1971, 1981 and 1991?

4 In France, what name is given to a patty of raw minced beef, often served with a raw egg yolk on top?

5 Name five politicians who were in the first Labour cabinet of 1997 and the last Labour cabinet of 2010.

QUIZ 250 — 6th September

1 Which American President was assassinated in 1865 at Ford's Theatre?

2 Which F is Santa Claus's brother in the 2007 movie?

3 How was Alexandra Legge-Bourke better known when she was nanny to Princes William and Harry?

4 In 1989, B&Q significantly and influentially broke British law by doing what?

5 In 'Thomas the Tank Engine' there are eight main characters numbered from 1-8. Thomas is Number 1. Name any five of the other seven. We just need the names of the engines, not their numbers.

QUIZ 251 — 7th September

1 An acorn is the nut of which tree?

2 Give any year in the life of Charles Darwin.

3 Which couple, who married in 2010, first acted on screen together in a 1992 film called 'Jamón Jamón'?

4 Which island nation is the world's leading producer of vanilla?

5 Name five US states with three or more of the same vowel in their name.

QUIZ 252 — 8th September

1 Which motorway links London and Leeds?

2 What sort of animal is a galah?

3 A man named John Pemberton produced the syrup for which soft drink in 1886?

4 What links ABBA in 1974 to Celine Dion in 1988?

5 Name five of the eleven MPs who joined the new political party Change UK in 2019.

QUIZ 249
1 Pacific Ocean (the island is administered by Chile)
2 Mother Nature
3 Tottenham Hotspur (League, League + FA Cup, League Cup, FA Cup, FA Cup)
4 Steak tartare
5 Gordon Brown, Harriet Harman, Peter Mandelson, Alistair Darling, Jack Straw, Nick Brown (Margaret Beckett left government in 2009)

QUIZ 250
1 Abraham Lincoln
2 Fred Claus
3 Tiggy (Legge-Bourke)
4 Opening on a Sunday
5 2-Edward, 3-Henry, 4-Gordon, 5-James, 6-Percy, 7-Toby, 8-Duck

QUIZ 251
1 Oak
2 1809-1882
3 Penelope Cruz and Javier Bardem
4 Madagascar
5 Alabama, Alaska, Arkansas, Tennessee, Mississippi, Colorado, Illinois, New Jersey, Virginia, West Virginia

QUIZ 252
1 M1
2 Bird (it's an Australian cockatoo)
3 Coca-Cola
4 Eurovision Song Contest winners (for Sweden and Switzerland)
5 Sarah Wollaston, Gavin Shuker, Heidi Allen, Anna Soubry, Ann Coffey, Chris Leslie, Chuka Umunna, Luciana Berger, Angela Smith, Joan Ryan, Mike Gapes

QUIZ 253 — 9th September

1 Who played Colonel Kurtz in 'Apocalypse Now'?

2 In Greece he was called Eros – what was he called in Rome?

3 Which news network, with various TV channels in different languages, has a name that means "The Island" in English?

4 Which city links the Tennessee Williams play 'A Streetcar Named Desire', the American TV series 'Tremé' and the Bond movie 'Live and Let Die'?

5 Name five of the six completed novels written by EM Forster.

QUIZ 254 — 10th September

1 Which British Crown Dependency has its capital at Douglas?

2 Who duetted with Janet Jackson at the Super Bowl 38 half-time show, ripping off part of her clothing in a controversial "wardrobe malfunction"?

3 In how many different years of the 20th century did someone who reigned as King or Queen of the United Kingdom die?

4 True or False? The Hungarian word 'Donaldkacsázás' literally means 'Donald Ducking' which is the practice of wearing a shirt but no trousers.

5 Name five independent countries that India has a land border with.

QUIZ 255 — 11th September

1 What does HBO stand for, as in the popular US cable channel?

2 Which chess piece always stays on squares of the same colour?

3 Which author wrote a story in which the ghost of Jacob Marley visits his former business partner Ebenezer Scrooge?

4 What might you expect to see being "born" at Babyland General Hospital in Cleveland, Georgia?

5 Name five of the six male tennis players who have won Grand Slam singles tournaments on all of grass, clay and hard courts. [up to 2022]

QUIZ 256 — 12th September

1 Myxomatosis is a disease which affects which animals?

2 What note is the bottom string of a standard guitar tuned to?

3 What is the maximum number of Friday 13ths that can occur in any one year?

4 The action of which bestselling novel, written by David Nicholls, begins on 15th July 1988?

5 Name the five previously Republican states that Joe Biden, for the Democrats, won from Donald Trump at the 2020 US presidential election.

QUIZ 253
1 Marlon Brando
2 Cupid
3 Al Jazeera
4 New Orleans
5 Where Angels Fear to Tread, The Longest Journey, A Room With a View, Howard's End, A Passage to India, Maurice

QUIZ 254
1 Isle of Man
2 Justin Timberlake
3 Five (1901, 1910, 1936, 1952, 1972 (Edward VIII))
4 True
5 Pakistan, China, Nepal, Bhutan, Bangladesh, Myanmar (not Sri Lanka – narrowly separated by the Palk Strait)

QUIZ 255
1 Home Box Office
2 Bishop
3 Charles Dickens
4 Cabbage Patch Kids
5 Jimmy Connors, Mats Wilander, Andre Agassi, Rafael Nadal, Roger Federer, Novak Djokovic

QUIZ 256
1 Rabbits
2 E
3 Three (February, March, November in a non leap year – every year has at least one Friday 13th)
4 One Day
5 Pennsylvania, Michigan, Wisconsin, Georgia, Arizona

QUIZ 257 — 13th September

1 At which fast food restaurant could you order a Chicken Royale or a Whopper?

2 What is the home country of the groundskeeper of Springfield Elementary School?

3 In the normal English spelling, what is the only national capital city in the world with three consecutive letters with a dot above them?

4 Which ice cream company was founded in 1978 by a Mr Cohen and Mr Greenfield?

5 Before Boris Johnson, name five of the last six UK Prime Ministers not to have attended fee-paying secondary schools. [Theresa May did spend some time at a fee-paying school, as well as a state school, so don't put her]

QUIZ 258 — 14th September

1 What F is the name of an edible fish and also means to behave awkwardly?

2 What is the designation of any US Air Force aircraft carrying the US Vice President?

3 Roger Federer, Muhammad Ali and Floyd Mayweather have sometimes been described as the GOAT. What, in this context, is GOAT?

4 Mary Anning became famous for her discoveries of fossils at which coastal town in Dorset?

5 Name five of the six U2 studio albums with a one or two word name. [up to 2022]

QUIZ 259 — 15th September

1 What does the L stand for in the charity, the RNLI?

2 The slogan 'Never Knowingly Undersold' was for many years associated with which store?

3 Whose film roles include Reggie Hammond, Norbit Rice, James 'Thunder' Early and Billy Ray Valentine?

4 What links The Trotters in 'Only Fools and Horses', Travis Bickle in 'Taxi Driver', Gordon Tracy from the 'Thunderbirds', Mr Bean, and The Beatles?

5 Since 1980, name five men with more than one Olympic 100 metres medal of any colour. [according to current official results, up to Tokyo Olympics in 2021]

QUIZ 260 — 16th September

1 Who wrote the novel 'Animal Farm'?

2 Which is the only US State Capital with a three-word name?

3 Iran broke off diplomatic relations with Great Britain in 1989 because of the publication of which book?

4 By what C was John Darwin better known when he hit the headlines in 2007?

5 Name five independent countries whose usual English name ends with the letter U.

QUIZ 257
1 Burger King
2 Scotland
3 Beijing
4 Ben and Jerry's
5 Gordon Brown, John Major, Margaret Thatcher, James Callaghan, Edward Heath, Harold Wilson

QUIZ 258
1 Flounder
2 Air Force 2
3 Greatest of all time
4 Lyme Regis
5 Boy, War, October, Achtung Baby, Zooropa, Pop

QUIZ 259
1 Lifeboat
2 John Lewis
3 Eddie Murphy
4 All have a yellow vehicle
5 Andre De Grasse, Usain Bolt, Justin Gatlin, Carl Lewis, Linford Christie, Maurice Greene, Ato Boldon, Frankie Fredericks

QUIZ 260
1 George Orwell
2 Salt Lake City (Utah)
3 The Satanic Verses (Salman Rushdie)
4 Canoe Man
5 Nauru, Palau, Guinea-Bissau, Peru, Tuvalu, Vanuatu

QUIZ 261 — 17th September

1 Who wrote the novel 'The Color Purple'?

2 On which gangster was the original 1932 film 'Scarface' based?

3 Which rodent is Canada's national animal?

4 Which US city is served by Louis Armstrong International airport?

5 Name five UK Top 10 singles by A-ha.

QUIZ 262 — 18th September

1 In which country is the wine brand Jacob's Creek based?

2 Which Republican did Bill Clinton defeat when he first became US President in 1992?

3 How long does one term for the Lord Mayor of London last?

4 Actress Mia Farrow has married twice - once to conductor Andre Previn and the other time to which Oscar-winning American star?

5 Name five official, EON series, Bond films that were an actor's first in the lead role. [up to 2022]

QUIZ 263 — 19th September

1 In which year did Neil Armstrong set foot on the moon?

2 Which pre-Euro currency ended its life with an exchange rate of 1936.27 to the Euro?

3 What name (first name and surname) links a Welsh rugby player born in 1985 to a fictional pirate?

4 On 23rd August 1994, what did the two members of the KLF burn, on the island of Jura, to the outrage of many?

5 Name the five EU capital cities that end with the letter N. [in the normal English spelling]

QUIZ 264 — 20th September

1 Which acclaimed TV drama featured characters called Paulie Walnuts, Meadow, Artie Bucco and Big Pussy?

2 What does IHOP stand for, as in the US based restaurant chain that specialises in breakfast foods?

3 What type of furniture is the Polyprop, an iconic item designed in 1963 and still in production today, and noted for its stackability?

4 Which artist was shot three times by a woman called Valerie Solanas on June 3rd 1968?

5 Name five US states that have four different vowels in them at least once. [Y is not in any context a vowel for this question]

QUIZ 261

1 Alice Walker
2 Al Capone
3 Beaver
4 New Orleans
5 Take On Me, The Sun Always Shines on TV, Train of Thought, Hunting High and Low, I've Been Losing You, Cry Wolf, The Living Daylights, Stay on These Roads, Analogue (All I Want)

QUIZ 262

1 Australia
2 George HW Bush
3 One year (Four years for the Mayor of London, a different position)
4 Frank Sinatra (in 1966, when she was 21 and he was 50 - she was never married to Woody Allen)
5 Dr No, On Her Majesty's Secret Service, Live and Let Die, The Living Daylights, GoldenEye, Casino Royale

QUIZ 263

1 1969
2 Italian Lira
3 James Hook
4 £1 million
5 Dublin, Tallinn, Berlin, Lisbon, Copenhagen

QUIZ 264

1 The Sopranos
2 International House of Pancakes
3 Chair
4 Andy Warhol (he survived)
5 Connecticut, Georgia, Louisiana, Minnesota, Rhode Island, South Carolina (Not allowing Pennsylvania)

QUIZ 265 — 21st September

1 Which country is the home of the famous car manufacturer Skoda?

2 Which British writer created the acclaimed 2022 TV drama 'Sherwood'?

3 Give any year in the life of the great artist Michelangelo.

4 Which British film from 1981 is the only Best Picture Oscar winner to contain all of the letters of the word "Oscar" in its title?

5 Name five London boroughs whose names have exactly six letters in their name.

QUIZ 266 — 22nd September

1 Which substance found on teeth is the hardest in the human body?

2 In 'The Simpsons', what breed is the dog Santa's Little Helper?

3 Which character beat alternatives such as Katy the Kangaroo, Elmo the Elephant and Newt the Gnu in a 1950s contest to find a new breakfast cereal mascot?

4 Who was the founder of the health technology company Theranos, who was found guilty of fraud in 2022?

5 Name five US Presidents since 1920 who have directly followed someone of their own party. [up to 2022]

QUIZ 267 — 23rd September

1 In HG Wells' 'The War of the Worlds', the alien invaders come from which planet?

2 Which building is supposed to be haunted by Lady Jane Grey, Edward V, Henry VI and Anne Boleyn, who all died there?

3 Which S is the American city where you would find the Gateway Arch?

4 What was Harold Wilson referring to in 1956 when he said: "Now Britain's strength, freedom and solvency apparently depend on the proceeds of a squalid raffle"?

5 Name five Top 3 UK singles for Whitney Houston.

QUIZ 268 — 24th September

1 Which witch lives in the woods near Burkittsville, Maine, according to a movie released in the UK at Halloween 1999?

2 What's the popular name for the section of the North Atlantic Ocean where, spookily, more than fifty ships and aircraft have disappeared?

3 In which month of the year does the Trooping the Colour ceremony take place?

4 Which javelin thrower was BBC Sports Personality of the Year in 1987?

5 Name five independent countries with names beginning with M and containing two or more Os in their common English name.

QUIZ 265

1 Czech Republic/ Czechia
2 James Graham
3 1475-1564 (he died one month short of his 89th birthday)
4 Chariots of Fire
5 Barnet, Camden, Harrow, Newham, Ealing, Bexley, Sutton, Merton

QUIZ 266

1 Enamel
2 Greyhound
3 Tony the Tiger
4 Elizabeth Holmes
5 George HW Bush, Gerald Ford, Lyndon B Johnson, Harry S Truman, Herbert Hoover, Calvin Coolidge

QUIZ 267

1 Mars
2 Tower of London
3 St. Louis
4 Premium Bonds
5 Saving All My Love for You, I Wanna Dance With Somebody, One Moment in Time, I Will Always Love You, I Have Nothing, It's Not Right But It's OK, My Love is Your Love, Higher Love (Kygo & Whitney Houston)

QUIZ 268

1 The Blair Witch
2 Bermuda Triangle
3 June (Second Saturday in June, and coincides with monarch's official birthday)
4 Fatima Whitbread
5 Moldova, Monaco, Mongolia, Montenegro, Morocco

QUIZ 269 — 25th September

1 What is the first name of the man who became Duke of Cambridge in 2011?

2 Which actor links 'Philadelphia', 'Interview with a Vampire' and 'Shrek 2'?

3 Which book was JR Hartley searching for in a Yellow Pages advert first shown in 1983?

4 Between December 1984 and September 1985, Frankie Goes to Hollywood, Jennifer Rush and Huey Lewis and the News all had UK Top 20 hits with three entirely different songs that had the same title. What was the title?

5 Name five of Spain's eight largest islands, by area.

QUIZ 270 — 26th September

1 What colour rabbit did Alice follow down the hole to Wonderland?

2 Which theatrical term describes blocking a fellow actor by standing in front of them?

3 What L is the common name in the UK for what is known in the USA as Spandex?

4 WAZA is an international body which provides leadership and organisation for various wildlife parks. WAZA stands for the World Association of Zoos and what?

5 By area, name five of the seven largest Greek islands?

QUIZ 271 — 27th September

1 Office workers can often be seen with a lanyard. What is a lanyard?

2 What kind of creature is a natterjack?

3 In 'The Lion King', what is the name of the young cub who goes on to become the eponymous Lion King?

4 Who was the youngest of the six central cast members in 'Friends'?

5 Name five independent countries which have land which is part of the Sahara Desert. [for simplicity, let's not count the disputed territory of Western Sahara]

QUIZ 272 — 28th September

1 Which comedian has been known as "The Big Yin"?

2 One of the largest public squares in the world, which landmark in China has a name which means "Gate of Heavenly Peace"?

3 What surname links a social-climbing TV character and a boy in a famous children's book who lives with his mother and four grandparents?

4 Which French military general said "all religions have been made by men"?

5 Name five independent countries whose English name starts with S and ends with A.

QUIZ 269
1 William (Prince William)
2 Antonio Banderas
3 Fly Fishing
4 The Power of Love
5 Mallorca, Tenerife, Fuerteventura, Gran Canaria, Lanzarote, La Palma, Menorca, Ibiza (followed by La Gomera)

QUIZ 270
1 White
2 Upstaging
3 Lycra
4 Aquariums
5 Crete, Euboea, Lesbos, Rhodes, Chios, Kefalonia, Corfu (followed by Lemnos, Samos, Naxos)

QUIZ 271
1 Rope worn around the neck to carry/display security card
2 Toad
3 Simba
4 Matthew Perry (6 months younger than Jennifer Aniston - both born in 1969)
5 Algeria, Chad, Egypt, Libya, Mali, Mauritania, Morocco, Niger, Sudan and Tunisia

QUIZ 272
1 Billy Connolly
2 Tiananmen Square
3 Bucket (Hyacinth and Charlie)
4 Napoleon Bonaparte
5 Saint Lucia, Samoa, Saudi Arabia, Serbia, Slovakia, Slovenia, Somalia, South Africa, Somalia, Syria

QUIZ 273 — 29th September

1 Which mythological creature features on the Vauxhall Motors logo?

2 In the 2004 film 'Starsky & Hutch' who played Starsky opposite Owen Wilson's Hutch?

3 Fittingly, who married former 'Doctor Who' actor Peter Davison's daughter in 2011?

4 Which very successful action film was released in the UK on the 9th August 1996, 36 days after it went on general release in the US?

5 Name five teams that have lost in the final of the men's UEFA European Championships. [up to 2022]

QUIZ 274 — 30th September

1 Which London Underground line is shown in red on tube maps?

2 In which American state is the original Disneyland?

3 Which British Prime Minister resigned because of the Suez Crisis?

4 What is the name of Will Smith's character in 'The Fresh Prince of Bel Air'? [first name and surname]

5 Name five cities that have hosted the Summer Olympics more than once.

QUIZ 275 — 1st October

1 Which gas makes up approximately 78% of Earth's atmosphere?

2 How many James Bond films did Pierce Brosnan star in?

3 In which country was Richard Leakey, who died in early 2022, a leading conservationist and civil servant?

4 In which country would you find the majority of the world's Walloons?

5 Apart from the Christmas special, each episode of the comedy series 'Extras' was named after the main guest celebrity in it. Name five of those episodes. [be careful, there are various celebrities who weren't the episode titles, think about the ones with the largest parts]

QUIZ 276 — 2nd October

1 What is calligraphy the art of?

2 1989's 'A Grand Day Out' was the first appearance of which inventor and his dog?

3 What surname links a character played by Dustin Hoffman in an Oscar-winning 1969 film and a character played by Stockard Channing in a hugely successful 1978 film?

4 What is the only planet in our Solar System whose name begins with a different letter in French and English?

5 Name five feature films directed by Christopher Nolan with a single word title. [up to 2022]

QUIZ 273
1 Griffin
2 Ben Stiller
3 David Tennant
4 Independence Day (was released on July 4th the USA) [note: it had a widespread "pre-release on the 3rd July]
5 Yugoslavia, USSR, West Germany/Germany, Belgium, Spain, Czech Republic/Czechia, Italy, Portugal, France, England

QUIZ 274
1 Central Line
2 California
3 Anthony Eden
4 Will Smith
5 Paris, London, Los Angeles, Tokyo, Athens (allow Stockholm, which hosted in 1912 and hosted equestrian events for Melbourne in 1956)

QUIZ 275
1 Nitrogen
2 Four (Goldeneye, Tomorrow Never Dies, The World is Not Enough, Die Another Day)
3 Kenya
4 Belgium (they are the French speaking ones)
5 Ben Stiller, Ross Kemp and Vinnie Jones, Kate Winslet, Les Dennis, Samuel L Jackson, Patrick Stewart, Orlando Bloom, David Bowie, Daniel Radcliffe, Chris Martin, Sir Ian McKellen, Jonathan Ross

QUIZ 276
1 Handwriting
2 Wallace and Gromit
3 Rizzo - the films are 'Midnight Cowboy' and 'Grease'
4 Earth (Terre in French)
5 Following, Memento, Insomnia, Inception, Interstellar, Dunkirk, Tenet ('Oppenheimer' due in 2023 - allow that)

QUIZ 277 — 3rd October

1 What colour is Winnie the Pooh's normal t-shirt in the Disney cartoon?

2 In which sport do nations compete in the Davis Cup?

3 Which animal provides the milk for Roquefort cheese?

4 In which country would you spend a dong?

5 Name five US Presidents between 1970 and 2020 who were in office while the UK has had a Labour Prime Minister.

QUIZ 278 — 4th October

1 What does a fletcher make?

2 If an adult male swan is called a cob what is an adult female swan called?

3 What TV show (later made into a film) follows the exploits of Will, Simon, Jay and Neil at Rudge Park Comprehensive?

4 Which M is a primitive but effective weapon developed by Finnish troops fighting against the USSR in the late 1930s, and named after the Soviet Foreign Minister?

5 Name any five non-UK capital cities of fully independent countries which are less than 500 miles by air from Heathrow Airport.

QUIZ 279 — 5th October

1 In which city does Batman live?

2 In the Solar System, what is the closest planet to the Sun?

3 After many nominations, who finally received a Best Director Oscar for 'The Departed'?

4 Which band is credited with the albums 'Intravenus de Milo', 'The Sun Never Sweats', 'Smell the Glove' and 'Break Like The Wind'?

5 Name five US states with at least one y in their name.

QUIZ 280 — 6th October

1 What A was the catchphrase of football hard man John Fashanu when he presented 'Gladiators'?

2 What word goes before the words "Enlightening the World" to give the name of a famous statue?

3 Which large mammal can be Indian, Black, White, Javan or Sumatran?

4 What three-word phrase does Hercule Poirot use for his brain, when he needs to exercise it to solve a murder?

5 Name five actors who appeared in more than 75 episodes of the US sitcom 'Parks and Recreation'.

QUIZ 277
1 Red
2 Tennis
3 Sheep (ewe)
4 Vietnam
5 Richard Nixon, Gerald Ford, Jimmy Carter, Bill Clinton, George W Bush, Barack Obama

QUIZ 278
1 Arrows
2 Pen
3 The Inbetweeners
4 Molotov cocktail
5 Paris, Brussels, Luxembourg, Amsterdam, Dublin, Bern (The Hague isn't the capital of the Netherlands, it's the seat of government.)

QUIZ 279
1 Gotham City
2 Mercury
3 Martin Scorsese
4 Spinal Tap (only 'Break Like The Wind' has actually been released, the others are mentioned in the movie)
5 Kentucky, Maryland, New Jersey, New York, Pennsylvania, Wyoming

QUIZ 280
1 Awooga!
2 Liberty (it is the official name of the Statue of Liberty)
3 Rhinoceros
4 Little grey cells
5 Amy Poehler, Nick Offerman, Aubrey Plaza, Aziz Ansari, Chris Pratt, Jim O'Heir, Retta, Rashida Jones, Adam Scott, Rob Lowe

QUIZ 281 — 7th October

1 What is the name of the line in darts from which the players throw?

2 What is tennis player Andy Murray's mother called?

3 Who wrote 'The Interpretation Of Dreams', published in 1899?

4 In standard London Monopoly, starting on Go, where would you end up if, on one turn, you threw double six, double one, and double six? [think about it]

5 Name five of the six Shakespeare plays with standard titles ending with the letter T.

QUIZ 282 — 8th October

1 Which is larger, in terms of area: Kuwait or Qatar?

2 On French taps, F is on the cold; what letter is on the hot tap?

3 Which Brit won a gold medal in figure skating at the 1980 Olympics?

4 What links Ben Elton, TS Eliot, Alan Ayckbourn, Jim Steinman and Richard Stilgoe, amongst others?

5 Name five ABBA UK Top 5 singles with titles ending with a vowel.

QUIZ 283 — 9th October

1 Which country is the native home of the redback spider?

2 Who would have killed you if you were a victim of patricide?

3 What word (for a book) comes from the Ancient Greek for "well-rounded education"?

4 Which novel was published on 8th June 1949, 34 years 10 months and 4 days before the opening of the book is set?

5 Name the five countries that border Argentina.

QUIZ 284 — 10th October

1 What was the currency of Germany before the Euro?

2 In the Disney film 'Dumbo', what kind of animal is Dumbo's friend Timothy?

3 Which sitcom had episodes called: 'The Changing Face of Rural Blamire', 'Deep in the Heart of Yorkshire' and 'Elegy for Fallen Wellies'?

4 What 1994 film, directed by Nicholas Hytner, had its title changed from the book on which it was based by adding in one word and taking away a Roman numeral? [allegedly to avoid confusing Americans...]

5 Name five official capital cities in Africa whose usual English names start with an A.

QUIZ 281
1 The oche
2 Judy
3 Sigmund Freud
4 Jail (for three doubles)
5 Hamlet, Romeo and Juliet, Twelfth Night, The Tempest, As You Like It, Love's Labour's Lost

QUIZ 282
1 Kuwait (6,880 sq mi to 4,473 sq mi)
2 C (for Chaud)
3 Robin Cousins
4 They've all provided lyrics for Andrew Lloyd Webber musicals
5 Waterloo, Mamma Mia, Fernando, Name of the Game, Take a Chance on Me, Chiquitita, Gimme Gimme Gimme, Knowing Me Knowing You

QUIZ 283
1 Australia
2 Your son/daughter - patricide is the killing OF a father
3 Encyclopaedia
4 1984 (the action starts on April 4 1984)
5 Chile, Bolivia, Paraguay, Brazil, Uruguay

QUIZ 284
1 Mark/Deutschmark
2 Mouse (Timothy Q Mouse)
3 Last of the Summer Wine
4 The Madness of King George - changed from 'The Madness of George III' to make clear to an American audience that it was about a king rather than a sequel
5 Algiers, Asmara, Addis Ababa, Accra, Antananarivo, Abuja

QUIZ 285 — 11th October

1 In the USA, how many cents are there in a dime?

2 In which city did Mark Chapman assassinate John Lennon in 1980?

3 Complete this Oscar Wilde quotation: "There is only one thing in life worse than being talked about, and that is ..." what?

4 What is the smallest member state of the EU, by both area and population?

5 Give the name of five Agatha Christie novels with "Murder" in the title. They have to be UK titles, and also not short stories or short story collections.

QUIZ 286 — 12th October

1 What sort of animal is the Warner Bros. cartoon character Pepé Le Pew?

2 What is the nickname of the Central Criminal Court in London?

3 Who founded the film and television production company Happy Madison?

4 Who was the first US President to be born in the 20th century? [to be clear, this means who became President first, rather than which US President was born first in the 20th century]

5 Laos is a landlocked country bordered by five other countries. Name them.

QUIZ 287 — 13th October

1 According to Adam and the Ants song 'Prince Charming', what is nothing to be scared of?

2 In which film does the titular character search for Snowflake, the missing mascot of the Miami Dolphins?

3 Which C, a complication of 'haematoma auris', is a condition most associated with rugby union forwards?

4 What aid to police work was invented by the medical student and policeman John Augustus Larson in California in 1921?

5 John Cazale's movie career consisted of five films between 1972 and 1978 (three starring Al Pacino), all of which were nominated for the Best Picture Oscar. Name four of them.

QUIZ 288 — 14th October

1 On which planet is there a volcano called Olympus Mons?

2 What is situated at the eastern end of the Champs-Élysées in Paris?

3 In ancient Greece, what were biremes, triremes and quadriremes?

4 What is the only capital city in the world whose name begins with the letter I?

5 Name five men who were Emperor of Rome at any point in the 1st century AD. [don't write Caesar, they're all Caesar, and so you don't waste an answer, Julius Caesar isn't one of them]

QUIZ 285
1 Ten
2 New York
3 Not being talked about
4 Malta (316 sq km and around 415k people, next is Luxembourg, then Cyprus)
5 The Murder on the Links, The Murder of Roger Ackroyd, The Murder at the Vicarage, Murder on the Orient Express, The ABC Murders, Murder in Mesopotamia, Murder is Easy, A Murder is Announced, Sleeping Murder

QUIZ 286
1 Skunk
2 The Old Bailey
3 Adam Sandler
4 John F Kennedy (1917)
5 China, Vietnam, Cambodia, Thailand, Myanmar (Burma)

QUIZ 287
1 Ridicule
2 Ace Ventura: Pet Detective
3 Cauliflower ear
4 Polygraph/Lie detector
5 The Godfather, The Godfather Part 2, Dog Day Afternoon, The Conversation, The Deer Hunter (He played Fredo in 'The Godfather' films)

QUIZ 288
1 Mars
2 The Place de la Concorde (The Arc de Triomphe is at the western end)
3 Ships – (the 'reme' part refers to the number of rows of oars)
4 Islamabad (Pakistan)
5 Augustus, Tiberius, Gaius/Caligula, Claudius, Nero, Galba, Otho, Vitellius, Vespasian, Titus, Domitian, Nerva, Trajan

QUIZ 289 — 15th October

1 With what did the farmer's wife cut off the tails of the three blind mice?

2 Who was on the English throne when the Spanish Armada attacked?

3 Which biblical figure had a height of six cubits and a span?

4 Which production team was behind the best selling album in the UK in both 1988 and 1989?

5 Name five capital cities of fully independent countries for which the usual name in English contains only the vowel O. [they can be official capitals, or, in one case, we will allow a de facto capital]

QUIZ 290 — 16th October

1 Which meat is the traditional centrepiece of an American Thanksgiving meal?

2 'Shakermaker' was the first Top 20 hit for which band?

3 What colour is the zero segment on a roulette wheel?

4 Which famous anti-slavery novel was written by abolitionist Harriet Beecher Stowe?

5 Name five counties of the Republic of Ireland with five letters or fewer in their name.

QUIZ 291 — 17th October

1 In which county in England is Lea & Perrins sauce made and bottled?

2 What surname links a land visited by Dorothy Gale to a famous director?

3 Which legendary star was born Lee Jun-fan in San Francisco in November 1940?

4 What links the novels 'Mrs Dalloway', 'Ulysses', 'Cosmopolis' and 'Saturday'?

5 Not including City of London, which isn't a borough, or City of Westminster, which is, name five London boroughs whose names contain more than one word.

QUIZ 292 — 18th October

1 What type of animal is Baloo in 'The Jungle Book'?

2 What is the most northerly capital city of an independent country in the world?

3 Who was the UK Prime Minister at the start of World War II?

4 What is the name of the small town in Sicily where Al Pacino's grandparents, who brought him up, were from?

5 Name five countries which are in both NATO and the G20.

QUIZ 289
1 A carving knife
2 Elizabeth I
3 Goliath
4 Stock Aitken Waterman – 'Kylie' by Kylie Minogue and 'Ten Good Reasons' by Jason Donovan
5 Colombo (de facto), London, Oslo, Porto Novo, Moscow, Stockholm, Tokyo

QUIZ 290
1 Turkey
2 Oasis
3 Green
4 Uncle Tom's Cabin
5 Cork, Kerry, Clare, Laois, Louth, Sligo, Cavan, Meath, Mayo

QUIZ 291
1 Worcestershire
2 Oz (Frank Oz is the director)
3 Bruce Lee
4 All set on one day
5 Kensington and Chelsea, Hammersmith and Fulham, Tower Hamlets, Richmond upon Thames, Kingston upon Thames, Waltham Forest, Barking and Dagenham

QUIZ 292
1 Bear
2 Reykjavik
3 Neville Chamberlain
4 Corleone. In 'The Godfather', Vito Corleone takes that name because he is from that town. The Pacino connection is pure coincidence
5 USA, Canada, UK, France, Germany, Italy

QUIZ 293 — 19th October

1 Which G can be a font, a type of novel, or a style of architecture?

2 The son of a former contestant on 'The X Factor', which entrepreneur who died in February 2022 set up the influential SBTV music channel?

3 Give any year in the life of Wild West outlaw Jesse James.

4 Who rowed in the 1980 University Boat Race, released a 2011 blues album called 'Let Them Talk', and was for a time one of the best paid TV actors in the world?

5 Name five of the eight individual, de facto leaders of the Soviet Union from 1922 from 1991.

QUIZ 294 — 20th October

1 Which city is furthest north: Prague, London or Vancouver?

2 In 1989 they had an 'Excellent Adventure'. What did they have in 1991?

3 What is the name of Donald Duck's miserly uncle?

4 How, according to their names, do you distinguish between the two types of sloth?

5 Name five full-length books written by George Orwell - not including pamphlets or articles, so there are six novels and three non-fiction books to choose from.

QUIZ 295 — 21st October

1 What was the first James Bond movie to star Daniel Craig?

2 Which W was the product launched by Vidal Sassoon in 1989 to ensure you never needed to take two bottles into the shower?

3 What news event of 2011 was initially reported with the code "Geronimo EKIA"?

4 What street in Salford did LS Lowry paint in 1957, three years before its name entered popular culture?

5 Name five professional football teams managed by either Nigel or Brian Clough. [up to start of 2022]

QUIZ 296 — 22nd October

1 Horror veteran Vincent Price provided a spoken narration for which Michael Jackson hit?

2 Which king would have been blown up had the Gunpowder Plot of Robert Catesby and Guy Fawkes been successful?

3 What does the W stand for in George W Bush?

4 Which K comes from a German word meaning "to smear" and is now used in English to describe something which is tacky, vulgar or over-sentimental, especially in art?

5 Name the first five cyclists to have won BBC Sports Personality of the Year.

QUIZ 293

1 Gothic
2 Jamal Edwards
3 1847-1882
4 Hugh Laurie
5 Vladimir Lenin, Josef Stalin, Georgy Malenkov, Nikita Khrushchev, Leonid Brezhnev, Yuri Andropov, Konstantin Chernenko, Mikhail Gorbachev

QUIZ 294

1 London
2 Bogus Journey (titles of first two 'Bill & Ted' movies)
3 Scrooge McDuck
4 Number of toes
5 Burmese Days, A Clergyman's Daughter, Keep the Aspidistra Flying, Coming Up for Air, Animal Farm and Nineteen Eighty-Four, ... non fiction - Down and Out in Paris and London, Homage to Catalonia, The Road to Wigan Pier

QUIZ 295

1 Casino Royale
2 Wash & Go
3 The killing of Osama Bin Laden - Geronimo was the code name of the operation, EKIA stands for Enemy Killed in Action
4 Coronation Street
5 Hartlepool United, Derby County, Brighton and Hove Albion, Leeds United, Nottingham Forest (all Brian), Burton Albion, Sheffield United, Mansfield Town (Nigel) [Both managed Derby County. Nigel has had two stints at Burton Albion]

QUIZ 296

1 Thriller
2 King James I
3 Walker
4 Kitsch
5 Tom Simpson, Chris Hoy, Mark Cavendish, Bradley Wiggins, Geraint Thomas

QUIZ 297 — 23rd October

1 Which "Witch" was flattened by a house in 'The Wizard of Oz'?

2 In which city would you find the headquarters of the Open University?

3 Which film from 1990 had the following tagline: "His story will touch you, even though he can't."?

4 'The Ring' magazine is considered the world's leading authority on which subject?

5 Name five films for which Jack Nicholson received an acting Oscar nomination. [can be Best Actor or Best Supporting]

QUIZ 298 — 24th October

1 At which university did Prince William and Kate Middleton meet?

2 What is the popular name for cowboy films mainly produced and directed by Italians, from the mid-1960s onwards?

3 Which Art Deco skyscraper was the world's tallest building for 11 months until the completion of the Empire State Building, found in the same city?

4 Which country is home to the River Kwai, as in the famous 'Bridge on the River Kwai'?

5 Name five of the ten outfield players who were in the official Team of the Tournament for the 1990 men's FIFA World Cup.

QUIZ 299 — 25th October

1 What type of vessel did Sean Connery command in 'The Hunt for Red October'?

2 Which band had hits with 'Fairground' and 'Money's Too Tight To Mention'?

3 With exactly how many test wickets did the great Muttiah Muralitharan retire?

4 Which Irish actor was nominated for a Best Actor Oscar eight times but never won the award?

5 Name five Beatles songs which reached Number 1 in the UK that have a title with four or more words. This can include songs which were part of Double-A sides, but not B-sides.

QUIZ 300 — 26th October

1 What is the first name of Beatrix Potter character Miss Puddleduck?

2 On which day of the week do Prime Minister's Questions take place in the UK?

3 Which US President's sister was Eunice Shriver?

4 In the context of the FIFA World Cup, what connects, amongst others: Scotland (1974), Brazil (1978), England (1982), New Zealand (2010)?

5 Name five official capital cities in Africa with names starting with an M.

QUIZ 297
1 Wicked Witch of the East
2 Milton Keynes
3 Edward Scissorhands
4 Boxing
5 Easy Rider, Reds, Terms of Endearment, A Few Good Men (all supporting), Five Easy Pieces, The Last Detail, Chinatown, One Flew Over the Cuckoo's Nest, Prizzi's Honour, Ironweed, As Good As It Gets, About Schmidt

QUIZ 298
1 St Andrews
2 Spaghetti Westerns
3 Chrysler Building
4 Thailand (or Siam, at the time)
5 Andreas Brehme, Paolo Maldini, Franco Baresi, Diego Maradona, Lothar Matthäus, Paul Gascoigne, Dragan Stojkovic, Jurgen Klinsmann, Roger Milla, Salvatore Schillaci (For some reason there were two goalkeepers, Sergio Goycochea, Luis Gabelo Conejo)

QUIZ 299
1 Submarine
2 Simply Red
3 800
4 Peter O'Toole (he was given an honorary Oscar for lifetime achievement in 2003)
5 From Me To You, I Want to Hold Your Hand, Can't Buy Me Love, A Hard Day's Night, We Can Work It Out, All You Need is Love, The Ballad of John and Yoko

QUIZ 300
1 Jemima
2 Wednesday
3 John F Kennedy
4 They all were knocked out of the competition without losing a game
5 Moroni, Malabo, Mbabane (executive capital of Eswatini), Maseru, Monrovia, Maputo, Mogadishu (of Comoros, Equatorial Guinea, Eswatini, Lesotho, Liberia, Mozambique, Somalia)

QUIZ 301 — 27th October

1 What, in Scotland, is a bridie?

2 How many humps does a Bactrian camel have?

3 Who was the Greek god of war?

4 Which former UK Poet Laureate was the author of the 'The Box of Delights'?

5 Name the five female acts - solo or groups - that won the main UK series of 'The X Factor' on its original ITV run.

QUIZ 302 — 28th October

1 What is the country of origin of the dessert tiramisu?

2 Which Andrew Lloyd Webber musical takes place entirely on roller skates?

3 The city of Istanbul used to be called Constantinople. What was Constantinople called before that?

4 In a 1992 film, Kristy Swanson was the first person to play which character, that went on to become much more successful and famous in a TV series that started in 1997?

5 Name five US states that have a border with Nevada.

QUIZ 303 — 29th October

1 If you are standing at the front of a ship, facing forwards in the direction of travel, would the starboard side be on your right or your left?

2 In Italy, what flavour ice cream would you get if you ordered "fragola"?

3 What is the name shared by a John Wayne film and an international transport business run by the Scotsman Brian Souter?

4 Which two countries in the world have as many 'a's in their name as consonants, and no other vowels?

5 Name five French whole numbers up to 25 which start with the same letter, when written out, as in English. [not including zero]

QUIZ 304 — 30th October

1 In 'Toy Story', who provides the voice of Woody the cowboy?

2 Which symbol is used on British road signs to indicate a zoo?

3 Which member of the British royal family was born on 21st April 1926 on Bruton Street in Mayfair, London?

4 What was the first track on Oasis' first album 'Definitely Maybe'?

5 Name five Grand Slam men's singles tennis champions of the open era (since 1968) with alliterative names (given first name and surname having the same first letter).

QUIZ 301
1 A pie/pastry
2 Two (a dromedary has one)
3 Ares, as opposed to Mars, his Roman counterpart
4 John Masefield
5 Leona Lewis, Alexandra Burke, Little Mix, Sam Bailey, Louisa Johnson

QUIZ 302
1 Italy
2 Starlight Express
3 Byzantium
4 Buffy the Vampire Slayer
5 California, Oregon, Idaho, Utah, Arizona

QUIZ 303
1 Right
2 Strawberry
3 Stagecoach
4 Panama, Canada
5 Trois, Six, Sept, Neuf, Treize, Seize

QUIZ 304
1 Tom Hanks
2 Elephant (even if the zoo doesn't have any elephants)
3 Queen Elizabeth II (Princess Elizabeth at the time)
4 Rock'n'Roll Star
5 Stan Smith, Arthur Ashe, Bjorn Borg, Boris Becker, Andre Agassi, Gaston Gaudio

QUIZ 305 — 31st October

1 Which has the larger population - North or South Korea?

2 Which famous historical figure has been played on film by the likes of Rod Steiger, Telly Savalas, Gary Oldman, David Bowie and Michael Palin?

3 In music, which note is one semitone higher than G sharp?

4 In London, what road runs directly from Parliament Square north to Trafalgar Square?

5 Name five chemical elements whose name begins with an A.

QUIZ 306 — 1st November

1 René Goscinny and Albert Uderzo created books with which legendary Gaulish warrior as the title character?

2 What is the English equivalent of the French words "anti-pellicule", often found on shampoo bottles?

3 In which year did Iraq invade Kuwait, leading to the First Gulf War?

4 What, or whom, do 'Loose Women' presenter Carol McGiffin and actress Billie Piper have in common?

5 Name five of the seven London boroughs which border the City of London. That includes the two that would touch it to the south, but for the River Thames.

QUIZ 307 — 2nd November

1 What is the most populous of the Channel Islands?

2 In August 2001, 'Groovejet (If This Ain't Love)', by Spiller featuring Sophie Ellis-Bextor, was the first song played on a prototype of which device?

3 Give any year in the life of Herman Melville, author of 'Moby Dick'.

4 In which year did legendary singer James Brown die on Christmas Day?

5 Name the five independent countries in Africa whose name begins with the letter G.

QUIZ 308 — 3rd November

1 In which country would one spend a shekel?

2 A member of ABTA in the UK would have what job?

3 What is the name of the British spacecraft which failed to land successfully on Mars on Christmas Day 2003?

4 Who became the 124th Emperor of Japan on Christmas Day in 1926?

5 Name five of the actors who have appeared in every single episode of 'Gavin and Stacey'. [up to 2022]

QUIZ 305
1 South Korea
2 Pontius Pilate
3 A (not A flat - that is the same as G sharp)
4 Whitehall
5 Actinium, Aluminium, Americium, Argon, Antimony, Arsenic, Astatine

QUIZ 306
1 Asterix
2 Anti-Dandruff
3 1990
4 Both were married to Chris Evans
5 City of Westminster, Camden, Islington, Hackney, Tower Hamlets, Southwark, Lambeth

QUIZ 307
1 Jersey - about 25,000 more than Guernsey
2 iPod
3 1819-1891
4 2006
5 (The) Gambia, Guinea, Guinea-Bissau, Gabon, Ghana

QUIZ 308
1 Israel
2 Travel agents
3 Beagle 2
4 Hirohito / Emperor Showa
5 Matthew Horne, Joanna Page, Ruth Jones, James Corden, Larry Lamb, Alison Steadman, Rob Brydon, Melanie Walters (no one else is close to appearing in all of them)

QUIZ 309 — 4th November

1 Which Scottish island group is further north: Orkney or Shetland?

2 How are Murdoc, Noodle, Russel and 2D better known?

3 Which English county town is an anagram of the word "dominates"?

4 How many individual squares are there on a standard Scrabble board?

5 Name the five Simon and Garfunkel studio albums, not including 'The Graduate' soundtrack.

QUIZ 310 — 5th November

1 Which furniture retailer was founded in 1943 by Ingvar Kamprad in Sweden?

2 The Davis, Weddell, Dumont d'Urville and Bellingshausen seas are all found off which continent?

3 What links Kenneth Williams, Brian Clough, David Frost and Tony Blair?

4 Which former Tottenham Hotspur player, who went on to great things, went a remarkable 24 Premier League games before being on a winning Spurs side?

5 Name five performers who have, according to IMDb, been in at least 20 of the 25 episodes broadcast of 'The Fast Show'.

QUIZ 311 — 6th November

1 Stalingrad is a former name of which Russian city?

2 'Leviathan' is a major work of which English author and philosopher?

3 What is the name of the pub in Edale which marks the start of the Pennine Way?

4 In 'Four Weddings and a Funeral', whose is the second wedding? [two names needed]

5 Name the four US states whose name ends with the letter O.

QUIZ 312 — 7th November

1 In which fictional village did 'Noel's House Party' take place?

2 Which of Queen Elizabeth's children has had the longest lasting marriage (from wedding day to divorce, or to the present day)?

3 What year saw the so-called 'great storm' in Britain, which Michael Fish famously failed to predict?

4 From the catalogue of which mail delivery service, established in 1935, can the following be ordered: Artificial rocks, Birdseed, Earthquake pills, Railroad track, Strait-Jacket ejecting bazooka, Instant icicle maker?

5 Name five non-capital cities that have hosted the Summer Olympics.

QUIZ 309
1 Shetland
2 Gorillaz
3 Maidstone
4 225
5 Wednesday Morning 3 AM; Parsley, Sage, Rosemary and Thyme; Sounds of Silence; Bookends; Bridge Over Troubled Water

QUIZ 310
1 IKEA (Stands for Ingvar Kamprad, Elmtaryd (the farm he grew up on), Agunnaryd (the nearby village))
2 Antarctica
3 All have been played by Michael Sheen
4 Gareth Bale
5 Paul Whitehouse, Charlie Higson, Arabella Weir, Simon Day, John Thomson, Caroline Aherne, Mark Williams, Eryl Maynard, Paul Shearer (Next are Maria McErlane and Colin McFarlane, with 15 and 14)

QUIZ 311
1 Volgograd (known as Tsaritsyn originally)
2 Thomas Hobbes
3 The Old Nags Head
4 Bernard and Lydia
5 Colorado, Idaho, New Mexico, Ohio

QUIZ 312
1 Crinkley Bottom
2 Princess Anne (to Timothy Laurence)
3 1987
4 Acme (in 'Looney Tunes')
5 St Louis, Antwerp, Los Angeles, Melbourne, Munich, Montreal, Barcelona, Atlanta, Sydney, Rio de Janeiro

QUIZ 313 — 8th November

1 What is the capital city of the Seychelles and the name of an Australian state?

2 Which drink's name comes from the Gaelic for "water of life"?

3 Where might you hear the words "Doors to manual and cross check"?

4 Which highly successful 2004 British film was described as a "rom-zom-com"?

5 Name five chemical elements whose name begins with an N.

QUIZ 314 — 9th November

1 Which 1999 movie features characters such as Jim, Oz, Kevin, and Finch?

2 What links: the Lithuanian word for sheep, a Scandinavian word for newspaper, the French word for opinion or advice, the Latin word for a bird, and a car rental company?

3 What TV comedy featured supporting characters called Super Hans, Dobbie, Johnson and Big Suze?

4 In 1992 Alvena Roy helped to compile a cookbook featuring recipes such as 'Fried Chicken Cooked in Pancake Batter', 'Peanut Butter and Banana Sandwiches' and 'Hamburgers in Sour Cream'. Whose chef had Alvena Roy been?

5 Name five Heads of Government (Taoiseach) of Ireland between 1990 and 2020.

QUIZ 315 — 10th November

1 On which side of your body is your appendix usually found?

2 What is the name of the world's second smallest sovereign state by area?

3 In 1893 the US Supreme Court ruled that what foodstuff should be classified as a vegetable, not a fruit?

4 In May 2022, at Garry Bridge in Perthshire, Frenchman Francois-Marie Dibon smashed a world record by doing what 765 times in a 24 hour period?

5 Name five artists who had five albums or more in the updated 2020 list by Rolling Stone magazine of the 500 Greatest Albums of All Time.

QUIZ 316 — 11th November

1 What kind of animals are TV characters Pinky and Perky?

2 In which American city would you visit the Smithsonian museums?

3 Which liqueur was supposedly first made in South America with avocados, but is now made with egg yolks, sugar and brandy?

4 The Vampire's Wife is a fashion label run by Susie Bick - which rock star is Susie Bick's husband?

5 Name five Blondie singles that went to Number 1 in either the UK or US (or both).

QUIZ 313
1 Victoria
2 Whisky (Uisge Beatha)
3 On an aeroplane
4 Shaun of the Dead
5 Neodymium, Neon, Neptunium, Nickel, Nihonium, Niobium, Nitrogen, Nobelium

QUIZ 314
1 American Pie
2 Avis
3 Peep Show
4 Elvis Presley
5 Charles Haughey, Albert Reynolds, John Bruton, Bertie Ahern, Brian Cowen, Enda Kenny, Leo Varadkar, Micheal Martin (who took over from Varadkar in 2020)

QUIZ 315
1 Right
2 Monaco
3 Tomato
4 Bungee jumping
5 The Beatles, Bob Dylan, Neil Young, Kanye West, The Rolling Stones, Led Zeppelin, Bruce Springsteen, David Bowie

QUIZ 316
1 Pigs
2 Washington D.C.
3 Advocaat
4 Nick Cave
5 Heart of Glass, Sunday Girl, Call Me, Atomic, The Tide is High, Rapture, Maria

QUIZ 317 — 12th November

1 Which rock band took their name from letters seen next to a power switch on a sewing machine?

2 What G is the name given to the act of buying a house by offering an amount greater than an offer that has already been accepted?

3 What is the name of the family of small birds Dicruridae? The Spangled variety is the only one found in Australia, but it has given its name to a common Australian word for a fool.

4 Which country contains the most easterly point of the European Union?

5 There are five left-handers among the 11 topscoring test cricket batsmen of all time. Name them.

QUIZ 318 — 13th November

1 What was the first name of Mr Schindler, of 'Schindler's List'?

2 What is the name of the internet payment system bought by eBay for $1.5 billion in 2002?

3 When making bread sauce, what should the onion be pierced with whilst boiling the milk to get the traditional flavour?

4 Which is the only US city to contain a royal palace that was used as an official residence by a reigning monarch?

5 Name five Winter Olympic host venues that begin with S. [main, named, host venue]

QUIZ 319 — 14th November

1 Which movie monster was found on Skull Island and brought to New York, where he climbed the Empire State Building?

2 Where would someone come from if they were described as Bajan?

3 In which decade is Halley's Comet next expected to be visible from Earth?

4 Who was Prime Minister of Britain from 1830 to 1834, perhaps now best known for supposedly once receiving a gift of Chinese tea scented with bergamot?

5 Name five of the first 10 performers inducted, in 1986, into the Rock and Roll Hall of Fame - not including the three pre-rock and roll "Early Influences". (Acts become eligible 25 years after the release of their first record.)

QUIZ 320 — 15th November

1 What is the first word of Kylie Minogue's 'I Should Be So Lucky'?

2 Which top-flight British football club were nicknamed "The Pensioners" in their early days (due to a famous local retirement home)?

3 What does IMDb stand for, as in the website imdb.com?

4 What are the only two independent countries in the world whose name, in the normal English spelling, ends in the letter T?

5 Name the four monarchs of England/Britain at the halfway point of a century, since 1500.

QUIZ 317
1 AC/DC
2 Gazumping
3 Drongo
4 Cyprus
5 Alastair Cook, Kumar Sangakkara, Brian Lara, Shivnarine Chanderpaul, Allan Border

QUIZ 318
1 Oskar (not to be confused with Robert Schindler, who founded Schindler's Lifts)
2 PayPal
3 Cloves
4 Honolulu - used by the monarchs of Hawaii in the 19th century
5 St Moritz, Sapporo, Squaw Valley, Sarajevo, Salt Lake City, Sochi

QUIZ 319
1 King Kong
2 Barbados
3 2060s
4 Earl Grey
5 Chuck Berry, James Brown, Sam Cooke, Ray Charles, Fats Domino, The Everly Brothers, Buddy Holly, Jerry Lee Lewis, Fats Domino, Elvis Presley

QUIZ 320
1 In (In my imagination)
2 Chelsea (the club changed the nickname to the much less imaginative "The Blues" in 1955)
3 Internet Movie Database
4 Egypt and Kuwait
5 Edward VI, George II, Victoria, George VI (1650, there was no monarch)

QUIZ 321 — 16th November

1 Apart from being a clouding of the eye, what kind of natural feature is a cataract?

2 How many times has Great Britain hosted the Winter Olympics?

3 In which 1979 James Bond film does Bond battle with Jaws on the cable car to Sugarloaf Mountain in Rio?

4 In which play by Anton Chekhov are the title characters called Olga, Maria and Irina?

5 Name five cities in the UK whose only vowel is an E. [for the purposes of the question, Y is not a vowel]

QUIZ 322 — 17th November

1 Which was faster - the fastest tennis ball ever served or the fastest cricket ball ever bowled?

2 Which famous site takes its name from the fact that it was restored by Pope Sixtus IV between 1477 and 1480?

3 Both 'West Side Story' and 'The Sound of Music' contain a song with what name?

4 Which football man, who died in 2015, had a career that involved being, at various times, a player, a coach, manager, director, chairman, television executive, union leader, presenter, analyst and match official?

5 Name five states on either side, directly, of the US/Mexico border.

QUIZ 323 — 18th November

1 Which car manufacturer makes the Yeti, the Octavia and the Fabia?

2 When Pol Pot took power there, he changed the name of Cambodia to what?

3 Which Ukrainian defeated Anthony Joshua in a 2021 boxing match?

4 Which English county has the motto "Floreat Salopia"?

5 South Africa has 11 official languages - name five of them.

QUIZ 324 — 19th November

1 In 'The Three Little Pigs', the house that survived the huffing and puffing of the Big Bad Wolf was made of what?

2 In which century was the French Revolution?

3 If X = 1 and Y = 4 then what is 2X + 3Y?

4 What name links several theatres, including one in Belfast, one on Shaftesbury Avenue in London, and one in Hammersmith, West London?

5 Name the first five male celebrities to have won 'Strictly Come Dancing'. [main series, not specials]

QUIZ 321
1 Waterfall
2 None
3 Moonraker
4 Three Sisters
5 Chester, Derby, Ely, Exeter, Leeds, Wells, Perth, Derry (allow, though officially called Londonderry), Newry

QUIZ 322
1 The fastest tennis ball
2 Sistine Chapel (Sacellum Sixtinum)
3 Maria
4 Jimmy Hill
5 California, Arizona, New Mexico, and Texas, Baja California, Sonora, Chihuahua, Coahuila, Nuevo León, and Tamaulipas

QUIZ 323
1 Skoda
2 Kampuchea
3 Oleksandr Usyk
4 Shropshire (it is sometimes known as Salop)
5 English, Afrikaans, Zulu, Xhosa, Ndebele, Northern Sotho, Sotho, Tsonga, Swazi, Tswana, Venda

QUIZ 324
1 Bricks
2 18th
3 14
4 Lyric
5 Darren Gough, Mark Ramprakash, Tom Chambers, Chris Hollins, Harry Judd

QUIZ 325 — 20th November

1 Which four-letter word can precede Roman Empire, Grail and Week?

2 Into which body of water does the Mississippi river empty? [Do not put Atlantic Ocean, which is the source ocean for this body of water].

3 In Ancient Rome, what was the purpose of the system called the hypocaust?

4 What was set up in 1954 as a network for exchanging TV programmes and news footage, but is most famous for the annual event it puts on which is viewed by several hundred million people?

5 Name five other English counties that border Wiltshire.

QUIZ 326 — 21st November

1 Which two words go before 'Hurry Love' and 'Always Get What You Want' in famous song titles?

2 Which chemical symbol is also the last word of Paul Simon's biggest UK solo hit single?

3 Who was the author of 'The House of Mirth', 'The Age of Innocence' and 'Ethan Frome'?

4 Construction began on which building in September 1941, 60 years to the day before another notable event in its history?

5 Name five of the first seven films for which Kate Winslet either won or was nominated for an acting Oscar. [either Best Actress or Best Supporting Actress]

QUIZ 327 — 22nd November

1 What is a Black Maria a slang term for?

2 Frederick Banting and Charles Best isolated which medically important substance in 1921?

3 What did the Sunday Pictorial newspaper change its name to in 1963?

4 What four-word phrase appears in the first line of the national anthem of Belize and the last line of the national anthem of the USA?

5 Aside from City of London, there are eight ceremonial counties of England with no motorways at all. Name five.

QUIZ 328 — 23rd November

1 What is the company Duracell known for producing?

2 Harry Ellis, Richard Thornburg and Al Powell are supporting characters in which film?

3 In which city was singer Annie Lennox born in 1954?

4 The first of the series is set during the Crusades, the second in the Renaissance, part 3 is set during the American Revolution. What is the name of this video game series?

5 Name five US Presidents with five-letter surnames. [not including Martin van Buren]

QUIZ 325
1 Holy
2 Gulf of Mexico
3 Underfloor heating/ central heating
4 Eurovision
5 Dorset, Somerset, Hampshire, Gloucestershire, Oxfordshire and Berkshire

QUIZ 326
1 You Can't
2 Al
3 Edith Wharton
4 The Pentagon
5 Sense and Sensibility, Titanic, Iris, Eternal Sunshine of the Spotless Mind, Little Children, The Reader, Steve Jobs

QUIZ 327
1 A police van
2 Insulin
3 Sunday Mirror
4 Land of the Free
5 Isle of Wight, Rutland, Norfolk, Suffolk, Northumberland, Dorset, Cornwall, East Sussex

QUIZ 328
1 Batteries
2 Die Hard (Nakatomi exec, reporter, police officer respectively)
3 Aberdeen
4 Assassin's Creed
5 John Adams, John Quincy Adams, John Tyler, Ulysses S Grant, Rutherford B Hayes, Richard Nixon, Barack Obama, Donald Trump, Joe Biden

QUIZ 329 — 24th November

1 Which band links Françoise Hardy, Ken Livingstone and Phil Daniels?

2 Which character from a classic Clive King children's novel lives at the bottom of a quarry near Barney's grandmother's house?

3 In the T20 quarter-final between Lancashire and Essex on July 8th 2022, by which wicketkeeper was batter Michael Pepper stumped? [surname only required]

4 Which character in a BBC sitcom was sacked as a security guard in the first episode and killed by a hit-and-run driver in the last?

5 Name five independent countries in Asia which are part of the Commonwealth. [as of 2022]

QUIZ 330 — 25th November

1 Which mammal is known as a leveret when it is under one year old?

2 In which century did Queen Elizabeth I die?

3 How long, in feet, is the playing surface of a full-size regulation snooker table?

4 Which fictional character, whose father is Scottish and mother Swiss, has the family motto 'Orbis Non Sufficit'?

5 Name the four standard sections of a symphony orchestra.

QUIZ 331 — 26th November

1 In the summer of 2022, Sadio Mané joined which club from Liverpool?

2 Digitalin is the name given to medicines extracted from which flower?

3 What opera by George Gershwin contains the songs 'Summertime' and 'It Ain't Necessarily So'?

4 How did Philippe Petit travel between the two World Trade Center towers in 1974?

5 Name five US states that have voted Republican at every election since 1972. [up to and including 2020 election]

QUIZ 332 — 27th November

1 Which European country's top football division is Serie A?

2 What word can go after Ashford, Ebbsfleet and Stratford in the names of railway stations?

3 Which writer, broadcaster and former Conservative MP ran the London Marathon in 2 hrs 32 minutes in 1985?

4 With a name meaning "students" how is the Islamic Emirate of Afghanistan better known?

5 Give five of the nine first names of the members of the singing Von Trapp family in 'The Sound of Music'? [seven children, one governess and one father]

QUIZ 329
1 Blur (all featured on Blur tracks)
2 Stig of the Dump
3 Phil Salt (Later in the game, Salt was caught on the boundary by Pepper)
4 Victor Meldrew
5 India, Pakistan, Sri Lanka, Bangladesh, Malaysia, Singapore, Brunei, Maldives

QUIZ 330
1 Hare
2 17th (1603)
3 12 feet
4 James Bond - "The World is not Enough"
5 Woodwind, Brass, Percussion, Strings

QUIZ 331
1 Bayern Munich
2 Foxglove
3 Porgy and Bess
4 On a high-wire/ tightrope
5 Alaska, Idaho, Kansas, North Dakota, Oklahoma, South Dakota, Utah, Wyoming (Maine and Nebraska have congressional districts so the vote can be more split. Don't include them.)

QUIZ 332
1 Italy
2 International
3 Matthew Parris
4 Taliban
5 Liesl, Friedrich, Louisa, Kurt, Brigitta, Marta, Gretl. Maria and Georg

QUIZ 333 — 28th November

1 What did comedian Eddie Izzard do 43 times in 51 days in 2009?

2 What is the name of the Japanese art of flower arranging?

3 At which school did Aldous Huxley teach George Orwell French?

4 How many principal ghost characters are there in 'A Christmas Carol' by Charles Dickens?

5 Name the first five regular hosts of 'Desert Island Discs'.

QUIZ 334 — 29th November

1 What kind of animal is the Beatrix Potter character Mr Tod?

2 Although the exact source of the Thames is occasionally disputed, it is definitely within which English county?

3 Which place, approximately 26 miles from Athens, was the site of a crucial Athenian victory over the Persian invaders in 490 BC?

4 In the list of the English names of full United Nations member states, there are only two letters that no country name begins with. One of those letters is X - no UN member state has a name beginning with the letter X. What is the other letter which is not the first letter of any UN member state's name?

5 Four properties on a standard British Monopoly board have names beginning with the letter P. Which squares?

QUIZ 335 — 30th November

1 What does a taxidermist do for a living?

2 Which US state has the longest border with Canada?

3 Which archaeological site near Woodbridge in Suffolk is the subject of the 2021 feature film 'The Dig'?

4 Which character did Tom Hardy partly model on Bartley Gorman, bare-knuckle boxer, self-styled "King of the Gypsies" and relative of Tyson Fury?

5 Name five UK Number 1 singles by the Spice Girls.

QUIZ 336 — 1st December

1 Lee Ryan and Simon Webbe were members of which boyband?

2 An American remake of which crime drama was given the title 'Fitz' when shown in the UK?

3 Which Polish city is known as Danzig in German?

4 Which London mainline station has a statue of rail pioneer Robert Stephenson outside it?

5 Name five US state capitals which have names which contain two or more words.

QUIZ 333
1 Running a marathon
2 Ikebana
3 Eton
4 Four (the ghosts of Christmas Past, Christmas Present, and Christmas Yet to Come, and Jacob Marley)
5 Roy Plomley, Michael Parkinson, Sue Lawley, Kirsty Young, Lauren Laverne

QUIZ 334
1 Fox
2 Gloucestershire
3 Marathon
4 W - Wales is not independent, Western Sahara is "disputed", not West Germany or Western Samoa (Western Samoa changed its name officially in 1997)
5 Pentonville Road; Pall Mall; Piccadilly; Park Lane

QUIZ 335
1 Stuff animals
2 Alaska
3 Sutton Hoo
4 Bane (in 'The Dark Knight Rises')
5 Wannabe, Say You'll Be There, 2 Become 1, Mama/Who Do You Think You Are?, Spice Up Your Life, Too Much, Viva Forever, Goodbye, Holler/Let Love Lead the Way

QUIZ 336
1 Blue
2 Cracker
3 Gdansk
4 Euston
5 Baton Rouge, Little Rock, Des Moines, Saint Paul, Jefferson City, Carson City, Santa Fe, Oklahoma City, Salt Lake City

QUIZ 337 — 2nd December

1 What colour were the covers of British passports from 1920 until 1988?

2 A satirical character played by the actress Diane Morgan is Philomena ... what?

3 What is the official national language of Zambia?

4 By what alternative name is the Dinorwig Power Station near Llanberis in Snowdonia better known?

5 In 1996, there was a major two-night concert at Knebworth in Hertfordshire where around 300,000 people watched nine big rock and dance acts of the era. Name five of the acts who performed.

QUIZ 338 — 3rd December

1 In which religion do followers observe the Four Noble Truths?

2 What name links a boat used by the diver Jacques Cousteau for almost 50 years with a form of Caribbean music?

3 Which Scottish football club was founded in 1874 from a school team?

4 Where is the Beetham Tower, one of the tallest buildings in the UK outside London?

5 Name five countries that have a land border with Turkey/Türkiye.

QUIZ 339 — 4th December

1 Whose published books include 'The English Roses', 'Mr Peabody's Apples' and 'Sex'?

2 What are La Boqueria in Barcelona and the Grand Bazaar in Istanbul?

3 Where in London would you find the Great Pagoda, designed by the architect William Chambers and erected in 1762?

4 In 2010, a photograph was discovered supposedly depicting the Wild West outlaw Billy the Kid playing which sport?

5 Name five independent states of Africa whose name begins with S.

QUIZ 340 — 5th December

1 McGill University is in which Canadian city?

2 What nickname (with a James Bond connection) is used for people from Wiltshire?

3 Adam Gilchrist had what object inside his batting glove while scoring a century in cricket's 2007 World Cup final?

4 Whose official home is the Istana Nurul Iman, the largest residential palace in the world?

5 Name five Prime Ministers of Australia between 2000 and 2020.

QUIZ 337
1 Blue
2 Cunk
3 English
4 Electric Mountain
5 Oasis, The Charlatans, Kula Shaker, Manic Street Preachers, Chemical Brothers, The Prodigy, Ocean Colour Scene, Cast, Bootleg Beatles

QUIZ 338
1 Buddhism
2 Calypso
3 Hamilton Academical
4 Manchester
5 Greece, Bulgaria, Georgia, Armenia, Azerbaijan, Iran, Iraq, Syria

QUIZ 339
1 Madonna
2 Markets
3 Kew Gardens (The pagoda in Battersea Park is the Peace Pagoda)
4 Croquet
5 Sao Tome and Principe, Senegal, Seychelles, Sierra Leone, Somalia, South Africa, South Sudan, Sudan (Swaziland is now called Eswatini)

QUIZ 340
1 Montréal
2 Moonrakers
3 Squash ball
4 Sultan of Brunei
5 Scott Morrison, Malcolm Turnbull, Tony Abbott, Julia Gillard, Kevin Rudd, John Howard

QUIZ 341 — 6th December

1 If January 1st is on a Friday at the start of a Leap Year, what day of the week will it fall on the next year?

2 What is the name of the Jewish New Year festival?

3 Which organisation has a Latin motto that roughly translates as "not apt to disclose secrets"?

4 Who was the first female host of the 'Radio 1 Breakfast Show'?

5 Name five of the ten largest regions of Italy, in terms of area. There are 20 regions in total. [tip - remember to think about all the parts that make up Italy]

QUIZ 342 — 7th December

1 What colour are number plates on the backs of cars in the UK?

2 Guillaume is the French equivalent of which English name?

3 What was the 1983 sequel to the film 'Saturday Night Fever' called?

4 Named after a biblical figure who lived for 969 years, what is the name of a champagne bottle which holds 6 litres?

5 The Texan amusement park Six Flags is named after the six nations that have historically held sovereignty over Texas. Name them. [clue - two of them are no longer nations today]

QUIZ 343 — 8th December

1 A Scottish country dance, where four couples face each other at the start, is called 'Strip the ...' what?

2 Which items of clothing worn by the comedian Jimmy Cricket had L and R on them (for Left and Right) but were worn the wrong way round?

3 A popular online meme shows which of the Muppets drinking tea?

4 The pilgrim's route known in English as the Way of St James ends up in which Spanish city?

5 Name five of the best-selling singles of the decade 2010-2019 in the UK. Song names, not artists. There might be more than one by the same artist.

QUIZ 344 — 9th December

1 In the early 2000s, Tom, the co-founder, would automatically be your first friend on which social networking site?

2 What does the first M in the film company MGM stand for?

3 Which adjective links a song by The Corrs to a femme fatale character in the 'Dick Tracy' comic strip?

4 Which architect and minister in Adolf Hitler's government was released from prison in 1966 and died on a visit to London in 1981?

5 Name five independent states with a common English name that contains no other vowels apart from "a". For avoidance of dispute, you're not allowed The Bahamas or Kyrgyzstan.

QUIZ 341
1 Sunday
2 Rosh Hashanah
3 The Magic Circle ("indocilis privata loqui")
4 Zoë Ball
5 Sicily, Piedmont, Sardinia, Lombardy, Tuscany, Emilia-Romagna, Apulia/Puglia, Veneto, Lazio, Calabria

QUIZ 342
1 Yellow
2 William
3 Staying Alive
4 Methuselah
5 Spain, France, Mexico, the Republic of Texas, the United States of America, and the Confederate States of America

QUIZ 343
1 Willow
2 Wellington boots
3 Kermit the Frog
4 Santiago de Compostela
5 Shape of You, Uptown Funk, Thinking Out Loud, Despacito, Perfect (also Sheeran), One Dance (Drake), Happy, All of Me (John Legend), Sorry, Rather Be

QUIZ 344
1 Myspace
2 Metro (Metro-Goldwyn-Mayer)
3 Breathless
4 Albert Speer
5 Canada, Chad, Ghana, Japan, Kazakhstan, Malta, Panama, Qatar

QUIZ 345 — 10th December

1 Which long-running British music weekly's final print issue was released in 2018?

2 Which bishop preached at the 2018 wedding of Prince Harry and Meghan Markle?

3 Which comedian won the 2013 Edinburgh Comedy Award with her show 'A Bic for Her'?

4 Chesley Sullenberger landed a plane on the Hudson River 2009 after it was struck by what?

5 Name five UK Top 10 hits for Roxette.

QUIZ 346 — 11th December

1 In which decade did the colour of the tennis balls used at Wimbledon change from white to yellow?

2 Which journalist and interviewer released a reggae album called 'Bass Lion' in 2010?

3 What does the phrase "Valar morghulis" mean in the TV series 'Game of Thrones'?

4 Until they were terminated in the year 2000, ferries from Folkestone in Kent travelled to which French port?

5 Name the five countries in Africa whose name begins with the letter E.

QUIZ 347 — 12th December

1 Olympic and Britannic were the sister ships of which early 20th century ocean liner?

2 What was a massive hit for Cardi B and Megan Thee Stallion in 2020?

3 By what unusual method can people cross the border between Sanlucar de Guadiana in Spain and Alcoutim in Portugal?

4 In December 2016, what was seen in the sandy areas of the Sahara Desert for the first time in over 37 years?

5 The Cotswolds lie across the boundaries of which six English counties?

QUIZ 348 — 13th December

1 Which colour can go before Dawn, Eye and Sonja to produce three film titles?

2 Which four-letter word is both the name of a Russian city on the banks of the river Kama, and a hairstyle?

3 The green wool traditionally associated with Robin Hood's costume was dyed by the dyers of which town?

4 Who designed the dress the future Queen Elizabeth II wore for her wedding in November 1947?

5 Up to and including the Tokyo Olympics in 2021, name five British sportspeople who have won four or more Olympic gold medals.

QUIZ 345

1 NME
2 Michael Curry
3 Bridget Christie
4 A flock of geese
5 The Look, It Must Have Been Love (twice), Listen to Your Heart, Dangerous, Joyride, Almost Unreal (lots of others which were Top 40 hits)

QUIZ 346

1 1980s
2 Martin Bashir
3 All men must die
4 Boulogne
5 Eritrea, Eswatini, Ethiopia, Equatorial Guinea, Egypt

QUIZ 347

1 Titanic
2 WAP
3 Zip wire
4 Snow
5 Gloucestershire, Oxfordshire (mainly), parts of Wiltshire, Somerset, Worcestershire and Warwickshire

QUIZ 348

1 Red
2 Perm
3 Lincoln
4 Norman Hartnell
5 Jason Kenny, Chris Hoy, Bradley Wiggins, Laura Kenny, Steve Redgrave, Ben Ainslie, Mo Farah, Matthew Pinsent, Paulo Radmilovic

QUIZ 349 — 14th December

1 The ordinary Gurkha soldiers who serve in the British army are mainly recruited from which country?

2 What is the first name of Alan Partridge's loyal assistant, played by Felicity Montagu?

3 According to an essay he wrote in 1946, what is the name of George Orwell's ideal pub?

4 What is the name of WWE wrestler The Undertaker's belly-to-belly finishing move?

5 Name five British women who won or were nominated for the Best Actress Oscar in the 1990s. [this starts with the 1991 ceremony for 1990 films so excludes Jessica Tandy and Pauline Collins from previous year, but includes 2000 for 1999]

QUIZ 350 — 15th December

1 In which decade were the first female priests ordained within the Church of England?

2 On BBC children's TV, Edd was a duck, Gordon was a gopher, but what kind of animal was Otis?

3 Which song plays over the opening credits of the film 'Dirty Dancing'?

4 In Greek mythology, what were the Symplegades?

5 There were seven main kingdoms of Anglo-Saxon England - name five of them. [all are names which survive in some way to this day]

QUIZ 351 — 16th December

1 Where did Dominic Cummings drive to on 12 April 2020?

2 Who was the last king of England made a Catholic saint?

3 Who co-authored 'The Communist Manifesto' with Karl Marx?

4 Which village in Nottinghamshire, famous for its fools, did Washington Irving introduce as a nickname for New York in 1807?

5 Name any five books of the New Testament of the Bible with a man's name for a title, other than the names used for the four gospels.

QUIZ 352 — 17th December

1 Algy Pug, Edward Trunk and Podgy Pig are friends of which fictional bear?

2 In the UK they are called wall plugs or rawlplugs - what are they called in the USA?

3 What was the name of the 1987 autobiography of the former MI5 intelligence officer Peter Wright?

4 Under what title was a video featuring 15-year-old Ghyslain Raza - one of the early viral YouTube videos - uploaded in 2006?

5 Name five national capitals whose English name begins with the letter R. They must be the capitals of independent countries.

QUIZ 349
1 Nepal
2 Lynn
3 The Moon Under Water
4 The Tombstone Piledriver
5 Emma Thompson (three times including one win), Miranda Richardson, Brenda Blethyn, Kristin Scott Thomas, Emily Watson, Helena Bonham Carter, Julie Christie, Judi Dench, Kate Winslet, Janet McTeer (allow Julianne Moore, who has British citizenship)

QUIZ 350
1 1990s
2 Aardvark
3 Be My Baby (by The Ronettes)
4 Clashing rocks (they clashed together whenever a ship passed between them)
5 Wessex, Mercia, Northumbria, Kent, Essex, East Anglia, Sussex

QUIZ 351
1 Barnard Castle
2 Edward the Confessor
3 Friedrich Engels
4 Gotham
5 Timothy, Titus, Philemon, James, Peter, Jude

QUIZ 352
1 Rupert Bear
2 Screw Anchors/Drywall anchors
3 Spycatcher
4 Star Wars Kid
5 Rabat, Reykjavik, Riyadh, Riga, Roseau, Rome

QUIZ 353 — 18th December

1 The patron saint of which country of the UK was one of the Twelve Apostles of Jesus?

2 What three words can go before 'Monkey', 'Squirrel' and 'Dinosaur', amongst others, in a series of children's books written by Fiona Watt?

3 What was the name of the plane flown by Charles Lindbergh for his solo flight across the Atlantic in 1927?

4 The titles of all but three of the 236 episodes of which sitcom begin with the same two words?

5 Name the first five British or Irish male cyclists to win one of cycling's three Grand Tours (Giro d'Italia, Tour de France, Vuelta a España).

QUIZ 354 — 19th December

1 Which genre of American music shares its name with plants from the genus Poa?

2 Which country did the Portuguese explorer Pedro Álvares Cabral sight on 22nd April 1500?

3 Which former 'Strictly Come Dancing' judge appeared in the video for Elton John's 'I'm Still Standing'?

4 Who wrote the book 'The One That Got Away' about the SAS patrol Bravo Two Zero, dropped behind enemy lines in Iraq in 1991?

5 Name the first five movies directed by Martin Scorsese which Robert De Niro appeared in.

QUIZ 355 — 20th December

1 According to the gospels, Jesus rode which animal into Jerusalem the week before his crucifixion?

2 Which anti-hero is played by Ryan Reynolds in a 2016 blockbuster?

3 The professional football team Schalke is based in which German city?

4 Which weekly magazine was founded by Scotsman James Wilson in 1843?

5 Name five counties on the Ireland/Northern Ireland border - on either side.

QUIZ 356 — 21st December

1 In which country were Terry Waite and John McCarthy held hostage before being released in 1991?

2 Which Rowan Atkinson film character first appeared in a series of adverts for Barclaycard?

3 Who scored two goals, including a spectacular overhead kick, in the 2018 Champions League final?

4 The cast of which Steven Spielberg film includes Ben Stiller, Burt Kwouk, Nigel Havers and John Malkovich?

5 Name five of the seven men's national teams which have appeared in all of the football, 50-over cricket and rugby union World Cup tournaments. [up to 2022]

QUIZ 353
1 Scotland
2 That's Not My
3 The Spirit of St Louis
4 Friends ("The one...")
5 Stephen Roche (Tour and Giro), Sean Kelly (Vuelta), Bradley Wiggins (Tour), Chris Froome (all three), Geraint Thomas (Tour)

QUIZ 354
1 Bluegrass
2 Brazil
3 Bruno Tonioli
4 Chris Ryan (not Andy McNab)
5 Mean Streets, Taxi Driver, New York New York, Raging Bull, The King of Comedy

QUIZ 355
1 Donkey
2 Deadpool
3 Gelsenkirchen
4 The Economist
5 Donegal, Leitrim, Cavan, Louth, Monaghan (south), Londonderry/ Derry, Fermanagh, Tyrone, Armagh, Down

QUIZ 356
1 Lebanon
2 Johnny English
3 Gareth Bale
4 Empire of the Sun
5 Australia, Canada, England, Ireland, New Zealand, Scotland, South Africa (strictly, the Ireland teams are slightly different as the cricket and rugby teams are all-Ireland but the football team is just the Republic, but allow).

QUIZ 357 — 22nd December

1 General Blight was the arch enemy of which children's TV character?

2 In which racquet sport could you perform a Danish wipe or a hairpin drop shot?

3 There was a total eclipse of the sun in which month of 1999?

4 What name links the patron saint of Milan to the first name of the American general who is said to have "invented" sideburns?

5 Name five of the nine independent countries whose name is English begins and ends in A.

QUIZ 358 — 23rd December

1 Which ITV drama series shown between 1999 and 2006 was set in Larkhall Prison?

2 What number Pennsylvania Avenue is the White House?

3 In July 2014, the Tower of London's moat was filled with around 900,000 what?

4 In 'The Catherine Tate Show', what is the teenager Lauren Cooper's catchphrase?

5 Not including any films in the 'Avatar' series, name five full-length feature films directed by James Cameron. [not short films, not documentaries]

QUIZ 359 — 24th December

1 You better watch out, you better not cry, you better not pout, I'm telling you why. Why?

2 Which Christmassy word is this an anagram of? IMEETLOTS

3 True or False? Jon Bon Jovi's first appearance on a record was singing 'R2-D2 We Wish You a Merry Christmas' on the 1980 Star Wars album 'Christmas in the Stars', an album that contained a Billboard Number 69 with 'What Can You Get a Wookie for Christmas (When He Already Owns a Comb)'.

4 Who wrote and directed 'The Mezzotint', the BBC's 2021 Christmas ghost story?

5 In the famous song 'The Twelve Days of Christmas', six of the gifts are birds. Name five of them. [you don't have to give the exact numbers, just name the birds]

QUIZ 360 — 25th December

1 The French version of Santa Claus is called 'Père ...' what?

2 The classic Irving Berlin song 'White Christmas' originally appeared in which 1942 film starring Bing Crosby and Fred Astaire?

3 What is the 8-day Jewish festival also known as 'The Festival of Lights'?

4 In the 'Bottom' Christmas Special, what does Eddie prepare instead of Brandy Butter?

5 Name any five of Santa's reindeer, not including Rudolph. This is according to the classic poem 'A Visit from St Nicholas'.

QUIZ 357
1 Bananaman
2 Badminton
3 August
4 Ambrose (Ambrose Burnside)
5 Angola, Algeria, Australia, Albania, Argentina, Antigua and Barbuda, Austria, Armenia, Andorra

QUIZ 358
1 Bad Girls
2 1600
3 [Ceramic] poppies
4 Am I bovvered?
5 Piranha II: The Spawning (accept any part of that!), The Terminator, Aliens, The Abyss, Terminator 2: Judgement Day, True Lies, Titanic

QUIZ 359
1 Santa Claus is Coming to Town
2 Mistletoe
3 TRUE
4 Mark Gatiss
5 A Partridge (in a Pear Tree), (Two) Turtle Doves, (Three) French Hens, (Four) Calling/Colly Birds, (Six) Geese (a-Laying), (Seven) Swans (A-Swimming)

QUIZ 360
1 Noel
2 Holiday Inn
3 Hanukkah
4 Vodka Margarine
5 Dasher, Dancer, Prancer, Vixen, Comet, Cupid, Donner (Dunder), Blitzen (Blixem)

QUIZ 361 — 26th December

1 Which country has the largest number of native Arabic speakers?

2 In the lyrics to the song 'Oh! Mr Porter', where did the singer originally want to travel to?

3 Which electronic band was formed by Ralf Hütter and Florian Schneider?

4 What is the previous name of HMP Manchester?

5 Name five of the six official James Bond films with the longest names, in terms of number of letters in title. [not 'Never Say Never Again' as not official]

QUIZ 362 — 27th December

1 The "Farage Garage" is a nickname given to the "inland border facility" next to which Kent town?

2 Mrs Keele and Mrs McClusky were head teachers at which fictional school?

3 Which university's Macintosh Building suffered a terrible fire in 2018?

4 What is the historic English name of the Maluku Islands that belong to Indonesia?

5 Name five winners of the Best Picture Oscar with a title of six letters or fewer. [up to ceremony in 2022]

QUIZ 363 — 28th December

1 Which university did King Charles III graduate from?

2 The border between Nepal and which country runs through Mount Everest?

3 In August 2016, which Russian hacking group breached the security of the World Anti-Doping Agency?

4 Kingsmarkham is the setting for many of the stories of which crime writer?

5 Give five whole numbers between two and 20 which have the same number of letters when written in English and French?

QUIZ 364 — 29th December

1 Which renowned female animated cartoon character first appeared in 'Dizzy Dishes' in 1930?

2 What lemur is the only extant member of the genus Daubentonia?

3 Which British boxer, born in Sheffield in 1986, was defeated by America's Terence Crawford in November 2020?

4 Who designed the wedding dress worn by the Duchess of Cambridge?

5 There have been six artists whose name contained the word 'Brothers' who have had UK Number 1s. Name five of them. [up to the end of 2021]

QUIZ 361
1 Egypt
2 Birmingham
3 Kraftwerk
4 Strangeways
5 On Her Majesty's Secret Service, The Man With the Golden Gun, The Living Daylights, The World is Not Enough, From Russia With Love, Diamonds Are Forever (next is 'Tomorrow Never Dies')

QUIZ 362
1 Ashford (Sevington Inland Border Facility)
2 Grange Hill
3 Glasgow
4 The Spice Islands
5 Wings, Hamlet, Marty, Gigi, Ben-Hur, Oliver!, Patton, Rocky, Gandhi, Crash, Argo, CODA

QUIZ 363
1 Cambridge
2 China (Tibet)
3 Fancy Bear
4 Ruth Rendell
5 Three, Five, Six, Nine, Ten, Fourteen

QUIZ 364
1 Betty Boop
2 Aye-aye
3 Kell Brook (not Amir Khan, who was born in Bolton in 1986, who lost to Crawford in 2019)
4 Sarah Burton
5 Johnston Brothers, Everly Brothers, Righteous Brothers, Walker Brothers, Outhere Brothers, Chemical Brothers

QUIZ 365 — 30th December

1 With which song did Robbie Williams and Nicole Kidman have the 50th Christmas Number 1?

2 The novel and TV drama 'Death Comes to Pemberley' was a sequel (sort of) to which classic novel?

3 In 1994, who voted for the first time in his life, presumably for himself, in an election that he won?

4 Which author, more famous for another children's story, wrote 'The Life and Adventures of Santa Claus' in 1902?

5 Different countries around the world greet the New Year at different times, depending on their timezone. Name five of the nine independent countries who greet the New Year earliest. [must be independent countries, and also a country is counted even if it is only a small part of that country in one of the earliest timezones]

QUIZ 366 — 31st December

1 What is Scotland's largest loch by surface area?

2 Who did Ray Wilson replace as the lead singer of Genesis in the 1990s?

3 In horse racing, what course hosts the 1000 Guineas and the 2000 Guineas?

4 In Greek mythology, who did the hero Theseus abandon on the island of Naxos?

5 At the 2014 Oscars, host Ellen DeGeneres took a selfie which became, at the time, the most retweeted picture in history. Besides herself, name five of the other eleven people in the picture. [mainly a selection of nominees and other major Hollywood stars]

QUIZ 367

And here are a couple more for extremely long days.

1 How many finger holes are there in a standard ten-pin bowling ball?

2 If you were to sail due south from Land's End in Cornwall, which country would you hit first?

3 Who was the main character in two sitcoms, both of which took their titles from traditional Christian wedding vows?

4 Which bird, with the Latin name hirundo rustica, is the main character in Oscar Wilde's ' The Happy Prince'?

5 Name the five sovereign states of Africa whose English name ends with the letter N.

QUIZ 368

1 By weight, what is the most common element in the Earth's crust?

2 Jon Ossoff and Raphael Warnock became senators for which US state in early 2021?

3 Which European city is served by two airports called Fiumicino and Ciampino?

4 'Tick, Tick... Boom!' is a 2021 biographical film about the man who died one day before the premiere, in 1996, of which musical he had written?

5 There have (up to 2021) been four Irish winners of the Nobel Prize for Literature. Name them. [for avoidance of any doubt, Eugene O'Neill is not counted]

QUIZ 365
1 Somethin' Stupid
2 Pride and Prejudice
3 Nelson Mandela
4 L. Frank Baum
5 Samoa, Kiribati, New Zealand, Fiji, Tonga, Russia, Nauru, Tuvalu, Marshall Islands

QUIZ 366
1 Loch Lomond (Loch Ness is, by volume)
2 Phil Collins
3 Newmarket
4 Ariadne
5 Bradley Cooper, Jared Leto, Jennifer Lawrence, Brad Pitt, Channing Tatum, Kevin Spacey, Angelina Jolie, Lupita Nyong'o, Peter Nyong'o Jr. (Lupita Nyong'o's brother), Julia Roberts and Meryl Streep

QUIZ 367
1 Three
2 Spain
3 Alf Garnett
4 Swallow
5 Benin, Cameroon, Gabon, Sudan, South Sudan

QUIZ 368
1 Oxygen
2 Georgia
3 Rome
4 Rent (he was Jonathan Larson)
5 WB Yeats, George Bernard Shaw, Samuel Beckett, Seamus Heaney

FAMILY-FRIENDLY QUIZZES

It's not that all the other questions are unsuitable, we promise, but this section is particularly designed to contain questions for children and teenagers to answer. That's not to say that it's all easy, or that there's nothing for adults and hardcore quizzers here, but if you want questions that are generally on the more straightforward side, this is a good place to start.

The chapter is divided into twenty-nine well-balanced quizzes, each containing four rounds of ten questions, on standard subjects like Geography, Science & Nature, Sport & Games, etc.

ROUND 1 — GEOGRAPHY

1 The Canary Islands are in which ocean?

2 When facing south, which compass point is directly to your right?

3 The river Severn flows through which channel to the Irish Sea?

4 Which country has the most native Spanish speakers?

5 In which large city is the neighbourhood of Interlagos?

6 What is the name of the thinnest and outermost layer of the Earth?

7 "Auld Reekie" is a nickname for which Scottish city?

8 Chalk and limestone belong to which group of rocks?

9 What is the name of the small EU member state which has Valletta as its capital?

10 Which mountain range extends from California up to Alaska, a distance of about 6,000 kilometres?

ROUND 2 — SCIENCE AND NATURE

1 Which class of animals are typically cold blooded with soft skin, and live in water and on land?

2 What is a barometer designed to measure?

3 What is the name of a trace of past life preserved in a rock or mineral?

4 Whose General Theory of Relativity was confirmed in May 1919?

5 How many legs does a crocodile have?

6 Rust is formed when moist air reacts with which transition metal?

7 What is a female fox called?

8 Enceladus is a moon of which planet?

9 Brown long-eared, fringe-lipped and Australian false vampire are species of which mammal?

10 Which Greek word meaning "indivisible" is used for particles that, until the 19th century, were thought to be the smallest parts of matter?

ROUND 1 — GEOGRAPHY
1 Atlantic
2 West
3 Bristol Channel
4 Mexico
5 São Paulo
6 The Crust
7 Edinburgh
8 Sedimentary
9 Malta
10 Rocky Mountains

ROUND 2 — SCIENCE AND NATURE
1 Amphibians
2 Air Pressure
3 Fossil
4 Albert Einstein
5 Four
6 Iron
7 Vixen
8 Saturn
9 Bat
10 Atom

ROUND 3 — ARTS

1 Harps and violins belong to which group of musical instruments?

2 In the 'Narnia' books, what kind of creature is Mr Tumnus?

3 What was the surname of the 19th century literary brothers called Jacob and Wilhelm?

4 In which city is the Sistine Chapel, with its famous ceiling painting by Michelangelo?

5 In music, which major scale has no sharps and no flats?

6 In the 'Winnie-the-Pooh' stories, what is the name of Roo's mother?

7 Whose opera, 'The Magic Flute', premiered in Vienna in September 1791?

8 What is the name of the large art gallery right next to the National Gallery in London?

9 What is the name of Sergei Prokofiev's 1936 composition about a boy and his encounter with a fierce creature in the woods?

10 How many separate "Planets" are there in Gustav Holst's 'The Planets' suite?

ROUND 4 — GENERAL KNOWLEDGE

1 Which word, from the French for "again", is given to an additional performance at the end of a concert?

2 Sun-Maid is a famous brand of what?

3 What's the 12th letter of the alphabet?

4 What seven-letter word can be a beginner's ski slope or a place where plants are grown?

5 In a traditional Eton mess, strawberries and whipped double cream are mixed with what other ingredient?

6 Which pizza is named after the woman who was Queen of Italy from 1878 to 1900?

7 What is the French for "Thursday"?

8 What term describes the result of transposing the first letters of two words, often to comedic effect?

9 How many vowels are there on the middle row of letters on a standard computer keyboard?

10 If you had just one of every current standard denomination of English coin and note, how much money would you have?

ROUND 3 — ARTS
1 Stringed Instruments
2 Faun
3 Grimm
4 Rome (accept Vatican City)
5 C
6 Kanga
7 Wolfgang Amadeus Mozart
8 National Portrait Gallery
9 Peter and the Wolf
10 Seven

ROUND 4 — GENERAL KNOWLEDGE
1 Encore
2 Raisins
3 L
4 Nursery
5 (Broken) Meringue
6 Margherita
7 Jeudi
8 Spoonerism
9 One (A)
10 £88.88

ROUND 1 — HISTORY AND POLITICS

1 In 1840, who married her cousin, Albert of Saxe-Coburg and Gotha?

2 Which European country had a revolution in 1789?

3 In November 1963, who was arrested and charged with the murder of President Kennedy?

4 What was the first name of the World War II military leader Field Marshal Montgomery?

5 What did climber George Mallory famously say when asked why he wanted to ascend Mount Everest?

6 The Tashkent Agreement of 1966 resolved a conflict between India and which other country?

7 What nickname was given to Louis XIV of France?

8 Winston Churchill was Prime Minister of the UK for how many separate periods?

9 Haile Selassie was Emperor of which country from 1930 to 1974?

10 The First Crusade took place towards the end of which century?

ROUND 2 — SCIENCE AND NATURE

1 What name is given to a living thing with a backbone?

2 By what one-word phrase is the process of induced hydraulic fracturing commonly known?

3 Max Planck, Guglielmo Marconi and Niels Bohr are past winners of which Nobel Prize?

4 If the father of a liger is a lion, then what is its mother?

5 Which chemical symbol is also the surname of a Bond villain?

6 What G is another common name for the wildebeest?

7 What is the name of the tube that connects a developing embryo to its placenta?

8 What colour is an adult beluga?

9 Also known as turf, what name is used for the spongy material formed by the partial decomposition of organic matter in wetlands?

10 The space telescope launched on Christmas Day 2021, designed to replace the Hubble, is named after which former NASA administrator?

ROUND 1 — HISTORY AND POLITICS
1 Queen Victoria
2 France
3 Lee Harvey Oswald
4 Bernard
5 Because it's there
6 Pakistan
7 The Sun King
8 Two
9 Ethiopia
10 11th century

ROUND 2 — SCIENCE AND NATURE
1 Vertebrate
2 Fracking
3 Physics
4 Tiger
5 No
6 Gnu
7 Umbilical cord
8 White
9 Peat
10 James Webb

ROUND 3 — POP CULTURE

1 In 2021, an extended version of which Taylor Swift song became, at ten minutes, the longest song to top the Billboard Hot 100?

2 Which 1983 novel by Walter Tevis inspired a hit Netflix miniseries from 2020 starring Anya Taylor-Joy?

3 In which 2021 film does Dev Patel play the part of King Arthur's nephew Gawain?

4 Which word links the titles of a UK Number 1 single by Madonna in 2006 and one by Justin Bieber in 2015?

5 In 'The Empire Strikes Back', what is the name of the swamp planet where Yoda lives?

6 What goes with 'Ratchet' in the title of a successful video game franchise?

7 In 2021, British student Francis Bourgeois gained fame on TikTok and Instagram for videos showing him taking part in which hobby?

8 Musician Tyler Okonma spoke in late 2021 about no longer using the stage name he'd first used as a child, as he thought he'd outgrown it. What is that stage name?

9 Which former Paris Saint-Germain football player gave his name to a song by the rapper Dave?

10 Which Foo Fighters frontman managed to return to complete a concert in Gothenburg in June 2015 despite breaking his leg near the start?

ROUND 4 — SPORT AND GAMES

1 The nickname of Brentford FC is the ... what?

2 Which catching position in cricket stands near the slips, but squarer?

3 How many people are in each boat for the Oxford-Cambridge Boat Race?

4 In golf, at what course in Northern Ireland did the men's 2019 British Open Championship take place?

5 Who is the Lev Yashin Award given to at the end of each football World Cup?

6 What is the maximum score in one game of tenpin bowling?

7 In Monopoly, which square is, unfortunately, landed on the most?

8 Knighted in 2022, which author co-founded Games Workshop with Steve Jackson and John Peake?

9 In chess, which pieces can be captured "en passant"?

10 Who scored Liverpool's second goal in the 2019 Champions League final against Tottenham Hotspur?

ROUND 3 — POP CULTURE
1 All Too Well
2 The Queen's Gambit
3 The Green Knight
4 Sorry
5 Dagobah
6 Clank
7 Trainspotting
8 Tyler the Creator
9 Thiago Silva
10 Dave Grohl

ROUND 4 — SPORT AND GAMES
1 Bees
2 Gully
3 Nine (eight rowers plus one cox)
4 Royal Portrush
5 Best goalkeeper
6 300
7 Jail
8 Ian Livingstone
9 Pawns
10 Divock Origi

ROUND 1 — POP CULTURE

1 Who had a 2013 Number 1 with 'Burn'?

2 New Zealander Temuera Morrison plays which character in the 'Star Wars' universe, who was given his own spin-off TV series in late 2021?

3 What was the title of Olivia Rodrigo's debut album, from 2021?

4 What title links a 2021 video game developed by Hazelight Studios, a song by Rob Base and DJ E-Z Rock, and a TV show associated with 'Strictly Come Dancing'?

5 In which 2021 game do players take on the role of Colt, an assassin stuck in a time loop?

6 What is the stage name of the award-winning singer-songwriter Anaïs Oluwatoyin Estelle Marinho?

7 In 2021, who directed the films 'The Last Duel' and 'House of Gucci'?

8 Ed Sheeran's 'Bad Habits' was Number 1 in the UK for much of July, August and September 2021. Whose single 'Shivers' directly followed it as Number 1?

9 Who directed an acclaimed film, released in the UK in 2022, which is named after the city where he was born in 1960?

10 If Seong Gi-hun is 456, what number is Oh Il-nam?

ROUND 2 — HISTORY AND POLITICS

1 A man named Casca is said to have struck the first blow in whose assassination?

2 St Denis was the first bishop and is the patron saint of which city?

3 Two sons of which King of England died in hunting accidents in the New Forest?

4 In which country did King Willem-Alexander succeed his mother Queen Beatrix in 2013?

5 Richard Arkwright and James Watt played major roles in which very progressive revolution?

6 What term is used for traditional Labour areas in the Midlands which voted Conservative in the 2019 UK General Election?

7 In 1907, which European country became the first in the world in which women could both vote and stand for office?

8 Who wrote in his diary on the 17th January 1912, "Great God this is an awful place"?

9 Who was the first person from an African country to be United Nations Secretary-General?

10 Bill DeBlasio became mayor of what city in 2014?

ROUND 1 — POP CULTURE
1 Ellie Goulding
2 Boba Fett
3 Sour
4 It Takes Two
5 Deathloop
6 Arlo Parks
7 Ridley Scott
8 Ed Sheeran
9 Kenneth Branagh (Belfast)
10 1 (001) (In 'Squid Game')

ROUND 2 — HISTORY AND POLITICS
1 Julius Caesar
2 Paris
3 William I
4 The Netherlands
5 The Industrial Revolution
6 Red wall
7 Finland
8 Captain R F Scott
9 Boutros Boutros-Ghali (Egyptian)
10 New York City

ROUND 3 — ARTS

1 In the books of Beatrix Potter, Simpkin and Tabitha Twitchit are what kind of animal?

2 What is the Welsh name for a festival with a name roughly meaning "sitting together"?

3 What middle initial links the authors Carr, Travers and James?

4 The son of which famous Impressionist painter was himself a renowned film director?

5 Jack Dawkins is the real name of which Charles Dickens character?

6 Pompey Bum is a character in which Shakespeare play?

7 What M is the name given to the modern experimental musical movement whose proponents include Steve Reich and Philip Glass?

8 The Booker Prize winners of 1974, 1983, 1999 and 2021 were born in which country?

9 In 2016, to mark the 90th anniversary of the first book, what new character was introduced to the world of Winnie-the-Pooh?

10 Which musical includes musical numbers called 'Solidarity', 'Merry Christmas, Maggie Thatcher' and 'Electricity'?

ROUND 4 — GENERAL KNOWLEDGE

1 How many completely enclosed areas are there within a hashtag symbol?

2 Which country's top-level domain is .ch?

3 Which French car manufacturer produced an iconic vehicle whose name means "two horses"?

4 What four-letter word starts and ends with the 14th letter of the alphabet, and has the 15th letter of the alphabet twice in between?

5 What colour is the circle at the centre of the RAF's roundel?

6 Which animal is on the logo of the car company Lamborghini?

7 From the Latin for "let it stand" what word gives the instruction to ignore a correction on a printed work?

8 Who were married at Westminster Cathedral on 29th May 2021?

9 If a digraph is a sound made up of two letters, what is a sound made up of three letters?

10 Which country held a referendum on its membership of the United Kingdom in 2014?

ROUND 3 — ARTS
1 Cats
2 Eisteddfod
3 L
4 Pierre-Auguste Renoir
5 The Artful Dodger
6 Measure for Measure
7 Minimalism
8 South Africa
9 Penguin
10 Billy Elliot

ROUND 4 — GENERAL KNOWLEDGE
1 One
2 Switzerland (it stands for Confoederatio Helvetica)
3 Citroen
4 Noon
5 Red
6 Bull
7 Stet
8 Boris and Carrie Johnson
9 Trigraph
10 Scotland

ROUND 1 — GEOGRAPHY

1 What is the British name for the body of water that the French call La Manche?

2 The Great Sphinx of Giza is in which country?

3 What word is in the capital city of both Trinidad and Tobago and Papua New Guinea?

4 Where in the UK would you find the word "ARAF" on roads?

5 Mount Kilimanjaro is which continent's highest mountain?

6 Ridges formed from rock debris deposited at the side of glaciers are called ... what?

7 The city of Istanbul is partly in Europe, and partly in which other continent?

8 Locations on the Earth's surface can be described using two coordinates: longitude and which other?

9 Which organisation, with the initials WMO, has a network of around 11,000 permanent weather stations around the world?

10 In 2018, an apostrophe was officially added to the name of which area on the coast of Cornwall by local councillors?

ROUND 2 — SCIENCE AND NATURE

1 Which land animal has the longest tail?

2 Consumption is a historical name for which infection disease?

3 Which company was founded by Martin Eberhard and Marc Tarpenning on July 1st 2003 (though someone else far richer is usually believed to be the founder)?

4 Initially associated with the outbreak of Covid-19 (an association later discredited) which mammal is also known as the scaly anteater?

5 On a flower, what is the name of the part of the stamen where pollen is produced?

6 What is the literal meaning of the dog breed "dachshund"?

7 What is the largest land mammal native to the UK?

8 Which creature has a name which comes from the Latin word for "pig-spine"?

9 Which Polish polymath published 'On the Revolutions of the Celestial Spheres' in 1543?

10 Sometimes considered the first computer programmer for her work on Charles Babbage's difference engine, who was the only daughter of Lord and Lady Byron?

ROUND 1 — GEOGRAPHY
1 The (English) Channel
2 Egypt
3 Port
4 Wales (ARAF means Slow)
5 Africa
6 Moraines
7 Asia
8 Latitude
9 World Meteorological Organisation
10 Land's End

ROUND 2 — SCIENCE AND NATURE
1 Giraffe
2 Tuberculosis
3 Tesla Inc
4 Pangolin
5 Anther
6 Badger dog
7 Red deer
8 Porcupine
9 (Nicolaus) Copernicus
10 Ada Lovelace

ROUND 3 — ARTS

1 Upright and baby grand are types of which musical instrument?

2 In the book by Eric Carle, on which day of the week does the Very Hungry Caterpillar pop out of its egg?

3 Which acclaimed musical by Lin-Manuel Miranda opened in London in late 2017?

4 Which city is home to Leonardo Da Vinci's 'The Last Supper' mural?

5 In the Bible, who had sons called Shem, Ham, and Japheth?

6 Which 19th century Dutch artist painted 'Self-Portrait with Bandaged Ear'?

7 William Blake wrote a famous poem about what sort of big cat?

8 In Roman mythology, Vesta was the goddess of which feature of the household?

9 What A is a poem where the first letter of each line spells out a message?

10 A kimono is a traditional Japanese ... what?

ROUND 4 — GENERAL KNOWLEDGE

1 Which European nationality goes before the word "roll" in the name of a thin sponge cake rolled up with jam?

2 Traditionally, Chinese chopsticks are made from which material?

3 With its website at abc.xyz, what is the name of the parent company of Google?

4 Mint sauce usually accompanies which roast meat?

5 Which pastry takes its name from the French word for "crescent"?

6 What E is the name for three dots to indicate that something is missing from a word, sentence or longer piece of text?

7 What date is St Stephen's Day, a public holiday in the UK?

8 In which county is the public school Winchester?

9 In which religion is the 'Bhagavad Gita' an important text?

10 If you asked for a "trombone" in an office in France, what would you be trying to get?

ROUND 3 — ARTS
1 Piano
2 Sunday
3 Hamilton
4 Milan
5 Noah
6 Vincent van Gogh
7 Tiger
8 The hearth/fireplace
9 Acrostic
10 Robe

ROUND 4 — GENERAL KNOWLEDGE
1 Swiss
2 Bamboo
3 Alphabet
4 Lamb
5 Croissant
6 Ellipsis
7 26th December
8 Hampshire
9 Hinduism
10 Paperclip

ROUND 1 — HISTORY AND POLITICS

1 Who did Winnie Madikizela marry in 1958?

2 "England expects that every man will do his duty" is a quote attributed to which military leader?

3 Charles Darwin set out on a scientific voyage in 1831 - on which ship?

4 What was the provisional capital of West Germany between 1949 and 1990?

5 In 2017, who became the first female Metropolitan Police Commissioner?

6 Which UK political party's emblem is a Welsh poppy?

7 Which country's "Reign of Terror" began on 5th September 1793?

8 The "Bay of Pigs" expedition was a failed invasion of which country?

9 Lord Russell was the last Prime Minister of which political party beginning with W?

10 Who was the first British woman to fly solo from England to Australia?

ROUND 2 — POP CULTURE

1 Dwayne Johnson is the voice of Maui, a Polynesian demi-god, in which 2016 Disney film?

2 What does the slogan "YOLO" stand for?

3 Lana Lang, Lex Luthor and Lois Lane are all closely associated with which superhero?

4 Who wore a dress made of slabs of raw meat to the 2010 MTV Video Music Awards in LA?

5 What kind of animals are Shenzi, Banzai and Ed in 'The Lion King'?

6 The Rum-Tum-Tugger is a character from which musical?

7 Which British grime artist's hits include 'Big For Your Boots' and 'Shut Up'?

8 Ed Sheeran featured on which rapper's 2017 hit song 'River'?

9 In the CBeebies series 'The Octonauts', what type of animal is Peso?

10 Whose 2016 album is called 'Lemonade'?

ROUND 1 — HISTORY AND POLITICS
1 Nelson Mandela
2 Admiral Horatio Nelson
3 The Beagle
4 Bonn
5 Cressida Dick
6 Plaid Cymru
7 France
8 Cuba
9 Whigs
10 Amy Johnson

ROUND 2 — POP CULTURE
1 Moana
2 You Only Live Once
3 Superman
4 Lady Gaga
5 Hyena
6 Cats
7 Stormzy
8 Eminem
9 Penguin
10 Beyoncé

ROUND 3 — SCIENCE AND NATURE

1 Which insect spreads malaria, which is widespread in sub-Saharan Africa?

2 Which D was a group of animals that included Sauropods and Theropods?

3 A substance that does not let light pass through it as described by what adjective?

4 Animals with no backbone, such as worms or arthropods, are known as … what?

5 Which common alloy is made from copper and tin?

6 In the binomial system used in taxonomy, how many names is each living organism given?

7 Trapdoor, Huntsman and Goliath Birdeater are examples of which type of creature?

8 What is the green pigment needed by plants for photosynthesis?

9 In 1876, Alexander Graham Bell patented the first … what?

10 Cashmere is a breed of what animal?

ROUND 4 — GENERAL KNOWLEDGE

1 What does the second B of the organisation the BBC stand for?

2 How many leaves does a shamrock have?

3 What, in internet slang, does LOL mean?

4 Philippe Suchard and Rodolphe Lindt, both from Switzerland, gave their name to businesses making what product?

5 What was the name of the supersonic passenger plane that could fly at speeds of up to 2,333 kilometres per hour?

6 Gilbert Baker, who died in 2017, created which famous symbol of the LGBT rights movement?

7 Which has the larger volume: a typical adult eyeball or a table tennis ball?

8 The Kindle bookreading device is made by which company?

9 Which European city name is found on the badge of Porsche cars?

10 Rhinotillexomania is the obsessive compulsion of putting your finger where?

ROUND 3 — SCIENCE AND NATURE
1 Mosquito
2 Dinosaurs
3 Opaque
4 Invertebrates
5 Bronze
6 Two
7 Spider
8 Chlorophyll
9 Telephone
10 Goat

ROUND 4 — GENERAL KNOWLEDGE
1 Broadcasting
2 Three
3 Laugh out loud
4 Chocolate
5 Concorde
6 Rainbow flag
7 Table tennis ball (33.5ml vs approx. 6.5ml for eyeball)
8 Amazon
9 Stuttgart
10 Up your nose

ROUND 1 — GEOGRAPHY

1 Which is the only country that Portugal has a land border with?

2 Siberia covers a large area of which country?

3 Which tributary of the Mississippi is the longest river in the USA?

4 Hesse, Saxony and Bavaria are states of which country?

5 Baffin Island is off which country's northeastern coastline?

6 Atatürk International Airport is the main international airport for which city?

7 The remains of ancient Babylon are in which modern-day country?

8 On which thoroughfare would you find the New York Stock Exchange?

9 What is the name of the wetland that the two channels of the Rhône delta flow through?

10 The ancient Via Dolorosa lies within which city?

ROUND 2 — HISTORY AND POLITICS

1 What was the name of the royal house that ruled England and Wales from 1485 to 1603?

2 What was the first surname to be repeated in the name of a US President?

3 In which century did Guy Fawkes die?

4 Who was Chairman of the Palestine Liberation Organisation from 1969 to 2004?

5 Which Roman emperor led the invasion and conquest of Britain in 43 AD?

6 Which "good king" was Duke of Bohemia from 921 to 935?

7 Which is the only one of the Seven Wonders of the Ancient World that is still intact?

8 What did the F stand for in the name of US President John F Kennedy?

9 Who was the last monarch of Great Britain born outside the United Kingdom?

10 What famous object in Italy stopped moving for the first time in its 800-plus year history in May 2008?

ROUND 1 — GEOGRAPHY
1 Spain
2 Russia
3 Missouri
4 Germany
5 Canada
6 Istanbul
7 Iraq
8 Wall Street
9 The Camargue
10 Jerusalem

ROUND 2 — HISTORY AND POLITICS
1 Tudor
2 Adams
3 17th century/1600s
4 Yasser Arafat
5 Claudius
6 Wenceslaus
7 The Great Pyramid of Giza
8 Fitzgerald
9 George II (Hanover, Germany)
10 The Leaning Tower of Pisa

ROUND 3 — ARTS

1 In the Harry Potter novels, what item of clothing allocates Houses to the new students?

2 What is the name for the highness or lowness of musical notes?

3 What is the name of the little girl visited by 'The Tiger Who Came to Tea'?

4 Which Yorkshire city hosts an international piano competition every three years?

5 How many undamaged arms does the Venus De Milo statue have?

6 What was the surname of a man named Nicholas in the title of a novel by Charles Dickens?

7 Which of the Planets in Gustav Holst's 'Planets' Suite is described as 'The Bringer of Old Age'?

8 Which author wrote the 'Just So Stories' including 'How the Leopard Got His Spots' and 'How the Camel Got His Hump'?

9 Susanna, Judith and Hamnet were the children of which 16th and 17th century playwright?

10 Who wrote operas with title characters called Wingrave, Herring, Bunyan, Budd and Grimes?

ROUND 4 — GENERAL KNOWLEDGE

1 What time is it eight hours before midnight?

2 What does the U in UFO stand for?

3 What paper size is exactly half the size of A2?

4 How many terminals does Stansted Airport have?

5 In the TV show 'Bluey', what is the name of Bluey's sister?

6 What Middle Eastern dip has crushed chickpeas as its main ingredient?

7 The Japanese toy Hello Kitty notably does not have what facial feature?

8 In France, what is 'Le Petit Robert'?

9 In the Bible, what is the fifth book of the New Testament?

10 What letter is shared in the spelling of all odd numbers in the English language?

ROUND 3 — ARTS
1 Hat (Sorting Hat)
2 Pitch
3 Sophie
4 Leeds
5 None
6 Nickleby
7 Saturn
8 Rudyard Kipling
9 William Shakespeare
10 Benjamin Britten

ROUND 4 — GENERAL KNOWLEDGE
1 4pm, 1600 hours
2 Unidentified
3 A3
4 One
5 Bingo
6 Hummus
7 Mouth
8 A dictionary
9 Acts
10 E

ROUND 1 — GEOGRAPHY

1 Sevenoaks and Canterbury are in which English county?

2 What colours are on the flag of Poland?

3 "Solo" is an anagram of the capital of which country?

4 In which city would you find the Scott Memorial and the Royal Mile?

5 A line showing points of the same height on a map is a ...?

6 Which EU member state has a picture of its country outline on its national flag?

7 The French city of Avignon is on which major river?

8 Which area of Britain became a UNESCO World Heritage Site in 2017?

9 Which two countries are separated by a demilitarised buffer zone along the 38th parallel?

10 A famous sea stack in the Orkney Islands is known as the Old Man of ... what?

ROUND 2 — MATHS

1 What name is given to the distance around a circle?

2 How is the fraction ½ written as a decimal?

3 On a clock face, how many degrees does the minute hand turn through in one minute?

4 What A was the counting frame that Victorian children used as a calculator?

5 If you wrote down the numbers from 1 to 10, what would be the antepenultimate number you would write?

6 What branch of mathematics deals with triangles?

7 How long does it take a cyclist travelling at 10 mph to travel 200 miles, assuming the cyclist takes an hour's break after every four hours cycling?

8 What is 150% of 250?

9 What is the first square number above 100?

10 Which letter is used in mathematics to represent the square root of minus one?

ROUND 1 — GEOGRAPHY
1 Kent
2 Red and White
3 Norway
4 Edinburgh
5 Contour
6 Cyprus
7 Rhône
8 Lake District
9 North and South Korea
10 Hoy

ROUND 2 — MATHS
1 Circumference
2 0.5
3 6
4 Abacus
5 8
6 Trigonometry
7 24 hours
8 375
9 121
10 i

ROUND 3 — POP CULTURE

1 In a 2012 movie, which title character decides he doesn't want to be a video game villain?

2 Which comedian plays Alan Partridge?

3 Whose 2017 album is called 'Reputation'?

4 In 2019, what became the most successful film of all time, worldwide?

5 Who is the featured vocalist on Mark Ronson's 2014 hit 'Uptown Funk'?

6 In a series of films, Jack Black is the voice of Po, an animal obsessed with which martial art?

7 Peter Quill is the main character in which hit film from 2014?

8 Which character is the protagonist of the 'Tomb Raider' games and films?

9 Who replaced Mary Berry as a judge on 'The Great British Bake Off' in 2017?

10 In 'The Simpsons', what is Principal Seymour Skinner's birth name?

ROUND 4 — SPORT AND GAMES

1 What is the name of the main show court at Wimbledon?

2 What sport takes place at a velodrome?

3 How many yards wide is a football goal?

4 What is the maximum number of rounds in a men's World Championship boxing match?

5 In which Spanish city were the 1992 Summer Olympics held?

6 How many players are there on a rugby union team?

7 What country is the company Nintendo based in?

8 What sport features sand traps called bunkers?

9 What does MLB stand for, as in the American sporting competition?

10 To the nearest mile, how long is a half-marathon?

ROUND 3 — POP CULTURE
1 Wreck-It Ralph
2 Steve Coogan
3 Taylor Swift
4 The Avengers: Endgame
5 Bruno Mars
6 Kung Fu
7 Guardians of the Galaxy
8 Lara Croft
9 Prue Leith
10 Armin Tamzarian

ROUND 4 — SPORT AND GAMES
1 Centre Court
2 Cycling
3 8
4 12
5 Barcelona
6 15
7 Japan
8 Golf
9 Major League Baseball
10 13 miles (13.1 miles)

ROUND 1 — HISTORY AND POLITICS

1 In May 2017, Emmanuel Macron was elected President of which country?

2 In which country of the UK was the Battle of Bannockburn fought?

3 In June 2018, who received over 600,000 likes for tweeting "But my emails."?

4 Which war, in which 4,600 soldiers died in battle, took place between 1854 and 1856?

5 Of the names of all the monarchs of England or Britain from 1066 onwards, which one comes first alphabetically?

6 Which empire lasted from 1299 to 1922, under the sovereignty of 36 sultans?

7 How many rows of benches are there on each side of the House of Commons?

8 The tomb of which pharaoh was discovered by Howard Carter in 1922?

9 What is the largest religion in Sri Lanka?

10 In the 1870s, the German archaeologist Heinrich Schliemann carried out a significant dig which uncovered (but all also caused great damage to) the remains of which ancient city?

ROUND 2 — SCIENCE AND NATURE

1 A creature described as a hexapod has how many legs?

2 Which noble gas shares its name with Superman's home planet?

3 Bats are the only mammals that can do what?

4 What is the main reproductive female in an ant colony called?

5 What, in carnivores, are carnassials, incisors and canines?

6 Named after the Greek god of fear, which is the larger of Mars's moons?

7 Extracted from pegmatite minerals, which metal is commonly used for the tips of darts?

8 Which Italian scientist created the first thermometer in around 1600?

9 In which country can you find CERN, the large particle physics laboratory?

10 What is the chemical symbol for sodium?

ROUND 1 — HISTORY AND POLITICS
1 France
2 Scotland
3 Hillary Clinton
4 Crimean War
5 Anne (the likes of Aethelred, Athelstan etc were before 1066)
6 Ottoman Empire
7 Five
8 Tutankhamun
9 Buddhism
10 Troy

ROUND 2 — SCIENCE AND NATURE
1 Six
2 Krypton
3 Fly
4 Queen
5 Teeth
6 Phobos
7 Tungsten
8 Galileo Galilei
9 Switzerland
10 Na

ROUND 3 — ARTS

1 Who, with Axel Scheffler, wrote 'The Snail and the Whale', 'Zog' and 'A Squash and a Squeeze'?

2 How many strings are there on a cello?

3 What name is given to a surface on which an artist mixes colours?

4 What job is held by the title character of a Rossini opera set in Seville?

5 On which birthday does Harry Potter discover he's a wizard?

6 Pablo Picasso's 'Guernica' was painted during which civil war?

7 In the book 'Charlie and the Chocolate Factory', how many genuine golden tickets are there?

8 What is the name of the Shakespeare work often known as "the Scottish play"?

9 Which author created the epic work 'Paradise Lost'?

10 Which of the 12 apostles of Jesus, according to the Gospel of John, didn't believe in the resurrection when first told of it?

ROUND 4 — GENERAL KNOWLEDGE

1 Which sign of the zodiac is represented by a lion?

2 How many sides are there on the British £1 coin introduced in 2017?

3 In the term GPS, what does the letter G stand for?

4 What kind of food item is a "butty"?

5 What make of car has had models called the Silver Cloud, Silver Ghost and Silver Shadow?

6 The word "graffiti" comes from the Italian for what?

7 Which month of the year comes last in alphabetical order?

8 At which supermarket can you earn Nectar points?

9 In the days of coal fires in the home, wallpaper cleaner was a typical household product. When the need for that disappeared, a Cincinnati-based company rebranded their wallpaper cleaner as what children's product?

10 Which celebrity's many tattoos include the Roman numeral VII and the words Romeo and Brooklyn?

ROUND 3 — ARTS

1 Julia Donaldson
2 Four
3 Palette
4 Barber
5 11th
6 Spanish Civil War
7 Five
8 Macbeth
9 John Milton
10 Thomas (Doubting Thomas)

ROUND 4 — GENERAL KNOWLEDGE

1 Leo
2 12
3 Global (Global Positioning System)
4 Sandwich
5 Rolls Royce
6 Writing/Scratching
7 September
8 Sainsbury's
9 Play-Doh
10 David Beckham

ROUND 1 — GEOGRAPHY

1 Which city is found on the eastern side of the Mersey estuary?

2 The Bosporus strait lies between which two continents?

3 Lake Chad is located at the southern fringes of which vast desert?

4 Aoraki is the highest mountain in New Zealand. How is this mountain also known?

5 Which European country's flag features a red and white chequered shield?

6 The Rock of Gibraltar is considered to be one of the Pillars of ... who?

7 What is the name of the highest mountain in Japan?

8 What is the IATA code for Paris's major international airport?

9 How many countries have a name in English which ends with the letter K?

10 What A is the name of the instrument used for measuring wind speed?

ROUND 2 — HISTORY AND POLITICS

1 What does the A stand for in the abbreviation NATO?

2 Jawaharlal Nehru was the first Prime Minister of which country?

3 What alliterative term is used for the group of men instrumental in the birth of the United States of America?

4 Juan Perón served as President of which South American country?

5 Which famous pioneer boarded The Beagle in December 1831?

6 What was former British Prime Minister Margaret Thatcher's maiden name?

7 What was the name of the grandson of Genghis Khan who ruled the Mongol Empire from 1260 to 1294?

8 How many years before the Great Fire of London was the Norman Conquest?

9 What relation was King Charles II of England to his successor, James II?

10 Between 1958 and 1962, countries including Jamaica and Barbados were part of the short-lived Federation of the ... what?

ROUND 1 — GEOGRAPHY
1 Liverpool
2 Europe and Asia
3 Sahara
4 Mount Cook
5 Croatia
6 Hercules
7 Mount Fuji
8 CDG
9 One (Denmark)
10 Anemometer

ROUND 2 — HISTORY AND POLITICS
1 Atlantic
2 India
3 Founding Fathers
4 Argentina
5 Charles Darwin
6 Margaret (Hilda) Roberts
7 Kublai Khan
8 600
9 Brother
10 West Indies

ROUND 3 — POP CULTURE

1 'The A-Team' and 'Small Bump' are early songs by which artist?

2 In which city is the district, famous for the film industry, known as Hollywood?

3 What TV quiz did Alexander Armstrong begin presenting with Richard Osman in 2009?

4 The 2012 movie 'Brave' is set in which country?

5 Who directed the movie 'The Dark Knight Rises'?

6 What is the country of birth of the rapper Iggy Azalea?

7 In which state is the cartoon 'South Park' set?

8 Which rap artist's album 'Damn.' won a Pulitzer Prize in 2018?

9 Who does Oscar Isaac play in 'Star Wars: The Force Awakens'?

10 How is the character Benjamin Tennyson better known in a successful cartoon series?

ROUND 4 — SCIENCE AND NATURE

1 What is the fruit of a horse chestnut tree called?

2 What does the "rex" part of the name tyrannosaurus rex mean?

3 Who co-founded Microsoft with Paul Allen?

4 What is the gas in a party balloon that can give you a squeaky voice?

5 Echolocation involves bats using which sense to locate nearby objects and prey?

6 On Earth, 100 Newtons is equivalent to how many kilograms?

7 The transparent cover to the human eye is the ... what?

8 What astronomical body was discovered by Clyde Tombaugh in 1930?

9 In 1709, the German physicist Daniel Fahrenheit made the first truly successful example of what item?

10 What is the name of the chemical element which was so called because it was the first to be produced artificially?

ROUND 3 — POP CULTURE
1 Ed Sheeran
2 Los Angeles
3 Pointless
4 Scotland (UK)
5 Christopher Nolan
6 Australia
7 Colorado
8 Kendrick Lamar
9 Poe Dameron
10 Ben 10

ROUND 4 — SCIENCE AND NATURE
1 Conker
2 King
3 Bill Gates
4 Helium
5 Hearing
6 10
7 Cornea
8 Pluto
9 Thermometer
10 Technetium

ROUND 1 — GEOGRAPHY

1 Brittany is in which European country?

2 What is the only English city to begin with the letter G?

3 What name is used in the USA for what the Mexicans call the Rio Bravo?

4 Which country has Mount Kosciuszko as its highest mountain?

5 Andorra has borders with how many countries?

6 Which country in the world has the longest coastline (including all its islands)?

7 New Street is the main railway station in which British city?

8 The flood-prone Ganges river is on which continent?

9 What is the world's only remaining Grand Duchy?

10 On the M40, what, specifically, are Warwick, Cherwell Valley, Oxford and Beaconsfield?

ROUND 2 — MATHS

1 How many hundreds are there in one thousand?

2 If a right angled triangle has two shorter sides of lengths 3cm and 4cm, how long is the hypotenuse?

3 What is the highest number under 100 with a seven letter name in English?

4 How many lines can be drawn across a square from one corner to another?

5 How many prime numbers are there between 90 and 100?

6 What name is given to angles between 180 and 360 degrees?

7 A train travelling at 60 mph enters a tunnel that is 5 miles long. The train is 1 mile long. How many minutes does it take the whole train to pass through the tunnel?

8 What is 37% of 200?

9 What is the product of 18 and 6?

10 How is the number 38 written in binary?

ROUND 1 — GEOGRAPHY
1 France
2 Gloucester
3 Rio Grande
4 Australia
5 Two
6 Canada
7 Birmingham
8 Asia
9 Luxembourg
10 Service stations

ROUND 2 — MATHS
1 Ten
2 5cm
3 70
4 Two
5 One (just 97)
6 Reflex angles
7 6 (60mph is 1 mile per minute. The front of the train has to travel 6 miles for the whole train to pass through the tunnel.)
8 74
9 108
10 100110

ROUND 3 — ARTS

1 What kind of animal is the Beatrix Potter character Jeremy Fisher?

2 There are two Tate galleries in London - one is called Tate Britain, the other is called ... what?

3 The Beatles met and formed in which English city?

4 "At that moment a curious crack sounded inside the statue" is a line from which Oscar Wilde short story?

5 What is the name of the town on the river Avon which is the home town of William Shakespeare?

6 La Scala in the Italian city of Milan is famous for which sort of entertainment?

7 What was the first name of the Hungarian composer Bartók?

8 Who, in Greek culture, were the nine goddesses of the arts?

9 'Under Milk Wood' is a drama by which Welsh poet?

10 Following the Great Fire of London, which architect designed the new St Paul's Cathedral?

ROUND 4 — GENERAL KNOWLEDGE

1 What is the 24th letter of the alphabet?

2 What kind of foodstuff is halloumi?

3 What is the title of the rank in the British army between lieutenant and major?

4 What first name links the news presenters Wark and Young?

5 Apa Sherpa was the first man to achieve which feat 20 times?

6 How is the processed, salted roe of the sturgeon better known?

7 What word completes the one-time motto of Google: "Don't be ..." what?

8 Which word connects cabbages and one of the only roads in the UK on which you can legally drive on the right hand side?

9 The Golden Spurtle is an annual award given in Scotland for the making of ... what?

10 In which crafting activity might you make use of an overlocker?

ROUND 3 — ARTS
1 Frog
2 Tate Modern
3 Liverpool
4 The Happy Prince
5 Stratford-upon-Avon
6 Opera/theatre
7 Béla
8 The Muses
9 Dylan Thomas
10 Sir Christopher Wren

ROUND 4 — GENERAL KNOWLEDGE
1 X
2 Cheese
3 Captain
4 Kirsty
5 Climbing Everest
6 Caviar
7 Evil
8 Savoy
9 Porridge
10 Sewing

ROUND 1 — HISTORY AND POLITICS

1 What was the name of the single European Currency launched in 1999?

2 Which ocean's name was coined by Ferdinand Magellan in the 16th century and means "peaceful sea"?

3 Jair Bolsonaro was elected as president of which country in late 2018?

4 In the early 20th century, suffragettes campaigned for voting rights for ... who?

5 What was the name of the system of racial segregation imposed in 1948 by the South African government?

6 In 1510, Goa became the principal Portuguese base in which country?

7 Pheasant Island, near the town of Hendaye is, for alternating six-month periods, under the governance of France and which other country?

8 In 1957, what became the first sub-Saharan African country to gain independence from a colonial power?

9 The Tyburn Tree, site of many medieval hangings, was nearest to the site of which modern London tube station?

10 Which American President coined the name United Nations?

ROUND 2 — POP CULTURE

1 In the film 'Frozen', what kind of creature is Sven?

2 Which superhero's alter ego is Tony Stark?

3 Which chart-topping musician shares his name with the generic term for a male duck?

4 In the Disney versions of 'Cinderella', what does the Fairy Godmother turn into a carriage?

5 Which singer had a 2003 hit with 'Crazy In Love'?

6 Which English singer of Kosovan origin had her first UK Number 1 single, 'New Rules' in 2017?

7 For which song did Adele win an Oscar, a Grammy and a Golden Globe?

8 In which classic film from 1939 did a man called Frank Morgan play the title character, actually quite a small part in the film?

9 'Strip That Down', 'Sign of the Times', and 'Slow Hands' have all been solo hits from former members of which boy band?

10 Sian Gibson, playing Kayleigh, is the co-star of which hit comedy?

ROUND 1 — HISTORY AND POLITICS
1 Euro
2 Pacific Ocean
3 Brazil
4 Women
5 Apartheid
6 India
7 Spain (under the Treaty of the Pyrenees)
8 Ghana
9 Marble Arch
10 Franklin D Roosevelt

ROUND 2 — POP CULTURE
1 Reindeer
2 Iron Man
3 Drake
4 Pumpkin
5 Beyoncé (featuring Jay-Z)
6 Dua Lipa
7 Skyfall
8 The Wizard of Oz
9 One Direction
10 Peter Kay's Car Share

ROUND 3 — ARTS

1 The Fringe is the name of the largest arts festival in the world, which takes place every year in which British city?

2 Who was the Italian composer of 'The Four Seasons'?

3 What is the name of the oldest sister in both the 'Narnia' books and the 'Swallows and Amazons' books?

4 In Roman mythology, which goddess is the wife of Jupiter?

5 In literature, the Carnegie medal is awarded to books written for what audience?

6 On what ship, according to myth, did Jason travel to Colchis to steal the Golden Fleece?

7 What was the name of the first son of Adam and Eve, making him, according to the Bible, the first human born?

8 In music, which is the highest of the main vocal ranges?

9 What is the main colour of Gustav Klimt's famous painting 'The Kiss'?

10 In Prokofiev's 'Peter and the Wolf', what large woodwind instrument represents Peter's grandfather?

ROUND 4 — SCIENCE AND NATURE

1 What name is given to the male of the hedgehog?

2 Which element has the chemical symbol K?

3 How, in the human body, is the mandible also known?

4 In which American state is the technological hub known as Silicon Valley?

5 What animal would be the father of a mule?

6 A naturally occurring catalyst that increases the rate of reaction of chemical processes in living things is known as a what?

7 What is the English name of the calcaneus, the largest bone of the foot?

8 In which organ would you find the Islets of Langerhans?

9 While the US employs the term astronaut, what is the Russian equivalent?

10 If you add 273 to an object's temperature in Celsius, you get its temperature in ... what?

ROUND 3 — ARTS
1 Edinburgh
2 Antonio Vivaldi
3 Susan
4 Juno (Hera in Greek mythology)
5 Children / Young People
6 Argo
7 Cain (of "and Abel" fame)
8 Soprano
9 Gold
10 Bassoon

ROUND 4 — SCIENCE AND NATURE
1 Boar
2 Potassium
3 Jawbone
4 California
5 Donkey
6 Enzyme
7 Heel bone
8 Pancreas
9 Cosmonaut
10 Kelvin

ROUND 1 — GEOGRAPHY

1 Tsavo and Serengeti are National Parks in which continent?

2 Which language is most widely spoken in the Canadian city of Montreal?

3 How many points are there on the Star of David?

4 Which American city is known as "The City of Brotherly Love"?

5 How many European countries lie on the Greenwich meridian?

6 The river Thames rises in which range of hills in England?

7 Which country is known as "The Land of the Rising Sun"?

8 In which country would you find the Blue Lagoon geothermal spa?

9 Which city is the capital of the Spanish region of Catalonia?

10 What is Europe's highest active volcano?

ROUND 2 — HISTORY AND POLITICS

1 How many US Presidents have there been called Bush?

2 In 1990, Helmut Kohl became the first chancellor of which reunified country?

3 Who resigned as a government spokesperson in December 2021 for her role in "partygate"?

4 What do the initials AV stand for in terms of a voting system?

5 Of which city did former Cabinet minister Andy Burnham become Mayor in 2017?

6 The Battle of Midway was one of the most important air battles of World War II. In which ocean is the Midway Atoll, after which it is named?

7 Which African country was known as the Gold Coast when it was a British colony?

8 What is the Afrikaans word for farmer, and the name of a war fought from 1899 to 1902?

9 Elizabeth Garrett Anderson was the first woman in Britain to qualify as ... what?

10 What is the emblem of the Labour Party in the UK?

ROUND 1 — GEOGRAPHY
1 Africa
2 French
3 Six
4 Philadelphia
5 Three (UK (England), France, Spain)
6 Cotswolds
7 Japan
8 Iceland
9 Barcelona
10 Etna

ROUND 2 — HISTORY AND POLITICS
1 Two
2 Germany
3 Allegra Stratton
4 Alternative Vote
5 Manchester
6 (North) Pacific
7 Ghana
8 Boer
9 Doctor
10 (Red) rose

ROUND 3 — ARTS

1 Who wrote 'David Copperfield' and 'Great Expectations'?

2 The theatre district of which city is known as Broadway?

3 The poems of TS Eliot were the basis for which musical?

4 Which Norwegian artist painted 'The Scream'?

5 How, in religion, is Siddhartha Gautama also known?

6 In which European city could you visit Anne Frank's house and museum?

7 Which two word Italian term is used to describe singing without any instrumental accompaniment?

8 Where can the so-called Raphael Rooms be found?

9 El Greco and Francisco Goya were artists of which nationality?

10 Who was the Greek goddess of Victory?

ROUND 4 — GENERAL KNOWLEDGE

1 According to the Bible, what kind of reptile tempts Eve to eat the forbidden fruit?

2 What is sandwiched between two biscuit slices in a Garibaldi?

3 Twitching is a name for what hobby?

4 According to the 1908 book 'Scouting for Boys', what is the two-word motto of the Scouts?

5 What banknote was withdrawn from circulation in the UK in March 1988?

6 The longest land border in the world is between the USA and which other country?

7 In which month is the first bank holiday of the year in the UK?

8 In Mexico, what is a papier-mâché donkey that children hit to reveal goodies within?

9 What is the Latin word for "therefore" and also a name for a rowing machine?

10 Searching for what word on Google will cause it to ask "Did you mean: nag a ram?"?

ROUND 3 — ARTS
1 Charles Dickens
2 New York
3 Cats
4 Edvard Munch
5 Buddha
6 Amsterdam
7 A cappella
8 The Vatican (accept Rome)
9 Spanish
10 Nike

ROUND 4 — GENERAL KNOWLEDGE
1 Snake
2 Currants/raisins
3 Birdwatching
4 Be prepared
5 £1 (one pound)
6 Canada
7 January
8 Piñata
9 Ergo
10 Anagram

ROUND 1 — GEOGRAPHY

1 What is the main language spoken in Hong Kong?

2 Designed by Renzo Piano, what is the name of London's tallest building?

3 Tango is an Argentine tradition - what is it?

4 What, by area, is the largest country in the world where English is an official language?

5 The National Gallery is situated on which square in London?

6 In which country does the river Rhine rise?

7 What is the name of Greece's highest mountain, the home of the gods in ancient Greek mythology?

8 Which so-called "sea" is a salt lake bordered by Jordan, Israel and the West Bank?

9 Which US state is furthest away from the national capital, Washington DC?

10 Ruins of what type of building can be seen at Lullingstone, Chedworth and Woodchester?

ROUND 2 — MATHS

1 How many sides does a nonagon have?

2 What is 12 x 4?

3 What is the missing number at the end of this sequence: 3, 11, 19, 27, ...?

4 What is the square root of 441?

5 What is the next prime number up after 7?

6 What is 16 + 96?

7 What S is defined as an unresolved mathematical expression of an nth root?

8 What is 86% of 450?

9 In a survey 100 people said they preferred margarine. 200 said they preferred butter. The remaining 700 said they had no clear preference. What percentage of people preferred margarine?

10 What is 24 cubed?

FAMILY-FRIENDLY 13

ROUND 1 — GEOGRAPHY
1 Cantonese (allow: Chinese)
2 The Shard
3 A dance
4 Canada
5 Trafalgar Square
6 Switzerland
7 Olympus
8 Dead
9 Hawaii
10 Roman villas

ROUND 2 — MATHS
1 Nine
2 48
3 35
4 21
5 11
6 112
7 Surd
8 387
9 10
10 13824

ROUND 3 — POP CULTURE

1 In 'Game of Thrones', what kind of creatures are Rhaegal, Viserion and Drogon?

2 In the children's TV show, what does Peppa Pig particularly enjoy jumping into?

3 K-Pop music originates from which country?

4 Which 'Simpsons' character has the largest Malibu Stacy doll collection in Springfield?

5 The 1998 film 'Ever After', starring Drew Barrymore, was a retelling of which fairytale?

6 Which children's TV show has characters including Koko, Wilson, Brewster, Hoot, Toot and Piper?

7 In the 1939 film 'The Wizard of Oz', what is the name of the Good Witch?

8 Which 'Strictly Come Dancing' judge retired from the show at the end of the 2016 series?

9 The fictional J Jonah Jameson is the editor of which newspaper?

10 Which children's TV series, revived in 2015, includes characters such as the Soup Dragon and the Iron Chicken?

ROUND 4 — SCIENCE AND NATURE

1 The adjective leonine refers to which animal?

2 Wombats are native to which country?

3 Which word is used to describe animals that generally sleep during the day?

4 What word describes the appearance of the moon from Earth when it is approaching full moon?

5 What is the name of the group of four muscles at the front of the thigh in the human body?

6 Which element of the periodic table comes last alphabetically?

7 What animal is sometimes known as the African antbear or the Cape anteater?

8 In pharmaceuticals, what does GSK stand for?

9 The two large bones in the human forearm are the ulna and the ... what?

10 3.4% of the atmosphere of which planet is made up of water vapour?

FAMILY-FRIENDLY 13

ROUND 3 — POP CULTURE
1 Dragons
2 Muddy puddles
3 South Korea
4 Waylon Smithers
5 Cinderella
6 Chuggington
7 Glinda
8 Len Goodman
9 The Daily Bugle
10 The Clangers

ROUND 4 — SCIENCE AND NATURE
1 Lion
2 Australia
3 Nocturnal
4 Waxing (vs Waning when it is moving away from appearing full)
5 Quadriceps (femoris)
6 Zirconium
7 Aardvark
8 GlaxoSmithKline
9 Radius
10 Mercury

ROUND 1 — GEOGRAPHY

1 In which mountain range is the world's tallest mountain?

2 The "Home Counties" surround which English city?

3 The river Loire widens into an estuary that discharges into which large bay?

4 Which island in the Pacific is known by its natives as Rapa Nui?

5 The Gobi Desert is in which continent?

6 Bodmin Moor is located entirely within which English county?

7 What is the name for the islands including Majorca, Minorca and Ibiza?

8 Which continent lies nearest to 0 degrees latitude and 0 degrees longitude?

9 What is the name of the only US state whose name begins with the letter D?

10 What is the main language spoken in Argentina?

ROUND 2 — HISTORY AND POLITICS

1 The Head of State of which country lives at the Kremlin?

2 How is the United Nations Children's Fund better known?

3 Since 1301, male heirs to the throne of England (or later, the UK) have held which title?

4 How long is one full term for a President of the USA?

5 "The Desert Fox" is a nickname that refers to which World War II general?

6 The Charge of the Light Brigade took place during which war?

7 Which country has had two Prime Ministers with the surname Trudeau?

8 Which French leader did the Duke of Wellington's army defeat decisively at the Battle of Waterloo?

9 In which century did construction begin on the Leaning Tower of Pisa?

10 Of whom did Winston Churchill say, "The Russian people were left floundering in the bog. Their worst misfortune was his birth: their next worst - his death."?

ROUND 1 — GEOGRAPHY
1 Himalayas
2 London
3 Bay of Biscay
4 Easter Island
5 Asia
6 Cornwall
7 Balearics
8 Africa
9 Delaware
10 Spanish

ROUND 2 — HISTORY AND POLITICS
1 Russia
2 UNICEF
3 Prince of Wales
4 Four years
5 Erwin Rommel
6 Crimean War
7 Canada
8 Napoleon Bonaparte (Napoleon I)
9 12th
10 Vladimir Lenin

ROUND 3 — ARTS

1 What were the magic words used in Ali Baba and the Forty Thieves to access the cave that contains the secret treasure?

2 In Greek legend, which creature did Theseus kill in the Labyrinth?

3 An iconic painting by Botticelli depicts which Roman goddess standing in a giant shell?

4 What is the surname of James, he of the Giant Peach?

5 Yo-Yo Ma is best known for playing which string instrument?

6 Which great artist completed 'The Last Supper' in 1498?

7 Who, in the Old Testament, is the brother of Moses?

8 Which hero supposedly shot an arrow through an apple on his son's head?

9 The Uffizi is a major attraction in Florence, Italy. What is it?

10 Who wrote the novel 'Tess of the D'Urbervilles'?

ROUND 4 — GENERAL KNOWLEDGE

1 What is the most common surname in the UK?

2 What does the K in the fast food restaurant KFC stand for?

3 Which birds are traditionally associated with the Tower of London?

4 Which word describes food prepared in accordance with Jewish dietary regulations?

5 Which London park contains Speakers' Corner and the Serpentine Lake?

6 What artistic part of Google.com did Dennis Hwang start designing in 2000?

7 St Peter is generally accepted as the first holder of which religious post?

8 Acorn, spaghetti and butternut are varieties of which vegetable?

9 What do the letters "TLDR" stand for in the context of a lengthy article online?

10 In France, what are crêpes and galettes?

ROUND 3 — ARTS
1 Open Sesame
2 Minotaur
3 Venus
4 Trotter
5 Cello
6 Leonardo Da Vinci
7 Aaron
8 William Tell
9 An art gallery
10 Thomas Hardy

ROUND 4 — GENERAL KNOWLEDGE
1 Smith
2 Kentucky
3 Ravens
4 Kosher
5 Hyde Park
6 Google Doodles
7 The Pope/Bishop of Rome
8 Squash
9 Too long, didn't read
10 Pancakes

ROUND 1 — HISTORY AND POLITICS

1 Mahatma Gandhi helped lead which country to independence from the British Empire?

2 The heavily guarded border dividing Europe's Eastern Bloc from the rest of the continent was called the Iron ... what?

3 Charles de Gaulle became which country's President in 1959?

4 A plutocracy is a system of government with which people in charge?

5 Immediately before becoming Prime Minister of the UK, Theresa May held which cabinet position?

6 As recorded by the Roman historian Suetonius, what kind of people said "Ave Caesar, morituri te salutant"?

7 Which general became a dictator in Spain as a result of the Spanish Civil War?

8 What was the tallest structure in the world between 1887 and 1930?

9 In the 1850s, which British political party emerged from a mixture of Whigs and radicals?

10 Who was the last Monarch of Great Britain not to succeed one of their parents?

ROUND 2 — POP CULTURE

1 'Teenage Dream' and 'Firework' are songs by which female artist?

2 What connects the entertainer Dwayne Johnson to a name often given to Gibraltar?

3 Dolly Parton is godmother to which MTV award winning singer - the child of another country singer?

4 Which Christmas-hating character, created by Dr. Seuss, was played by Jim Carrey in a 2000 film?

5 In 2017, which singer held nine of the top 10 positions simultaneously in the UK singles chart?

6 In the title of a 2017 film, how many billboards are 'Outside Ebbing, Missouri'?

7 Which dinosaur character made his debut in 'Super Mario World' in 1990?

8 Actress Lily James played Lady Rose in which popular TV drama?

9 The name of which animated character is derived from Japanese onomatopoeic words for an electric sparkle sound and the sound small mice make?

10 Who released the album 'Melodrama' in 2017?

ROUND 1 — HISTORY AND POLITICS
1 India
2 Curtain
3 France
4 The rich
5 Home Secretary
6 Gladiators
7 (Francisco) Franco
8 The Eiffel Tower
9 The Liberal party
10 King George VI

ROUND 2 — POP CULTURE
1 Katy Perry
2 The Rock
3 Miley Cyrus
4 The Grinch
5 Ed Sheeran
6 Three
7 Yoshi
8 Downton Abbey
9 Pikachu
10 Lorde

ROUND 3 — SCIENCE AND NATURE

1 The letters "FEAR FIG" can be rearranged to make the name of which mammal?

2 Originally coined by Richard Dawkins, which word is now used to describe an online concept that spreads rapidly across social media?

3 What are a dolphin's broad, paddle-like front limbs called?

4 True or False? In 2009, the scientist Stephen Hawking threw a party at Cambridge University which nobody went to. This is because he didn't announce the details until after the date as the party was for time travellers.

5 The two main components of steel are carbon and what?

6 In taxonomy, the names of species are given in which language?

7 What is the full name of the LHC, the world's largest particle accelerator?

8 Which hormone stimulates the human liver to release more glucose?

9 Ungulates is an order of animals that typically have what sort of feet?

10 The Y2K problem, relating to computers' abilities to deal with dates after 1999, was popularly known by what other name?

ROUND 4 — GENERAL KNOWLEDGE

1 A phrase in English meaning something is very hard to find is "like finding a needle in a ..." what?

2 In 1945, which car manufacturer started to make the Beetle?

3 Which animal is consulted for a seasonal weather forecast every February 2nd in Punxsutawney, Pennsylvania?

4 What would you be afraid of if you suffered from hippophobia?

5 Which month of the year is named after the Roman God of War?

6 What common English word is the Latin for "he leaves"?

7 What symbol goes above the number 5 on a standard UK keyboard?

8 The name Peggy is, somewhat counterintuitively, derived from which girl's name?

9 In the sentence "The quick brown fox jumps over the lazy dog" which word is the preposition?

10 On a standard clock, how many times between midnight and midday will the minute hand cross the hour hand?

ROUND 3 — SCIENCE AND NATURE

1 Giraffe
2 Meme
3 Flippers
4 True
5 Iron
6 Latin
7 Large Hadron Collider
8 Adrenaline
9 Hooves
10 Millennium Bug

ROUND 4 — GENERAL KNOWLEDGE

1 Haystack
2 Volkswagen
3 Groundhog
4 Horses
5 March
6 Exit
7 % (per cent)
8 Margaret
9 Over
10 11 (one for every hour, except for midnight and midday when they don't cross)

ROUND 1 — HISTORY AND POLITICS

1 1969 saw the first manned expedition to which body in the Solar System?

2 Who became the first President of the USA in 1789?

3 In June 1960, Congo gained independence from which European country?

4 The English translation of the rallying cry of the French Revolution is "Liberty, Equality, ..." what?

5 How many English monarchs were called Henry?

6 What was the name of Robert Stephenson's pioneering 1829 steam locomotive?

7 What school did Boris Johnson and David Cameron attend?

8 At the Battle of Blood River in 1838, the Boers won victory against which people?

9 In 1893, which was the first country to grant women the vote?

10 Who became Lord Mayor of London in 1397?

ROUND 2 — SPORT AND GAMES

1 In rock-paper-scissors, which gesture beats scissors?

2 The roads of which city-state are turned into a Formula One race track every year?

3 Who replaced Sir Alex Ferguson as manager of Manchester United?

4 What sport do the Jacksonville Jaguars and the Chicago Bears play?

5 What major golf tournament takes place every year at Augusta National in Georgia?

6 What is the most valuable property on a London Monopoly board?

7 Which European capital city is the host of the 2024 Summer Olympics?

8 In the original card game Happy Families, what is the name of the baker?

9 Which annual football match is traditionally contested between the Premier League champions and the FA Cup winners?

10 In basketball, what name is given to the violation of the rules where a player moves one or both of their feet illegally?

ROUND 1 — HISTORY AND POLITICS
1 The Moon
2 George Washington
3 Belgium
4 Fraternity
5 Eight
6 Rocket
7 Eton College
8 Zulus
9 New Zealand
10 Richard "Dick" Whittington

ROUND 2 — SPORT AND GAMES
1 Rock
2 Monaco (accept Monte Carlo)
3 David Moyes
4 American football
5 The Masters
6 Mayfair
7 Paris
8 Mr Bun
9 Community Shield
10 Travelling

ROUND 3 — ARTS

1 What kind of musical instrument is a timpani?

2 What is the name of Paddington Bear's aunt in Peru?

3 In 2020, 17 year-old Fang Zhang was the winner of which biennial competition, which has previously been won by Nicola Benedetti and Sheku Kanneh-Mason?

4 In musical notation, what is a quarter of a semibreve?

5 Andromache is the wife of which Trojan hero?

6 In the book of the same name, what is the name of 'The Hobbit'?

7 What nationality were the artists Wassily Kandinsky and Kazimir Malevich?

8 Which word, meaning "I have found it!", is the mathematician Archimedes famous for shouting?

9 Roald Dahl's 'The Twits' was written, in part, to express his hatred of ... what?

10 Scottish actor Tony Curran played which painter in 'Doctor Who', in an episode where he travels through time at the end of the episode to see the acclaim in which his work is held in the modern day?

ROUND 4 — SCIENCE AND NATURE

1 Which force makes apples fall from trees to the ground?

2 What M is the red-hot, treacly, melted rock deep inside earth?

3 What is the common name for the bird also known as Columba livia or rock dove?

4 If Domain is the highest ranked main taxonomic group, what is the lowest ranked?

5 Elsa Einstein, wife of Albert Einstein, was born with what surname?

6 In what scale does water boil at 220 degrees?

7 What common canine activity is a Basenji dog not able to do?

8 In the human body, what connects muscles to bones?

9 In Pythagoras' Theorem, relating to the sides of a right-angled triangle, A squared plus B squared equals ... what?

10 Which mineral is graded at 10 on the Mohs Scale?

ROUND 3 — ARTS
1 Drum
2 Lucy
3 BBC Young Musician
4 Crotchet
5 Hector
6 Bilbo Baggins
7 Russian
8 Eureka
9 Beards
10 Vincent van Gogh

ROUND 4 — SCIENCE AND NATURE
1 Gravity
2 Magma
3 Pigeon
4 Species
5 Einstein
6 Fahrenheit
7 Bark
8 Tendons
9 C Squared
10 Diamond

ROUND 1 — GEOGRAPHY

1 Which English county describes itself as "The Garden of England" on road signs?

2 Lake Chad and Lake Malawi are on which continent?

3 What island goes with Tobago to make the name of a country in the Caribbean?

4 The Bering Strait separates which two countries?

5 In London, what is a Hackney carriage better known as?

6 Which country was an observer state for many years before joining the United Nations on 10th September 2002?

7 In which country are the cities of Turin, Florence and Milan?

8 Which American state comes second in alphabetical order?

9 Nakuru, Kisumi and Mombasa are cities in which African country?

10 The Waikato is the longest river in which country?

ROUND 2 — SCIENCE AND NATURE

1 Which planet of the solar system comes first in alphabetical order?

2 Which metal had the chemical symbol Cu?

3 Where might you see arches, loops and whorls?

4 What did the Hungarian László Bíró invent in 1931?

5 What winged creatures does a lepidopterist study?

6 What is the Latin name for the calf bone?

7 Brass is an alloy of copper and which other metal?

8 In a microwave oven, what name is given to the part that produces the microwaves?

9 As in a type of electromagnetic wave that is essential for photosynthesis, what does UV stand for?

10 Which gas makes up most of the atmosphere on Mars?

ROUND 1 — GEOGRAPHY

1 Kent
2 Africa
3 Trinidad
4 USA and Russia
5 Black cab/Taxi
6 Switzerland
7 Italy
8 Alaska
9 Kenya
10 New Zealand

ROUND 2 — SCIENCE AND NATURE

1 Earth
2 Copper
3 Fingerprints
4 Ballpoint pen
5 Butterflies (and moths)
6 Fibula (not femur)
7 Zinc
8 Magnetron
9 Ultra-Violet
10 Carbon dioxide

ROUND 3 — HISTORY AND POLITICS

1 In which century was the English Civil War?

2 How was King Robert I of Scotland commonly known?

3 What has been the most common first name for a President of the USA?

4 Papua New Guinea established independence from which country in 1975?

5 Which modern city was the first capital of the Roman province of Britannia?

6 Which MP for South West Norfolk became the UK Foreign Secretary in September 2021?

7 Abraham Lincoln, as President of the USA, represented which political party?

8 King Idris, who reigned from 1951 to 1969, was the first and only king of which country?

9 Sir Alexander MacEwen was, in 1934, the first leader of which political party?

10 Which English monarch was preceded by his brother Richard and followed by his son Henry?

ROUND 4 — GENERAL KNOWLEDGE

1 In which month of the year is Valentine's Day?

2 What word can go before mess, rifles, fives and boating song?

3 Kissing what Irish monument is meant to give someone great speaking powers?

4 In which country was the businessman Elon Musk born?

5 What is the name of the energy drink that "gives you wings"?

6 Wing Commander is a rank in which branch of the armed forces?

7 The traditional Margherita pizza is topped with the leaves of what herb?

8 In which London building is The Strangers' Gallery?

9 The futon is a furniture item invented in which country?

10 If you were interested in rolling stock numbers, you would be a ... what?

ROUND 3 — HISTORY AND POLITICS
1 17th
2 Robert the Bruce
3 James
4 Australia
5 Colchester
6 Liz Truss
7 Republican
8 Libya
9 Scottish National Party
10 John – (Henry IV and Henry VII both also preceded by Richard and followed by Henry, but the Richards were not their brothers)

ROUND 4 — GENERAL KNOWLEDGE
1 February
2 Eton
3 Blarney Stone
4 South Africa
5 Red Bull
6 Royal Air Force
7 Basil
8 The Houses of Parliament
9 Japan
10 Trainspotter

ROUND 1 — HISTORY AND POLITICS

1 The pharaohs ruled which ancient kingdom?

2 To which decade in the UK is the adjective "Swinging" most often applied?

3 The Russian Civil War pitted the White Army against which other army?

4 Who is Britain's second longest reigning monarch?

5 What was discovered in 1928 by Alexander Fleming?

6 Complete the saying attributed to the Roman general Julius Caesar: "I came, I saw, I ..."?

7 Who was King of England, Scotland and Ireland during the Great Fire of London and the Great Plague?

8 Genghis Khan was the warlord leader of which empire?

9 What is the name usually used by historians to describe the series of conflicts between England and France which ran from 1337 to 1453?

10 In the 1750s, which American inventor carried out experiments with kites to prove that lightning was electricity?

ROUND 2 — SCIENCE AND NATURE

1 Anacondas are snakes which are native to which continent?

2 Which is the only planet in the Solar System that is less dense than water?

3 Which H is a protein found in red blood cells that helps to transport oxygen around the body?

4 Iron oxide in the dust on Mars makes the planet appear which colour?

5 A Pascal is the SI unit used to measure what?

6 Which English naturalist took notes on the nature of the Galápagos Islands in 1835?

7 Which M is the animal also known as a sea cow?

8 The world's first ever cloned sheep was named after which singer?

9 Home to the largest lizards in the world, the island of Komodo is part of which country?

10 What organ in the body breaks down amino acids from food, producing urea?

ROUND 1 — HISTORY AND POLITICS
1 Egypt
2 Sixties
3 Red Army
4 Queen Victoria
5 Penicillin
6 Conquered
7 Charles II
8 Mongol
9 Hundred Years' War
10 Benjamin Franklin

ROUND 2 — SCIENCE AND NATURE
1 South America
2 Saturn
3 Haemoglobin
4 Red
5 Pressure
6 Charles Darwin
7 Manatee
8 Dolly Parton
9 Indonesia
10 Liver

ROUND 3 — ARTS

1 How many people are there in an octet?

2 What does "V&A" stand for in the name commonly used for the famous London museum?

3 'The Persistence of Memory' is a renowned painting by which Spanish artist?

4 Who is the author of the 'Artemis Fowl' series of books?

5 What is the name of the middle book of JRR Tolkien's 'The Lord of the Rings' trilogy?

6 Which common expression taken from Latin means "In good faith"?

7 'The Mysterious Affair at Styles' was the first book to feature which detective?

8 Which relative did James McNeill Whistler famously paint in 1871?

9 Michelangelo's 'The Creation of Adam' can be seen on the ceiling of which chapel?

10 'The Curious Incident of the Dog in the Night-Time' takes its name from a line spoken by which fictional character?

ROUND 4 — GENERAL KNOWLEDGE

1 What goes after straw, blue and rasp in the names of fruit?

2 The patron saint's days of both Wales and Ireland fall in which month?

3 What household items can be open coil, pocket sprung or memory foam?

4 Which website founded by Pierre Omidyar has described itself as "the world's largest online marketplace"?

5 On what day of the week is The Observer newspaper published in the UK?

6 What is the fourth from last letter of the Roman alphabet?

7 Numismatics is the study and collection of what?

8 How many months of the year have exactly the same spelling in French and in English?

9 Which seven-letter word is the longest word in the list of 100 most frequently used words in written English?

10 A deltiologist is the name of a person who studies and collects which objects?

ROUND 3 — ARTS
1 Eight
2 Victoria and Albert
3 Salvador Dali
4 Eoin Colfer
5 The Two Towers
6 Bona fide
7 Hercule Poirot
8 His mother
9 Sistine Chapel
10 Sherlock Holmes

ROUND 4 — GENERAL KNOWLEDGE
1 Berry
2 March
3 Mattresses
4 eBay
5 Sunday
6 W
7 Coins
8 None
9 Because
10 Postcards

ROUND 1 — GEOGRAPHY

1 On which continent would you find the Yangtze and Mekong rivers?

2 Tasmania is separated from the Australian mainland by which Strait?

3 Which Alpine country is made up of member states called cantons?

4 The island of Zanzibar is part of which African nation?

5 The Drakensberg mountain range is in South Africa and which other country?

6 What is the tallest mountain in the Southern Hemisphere?

7 Chesil Beach is an 18-mile long barrier beach in which English county?

8 Portobello is a beach resort located just to the north of which British city?

9 What is the modern name of territory formerly known as British Honduras?

10 Name one of the cities at either end of the Suez Canal.

ROUND 2 — HISTORY AND POLITICS

1 What name is given to the parliamentarians who fought against the Cavaliers in the English Civil War?

2 Which country's Declaration of Independence was approved in July 1776?

3 Who was the Soviet leader during World War II?

4 What was the surname of the Portuguese explorer who led the expedition which first circumnavigated the world?

5 Which continent had its first cash machines installed in January 1997?

6 In what decade was the former British Prime Minister Tony Blair born?

7 Who became President of Zimbabwe in 1987?

8 Which goddess was the wife and sister of the Egyptian God Osiris?

9 Which modern state declared independence from Pakistan in 1971?

10 What V is the name given to the non-violent revolution in Czechoslovakia in 1989?

ROUND 1 — GEOGRAPHY
1 Asia
2 Bass
3 Switzerland
4 Tanzania
5 Lesotho
6 Aconcagua
7 Dorset
8 Edinburgh
9 Belize
10 Suez and Port Said

ROUND 2 — HISTORY AND POLITICS
1 The Roundheads
2 USA
3 Joseph Stalin
4 Magellan
5 Antarctica
6 1950s
7 Robert Mugabe
8 Isis
9 Bangladesh
10 Velvet Revolution

ROUND 3 — SCIENCE AND NATURE

1 The Great Red Spot is a huge storm on the surface of which planet?

2 In sublimation, a heated substance changes from a solid to what?

3 The deafening bang when an aircraft reaches supersonic speed has what two-word name?

4 How many canine teeth would you expect a healthy adult human to have?

5 In fish such as sharks and rays, of what flexible substance is the endoskeleton made?

6 What are the subatomic particles which have a negative electrical charge?

7 In an electrical circuit, what do the letters LED stand for?

8 In a computer, how many bits are there in a byte?

9 The unit of power, whose symbol is W, is named after which scientist?

10 What is the alternative name for vitamin B1?

ROUND 4 — SPORT AND GAMES

1 In which cycling Grand Tour does the leader traditionally wear a yellow jersey?

2 In which sport would players use woods, irons and wedges?

3 Which is the slowest Olympic swimming stroke?

4 On a standard dartboard, what number is on the right-hand side of 20 as you look at the board?

5 Which sportswoman married the tech billionaire Alexis Ohanian in November 2017?

6 What U is a word linking a team sport that uses a frisbee and a combat sport that takes place in an octagon?

7 Which two teams compete in rugby union's Calcutta Cup?

8 How many pockets does a snooker table have?

9 United Nations Space Command combats the alien Covenant in which series of video games?

10 At the 2020 Tokyo Olympics, in which event did competitors ride horses that were randomly allocated to them?

ROUND 3 — SCIENCE AND NATURE
1 Jupiter
2 Gas
3 Sonic Boom
4 Four
5 Cartilage
6 Electrons
7 Light-Emitting Diode
8 8
9 James Watt
10 Thiamine

ROUND 4 — SPORT AND GAMES
1 Tour de France
2 Golf
3 Breaststroke
4 1
5 Serena Williams
6 Ultimate
7 England and Scotland
8 Six
9 Halo
10 Modern Pentathlon

ROUND 1 — GEOGRAPHY

1 Which organisation has a flag that features a map of the world surrounded by olive branches?

2 In which English county is the area known as the Potteries?

3 The ancient city of Petra is in which modern day country?

4 What is the first letter in the name of three of the four smallest capital cities in Europe?

5 Which US State comes first in alphabetical order?

6 In which European city is the famous thoroughfare called Las Ramblas?

7 What is the name of the large square-mouthed bay which separates Norfolk from Lincolnshire?

8 What is the only Asian country the Equator passes through?

9 Angkor Wat is a temple complex in which country?

10 Which Scottish mountain range is named after the fifth highest mountain in the range?

ROUND 2 — SCIENCE AND NATURE

1 The first two elements in the periodic table began with which letter?

2 What is the most populous species of bird in the world?

3 The bright red fungus Clathrus archeri is sometimes known as the Octopus stinkhorn, and also by what other evocative name?

4 What is measured on the Richter Scale?

5 Experiments with a tin can and an air blower helped push Christopher Cockerell to invent ... what?

6 What is the tallest breed of dog?

7 Charles Babbage's "difference engine" is an early type of ... what?

8 The region of space where conditions are "just right" to contain life is called ... what?

9 In the USA, which broadcaster and scientific educator is known as "The Science Guy"?

10 What type of fly carries and transmits deadly diseases such as sleeping sickness?

ROUND 1 — GEOGRAPHY

1 UN
2 Staffordshire
3 Jordan
4 V (Vatican City, Vaduz and Valletta (the other is San Marino))
5 Alabama
6 Barcelona
7 The Wash
8 Indonesia
9 Cambodia
10 Cairngorms (named after Cairn Gorm)

ROUND 2 — SCIENCE AND NATURE

1 H
2 Chicken (about 25 billion)
3 Devil's fingers
4 Earthquakes
5 Hovercraft
6 Great Dane
7 Computer
8 The Goldilocks Zone
9 Bill Nye
10 Tsetse fly

ROUND 3 — ARTS

1 In the books of Arthur Conan-Doyle, which London thoroughfare was the home of consulting detective Sherlock Holmes?

2 Which book by F. Scott Fitzgerald features the characters Nick Carraway and Jordan Baker?

3 Which title character in a popular children's book had the catchphrase "I'll 'ave that"?

4 In 1824, which deaf composer was on stage for the premiere of his Ninth Symphony?

5 Which novel by Daniel Defoe was inspired by the true story of Alexander Selkirk, who was marooned on a Pacific island?

6 What nationality were the authors Victor Hugo and Alexandre Dumas?

7 In what century did the Art Movement known as The Pre-Raphaelite Brotherhood come into being?

8 In 'Treasure Island', what was Long John Silver's job on the Hispaniola?

9 In Greek Mythology, who had a "face that launched a thousand ships"?

10 What name links the daughter of Henry I, who fought her cousin Stephen for the throne of England, and a novel by Roald Dahl about the daughter of Mr and Mrs Wormwood?

ROUND 4 — GENERAL KNOWLEDGE

1 The 100th day of the year, in the Gregorian calendar, is in which month?

2 In Judaism, a boy's coming of age ritual is a Bar Mitzvah. Which word replaces "Bar" in a girl's equivalent ritual?

3 What piece of garden equipment gives its name to a race where one person holds a team-mate's ankles, and that one walks on their hands?

4 The hood is the name in US English for which part of a car?

5 Deva was the Roman name of which English city?

6 Which word can go before water, bread and stream, and after caustic and baking?

7 Who became Chief Medical Officer for England in 2019?

8 What colour berets would you associate with US Army Special Forces?

9 On an Ordnance Survey map, what is represented by an "H" in a circle?

10 In western astrology, which is the only star sign not depicted by an animal or person?

ROUND 3 — ARTS
1 Baker Street
2 The Great Gatsby
3 Burglar Bill
4 Ludwig van Beethoven
5 Robinson Crusoe
6 French
7 19th
8 Cook
9 Helen of Troy (the line was actually written by Marlowe, in 'Doctor Faustus')
10 Matilda

ROUND 4 — GENERAL KNOWLEDGE
1 April
2 Bat
3 Wheelbarrow
4 Bonnet
5 Chester
6 Soda
7 Chris Whitty
8 Green
9 Heliport
10 Libra

ROUND 1 — HISTORY AND POLITICS

1 Ronald Reagan was President of which country in the 1980s?

2 What was the Roman name for London?

3 Which French leader was burned at the stake in 1431, and later made a saint?

4 The island of Pitcairn was settled in the eighteenth century by mutineers originally from which ship?

5 At Prime Minister's Question Time on 26th January 2022, Boris Johnson called Keir Starmer "a lawyer, not a ..." what?

6 Which country has the longest written constitution in the world?

7 In ancient Rome, what were Mirmillones and Retiarii?

8 What name is given to the period in Britain between 1811 and 1820 when the Prince of Wales ruled but was not yet king?

9 King William III was born in 1650 in which city of The Netherlands?

10 Who declared himself Haiti's President for Life in 1964?

ROUND 2 — SCIENCE AND NATURE

1 Which is the only continent where giraffes are found in the wild?

2 What two-letter symbol represents the chemical element gold?

3 Used to connect many devices to a computer, USB stands for "Universal ..." what?

4 From what lunar module did Neil Armstrong step onto the surface of the Moon?

5 What is the name of the largest species of land crab?

6 Which word did British palaeontologist Sir Richard Owen coin in 1842?

7 The word plumber derives from the Latin word for which element?

8 What was the name of the world's first communication satellite, launched in 1962?

9 Which organ in the human body produces the hormone insulin?

10 Which seabird similar to the penguin has a name which derives from the French for William?

ROUND 1 — HISTORY AND POLITICS
1 USA
2 Londinium
3 Joan of Arc
4 The Bounty
5 Leader
6 India
7 Gladiators
8 Regency
9 The Hague
10 François "Papa Doc" Duvalier

ROUND 2 — SCIENCE AND NATURE
1 Africa
2 Au
3 Serial Bus
4 Eagle
5 Coconut crab
6 Dinosaur
7 Lead (Plumbum)
8 Telstar
9 Pancreas
10 Guillemot

ROUND 3 — SPORT AND GAMES

1 Yorker, bouncer and beamer are types of delivery in which team sport?

2 Which martial art has a name that literally means "empty hand" in Japanese?

3 In the 2003-04 English Premier League season, which football team finished unbeaten, earning the nickname "The Invincibles"?

4 In 1986, Greg LeMond became the first non-European to win which annual sporting event?

5 The Yankees and the Giants are the two main baseball teams of which city?

6 Which of the four Grand Slam tennis tournaments is played on clay?

7 Who missed a penalty for the England women's football team in the semi-final of the 2019 World Cup?

8 In the video game franchise, what do the letters GTA stand for?

9 Walter Morrison designed the Pluto Platter flying disc, which is now much better known as a ... what?

10 What is the surname of the first biological father and son to both win the English Premier League title?

ROUND 4 — GENERAL KNOWLEDGE

1 How many "legs" does the Eiffel Tower have?

2 In which month of 2020 did the UK begin its first Covid-19 "lockdown"?

3 What word is used for the highest rating that can be given to a school in an Ofsted report?

4 Which letter of the NATO phonetic alphabet is represented by the name of a province of Canada?

5 Where on his body would a gentleman traditionally wear a cummerbund?

6 There are two umpires on a cricket pitch - one behind the stumps at the bowler's end and the other in which fielding position?

7 According to the Marriage Act of 1949, how many times should the Banns be read out in the weeks leading up to a marriage in England?

8 The viral online challenge of 2014 which raised vast sums of money for research into ALS was known as the WHAT challenge?

9 Under a car's bonnet, what is used to check the engine oil level?

10 Which word links a style of newspaper, John F Kennedy and a type of pastry?

ROUND 3 — SPORT AND GAMES

1 Cricket
2 Karate
3 Arsenal
4 Tour de France
5 New York
6 French Open
7 Steph Houghton
8 Grand Theft Auto
9 Frisbee
10 Schmeichel

ROUND 4 — GENERAL KNOWLEDGE

1 Four
2 March
3 Outstanding
4 Q
5 Round his waist
6 Square Leg
7 Three times
8 Ice Bucket
9 Dipstick
10 Berliner

ROUND 1 — GEOGRAPHY

1 What is the capital city of Turkey/ Türkiye?

2 Which is the only ceremonial county of England with a one syllable name?

3 The tallest mountain in the Southern Hemisphere, Aconcagua, is in which mountain range?

4 Split is a city in which country?

5 Which African country has its capital city at Juba?

6 Mebyon Kernow, formed in 1951, seeks independence for which English county?

7 In which country is the ruined city of Pompeii?

8 What is the last letter of the name of the capital city of Belgium?

9 In which modern country is the holy Muslim city of Mecca situated?

10 Which country takes its name from the Latin word for silver?

ROUND 2 — HISTORY AND POLITICS

1 Which prison in Paris is strongly associated with the French Revolution?

2 Who was the American President immediately before Barack Obama?

3 In which century was Macbeth king of Scotland?

4 Which city was renamed Ho Chi Minh City in 1975?

5 In which East European country was the Solidarnosc party set up in 1980?

6 The Boxer Uprising was a rebellion in which country?

7 In 1945, who followed Winston Churchill as Prime Minister of the UK?

8 Leo Varadkar became the leader of which European country's government in June 2017?

9 What is the name of Scotland's oldest university?

10 Astronomer Tycho Brahe replaced a missing bit of what body part with a metal prosthetic?

ROUND 1 — GEOGRAPHY
1 Ankara
2 Kent
3 Andes
4 Croatia
5 South Sudan
6 Cornwall
7 Italy
8 S
9 Saudi Arabia
10 Argentina

ROUND 2 — HISTORY AND POLITICS
1 Bastille
2 George W Bush
3 11th
4 Saigon
5 Poland
6 China
7 Clement Attlee
8 Ireland (he became Taoiseach)
9 St Andrews
10 Nose

ROUND 3 — ARTS

1 Whose collections of poetry were called 'Rhyme Stew', 'Dirty Beasts' and 'Revolting Rhymes'?

2 What is the name of the winged horse ridden by Bellerophon in Greek mythology?

3 In Prokofiev's 'Peter and the Wolf', which instrument represents the character of the Wolf?

4 Artists Pablo Picasso and Vincent van Gogh both died in which country?

5 What can't giraffes do, according to the title of a book by Giles Andreae?

6 'Swan Lake' and 'The Nutcracker' are ballets by which Russian composer?

7 What general word is used to describe poetry that is made up of five "feet"?

8 Which of the Famous Five, based on Enid Blyton herself, is the owner of the dog Timmy?

9 A translation of which children's book is the only book published in Latin to make it to the New York Times Bestseller List?

10 French artist Yves Klein created and registered a shade of which colour, and made a series of paintings exclusively in that shade?

ROUND 4 — GENERAL KNOWLEDGE

1 What B does the conductor of an orchestra hold in their hand to direct a musical performance?

2 Until 1987, it was compulsory in the UK to have a licence for what?

3 When written as words, which of the numbers 1 to 10 is first alphabetically?

4 In Britain, SAGE stands for Scientific Advisory Group for ...?

5 Which local crime prevention scheme started in the UK in the village of Mollington, Cheshire in 1982?

6 In the lyrics of the song 'I Can Sing a Rainbow', what is the third colour that is mentioned?

7 According to the popular World War I song, 'It's a long way to ...' where?

8 The usual layout of a computer keyboard in the UK is called QWERTY after the first six letters of the top line of letters. What is the usual keyboard layout called in Germany?

9 Which decimal coin was withdrawn from circulation in the UK in December 1984?

10 What is the name of Jeremy Corbyn's climate sceptic brother?

ROUND 3 — ARTS
1 Roald Dahl
2 Pegasus
3 French horn
4 France
5 Dance
6 Piotr Tchaikovsky
7 Pentameter
8 George
9 Winnie-the-Pooh
10 Blue

ROUND 4 — GENERAL KNOWLEDGE
1 Baton
2 Dogs
3 Eight
4 Emergencies
5 Neighbourhood Watch
6 Pink
7 Tipperary
8 QWERTZ
9 Halfpenny
10 Piers

ROUND 1 — GEOGRAPHY

1 In which Brazilian city is Sugarloaf Mountain?

2 After England, which country of the United Kingdom has the most cities?

3 The provinces of Ireland are Leinster, Munster, Ulster and ... which other?

4 What does the Statue of Liberty hold in her right hand?

5 Machu Picchu is a historic site in Peru. Which ancient civilization developed it?

6 The national flags of both Bhutan and Wales depict which mythical creature?

7 The volcano Mount St Helens is in which American state?

8 The Witch of Wookey Hole, near Wells in Somerset, is what kind of geographical feature?

9 How many African countries have a coastline on the Mediterranean?

10 The island of Ushant contains the most north-westerly point of which country?

ROUND 2 — HISTORY AND POLITICS

1 Who is the only king of England to have had six wives?

2 Which ocean did Christopher Columbus cross in 1492?

3 What is the most common name for kings of France?

4 In the 1960s, the Beeching Reports related to what aspect of British life?

5 Benito Mussolini led which country during World War II?

6 New Amsterdam is a former name of an area of which city?

7 The nobleman El Cid, who fought against the Moors, is a national hero of which country?

8 Who was famously depicted on posters during World War I declaring "Your Country Needs You!"?

9 Which Sherpa was the first man, alongside the explorer Edmund Hillary, to climb Everest?

10 In which year did Japanese forces attack Pearl Harbor?

ROUND 1 — GEOGRAPHY
1 Rio de Janeiro
2 Scotland
3 Connacht
4 Torch
5 Inca
6 Dragon
7 Washington
8 Stalagmite/Icicle
9 Five
10 France

ROUND 2 — HISTORY AND POLITICS
1 Henry VIII
2 Atlantic
3 Louis
4 Railways
5 Italy
6 New York City
7 Spain
8 Lord Kitchener
9 Tenzing Norgay
10 1941

ROUND 3 — SCIENCE AND NATURE

1 How many people have stood on the surface of the planet Mars?

2 Which island, whose unique wildlife includes lemurs, separated from the African continent around 95 million years ago?

3 Which L is the scientific name for the voice box?

4 In 1999, what user-friendly name was given to widely used wireless networking protocol IEEE 802.11?

5 Which large bird native to Africa has the fastest land speed of any bird?

6 Billies and nannies are the names given to the males and females of which animal?

7 What does the Beaufort Scale measure?

8 How many audio channels do stereo recordings have?

9 Ethanol contains atoms of carbon, hydrogen and which other element?

10 What is the male part of a flower called?

ROUND 4 — SPORT AND GAMES

1 Crews in the Oxford and Cambridge University Boat Race wear tops in light or dark shades of which colour?

2 In a standard UK Monopoly set, the money is made up of notes of how many different values?

3 As well as the 100 metres, what other individual event did Usain Bolt win at Beijing 2008, London 2012 and Rio 2016?

4 In which winter sport do competitors compete lying on their back?

5 Tacking is an important part of which Olympic sport?

6 In which city is the football club Benfica based?

7 In road cycling, what French name is given to the main group of riders?

8 The foible is a part of which item of sporting equipment?

9 When compiling a maximum 147 snooker break, how many balls do you have to pot in total?

10 In which game, invented at Cambridge University, might players squidge those playing pieces which are not squopped?

ROUND 3 — SCIENCE AND NATURE
1 None
2 Madagascar
3 Larynx
4 Wi-Fi
5 Ostrich
6 Goat
7 Wind speed
8 Two
9 Oxygen
10 Stamen

ROUND 4 — SPORT AND GAMES
1 Blue
2 Seven
3 200m
4 Luge
5 Sailing
6 Lisbon
7 Peloton
8 Fencing sword
9 36
10 Tiddlywinks ["squidging" is the act of flipping winks and a wink is "squopped" where covered by another wink]

ROUND 1 — HISTORY AND POLITICS

1 Which political party has produced the most British Prime Ministers?

2 The Vietnam War took place on which continent?

3 What is the name of the French national anthem?

4 Which Emperor of Japan died in January 1989?

5 Which monarch was depicted on the Penny Black, the world's first adhesive postage stamp?

6 The Treaty of Tordesillas divided South America between which countries?

7 Catherine the Great was Empress of which country from 1762 until 1796?

8 Who killed the notorious outlaw Billy the Kid?

9 How else was the 1st century Roman Emperor Gaius known?

10 Whom did the Vikings believe was ruler of the Gods?

ROUND 2 — GEOGRAPHY

1 Which country contains Indira Gandhi International Airport?

2 In the UK, an area designated as an AONB is an 'Area of Natural ...' what?

3 Which Australian state is known as the "Apple Isle"?

4 Halifax is the capital of which Canadian province?

5 Which ocean does the Limpopo river drain into?

6 What is the name of the intercity passenger train system in the USA?

7 In which British city is the Bullring shopping centre?

8 What city is home to the U-Bahn rapid transit system?

9 Which site in Romania is sometimes known as "Dracula's Castle"?

10 Elbow Beach and Horseshoe Bay are located on which island in the North Atlantic Ocean?

ROUND 1 — HISTORY AND POLITICS
1 Conservative
2 Asia
3 La Marseillaise
4 Hirohito/Showa
5 Queen Victoria
6 Spain and Portugal
7 Russia
8 Pat Garrett
9 Caligula
10 Odin/Woden

ROUND 2 — GEOGRAPHY
1 India
2 Beauty
3 Tasmania
4 Nova Scotia
5 Indian
6 Amtrak
7 Birmingham
8 Berlin
9 Bran Castle
10 Bermuda

ROUND 3 — ARTS

1 In 'Peter Pan' who is Wendy's youngest brother?

2 Who wrote 'The Creakers' and 'The Christmasaurus'?

3 Edward Elgar's 'Variations on an Original Theme' is commonly known by what name?

4 What is the name of the land populated by very tiny people in Gulliver's Travels?

5 What adjective is used to describe 'Jude' in the title of a Thomas Hardy novel?

6 In the Bible, which book of the Old Testament comes between Genesis and Leviticus?

7 What Q is, in poetry, a four-line stanza?

8 Before it was a gallery, what did Paris's famous Musée D'Orsay serve as?

9 What did the Vikings call female deities supposed to collect men who had died heroically in battle?

10 Which German composer's Third Symphony is often called 'The Scottish Symphony'?

ROUND 4 — GENERAL KNOWLEDGE

1 In the summer of 2020, the scheme devised by chancellor Rishi Sunak was called 'Eat Out to ...' what?

2 Which three-letter abbreviated name is also a ranking system in some martial arts?

3 Which word links a rank in the army and a type of punishment intended to cause physical pain?

4 On twitter, a 'verified' badge contains a small tick on what colour background?

5 In the nursery rhyme 'Sing a Song of Sixpence', which birds are baked in a pie?

6 Listing the London Underground lines alphabetically, which comes first?

7 What paper size is 148 by 210 millimetres?

8 In which Scottish city is Heriot-Watt University located?

9 How many circles are there on a traditional Connect Four grid?

10 According to the nursery rhyme 'Hey Diddle Diddle', the dish ran away with ... what?

ROUND 3 — ARTS
1 Michael
2 Tom Fletcher
3 Enigma Variations
4 Lilliput
5 Obscure
6 Exodus
7 Quatrain
8 A railway station - it was the Gare D'Orsay
9 Valkyries
10 Felix Mendelssohn

ROUND 4 — GENERAL KNOWLEDGE
1 Help Out
2 Dan
3 Corporal
4 Blue
5 Blackbirds
6 Bakerloo
7 A5
8 Edinburgh
9 42
10 The spoon

ROUND 1 — SCIENCE AND NATURE

1 Which chemical element has the atomic number 2?

2 Veal is meat which comes from which animal?

3 Why is sodium fluoride often added to toothpaste?

4 Who was the third man to walk on the Moon?

5 Who is credited with formulating the first periodic table of the elements?

6 The bird with the widest wingspan, which can be around 3 metres, is the Wandering ... what?

7 What is controlled by a rheostat?

8 The human genome project was an attempt to identify all 3 billion base pairs of what sort of molecule?

9 Tanning of the skin is caused by what type of radiation?

10 At 4.2 light years distance, which star is closest to the Sun?

ROUND 2 — HISTORY AND POLITICS

1 What was the first name of Queen Elizabeth II's mother?

2 In which century did England have two kings called James?

3 The Shoguns ruled which country for much of the period between the 12th and the 19th century?

4 Which position has been held by Thomas Becket, Thomas Cranmer and Rowan Williams?

5 Apart from Wilson, what other surname has been shared by a British Prime Minister and US President?

6 Which former South Korean Foreign Minister became UN Secretary-General in 2007?

7 The 'Defenestrations Of Prague' were historical events involving protesters throwing their opponents ... where?

8 Kwame Nkrumah was the first President of which African country?

9 Harriet Tubman was an important figure in what 19th century American network?

10 Known as 'El Libertador', who led independence movements throughout South America?

ROUND 1 — SCIENCE AND NATURE
1 Helium
2 Calf/cow
3 To strengthen enamel
4 Pete Conrad
5 Dmitri Mendeleev
6 Albatross
7 Electric current
8 DNA
9 Ultra-Violet
10 Proxima Centauri

ROUND 2 — HISTORY AND POLITICS
1 Elizabeth
2 17th
3 Japan
4 Archbishop of Canterbury
5 Johnson
6 Ban Ki-moon
7 Out of a window
8 Ghana
9 Underground Railroad
10 Simon Bolivar

ROUND 3 — POP CULTURE

1 On film, what has been Pink, starring Peter Sellers, and Black, starring Chadwick Boseman?

2 Whose 2021 divorce from Simon Konecki provided much of the subject matter for her fourth album?

3 Set in the year 2560, what is the name of the 2021 instalment in the 'Halo' series of games?

4 Which London-born actor was Oscar-nominated for his role as Ruben Stone in 'Sound of Metal'?

5 Which word links a 1995 Number 1 single for Celine Dion, a 1967 James Bond film, and a 2021 Richard Osman novel?

6 Which celebrity couple married in Las Vegas in July 2022, more than 18 years after calling off their first engagement?

7 What legendary Englishman did Taron Egerton play in a 2018 film directed by Otto Bathurst?

8 Which M was a puppet character who first appeared on BBC in 1946, with friends including Crumpet the Clown and Mr Peregrine Esquire the Penguin?

9 Whose 100th birthday did People magazine, unfortunately, celebrate, in January 2022?

10 What three words appear on screen at the end of Looney Tunes cartoons?

ROUND 4 — SPORT AND GAMES

1 In football, which team do Barcelona play in "El Clásico"?

2 What is the minimum number of points in a conventional (not final set) tennis tie-break?

3 Which tile-based game gets its name from the Chinese for "sparrows"?

4 What is the surname of the Indian fast bowler, known for his unorthodox style, who made his test debut in 2018 and whose first name is Jasprit?

5 In rugby league, how many players make up the forwards in one team?

6 True or False? Andy Murray rapped on a 2009 song by the Bryan Brothers Band called 'Autograph'. His lines include "During Wimbledon, it really gets crazy; my hand cramps up and my mind gets hazy".

7 In football, how high, in feet, should the crossbar be? (the lower edge of the crossbar specifically)

8 Which online word game, which became wildly popular in late 2021, was devised by Josh Wardle?

9 Which baseball team was previously named the Highlanders?

10 What is the highest possible break, theoretically, that can be achieved in a frame of snooker?

ROUND 3 — POP CULTURE
1 Panther
2 Adele
3 Halo Infinite
4 Riz Ahmed
5 Twice (Think Twice, You Only Live Twice, The Man Who Died Twice)
6 Jennifer Lopez and Ben Affleck
7 Robin Hood
8 Muffin the Mule
9 Betty White (she died in late Dec 2021)
10 That's All Folks

ROUND 4 — SPORT AND GAMES
1 Real Madrid
2 Seven (there are now ten-point tie-breaks to decide final sets)
3 Mah jong
4 Bumrah
5 Six (two props, one hooker, two second row forwards and a loose forward or lock)
6 True
7 8 feet
8 Wordle
9 New York Yankees
10 155 (if your opponent fouls and leaves you a free ball, you can pot a colour worth 1, pot the black, then pot the first red)

ROUND 1 — GEOGRAPHY

1 Which body of water separates Ireland from Great Britain?

2 What was the currency of Cyprus before it was replaced by the Euro in 2008?

3 What is the capital city of the country of Jordan?

4 Which Central American country has a name which means "The Saviour"?

5 In which country of the United Kingdom are the Mountains of Mourne?

6 The Gulf of Bothnia is between Sweden and Finland. Which sea is it part of?

7 Which fruit is banned from public transport in Singapore due to its disgusting smell?

8 In which US state is the famous Mount Rushmore, with its carved presidential likenesses?

9 Which province in the north of Canada was created for the Inuit?

10 In which country are the ancient sites of Delphi and Olympia?

ROUND 2 — SCIENCE AND NATURE

1 What name is given to the tail of a fox?

2 To the nearest light year, 20 trillion kilometres is equivalent to how many light years?

3 The ability of a substance to restrict the flow of electric current is known as ... what?

4 A breed of small horse is named after which group of Scottish islands?

5 Birds (beginning with F) identified by Charles Darwin which helped him explain evolution are called "Darwin's ..." what?

6 What is the largest artery in the human body?

7 Named after a German scientist who died in 1832, what scale is used to measure a mineral's hardness?

8 When animals pass the winter in a state of inactivity or sleep they are said to do what?

9 The Australian pelican is noted for what characteristic amongst all birds?

10 What life-changing procedure was first performed by Dr Christiaan Barnard in 1967?

ROUND 1 — GEOGRAPHY
1 Irish Sea
2 Pound
3 Amman
4 El Salvador
5 Northern Ireland
6 Baltic Sea
7 Durian
8 South Dakota
9 Nunavut
10 Greece

ROUND 2 — SCIENCE AND NATURE
1 Brush
2 Two
3 Resistance
4 Shetlands
5 Finches
6 Aorta
7 Mohs Scale
8 Hibernate
9 Largest bill
10 Heart transplant

ROUND 3 — ARTS

1 How would you usually play the musical instrument the lute?

2 The Sainsbury Wing was added to which London gallery in 1991?

3 A famous play by George Bernard Shaw is 'Androcles and the ...' what?

4 In the 'Narnia' books, what is the name of the castle where the kings and queens of Narnia rule?

5 In the classic children's book, Peter Rabbit steals vegetables from whose garden?

6 Richard Wagner's 1843 opera is titled 'The Flying ...' what?

7 The Kelpies are a pair of 30 metre-high sculptures in Falkirk, each depicting the head of which animal?

8 Hiccup is a teenage Viking in which series of books by Cressida Cowell?

9 "When a man is tired of London, he is tired of life" - words attributed to which author?

10 What unlikely occurrence links the children's book 'Tom's Midnight Garden' to George Orwell's '1984'?

ROUND 4 — GENERAL KNOWLEDGE

1 What is the name of the youngest level in the UK Girlguiding movement, for girls aged five to seven?

2 Which actor lost a libel case to The Sun newspaper in November 2020?

3 Which Nobel prize was won by Mother Teresa in 1979?

4 In the branch of the British police known as CID, what does the I stand for?

5 What three-letter word can mean a short haircut or to move up and down in water?

6 How many furlongs are there in a mile?

7 Which punctuation mark is also the name of a type of butterfly?

8 In the Bible, which of the three Wise Men brought the gift of frankincense?

9 What is the only country name used in the current NATO phonetic alphabet?

10 What word is both an informal name for a helicopter and a classic children's bicycle?

ROUND 3 — ARTS
1 Pluck it
2 National Gallery
3 Lion
4 Cair Paravel
5 Mr McGregor
6 Dutchman
7 Horse
8 How to Train Your Dragon
9 Samuel Johnson
10 The clock strikes 13

ROUND 4 — GENERAL KNOWLEDGE
1 Rainbow
2 Johnny Depp
3 Peace
4 Investigation
5 Bob
6 Eight
7 Comma
8 Caspar
9 India
10 Chopper

ROUND 1 — GEOGRAPHY

1 The shortest ferry crossing over the English Channel goes from Dover to where?

2 Which tiny country is found in the Pyrenees?

3 Which transport service launched in the UK in late 2003, renowned for its advertised £1 fares?

4 In which English county would you find Luton Airport?

5 What is the name of the capital city of Morocco?

6 On what day is the Chicago River traditionally dyed green?

7 Which area in London is bounded by High Holborn, Kingsway, The Strand, and Charing Cross Road, although the name is commonly used to refer to the open area at its centre?

8 What is the name of the currency in Kenya, Uganda and Somalia?

9 In which English county would you find the town of Lichfield?

10 For the majority of the year, how far behind the UK is the time in Los Angeles?

ROUND 2 — SCIENCE AND NATURE

1 Water contains two hydrogen atoms and one ... what?

2 By what name is the upper portion of the skull known?

3 What is the SI base constant representing the amount of substance?

4 What silvery-white metal is found in limestone and chalk, as well as occurring in animal bones and teeth?

5 The European Organization for Nuclear Research, known as CERN, is based on the outskirts of which European city?

6 What chemical element has the symbol Mn?

7 What D is the name that the plant Belladonna is also commonly known as?

8 What two-word term describes the temperature of -273.15 Celsius?

9 What U is the fleshy extension which hangs above the throat at the back of the soft palate?

10 What word describes a tree or shrub that sheds its leaves seasonally?

ROUND 1 — GEOGRAPHY
1 Calais
2 Andorra
3 Megabus
4 Bedfordshire
5 Rabat
6 St Patrick's Day/17th March
7 Covent Garden
8 Shilling
9 Staffordshire
10 8 hours

ROUND 2 — SCIENCE AND NATURE
1 Oxygen atom
2 Cranium
3 Mole
4 Calcium
5 Geneva
6 Manganese
7 Deadly Nightshade
8 Absolute Zero
9 Uvula
10 Deciduous

ROUND 3 — ARTS

1 In the children's book 'We're Going on a Bear Hunt', where do the children find the bear?

2 What name links an iconic sculpture by Auguste Rodin with a world famous painting by Gustav Klimt?

3 The character Esmeralda is a main character in which novel by Victor Hugo?

4 The name of which craft material means "chewed paper" in French?

5 Which composer's Piano Sonata Number 14 is better known as the 'Moonlight Sonata'?

6 A man called Daniel Handler has written popular children's books under what pen-name?

7 Which word describes the rabbit in the title of a classic children's book by Margery Williams?

8 The Turbine Hall, a cavernous area used for displaying specially commissioned works, can be found at which art gallery?

9 How would a ballet dancer be standing if they were 'en pointe'?

10 What is the occupation of Colin Creevey's father in the Harry Potter books?

ROUND 4 — GENERAL KNOWLEDGE

1 On a QWERTY computer keyboard, which is the only vowel not found on the top row of letters?

2 Which meat is traditionally used in a pasta carbonara dish?

3 If omicron means little o, what means big O?

4 The logo of which British film company featured a man hitting a gong?

5 The CPI is the index that measures inflation in the UK - for what does the letter C stand?

6 What is the name of the girl offering advice in the song 'There's a Hole in My Bucket'?

7 Taking its name from the Sanskrit for "union", what type of exercise has poses including "plank", "lotus" and "downward facing dog"?

8 In British education, A-Levels were introduced in which decade?

9 Which C is the British convenience store and supermarket group founded by Colin Graves in 1986?

10 Pandiculation is the act of doing what whilst yawning?

ROUND 3 — ARTS
1 In a cave
2 The Kiss
3 The Hunchback of Notre-Dame
4 Papier-mâché
5 Ludwig van Beethoven
6 Lemony Snicket
7 Velveteen
8 Tate Modern
9 On the tips of their toes
10 Milkman

ROUND 4 — GENERAL KNOWLEDGE
1 A
2 Bacon/Pancetta
3 Omega
4 Rank
5 Consumer
6 Liza
7 Yoga
8 1950s
9 Costcutter
10 Stretching

ROUND 1 — GEOGRAPHY

1 The river Tagus flows through Spain and which other country?

2 What is the second largest continent in terms of both area and population?

3 What is the capital of the Czech Republic/Czechia?

4 What name is given to a U-shaped body of water formed when a wide meander from the main stem of a river is cut off?

5 What famous waterfall lies on the border between Zambia and Zimbabwe?

6 Brooklyn, Staten Island and Queens are boroughs of which city?

7 In which country is the city of Melbourne?

8 What Greek town, on the slopes of Mount Parnassus, was believed, in ancient times, to be the centre of the world?

9 Which country's flag, adopted in 1994, has six colours: black, yellow, green, red, white and blue?

10 What E is the name for the body of water where a river widens to enter the sea?

ROUND 2 — POP CULTURE

1 Who plays Belle in the 2017 live-action remake of 'Beauty And The Beast'?

2 Marshall Mathers is the real name of which rapper?

3 Who plays Batman in 'The Dark Knight' trilogy of films?

4 A flag hoisted by ships when they are ready to sail out to sea shares its name with which children's television programme?

5 In 2015, which British singer had her first UK Number 1 single as a solo artist with 'Hold My Hand'?

6 Which animated dog on CBeebies runs an activity club attended by a young octopus, crocodile, hippo, rhino and mouse?

7 Dave Myers and Si King are better known as which TV culinary duo?

8 Which animated film from 2009 is about an elderly widower called Carl Fredricksen?

9 What did the I originally stand for in ITV?

10 What is the stage name of Charlotte Aitchison, whose singles include 'Boys' and 'Boom Clap'?

ROUND 1 — GEOGRAPHY
1 Portugal
2 Africa
3 Prague
4 Oxbow Lake
5 Victoria Falls
6 New York
7 Australia
8 Delphi
9 South Africa
10 Estuary

ROUND 2 — POP CULTURE
1 Emma Watson
2 Eminem
3 Christian Bale
4 The Blue Peter
5 Jess Glynne
6 Duggee
7 The Hairy Bikers
8 Up
9 Independent
10 Charli XCX

ROUND 3 — ARTS

1 In art, what colour is produced when blue and yellow paints are mixed?

2 According to the title of a Roald Dahl book, who is the Champion of the World?

3 Who was the Norse god of thunder?

4 "Second to the right, and straight on till morning" are the directions to which faraway place in 'Peter Pan'?

5 The bars of a xylophone are traditionally made from which material?

6 In what language did Virgil write the epic poem 'The Aeneid'?

7 The European Anthem is set to the music of the 'Ode to Joy' by which composer?

8 Which Spanish artist, born in 1881, had blue, rose and Cubist periods?

9 Igor Stravinsky wrote a ballet inspired by which season?

10 Which Harry Potter book was split into two parts when made into films?

ROUND 4 — GENERAL KNOWLEDGE

1 On which continent is the world's largest rainforest?

2 What is the common unit used for measuring the height of horses?

3 In the New Testament, what is traditionally the second of the Gospels?

4 McDonald's and KFC were founded in which country?

5 Under which sign of the zodiac does New Year's Day fall?

6 Which sandwich traditionally includes chicken or turkey with bacon, and uses three slices of toasted bread?

7 Which Tottenham Hotspur player shared the 2021-22 Premier League Golden Boot with Mo Salah?

8 In which month does the Hindu festival Holi take place?

9 Which sauce is named after the Houses of Parliament?

10 In what decade was the National Curriculum introduced to England, Wales and Northern Ireland?

ROUND 3 — ARTS
1 Green
2 Danny
3 Thor
4 Neverland
5 Wood
6 Latin
7 Ludwig van Beethoven
8 Pablo Picasso
9 Spring (The Rite of Spring)
10 Harry Potter and the Deathly Hallows

ROUND 4 — GENERAL KNOWLEDGE
1 South America
2 Hands
3 Mark
4 USA
5 Capricorn
6 Club sandwich
7 Son Heung-min
8 March
9 HP Sauce
10 1980s (1988)

ROUND 1 — HISTORY AND POLITICS

1 The International Court of Justice sits in The Hague - in which country?

2 Algeria gained independence from which country in 1962?

3 The fourth, and youngest, son of King Aethelwulf, which renowned English ruler was king of Wessex from 871 to 899 AD?

4 On 3rd December 1989, which war was declared over by the USA and the USSR?

5 Which Italian volcano's last major eruption, which claimed the lives of 44 people, was in 1944?

6 In 1791, the Brandenburg Gate was completed in which German city?

7 Who narrowly defeated Richard Nixon to become American President in 1960?

8 Britain had how many different reigning female monarchs in the 20th century?

9 Which number Apollo mission took Neil Armstrong, Michael Collins and Buzz Aldrin to the Moon?

10 How many kings of England have there been called Robert?

ROUND 2 — MATHS

1 Which shape has eight sides?

2 How many degrees are there in a right-angle?

3 How long does it take a train travelling at 80 mph to travel 20 miles?

4 What number is represented by the expression "a baker's dozen"?

5 What do you get if you add up the whole numbers from 1 to 10 inclusive?

6 What is the next number in this sequence: 1,4,9,16,25,36,49, ... ?

7 How many hours are there between 7pm on Friday and 3am on Monday?

8 What is the highest number that does not need the letter N when you spell it out in English?

9 When it is a quarter past five, how many degrees from north is the minute hand pointed?

10 In a survey 1/10 of people said they preferred red sauce. 2/5 said they preferred blue sauce. The remaining 90 said they had no clear preference. How many people preferred red sauce?

ROUND 1 — HISTORY AND POLITICS
1 The Netherlands
2 France
3 Alfred
4 Cold War
5 Vesuvius
6 Berlin
7 John F Kennedy
8 Two (Victoria and Elizabeth II)
9 Apollo 11
10 None

ROUND 2 — MATHS
1 Octagon
2 90
3 15 minutes
4 Thirteen
5 55
6 64
7 56
8 88
9 90
10 18

ROUND 3 — POP CULTURE

1 In which film does Hugh Grant play the faded, narcissistic actor Phoenix Buchanan?

2 What can be a video game hedgehog or a type of screwdriver used in 'Doctor Who'?

3 Rapper Big Sean, dancer Ricky Alvarez, comedian Pete Davidson and rapper Mac Miller are all referenced in the 2018 single 'thank u next' by which artist?

4 What is the name of the male protagonist in 'The Legend of Zelda' series of video games?

5 'Bodak Yellow' was a Top 40 hit for which American rapper in 2017?

6 Which animated 2013 hit movie is based on the fairytale 'The Snow Queen'?

7 Reggie Yates provided the voice of which TV mouse?

8 The role playing game 'Skyrim' is about a quest to destroy what type of mythical creature?

9 'Channel Orange' and 'Blonde' are albums by which American musician?

10 What connects: Pyramid, Other and West Holts among others?

ROUND 4 — SCIENCE AND NATURE

1 Which two-word term was first used by astronomer Fred Hoyle to describe the origin of the universe?

2 Which order of mammals contains all humans and apes?

3 What is the name of a chemical substance that cannot be broken down any further?

4 The three basic cloud forms are cumulus, stratus and ... what?

5 Which metal has the chemical symbol Pb?

6 What name is given to a baby seal?

7 What A is the scientific name for the white of an egg?

8 Castor and Pollux are the two brightest stars in which constellation?

9 Alopecia is a condition causing the loss of what from the body?

10 How many pairs of chromosomes are there in each human cell?

ROUND 3 — POP CULTURE
1 Paddington 2
2 Sonic
3 Ariana Grande
4 Link
5 Cardi B
6 Frozen
7 Rastamouse
8 Dragon
9 Frank Ocean
10 Stages at Glastonbury festival

ROUND 4 — SCIENCE AND NATURE
1 Big Bang
2 Primates
3 Element
4 Cirrus
5 Lead
6 Pup
7 Albumen
8 Gemini
9 Hair
10 23

READY-MADE QUIZZES

For this chapter, we're drawing on all our experience running fun, varied quizzes. There are 50 quizzes here, each comprising 40 questions spread across four rounds. Each quiz contains a selection of rounds that are constructed around a format, rather than a single subject.

Each round has rules that will help you answer the questions, and sometimes we'll give precise guidance as to what form a particular answer should take (e.g. first name and surname required) so that the answer fits the rules of the round.

It is a good idea to get to grips with the rules of a round before you have a go at it, as the rules will help you figure out some answers you might not otherwise get.

Rather than repeat the introduction to each round every time, here is a rundown of the round introductions:

ALPHABET

We give you the first letter of each answer. Some of the answers may have more than one word, but the letter provided is just the first letter of the entire answer.

FOLLOW ON

Each answer has one letter or number more than the previous answer (the number specifically doesn't include spaces or punctuation marks, only letters or numbers). So, if the answer to Question 1 has one letter, Question 2 will have a two-letter answer, etc.

THE CHAIN

In The Chain, the last letter of one answer will be the first letter of the next answer, all the way to the end (with the last letter of the final answer being the first letter of the first answer). Note that more than one answer can begin or end with the same letter.

MISSING LINK

The first nine answers in this round will be united by a common link, and then Question 10 will ask you what that link is.

MYSTERY YEAR

All the questions will be about events that took place in the same year, and then Question 10 will ask you to pin down the Mystery Year.

DOUBLE TROUBLE

In Double Trouble, there are 15 questions. Seven of the answers appear twice. That's the "double". However, there is one rogue answer which does not have a pair – that's the "trouble". Some answers might not be immediately obvious, but you may be able to work them out by pairing them with another answer.

54321

In 54321, there are five questions. For the first question, you give 5 answers, for the second 4 answers, for the third 3 answers, for the fourth 2 answers and for the fifth 1 answer.

CULTURE CLASH

This round is a mixture of what gets described as lowbrow and highbrow, sometimes all in the same question. A wide range of topics are covered, including TV, film, music, art, classical music, history, and literature, and more.

UP AND DOWN

Whenever it appears, this is always the final round, and so it is time to gently squeeze up the jeopardy by changing the scoring: PLUS one point for each correct answer and MINUS one point for each incorrect answer, but no points up or down for a blank/non-answer.

Or you could try using a Wipeout format: each answer is worth one point as usual, but a single incorrect answer means you lose all your points in the round (but blanks/non-answers are allowed).

Or of course you could use it as a standard General Knowledge round.

ROUND 1 — ALPHABET

1 Which D is another name for bumper cars at a funfair?

2 Which A is the American state which has Little Rock as the state capital?

3 Eduardo Saverin became a billionaire via his involvement with the foundation of which F?

4 What G is a carved stone grotesque figure designed to spray water away from the side of a building?

5 Of which L was Richard Bingham, born in 1934, the 7th Earl?

6 Which Q was the producer of the biggest selling album of all time?

7 What R is a two-word term first used by Lauren Bacall on seeing her husband Humphrey Bogart and various friends returning from Las Vegas in a dishevelled state?

8 Which V is the name of the plastic horn that came to prominence during the 2010 men's FIFA World Cup?

9 What W is a first name that links Boyd, Guthrie and Woodpecker?

10 What B is the name of the lowest compartment of a ship, below the waterline as well as being a general term for nonsense?

ROUND 2 — FOLLOW ON

1 What was the nickname of the astronaut Edwin Aldrin?

2 Which singer from New Zealand released the single 'Solar Power' in 2021?

3 Native to North America, which canine has the taxonomic name canis latrans?

4 What is the name of a Spanish political party with a name meaning "We can"?

5 'Save the World', 'Creative' and 'Battle Royale' are the three modes of which hit video game?

6 Which US civil rights leader and congressman, who died in 2020, shared his name with a British department store?

7 Who was the second female Home Secretary of the UK?

8 Taking its title from a line in 'Romeo and Juliet', which novel by David Nicholls was published in 2019?

9 Whose film roles include Winnie Mandela, Tia Dalma and Eve Moneypenny?

10 A famous painting by John William Waterhouse, based on a poem by Tennyson, is 'The ...' who?

ROUND 1 — ALPHABET
1 Dodgems
2 Arkansas
3 Facebook
4 Gargoyle
5 Lucan
6 Quincy Jones (Thriller)
7 Rat Pack ("You look like a goddamn rat pack")
8 Vuvuzela
9 Woody (Woody Boyd in 'Cheers')
10 Bilge

ROUND 2 — FOLLOW ON
1 Buzz
2 Lorde
3 Coyote
4 Podemos
5 Fortnite
6 John Lewis
7 Theresa May (after Jacqui Smith. Priti Patel 4th.)
8 Sweet Sorrow
9 Naomie Harris
10 Lady of Shalott

ROUND 3 — MYSTERY YEAR

1 On August 6 of the mystery year, Tim Berners-Lee launched the first ever example of what?

2 Patrick Bateman, the serial-killing Wall Street banker, is the central character of which novel by Bret Easton Ellis, published in the mystery year?

3 Which Nottingham Forest and England defender scored a decisive own goal in the FA Cup final of the mystery year?

4 Macaulay Culkin featured in the video to which Michael Jackson song, which was a hit in November of the mystery year?

5 Hugh Callaghan, Patrick Hill, Gerard Hunter, Richard McIlkenny, William Power and John Walker were freed on March 14 of the mystery year. How were they collectively known?

6 In August of the mystery year, which Communist leader was put under house arrest when he went on holiday in the Crimea?

7 In November of the mystery year, 'The Fly' by U2 became the first new British Number 1 single for seventeen weeks. What single did it replace at Number 1?

8 Who jumped 8.95 metres to break the men's world long jump record at the World Championships in the mystery year?

9 Which "Operation", involving air strikes on Iraq, began on January 16th of the mystery year?

10 What is the mystery year?

ROUND 4 — UP AND DOWN

1 Which is the only day of the week that begins with the same letter in both French and English?

2 In which Bavarian city has Oktoberfest taken place almost every year since 1810?

3 According to legend, which creatures did St Patrick banish from Ireland?

4 What is the English for the Latin word "albus", from which the word albumen is derived?

5 In the United Kingdom, what is the longest month of the year?

6 What is the name shared by a region in the Peloponnese, a former retail group owned by Philip Green and a play by Tom Stoppard?

7 As well as founding Singapore, Stamford Raffles also founded which London tourist attraction near Regent's Park?

8 Which word for favouritism comes from the Latin for nephew?

9 What year was 100 years before 90 AD? [Think long and hard about it!]

10 What nickname connects former footballer Ron Harris and the name of an iconic bicycle of the 1970s?

ROUND 3 — MYSTERY YEAR
1 A web page/website
2 American Psycho
3 Des Walker
4 Black Or White
5 The Birmingham Six
6 Mikhail Gorbachev
7 '(Everything I Do) I Do It For You' by Bryan Adams (which had been at the top for sixteen weeks)
8 Mike Powell
9 Desert Storm
10 1991

ROUND 4 — UP AND DOWN
1 Saturday (Samedi)
2 Munich
3 Snakes
4 White
5 October (October has 31 days, just like many other months, but since the clocks are put back in October, the month lasts 31 days and one hour)
6 Arcadia
7 London Zoo
8 Nepotism
9 11 BC – there was no year zero
10 Chopper

ROUND 1 — ALPHABET

1 Which J typically has 7 people in Hong Kong, 15 in Scotland, and 12 in England and most of the rest of the world?

2 What Q is the Spanish word for "what", which was the catchphrase of Manuel in 'Fawlty Towers'?

3 Which W is, fittingly, the name of the Tyneside town which grew up around the most easterly point of Hadrian's Wall?

4 Which E is the five-letter first name of the Bond supervillain Blofeld?

5 Which C is a device used in filmmaking to assist in the synchronising of picture and sound?

6 What O is a common skateboarding trick where the rider and board leap into the air without the use of the rider's hands?

7 Which Y did Elton John say "Goodbye" to in a ballad released in 1973?

8 Which D was a 1980s cartoon featuring characters including Hank, Eric, Presto, Bobby, Uni, and Venger?

9 Which M was, originally, available in Pink for Roast Beef, Blue for Smokey Bacon, Yellow for Pickled Onion and Orange for Prawn Cocktail?

10 Which G is the 4th most populated district in Seoul in South Korea, and in 2012 was the site of the second Nuclear Security Summit?

ROUND 2 — CULTURE CLASH

1 The name of what entertainment, first popularised in Japan, can be translated into English as "empty orchestra"?

2 Superman's alter ego Clark Kent is a journalist for which newspaper?

3 The musical 'Miss Saigon' is based on which Puccini opera?

4 Which company won the contract to run the UK National Lottery when it started in 1994?

5 Which film starring Michael Douglas and Kathleen Turner is not - despite its title - about a series of civil wars in 15th century England?

6 What family name links the films 'Ice-Cold in Alex' and 'Whistle down the Wind' to the 90s rock band Kula Shaker?

7 A man called Antonio and an object called Antonia are the title characters in which bestselling novel?

8 What is the official FM frequency range of BBC Radio 2?

9 Which former footballer played the role of Monsieur de Foix in the 1998 film 'Elizabeth'?

10 The many characters of which comedian include Tony Ferrino, Pauline Calf and Tommy Saxondale?

ROUND 1 — ALPHABET
1 Jury (in Scotland, criminal juries have 15 people, and civil trials have a jury of 12 people)
2 Que
3 Wallsend
4 Ernst
5 Clapper Board
6 Ollie
7 Yellow Brick Road
8 Dungeons & Dragons
9 Monster Munch
10 Gangnam (of 'Gangnam Style' fame)

ROUND 2 — CULTURE CLASH
1 Karaoke
2 Daily Planet
3 Madame Butterfly
4 Camelot
5 The War of the Roses
6 Mills (John, Hayley, Crispian Mills)
7 Captain Corelli's Mandolin
8 88-91 FM
9 Eric Cantona
10 Steve Coogan

ROUND 3 — 54321

1 Name five of the six British monarchs since 1066 with the longest reign. We're talking Kings and Queens of Great Britain or of just England.

2 Name the first four Martin Scorsese movies nominated for the Best Picture Oscar which didn't win.

3 Jelly Baby or Only Maybe? The six Jelly Babies all have their own names, according to Bassetts. Which of these are real Jelly Baby names? a) Billy b) Boofuls c) Brilliant

4 Guess the Year. a) Ruslana wins the Eurovision Song Contest for Ukraine, The new Scottish Parliament Building is used for its first meeting of the Scottish Parliament. b) Elvis Presley performs his last ever concert, Orlando Bloom is born, Jimmy Carter is inaugurated as US President.

5 What does the word "grimalkin" mean? a) A highly coloured waistcoat, especially as worn by prefects at Eton College b) The fee paid at a baptism c) A bossy old woman

ROUND 4 — DOUBLE TROUBLE

1 What is the capital and largest city of the state of Massachusetts?

2 Which Channel 4 TV series made stars of Dev Patel, Daniel Kaluuya and Nicholas Hoult?

3 On May 31st 1993, which band did Alan McGee sign after watching them play at King Tut's Wah Wah Hut in Glasgow?

4 Which word goes before 'fiction' to describe low quality literature printed on cheap paper?

5 Which surname links an actress named Carey to a character in James Joyce's 'Ulysses' named Buck?

6 In Greek mythology, which river forms the boundary between the Earth and the Underworld?

7 In William Shakespeare's 'The Tempest', what is the name of the daughter of Prospero?

8 Which Irish surname is used for a type of stew traditionally prepared by hobos at the start of the 20th century?

9 Which American rock band's biggest hit was 'More than a Feeling'?

10 Which word is used for the juice vesicles of a citrus fruit?

11 What term is used for an informal golf game where players compete for money on each individual hole?

12 What name is used in the USA for a warning given by police to criminal suspects, advising them of their rights?

13 Which comedy, in which its female protagonist often talks to camera, won the Golden Globe for Best Television Series in 2020?

14 Which drinks brand once used the slogan "For people who don't like water"?

15 Discovered in 2012, what is the smallest known moon of the dwarf planet Pluto?

ROUND 3 — 54321
1 Elizabeth II, Victoria, George III, Henry III, Edward III, Elizabeth I
2 Taxi Driver, Raging Bull, GoodFellas, Gangs of New York
3 a) Made up b) Real (lime flavour) c) Real (strawberry flavour)
4 a) 2004 b) 1977
5 c) A bossy old woman

ROUND 4 — DOUBLE TROUBLE
1 Boston	11 Skins
2 Skins	12 Miranda
3 Oasis	13 Fleabag
4 Pulp	14 Oasis
5 Mulligan	15 Styx
6 Styx	
7 Miranda	
8 Mulligan	
9 Boston	
10 Pulp	

ROUND 1 — ALPHABET

1 Which S is a detail given away in advance of a TV show or film which reveals more of the plot than wished for?

2 Which T is the product whose logo is a picture of the Matterhorn with a bear on it?

3 What M is a word commonly used for a misheard lyric or phrase?

4 What P is a luxury knitwear manufacturer and, in its plural, a stackable potato chip?

5 Which L is the Egyptian city which is the site of the ancient city of Thebes?

6 What I was, in 1990, the first hip-hop song to top the US Billboard charts? (not counting 'Rapture' by Blondie in 1981, which has a short rapped section)

7 Which A is the name of Sebastian Flyte's teddy bear in 'Brideshead Revisited'?

8 Which B is the largest borough of London by area?

9 Which V is one of the classic sauces of French cuisine, getting its name from the French for "velvet"?

10 Which R is a breakfast cereal for which the Rolling Stones recorded a short song used on an advert in 1964?

ROUND 2 — FOLLOW ON

1 Which word links a cartilaginous fish to actors called Winstone and Liotta?

2 In which TV comedy do Robert Webb and David Mitchell star as Andrew Donnelly and Stephen Nichols?

3 Which five-letter acronym is widely used for the President of the USA?

4 Which word is both a fairy-like mythical creature and a colourless fizzy drink made by Coca-Cola?

5 Taken from the surname of the man after whom another country in South America is named, what is the currency of Venezuela?

6 The athletes Nijel Amos, Amantle Montsho and Isaac Makwala come from which southern African country?

7 Which Booker Prize-winning novel by Ian McEwan takes its name from a European capital city?

8 An acclaimed album from the late 90s was 'The Miseducation of ...' who?

9 What game, using red and yellow checkers and an upright blue gameboard with 42 holes in it, was first sold by Milton Bradley in 1976?

10 Which Oscar winner became co-owner of the South Sydney Rabbitohs rugby league team in 2006?

ROUND 1 — ALPHABET
1 Spoiler
2 Toblerone
3 Mondegreen
4 Pringle/Pringles
5 Luxor
6 Ice Ice Baby
7 Aloysius
8 Bromley
9 Velouté
10 Rice Krispies

ROUND 2 — FOLLOW ON
1 Ray
2 Back
3 POTUS
4 Sprite
5 Bolivar (named after Simon Bolivar)
6 Botswana
7 Amsterdam
8 Lauryn Hill
9 Connect Four
10 Russell Crowe

ROUND 3 — MYSTERY YEAR

1 The first commercial flight of which supersonic aircraft took place in January of the mystery year?

2 Who succeeded Harold Wilson as Prime Minister when he resigned in the mystery year at the end of his second term in office?

3 Which South American country was ruled by general Jorge Videla and his military junta after a coup d'état in the mystery year?

4 Which computer company was founded by Steve Jobs and Steve Wozniak in the mystery year?

5 Who won a bronze medal for Great Britain in the men's 10,000 metres at the Olympics of the mystery year, his country's only track and field medal of the whole Games?

6 Which band had a hit single with 'New Rose' in the mystery year, often considered the UK's first punk single?

7 Against which country did the UK fight the Cod Wars, which ended in June of the mystery year?

8 What was the title of Chicago's only UK Number 1 single, which reached the top in the mystery year?

9 Which African country joined the UN on December 1st of the mystery year, just over a year after gaining independence from Portugal?

10 What is the mystery year?

ROUND 4 — UP AND DOWN

1 What did the C originally stand for in the (motoring) organisation RAC plc?

2 In which country is the town of Hamelin, famous for the story of the Pied Piper of Hamelin?

3 On what day of the week do Americans celebrate Thanksgiving?

4 What is the name of the apparatus used in piston engines to operate poppet valves that control the flow of fuel intake and exhaust?

5 What name is shared by an 80s computer and a female friend in Spain and Portugal?

6 What was the name of the yacht Robert Maxwell fell off, or jumped off, or was pushed off, in November 1991?

7 In which European capital city would you find the headquarters of the Spanish Riding School?

8 On the Olympic flag, what colour is the middle of the five rings?

9 Which producer of films such as 'Chariots of Fire', 'F/X – Murder By Illusion', and 'Hook', was killed in a tragic car crash in August 1997?

10 What links the number "four" in English, "four" in German, "three" in Italian, and "five" in Spanish?

ROUND 3 — MYSTERY YEAR
1 Concorde
2 James Callaghan
3 Argentina
4 Apple
5 Brendan Foster
6 The Damned
7 Iceland
8 If You Leave Me Now
9 Angola
10 1976

ROUND 4 — UP AND DOWN
1 Club (Royal Automobile Club)
2 Germany
3 Thursday
4 Camshaft
5 Amiga
6 Lady Ghislaine
7 Vienna
8 Black
9 Dodi Fayed (he died alongside Diana, Princess of Wales)
10 They have the same number of letters in the word as the number itself (German: four = Vier; Italian: three = Tre, Spanish: five = Cinco).

ROUND 1 — ALPHABET

1 What S is an English word commonly used for stealing fruit, particularly apples?

2 In Morse Code, the letter E is symbolised by one of what D?

3 In Morse Code, the letter T is symbolised by one of what D?

4 What M is a bird common in the UK which is considered one of the most intelligent of all animals, and indeed the only non-mammal to be able to recognise itself in a mirror?

5 What O is a circular opening in a wall or a dome which takes its name from the Latin for eye?

6 What F is a name used for a stock character exemplified in films by the likes of Lana Turner, Ava Gardner and Rita Hayworth, as well as being the title of a Velvet Underground song and a Britney Spears album?

7 What is a state of India created in 1937 as United Provinces, but given its current name, which has the same initials, in 1950?

8 What P is the French name given for glasses which are supported without the need for earpieces?

9 What Y was the title of Kanye West's 6th studio album, a pun on his own nickname and the name of an even more revered figure?

10 What A is a Neil Young song, the second part of a ship hijacked by Somali pirates in 2009, and the name of Patricia Arquette's character in 'True Romance'?

ROUND 2 — CULTURE CLASH

1 Which Rolling Stones song contains the line "I have to turn my head until my darkness goes"?

2 What is the name of the daily music quiz hosted by Ken Bruce on his BBC Radio 2 show?

3 The film 'The Greatest Showman' is based on the life of which legendary entertainer?

4 When Tears For Fears re-released 'Everybody Wants to Rule the World' in 1986, the word "Rule" was replaced by which other word?

5 Stephen Sondheim's musical 'Sunday in the Park with George' is based on a painting by which artist?

6 What title links a 2002 book by John Gray with a 1971 film starring Dustin Hoffman?

7 Which bird, as referenced in mythology, song and poems, is said to be silent through most of its life and then makes a beautiful noise just before it dies?

8 In English, how are the Erinyes of Greek mythology commonly known?

9 What was the only film in which Robert De Niro and Marlon Brando appeared on screen at the same time?

10 The 'Blue Peter' ship logo was designed by whom?

ROUND 1 — ALPHABET

1 Scrumping
2 Dot
3 Dash
4 Magpie
5 Oculus
6 Femme Fatale
7 Uttar Pradesh
8 Pince-nez
9 Yeezus (Yeezy and Jesus)
10 Alabama (the ship is Maersk Alabama)

ROUND 2 — CULTURE CLASH

1 Paint it, Black
2 PopMaster
3 PT Barnum
4 Run (it was for Sport Aid)
5 Georges Seurat
6 Straw Dogs
7 Swan
8 The Furies
9 The Score (They played the same person in 'The Godfather' series, in different films)
10 Tony Hart

ROUND 3 — FOLLOW ON

1 What is the common English name for the tree of the generic name Fraxinus?

2 In rugby union, what is formed when, in open play, at least one player from each side bind onto each other with the ball on the ground between them?

3 What is the surname of the English romantic poet portrayed by Ben Whishaw in the film 'Bright Star'?

4 Complete the 1990s advertising slogan: "Like the Murphy's, I'm not ..." what?

5 Which actress, comedian and activist played Clarissa Mullery in 'Silent Witness' from 2013 to 2020?

6 Who was the title character in a novel by Thomas Hughes about schooldays at Rugby public school?

7 In the British football pools, what two-word name is given to a result which is not nil-nil but in which the teams have the same number of goals?

8 Which former Olympic gymnast won 'Strictly Come Dancing' in 2012?

9 What cocktail of Guinness and champagne shares its name with the biggest hit single for Alannah Myles?

10 Which Michael Crichton book was turned into a successful 1993 movie starring Richard Attenborough and Jeff Goldblum?

ROUND 4 — UP AND DOWN

1 'Listen with Mother', a radio show that ran on BBC Radio for over 30 years, always began with what four-word phrase?

2 Which former British Cabinet minister was "Aristocracy Coordinator" on the film 'Four Weddings & a Funeral'?

3 In which year's men's FIFA World Cup final did the same player score a goal and then get sent off? [not including 2022 competition]

4 What did British explorer Sir Ranulph Fiennes do seven times, in seven days, on seven continents in 2003?

5 In which country is the second highest mountain in Africa?

6 In the first 'Star Wars' film, what is the name of the bounty hunter shot and killed by Han Solo in the cantina?

7 Apart from 'Chicago', which other winner of the Best Picture Oscar has a one-word title that is the name of the city where the film is set? [up to 2022]

8 Which politically outspoken comic strip does Garry Trudeau write and draw?

9 With a similar name to a green space in London, who was the Admiral whose command Nelson was said to have ignored at the Battle of Copenhagen by holding his telescope to his blind eye?

10 Followers of which religion celebrate the festival of Purim?

ROUND 3 — FOLLOW ON
1 Ash
2 Ruck (with a maul, the ball is not on the ground)
3 Keats (as opposed to Byron)
4 Bitter
5 Liz Carr
6 Tom Brown
7 Score Draw
8 Louis Smith
9 Black Velvet
10 Jurassic Park

ROUND 4 — UP AND DOWN
1 Are you sitting comfortably?
2 Amber Rudd
3 2006 (Ziendine Zidane)
4 Run a marathon
5 Kenya
6 Greedo
7 Casablanca
8 Doonesbury
9 Hyde Parker
10 Judaism

ROUND 1 — ALPHABET

1 What J is a mild cow's cheese manufactured in Norway since around 1956?

2 What F is a city in Portugal whose airport is commonly used for holidaymakers to the Algarve?

3 What D is the Roman equivalent of the Greek goddess Artemis?

4 Which O is the term for any professional theatre venue in New York City with a seating capacity between 100 and 499?

5 What G was a UK Number 1 single of 1970 recorded by a man who was then 50 and who died in 2012?

6 What U is the name given to the extreme and fanatical supporters of Italian football clubs such as Lazio and AS Roma?

7 What M was the comedy sketch show of the 80s and 90s featuring Punt, Newman, Dennis and Baddiel?

8 What A is software created by Dr Andy Hildebrand which was first famously used by Cher in 1998 and is now widely used throughout popular music?

9 Which B is a form of yoga named after its founder which began in the early 70s and is practised in high heat?

10 What T was the surname of a French neurologist who gave his name to a condition which he, in 1884, called a "maladie des tics"?

ROUND 2 — FOLLOW ON

1 Which letter of the alphabet is used in the TV series 'Line of Duty' as code for the corrupt senior police officer linked to organised crime?

2 What name links the comedian Burnham to the Portuguese water dog owned by the Obamas who died in 2021?

3 Starring Lesley Manville and Peter Mullan, which acclaimed TV comedy written by Stefan Golaszewski ran for three series on BBC Two from 2016 to 2019?

4 Which programming language shares its name with the most populous island in the world?

5 What is the surname of the main character in 'Avatar', as well as being the nickname of the pilot who landed a plane in the Hudson river?

6 Of all the teams that have played in the English Premier League since 1992, which has, in its usual form, the shortest name?

7 Which operetta with music by Leonard Bernstein, based on a novel by Voltaire, features musical numbers 'The Best of All Possible Worlds' and 'Glitter and Be Gay'?

8 Which small New World monkey native to South America has species including Emilia's, Buffy-tufted and Santarem?

9 Who was the MP for Tooting from 2005 and 2016?

10 Which renowned musician has been in The Cribs, Modest Mouse, The Pretenders, The The, Electronic and The Smiths?

ROUND 1 — ALPHABET
1 Jarlsberg
2 Faro
3 Diana
4 Off-Broadway
5 Grandad (Clive Dunn)
6 Ultras
7 Mary Whitehouse Experience
8 Auto-Tune
9 Bikram
10 Tourette (Georges Gilles de la Tourette)

ROUND 2 — FOLLOW ON
1 H
2 Bo
3 Mum
4 Java
5 Sully (Chesley Sullenberger was the pilot)
6 Fulham
7 Candide
8 Marmoset
9 Sadiq Khan (He left that post to become Mayor of London)
10 Johnny Marr

ROUND 3 — MYSTERY YEAR

1 Betty Boothroyd became the first woman to be elected to which post in the mystery year?

2 Which American singer, who had worked with South African musicians previously, became the first to tour South Africa after the lifting of the cultural boycott in the mystery year?

3 Two of Britain's most famous comedians died over the same weekend in April of the mystery year; one was Benny Hill, the other the star of 'Up Pompeii!'. What was his name?

4 In which month of the mystery year was Black Wednesday, when the British government was forced to withdraw the pound from the ERM?

5 The first ever goal of which league was scored by Brian Deane of Sheffield United on August 15th of the mystery year?

6 Which British runner won the women's 400m hurdles gold medal at the Barcelona Olympics in the mystery year?

7 What was the name of the classic hip-hop album, containing 'Nothing But a 'G' Thang' released by Dr Dre in the mystery year?

8 Who replaced Javier Perez de Cuellar as Secretary-General of the United Nations in January of the mystery year?

9 In a speech at the Guildhall, with which two-word Latin term did Queen Elizabeth II describe the mystery year?

10 What is the mystery year?

ROUND 4 — UP AND DOWN

1 How many strings are there on a violin?

2 What is the name of the monument on Whitehall in London which has a name meaning "empty tomb"?

3 How many signs of the zodiac begin with the letter A?

4 According to the Bible on what number day did God create the beasts of the Earth?

5 From 1966 to 1987, who was the only inmate at Spandau Prison?

6 How many denominations of Euro banknotes are there?

7 In what town in Lancashire were there 4000 holes, according to 'A Day in the Life', from 'Sgt. Pepper's Lonely Hearts Club Band'?

8 Which earldom, unused since 1066, was given to Prince Edward in 1999?

9 What semi-aquatic mammal is on the reverse of the original Australian 20 cent coin (issued in 1966 and still in circulation)?

10 According to followers of witchcraft, what is the optimum number of witches in a coven?

ROUND 3 — MYSTERY YEAR
1 Speaker of the House of Commons
2 Paul Simon
3 Frankie Howerd
4 September
5 The Premier League/Premiership
6 Sally Gunnell
7 The Chronic
8 Boutros Boutros-Ghali
9 Annus horribilis
10 1992

ROUND 4 — UP AND DOWN
1 Four
2 The Cenotaph
3 Two (Aries, Aquarius)
4 Fifth day
5 Rudolf Hess (two others were released in 1966, and Hess died in 1987)
6 Seven
7 Blackburn
8 Wessex
9 (Duck-billed) Platypus
10 13 (a coven can be any number of 3 and over, but traditionally 13 is optimum)

ROUND 1 — ALPHABET

1 What T is the common name of the tropical hardwood tree Tectona grandis, renowned for its toughness?

2 Which B is a British brand of clothing and equipment whose name comes from the German for "mountain house"?

3 What C are coverings for the leg area widely used in horse-riding, though the word can also be used as a general term for a collection of gentlemen?

4 What E is the point directly above where the fault begins to rupture during an earthquake?

5 Which H is an animal also called the ratel, known for its ferocious aggression?

6 What K is a dish of fermented vegetables which is Korea's national dish?

7 What O is the London school Tony Blair sent his children to, as well as being a word for the art of speechmaking?

8 What L is the adjective that goes before "Jesse James" in a bold statement in a massive hit by Snap, and before "Gangster" in a bold statement in a massive hit by Ini Kamoze?

9 What Q, the Latin for "of whom", is the minimum number of people necessary for a body to conduct its business?

10 What P is the tourist village in Northwest Wales designed by Clough Williams-Ellis?

ROUND 2 — CULTURE CLASH

1 In Greek mythology, what was Medusa's hair made of?

2 Which Irish author, played on film by Stephen Fry, had the middle names Fingal O'Flahertie Wills?

3 Which awards were created by American John Wilson to recognise the year's "worst" acting and film-making?

4 What was the name of the king murdered by Macbeth in the Shakespeare play?

5 Who wrote the theme for TV-AM and many commercials, but is best known for a musical version of HG Wells' 'The War of The Worlds'?

6 Who took over from Sue Lawley as the presenter of Radio 4's 'Desert Island Discs' in 2006?

7 What was Madonna's first UK Number 1 single, which appeared in the 1985 film 'Desperately Seeking Susan'?

8 What surname links Tom Hanks' character in 'Philadelphia' to Scott Bakula's character in the TV show 'Quantum Leap'?

9 In the book 'A Clockwork Orange', by Anthony Burgess, who is Alex's favourite composer?

10 What name is common to the King of Persia defeated at the Battle of Marathon and the contestant who came third in the first UK series of 'Pop Idol'?

ROUND 1 — ALPHABET
1 Teak
2 Berghaus
3 Chaps
4 Epicentre
5 Honey Badger
6 Kimchi
7 Oratory
8 Lyrical
9 Quorum
10 Portmeirion

ROUND 2 — CULTURE CLASH
1 Snakes
2 Oscar Wilde
3 The Golden Raspberry Awards or Razzies
4 Duncan
5 Jeff Wayne
6 Kirsty Young
7 Into The Groove
8 Beckett (Andrew Beckett and Dr Sam Beckett)
9 Ludwig van Beethoven
10 Darius (Darius the Great and Darius Campbell Danesh)

ROUND 3 — 54321

1 In what month do each of these events normally take place? a) US Presidential Elections b) US Open tennis final (women's and men's) c) Thanksgiving in Canada d) Peak of the Perseid Meteor Shower e) Burns Night

2 The UK had four different Prime Ministers in the 1950s. Name them.

3 For each of these people, identify what they were the "Last" of: (a) Dave Lister; (b) Uncas; (c) Idi Amin.

4 Wales contains three National Parks - name two of them.

5 Conundrum: this an anagram of which word? MARRYPOET

ROUND 4 — DOUBLE TROUBLE

1 Which car manufacturer made the Granada, the Cortina, the Sierra, the Escort and the Mondeo?

2 Which comic character, whose real name is Dick Grayson, is the "Boy Wonder"?

3 Who, in the Disney cartoon, is the chipmunk brother of Dale?

4 Which song by The Cars was used at Live Aid for a montage of victims of the Ethiopian famine?

5 What is the name of the prison in the sitcom 'Porridge'?

6 Which UK band had Number 1 hits called 'Tiger Feet', 'Lonely This Christmas' and 'Oh Boy'?

7 If the first is made of straw, the second of sticks, what is the third made of?

8 Which word can be synonymous with both "fry" and "crisp", depending on which country you're in?

9 What is the surname of the English rugby union player George and his father, coach and former rugby league star Mike?

10 If someone has a bad reputation, their name is said to be which substance, beloved of hippopotamuses?

11 What is the name of the person to whom Kevin Rowland contemptuously sings in the Dexys Midnight Runners song 'There, There, My Dear'?

12 In sport, which word links a straight-batted offensive shot in cricket with a long tee shot in golf?

13 Which neo-noir film starring Joseph Gordon-Levitt was the directorial debut of Rian Johnson?

14 Named after a 19th century philanthropist, the art school of University College, London, is known as the ... what?

15 The Keats poem that begins "My heart aches ..." is an 'Ode to' which small bird, famed for its song?

ROUND 3 — 54321

1 a) November b) September c) October d) August e) January
2 Clement Attlee, Winston Churchill, Anthony Eden, Harold Macmillan
3 (a) Last Human (according to the novel based upon 'Red Dwarf'); (b) The Last of the Mohicans; (c) The Last King of Scotland (in the book and film)
4 Snowdonia, Brecon Beacons, Pembrokeshire Coast
5 TEMPORARY

ROUND 4 — DOUBLE TROUBLE

1 Ford	11 Robin
2 Robin	12 Drive
3 Chip	13 Brick
4 Drive	14 Slade
5 Slade	15 Nightingale
6 Mud	
7 Brick/s	
8 Chip	
9 Ford	
10 Mud	

ROUND 1 — ALPHABET

1 Which K is the US State in which the businessman Colonel Harland Sanders died in 1980?

2 What E is both the first name of a former 'Baywatch' actress and the actual first name of the author of the 'Fifty Shades of Grey'?

3 Which Q is a game which involves throwing rings with the aim of landing the ring over or near a spike or pin in the ground?

4 Which B is the more common name for the condition of nocturnal enuresis?

5 Which R is the sauce created by Levi Roots, who came to prominence when he received funding on 'Dragon's Den'?

6 What F is the brand name of a piece of gardening equipment invented by Karl Dahlman in 1964 after he saw how a hovercraft worked?

7 What I is, specifically and originally, an athletics conference composed of sports from teams from 8 prestigious educational establishments?

8 Which C is the company that has as one of its trademarks the so-called "Dynamic Ribbon"?

9 What S is a British charity founded in 1953 by a vicar called Chad Varah?

10 What T is a medical condition caused by prolonged exposure to damp and unsanitary ground conditions, which became particularly prevalent in World War I?

ROUND 2 — FOLLOW ON

1 Which word can be a Chinese beer, a surname denoting illegitimacy in 'Game of Thrones', and a rapper whose biggest hit was 'Informer'?

2 Alphonso, Haden, Kent and Tommy Atkins are cultivars of which fruit?

3 What was the actual surname of the three 19th century authors who used the pseudonymous first names Currer, Ellis and Acton, and the surname Bell?

4 Of which country did former footballer George Weah become President in 2018?

5 Thought to be the most commonly fractured in the human body, which bone's medical name comes from the Latin for "little key"?

6 In 1988, who was the first British golfer to win the Masters at Augusta?

7 Which first-person shooter video franchise released the title 'Black Ops Cold War' in late 2020?

8 Which British-Swedish pharmaceutical company, founded by a merger in 1999, has its headquarters at the Cambridge Biomedical Campus?

9 Reaching Number 2 in the UK and the USA, what was the lead single from Dua Lipa's second studio album 'Future Nostalgia'?

10 Which Oscar-nominated film from 2019 was based, in part, on the director's own divorce from the actress Jennifer Jason Leigh?

ROUND 1 — ALPHABET
1 Kentucky (he is the KFC Colonel)
2 Erika
3 Quoits
4 Bedwetting
5 Reggae Reggae Sauce
6 Flymo
7 Ivy League
8 Coca-Cola
9 Samaritans (not Shelter, which was founded in 1966)
10 Trench foot

ROUND 2 — FOLLOW ON
1 Snow
2 Mango
3 Brontë
4 Liberia
5 Clavicle
6 Sandy Lyle (not Nick Faldo who won it in 1989 and 1990)
7 Call of Duty
8 AstraZeneca
9 Don't Start Now
10 Marriage Story (directed by Noah Baumbach)

ROUND 3 — MYSTERY YEAR

1 Linking the towns of Aranoutes and Biesma, the first tunnel under which mountain range was completed in the mystery year?

2 Jim Lovell and Fred Haise were two of the astronauts on which craft launched towards the moon, but not reaching it, in April of the mystery year?

3 What was the title of the song with which Dana won the Eurovision Song Contest for Ireland in the mystery year?

4 In September of the mystery year, Salvador Allende was elected President of which South American country?

5 The album released by Cat Stevens in November of the mystery year was 'Tea for the ...' who?

6 The first jumbo jet carrying fare-paying passengers landed at which airport in January of the mystery year?

7 The importation of pets was banned after an outbreak of which disease in Newmarket in March of the mystery year?

8 Who released his first solo album on the Apple label in the mystery year, a few days after announcing his former group had disbanded?

9 Peter Bonetti was in goal as England lost 3-2 to which country in the quarter final of the football men's FIFA World Cup in the mystery year?

10 What is the mystery year?

ROUND 4 — UP AND DOWN

1 How many pence were there in an old pound, before decimalisation?

2 What name is given to the longest side of a right-angled triangle?

3 In French, which day of the week comes last in alphabetical order?

4 Les Paul was famous for playing, and creating, what kind of instruments?

5 Which short word can go after Brazil, monkey and pine?

6 On a standard British computer keyboard, what symbol is on the same key as the number 1?

7 If you add up all the numbers in a normal sized completed sudoku, what do you get?

8 What was the name of the Salvation Army orphanage on Beaconsfield Road in Woolton, near to John Lennon's childhood home?

9 In the UK, what may not be sounded for longer than four seconds at a time; more often than every three minutes; or within 50 metres of a school during school hours, and places of worship on Sundays or any other day of worship?

10 My old man's a dustman, He wears a dustman's hat ... but what kind of trousers does he wear, and where does he live?

ROUND 3 — MYSTERY YEAR
1 The Pyrenees
2 Apollo 13
3 All Kinds of Everything
4 Chile
5 Tillerman
6 London Heathrow
7 Rabies
8 Paul McCartney
9 West Germany
10 1970

ROUND 4 — UP AND DOWN
1 240
2 Hypotenuse
3 Vendredi (French for Friday)
4 Guitars (electric)
5 Nut
6 ! (the exclamation mark)
7 405 (45x9)
8 Strawberry Field (which inspired the song 'Strawberry Fields Forever')
9 Ice cream van chimes
10 He wears cor blimey trousers, And he lives in a council flat

ROUND 1 — CHAIN

1 Which 2020 TV drama starred its writer Michaela Coel as Arabella?

2 What is, along with Liechtenstein, one of two doubly landlocked independent countries in the world? [meaning every country that surrounds it is also landlocked]

3 Margaret Hale is the protagonist of which novel by Elizabeth Gaskell set in the fictional town of Milton?

4 What name links a chain of steak restaurants, a novel by Peter Ackroyd and a leading architect of London?

5 Derived from a Japanese word meaning "human-powered vehicle", what name is given to a passenger cart usually pulled by one person?

6 Which song about a girl called Marie-Claire was the only UK Number 1 single for Peter Sarstedt?

7 What is one of the three largest ethnic groups in Nigeria along with Hausa and Igbo?

8 What name is given to a bridge that transports a watercourse over a valley?

9 Which North African dish, a slow-cooked stew, is named after the large earthenware pot it is cooked in?

10 In the biblical book of Samuel, what is the name of the high priest who trains Samuel?

ROUND 2 — CULTURE CLASH

1 Which famous mask-wearing duo announced they would be breaking up on 22nd March 2021?

2 Who wrote the novel 'The Great Divorce', whose title echoes William Blake's 'The Marriage of Heaven and Hell'?

3 John Green wrote which bestseller, turned into a hit 2014 movie?

4 What first name links characters played by Anne Baxter in a 1950 film and Sandra Oh in a TV series which began in 2018?

5 For which film was the Aerosmith song 'I Don't Want to Miss A Thing' originally written?

6 A pun on the title of a John Steinbeck novel, what is the title of the 2019 documentary series about the Wu-Tang Clan?

7 From which musical do the songs 'On My Own', 'Master of the House' and 'Do You Hear the People Sing?' come?

8 Give a year in the life of the composer George Handel.

9 What song do these lyrics come from? "Lonely rivers sigh 'wait for me, wait for me', I'll be coming home, wait for me".

10 The actor who starred as Richie Tozer in the 2021 Russell T Davies drama 'It's a Sin' is the frontman of which pop group, which shares its name with another Russell T Davies show?

ROUND 1 — CHAIN

1 I May Destroy You
2 Uzbekistan
3 North and South
4 Hawksmoor (the architect is Sir Nicholas Hawksmoor)
5 Rickshaw (nowadays, rickshaws are often pulled by bikes or motorised)
6 Where Do You Go To (My Lovely)?
7 Yoruba
8 Aqueduct
9 Tagine
10 Eli

ROUND 2 — CULTURE CLASH

1 Daft Punk (Guy-Manuel de Homem-Christo, Thomas Bangalter)
2 CS Lewis
3 The Fault in Our Stars
4 Eve (in All About Eve and Killing Eve)
5 Armageddon
6 Of Mics and Men
7 Les Misérables
8 1685-1759
9 Unchained Melody
10 Years and Years

ROUND 3 — FOLLOW ON

1 Which character has been played in movies by Bernard Lee, Robert Brown, Judi Dench and Ralph Fiennes?

2 By what abbreviated name was politician Marjorie Mowlam generally known?

3 What name describes a follower of an early 1960s teenage style, associated with scooters, parkas, and fighting the rockers?

4 What is the name of the fashion magazine for which Betty Suarez worked in 'Ugly Betty'?

5 In which Italian town was Leonardo da Vinci born?

6 What element has the chemical symbol C?

7 What is the name of the disease commonly known as German Measles?

8 Which city is the capital of Serbia?

9 What does Paddington Bear like to have in his sandwiches?

10 Which large body of wetlands can be found in southern Florida?

ROUND 4 — UP AND DOWN

1 Monza is the location of the Formula 1 Grand Prix racing circuit in which country?

2 Are polar bears native to A) the Arctic or B) Antarctica?

3 Issued by Scottish and Northern Irish banks, what is the highest denomination of banknote in circulation in the UK?

4 The name of which US state ends with three consecutive vowels?

5 What goes missing from the Natural History Museum according to the title of a 1975 comedy film starring Derek Nimmo and Peter Ustinov?

6 At the 2012 Olympic Opening Ceremony, Kenneth Branagh read out a Shakespeare passage originally spoken by which character in 'The Tempest'?

7 Which musical instrument does the singer-songwriter Joanna Newsom mainly play?

8 What scorching feat did Antonio Restivo do to a height of 26ft 5in in Las Vegas in January 2011, setting a world record?

9 What actually is a scarlet pimpernel, from which the fictional character takes his name?

10 In Scotland, what have been named, amongst other things, Sir Andy Flurry and Gritty Gritty Bang Bang?

ROUND 3 — FOLLOW ON

1 M (in the Bond movies)
2 Mo
3 Mod
4 Mode
5 Vinci
6 Carbon (not Cobalt or copper)
7 Rubella
8 Belgrade
9 Marmalade
10 Everglades

ROUND 4 — UP AND DOWN

1 Italy
2 A) Arctic (Arctic gets its name from the Greek word for bear (Arktos). The two regions take their names from either "The place with bears" or "The place without bears")
3 £100
4 Hawaii
5 Dinosaur
6 Caliban
7 Harp
8 Breathe fire
9 Flower
10 Salt-spreading trucks

ROUND 1 — CHAIN

1 What can go before 'Nurse', 'Camping' and 'Cruising' in the titles of films in a famous comedy series?

2 As well as being the name of a country, what is the third longest river in Africa?

3 From the Latin for "rest", what is the name of a Catholic mass for the dead (as well as being the title of a hit single by the London Boys)?

4 As revealed in the song 'Let it Be', what was the first name of Paul McCartney's mother?

5 What is the name of a mountain bike manufacturer, a Skoda car, and a Nepalese airline?

6 Which peninsula and former island, where you'd find Broadstairs, Margate and Ramsgate, contains the most westerly point of Kent?

7 Will Bayley, who appeared on 'Strictly Come Dancing' in 2019, is the 2016 Paralympic champion in which sport?

8 What follows the word "Cullen" in the name of a Scottish soup made of smoked haddock, potatoes and onions?

9 What is the surname of both the first and the fourth President of Kenya?

10 Which highly toxic element, with chemical number 33, goes with "Old Lace" in the name of a film and in a cocktail made with gin?

ROUND 2 — MISSING LINK

1 What is the royal title of Sarah Ferguson?

2 What is the nickname of the title schoolmaster of Brookfield school in a novel by James Hilton?

3 Which word meaning dolphin was the title given to the heir apparent to the French throne?

4 Which college of Oxford University was founded by William of Wykeham in 1739 (making its name somewhat inappropriate these days)?

5 'Suicide is Painless' was the theme song to which extremely popular US sitcom?

6 Which 1987 Stanley Kubrick film portrays the Vietnam War from the perspective of US Marines?

7 What is the French verb which means "to jump"?

8 In 'Gulliver's Travels', the little people of Lilliput are split into two factions - the Little Enders and the Big Enders - and are at war over the correct way to eat which common breakfast food?

9 Which two-word term, referring to someone's heyday or youth, was the title of a 1954 musical by Julian Slade involving a piano that makes people dance?

10 What is the missing link?

ROUND 1 — CHAIN

1 Carry On
2 Niger
3 Requiem
4 Mary
5 Yeti
6 Isle of Thanet (not actually an island anymore)
7 Table Tennis
8 Skink (Cullen Skink)
9 Kenyatta (Jomo Kenyatta and his son Uhuru Kenyatta)
10 Arsenic (Arsenic and Old Lace)

ROUND 2 — MISSING LINK

1 Duchess of York
2 Mr Chips (the character's name is Mr Chipping)
3 Dauphin
4 New College
5 M*A*S*H
6 Full Metal Jacket
7 Sauter
8 Boiled Eggs
9 Salad Days
10 Potatoes (most of the potatoes should be obvious but a couple perhaps are a bit devious: Dauphin(oise), Sauté(r))

ROUND 3 — MYSTERY YEAR

1 10th January of the mystery year saw the launch of the electric tricycle the C5. Which computer millionaire was the man behind its development and manufacture?

2 What was the name of the boat owned by Greenpeace which was sunk in Auckland Harbour by French secret service agents in the mystery year?

3 The mystery year saw Europe beat the United States for the first time in 28 years to win which prestigious sporting tournament?

4 Mouth, Data, Chunk and Sloth were characters in which adventure film, released in the mystery year?

5 The mystery year saw the release of 'Rocky IV' in the US. Who was Rocky's opponent in the film, played by Dolph Lundgren?

6 In October of the mystery year, which Hollywood star, born Roy Harold Scherer Jr, became the first major celebrity to die of an AIDS-related illness?

7 In which stadium did the UK staging of Live Aid take place in July of the mystery year?

8 The mystery year saw 'The Dukes of Hazzard' end its run on American television. Which role did Catherine Bachman play?

9 Wayne Rooney was born in the mystery year. Which side did he score against to become the Premiership's youngest ever goalscorer when still just 16?

10 What is the mystery year?

ROUND 4 — UP AND DOWN

1 In the UK, how many pounds are there in a stone?

2 Which words, often seen on road signs, literally mean "butt of the sack" (in French) when translated into English?

3 The Opening Ceremony for the 1992 Summer Olympic Games had to be changed from the original plan because of whose death, eight months before the event?

4 What five-letter name describes the small mallet used to indicate that an item has been sold in an auction?

5 In 2022, who was the first Black woman to serve on the US Supreme Court?

6 Who was the first human resident of the White House to have been born in the 21st century?

7 Which West End play, based on an award-winning film, had souvenir t-shirts for sale which included the words "Ethel the pirate's daughter"?

8 Which religion with around 30 million adherents was founded in the 16th century by Guru Nanak?

9 From 1978 to 1988, Sir Isaac Newton was the last man to appear on what in England and Wales?

10 If you put your trousers on inside out and back to front, where does the entrance to your right hand back pocket end up? Your answer needs to specify Left or Right; Back or Front; Inside or Outside.

ROUND 3 — MYSTERY YEAR
1 Sir Clive Sinclair
2 Rainbow Warrior
3 The Ryder Cup
4 The Goonies
5 Ivan Drago
6 Rock Hudson
7 Wembley Stadium
8 Daisy Duke
9 Arsenal
10 1985

ROUND 4 — UP AND DOWN
1 14
2 Cul-de-Sac
3 Freddie Mercury (who'd have sung 'Barcelona' with Montserrat Caballe)
4 Gavel
5 Ketanji Brown Jackson
6 Sasha (Natasha) Obama
7 Shakespeare in Love
8 Sikhism
9 The £1 note
10 Right Front Inside (we promise! Try it)

ROUND 1 — CHAIN

1 Which landmark is on Salisbury Plain, 2 miles west of Amesbury?

2 Which East African country, with a coastline on the Red Sea, achieved full independence in 1993?

3 Which former Home Secretary was married, in the 1990s, to the author and journalist AA Gill? [first name and surname both required]

4 The "Belles" are the women's football team in which South Yorkshire city?

5 Dustin Hoffman won his second Best Actor Oscar for his performance in which 1988 film, also starring Tom Cruise?

6 Which first name links the actress Watts, the tennis player Osaka and the model Campbell?

7 What is the correct name of the last stage of an insect's development (also known as the adult phase)?

8 In 1979, Pink Floyd released the album 'The Wall', but which album did Michael Jackson release in 1979?

9 In publishing and graphic design, what is the two-word name of the nonsense Latin used as placeholder text before the final copy is available?

10 Which beloved Judy Garland film contains 'The Trolley Song' and 'Have Yourself a Merry Little Christmas'?

ROUND 2 — CULTURE CLASH

1 Who performed the title track to 'The Man With The Golden Gun'?

2 As a teenager the composer Stephen Sondheim was mentored by which great lyricist?

3 What is the first book of the Old Testament with a name that does not end in S?

4 Which of Beethoven's symphonies contains the famous 'Ode to Joy' chorus, which is also the official anthem of the European Union?

5 What first name is shared by the composers Prokofiev and Rachmaninov?

6 Which band, fronted until 1988 by Fish, took their name from a book by J.R.R. Tolkien?

7 Who is the Oliver referred to in the Elvis Costello song 'Oliver's Army'?

8 Which Shakespeare play has a title consisting of three words, each beginning with the same letter?

9 Now better known as an actress, who sang the UK entry in the Eurovision Song Contest in 1991, 'A Message To Your Heart'?

10 What is the name of the criminal family in 'The Goonies', and also a Scottish group proclaimed by NME to be "the best new band in Britain" in 2006?

ROUND 1 — CHAIN
1 Stonehenge
2 Eritrea
3 Amber Rudd
4 Doncaster
5 Rain Man (His first Best Actor Oscar was for 'Kramer Vs Kramer')
6 Naomi
7 Imago
8 Off the Wall
9 Lorem ipsum
10 Meet Me in St Louis

ROUND 2 — CULTURE CLASH
1 Lulu
2 Oscar Hammerstein
3 Deuteronomy
4 Ninth (also known as the Choral Symphony)
5 Sergei
6 Marillion (the book being 'The Silmarillion')
7 Oliver Cromwell
8 Love's Labour's Lost
9 Samantha Janus/Womack
10 The Fratellis

ROUND 3 — 54321

1. Club or Snub: Which of these are real club football teams, which are made up? A) Total Clean, in Peru b) The Strongest, of Bolivia c) O'Higgins, of Chile d) Bad Losers, of Colombia e) Young Boys, of Switzerland.

2. Not including the city-states of Singapore and Vatican City, name the four independent countries in the world where the capital city is the name of the country, in English, followed by the word city.

3. Name three of the four acts to have had a UK Number 1 with 'Unchained Melody'?

4. Two authors to identify, both with a middle name beginning with the letter K. a) The author of 'Three Men in a Boat', whose middle name is Klapka; b) The author of 'Fantastic Beasts' and 'The Casual Vacancy' amongst other things, whose middle name is Kathleen (although it is really only a pseudonym).

5. Put these four people in order of age, starting from the youngest: Jo Brand, Michael McIntyre, Jimmy Carr, Jack Dee

ROUND 4 — DOUBLE TROUBLE

1. Which of David and Victoria Beckham's children was named after a member of So Solid Crew?

2. Which Ford family car replaced the Cortina and was replaced itself by the Mondeo?

3. What board game, also known as Reversi, is played with 64 identical black and white discs on an 8x8 board?

4. Two Polish brothers, born with the surname Czyz, changed their surname and founded a famous American record label which they gave their adopted surname to. What is that name?

5. What low cost airline was founded in 1998 by British Airways, before being bought out by a rival in 2002?

6. What is the name of the Indian Premier League (IPL) men's cricket franchise based in Mumbai?

7. What is the name of the song by the artist Moby which sampled the theme to the show 'Twin Peaks'?

8. Royal Crown Derby, Royal Worcester and Royal Doulton are well known manufacturers of what?

9. What Ocean are the Azores, St Helena and Ascension Island in?

10. Which Shakespearean character has been played famously by Paul Robeson and Laurence Fishburne and in more recent times by Adrian Lester and Lenny Henry?

11. Which musical, co-written by members of ABBA, contains the songs 'I Know Him So Well' and 'One Night in Bangkok'?

12. At Mardi Gras in New Orleans, what name is given to 38 tribes who dress up in elaborate costumes influenced by Native American culture?

13. In the USA, what word can go before Ancha, Blanca, Estrella, Madre and Nevada in the names of mountain ranges?

14. What Virgin brand was founded in 1984 and has its head office in Crawley, West Sussex?

15. In the NATO phonetic alphabet, which word, apart from India, has three syllables and only five letters?

ROUND 3 — 54321

1. a) Club b) Club c) Club d) Snub e) Club
2. Kuwait, Guatemala, Mexico, Panama
3. Jimmy Young (1955), Righteous Brothers (1990), Robson & Jerome (1995), Gareth Gates (2002)
4. a) Jerome K Jerome b) J K Rowling
5. McIntyre (1976), Carr (1972), Dee (1962), Brand (1957)

ROUND 4 — DOUBLE TROUBLE

1. Romeo
2. Sierra
3. Othello
4. Chess (Records)
5. Go
6. Indians
7. Go
8. Porcelain (accept Crockery etc)
9. Atlantic
10. Othello
11. Chess
12. Indians
13. Sierra
14. Atlantic
15. Romeo

ROUND 1 — ALPHABET

1 What A was, somewhat alarmingly, the substance used for fake snow in the film 'The Wizard of Oz'?

2 What V is another name for the card game Blackjack, taken from the French translation of the ideal score in the game?

3 What W is the first name of a character played by Jamie Lee Curtis in a 1988 British comedy?

4 Which U is the fourth largest city in the Netherlands, which saw a series of important treaties in 1713?

5 Which S is a New York neighbourhood which takes its name both from an area of London and also from its geographical location?

6 Which P is a craze of the early 2010s which involves lying inert and face down in an incongruous location?

7 What K is a controversial film from 1995, as well as being a song title used by MGMT and by Kylie Minogue with Robbie Williams?

8 What N "quoth the Raven", in the famous poem by Edgar Allan Poe?

9 Which F is the name given to a stylised lily used as a decorative design or symbol?

10 What B, originally with a meaning closer to parody or caricature, is now more commonly a form of bawdy cabaret entertainment of which singer Paloma Faith is a known former exponent?

ROUND 2 — FOLLOW ON

1 Which twin brother, who has an L on his green cap, was played in a 1993 film by John Leguizamo?

2 Which domesticated South American mammal, smaller than the llama, has two species, the Suri and the Huacaya?

3 Which medication, traditionally used to combat malaria, is also the ingredient that gives tonic water its bitter taste?

4 Alastair, David, Nicola, Timothy, the four grandchildren of horse breeder Tommy Barron, gave their names to which Grand National-winning racehorse?

5 Which word links Michael and Gabriel to the anglicised form of a North Russian city?

6 Who was the UK Chancellor of the Exchequer from July 2019 to February 2020, the first person of Asian origin to hold the role?

7 On which mountain in Provence did the cyclist Tom Simpson die during a Tour de France stage in 1967?

8 What is the name of the sinister tone poem by the composer Camille Saint-Saëns which was adapted for the theme music to 'Jonathan Creek'?

9 Which long-standing British department store group was bought by Mike Ashley's Sports Direct group in 2018?

10 Who first won the Booker Prize for 'The Blind Assassin' in 2000, though she was also the co-winner 19 years later? [first name and surname required]

ROUND 1 — ALPHABET
1 Asbestos
2 Vingt-un (allow Vingt-et-un, though that's slightly different)
3 Wanda (in 'A Fish Called Wanda')
4 Utrecht
5 SoHo (standing for South of Houston Street)
6 Planking
7 Kids
8 Nevermore
9 Fleur-de-lys
10 Burlesque

ROUND 2 — FOLLOW ON
1 Luigi
2 Alpaca
3 Quinine
4 Aldaniti (the name came from the first two letters of each of their names. Aldaniti won the 1981 National, ridden by Bob Champion)
5 Archangel
6 Sajid Javid (He was followed by Rishi Sunak)
7 Mont Ventoux
8 Danse macabre
9 House of Fraser
10 Margaret Atwood (co-winner for 'The Testaments' with Bernardine Evaristo)

ROUND 3 — MYSTERY YEAR

1 Which television series, filmed in Portmeirion, Wales, finished in the mystery year?

2 Which famous cosmonaut was killed in a training flight in the mystery year?

3 In March of the mystery year, the My Lai Massacre was an infamous incident in which war?

4 Which beloved sitcom set in Walmington-on-Sea was first broadcast in the mystery year?

5 Who set a world long jump record of 8.90m in the mystery year, a record that stood for 23 years?

6 What was the seasonal name given to the period of reforms implemented in Czechoslovakia in the mystery year, which were halted by a Soviet invasion in August?

7 In which film released in the mystery year did Zero Mostel and Gene Wilder set out to create a Broadway flop?

8 Which brother of a former US President was assassinated in the mystery year during his campaign for the presidency?

9 Which singer, born in the mystery year, found success with the 1999 album 'White Ladder'?

10 What is the mystery year?

ROUND 4 — UP AND DOWN

1 In the UK, how many pints are there in a gallon?

2 STV, PR, and Condorcet are all methods that would be familiar to a psephologist. What is psephology the study of?

3 What is the name of the Christian feast which is on the 12th day of Christmas?

4 In the famous brand WD-40, what does the WD stand for?

5 Paul Vasquez, who died in 2020, was a viral sensation in 2010 for his ecstatic response to seeing which natural phenomenon in Yosemite National Park?

6 Which is the only sign of the zodiac with the same first letter as one of the months it falls within?

7 Which Joni Mitchell song was inspired by reading a passage from Saul Bellow's 'Henderson the Rain King' while flying in a plane?

8 Which English city was stripped of UNESCO World Heritage status in 2021?

9 Which market town in Norfolk shares its name with a slang term meaning to insult someone?

10 In what discipline was the first World Championship held at the Bath & West Showground in 1977, and has been held every two to three years since in countries such as New Zealand, England, Ireland, Australia, Wales and Norway?

ROUND 3 — MYSTERY YEAR
1 The Prisoner
2 Yuri Gagarin
3 Vietnam War
4 Dad's Army
5 Bob Beamon
6 The Prague Spring
7 The Producers
8 Robert F. (Bobby) Kennedy
9 David Gray
10 1968

ROUND 4 — UP AND DOWN
1 Eight
2 Elections and Voting Systems (STV is Single Transferable Vote; PR is Proportional Representation).
3 Epiphany
4 Water Displacement
5 (Double) rainbow
6 Aries (April)
7 Both Sides, Now (she was looking at clouds from both sides, now)
8 Liverpool
9 Diss
10 Sheep shearing

ROUND 1 — CHAIN

1 What is the currency of Liechtenstein, Switzerland and many parts of Africa?

2 What title links a film featuring the voices of Owen Wilson and Paul Newman with a hit single by Gary Numan?

3 In which film from 1994 did Keanu Reeves play Jack Traven?

4 Which much loved character was portrayed by the actor James Buckley in the 2010 comedy drama prequel 'Rock and Chips'?

5 What name links the Lord Chancellor of England in the reign of Edward VI with the full name of a very wealthy boy played by Macaulay Culkin in a 1994 movie?

6 As well as being the name of a character in 'Much Ado About Nothing' what word is the title of songs by Chad Kroeger, Enrique Iglesias and Mariah Carey?

7 What is the name of Jon Arbuckle's dog in the 'Garfield' comic strip?

8 Provide the next three words of this quote: "This is 29 Acacia Road, and this is Eric, the schoolboy who leads an amazing double life. For when Eric eats a banana an amazing transformation occurs ..."?

9 What title links a Bruce Springsteen album to an Alexander Payne film starring Bruce Dern?

10 Also her nickname, what was the title of Alison Moyet's 1984 debut solo album?

ROUND 2 — CULTURE CLASH

1 Which British company, best known for designing digital radios, shares its name with a 1989 hit for The Lightning Seeds?

2 What is the name of an apolitical subgenre of reggae, celebrated in a song by The Clash and a film in Steve McQueen's 2020 'Small Axe' series?

3 Carnac in France is known as the site of over 1,000 of which unusual feature?

4 What was the haircut, very popular around the turn of the century, popularised by the likes of Travis singer Fran Healy and named after an area of East London?

5 The title of which beloved 1988 Robert De Niro film can be found inside the name of a British band which had a 1980 Number 1 single and another, massive, Number 1 in 1982?

6 The UK's best selling album was the same in both 1991 and 1992. What was its one-word title?

7 What is the surname of the father and son poets Ian and Andrew, the father being the poet in residence for Barnsley FC, the son having won the Guardian first book prize in 2015?

8 As well as being the name of a real place which is now in Jordan, what is the name of a 2004 novel by Marilynne Robinson and the fictional theocratic nation in Margaret Atwood's 'The Handmaid's Tale'?

9 What was the name of the UK sitcom, sometimes compared to 'Friends', written by Steven Moffat and starring Jack Davenport, Sarah Alexander, Ben Miles and Gina Bellman?

10 Which senior politician surprisingly chose Benny Hill's 'Ernie, the Fastest Milkman in the West' as a Desert Island Disc in May 2006?

ROUND 1 — CHAIN

1 Franc
2 Cars
3 Speed
4 Del Boy Trotter
5 Richard Rich (the movie Richie Rich)
6 Hero
7 Odie
8 Eric is Bananaman
9 Nebraska
10 Alf

ROUND 2 — CULTURE CLASH

1 Pure
2 Lover's Rock
3 Standing stones/Menhirs
4 Hoxton fin
5 Midnight Run (Inside Dexys Midnight Runners)
6 Stars (Simply Red)
7 McMillan
8 Gilead
9 Coupling
10 David Cameron

ROUND 3 — FOLLOW ON

1 Which initials link O'Rourke, the American writer; Proby, a 60s rock'n'roll singer; and a character in the children's show 'Byker Grove'?

2 In the world of sport, in Chicago, they're White, in Boston they're Red. What?

3 What connects the surname of a character from 'Friends' and an internet search engine?

4 Which word is in a 1970 hit for John Lennon, a 1997 hit for Radiohead and a 1983 Number 1 for Culture Clash?

5 Which English public school shares its name with a size of cricket bat just below adult size?

6 Which one-woman show won a Fringe First award at the 2013 Edinburgh Festival before transferring to TV three years later?

7 Which constituency did Margaret Thatcher represent in parliament?

8 What is the third book of the Old Testament?

9 At which UK theme park would you visit the Lost City, Calypso Quay, and Canada Creek?

10 Which British town, with a nearby village of Pilton, is believed to have been visited by Joseph of Arimathea and to be the resting place of King Arthur?

ROUND 4 — MISSING LINK

1 In the UK, the telecommunications brand EE was formed by the merger of T-Mobile and which other company?

2 Which mountain in modern Turkey/ Türkiye is traditionally considered to be the resting place of Noah's Ark?

3 Which British Crown Colony was replaced in 1957 by the Dominion in Ghana, which would, in 1960, become the Republic of Ghana?

4 Whose last published book, in 1881, was 'The Formation of Vegetable Mould Through the Action of Worms'? (he is better known for a book from 22 years earlier)

5 In the musical 'Guys and Dolls', what is the name of Nathan Detroit's fiancée?

6 Which surname links the father-and-son New Zealand cricketers Lance and Chris?

7 In medieval times, which Scottish city was called St John's Toun by its inhabitants?

8 Who directed films such as 'Tootsie' and 'Out of Africa'? [it is the first name that will help with the link here]

9 William Lamb, the British Prime Minister from 1835 to 1841, was known as Viscount ... what?

10 What is the missing link?

ROUND 3 — FOLLOW ON
1 PJ
2 Sox (baseball teams)
3 Bing
4 Karma (Instant Karma, Karma Police, Karma Chameleon)
5 Harrow (between Size 6 and Short Handle)
6 Fleabag
7 Finchley
8 Leviticus
9 Thorpe Park
10 Glastonbury

ROUND 4 — MISSING LINK
1 Orange
2 Mount Ararat
3 The Gold Coast
4 Charles Darwin (In 1859 he published 'On the Origin of Species')
5 Miss Adelaide
6 Cairns
7 Perth (the name lives on in its football team St Johnstone)
8 Sydney Pollack
9 Melbourne
10 Australian towns and cities

ROUND 1 — CHAIN

1 In April 2021, who was sacked as manager of Tottenham Hotspur? [first name and surname required]

2 Featuring guest star Billy Ray Cyrus, Lil Nas X had a massive hit in 2019 with which song?

3 What is the shared name of rivers that run through Rostov, Sheffield and Aberdeen?

4 Which British comedian was the main presenter of 'The Mash Report' from 2017 to 2021?

5 As well as being a generic name for a two-seater sports car, which make of Tesla car was launched into space in 2018?

6 Which French stew, with a name derived from the word for "to stir up", gave its name to a 2007 Pixar film?

7 In 1265, a major battle of the Second Barons' War took place near which town in Worcestershire?

8 Which English fashion designer, instrumental in the development of the miniskirt, was made a Dame in 2015?

9 Originally called the imitation game, the test of a machine's ability to display intelligent behaviour is named after which scientist? [only surname required]

10 Which song title links Faithless in 1998 and Pink in 2004?

ROUND 2 — MISSING LINK

1 Which month is so named as it was originally the eighth month of the year?

2 Grog is traditionally made by mixing which spirit with water?

3 Who is Stewart Lee's former comedy partner, known for his 'Leicester Square Theatre Podcast'?

4 What does Benjamin Braddock "crash" at the end of the film 'The Graduate'?

5 Based in Devon, Axminster is a company particularly associated with making which household furnishings?

6 What, apart from people, run through the Spanish City of Pamplona during the Fiesta of San Fermín?

7 In the 'Lord of the Rings', what type of being is Gimli?

8 What is the first name of the character played by Kate Winslet in the 1997 film 'Titanic'?

9 In which British city was Gary Lineker born on 30th November 1960?

10 What is the missing link?

ROUND 1 — CHAIN
1 José Mourinho
2 Old Town Road
3 Don
4 Nish Kumar
5 Roadster
6 Ratatouille
7 Evesham
8 Mary Quant
9 Turing
10 God is a DJ

ROUND 2 — MISSING LINK
1 October
2 Rum
3 (Richard) Herring
4 Wedding (of Elaine Robinson to Carl Smith)
5 Carpets
6 Bulls
7 Dwarf
8 Rose
9 Leicester
10 They can all be preceded by "Red" (Most of the "Red" connection should be obvious enough. The "Red Wedding" is from 'Game of Thrones')

ROUND 3 — MYSTERY YEAR

1 An opera house on Bennelong Point in which city was opened by Queen Elizabeth II in the mystery year?

2 'Breathe', 'Money' and 'Time' are all tracks from which famous concept album released in the mystery year?

3 The speed limits on British motorways were reduced to 50 mph as a result of which crisis in the mystery year?

4 The modern version of which bridge was opened in the mystery year, its predecessor having been sold to a man from Arizona?

5 Ireland, Denmark and the UK joined which organisation in the mystery year?

6 Which female tennis star won the 'Battle of the Sexes' against Bobby Riggs in the mystery year?

7 Which country's monarchy was abolished in the mystery year, six years after King Constantine II was forced to recognise a military junta?

8 Which musician released the classic album 'Innervisions' in August of the mystery year?

9 In Kingston, Jamaica, which heavyweight boxer knocked out Joe Frazier in Round 2 to become world champion in January of the mystery year?

10 What is the mystery year?

ROUND 4 — UP AND DOWN

1 How many zeros do you get when you write out the digits for 10 million?

2 What is the only US State with a name that includes none of the letters in George W Bush?

3 Commemorating the date in 1865 when all enslaved people in Texas were proclaimed free, what is the commonly used one-word name for June 19th in the USA? In 2021, it became the first federal holiday established since Martin Luther King Jr Day was signed into law in 1983.

4 Which of these websites was launched first? Facebook, Twitter, or LinkedIn

5 What surname links the Englishman most famous for his limericks and an American who founded a corporate aircraft company?

6 Mary Lou McDonald and Michelle O'Neill represent which political party?

7 Which Hungarian-born American newspaper magnate who died in 1911 gave his name to a group of prizes established in 1917 which are held in great esteem to this day?

8 What do you fear if you suffer from panphobia?

9 In reference to a notorious 17th century figure, how is the right-wing political blogger Paul Staines better known?

10 Johnny's mother has three children. The oldest is called April. The next child is called May. What is the third child called?

ROUND 3 — MYSTERY YEAR
1 Sydney
2 Dark Side of the Moon (by Pink Floyd)
3 The Oil Crisis
4 London Bridge (the previous bridge was bought by Robert P. McCulloch)
5 The European Economic Community (EEC)
6 Billie Jean King
7 Greece
8 Stevie Wonder
9 George Foreman
10 1973

ROUND 4 — UP AND DOWN
1 Seven
2 Indiana
3 Juneteenth
4 LinkedIn (2003) (Facebook (2004), Twitter (2006))
5 Lear
6 Sinn Féin
7 Joseph Pulitzer
8 Everything
9 Guido Fawkes
10 Johnny

ROUND 1 — CHAIN

1 Which character was played by Ian Holm when he was old and by Martin Freeman when he was younger? [first and surname required]

2 Which independent country became around 250,000 square miles smaller in 2011?

3 Which species of whale possesses a large single "tusk" that juts out from its canine tooth?

4 In which 1991 computer puzzle game would you find floaters, blockers, climbers, bombers, builders, bashers, miners and diggers?

5 What is the name for a collection of broken rock fragments on a mountainside that have gathered over time?

6 What is the name of both Iron Maiden's mascot and the dog belonging to Martin Crane in 'Frasier'?

7 Which type of missile takes its name from the taxonomic name of the flying fish?

8 Which African country's capital is Lomé?

9 Which phrase links a Top 10 single by the Kaiser Chiefs with a comic catchphrase spoken by the actress Maggie Wheeler?

10 What is the word linking a fish to a dance move which looks similar to someone sneezing into the crook of their elbow?

ROUND 2 — CULTURE CLASH

1 Which district of London gave its name to a group of writers and intellectuals including Virginia Woolf and EM Forster?

2 What British satirical website (which would later become a TV show) was founded in 2007 by the journalists Paul Stokes and Neil Rafferty?

3 EL James developed 'Fifty Shades of Grey' from stories she originally produced as fan fiction inspired by which series?

4 What is the first song in the musical movie 'Oliver!'?

5 What Italian term is used for when a stringed orchestral instrument is plucked with the fingers, rather than played with the bow?

6 Which "American folk opera" is set in Catfish Row, Charleston?

7 What name is shared by two Greek heroes of the Trojan War, one the son of King Telamon, the other the son of King Oileus?

8 The life and works of Pauline Boty, one of the founders of the British pop art movement, who also appeared in the film 'Alfie', is a major inspiration of which 2016 novel by Ali Smith?

9 In the movie 'High Plains Drifter', which actor plays The Stranger, who renames a town Hell and also paints it entirely red?

10 In 1964, a 17-year-old David Jones appeared on TV as the founder of The Society for the Prevention of Cruelty to Long-haired Men. By what stage name was David Jones best known?

ROUND 1 — CHAIN
1 Bilbo Baggins
2 Sudan (on the independence of South Sudan)
3 Narwhal
4 Lemmings
5 Scree
6 Eddie
7 Exocet (from "Exocoetidae")
8 Togo
9 Oh My God (Maggie Wheeler played Janice in 'Friends')
10 Dab

ROUND 2 — CULTURE CLASH
1 Bloomsbury
2 The Daily Mash ('The Mash Report' was the show)
3 Twilight
4 Food, Glorious Food!
5 Pizzicato
6 Porgy and Bess
7 Ajax
8 Autumn
9 Clint Eastwood
10 David Bowie

ROUND 3 — 54321

1 Name five novels by the author Ian McEwan from between 1995 and 2010.

2 Name the four Take That UK Number 1 singles that do not feature Gary Barlow on lead vocals. [up to 2022]

3 What three independent countries have names that begin with a letter that no other country begins with (assuming normal English spelling)?

4 Viking or Not to My Liking: are these real or made up characters from Scandinavian history? a) Harald Badfish b) Eric Greycloak

5 Conundrum: Of which common English word is this an anagram? TENSEMINT

ROUND 4 — DOUBLE TROUBLE

1 What is the traditional name for a group of lions?

2 Which coastal city is the second largest in Croatia, and the largest in the region of Dalmatia?

3 On July 20, 1976, Viking 1 successfully landed on the surface of which planet?

4 Which day of the week is called Domingo in Spanish and Portuguese?

5 Traditionally, the second highest taxonomic rank is Kingdoms. What is the English name of the Kingdom to which humans and other mammals belong?

6 What was, in 2007, the title of Ricky Gervais' third stand-up comedy tour?

7 Give the next word in this famous quote from former Spurs and Northern Ireland football captain Danny Blanchflower; "The great fallacy is that the game is first and last about winning. It is nothing of the kind. The game is about ..." what?

8 A traditional dessert, in which a banana is placed in a long dish, cut lengthwise and then has three scoops of icecream added to it, is a Banana ... what? [there are, occasionally, different names for this dessert, but give the one that fits the round]

9 A 1999 film directed by Oliver Stone about the world of American Football is 'Any Given ...'?

10 Which battle of 490 BC was the culmination of King Darius of Persia's failed attempt to subjugate Greece?

11 Which song from the film 'Selma', by John Legend and Common, won the Academy Award for Best Song in 2015?

12 What is the former name, in the UK, of the Snickers bar?

13 When he moved to Los Angeles, the Hawaiian singer Peter Hernandez changed his first name to Bruno, and his second name to ... what?

14 What has been a film twice, a TV series, a successful musical, and, with its title song, a Number 1 hit for Irene Cara?

15 Which annual celebration, which takes place in London on either the last Saturday of June or first Saturday of July, is the only annual event to close Oxford Street?

ROUND 3 — 54321
1 Solar, On Chesil Beach, Saturday, Atonement, Enduring Love, Amsterdam. Any of his other novels are from either before or after those times.
2 Babe, Everything Changes, Never Forget, Shine
3 Oman, Qatar, Yemen
4 a) Made up b) Real
5 SENTIMENT

ROUND 4 — DOUBLE TROUBLE

1 Pride	11 Glory	
2 Split	12 Marathon	
3 Mars	13 Mars	
4 Sunday	14 Fame	
5 Animals	15 Pride	
6 Fame		
7 Glory		
8 Split		
9 Sunday		
10 (Battle of) Marathon		

ROUND 1 — CHAIN

1 In which city would you find the football clubs Hibernian and Heart of Midlothian?

2 What was the Roman name for Ireland? [Q1 might be some help]

3 Which word for a vital piece of diving equipment was also the name of a Jethro Tull album and of a musical act who had a hit with 'Strange & Beautiful'?

4 Which river, sacred to Hindus and one of the largest on earth, rises in the Himalayas and empties into the Bay of Bengal?

5 What is the former English name of the country which officially changed its name to Eswatini in 2018?

6 Which first name links the American actor Benedict and the British actor/author Bogarde?

7 What was the surname of the Russian abstract artist who taught at the Bauhaus, is commemorated in a 2014 Google Doodle, and who died in France in 1944?

8 According to the title of a Supremes song written by Holland-Dozier-Holland, covered by Phil Collins in 1982, what did Mama say?

9 What is the common three-word name for the King of England from 1042 to 1066, whose death prompted the Norman invasion?

10 The title of a 2005 thriller directed by Wes Craven, which term is commonly used for a commercial flight where you depart at night and arrive the next morning?

ROUND 2 — MISSING LINK

1 Which bank, famous for its golden griffin logo, was taken over and renamed HSBC in 1992?

2 Who was Archbishop of Canterbury from 2002 to 2012?

3 Which energy drink was launched in Europe by Dietrich Mateschitz in 1987?

4 According to the gospel of Matthew in the New Testament, in which river did John baptise Jesus?

5 Which former Sex Pistols manager had a hit song of his own with 'Buffalo Gals'?

6 Which German tennis player, who reached Number 2 in the world, won the silver medal in the men's singles at the 2000 Olympics?

7 What is both the name of a flower sacred to Hinduism and Buddhism and the title of a 1998 song by the band REM?

8 Which tone poem by composer Richard Strauss was written to describe the experience of climbing a mountain in a large European range?

9 Which American actress won an Academy Award for Best Supporting Actress for her role in 'The Fisher King'?

10 What is the missing link?

ROUND 1 — CHAIN
1 Edinburgh
2 Hibernia
3 Aqualung
4 Ganges
5 Swaziland
6 Dirk
7 Kandinsky (Wassily Kandinsky)
8 You Can't Hurry Love
9 Edward the Confessor
10 Red Eye

ROUND 2 — MISSING LINK
1 Midland
2 Rowan Williams
3 Red Bull
4 Jordan
5 Malcolm McLaren
6 Tommy Haas
7 Lotus
8 An Alpine Symphony
9 Mercedes Ruehl
10 Formula 1 teams (past and present)

ROUND 3 — MYSTERY YEAR

1 In which English south coast town was Britain's first major nudist beach established in the mystery year?

2 Art Garfunkel had a UK Number 1 record in the mystery year that was the theme song to which animated film about rabbits?

3 In March of the mystery year, Maurice Bishop led a successful coup in which island nation?

4 Which bassist of the Sex Pistols died of a heroin overdose in February of the mystery year?

5 In which country did Ayatollah Khomeini seize control in the mystery year?

6 By what numerical nickname was Sir Anthony Blunt known? He was revealed in the mystery year to have been a Russian spy.

7 In the mystery year an Albanian woman born in 1910 won the Nobel Peace Prize. How was she commonly known?

8 Which team did West Indies defeat in the second men's cricket World Cup Final at Lord's in the mystery year?

9 Whom did Margaret Thatcher replace as British Prime Minister in the mystery year?

10 What is the mystery year?

ROUND 4 — UP AND DOWN

1 The chocolate manufacturers Cadbury's, Rowntree and Fry's were all founded by members of which religious movement?

2 In maths, if a fraction has the denominator on the bottom, what is on the top?

3 John Glen directed five films in which long-running British film franchise, the most of any single director?

4 What is the single most commonly used word in the English language, accounting for one in 16 words used in writing? [based on analysis of Oxford English Corpus]

5 Sharing his name with a US President, which Liverpool and Arsenal player was the first British Asian to play in the Premier League?

6 As coined by the feminist scholar Moya Bailey, what ten-letter portmanteau words is used for prejudice specifically directed at Black women?

7 What nickname links the loyalist paramilitary Johnny Adair, the fictional character Buford Tannen and the former England rugby captain Lewis Moody?

8 What informal term for someone behaving erratically derives from a Latin word which roughly translates as "moonstruck"?

9 What nine-letter word is used in the conspiracy theory that long-lasting condensation trails are deliberately left in the sky by some aircraft, causing harm to the public?

10 Though she admitted the content was "nothing special", how did Eimi Haga, a Japanese student, ensure she received top marks on an essay about a visit to the Ninja Museum of Igaryu?

ROUND 3 — MYSTERY YEAR
1 Brighton
2 Watership Down (the song is called 'Bright Eyes')
3 Grenada
4 Sid Vicious (Simon John Ritchie)
5 Iran
6 The Fourth Man (he was part of the Cambridge Spy Ring which also included Kim Philby, Donald Maclean and Guy Burgess)
7 Mother Teresa (of Calcutta)
8 England
9 James Callaghan
10 1979

ROUND 4 — UP AND DOWN
1 Quakers
2 Numerator (accept: Nominator)
3 James Bond
4 The
5 Jimmy Carter (he played in Division 1 for Liverpool, in the Premier League for Arsenal)
6 Misogynoir
7 Mad Dog
8 Lunatic
9 Chemtrail
10 She wrote it in invisible ink

ROUND 1 — CHAIN

1 In 2012, who became the first British cyclist to win the Tour de France?

2 Which word links a 2016 cartoon starring Matthew McConaughey as entrepreneur Buster Moon with a song title used by Ed Sheeran, Travis and The Carpenters?

3 Speke's, Grant's and Thomson's are species of which African mammal?

4 What is the Spanish form of the word "Stephen"?

5 Which 1841 musical by Giuseppe Verdi about a Babylonian king contains 'Chorus of the Hebrew Slaves'?

6 Which actress played Juliet in Franco Zeffirelli's 1968 film of 'Romeo & Juliet'?

7 Also known as the vitellus, what is the common name of the nutrient-bearing part of the egg?

8 Which member of Destiny's Child was a judge on the UK version of 'The X Factor' in 2011?

9 Which historic region of Croatia has given its name to a black and white spotted dog?

10 In a famous novel by Herman Melville, what is the name of the captain of the Pequod?

ROUND 2 — CULTURE CLASH

1 Which singer's film roles include The Acid Queen in 'Tommy' and 'Aunty Entity' in 'Mad Max Beyond Thunderdome'?

2 The '1812 Overture' by Tchaikovsky features portions of the national anthems of Russia and which other country?

3 The book 'Home School', in which the married couple Benjamin and Elaine educate their children at home, was the title of the belated sequel to which 1963 novella?

4 Give any year in the life of Ludwig van Beethoven.

5 Which English comedian's shows include 'Content Provider, 'Snowflake/Tornado' and '41st Best Stand-Up Ever!'?

6 In musical notation, how many horizontal lines are used in a normal stave?

7 What title links a 1972 David Bowie song to a 1984 Jeff Bridges film?

8 What surname links the American author Kate, whose works include 'The Awakening', and the Polish composer Frederic, whose famous works include 'Nocturnes'?

9 In the book and TV series 'Normal People', the two central characters are from which county in the west of Ireland?

10 Which Oscar-winning British actress was the first person to play the role of Sally Bowles in 'Cabaret' on the West End stage, in 1968?

ROUND 1 — CHAIN

1 Bradley Wiggins
2 Sing
3 Gazelle
4 Esteban (accept: Estevan)
5 Nabucco
6 Olivia Hussey
7 Yolk
8 Kelly Rowland
9 Dalmatia
10 Ahab

ROUND 2 — CULTURE CLASH

1 Tina Turner
2 France
3 The Graduate
4 1770-1827
5 Stewart Lee
6 Five
7 Starman
8 Chopin
9 Sligo
10 Judi Dench

ROUND 3 — MYSTERY YEAR

1 Which cartoon was first seen on 'The Tracey Ullman Show' in America on 19 April of the mystery year?

2 Both born in May of the mystery year, Andy Murray and Novak Djokovic would go on to be famous names in which sport?

3 In October of the mystery year, which British weatherman assured viewers that the worst of an impending storm would affect Spain and France?

4 On 3 January of the mystery year, a soul singer became the first woman to be inducted into America's Rock and Roll Hall of Fame. Who was she?

5 Where in Russia did the German student Mathias Rust famously land his plane on May 28 of the mystery year?

6 The novelist Paul Sheldon and nurse Annie Wilkes are characters in which Stephen King book, published in the mystery year, which was later turned into a film starring James Caan and Kathy Bates?

7 On 9 December of the mystery year, which England cricket captain had a famous row with Shakoor Rana?

8 Which classic film from the mystery year featured appearances from Mel Smith, Billy Crystal, Peter Cook, Peter Falk, and Andre the Giant?

9 In 'Dirty Dancing', screened in the mystery year, Frances "Baby" Houseman famously carried which large fruit?

10 What is the mystery year?

ROUND 4 — UP AND DOWN

1 Which letter is in the name of more months of the year than any other (only count each letter once for each month)?

2 In May 2020, Costa Rica became the first Central American country to legalise what?

3 What first name links a fictional lawyer, a biblical king and the boxer better known by his nickname Canelo?

4 Which is the only suit in a pack of cards that is not mentioned in a Beatles song title?

5 What's the common factor: a city in northeast India, England's Whig Prime Minister in the early 1830s, and a red bush?

6 In 'Byker Grove', PJ, played by Ant McPartlin, was blinded while taking part in which activity?

7 What New York landmark was known as Longacre Square until 1904?

8 In the Catholic church, what is the 18-letter word for "the change of the whole substance of bread into the substance of the Body of Christ and of the whole substance of wine into the substance of his Blood"?

9 Taunton man Matthew Robson was able to put a deposit down on his first home in 2020 by selling off the collection of gifts his dad had given him every year of his life - each gift was an 18-year old ... what?

10 On 8th December, what was the name of the second person, after Margaret Keenan, to receive the Covid-19 Pfizer vaccine at University Hospital, Coventry?

ROUND 3 — MYSTERY YEAR

1 The Simpsons
2 Tennis
3 Michael Fish
4 Aretha Franklin
5 Red Square in Moscow
6 Misery
7 Mike Gatting
8 The Princess Bride
9 Watermelon
10 1987

ROUND 4 — UP AND DOWN

1 R (eight months)
2 Same-sex marriage
3 Saul (Saul Goodman (Better Call Saul), King Saul; Saul "Canelo" Alvarez)
4 Spades (Lucy in the Sky with Diamonds, Sergeant Peppers' Lonely Hearts Club Band)
5 Teas named after them (Darjeeling, Earl Grey, Rooibos)
6 Paintballing
7 Times Square
8 Transubstantiation
9 Whisky (Macallan 18-year single malt) (In total, the father spent about £5000 on them, they were now worth over £40,000)
10 William Shakespeare (from Warwickshire. He died in 2021)

ROUND 1 — ALPHABET

1 Which is the only independent country on the equator whose name begins, in English, with the letter E?

2 What D are "momo" in Nepalese cuisine?

3 Which H is a type of humorous American blues song which is also a synonym for nonsense?

4 What J is the peninsula that forms the part of Denmark which is on the European mainland?

5 What R is the name of the German shepherd dog that starred in 27 Hollywood films from 1922 to 1931?

6 Which O is the author whose 1985 bestseller was called 'The Man Who Mistook His Wife for a Hat'?

7 What K is the name of former red light districts in both Sydney and London?

8 The police unit AC-12 is at the centre of which hit TV series beginning with L?

9 In the King James Version, what is the only book of the Bible that begins with I?

10 Which F is [as of 2022] England's most capped footballer of all time, an achievement all the more impressive considering they were homeless for part of their career?

ROUND 2 — FOLLOW ON

1 Sometimes called the arobase or strudel, the symbol found above the apostrophe on a Windows keyboard is usually pronounced as which short word?

2 Which seven-piece band was the best selling act in the world in 2020?

3 What is the better known name of the Avtomat Kalashnikova, on which two years of design work began in 1945?

4 In chess, the player with which colour pieces starts?

5 Which city in south-eastern Spain has a name one letter different from the Anglo-Saxon kingdom that was next to Wales?

6 In 2004, which UK supermarket chain was acquired by Morrisons, with most of its 400+ shops being rebranded?

7 Which actor took the title role in the TV series 'Sharpe's Rifles' after Paul McGann injured himself playing football just before filming?

8 Which long-running British television programme is based on the French show 'Des chiffres et des lettres'?

9 In 1981, the character Mario first appeared in the guise of Jumpman. What was the game?

10 Which English band, whose first UK hit was in 1981, took their name from the French for "Fashion Update"?

ROUND 1 — ALPHABET
1 Ecuador (not Equatorial Guinea)
2 Dumplings
3 Hokum
4 Jutland
5 Rin Tin Tin
6 Oliver Sacks
7 Kings Cross
8 Line of Duty
9 Isaiah
10 Fara Williams

ROUND 2 — FOLLOW ON
1 At (it's @)
2 BTS
3 AK-47 (it was finished in 1947)
4 White
5 Murcia (the kingdom was Mercia)
6 Safeway
7 Sean Bean
8 Countdown
9 Donkey Kong
10 Depeche Mode

ROUND 3 — MYSTERY YEAR

1 Which 77 year-old American became the world's oldest astronaut in the mystery year?

2 The UK Poet Laureate, who wrote 'Crow', 'Tales From Ovid' and 'The Iron Man' died on 28 October of the mystery year. Who was he?

3 'Who Wants To Be A Millionaire?' first appeared on British television screens in September of the mystery year. It was named after a song written by which famous songwriter?

4 Which French midfielder scored the third and last goal of the final of the men's FIFA World Cup in the mystery year?

5 Which band's UK Number 1 singles in the mystery year included 'Under the Bridge' and 'Bootie Call'?

6 The Petronas Towers, which became the world's tallest skyscrapers in the mystery year, are located in which Asian capital city?

7 The American terrorist Theodore Kaczynski was sentenced to life imprisonment in the mystery year. By what nickname was he better known?

8 Which film, released in the mystery year, concerned Mr Burbank who lived in Seahaven?

9 Who was famously described as "that woman" in a White House press conference on 26 January of the mystery year?

10 What is the mystery year?

ROUND 4 — UP AND DOWN

1 What name links an ice lolly, a company set up by Eric Yuan which boomed in 2020, and a song by Fat Larry's Band?

2 Which town in California has the town motto: "It's not our fault"?

3 Which four letters are pronounced differently in a five-letter word beginning with the letter T, a six-letter word beginning T-H, and seven-letter word beginning with T-H-R?

4 The activist Tarana Burke is associated with the first use of which phrase on social media in 2006, though it would come to wider prominence as a hashtag more than a decade later?

5 What is the female equivalent of a Henry vacuum cleaner?

6 The Ecumenical Patriarch of Constantinople is recognised as the head of what religious body?

7 At the funeral in 2006 of "Crocodile Hunter" Steve Irwin, what word was spelt out in flowers by staff at Australia Zoo?

8 What word meaning "disappointed" is derived from the so-called sport of cockfighting?

9 In 1987, which Michael Jackson album was the best selling album in the UK, though, perhaps surprisingly, not in the USA?

10 Which popular brand was created by a German Second World War doctor after he injured his ankle skiing?

ROUND 3 — MYSTERY YEAR
1 John Glenn
2 Ted Hughes
3 Cole Porter
4 Emmanuel Petit
5 All Saints
6 Kuala Lumpur
7 Unabomber
8 The Truman Show
9 Monica Lewinsky
10 1998

ROUND 4 — UP AND DOWN
1 Zoom
2 San Andreas
3 OUGH
4 Me Too
5 Hetty
6 Eastern Orthodox Church
7 Crikey
8 Crestfallen
9 Bad
10 Dr Martens (Dr Klaus Maertens. He found the standard army issue boots uncomfortable)

ROUND 1 — CHAIN

1 Lewis Hamilton won his first Formula 1 World Championship driving for which team?

2 Which word, used figuratively to mean a "low point", is the opposite of zenith?

3 Audrey Hepburn won the Best Actress Oscar for her performance in which film?

4 Which city just to the south of Tokyo is the second largest in Japan?

5 Which bitter Italian orange spirit, now made by Campari but roughly half as alcoholic as Campari itself, is often mixed with prosecco and soda water to make a Spritz?

6 What name links a former editor of The Sun and the actor who plays Mick in 'Gavin and Stacey'? [first and surname required]

7 What was the title of a 2014 Number 1 hit single for Jessie J, Ariana Grande and Nicki Minaj?

8 Which film role links Morgan Freeman, George Burns and Alanis Morissette?

9 Which fish, also known as the pompadour fish and native to the Amazon river, shares its name with a throwing event which has a men's world record of 74.08 metres? [as of 2022]

10 Which historic city on the coast of Massachusetts is infamous for its 1692 Witch Trials?

ROUND 2 — MYSTERY YEAR

1 On May 14th of the mystery year, Piers Morgan was sacked as the editor of which newspaper for a scandal involving faked pictures?

2 In the Super Bowl of the mystery year, known for its halftime show "wardrobe malfunction", which team, led by Tom Brady, defeated Carolina Panthers?

3 Jean-Bertrand Aristide was overthrown as President of which Caribbean country in February of the mystery year?

4 Which "special one" was appointed as manager of Chelsea in June of the mystery year?

5 In which romantic drama screened in the mystery year did Ryan Gosling and Rachel McAdams play Noah Calhoun and Allie Hamilton?

6 What is the name of the convenor of the Scottish Socialist Party who resigned in the mystery year?

7 In which county is the village of Boscastle, where severe flooding occurred in August of the mystery year?

8 The final episode of which New York-based sitcom drew 8.6 million viewers on Channel 4 in May of the mystery year?

9 What is the better known name of the broadcaster born John Ravenscroft in 1939, and who died in Peru in November of the mystery year?

10 What is the mystery year?

ROUND 1 — CHAIN
1 McLaren (in 2008)
2 Nadir
3 Roman Holiday
4 Yokohama
5 Aperol
6 Larry Lamb
7 Bang Bang
8 God (in 'Bruce Almighty', 'Oh, God!' and 'Dogma')
9 Discus
10 Salem

ROUND 2 — MYSTERY YEAR
1 The Daily Mirror
2 New England Patriots
3 Haiti
4 José Mourinho
5 The Notebook
6 Tommy Sheridan
7 Cornwall
8 Friends
9 John Peel
10 2004

ROUND 3 — FOLLOW ON

1 Which 2020 animated feature stars Jamie Foxx as the voice of Joe Gardner, and is the first Pixar film to have an African-American in the lead role?

2 Which arboreal Australian marsupial eats eucalyptus and sleeps for around 20 hours a day?

3 Which popular tourist city on the Yucatán Peninsula is at Mexico's easternmost point?

4 Which brand of effervescent vitamin drink, which comes in a variety of flavours, has used the slogan, "You, but on a really good day"?

5 In 2021, which skateboarder became, at 13, the youngest person to win a medal for Great Britain at the Olympics?

6 What started out as Buchanan, Donaghy and Buena, at one point was Range, Ewen and Berrabah, then became Buchanan, Donaghy and Buena again?

7 What is the Spanish name of the 1856 painting by Diego Velasquez which, in English, means "the ladies in waiting"?

8 In 480 BC, as depicted in the film '300', which narrow coastal pass was the site of a famous battle in which a small number of Greek soldiers resisted the Persian army?

9 Married to her colleague Ed Balls, who was the Shadow Home Secretary from 2011 to 2015, a role to which she was re-appointed in 2021?

10 Which English home county's flag features a stag on a yellow background, surrounded by blue and white wavy lines?

ROUND 4 — UP AND DOWN

1 Graylag, Barnacle and Canada are all species of which bird?

2 Sagitta is the Latin word for which projectile?

3 In which country is El Alto, said to be the highest major city in the world?

4 In non-leap years, what's the only month that begins on the same day of the week as January?

5 What two-word term links a fictional pirate ship and the nickname of the legendary Portuguese footballer Eusebio?

6 Which type of coffee takes its name from the colour of the clothes of an Italian order of monks, who themselves get their name from the Italian for "hood"?

7 In most years, around 12% of marriages in Scotland take place in which village?

8 For the crime of failing to report for military service, which notorious brothers were, in 1952, amongst the last people imprisoned in the Tower of London?

9 Who is an Apgar score used to assess?

10 Named after an 18th century woman, which hairstyle, versions of which are worn by both men and women, involves a large volume of hair above the forehead?

ROUND 3 — FOLLOW ON

1 Soul
2 Koala
3 Cancún
4 Berocca
5 Sky Brown
6 Sugababes
7 Las Meninas
8 Thermopylae
9 Yvette Cooper
10 Hertfordshire (representing a hart and a ford)

ROUND 4 — UP AND DOWN

1 Goose
2 Arrow
3 Bolivia
4 October
5 Black Pearl
6 Cappuccino (Capuchins)
7 Gretna Green
8 Kray Twins
9 Newborn babies (appearance, pulse, grimace, activity, respiration - a backronym)
10 Pompadour

ROUND 1 — CHAIN

1 Who scored England's first three goals of Euro 2020?

2 In 'Game of Thrones' what is the name of Jon Snow's albino direwolf?

3 Which radioactive metal is named after the Norse God of Thunder?

4 Hastings Banda, who died in 1997, was the first President of which African country?

5 What was the debut album released by rapper Nas in 1994, now considered one of the greatest in hip-hop history?

6 Named after a French physicist, what is the SI Unit of electric charge?

7 Big Daddies, in the dystopian underwater city of Rapture, are characters in which series of video games?

8 Which small orange citrus fruit, with a name derived from Cantonese, was introduced to Europe in 1846 by Robert Fortune?

9 Who appeared in 'Easy Rider', choreographed David Bowie's 'Glass Spider' tour, and had a massive hit with the song 'Mickey'?

10 What is the job that links Samuel Johnson, Noah Webster and Susie Dent?

ROUND 2 — MISSING LINK

1 The 2020 documentary series 'The Last Dance' focused on the career of which basketball legend, who wore the number 23 for the Chicago Bulls?

2 The four ghosts in the video game 'Pac-Man' are called Blinky, Pinky, Inky and ... what?

3 What is the name of the test cricket ground which can be found in West Bridgford, Nottingham?

4 Julie Christie won the Best Actress Oscar for her role as Diana Scott in which 1965 film?

5 Which American state contains Columbus, Cleveland and Cincinnati?

6 Which online bookstore shares its name with a member of a mythological tribe of female warriors?

7 What was the title of the film in which James Dean had his first starring role, released in 1955?

8 What is the title of the only solo UK Number 1 single by the Irish singer Enya?

9 What was the name of the wife of the singer Bobby Darin, also known for being in the title of a song from the film 'Grease'? [it's the surname that helps you get the link]

10 What is the missing link?

ROUND 1 — CHAIN
1 Raheem Sterling
2 Ghost
3 Thorium
4 Malawi
5 Illmatic
6 Coulomb
7 BioShock
8 Kumquat
9 Toni Basil
10 Lexicographer

ROUND 2 — MISSING LINK
1 Michael Jordan
2 Clyde
3 Trent Bridge
4 Darling
5 Ohio
6 Amazon
7 East of Eden
8 Orinoco Flow
9 Sandra Dee
10 Rivers

ROUND 3 — MYSTERY YEAR

1 What was the name of the flagship of Henry VIII raised from the seabed in the mystery year?

2 The Jam made their final TV appearance on which Channel 4 music show in the mystery year?

3 What is the name of England's record wicket taker in men's test cricket, who was born on 30th July of the mystery year?

4 In a film from the mystery year directed by Steven Spielberg, what does 'E.T.' stand for?

5 On which common in Berkshire were there mass protests, particularly by women, against the use of cruise missiles in the mystery year?

6 What is the family name of the royal family of Monaco, of which Princess Grace died in a car crash in September of the mystery year?

7 Future President Lech Walesa was released from prison in which country in the mystery year?

8 Which future England captain scored the fastest goal in the mystery year's FIFA World Cup?

9 What was the name of the Argentinian cruiser sunk by a British submarine on 2nd May in the mystery year?

10 What is the mystery year?

ROUND 4 — UP AND DOWN

1 What Saint's Day is observed on 6th December in Western Europe and 19th December in Eastern Christianity?

2 Which acclaimed TV show ended in 2015 by showing a classic Coca-Cola advert of the 1970s?

3 An American team led by Nicholas Clinch was the first, in 1967, to climb Mount Vinson, the highest peak on which continent?

4 In which US city is the building known as Hitsville USA?

5 Gail Bradbrook, Simon Bramwell and Roger Hallam founded which environmental protest movement in 2018?

6 What name links a bestselling brand of Scotch whisky to a Radio 2 DJ?

7 What word was removed from the standard vocabulary used by umpires at Wimbledon in 2019?

8 Which London Underground line has most stations south of the River Thames?

9 What is a common word for an ice cream cone in Scotland and Ireland, as well as a once popular feature of Facebook?

10 Who finished third in the Miss Alaska pageant in 1984?

ROUND 3 — MYSTERY YEAR

1 The Mary Rose
2 The Tube
3 James Anderson
4 (The) Extra-Terrestrial
5 Greenham Common
6 Grimaldi
7 Poland (he was president from 1990 to 1995)
8 Bryan Robson (after 27 seconds against France)
9 General Belgrano
10 1982

ROUND 4 — UP AND DOWN

1 St Nicholas' Day
2 Mad Men
3 Antarctica
4 Detroit (original headquarters of Motown)
5 Extinction Rebellion
6 Johnnie Walker
7 Miss (or Mrs) (They no longer used "Miss" before female players' surnames, instead just using their surnames as they do for the men. So "Game Williams" rather than "Game Miss Williams")
8 Northern Line
9 Poke
10 Sarah Palin

ROUND 1 — CHAIN

1 On which island is Combermere School, attended by the likes of cricketer Carlos Brathwaite and singer Rihanna?

2 Which composer of musicals such as 'Into the Woods' and 'Company' published a book of crossword puzzles in 1980?

3 Which tidal island and World Heritage Site off the coast of Normandy was the model for Minas Tirith in Peter Jackson's film 'The Return of the King'?

4 If dogs are canine and foxes are vulpine, what are wolves?

5 In which TV comedy, which ran from 2011 to 2017, did Matt LeBlanc play Matt LeBlanc?

6 From the Greek for "narrow writing", what term is used for the person in a courtroom who takes notes in shorthand?

7 Which word links a moon of Saturn to a large flightless bird found in South America?

8 What is the name of author Laurie Lee's sequel to 'Cider With Rosie'?

9 Steamboat, in Yellowstone National Park, is the world's tallest example of which spectacular phenomenon?

10 Which game using tiles, which has similarities to Mah Jong and Rummy, was invented by Ephraim Hertzano in the 1940s?

ROUND 2 — MISSING LINK

1 Who, in the New Testament, is the author of epistles to the Romans and the Galatians?

2 What is the French version of the English name Peter?

3 What mythical bird features in the title of the fifth Harry Potter book?

4 What is the middle name of Mr Burns, Homer's employer in The Simpsons?

5 Which singer and trained pilot died in his own aircraft in October 1997?

6 Which British car company, founded in 1905, merged with Morris in 1952?

7 Which town in Kent is on the site of the Roman fort of Dubris?

8 Which comedy series created by Donald Glover won the Golden Globe for Best Television Series - Musical or Comedy in 2017?

9 Which US President features on a 5 dollar note?

10 What is the missing link?

ROUND 1 — CHAIN
1 Barbados
2 Stephen Sondheim
3 Mont St-Michel
4 Lupine
5 Episodes
6 Stenographer
7 Rhea
8 As I Walked Out One Midsummer Morning
9 Geyser (Steamboat Geyser)
10 Rummikub

ROUND 2 — MISSING LINK
1 Saint Paul (of Tarsus)
2 Pierre
3 Phoenix ('Harry Potter and The Order of the Phoenix')
4 Montgomery
5 John Denver
6 Austin Motor Company
7 Dover
8 Atlanta
9 Abraham Lincoln
10 US State Capitals

ROUND 3 — 54321

1 If all the countries in the world were listed in alphabetical order, which five would come last? [we're talking their normal English name, and as it happens they are all one-word names]

2 The "Million Dollar Quartet" is the name given to recordings made on Tuesday December 4, 1956 in the Sun Record Studios in Memphis, Tennessee. Name the four members of that quartet.

3 Which three full length animated movies from the Disney Animation Canon (not including Pixar) are set in France? [up to 2022]

4 Salvador Dali or Salvador Hardly: Are these real or made up titles of Dali works? a) Dream Caused by the Flight of a Bee around a Pomegranate a Second Before Awakening b) Statue of Dragon Dismantled by Wine-Drinking Infants.

5 True or False? The Kiwi is the only bird that can catch syphilis.

ROUND 4 — DOUBLE TROUBLE

1 What is England's smallest city apart from the City of London?

2 Which company is the official supplier of balls for the rugby union World Cup?

3 What is the title of the acclaimed 2010 novel written by Jonathan Franzen?

4 Which award for political writing was given in 2020 to Janice Turner?

5 What is the name of the traditional headwear of bishops in the Church of England?

6 What is the common name of the US bank whose logo constitutes its name next to four blue quadrilaterals?

7 The French political party 'En Marche', the Israeli party 'Kadima' and the Italian newspaper 'Avanti', all have names which roughly translate as which word?

8 What is the name of an impact crater on Mars, 98 km in diameter, taking its name from the surname of an English science fiction writer who died in 1946?

9 What word links a member of the 'Paw Patrol' who wears a blue uniform and a single, originally from the soundtrack to 'Midnight Express', released by Giorgio Moroder?

10 Which English city began as the Roman settlement of Derventio?

11 Which track on the Beyoncé album 'Lemonade' featured a co-write and performance from the English singer James Blake?

12 What is the first name of the artist Mr Prousch, who married, and has been the longtime professional partner of, Mr Passmore?

13 What is the name of the English river that broadens into an estuary at Ipswich and then flows into the North Sea at Felixstowe?

14 The most famous example of which kind of horse race, named after an 18th century aristocrat, takes place in Surrey on the first Saturday of June each year?

15 In the film 'Braveheart', what is the last word William Wallace shouts before he is beheaded?

ROUND 3 — 54321
1 Zimbabwe, Zambia, Yemen, Vietnam, Venezuela
2 Elvis Presley, Jerry Lee Lewis, Johnny Cash, Carl Perkins
3 The Hunchback of Notre Dame, The Aristocats, Beauty and the Beast
4 a) Real b) Made-up
5 False

ROUND 4 — DOUBLE TROUBLE
1 Wells
2 Gilbert
3 Freedom
4 Orwell (Prize)
5 Mitre
6 Chase (JP Morgan Chase)
7 Forward
8 Wells
9 Chase
10 Derby
11 Forward
12 Gilbert (of Gilbert and George)
13 Orwell
14 Derby (The Epsom Derby being the most famous)
15 Freedom

ROUND 1 — CHAIN

1 What name links a Brazilian footballer who joined Manchester United in 2018 to a man who said "Right" in a song?

2 Which first name has been shared by two of the first six main hosts of 'Countdown'?

3 Although "arrêt" is occasionally seen, which word do you usually see on a French road sign telling you to stop?

4 Also known as Princess Toadstool, who is the ruler of the Mushroom Kingdom?

5 What is the name of the annual Muslim pilgrimage to Mecca in Saudi Arabia?

6 In lawn bowls, what name is given to the small target ball?

7 Which model was married to the musician Jamie Hince from 2011 to 2016?

8 What is the name of a Mediterranean wind which heads north from the Sahara and can, in the summer season, reach hurricane speeds in North Africa and Southern Europe?

9 In World War II, which city in Nebraska gave its name to one of the landing beaches on D-Day?

10 What was the title of the instrumental theme music to 'Beverly Hills Cop', named after the main character?

ROUND 2 — MISSING LINK

1 Which city preceded Canberra as the capital of Australia?

2 Which actor played the title role in the TV series 'Dr Kildare'?

3 In the British Army, what rank comes between captain and lieutenant-colonel?

4 Which environmental complex near St Austell in Cornwall was conceived by Tim Smit?

5 What was the surname of Beach Boys members Brian, Carl and Dennis?

6 In which month does the World Snooker Championship usually finish?

7 Which family-owned Somerset cider firm, founded in 1904, uses the slogan "People who care about cider"?

8 Named after comedian Bill Hicks' school band, what was the name of The Bluetones' third UK Top 10 single?

9 Which actor played Tyler Durden in the film 'Fight Club'?

10 What is the missing link?

ROUND 1 — CHAIN
1 Fred
2 Des (Des O'Connor and Des Lynam)
3 Stop
4 Princess Peach
5 Hajj
6 Jack
7 Kate Moss
8 Sirocco
9 Omaha
10 Axel F (By Harold Faltermeyer)

ROUND 2 — MISSING LINK
1 Melbourne
2 Richard Chamberlain
3 Major
4 The Eden Project
5 Wilson
6 May (starts in April, ends on May Bank Holiday. Was different in 2020)
7 Thatchers
8 Marblehead Johnson
9 Brad Pitt
10 British Prime Ministers

ROUND 3 — FOLLOW ON

1 Which TV show's hosts have included James May, Chris Evans, Matt LeBlanc and Andrew Flintoff?

2 In a comic strip created by Jim Davis, what is the name of Jon Arbuckle's cat?

3 Which county cricket team plays its first class home matches at Lord's?

4 Taking its name from the title of a Charles Kingsley novel, what is the only place name in England with an exclamation mark in its title? [the exclamation mark doesn't count for number of characters in answer]

5 A US Number 1 single, what was the 2017 breakthrough hit for rapper Cardi B?

6 What term is used for someone who draws, studies or produces maps?

7 Dry ice is the solid form of which compound?

8 Which England cricketer, born in 1985, married her team-mate Natalie Sciver in 2022?

9 The plot of which 1924 novel by EM Forster hinges on an incident at the Marabar Caves?

10 Which English cheese is used for the annual Cooper's Hill Cheese-Rolling and Wake?

ROUND 4 — UP AND DOWN

1 Where did Ever Given get stuck on 24th March 2021?

2 Herrero is the Spanish version of which common English surname?

3 Which adjective describes the "lion" in the Royal Banner of Scotland?

4 Which London thoroughfare is believed to take its name from a type of collar which was popular in the 17th century, as a landowner in the area had made a fortune from these collars?

5 The Arctic island of Novaya Zemlya was for many years used by the Russian government for what purpose?

6 Chef Auguste Escoffier created both a dessert and a dish involving thinly-sliced bread for which performer?

7 Sharing its title with a name in a Thomas Hardy title, what is the penultimate book of the New Testament?

8 A sandbar at the mouth of the estuary of the river Camel in Cornwall gives its name to one of the region's most popular beers. What is it?

9 Hermione Farthingale was an early girlfriend of which music legend? The colour of her hair is mentioned in one of his most famous songs.

10 At every general election since 1929, a number of Labour MPs have been elected not just as members of the Labour Party but also as members of which party (which shares its name with a supermarket)?

ROUND 3 — FOLLOW ON

1 Top Gear
2 Garfield
3 Middlesex
4 Westward Ho!
5 Bodak Yellow
6 Cartographer
7 Carbon dioxide
8 Katherine Brunt
9 A Passage to India (The Marabar Caves are fictional)
10 Double Gloucester (Cooper's Hill is in Gloucestershire)

ROUND 4 — UP AND DOWN

1 The Suez Canal
2 Smith
3 Rampant
4 Piccadilly (collars called Piccadills)
5 Nuclear testing
6 Nellie Melba (Peach Melba and Melba Toast)
7 Jude
8 Doom Bar
9 David Bowie (The girl with the mousy hair)
10 Co-operative Party (they are officially Labour Co-op candidates)

ROUND 1 — ALPHABET

1 What G is the surname of Tom and Barbara, a couple who try to live off the land in a 1970s sitcom?

2 Which L played Cinderella in the 2015 live-action film version of the story?

3 On Christmas Day 1950, what S was taken from Westminster Abbey by the students Ian Hamilton, Gavin Vernon, Kay Matheson, and Alan Stuart?

4 What V is a medieval French word used in English that can be used to describe fictional characters such as Passepartout, Kato, Alfred Pennyworth and Reginald Jeeves?

5 What T is a kind of cruise missile which shares its name with a type of axe used by Native Americans?

6 What Q is a 2000 film starring Geoffrey Rush and Kate Winslet as well as being the name given to the spiny barbs of porcupines?

7 What M is the name for a type of small round defensive fort built around the British Empire from the 19th century onwards, and found at various points on the English coast?

8 What V, meaning "let's go" is a word associated with Rafael Nadal on the tennis court?

9 What Z is a UK website launched in 2008 whose main competitor is called Rightmove?

10 Which A is the footballer who had a child with Little Mix member Leigh-Anne Pinnock, born on Monday 23rd August 2021?

ROUND 2 — CULTURE CLASH

1 Which 1942 Christmas song is the internationally best selling single of all time?

2 The songs 'Somewhere', 'Tonight' and 'Maria' come from which Leonard Bernstein musical?

3 What is the name of both the 2019 Netflix series and video game franchise based on the fantasy writings of Andrzej Sapkowski?

4 For which 1990 film did Madonna record the Oscar-winning song 'Sooner or Later'?

5 As well as holding a PhD in neuroscience in real life, Mayim Bialik played neurobiologist Amy Farrah Fowler in which TV show?

6 Which opera singer's name literally means "Calm Sunday"?

7 Which Hollywood legend appeared as Martha Levinson in the third series of 'Downton Abbey'?

8 Give any year in the life of Isaac Newton.

9 Ernest Cline, author of 'Ready Player One' which was adapted for the big screen by Steven Spielberg, published a sequel to the book in November 2020. What is the name of the sequel?

10 Das Rheingold is the name of the first part of which famously long musical cycle?

ROUND 1 — ALPHABET
1 Good (The Good Life)
2 Lily James
3 Stone of Scone (accept: Stone of Destiny, or just "Stone")
4 Valet
5 Tomahawk
6 Quills
7 Martello/Martello Tower
8 Vamos!
9 Zoopla
10 Andre Gray (not Alex Oxlade-Chamberlain, who had a child with Little Mix member Perrie Edwards, born on Saturday 21st August 2021)

ROUND 2 — CULTURE CLASH
1 White Christmas
2 West Side Story
3 The Witcher
4 Dick Tracy
5 The Big Bang Theory
6 Placido Domingo
7 Shirley MacLaine
8 1642-1727
9 Ready Player Two
10 The Ring Cycle (by Wagner)

ROUND 3 — FOLLOW ON

1 The flag of which European country has two horizontal stripes, the top one white and the bottom one red?

2 Which Beatles classic was written by Paul McCartney to comfort John Lennon's son Julian?

3 Darragh Ennis joined the cast of which quiz show as "The Menace" in 2020?

4 Which British author wrote the 'Regeneration' trio which also includes 'The Eye in the Door' and 'The Ghost Road'?

5 Which band's album 'Eyes Open' was the best selling in the UK in 2006?

6 Which former rugby player, nicknamed "The Iceman" was the 2021 PDC World Darts champion?

7 Northwest of Buffalo, which landmark, consisting of Horseshoe, American and Bridal Veil, spans the border between New York state and Ontario province?

8 Featuring Nicki Minaj and Ty Dolla Sign, what was the 2019 breakthrough hit for rapper Megan Thee Stallion?

9 Which 19th century British scientist, amongst other things, discovered benzene and established that magnetism could affect rays of light?

10 Which award-winning 1959 play by Lorraine Hansberry takes its title from the poem 'Harlem' by Langston Hughes?

ROUND 4 — UP AND DOWN

1 What is the most common surname in the Republic of Ireland?

2 What is the name of the American businesswoman and political technology teacher who founded the online security firm Hacker House?

3 In March 2020, Luxembourg became the first country in the world to make what completely free?

4 Erasmus University is located in which European City?

5 Which word can go after Keith and Karl and before Myth and Outfitters?

6 Which town in Ulster County, New York, is actually about 60 miles away from the farm which most people associate its name with?

7 Which old brand of British non-filter cigarettes takes its name from a nautical device used for multiplying the force of sailors hauling ropes and cables?

8 Which disease, widely spread by sailors, was called the "French disease" in Italy and Germany, the "Italian disease" in France, the "Spanish disease' in the Netherlands and the "Polish disease" in Russia?

9 Which character in 'Dad's Army' did writer Jimmy Perry model on himself and his time in the Home Guard?

10 What does the Spanish word "matador", used for bullfighters, actually mean in English?

ROUND 3 — FOLLOW ON
1 Poland
2 Hey Jude
3 The Chase
4 Pat Barker
5 Snow Patrol
6 Gerwyn Price
7 Niagara Falls
8 Hot Girl Summer
9 Michael Faraday
10 A Raisin in the Sun

ROUND 4 — UP AND DOWN
1 Murphy
2 Jennifer Arcuri
3 Public transport
4 Rotterdam (not to be confused with the Erasmus Scheme)
5 Urban
6 Woodstock (the Woodstock Festival was at Max Yasgur's farm at Bethel, about 60 miles from Woodstock)
7 Capstan
8 Syphilis
9 (Private) Pike
10 Killer

ROUND 1 — CHAIN

1 Which tiny boy is the title character of what is thought to be the first fairytale printed in English?

2 Which area in East London shares its name with the device used to play a stringed instrument?

3 Which large marine mammal, with an Atlantic and Pacific subspecies, is the only living creature in the genus Odobenus?

4 What was The Beatles' second UK Number 1 and remains their best selling single in Britain?

5 Which video game company, founded in France, is responsible for games such as 'Assassin's Creed', 'Prince of Persia' and 'For Honor'?

6 Which Queen of the Fairies gives her name to the largest moon of Uranus?

7 Which city contains around 40% of the population of Alaska?

8 Not to be confused with the study of the history of words, what is the study of insects called?

9 What is the name of the heroine of the operetta 'The Mikado', as well as being a type of twisted donut?

10 Which type of fish is also the name of a haircut described as "business at the front, party at the back"?

ROUND 2 — MISSING LINK

1 Which rapper was born Stanley Burrell in 1962 and is particularly famous for his extravagant dancing and enormous trousers?

2 'Central Perk' is the name of the coffee shop in which hugely popular sitcom?

3 Which word links an Adobe software platform, a cleaning product, a DC Comics superhero and a type of "mob" who suddenly perform in public places?

4 What was the nickname of the American basketball player Earvin Johnson, part of the 1992 USA "Dream Team"?

5 What was the name of the TV show which always ended with presenter Ron Pickering shouting "Away You Go!"?

6 What is the name of a historical region in central Europe which takes up two-thirds of the current Czech Republic/ Czechia?

7 Which HG Wells short story, about a scientist called David Griffin, was made into a film starring the voice of Claude Rains?

8 Which word meaning an oblique hint or an indiscreet suggestion comes from the Latin for "nodding at"?

9 In the 1980 Winter Olympics, the match between the United States and the USSR is known as the "... on Ice"?

10 What is the missing link?

ROUND 1 — CHAIN
1 Tom Thumb
2 Bow
3 Walrus
4 She Loves You
5 Ubisoft
6 Titania
7 Anchorage
8 Entomology (words is "Etymology")
9 Yum Yum
10 Mullet

ROUND 2 — MISSING LINK
1 MC Hammer
2 Friends
3 Flash
4 Magic (Johnson)
5 We Are The Champions
6 Bohemia
7 The Invisible Man
8 Innuendo
9 Miracle
10 Queen songs (Hammer to Fall, Friends will be Friends, Flash, A Kind of Magic, We are the Champions, Bohemian Rhapsody, The Invisible Man, Innuendo, The Miracle)

ROUND 3 — MYSTERY YEAR

1 Which horse, later to be stolen, won the Derby by a record margin in the mystery year?

2 Which heavy metal band released the album 'No Sleep 'Til Hammersmith' in the mystery year?

3 Who succeeded Valéry Giscard d'Estaing as French President in the mystery year?

4 Whom did John Hinckley Jr. shoot in Washington D.C. in the mystery year?

5 Which man, who managed Liverpool FC for 15 years, died in the mystery year?

6 Which band won the Eurovision Song Contest in the mystery year with 'Making Your Mind Up'?

7 Which event in St Paul's Cathedral was watched by an estimated 750 million people on television in the mystery year?

8 Muhammad Ali lost his final professional bout in December of the mystery year - to whom?

9 In the film 'Mommie Dearest', released in the mystery year, Faye Dunaway played which Hollywood legend?

10 What is the mystery year?

ROUND 4 — UP AND DOWN

1 As well as being a place in southwest London, what was the name of the first nonhuman hominid launched into space?

2 Sharing its name with a town in Clackmannanshire, what is the currency of Brunei?

3 Whose 2019 autobiography, co-written with Alexis Petridis, is called 'Me'?

4 What is the name of the California desert resort city which gave its name to an acclaimed time-travel comedy of 2020?

5 What is the name of the raised section of the A40 in London which is mentioned in songs by The Clash and Blur, amongst others?

6 Which ancient city sat by the mouth of the River Scamander?

7 The steam locomotive built in 1923 and named after the London-to-Edinburgh train service is the Flying ... what?

8 In which English county is the Minack Theatre, an open-air venue which is perched on cliffs over the sea?

9 Which ship, now a major tourist attraction, sank less than a mile into its maiden voyage on 10th August 1628?

10 Which word links a team managed by Roy Hodgson in 2004, a shipping forecast area and a medieval warrior?

ROUND 3 — MYSTERY YEAR
1 Shergar
2 Motörhead
3 François Mitterrand
4 Ronald Reagan
5 Bill Shankly
6 Bucks Fizz
7 The marriage of Prince Charles and Princess Diana
8 Trevor Berbick
9 Joan Crawford
10 1981

ROUND 4 — UP AND DOWN
1 Ham
2 Dollar
3 Elton John
4 Palm Springs
5 The Westway
6 Troy
7 Scotsman
8 Cornwall
9 Vasa
10 Viking

ROUND 1 — CHAIN

1 Which defunct Swedish car manufacturer's name was short for Svenska Aeroplan Aktiebolaget?

2 In 'The Flintstones', what is the name of Barney and Betty Rubble's son?

3 Who, in 'Peter Pan', is the boatswain of the Jolly Roger? [your answer should include his title, not just his surname]

4 Which mountain in Russia is the highest in Europe?

5 Residents of which English city are known as "Mackems"?

6 Which rapper's 2021 album is called 'We're All Alone in This Together'?

7 Who became leader of the UK Liberal Democrats in 2020?

8 What was the name of the only UK Number 1 for the Scottish band The Bluebells?

9 Which West African country between Ghana and Benin is one of the narrowest in the world, little more than 70 miles wide?

10 What is the surname of an American lift pioneer and the first name of an American soul pioneer?

ROUND 2 — CULTURE CLASH

1 What instrument's A note does an orchestra usually tune itself up to?

2 The name of which wolf in 'The Jungle Book' was taken by leaders in the cub scout movement?

3 What two-word title links a song by Arcade Fire and a TV show created by Charlie Brooker?

4 From which Rodgers and Hammerstein musical does the song 'Oh What a Beautiful Mornin'' come?

5 What title links a 2004 song by Annie with a 2015 TV series created by Michaela Coel?

6 The song 'Moon River' originally comes from which film?

7 Played by Bradley Cooper and Dirk Benedict, how is Templeton Peck better known?

8 What is the English title of the work by Mozart called 'Eine kleine Nachtmusik', which is also the name of a Stephen Sondheim musical?

9 What is a former polite term of address for women, prominent in Arthur Miller's 'The Crucible' as well as being how you might describe either Bill Oddie, Graeme Garden or Tim Brooke-Taylor?

10 Which band's 7th studio album was released in November 1980, its 8th in November 1981, and its 9th in November 2021?

ROUND 1 — CHAIN
1 Saab
2 Bamm-Bamm
3 Mr Smee
4 Elbrus
5 Sunderland
6 Dave
7 Ed Davey
8 Young at Heart
9 Togo
10 Otis (Elisha Graves Otis and Otis Redding)

ROUND 2 — CULTURE CLASH
1 Oboe
2 Akela
3 Black Mirror
4 Oklahoma!
5 Chewing Gum
6 Breakfast at Tiffany's
7 Face (Faceman)
8 A Little Night Music
9 Goody
10 ABBA (Super Trouper, The Visitors, Voyage)

ROUND 3 — FOLLOW ON

1 Which music genre, a precursor to reggae, is also associated with the 2 Tone movement in the UK in the late 70s?

2 Dermatology is the branch of medicine dealing with which organ of the body?

3 Which town near Perth was the historic capital of Scotland, and shares its spelling with a baked good usually taken with jam and cream (or cream and jam)?

4 Lindsey Vonn, Alberto Tomba and Franz Klammer achieved success in which sport?

5 Which nickname links the musician Benjamin Crothers and the performer John Larkin, whose biggest UK hit includes the words "Ski-Ba-Bop-Ba-Dop-Bop"?

6 Which sweets have been advertised with the slogan "Touch the rainbow, taste the rainbow"?

7 What is the last word spoken in the film 'Star Wars: The Rise of Skywalker'?

8 Which Great Dane puppy, the nephew of his show's title character, has catchphrases like "Lemme at 'em!" and "Puppy Power!"?

9 What is the name of the tallest mountain in England?

10 What was the title of Geri Halliwell's debut album, a portmanteau word from the Greek for "split" and "sound"?

ROUND 4 — UP AND DOWN

1 Which was faster - A) the fastest cricket ball ever bowled or B) the fastest tennis ball ever served?

2 Who was Prime Minister of the UK when Arsène Wenger became Arsenal manager?

3 In Scottish traditional dress, what is a sgian dubh?

4 What was decriminalised in Northern Ireland on October 22nd 2019?

5 In 2011, the Duke and Duchess of Cambridge drove away from Buckingham Palace after their wedding in what make of car?

6 Which John Hughes film is set on Saturday March 24th 1984 at Shermer High School in Illinois?

7 Who was King of England 1000 years ago?

8 At the first Modern Olympics, in 1896, what medal did competitors receive for coming second?

9 Which British actor starred as Chris Washington in the 2017 hit film 'Get Out'?

10 The Mevlevi order of ascetics, who practise sufi spinning in remembrance of God, are nicknamed the whirling ... what?

ROUND 3 — FOLLOW ON

1 Ska
2 Skin
3 Scone (Prons: skoon, skone, skon)
4 Skiing (Alpine skiing)
5 Scatman (Scatman Crothers and Scatman John)
6 Skittles
7 Skywalker (Rey says her name is "Rey Skywalker")
8 Scrappy-Doo
9 Scafell Pike
10 Schizophonic

ROUND 4 — UP AND DOWN

1 B) The fastest tennis ball
2 John Major
3 Knife
4 Abortion
5 Aston Martin
6 The Breakfast Club
7 Canute
8 Bronze
9 Daniel Kaluuya
10 Dervishes

ROUND 1 — ALPHABET

1 What F can describe something injected into the skin, someone who takes an empty seat at an awards ceremony, and an unmemorable track on an album?

2 What G is the name of the UK tax incentive originally introduced in 1990 which allows people donating to charity to do so tax-effectively?

3 Which D has been played by Patrick Swayze, Craig McLachlan, Richard Gere and John Travolta?

4 Improving on the initial work of Thomas Edison, the inventor Lewis Howard Latimer made a significant contribution to the development of which L?

5 In the canonical hours of Christian liturgy, what V is the name of the sunset evening prayer service?

6 Which P was Britain's first Black cabinet member?

7 What M was the surname of the inventor of the first commercial synthesizer?

8 By what K was the combative masked entertainer Peter Thornley better known in his 1970s heyday?

9 What I is an area of East London surrounded on three sides by one of the largest meanders of the River Thames?

10 What Z is the name of singer Lauryn Hill's first child (born in 1997), a word that appears in the title of one of the most famous songs by the child's deceased grandfather?

ROUND 2 — FOLLOW ON

1 In 'The Big Lebowski', which item of furnishing do thugs steal from Jeffrey Lebowski's home?

2 Which type of fish is also a medieval weapon and a move in diving and gymnastics?

3 Which country won the men's cricket World Cup in 1983 and 2011?

4 Which word (apart from "The") is in the nicknames of New Jersey and of Kent?

5 In 1990, Dave Grohl replaced Chad Channing as the drummer in which band?

6 Chris Pine, Ben Affleck and Harrison Ford have all starred on the big screen as which CIA analyst?

7 The ship, which fought in the Battle of Trafalgar, painted by JMW Turner in 1837, was the HMS ... what?

8 Which chemical element, with atomic number 15, takes its name from the Greek for "light-bearing"?

9 Which Boston beer is named after a Founding Father of the USA who was a cousin of the second President?

10 Which Nobel Prize-winning author, born Chloe Ardelia Wofford, wrote novels including 'Sula', 'Jazz', 'Home' and 'Beloved'?

ROUND 1 — ALPHABET
1 Filler
2 Gift Aid
3 Danny Zuko
4 Lightbulb (he invented carbon filament - Edison had only invented paper filament, which burnt out quickly)
5 Vespers
6 Paul Boateng (2002 Chief Secretary to the Treasury)
7 Moog (Robert)
8 Kendo Nagasaki
9 Isle of Dogs
10 Zion (Hill has her own song called 'To Zion' but the grandfather in question is Bob Marley - 'Iron Lion Zion')

ROUND 2 — FOLLOW ON
1 Rug
2 Pike
3 India
4 Garden (The Garden State and The Garden of England)
5 Nirvana
6 Jack Ryan
7 Temeraire (as in 'The Fighting Temeraire')
8 Phosphorus
9 Samuel Adams
10 Toni Morrison

ROUND 3 — MYSTERY YEAR

1 In September of the mystery year Paula Yates died aged 40. Two years earlier, she had discovered that her real father was which TV presenter?

2 On February 12 of the mystery year, the creator of 'Peanuts' died. What was his name?

3 Denise Lewis won an Olympic gold medal in the mystery year - in which event?

4 George W Bush was confirmed as the next US President in the mystery year, after a recount was prematurely brought to a close in which state?

5 "They have a plan, but not a clue" was the tagline to which George Clooney film, directed by the Coen Brothers, released in the mystery year?

6 Craig Phillips won the first ever UK 'Big Brother' which was televised in the mystery year. Who came second?

7 Inspector Morse's first name was revealed in the book 'The Remorseful Day', published in the mystery year. What was it?

8 In May of the mystery year, a baby girl named Astha became the one billionth citizen of which country?

9 Which American punk band released the album 'Conspiracy of One' in the mystery year?

10 What is the mystery year?

ROUND 4 — UP AND DOWN

1 In the Christmas song, what are Frosty the Snowman's eyes made out of?

2 According to legend, which 5th century saint is said to have described the Holy Trinity using the three leaves of a shamrock?

3 In the first name and surname (combined) of the UK's first female Prime Minister, which vowel appears three times in total?

4 The M96 motorway in Gloucestershire is not open to the general public, as it is used for training … who?

5 Who wrote, directed and starred in the 1921 silent film 'The Kid'?

6 Who scored the only goal as Italy beat England at Wembley in 1973?

7 In which show did Ricky Gervais's co-writer Stephen Merchant play the agent Darren Lamb?

8 Mainly used for chariot racing, which entertainment venue in ancient Rome was over 600 metres long?

9 What is the profession of the film characters Jonathan Mardukas, Andy Dufresne and Leo Bloom?

10 In 1981, Terry Wogan set a record for the longest ever WHAT seen on live television?

ROUND 3 — MYSTERY YEAR
1 Hughie Green (not Jesse Yates who brought her up as his daughter)
2 Charles Schulz
3 Heptathlon
4 Florida
5 O Brother, Where Art Thou?
6 Anna Nolan (accept: 'Anna')
7 Endeavour
8 India
9 The Offspring
10 2000

ROUND 4 — UP AND DOWN
1 Coal
2 Patrick
3 A
4 Firefighters
5 Charlie Chaplin
6 Fabio Capello
7 Extras
8 Circus Maximus
9 Accountant
10 Golf putt

ROUND 1 — ALPHABET

1 Which R is the German word for "backpack"?

2 Which L is the northernmost province of South Africa, named after the river that forms part of South Africa's border with Botswana and Zimbabwe?

3 What P is a sleeveless girl's garment which gave its name to a famous theatrical ship?

4 Which C is the republic in the centre of Africa whose capital is Bangui?

5 What A is a legendary island from Arthurian legend, a song by Roxy Music and the surname of an American teen idol of the 1950s?

6 What T is the more common term for a funambulist?

7 What W was the surname of Albert, Harry, Sam, and Jack, founders of a famous film studio?

8 Which M is the Shakespeare player featuring the brother and sister Claudio and Isabella, as well as the sinister character Angelo?

9 What H refers to a type of head covering traditionally worn by Muslim women, but can also refer to modest Muslim styles of dress in general?

10 What V was the surname of John, a British logician and philosopher whose main invention was introduced in his 1881 book 'Symbolic Logic'?

ROUND 2 — CULTURE CLASH

1 Which God is the father of Greek hero Heracles, also known as Hercules?

2 Which King of England is popularly believed to have composed the song 'Greensleeves', although the evidence to prove it is very limited?

3 Who played agent Jack Bauer in the TV series '24'?

4 In the 'Feeding of the Five Thousand' miracle, as told in all four gospels, how many loaves of bread did Jesus manage to break up and distribute amongst the crowd?

5 How many planets are represented by pieces of music in Gustav Holst's The Planets suite?

6 Which is the only day of the week that takes its English name from a Roman God?

7 Which singer takes her stage name from the queen who, according to legend, founded the city of Carthage?

8 Which female singer became famous after starring in the 1998 series, 'The Cruise'?

9 Which British composer's 7th Symphony was entitled 'Sinfonia Antarctica'?

10 According to the song 'We Wish You A Merry Christmas', what dish do we wish to be brought and do we, apparently, all like so much that "we won't go until we get some"?

ROUND 1 — ALPHABET
1 Rucksack
2 Limpopo
3 Pinafore (as in Gilbert and Sullivan's 'HMS Pinafore')
4 Central African Republic
5 Avalon
6 Tightrope walker
7 Warner
8 Measure for Measure
9 Hijab
10 Venn

ROUND 2 — CULTURE CLASH
1 Zeus
2 Henry VIII
3 Kiefer Sutherland
4 Five (and two fish)
5 Seven (he did not write one for The Earth, and Pluto had not yet been discovered when the suite was written)
6 Saturday (Saturn)
7 Dido (the singer's full name is Dido Florian Cloud de Bounevialle Armstrong)
8 Jane McDonald
9 Ralph Vaughn Williams
10 Figgy Pudding

ROUND 3 — 54321

1 Name any five of the six independent countries of the world which have names in English ending with -stan.

2 Carnivore or Herbivore? a) Dolphin b) Tasmanian Devil c) Fruit Bat d) Platypus

3 Gangster or Prankster: are these real or made-up gangsters in early 20th century America? a) Waxey Gordon b) Toots Van Hoogstraten c) Pudgy Dunn

4 a) True or False? German football coach and former player Wolfgang Wolf was the manager of VfL Wolfsburg in the Bundesliga from 1998-2003. b) True or False? In 2014, between 8:30am and 1:30pm on the day of the major university entrance exam, Uzbekistan shut down the entire country's internet to prevent cheating.

5 Conundrum: this an anagram of which word? AMHERGRUB

ROUND 4 — DOUBLE TROUBLE

1 Which word follows Barton, Wroxham and Hickling in the names of bodies of water in East Anglia?

2 What is the name of the bottom part of a tooth, below the gumline?

3 The chamber used to transport deep sea divers from the surface to the depths and back again is called a diving ... what?

4 In the book of 'Genesis', when she looks upon Sodom, Lot's Wife turns into a pillar of ... what?

5 Nicholas Breakspear is the only English, and Jorge Mario Bertoglio the only Argentinean ... what?

6 By what surname was the character played by Jack O'Connell in the TV show 'Skins' known?

7 In a successful US hip-hop duo, how was Cheryl James, whose partner was Sandra Denton aka Pepa, better known?

8 In music theory, what is the name, which can be either major or minor, of the group of pitches in which a piece is performed?

9 Which Joni Mitchell song from the album 'Blue' contains the line "It's coming on Christmas, they're cutting down trees"?

10 Who goes with 'Peele' in the name of a renowned American sketch comedy duo?

11 What is the first name of Joaquin Phoenix's first son, born in 2020, with the actress Rooney Mara?

12 The poet whose 'An Essay on Criticism' contains the line "To err is Humane; to Forgive, Divine" is Alexander ... who?

13 What is the surname of Chris and Stuart, a father and son who have played cricket for England?

14 What do the fictional characters Monica Geller and Richard Boarst do for a living?

15 Which word is in the title of a novel by Ernest Hemingway, a Number 1 single by Anita Ward and a US sitcom set at Bayside High School?

ROUND 3 — 54321
1 Afghanistan, Kazakhstan, Kyrgyzstan, Pakistan, Tajikistan, Turkmenistan
2 a) Carnivore b) Carnivore c) Herbivore d) Carnivore
3 a) Gangster b) Prankster d) Gangster
4 A) True b) True
5 HAMBURGER

ROUND 4 — DOUBLE TROUBLE
1 Broad
2 Root
3 Bell
4 Salt
5 Pope
6 Cook
7 Salt
8 Key
9 River
10 Key (Keegan-Michael Key and Jordan Peele)
11 River
12 Pope
13 Broad
14 Cook (in 'Friends' and in 'The Cook, The Thief, His Wife and Her Lover')
15 Bell (For Whom the Bell Tolls, Ring My Bell, Saved by the Bell)

ROUND 1 — CHAIN

1 Which European language, when it is "Double", becomes unrecognisable gibberish?

2 Which airship was destroyed on May 6, 1937 in New Jersey, resulting in 36 fatalities?

3 Which tree-like creature is voiced by Vin Diesel in Marvel Universe films?

4 Which Middle Eastern condiment is made from grinding sesame seeds?

5 Which song from 'Frozen 2' was performed over the closing credits by the band Panic! At the Disco?

6 What name links an interplanetary space probe and the 2020 game in the 'Animal Crossing' series?

7 What is the three-letter name for the area of a Bishop's jurisdiction?

8 Which song by The Commodores was a hit when covered by Faith No More in 1992?

9 Whip-Ma-Whop-Ma-Gate, Shambles and Minster Close are thoroughfares in which English city?

10 Which word goes before Rock and Cudi in musicians, and also Gavilan and Galahad in the names of boxers?

ROUND 2 — MISSING LINK

1 Which crime drama starred Robbie Coltrane as Dr Edward "Fitz" Fitzgerald?

2 What Israeli port is famous for exporting oranges and gives its name to an excellent delivery in cricket?

3 Which Italian freedom fighter of the 19th century was given the nickname "Hero of the Two Worlds" because of his achievements in both Europe and South America?

4 What was the name of the dynasty that ruled France from the late 16th century until their downfall in the French Revolution in the late 18th century?

5 By what name are small blocks of data placed on a user's device by the web browser commonly known?

6 Which Major League baseball team, which won the World Series in 2020, moved from Brooklyn to Los Angeles in 1958?

7 What is the name, taken from a combined name for New Zealand and Australian forces, used to commemorate the landing at Gallipoli on 25th April?

8 Which German polymath who died in 1716 developed the main ideas of calculus simultaneously with, but independently of, Isaac Newton?

9 In the human body, gastrin and secretin are hormones which aid and regulate what process?

10 What is the missing link?

ROUND 1 — CHAIN
1 Dutch
2 Hindenburg
3 Groot
4 Tahini
5 Into the Unknown
6 New Horizons
7 See
8 Easy
9 York
10 Kid

ROUND 2 — MISSING LINK
1 Cracker
2 Jaffa
3 Giuseppe Garibaldi
4 Bourbon
5 Cookies
6 Los Angeles Dodgers
7 Anzac Day
8 Gottfried Leibniz
9 Digestive process/Digestion
10 Biscuits (and biscuit-like cakes, as Jaffa cakes are, of course, actually cakes, not biscuits)

ROUND 3 — MYSTERY YEAR

1 Of which African country was Jomo Kenyatta the first Prime Minister when it gained independence in the mystery year?

2 On 8th August in the mystery year, Jack Mills was going about his business as a driver just south of Leighton Buzzard when he got caught up in which famous incident?

3 How many times does the word 'Mad' appear in the title of the all-star comedy released in the mystery year featuring the likes of Spencer Tracy, Phil Silvers and Buster Keaton?

4 Stephen Ward, Mandy Rice-Davies and Christine Keeler were implicated in the resignation of which cabinet minister in the mystery year?

5 Which civil rights leader was murdered by Byron De La Beckwith in June of the mystery year?

6 Which Italian car manufacturer, with a bull as its logo, was founded, to compete with Ferrari, in the mystery year?

7 Which tunnel under the Thames opened in November of the mystery year?

8 Which song, written by Bob Dylan, was released as a single by Peter, Paul and Mary and became an anthem for the civil rights movement in the mystery year?

9 Who was the first man to commit a homicide live on television in the mystery year?

10 What is the mystery year?

ROUND 4 — UP AND DOWN

1 Who, in 2022, became the youngest solo artist to headline the Pyramid Stage at Glastonbury?

2 In central Europe, Krampusnacht is the day before the feast day of which saint?

3 "It is better to light a candle than to curse the darkness" is a motto associated with which charity organisation?

4 What is the highest number in Roman numerals that can be correctly written using only Xs?

5 Fleet Street in London is named after what kind of natural feature?

6 How is the rapper and activist Kingslee McLean Daley better known?

7 Which area of South London is named after a structure first erected in Hyde Park in 1851?

8 In which English county is royal residence Sandringham House?

9 Which daughter of King Priam of Troy had the gift of prophecy, though was cursed that the prophecies would never be believed?

10 What is the three-word catchphrase of Matthew McConaughey, which he first used in the movie 'Dazed & Confused' and also said in his Oscar acceptance speech?

ROUND 3 — MYSTERY YEAR

1 Kenya
2 The Great Train Robbery (he was the driver of the train, assaulted by the robbers)
3 Four (It's a Mad, Mad, Mad, Mad World)
4 John Profumo (Secretary of State for War)
5 Medgar Evers
6 Lamborghini
7 The Dartford Tunnel (also known as the Dartford Crossing)
8 Blowin' in the Wind
9 Jack Ruby (killing Lee Harvey Oswald)
10 1963

ROUND 4 — UP AND DOWN

1 Billie Eilish
2 St Nicholas
3 Amnesty International
4 30 (40 is XL)
5 A river
6 Akala
7 Crystal Palace
8 Norfolk
9 Cassandra
10 Alright alright alright!

ROUND 1 — CHAIN

1 Which 1995 crime film contained the first scene in which Robert De Niro and Al Pacino shared screen time?

2 Which coastal city is the second largest in Israel, behind Jerusalem?

3 Which 1981 single by Ultravox spent four consecutive weeks at Number 2 in the charts?

4 Which term, from the Latin for "from the earlier", refers to an argument that comes from previous experience rather than empirical evidence?

5 Which colour of the rainbow takes its name from a natural dye from India?

6 Which left-wing columnist's books include 'Chavs', 'The Establishment' and 'This Land'?

7 What term is used for a dominant adult male gorilla?

8 Which men's Olympic cycling event was won by Chris Hoy in 2008 and 2012, and by Jason Kenny in 2016 and 2021?

9 Which city is the name of a 1975 film and a later TV series set around the country music industry?

10 Which drawing toy, invented by Frenchman André Cassagnes, comprises a grey screen in a red frame?

ROUND 2 — CULTURE CLASH

1 The Pogues had a 'Rainy Night' and Edgar Wright directed a 'Last Night' - where?

2 Which word links the titles of a 1786 opera by Mozart, a 2018 novel by Tayari Jones and a 2019 film directed by Noah Baumbach?

3 Two characters in which 1997 action film are named after two half-brothers in Greek mythology who are the sons of Leda?

4 Which word links a book in the 'Mr Men' series, a song by James Arthur and a quiz show presented by Rick Edwards?

5 Which flowering plant goes with 'Bush' in a Vincent Van Gogh painting, with 'Time' in a band fronted by Stephen Duffy and with 'Wine' in a song by Elkie Brooks?

6 Prospect Garden, the former home of film director Derek Jarman, is situated on which headland in south-east England?

7 The Roman author Seneca's 'Apocolocyntosis' (meaning 'Pumpkinification') is a satirical attack on which Roman emperor, famously played by Derek Jacobi on TV?

8 What surname links the 18th century owner of a brewery at Leuven with a cafe owner in the French town of Nouvion?

9 Jacqueline du Pré and Pablo Casals are famous for playing which instrument?

10 Who fulfilled a lifelong stated ambition by appearing in the last ever printed edition of The Dandy, leading the comic's famous characters in a singalong of one of his most famous songs?

ROUND 1 — CHAIN
1 Heat
2 Tel Aviv (Tel Aviv-Yafo)
3 Vienna
4 A priori
5 Indigo
6 Owen Jones
7 Silverback
8 Keirin
9 Nashville
10 Etch A Sketch

ROUND 2 — CULTURE CLASH
1 Soho
2 Marriage (The Marriage of Figaro, An American Marriage, Marriage Story)
3 Face/Off (Castor Troy and his brother Pollux)
4 Impossible
5 Lilac
6 Dungeness
7 Claudius
8 Artois (Sebastian Artois, Rene Artois in 'Allo, Allo')
9 The 'cello
10 Paul McCartney – leading 'Hey Jude'

ROUND 3 — FOLLOW ON

1 How is the unfortunate condition bromhidrosis, or osmidrosis - particularly unfortunate and unwanted on a packed train - known in its usual acronym?

2 What word was added to "Le" to give the nickname of Southampton footballer Matthew Le Tissier?

3 What is the capital of Latvia?

4 Boadicea was the queen of which tribe in early Roman Britain?

5 "Today Is Saturday; Watch And Smile." What classic TV show are these words associated with?

6 Who was the Republican presidential candidate at the 1996 US election?

7 What is a dark brown food paste made from yeast extract which is very popular in Australia?

8 What was the name of a band famous for a massive 90s novelty hit whose name comes from the Spanish for "those from the river"?

9 Which city, the 11th largest urban area in the UK, is situated on its own island?

10 Which US state was the birthplace of Morgan Freeman, Oprah Winfrey, Tennessee Williams and Elvis Presley?

ROUND 4 — UP AND DOWN

1 The line "Shake it like a polaroid picture" comes from which UK Top 10 single?

2 What is the name of the Hindu spring festival in which participants throw coloured water and powders on each other?

3 The US Bullion Depository is found in which famously secure army post?

4 In which Australian soap opera did Danni Minogue play the part of Emma Jackson?

5 In Roman mythology, who was the God of doorways and beginnings?

6 The original nickname for descendants of the early Dutch settlers, which word is referenced in the name of a New York NBA basketball team?

7 The Soviet Union's International Peace Prize was renamed as the Lenin Prize in 1957 - what had it been called before that?

8 The American boxing announcer Michael Buffer has trademarked what phrase?

9 The rod of Asclepius is an international symbol of which profession?

10 Which Conservative MP was suspended from the party whip after agreeing to appear on 'I'm a Celebrity ... Get Me Out of Here' in 2012?

ROUND 3 — FOLLOW ON
1 B.O. (short for 'Body odour')
2 God
3 Riga
4 Iceni
5 TISWAS - it's an acronym, and was the official title of the show
6 Bob Dole
7 Vegemite
8 Los Del Rio - they did 'Macarena'
9 Portsmouth - it is on Portsea Island
10 Mississippi

ROUND 4 — UP AND DOWN
1 Hey Ya!
2 Holi
3 Fort Knox
4 Home and Away
5 Janus
6 Knickerbocker (New York Knicks)
7 The Stalin Prize
8 Let's get ready to rumble!
9 Medicine
10 Nadine Dorries

ROUND 1 — CHAIN

1 Which word links the back of the lower leg to a baby cow?

2 What surname links the film dynasty containing Henry, Jane, Peter and Bridget?

3 What is the state capital of South Australia?

4 What is the name of the king of England from 975 to 978 recognised as a saint and known as "The Martyr"?

5 Sharing its name with an item used for household cleaning, what is the name of the compact crossover SUV produced by the Romanian company Dacia?

6 Which bird, with the Latin name Corvus frugilegus, is marked out from similar birds by the white featherless area on its face?

7 From a Hebrew word meaning "gathering", what is the name of a collective in Israel traditionally based on agriculture?

8 Which Irish puppet duo had a UK Top 10 hit in 1995 with 'Them Girls, Them Girls'?

9 Which peninsula in Turkey/Türkiye, whose name is the Italian form of the Greek for "beautiful city", was the site of a famous military campaign in the First World War?

10 In the Old Testament, who is the son of Abraham and Sarah, and the father of Jacob?

ROUND 2 — MISSING LINK

1 Who co-wrote 'Gavin and Stacey' with James Corden? [first name fits the link here]

2 Who were infamously described as "Enemies of the People" in a Daily Mail headline from 4th November 2016?

3 What name did Bob Dylan give to the first volume of his memoirs, first published in 2004?

4 Which Shakespearean tragedy is about a Roman general who presents the Queen of the Goths as a slave to the new Roman emperor? [first word of the answer fits the link here]

5 Which rugby union player, who died in 2015, scored four tries against England in the semi-final of the 1995 World Cup? [first name fits the link here]

6 What amateur English football team of the 19th century popularised football around the world to such an extent that Real Madrid took their white strip and a major Brazilian club named itself after them?

7 What is the name of the Apple equivalent of Microsoft Excel?

8 A question famously asked in the film 'Monty Python's Life of Brian' is "What have the ... ever done for us?". Who?

9 Mike Rutherford and Tony Banks were two of the founding members of which British rock band, formed at Charterhouse School?

10 What is the missing link?

ROUND 1 — CHAIN

1 Calf
2 Fonda
3 Adelaide
4 Edward
5 Duster
6 Rook
7 Kibbutz
8 Zig and Zag
9 Gallipoli
10 Isaac

ROUND 2 — MISSING LINK

1 Ruth Jones
2 Judges (three high court judges who had ruled that the UK Government would require the consent of Parliament to give notice of Brexit)
3 Chronicles (Volume 1)
4 Titus Andronicus
5 Jonah Lomu
6 Corinthians
7 Numbers
8 Romans
9 Genesis
10 Books of the Bible (both New and Old Testament)

ROUND 3 — FOLLOW ON

1 What letters appear at the start of all postcodes in the city of Edinburgh?

2 Morten Harket was the lead vocalist of which Norwegian band?

3 How is the Shaftesbury Memorial in Piccadilly Circus more commonly known?

4 Austin is the capital of which US state?

5 What is another word for jellied gasoline, a flammable liquid fuel weapon invented in 1942?

6 Which country's national parliament is called the Althing?

7 With which item of furniture would you associate Peter, Susan, Edmund and Lucy?

8 Along with Mecca and Medina, what is the other holy city in Islam?

9 Dennis Coles, Russell Diggs, Gary Grice and Clifford Smith are the somewhat prosaic actual names of members of which hip-hop collective, whose classic debut album had the subtitle '36 Chambers'?

10 Who became US President in 1977?

ROUND 4 — UP AND DOWN

1 According to an old proverb, having which condiment with mutton is the sign of a glutton?

2 The Red Arrows usually fly as a formation of how many planes?

3 Which international charity was founded at the Church of Saint Mary the Virgin, Oxford in 1942?

4 The International Date Line passes through the middle of which ocean?

5 Which country's national flag was inspired by a legend of a national chief whose blood spilled to the edges of the white sheet in which he was wrapped?

6 Which model community on the Wirral was built by a soap company to accommodate its workers?

7 What phrase links a gangland event in Chicago on 14th February 1929 to a classic boxing match between Sugar Ray Robinson and Jake La Motta on 14th February 1951?

8 Later proved to be a hoax, what name was famously given to the fossilised remains supposedly discovered in Sussex in 1912?

9 Which charitable organisation was founded in 1930, with its first establishment opening later that year at Pennant Hall in North Wales?

10 In the 1920s and 30s, British archaeologist Leonard Woolley excavated the remains of a ziggurat in which ancient city, in what is now southern Iraq?

ROUND 3 — FOLLOW ON
1 EH
2 a-ha
3 Eros
4 Texas
5 Napalm
6 Iceland
7 Wardrobe (they're the children in 'The Lion, The Witch and The Wardrobe')
8 Jerusalem
9 Wu-Tang Clan (they are Ghostface Killah, RZA, GZA and Method Man)
10 Jimmy Carter

ROUND 4 — UP AND DOWN
1 Mustard
2 Nine
3 Oxfam
4 Pacific
5 Latvia
6 Port Sunlight
7 Saint Valentine's Day Massacre
8 Piltdown Man
9 YHA (Youth Hostels Association)
10 Ur

ROUND 1 — ALPHABET

1 What R is the Latin word for queen as well as being the capital city of the Canadian province of Saskatchewan?

2 What O is the name of a character in 'Buffy the Vampire Slayer', 'Auf Wiedersehen, Pet' and 'American Pie' as well as being the title character in a 2013 movie prequel to a 1939 classic?

3 Which L is an Australian bird notable for its ability to mimic natural and artificial sounds, including the calls of other animals?

4 By what H is the literary and film character Natty Bumppo also known?

5 What Y is the state of Mexico which shares its name with the larger peninsula on which it is situated?

6 Which B, the star of the TV drama 'Pose', wore a fitted tuxedo jacket and a velvet gown to the 2019 Oscars?

7 After the ostrich, what C is the second heaviest bird in the world?

8 What I was the literary discussion group in Oxford of which JRR Tolkien and CS Lewis were members, as well as a term used for slight suspicions?

9 Which D is the award-winning sitcom created by Lisa McGee, which has 'Dreams' by the Cranberries playing over its end credits?

10 What E is, confusingly, the middle name of former Liverpool star Mark Walters?

ROUND 2 — MISSING LINK

1 What is the Latin name, as used in Catholic mass, for the mother of Jesus?

2 Which singer-songwriter who died in 2016 was, between the years of 1993 and 2000, often known as Tafkap?

3 In a pack of playing cards, which card is ranked between the 10 and the Queen, for each suit?

4 Which former beauty queen won the Best Actress Oscar for her role in the film 'Monster's Ball'?

5 In Rudyard Kipling's 'The Jungle Book', what type of animal is Bagheera?

6 Courtney Love was the lead singer of which rock band?

7 In Judaism, what name is given to the day of rest?

8 What is the suffix of the NBA basketball team that comes from Orlando?

9 On a tarot card, a skeleton riding a horse symbolises what?

10 What is the missing link?

ROUND 1 — ALPHABET
1 Regina
2 Oz
3 Lyrebird
4 Hawkeye (in 'The Last of the Mohicans')
5 Yucatan
6 Billy Porter
7 Cassowary
8 Inklings
9 Derry Girls
10 Everton

ROUND 2 — MISSING LINK
1 Maria
2 Prince (he changed his name to a symbol, and was often "The Artist Formerly Known As Prince", often abbreviated to "TAFKAP")
3 Jack
4 Halle Berry
5 Panther
6 Hole
7 Sabbath (or Shabbat)
8 Magic (Orlando Magic)
9 Death
10 Black (a "Black Maria" is a slang term for a police van)

ROUND 3 — FOLLOW ON

1 What is the name of the Italian river which runs through Turin and was known as the Padus in Roman times?

2 In JRR Tolkien's 'The Lord of the Rings', of what species are Shagrat and Gorbag?

3 What famous film role was played by a Cairn Terrier called Terry?

4 What was the surname of the main family in the children's TV show 'Button Moon'?

5 Which town in Sussex grew up around an abbey built to mark the site of the Battle of Hastings?

6 The Faeroe Islands are an island group belonging to which country?

7 Who was head of the United Nations Monitoring, Verification and Inspection Commission in Iraq from 2000 to 2003? [first name plus surname]

8 Which term refers to the music style popular in the 1950s in which First World War pop tunes were played on out-of-tune pianos?

9 What is the former name of the sweet now known as Starburst?

10 Which song from the 90s begins with the lines: "We'll be singing, When we're winning, We'll be singing"?

ROUND 4 — UP AND DOWN

1 Who first called Princess Diana "The People's Princess" on television after her death?

2 The two official languages of Finland are Finnish and which other?

3 Which newspaper's literary supplement first appeared in 1902, before being published separately from 1914 onwards?

4 'No Such Thing As A Fish' is a podcast by the "elves" who research which TV show?

5 Which chain of holiday camps opened its first site at Brean Sands near Weston-Super-Mare in 1946?

6 In which city were Sergei and Yulia Skripal poisoned in 2018?

7 The grounds of Castlewellan, Cliveden House, Chatsworth House and Hampton Court Palace all have notable examples of which elaborate feature?

8 Which column in 'Private Eye' is named after tiny constituencies which could be corruptible?

9 Historically, which colloquial term was used for groups that snatched people for enforced military service?

10 Rock band The Doors took their name from an essay collection called 'The Doors of Perception' by Aldous Huxley, who himself took that phrase from within 'The Marriage of Heaven and Hell' by which English author who lived from 1757 to 1827?

ROUND 3 — FOLLOW ON
1 Po
2 Orc
3 Toto
4 Spoon
5 Battle
6 Denmark
7 Hans Blix
8 Honky-Tonk
9 Opal Fruits
10 Tubthumping

ROUND 4 — UP AND DOWN
1 Tony Blair
2 Swedish
3 The Times
4 QI
5 Pontins
6 Salisbury
7 Maze
8 Rotten Boroughs
9 Press gang
10 William Blake

ROUND 1 — CHAIN

1 Closely related to the baboon and known for its extraordinary colouring, what is the world's largest monkey?

2 What is the name of Edinburgh's main port (as featured in the title of an album by The Proclaimers)?

3 How else is the French harp commonly known?

4 Which coastal city is the largest in the Mexican state of Guerrero?

5 What is the name of the strait between Denmark and Sweden crossed by a famous bridge?

6 What is the surname of an English folk singer, the given name of a Canadian rapper and the first name of a fictional doctor?

7 What city in England is also the name of an Oxford college founded in 1314?

8 Which popular website, used for social networking, entertainment and news, was founded in 2005 by Steve Huffman and Alexis Ohanian?

9 What surname adorns skyscrapers in Istanbul, New York and Chicago?

10 Damson, Moyer and Mirabelle are varieties of which kind of fruit?

ROUND 2 — CULTURE CLASH

1 Which word links an Arnold Schwarzenegger film and an Adidas football boot designed by former Liverpool star Craig Johnston?

2 In which song from 'West Side Story' is the song's title sung 29 times?

3 In the name of the music festival founded by Peter Gabriel, what does WOMAD stand for?

4 Which British sitcom used the Irving Berlin song 'What'll I Do' as its theme music?

5 There are six books of the Old Testament with names which begin with the letter J. Which is the first of them?

6 Which Beatles film, which had an accompanying soundtrack album, was first shown on Boxing Day 1967?

7 In 2018, which musician began answering questions from fans on a website called 'The Red Hand Files' (named after a 1994 song of his)?

8 What is a fictional Marvel Universe organisation, a many-headed Greek beast and the name of a Greek island?

9 Benjamin Britten's 'Young Person's Guide to the Orchestra' was adapted from a piece of music by which much earlier English composer?

10 The terrifying Count Duckula first appeared in which other TV cartoon?

ROUND 1 — CHAIN
1 Mandrill
2 Leith
3 Harmonica
4 Acapulco
5 Oresund (Øresund or Öresund)
6 Drake (Nick Drake, Drake, Drake Ramoray)
7 Exeter
8 Reddit
9 Trump
10 Plum

ROUND 2 — CULTURE CLASH
1 Predator
2 Maria
3 World of Music, Arts and Dance
4 Birds of a Feather
5 Joshua
6 Magical Mystery Tour
7 Nick Cave
8 Hydra
9 Henry Purcell
10 Danger Mouse

ROUND 3 — MYSTERY YEAR

1 Which American city suffered its second huge earthquake of the 20th century in October of the mystery year?

2 Where did British police arrest 250 protesters for celebrating the Summer Solstice on June 21st of the mystery year?

3 Executed on Christmas day of the mystery year, Nicolae Ceaușescu is the former president of which country?

4 Which former CIA boss was sworn in as the 41st US President in January of the mystery year?

5 In which round did Mike Tyson stop Frank Bruno in a heavyweight bout in February of the mystery year?

6 In July of the mystery year, France celebrated 200 years since the storming of which Paris prison?

7 In the mystery year, which American reached the semi-finals (her 52nd Grand Slam semi-final appearance) in her final Wimbledon appearance?

8 The opening track on which band's eponymous debut album, released in the mystery year, was 'I Wanna Be Adored'?

9 Soviet forces completed their withdrawal from which country on 15th February of the mystery year?

10 What is the mystery year?

ROUND 4 — MISSING LINK

1 Complete the title of this 1973 album by a famous American singer-songwriter: 'There Goes Rhymin ...'?

2 Which King of England, Ireland and Scotland died in exile in 1701? [we need regnal number, either English/Irish or Scottish]

3 The P in the Dutch football team PSV Eindhoven stands for which multinational company?

4 What is the name of the home stadium of Birmingham City FC?

5 Who presented the shows 'Double Dare' and 'Run the Risk' on Children's BBC?

6 Who was the title character in the second book in Reverend W. Awdry's 'The Railway Series' (he would go on to be the main character in the series)?

7 What is the capital of the nation of Antigua and Barbuda?

8 Which teaching hospital in central London, founded in 1123, was the location for the initial meeting between Arthur Conan-Doyle's Sherlock Holmes and Dr Watson?

9 What did a heckler shout towards Bob Dylan at the Manchester Free Trade Hall in 1966 which prompted him to reply "I don't believe you ... you're a liar"?

10 What is the missing link?

ROUND 3 — MYSTERY YEAR
1 San Francisco
2 Stonehenge
3 Romania
4 George HW Bush
5 Fifth round (he stopped him in the third round of their second fight seven years later)
6 The Bastille (Bastille Day is July 14th)
7 Chris Evert
8 The Stone Roses
9 Afghanistan
10 1989

ROUND 4 — MISSING LINK
1 Simon
2 James II of England and Ireland/James VII of Scotland
3 Philips
4 St Andrew's
5 Peter Simon
6 Thomas the Tank Engine
7 St John's
8 St Bartholomew's/Barts
9 Judas
10 The Apostles (accept: Saints)

ROUND 1 — CHAIN

1 The constellation Ophiuchus is sometimes considered the 13th sign of the ... what?

2 The 2020 Netflix series 'The Queen's Gambit' is about a prodigy in which game?

3 The brothers Ron and Russell Mael are the two members of which cult pop group?

4 Which term for knockabout comedy comes from a device consisting of two slats of wood and the sound it makes when hitting an actor?

5 Which male doll was introduced by Mattel in 1961 as a counterpart to his even more famous female companion?

6 Which biblical king gives his name to a 15 litre bottle of champagne?

7 Which Brazilian striker, who later went into politics, was Player of the Tournament at the 1994 FIFA World Cup?

8 If, in an Indian restaurant, you ordered "Bhindi bhaji", which vegetable, also known as Ladies' fingers, would be the main ingredient?

9 Rheboks and springboks are types of which animal?

10 What is the actor Martin Sheen's birth surname?

ROUND 2 — CULTURE CLASH

1 Who was Andrew Lloyd Webber's lyrical partner for the musicals 'Jesus Christ Superstar' and 'Evita'?

2 Thelonious Monk was a famous jazz musician and composer. With which instrument is he most associated?

3 Which virtuoso deaf percussionist was born in Aberdeen in 1965?

4 In the Bible, what was the first of the ten plagues inflicted upon the Egyptians by God?

5 'Nobody Does it Better' by Carly Simon is the theme song from which James Bond film?

6 The character Deena Jones in the Oscar-winning film 'Dreamgirls' is based on which American singer?

7 Who completes the line-up of the three tenors alongside Pavarotti and Domingo?

8 Who played the artist Jan Vermeer in the 2003 film 'Girl with a Pearl Earring'?

9 From which classic song, sung by Frank Sinatra and Ella Fitzgerald amongst others, does this lyric come? "Your looks are laughable, unphotographable, yet you're my favourite work of art."

10 What title links a critically acclaimed 1946 Alfred Hitchcock film and a critically panned 2009 film about a dead rapper?

ROUND 1 — CHAIN

1 Zodiac
2 Chess
3 Sparks
4 Slapstick
5 Ken (accept: Kenneth Sean Carson, his full name)
6 Nebuchadnezzar
7 Romario (not Ronaldo, who won it in 1998)
8 Okra
9 Antelope
10 Estévez (he is Ramon Estévez – his acting sons are Charlie Sheen and Emilio Estévez)

ROUND 2 — CULTURE CLASH

1 Tim Rice
2 Piano
3 Evelyn Glennie
4 Rivers and water turning to blood
5 The Spy Who Loved Me
6 Diana Ross
7 José Carreras
8 Colin Firth
9 My Funny Valentine
10 Notorious

ROUND 3 — 54321

1 Name any five of the countries that participated in the first ever Eurovision Song Contest in 1956.

2 Tube or Boob: ae these real or made up London tube stations? a) Hatton Gardens b) Kenton c) Kew Gardens d) Upney

3 Name the three people who led the Labour Party in 1994.

4 By the end of the Second World War, Churchill had lost an election, and Roosevelt was dead. Name their successors as UK Prime Minister and US President.

5 What common word is this an anagram of? MAPCHANGE

ROUND 4 — DOUBLE TROUBLE

1 Argentina derives its name from the Latin for which element?

2 In which capital city is the commune known as Freetown Christiania?

3 Which artist had hits with 'Morning Papers', '1999' and 'Purple Rain'?

4 What name for a large male deer is used for a human male who is about to marry?

5 What was the regal nickname used by the British boxer Naseem Hamed?

6 Which element has the atomic number 22?

7 What title links a song by The Rolling Stones and the American singer D'Angelo?

8 Which Japanese optics manufacturer takes its name from a mountain in Greece?

9 Having gone through a few different name changes, what word did the Beatles remove from their name in 1960, thus becoming The Beatles from then on?

10 In Greek mythology, whose theft of Helen from her husband Menelaus started the Trojan War?

11 What was the name of the Duke of Wellington's warhorse, which he rode at the Battle of Waterloo?

12 Muscovado and Demerara are different types of which specific foodstuff?

13 In the title of a 2013 film starring Gerard Butler and Morgan Freeman, what "has fallen"?

14 Which city hosted the rugby union men's World Cup final in 2007 and the football men's World Cup final in 2007?

15 Which song by David Guetta featuring Sia was a huge hit in 2011 and 2012?

ROUND 3 — 54321
1 Belgium, France, (West) Germany, Italy, Luxembourg, Netherlands, Switzerland
2 a) Made up b) Real (Bakerloo) c) Real (District) d) Real (Upney)
3 John Smith, Margaret Beckett, Tony Blair (Beckett in interim after John Smith's death)
4 Clement Attlee, Harry S Truman
5 Champagne

ROUND 4 — DOUBLE TROUBLE
1 Silver
2 Copenhagen
3 Prince
4 Stag
5 Prince
6 Titanium
7 Brown Sugar
8 Olympus
9 Silver (they'd been the Silver Beetles and then the Silver Beatles)
10 Paris
11 Copenhagen
12 Brown Sugar
13 Olympus
14 Paris
15 Titanium

ROUND 1 — ALPHABET

1 Which H is a fairytale character played by Chris Hemsworth which is also the name of a dangerous spider?

2 Which G was the longest-lived Republican US President?

3 What F will the protagonist in a Beach Boys song have until her father confiscates her Ford Thunderbird car?

4 Which E is the London borough that extends furthest to the north?

5 Which D, a much-loved blonde American music star born in 1946, who had a successful acting as well as singing career, published the autobiography 'My Life and Other Unfinished Business' in 1994?

6 Which C is the 2011 Steven Soderbergh film which soared up streaming charts in early 2020?

7 Named after a 19th century botanist, what B is the two-word term which describes the random movement of particles suspended in a fluid?

8 By what T is lateral epicondylitis, an acute inflammation of the tendons that join the forearm muscles, better known?

9 Which P is the town in Yorkshire which has a name meaning "broken bridge"?

10 Which L is a dance from Brazil which achieved worldwide popularity when a song with its name was released in 1989?

ROUND 2 — FOLLOW ON

1 What name links a 2017 Pixar film with the nickname of fashion designer Gabrielle Chanel?

2 The shallot is a variety of which vegetable?

3 Which Italian region has neither a coastline nor a border with any other country?

4 A phrase uttered when a judge enters a courtroom, what was the debut UK Top 10 single for the band 'Blue'?

5 Which English sportscar manufacture was established in 1973 in its namesake Surrey town?

6 Which French football star left Manchester United in 2012 and rejoined in 2016?

7 What name [first and surname] links the director of films such as 'Frankenstein' with an English shock jock?

8 In which film does Julia Roberts play the film star Anna Scott?

9 Which US state, with its capital at Charleston, was the only state to form during the Civil War by separating from a Confederate state?

10 Who was the Booker Prize-winning author of 'Hotel du Lac'?

ROUND 1 — ALPHABET
1 Huntsman
2 George HW Bush (94, narrowly beating Gerald Ford (93), Jimmy Carter (Democrat) older than both)
3 Fun, Fun, Fun
4 Enfield
5 Dolly Parton
6 Contagion
7 Brownian Motion
8 Tennis Elbow
9 Pontefract
10 Lambada

ROUND 2 — FOLLOW ON
1 Coco
2 Onion
3 Umbria
4 All Rise
5 Caterham
6 Paul Pogba
7 James Whale
8 Notting Hill
9 West Virginia (separated from Virginia)
10 Anita Brookner

ROUND 3 — MYSTERY YEAR

1. On February 11 of the mystery year, which man was released from Robben Island prison?

2. Rex Harrison died in the mystery year. In which film did he play Professor Henry Higgins?

3. The mystery year saw the United Kingdom join the ERM. What did ERM stand for?

4. On February 10 of the mystery year, which 42-1 underdog sensationally knocked out Mike Tyson in a heavyweight boxing match in Tokyo?

5. The mystery year saw Mary Robinson become the first female President of which country?

6. François Omam-Biyik scored the first goal of the FIFA World Cup in the mystery year - for which African country?

7. Which band released the seminal hip-hop album 'Fear of a Black Planet' in the mystery year?

8. Manuel Noriega surrendered to American forces on January 3 of the mystery year. Of which Central American country was he the military leader?

9. The mystery year saw the first episode of 'One Foot In The Grave'. Who played Patrick Trench in the show?

10. What is the mystery year?

ROUND 4 — MISSING LINK

1. Which word represents O in the NATO Phonetic Alphabet?

2. Which great cricketing family includes Graeme, his brother Peter, and Peter's son Shaun?

3. In which film does Larenz Tate play Quincy Jones, Richard Schiff play Jerry Wexler and Jamie Foxx play the title character?

4. Which word describes a distinctive v-shaped pattern, resembling a broken zigzag, used on fabrics such as wool?

5. Which baseball player, who began his career with the Los Angeles Angels in 2011, won the American League MVP Award in 2014, 2016 and 2019?

6. Which band's UK hits include 'Susan's House' and 'Mr E's Beautiful Blues'?

7. Which graphic designer created the famous title sequences for the likes of 'Psycho', 'Vertigo' and 'North by Northwest'?

8. Who replaced Gordon Jackson as the MSP for Glasgow Govan in 2007?

9. Complete this piece of sitcom dialogue: "Your name will also go on the list. What is it?" "Don't tell him, ..."?

10. What is the missing link?

ROUND 3 — MYSTERY YEAR
1. Nelson Mandela
2. My Fair Lady
3. Exchange Rate Mechanism
4. James "Buster" Douglas
5. The Republic of Ireland
6. Cameroon
7. Public Enemy
8. Panama
9. Angus Deayton
10. 1990

ROUND 4 — MISSING LINK
1. Oscar
2. Pollock
3. Ray
4. Herringbone
5. Mike Trout
6. Eels
7. Saul Bass
8. Nicola Sturgeon
9. Pike (in 'Dad's Army')
10. Fish

ROUND 1 — CHAIN

1. What is the current full name of the political party founded on 8 January 1912 in Bloemfontein, whose first President was John Dube?

2. What was the name of the first space station launched and operated by the USA, which orbited the Earth from 1973 to 1979?

3. Which huge German battleship, named after a prominent 19th century statesman, sank on 27 May 1941?

4. What Cole Porter musical is a musical updating of the Shakespeare play 'The Taming of the Shrew'?

5. In the book and cartoon 'Watership Down', what is the name of the police state run by General Woundwort?

6. The Southern Tamandua and the Northern Tamandua are species of what kind of animal?

7. A famous painting by Diego Velasquez which is at the National Gallery in London is known as 'The ... Venus' [your answer is the word that fills the space]?

8. What is the capital city of Armenia?

9. How is the British record producer Shahid Khan, whose hits include 'La La La', better known?

10. Which Japanese brand, which began in 1887, is the largest piano manufacturer in the world?

ROUND 2 — CULTURE CLASH

1. Who was played by Austin Butler in a 2022 film directed by Baz Luhrmann?

2. Made into an Oscar-nominated film in 2018, 'If Beale Street Could Talk' is a novel by which American writer?

3. What name links a former Liverpool manager and the car salesman played by Tony Caunter in 'EastEnders'?

4. Who is the rapper, poet, podcaster and actor born David Meads, taking his stage name from an unfinished Edward Lear nonsense poem?

5. Which word, derived from a 2000 song but sometimes falsely thought to be a portmanteau, was first used in a derogatory fashion by Nas, insulting Jay Z in his 2001 dis track 'Ether', though it didn't enter the OED until 2017?

6. Which adventure novel has the subtitle 'The Adventures of David Balfour'?

7. Which performer and civil rights activist, who died in 1975, became, in 2021, the first black woman to be laid to rest in France's Pantheon?

8. Matthew Bourne's ballet 'The Car Man' had a story based on the book 'The Postman Always Rings Twice' by James L Cain and music based on an opera by whom?

9. What name and initial is shared by a leading African-American statesman of the early 20th century and a bandleader who played on many of the great Stax records of the 60s?

10. Who does the young actress Vivien Lyra Blair play in the 2022 TV series 'Obi-Wan Kenobi'?

ROUND 1 — CHAIN
1. African National Congress
2. Skylab
3. Bismarck
4. Kiss Me, Kate
5. Efrafa
6. Anteater
7. Rokeby
8. Yerevan
9. Naughty Boy
10. Yamaha

ROUND 2 — CULTURE CLASH
1. Elvis Presley (in 'Elvis')
2. James Baldwin
3. Roy Evans
4. Scroobius Pip (the poem is 'The Scroobious Pip')
5. Stan
6. Kidnapped (by Robert Louis Stevenson)
7. Josephine Baker
8. Georges Bizet (Carmen)
9. Booker T (Booker T Washington and Booker T Jones)
10. Princess Leia (Leia Organa)

ROUND 3 — FOLLOW ON

1 Who led the Sunshine Band to three UK top ten singles in the 1970s?

2 What is the name of the John Lennon song where he gives a long list of things he doesn't believe in, including yoga, Jesus, Kennedy and Beatles?

3 In 'Gone With the Wind' what is the name of the O'Hara family home?

4 What is the first name of the Vietnamese-American writer Vuong, and the given surname of the American singer Frank?

5 Which London borough contains the postcodes W5 and W13?

6 Who sang the American national anthem at Barack Obama's 2013 inauguration? [mononymous stage name will get you to correct number of letters]

7 In which city does the Blue Nile meet the White Nile?

8 Who founded the company Amstrad in 1968?

9 In which Alabama city did Rosa Parks refuse to give up her bus seat on 1st December 1955?

10 Which US state contains the geographic centre of the North American continent?

ROUND 4 — MISSING LINK

1 Marble Hill is the one area of which New York borough that is not on the island with which the borough shares its name?

2 What is the common name of the unpleasant sensation in the chest which is also known as pyrosis, cardialgia or acid indigestion?

3 In each 365-day year, there are 8,760 what?

4 Which luxury fashion house was founded in 1912 by Italian brothers called Mario and Martino?

5 Complete this online tribute to the pioneering American scientist Katherine Johnson, who died in 2020: "She was a badass mathematician till the very end, waiting until she was 101 so she would die in her ..." what?

6 Which character from 'Seinfeld' was based on writer Larry David's real next door neighbour?

7 In two successive UK Number 1 singles of the 1970s, which two-word phrase goes before "let me go" in one of them, and before "here I go again" in the other one?

8 Though first used mockingly in 1906 by the journalist Charles E. Hands, which word was embraced, and widely used, by women in the UK seeking the vote?

9 Which nickname was used for the likes of Benazir Bhutto and Indira Gandhi, but is most associated with the first female Prime Minister of the UK?

10 What is the missing link?

ROUND 3 — FOLLOW ON
1 KC (Harry Wayne Casey)
2 God
3 Tara
4 Ocean
5 Ealing
6 Beyoncé
7 Khartoum
8 Alan Sugar
9 Montgomery
10 North Dakota

ROUND 4 — MISSING LINK
1 Manhattan
2 Heartburn
3 Hours
4 Prada
5 Prime
6 (Cosmo) Kramer
7 Mamma mia (in 'Bohemian Rhapsody' and 'Mamma Mia')
8 Suffragette
9 Iron Lady
10 Meryl Streep films

ROUND 1 — ALPHABET

1. Which I is a parrot in a Disney film and one of the great Shakespearean villains?

2. Ghostface Chillah is the name of the mascot of which S?

3. What O is the name that comes before the words "A Biography" to give the name of a Virginia Woolf novel about the adventures of a poet who changes from man to woman and lives for centuries?

4. With the headline being "That's Yer Allotment", England football manager Graham Taylor was cruelly portrayed as which T on the front cover of The Sun in 1993?

5. What H is the common name of plants of the genus Heracleum which are increasingly found by the side of paths in the UK and which can cause serious skin inflammations?

6. Which B is a town renamed in 1929 for its part in prolonging the life of George V, though, apocryphally, he expressed distaste for it on his deathbed?

7. What E is the surname of an actor known for playing a cop in an acclaimed British TV series and a gangster in an acclaimed American series, as well being the name of Italy's third biggest island?

8. What Z is the name given to a vehicle used, particularly at ice hockey matches, to smooth and resurface ice?

9. In his Christmas special 'Knowing Me Knowing You', Alan Partridge, when asked for his theological views, said that God was a what, beginning with G?

10. Which W, set in the world of Azeroth, is one of the highest grossing video games of all time?

ROUND 2 — FOLLOW ON

1. What "is the loneliest number", according to a song written by Harry Nilsson?

2. Who is Simba's malevolent uncle, voiced by Jeremy Irons and, later, by Chiwetel Ejiofor?

3. The largest salamander in the world is native to which country?

4. What shared pseudonymous surname linked punk rockers Tommy, Dee Dee, Johnny and Joey?

5. Which British swimmer won the men's 200m freestyle at the 2020 Tokyo Olympics (in 2021)?

6. The capital of Paraguay, Asunción, is at the confluence of the Pilcomayo and which other major river?

7. Chloe Zhao won the Best Director Oscar for which 2020 film starring Frances McDormand?

8. Which mapping system, which divides the world into 3m by 3m squares, was founded by Chris Sheldrick, Jack Waley-Cohen and Mohan Ganesalingam in 2013?

9. Which American former world middleweight boxing champion had the nickname "Second To"?

10. Which occasional character in 'Friends' had first appeared as a waitress in the US sitcom 'Mad About You'?

ROUND 1 — ALPHABET
1. Iago
2. Snapchat
3. Orlando
4. Turnip
5. Hogweed (common and giant)
6. Bognor Regis (as in 'Bugger Bognor')
7. Elba (Idris Elba in 'Luther' and 'The Wire')
8. Zamboni
9. Gas
10. World of Warcraft

ROUND 2 — FOLLOW ON
1. One
2. Scar
3. China
4. Ramone (The Ramones)
5. Tom Dean
6. Paraguay
7. Nomadland
8. what3words
9. Michael Nunn (as in "Second to none")
10. Ursula Buffay (Phoebe's twin sister, also played by Lisa Kudrow)

ROUND 3 — MYSTERY YEAR

1 The Dallas Cowboys became the first team to win which sporting event three times in four seasons in the mystery year?

2 John Howard was elected Prime Minister of which country for the first time in the mystery year?

3 Which British actor played the title character in 'Doctor Who' for the only time in a one-off special in the mystery year?

4 The computer Deep Blue beat which world chess champion for the first time in February of the mystery year?

5 In the grounds of which country house (later a venue for a Robbie Williams concert) did Oasis play two massive concerts in August of the mystery year?

6 In May of the mystery year, on which mountain, the highest in the world, did a sudden storm lead to the death of eight people?

7 Which rapper and actor died in September of the mystery year, a few days after being shot in Las Vegas?

8 Which unusual sheep was revealed to the world on July 5th at the Roslin Institute in Scotland in the mystery year?

9 Which team was defeated by Germany in the final of the European Football Championships at Wembley in June of the mystery year?

10 What is the mystery year?

ROUND 4 — UP AND DOWN

1 Leigh Delamare is a service station on which British motorway?

2 The Celtic festival Samhain, meaning "end of summer", is one of the origins of which modern celebration day?

3 The Fabian Society is linked with the formation and history of which political party?

4 What, in Greek mythology, is the name of the snake-like monster slayed by Hercules for the second of his Labours?

5 Enero is the Spanish word for which month?

6 In July 2016, a piece of music called 'A Glorious Dawn' was the first vinyl record to play ... where?

7 Who presented the BBC Radio 4 show 'Home Truths' from 1998 until his death in 2004?

8 Which fictional cowboy hero was created in 1904 by the author Clarence E Mulford?

9 In America, the so-called "Twinkie defence" is associated with the killing of George Moscone and which other American politician?

10 A statue of which character pushing a barrow was unveiled on Grafton Street in Dublin in June 1988?

ROUND 3 — MYSTERY YEAR
1 The Super Bowl
2 Australia
3 Paul McGann
4 Garry Kasparov
5 Knebworth House
6 Mount Everest
7 Tupac Shakur
8 Dolly the Sheep
9 Czech Republic (2–1)
10 1996

ROUND 4 — UP AND DOWN
1 M4
2 Halloween
3 Labour
4 Hydra
5 January
6 In space
7 John Peel
8 Hopalong Cassidy
9 Harvey Milk
10 Molly Malone

ROUND 1 — CHAIN

1 Who committed suicide in Berlin on 30 April 1945, less than two days after marrying her new husband?

2 Living from 1503 to 1566, who is best known for his book 'Les Propheties'?

3 What 2005 film starring the likes of Bruce Willis and Jessica Alba shares its name with a common nickname for Las Vegas?

4 In the play 'Hamlet' what is the name of the dead former jester at the royal palace Elsinore?

5 Which former leader was, contrary to his official biography (which states that he was born on Mount Paektu), born in the Soviet village of Vyatskoye in 1941?

6 A'a and pahoehoe are forms of what substance?

7 What is the commonly used, shortened name for a unit of electrical current?

8 Which US territory has a name meaning "rich port"?

9 What, at around 15cm long and 13cm wide is the largest of its kind in the animal kingdom, but also the smallest relative to the size of the creature it comes from?

10 Which country's official name is the Hellenic Republic?

ROUND 2 — CULTURE CLASH

1 American actress-singer Andra Day secured an Oscar nomination in 2021 for playing which figure - whose nickname ends with the actress's surname?

2 Which news website has a name which comes from the Greek for "Worthy"?

3 The novel 'The Noise of Time', by Julian Barnes, is about the life of which great Russian 20th century composer?

4 Which great New York actor's father was an acclaimed abstract artist, whose work was exhibited at the Guggenheim? The son's 1993 directorial debut was dedicated to him.

5 The popular "Tailenders" podcast stars DJ Greg James, cricketer James Anderson and Felix White, a former member of which band?

6 Who received the Pulitzer Prize for Drama in 1979 and was nominated for an Academy Award for Best Supporting Actor in 1983?

7 What was the name of the Netflix series created by Spike Lee, based on his 1986 film of the same name?

8 The third album by which British band takes its name, almost exactly, from a poem by Wilfred Owen which begins "What passing-bells for these who die as cattle?"?

9 Famously depicted in the 1964 painting 'The Problem We All Live With' by Norman Rockwell, what is the name of the 6-year old Black girl who attended the all-white William Frantz Elementary School on 14th November 1960?

10 Which classical musician was the first official busker in London Underground stations in 2001?

ROUND 1 — CHAIN
1 Eva Braun
2 Nostradamus
3 Sin City
4 Yorick
5 Kim Jong-Il
6 Lava
7 Amp
8 Puerto Rico
9 Ostrich egg
10 Greece

ROUND 2 — CULTURE CLASH
1 Billie Holiday (Lady Day)
2 Axios
3 Dmitri Shostakovich
4 Robert De Niro (his father was Robert De Niro Sr)
5 The Maccabees
6 Sam Shepard
7 She's Gotta Have It
8 The Libertines (the poem is 'Anthem for Doomed Youth'. The album is 'Anthems for Doomed Youth')
9 Ruby Bridges
10 Julian Lloyd Webber (all money thrown into his cello case went to the Prince's Trust charity)

ROUND 3 — FOLLOW ON

1 Which vowel is least frequently used in the English language?

2 In 1999, Dylan Jones took over as editor of the UK edition of which men's magazine?

3 What name is given to the vaccine, routine for all children in the UK until 2005, used to combat tuberculosis?

4 What river flows through the city of Durham before entering the sea in Sunderland?

5 Which word links a 1973 Oscar-winning film, an elvish sword used by a hobbit, and a Geordie musician born in 1951?

6 Apart from the Vatican City and Rome, the two capital cities closest to each other in Europe are Bratislava, in Slovakia, and which other capital city, just 50 km away?

7 Which brewery and pub chain, founded by James Watt and Martin Dickie in 2007, is based in Ellon, Scotland?

8 Which board game, one of the best selling in the world, was designed by Alfred Mosher Butts in 1938?

9 What is the name of the family home of Max De Winter in Daphne Du Maurier's novel 'Rebecca'?

10 What phrase was popularised by the architect Ludwig Mies van der Rohe to explain his minimalist architectural style?

ROUND 4 — UP AND DOWN

1 How long is a half marathon in kilometres, to the nearest kilometre?

2 In which county is the village of Holme, near the lowest point in Great Britain?

3 In 2020, British historian David Olusoga conducted an interview with which former US President?

4 Although nowadays it is a name for a missile, what, originally, was a tomahawk?

5 What circus was founded in Canada in 1984 by the former street performers Guy Laliberté and Gilles Ste-Croix?

6 In 2018, Ross Edgley became the first person to swim round what island?

7 Founded in 1472, Monte dei Paschi di Siena is the world's oldest surviving ... what?

8 What do women of the Kayan Lahwi tribe of Burma traditionally wear around their necks?

9 What kind of motor vehicle derives its name from the Latin for "walk"?

10 Which organisation was established by Mary Tealby in 1860 as the Temporary Home for Lost and Starving Dogs?

ROUND 3 — FOLLOW ON
1 U
2 GQ
3 BCG
4 Wear (not Tyne or Tees)
5 Sting
6 Vienna
7 BrewDog
8 Scrabble
9 Manderley
10 Less is more

ROUND 4 — UP AND DOWN
1 21 (21.0975 kilometres (13 miles 192.5 yards))
2 Cambridgeshire
3 Barack Obama
4 An axe
5 Cirque du Soleil
6 Britain
7 Bank
8 Brass coils
9 Ambulance
10 Battersea Dogs and Cats Home

ROUND 1 — ALPHABET

1 What F is a term for a handyman from the Latin for "do everything"?

2 What J were Chris Cromby and Jemma Abbey, a pop double-act who memorably performed on stage in Riga, Latvia on 24 May 2003?

3 On 30 January 2020, a bronze statue of which B was unveiled outside the Main Stand at Anfield?

4 What V is the name used by the American actor who was born Mark Sinclair Vincent in 1967?

5 Which K is the British brand of bread that was temporarily rebranded during the 2012 Diamond Jubilee celebrations?

6 What L is the largest city, by population, in California with a name that doesn't derive from Spanish?

7 Which P is the 1960 psychological/horror thriller about a voyeuristic serial killer obsessed with his parents, made by one of the greatest British directors? The main character is played by Carl Boehm and the answer is not 'Psycho'.

8 What T, from the Italian for "cushion", is a landform made of sand connecting an island to a mainland?

9 What H is the most widely spoken language in Nigeria, mainly in the north of the country?

10 Which D, a much-loved blonde American music star born in 1945, who had a successful acting as well as singing career, published the autobiography 'Face It' in 2019?

ROUND 2 — FOLLOW ON

1 By what abbreviation is the controversial insecticide Dichlorodiphenyltrichloroethane better known?

2 Which island nation retained their men's Olympic Rugby Sevens title in 2021?

3 In 'Calvin and Hobbes', Hobbes is a stuffed ... what?

4 Which footwear manufacturer was named after a type of South African antelope?

5 Which Irish band, whose debut album reached Number 1 in the UK in 2021, is fronted by Elijah Hewson, the son of U2's Bono?

6 In 2021, Sandra Mason became the first President of which country?

7 Enniskillen is the county town of which county of Northern Ireland?

8 Esther Greenwood is the main character of which semi-autobiographical novel from 1963?

9 Which England player joined Manchester United from Borussia Dortmund in the summer of 2021?

10 Whose book 'How to Build a Girl' was turned into a 2019 film starring Beanie Feldstein?

ROUND 1 — ALPHABET
1 Factotum
2 Jemini
3 Bob Paisley (in the statue, he is carrying Emlyn Hughes off the pitch)
4 Vin Diesel
5 Kingsmill (it became Queensmill)
6 Long Beach
7 Peeping Tom (directed by Michael Powell)
8 Tombolo
9 Hausa
10 Debbie Harry

ROUND 2 — FOLLOW ON
1 DDT
2 Fiji
3 Tiger
4 Reebok
5 Inhaler
6 Barbados
7 Fermanagh
8 The Bell Jar (by Sylvia Plath)
9 Jadon Sancho
10 Caitlin Moran

ROUND 3 — MYSTERY YEAR

1 What is the name of the free internet encyclopaedia service that first went online in January of the mystery year?

2 Ariel Sharon was elected Prime Minister of which country in February of the mystery year?

3 What was the first single released by the band Hear'Say, which reached Number 1 in the UK in March of the mystery year?

4 Which British actor played Meriadoc Brandybuck in 'The Lord of the Rings: the Fellowship of the Ring', released in December of the mystery year?

5 Which New York band released their acclaimed debut album 'Is This It' in the mystery year?

6 In the mystery year, in the wake of 9/11, the US and its allies invaded which country with the intention of toppling the country's ruling Taliban?

7 What was the name of the Russian space station launched 15 years previously that was deliberately brought down to Earth in March of the mystery year?

8 Which former Conservative politician was jailed for four years for perjury in July of the mystery year?

9 Which 35-year-old was voted PFA Players' Player of the Year in the mystery year after helping Manchester United to their third successive Premier League title?

10 What is the mystery year?

ROUND 4 — UP AND DOWN

1 In the history of Test cricket, what is the most common way for a batsman to get out?

2 Who was President of the USA when Elizabeth II became Queen of the United Kingdom?

3 In what event did men called Jimmy White, Charlie Wilson and John Daly participate on 8th August 1963?

4 Who is the patron saint of music?

5 For which film set in space did the Mexican director Alfonso Cuaron win his first Oscar?

6 Whose first children's book is called 'The Racehorse Who Wouldn't Gallop'?

7 Which Scottish river shares its name with one member of a US crime duo who died in 1934?

8 What, according to Greek mythology, was the eternal punishment of Tantalus in the Underworld?

9 In 2018, the owner of which English football club was killed in a helicopter crash?

10 Which tree that produces a popular nut is named after a Scottish-Australian chemist and politician?

ROUND 3 — MYSTERY YEAR
1 Wikipedia
2 Israel
3 Pure and Simple
4 Dominic Monaghan
5 The Strokes
6 Afghanistan
7 Mir
8 Jeffrey Archer
9 Teddy Sheringham
10 2001

ROUND 4 — UP AND DOWN
1 Caught
2 Harry S Truman
3 Great Train Robbery
4 Cecilia
5 Gravity
6 Clare Balding
7 Clyde (Bonnie and Clyde)
8 Grasping at fruit he couldn't reach
9 Leicester City (Vichai Srivaddhanaprabha)
10 Macadamia

ROUND 1 — CHAIN

1 What name, which is also the title of a rock opera by The Who, is a slang name given to soldiers in the British army?

2 Which world-famous university is situated in New Haven, Connecticut?

3 What name links a fictional hamster and a swashbuckling Hollywood actor born in Hobart, Tasmania?

4 Who was leader of the Soviet Union from 1964 to 1982? [first name and surname for the link]

5 What word links a species from 'Star Trek' and the Roman equivalent of the Greek god Hephaistos?

6 Born in Trinidad and Tobago, whose hits include 'Super Bass' and 'Anaconda'?

7 What 2013 movie about a businessman who died in 2012 starred Ashton Kutcher as the title character?

8 Which English football club is known as "The Blades"?

9 What word links a river in Devon with the name given to Dublin's suburban train system?

10 Which 2020 Christopher Nolan film stars John David Washington as the Protagonist?

ROUND 2 — CULTURE CLASH

1 "The last man on Earth is not alone" is the tagline of which 2007 Will Smith film?

2 In Japan, which form of traditional theatre has a name that means "song, dance, skill"?

3 Who played the artist Andy Warhol in a 1996 film, having previously included a song called 'Andy Warhol' on an album from 1971?

4 Which acclaimed choreographer's works include dance versions of 'Edward Scissorhands' and 'Dorian Gray'?

5 What name links a ship used by Ernest Shackleton and the ninth of Edward Elgar's 'Enigma' variations?

6 Which Nirvana song takes its name from a drink extracted from the plant mentha pulegium?

7 Who played Hercule Poirot in the 2022 film adaptation of 'Death on the Nile'?

8 For 'The Comic Strip Presents' in 1990, which artist performed a tribute to Ken Livingstone that included the lyrics "Who is the funky sex machine? Ken!"?

9 In 2014, Mike Leigh made a film about which famous British artist?

10 23 and 25 Brook Street, in London, both have blue commemorative plaques, to which two contrasting musical figures?

ROUND 1 — CHAIN
1 Tommy
2 Yale
3 Errol
4 Leonid Brezhnev
5 Vulcan
6 Nicki Minaj
7 Jobs (not 'Steve Jobs' which starred Michael Fassbender)
8 Sheffield United
9 DART
10 Tenet

ROUND 2 — CULTURE CLASH
1 I Am Legend
2 Kabuki
3 David Bowie
4 Matthew Bourne
5 Nimrod
6 Pennyroyal Tea
7 Kenneth Branagh
8 Kate Bush
9 JMW Turner
10 Jimi Hendrix and Georg Handel

ROUND 3 — FOLLOW ON

1 Which consonant is most frequently used in the English language?

2 What is the surname of the most famous film character played by the actor Joseph Wiseman (in 1962)?

3 What meat shares its name with one of the sons of Noah, in the book of 'Genesis', and with a word for an overdramatic actor?

4 Which US state, taking its name from the Iroquois for "great river", is known as The Buckeye State?

5 Which vegetable links song titles by The Beatles, The Shins and Marvin Gaye?

6 Which band released their own beer, named Mmmhops, in early 2013?

7 What was the nickname of the character played by Jonny Lee Miller in 'Trainspotting'?

8 In which eerie town in Connecticut does Joanna Eberhart live in a 1972 satirical novel by Ira Levin?

9 Which city on the shore of Lake Erie is home to the Rock'n'Roll Hall of Fame?

10 Along with Eisenhower, which other US President has the longest surname?

ROUND 4 — UP AND DOWN

1 What is the name of Fred and Wilma Flintstone's daughter?

2 What was Take That's first UK Number 1 single of the 2000s?

3 Which word first appeared on the Waldseemüller world map in 1507?

4 Which priceless artefacts were discovered in the Qumran Caves in the 1940s and 1950s?

5 What name connects bridges in Oxford, Cambridge and Venice?

6 In Sweden and other parts of Europe, which textile is commonly known as "Manchester"?

7 What is the official national working language of Ethiopia?

8 In the USA, what kind of agency was founded in 1850 by Allan Pinkerton?

9 What does the letter A stand for in the name of BASE jumping?

10 Manchester University's 1975 'University Challenge' team famously answered questions by giving the names of ... who?

ROUND 3 — FOLLOW ON
1 T
2 No (Dr No)
3 Ham
4 Ohio
5 Onion (Glass Onion, Know Your Onion, The Onion Song)
6 Hanson
7 Sick Boy
8 Stepford
9 Cleveland
10 Washington (George Washington)

ROUND 4 — UP AND DOWN
1 Pebbles
2 Patience
3 America
4 Dead Sea Scrolls
5 Bridge of Sighs
6 Corduroy
7 Amharic
8 Detective agency
9 Antenna
10 Famous Marxists

ROUND 1 — CHAIN

1 What semi-hard European cheese was the most popular in the world for many centuries, due to its qualities of travelling and ageing well?

2 Which six piece band, which combined two other bands, had members including James Bourne, Tom Fletcher, Matt Willis and Harry Judd?

3 What common flower is also known as the cankerwort, blowball, Irish daisy, wet-a-bed and lion's tooth?

4 What word links the literary character Mr Pooter with the name Odysseus gives when the Cyclops asks him his name?

5 Which French fashion designer who died in 2008 was played in a 2014 film by the actor Gaspard Ulliel?

6 The films 'Hannah and her Sisters', 'The Ice Storm' and 'Planes, Trains and Automobiles' are all set around which celebration in the USA?

7 According to the Trojan priest Laocoön in 'The Aeneid', who should you beware of when they are bearing gifts?

8 What country, with its capital Ljubljana, became independent in January 1992, joined the EU in 2004 and started using the Euro in 2007?

9 What film contains the following line: "You know, my mother never had time for me. When you're the middle child in a family of 5 million, you don't get any attention."?

10 What is the name of the Belgian port which was the site of a ferry disaster on 6th March 1987?

ROUND 2 — MISSING LINK

1 What Morse code distress signal would you send out with three dots, three dashes, three dots?

2 What extremely useful item has a name derived from the Latin for "little shade"?

3 In physics, which W is defined as the product of force and displacement?

4 In 'The Deer Hunter', which frightening game are Nick and Steven forced to play when imprisoned in Vietnam?

5 What are the 19th & 13th letters of the English alphabet?

6 What three-word phrase links the title of a Madonna single with a phrase used by football commentator Andy Gray after a spectacular piece of play?

7 Cecil Rhodes founded the company De Beers in 1888 to specialise in mining ... what?

8 Which Jamaican slang term for a rebellious youth gave its name to a 1980 film about a roadie for The Clash?

9 Which 2007 thriller stars Shia LaBeouf as a teenager spying on his neighbours in suburban America?

10 What is the missing link?

ROUND 1 — CHAIN
1 Edam
2 McBusted (combining McFly and Busted)
3 Dandelion
4 Nobody
5 Yves Saint Laurent
6 Thanksgiving
7 Greeks
8 Slovenia
9 Antz
10 Zeebrugge (the capsizing of the Herald of Free Enterprise)

ROUND 2 — MISSING LINK
1 SOS
2 Umbrella
3 Work
4 Russian Roulette
5 S & M
6 Take a Bow (Gray used to say "Take a bow, son")
7 Diamonds
8 Rude Boy
9 Disturbia
10 The titles of Rihanna songs

ROUND 3 — MYSTERY YEAR

1 Prince Charles (as he was then) almost died on 10 March of the mystery year after being caught in an avalanche near which Swiss ski resort, favoured by the Royal Family?

2 Graeme Hick made history on 6th May of the mystery year when he scored 405 not out in a county cricket match. Which county was he playing for?

3 On 12 April of the mystery year which 60s singer was elected Mayor of Palm Springs, California?

4 Which actor, born on 10 April of the mystery year, played David in 'Artificial Intelligence' and Cole Sear in 'The Sixth Sense'?

5 Robin Beck's 'First Time', a UK Number 1 in the mystery year, was originally recorded for an advert for which company?

6 In the US presidential election in the mystery year, Lloyd Bentsen was the running mate of which losing Democrat?

7 35 people died on 12th December of the mystery year when two packed commuter trains collided outside which busy south London train station?

8 On 16 March of the mystery year, Iraqi forces carried out a poison gas attack on which Kurdish town 150 miles north-east of Baghdad?

9 The mystery year saw all four Men's Singles Grand Slam titles won by Swedish tennis players. Stefan Edberg won at Wimbledon, but which player won the other three?

10 What is the mystery year?

ROUND 4 — UP AND DOWN

1 A railway bridge over which Scottish waterway was made a UNESCO World Heritage Site in 2015?

2 In Greek mythology, Morpheus is the god of ... what?

3 Stonehenge and Dover Castle (and many other important sites) are looked after by which organisation?

4 Which word was both the title of a Wham! hit and, with the number 90 added to it, a hit for George Michael as a solo artist?

5 What, in Athens, was an "ostrakon", from which we get the word ostracism?

6 How is the section of the A39 between Barnstaple in Devon and Fraddon in Cornwall known?

7 At the 1998 Brit Awards, John Prescott had a bucket of water thrown over him by a member of which band?

8 Otto Rohwedder invented which innovative product, which some say has rarely been bettered?

9 'Cradle to Grave' was a 2015 comedy drama based on the childhood of which DJ and presenter?

10 What is the area, flooded about 8000 years ago, that linked Britain by land to Europe?

ROUND 3 — MYSTERY YEAR
1 Klosters
2 Worcestershire (against Somerset)
3 Sonny Bono (accept: Sonny)
4 Haley Joel Osment
5 Coca-Cola
6 Michael Dukakis
7 Clapham Junction
8 Halabja
9 Mats Wilander
10 1988

ROUND 4 — UP AND DOWN
1 Firth of Forth
2 Dreams
3 English Heritage
4 Freedom
5 A pot fragment
6 Atlantic Highway
7 Chumbawamba
8 Bread-slicing machine
9 Danny Baker
10 Doggerland

ROUND 1 — ALPHABET

1 What K is a game using marbles and straw first marketed by the Ideal Toy Company in 1967?

2 What S is a seven-letter word, most prominently used in recent times, for a beer that is not too strong and not too distinctly flavoured, and therefore easy to drink over the course of an evening?

3 What M is the most famous voice provided by Julie Kavner?

4 What C is the Cumbria town which was the birthplace of William Wordsworth?

5 What A is the country whose capital is Algiers?

6 Which T is the name of an animal in the title of an influential novel by Henry Williamson?

7 What W was the person beheaded at Whitehall on 29th October 1618?

8 Which P is a ligament or tendon in the neck that helps sheep or cattle hold their head up, and is referenced in a classic children's nursery rhyme?

9 What L is a small French town near the Pyrenees which, because of an event in 1858, receives as many as 5,000,000 visitors every year?

10 Which J is a singer who drowned in the Wolf River, Memphis in May 1997?

ROUND 2 — CULTURE CLASH

1 In which fictional village is 'The Archers' set?

2 Which actress who appeared on 'Celebrity Big Brother' played Karla Fry in 'Beverly Hills Cop 2'?

3 Who is the Shakespearean title character betrayed by his close confidant Iago?

4 By what nickname was Corporal Walter O'Reilly known in the film and TV series 'M*A*S*H'?

5 Stanley Kubrick's film 'The Shining' was based on a book by which author?

6 Which DJ, born in 1946, was famous for presenting 'Our Tune' on Radio 1?

7 Frank Lloyd Wright and Charles Rennie Mackintosh built up great reputations in which field?

8 The finale of the William Tell overture by Rossini was used as the theme tune to which popular TV and radio cowboy show in the 20th century?

9 Who succeeded Ted Hughes as the British Poet Laureate in 1999?

10 What surname links the murderer of the playwright Joe Orton, the maiden name of Alma Baldwin in 'Coronation Street', a British film historian, and the maiden name of the Spice Girl who had the most UK solo Number 1s?

ROUND 1 — ALPHABET
1 KerPlunk
2 Session
3 Marge Simpson
4 Cockermouth
5 Algeria
6 Tarka (of "the Otter" fame)
7 Walter Raleigh
8 Paddywhack (... knick-knack paddywhack, Give the dog a bone, This old man came rolling home.)
9 Lourdes
10 Jeff Buckley

ROUND 2 — CULTURE CLASH
1 Ambridge
2 Brigitte Nielsen
3 Othello
4 Radar
5 Stephen King
6 Simon Bates
7 Architecture
8 The Lone Ranger
9 Andrew Motion
10 Halliwell (Kenneth, Alma, Leslie, Geri)

ROUND 3 — 54321

1 Name any five of the seven top wine producing countries (so not exports, but wine produced in total in that country).

2 Identify the movies from the synopses given: a) Hugh Grant plays a tongue-tied posh Englishman who falls for an American at a series of social functions b) Hugh Grant plays a tongue-tied posh Englishman who falls for a Londoner whilst trying to run the country c) Hugh Grant plays a tongue-tied posh Englishman who falls for a Welsh girl whilst trying to complete a geographical survey d) Hugh Grant plays a devious and smooth-talking posh Englishman who frames a lovable bear for a crime he didn't commit.

3 Answer the clues using the letters to help you: e.g. JCS: came down from Heaven in a motorcar = Jesus Christ Superstar. a) AITI: hurl abuse at a wounded person b) JD: Lucky biscuit c) LOTSW: no more plonk until next June

4 Tree-high or Knee-high: are the following grown on trees up high or on shrubs/bushes/in the ground lower down? a) Kiwi fruit b) Cabbage

5 Put these three London buildings in order of height, starting from the highest a) The Gherkin (St Mary Axe) b) 1 Canada Square (Canary Wharf) c) 60 Cleveland Street (BT Tower).

ROUND 4 — DOUBLE TROUBLE

1 Arthur Wellesley was the first Duke of ... where?

2 What was the first name of the First Lady of the USA from 2009 to 2017?

3 A letter in which someone informs their partner they've found a new lover is traditionally called a "Dear ..." what?

4 What was the surname of the first man, along with Tenzing Norgay, to climb Mount Everest?

5 Which surname links the snooker player known as "The Sheriff of Pottingham" and the broadcaster known as "Diddy"?

6 In Australian cricket, which girl's name is a slang term for when a bowler takes five wickets?

7 What is the fourth Cardinal Virtue along with Justice, Fortitude and Temperance?

8 What is the surname of the main character, a butler, in Kazuo Ishiguro's 'The Remains of the Day'?

9 Tim Minchin wrote the music and lyrics for which 2010 musical, based on a popular book?

10 In The Wombles band, which of the Wombles played lead guitar?

11 In the title of a famous Australian song, what is the slang term for a bag of swag?

12 What place name links one of the largest cities in New Zealand, one of the largest cities in Canada, and one of the largest towns in Scotland?

13 Which English monarch had the nickname Lackland?

14 England had two players in their 1986 men's FIFA World Cup squad who both had the same first name, Gary - and which surname?

15 What is the first name of actress Mia Farrow's sister, about whom John Lennon wrote a famous song?

ROUND 3 — 54321

1 Italy, France, Spain, USA, Australia, Argentina, China

2 a) Four Weddings And A Funeral b) Love Actually c) The Englishman Who Went Up A Hill But Came Down A Mountain d) Paddington 2

3 a) Add Insult to Injury b) Jammy Dodger c) Last of the Summer Wine

4 a) Trees (on vines) b) Knee high (from plants)

5 b, c, a (Canary Wharf at 235m; BT Tower at 191m; The Gherkin at 180m)

ROUND 4 — DOUBLE TROUBLE

1 Wellington
2 Michelle
3 John
4 Hillary (Sir Edmund Hillary)
5 Hamilton (Anthony Hamilton, David Hamilton)
6 Michelle ("Five-for" as in "Michelle Pfeiffer")
7 Prudence
8 Stevens
9 Matilda (book by Roald Dahl)
10 Wellington
11 Matilda (in 'Waltzing Matilda')
12 Hamilton
13 John
14 Stevens
15 Prudence (Dear Prudence)

ROUND 1 — CHAIN

1 A Hindi word for "rule", how is the period in India between 1858 and 1947 commonly known? [do not include the word "The"]

2 In a 2002 single, despite the superficial trappings of fame (e.g. rocks), the artist commonly known as J-Lo was keen to point out that she was still ... who?

3 What flightless bird lays the largest egg compared to its body size of any species of bird in the world?

4 What is the third most populous country in Asia?

5 Who, in the famous novel, is the oldest of the Three Musketeers, and shares his name with a mountain and peninsula in Greece?

6 What is a 26 minute song suite of nine parts, split on record into two sections, which was written by three members of a British band as a tribute to a former band member?

7 Fittingly, the most famous song written by a man called Walter Kent was about avian activity above a famous coastal feature of which town?

8 What links a US state capital, an English naval hero and a famous bicycle company?

9 What is the name of Japan's second largest island, on which the largest city is Sapporo?

10 For which film, starring amongst others his nephew Oliver, did Carol Reed win the Oscar for Best Director?

ROUND 2 — MISSING LINK

1 The two basic ingredients of a screwdriver cocktail are vodka and ... what?

2 Which river, specifically, begins at Lake Tana in Ethiopia and flows to the city of Khartoum before converging with another river?

3 What was the name of New York's John F Kennedy Airport until 1963?

4 What first name links the rapper Scott and the drummer Barker?

5 What is the name of creatures in the 1984 film 'Gremlins' whose name means "evil spirit" in Cantonese?

6 What was the name of the first book published by psychotherapist Arthur Janov in 1970?

7 Which American state is second largest by both size and population?

8 According to the New Testament, in which town (now a city within Israel) did Jesus spend his childhood?

9 Which Archduke of Austria was assassinated on 28 June 1914?

10 What is the missing link?

ROUND 1 — CHAIN
1 Raj
2 Jenny from the Block
3 Kiwi
4 Indonesia (after China and India)
5 Athos
6 Shine On You Crazy Diamond (by Pink Floyd)
7 Dover ((There'll Be Bluebirds Over) The White Cliffs of Dover)
8 Raleigh
9 Hokkaido
10 Oliver! (Oliver Reed, who played Bill Sykes, was Carol Reed's nephew)

ROUND 2 — MISSING LINK
1 Orange juice
2 The Blue Nile
3 Idlewild
4 Travis
5 Mogwai
6 The Primal Scream
7 Texas
8 Nazareth
9 Franz Ferdinand
10 Scottish bands

ROUND 3 — MYSTERY YEAR

1 Broadcast on 11 February of the mystery year, in an episode of which series did a character book the performer Cowboy George, only to get Boy George and his band Culture Club instead?

2 January 24 of the mystery year saw the death of the science fiction writer L. Ron Hubbard. Which religion, very popular with celebrities, did he found in the 1950s?

3 The SS United States held the record for fastest crossing of the Atlantic until 29 June of the mystery year, when its record was beaten by which British businessman?

4 Which band's third album 'The Queen is Dead' was released in June of the mystery year?

5 Which Leicester-born English striker was the top scorer at the men's FIFA World Cup in the mystery year, with six goals?

6 The mystery year saw a major fire in the King's Apartments at which royal palace located on the Thames about 12 kilometres south-west of central London?

7 Which actor was voted Mayor of the Californian town of Carmel in April of the mystery year?

8 Dick Scobee and Christa McAuliffe were among those to die when which space shuttle crashed on 28 January of the mystery year?

9 In December of the mystery year it was announced by the government that what were being phased out of Britain's coal mines in favour of electronic detectors?

10 What is the mystery year?

ROUND 4 — UP AND DOWN

1 Which is higher - A) the record for most skips over a rope in 24 hours by one person or B) the number of shots in the longest ever tennis rally?

2 In the TV show 'Pop Idol: the Rivals', the winning girl group was named 'Girls Aloud'. What name was given to the short-lived winning boy band?

3 In a British General Election, a candidate receives their £500 deposit back if they manage to gain at least what percentage of the vote?

4 Which offshore radio station was founded by Ronan O'Rahilly in 1964?

5 The Bangor Broken Broomsticks and Holyrood Hippogriffs are among the teams associated with which originally fictional sport?

6 The title of a famous book by Lynne Truss is 'Eats, Shoots and Leaves: The Zero Tolerance Approach to ...' what?

7 In darts, the name of which Chinese city can describe hitting a single, double and triple of the same number?

8 At the 2015 General Election, Mhairi Black became the youngest member of the House of Commons - what party did she represent?

9 Which story in the book of Genesis explains the origin of different languages?

10 Tom Blower was, in 1947, the first person to successfully swim between which two countries of the UK?

ROUND 3 — MYSTERY YEAR
1 The A-Team
2 Church of Scientology
3 Richard Branson (in Virgin Atlantic Challenger)
4 The Smiths
5 Gary Lineker
6 Hampton Court Palace
7 Clint Eastwood
8 Challenger
9 Canaries (formerly used to detect the escape of any poisonous gases)
10 1986

ROUND 4 — UP AND DOWN
1 A) 168,394 skips (vs 51,283 shots)
2 One True Voice
3 5%
4 Radio Caroline
5 Quidditch (aka Quadball)
6 Punctuation
7 Shanghai
8 SNP (Scottish National Party)
9 Tower of Babel
10 Scotland & Northern Ireland

ROUND 1 — CHAIN

1 The westernmost point of Africa is in which country?

2 Which 1955 Disney film (remade in 2019) was based on a magazine article called 'Happy Dan, The Cynical Dog'?

3 Which magical artefact in 'The Lord of the Rings' is also the name of a big data analytics company co-founded by Peter Thiel?

4 Who served as leader of the Scottish Conservative party from 2011 to 2019?

5 What can be a bird in the Corvid family, a culinary tool and the title character in a ballet by Piotr Tchaikovsky from 1892?

6 Wild Blue Yonder, Old Gay Hill Red China and American Beauty are cultivars of which flower?

7 Which animal, in the monotreme order, is also sometimes known as the spiny anteater?

8 From the Latin for "sustenance", which word is commonly used in the USA for financial support after a marital celebration?

9 Which chain of restaurants, renowned for its conveyor belts, was founded by Simon Woodroffe in 1997?

10 Which state of the USA is known as the 'Land of Lincoln'?

ROUND 2 — CULTURE CLASH

1 The video for which Coldplay song features Chris Martin walking in slow motion at Studland Bay?

2 Which author's books include 'The Bell', 'Under the Net' and 'The Severed Head'?

3 E.H. Shepard is known for illustrating 'Winnie-the-Pooh', as well as which famous children's book by Kenneth Grahame?

4 In the French version of Disney's 'Snow White and the Seven Dwarfs', which of the dwarfs is called Atchoum?

5 The acclaimed 2015 film 'Carol' was based on which novel by Patricia Highsmith?

6 Which dance act, whose members would go on to form the rock band Doves, had a 1993 hit with 'Ain't No Love (Ain't No Use)'?

7 What is both the name of an alien race in 'Doctor Who' and also the name of the mother of Caliban in Shakespeare's 'The Tempest'?

8 Who was the only member of the Monty Python team not to attend Oxford or Cambridge University?

9 What is the first word of the Oasis hit 'Wonderwall'?

10 What name links a Top 10 UK hit single for The Proclaimers and a radio show that ran from 1946 to 2004?

ROUND 1 — CHAIN
1 Senegal
2 Lady and the Tramp
3 Palantir
4 Ruth Davidson
5 Nutcracker
6 Rose
7 Echidna
8 Alimony
9 YO! Sushi
10 Illinois

ROUND 2 — CULTURE CLASH
1 Yellow
2 Iris Murdoch
3 The Wind in the Willows
4 Sneezy
5 The Price of Salt
6 Sub Sub
7 Sycorax
8 Terry Gilliam
9 Today
10 Letter from America

ROUND 3 — FOLLOW ON

1 If f means "play loudly" on a musical score, what letter means "play quietly"?

2 What is the chemical formula for carbon monoxide, as well as being the postcode for a large area of Essex?

3 What began at midnight on 1st August 1981 with the Buggles' 'Video Killed The Radio Star'?

4 What is the name of a 2011 first-person shooter as well as the name of the virus in the film '28 Days Later'?

5 Complete the name of the Cambridge college; Gonville and ... what?

6 What kind of mustelid is Trufflehunter in 'Prince Caspian' and Tommy Brock in Beatrix Potter's 'The Tale of Mr Tod'?

7 In January 2002, what snack almost proved too difficult for George W Bush to handle?

8 Which root, long associated with magical rituals, is also the name of one of the 'Defenders of the Earth' in the 80s TV cartoon?

9 Maxi Jazz and Sister Bliss were members of which successful British dance band?

10 Which goalkeeper, known as the "Hero of Munich" died in February 2020 aged 87?

ROUND 4 — UP AND DOWN

1 Which cover of an Otis Redding song was, in 1967, Aretha Franklin's first UK Top 10 single?

2 The title of ex-Prime Minister David Cameron's autobiography is 'For the ...' what?

3 For how many games was Sam Allardyce manager of the England men's national football team?

4 After London Heathrow, which UK airport has the most terminals?

5 What is the English meaning of the word "Bolsheviks"?

6 In Greek mythology, which Trojan hero was the oldest son of Priam and husband of Andromache?

7 Which word meaning "of poor quality" was popularised by George Harrison in the film 'A Hard Day's Night'?

8 Who made a huge rotating wheel for the World's Columbian Exposition of 1893?

9 Which kind of animal is Fenton, the star of a viral video from 2011?

10 In a 1984 film, which physical activity has been banned in the small American town of Bomont?

ROUND 3 — FOLLOW ON
1 p (standing for "piano")
2 CO (for Colchester)
3 MTV
4 Rage
5 Caius (it is pronounced "Keys")
6 Badger
7 Pretzel
8 Mandrake
9 Faithless
10 Harry Gregg

ROUND 4 — UP AND DOWN
1 Respect
2 Record
3 One
4 Manchester
5 Majority
6 Hector
7 Grotty
8 George Ferris
9 Dog (black labrador)
10 Dancing (in 'Footloose')

ROUND 1 — ALPHABET

1 In a 1980s cartoon about the character Dogtanian, what M, specifically, were Porthos, Athos and Aramis?

2 What T is a short and repetitively named British band whose main member is Matt Johnson?

3 Which B was, in July 2019, a somewhat surprising nominee for New Zealander of the Year?

4 Which C is a city in Tennessee brought to international fame by a 1941 Glenn Miller song inspired by a train ride?

5 Born Ashley Charles, what D is the South London DJ who presented 'Sounds Like Friday Night' with Greg James?

6 Which G is the director whose first two feature films, from 2017 and 2019, were nominated for the Best Picture Oscar?

7 What J is the term for nationalism coined by the British radical George Holyoake in 1878, taken from a minced oath used in a patriotic song of the time?

8 What R is the film in which Ewan McGregor played the notorious Barings Bank employee Nick Leeson?

9 From the Italian words for "play on the harp", what A is a term given to a chord broken into a sequence of notes?

10 What P was the eight-letter name given to a scandal involving the Conservative minister Andrew Mitchell?

ROUND 2 — FOLLOW ON

1 Which of the Roman numerals comes first in alphabetical order?

2 In French, which word can mean "Yes" but also "If"?

3 Which measure of thermal insulation is used in rating duvets?

4 Which Netflix comedy-drama was a fictionalised account of the 'Gorgeous Ladies of Wrestling' professional wrestling circuit?

5 Which word links a type of dhal in Punjabi cuisine and the title otter in a novel by Henry Williamson?

6 What is the name of 2020's so-called "Covid comedy" starring David Tennant and Michael Sheen as fictionalised versions of themselves?

7 Which white wine grape, commonly grown in England, takes its name from the Roman god of wine?

8 Who was the drummer with The White Stripes?

9 Who became the Prime Minister of Pakistan in 2018?

10 Mintonette was the name of an early version of which team ball sport?

ROUND 1 — ALPHABET
1 Muskehounds
2 The The
3 Ben Stokes (his father was from New Zealand)
4 Chattanooga (as in 'Chattanooga Choo Choo')
5 Dotty
6 Greta Gerwig ('Lady Bird' and 'Little Women')
7 Jingoism
8 Rogue Trader
9 Arpeggio
10 Plebgate

ROUND 2 — FOLLOW ON
1 C
2 Si
3 Tog
4 GLOW
5 Tarka (Tarka dhal and 'Tarka the Otter')
6 Staged
7 Bacchus
8 Meg White
9 Imran Khan
10 Volleyball

ROUND 3 — MYSTERY YEAR

1 Which German car manufacturer purchased Rover from British Aerospace in the mystery year?

2 Which former US First Lady died in May of the mystery year, aged 64?

3 What was the name of the American skater clubbed on her knee by an assailant in the run-up to the Winter Olympics in the mystery year?

4 A man called Marmaduke Wetherell was involved in the faking of a photograph which was shown to be a hoax in March of the mystery year, which had previously been held up as proof of which creature?

5 Which Welsh rock band released the album 'The Holy Bible' in August of the mystery year?

6 Which painting by Edvard Munch was stolen, in Oslo, in February of the mystery year, though it was recovered in May?

7 What is the name of the restaurant in Islington at which Tony Blair and Gordon Brown allegedly met for a meal in the mystery year during which, it has been claimed, they made a deal about who would lead the Labour Party?

8 What was the title of the debut single by Whigfield which replaced Wet Wet Wet's 'Love is All Around' at Number 1 in the UK singles charts in September of the mystery year?

9 At which Grand Prix did both Roland Ratzenberger and Ayrton Senna die in the mystery year?

10 What is the mystery year?

ROUND 4 — UP AND DOWN

1 In the USA, what age must a person be in order to be a senator?

2 What nickname was given to the suspected serial killer Albert DeSalvo?

3 From 1972 until 2008, Robert Robinson was the regular host of which long-running Radio 4 quiz?

4 One of the most sacred sites in Islam, the Kaaba has a name that is the Arabic word for which shape?

5 What was the first Oasis UK Number 1 single to feature Noel Gallagher on lead vocal?

6 The Great Aletsch is the largest example of what in the Alps?

7 In the King James version, what is the most common letter for a book of the Bible to begin with?

8 What was the name of the enquiry into the British press which took place in 2011 and 2012?

9 A grotesque imp, carved into the wall of the cathedral, has become a popular mascot in which English city?

10 The first road built to a motorway standard in the UK was a bypass of which town (now a city)?

ROUND 3 — MYSTERY YEAR
1 BMW
2 Jacqueline Bouvier Kennedy Onassis
3 Nancy Kerrigan
4 The Loch Ness monster
5 Manic Street Preachers
6 The Scream
7 Granita
8 Saturday Night
9 San Marino Grand Prix
10 1994

ROUND 4 — UP AND DOWN
1 30
2 Boston Strangler
3 Brain of Britain
4 Cube
5 Don't Look Back in Anger
6 Glacier
7 J
8 Leveson Enquiry
9 Lincoln
10 Preston

ROUND 1 — CHAIN

1 What was the title of Britney Spears' second album, and the lead single from it?

2 Which American state has land borders with the Canadian provinces of both Quebec and Ontario?

3 Which singer, who's had more than fifteen UK Top 40 singles, wore the "Daisy" costume in the first British series of 'The Masked Singer'?

4 Which American underwear manufacturer was founded in 2000 by Sara Blakely?

5 What phrase, associated with pirates, is the title of a 1942 film, a former Radio 4 panel show, and a track on Coldplay's 2015 album 'A Head Full of Dreams'?

6 From the French for allocating, what name is given to the system of sorting patients according to their need for care?

7 Which French artist, famous for his portraits of ballerinas, was born in 1834 and died in 1917?

8 Whose congratulations prompted Sadiq Khan to joke, on becoming Mayor of London; "You wait ages for a Pakistani bus driver's son to come along, then two come along at once"?

9 Which country in Africa has exactly the same name, in English, as its capital city?

10 In Greek mythology, which daughter of Inachus was turned into a cow by Zeus?

ROUND 2 — CULTURE CLASH

1 As featured in the movie '300', Leonidas was a King of which Ancient Greek city-state?

2 Who wrote the theme music for 'Last of the Summer Wine', 'To the Manor Born' and 'Blankety Blank', among many others?

3 Which French artist is portrayed by John Leguizamo in the film 'Moulin Rouge!'?

4 Max Detweiler and Baroness Schrader are supporting characters in which musical?

5 In Greek mythology, who are Clotho, Lachesis and Atropos?

6 Which of the words in Queen's 'Bohemian Rhapsody' refers to a traditional Italian clown character?

7 Which maverick artist created 'Mr. Natural' and 'Fritz the Cat'?

8 The sister of which English Pre-Raphaelite artist wrote the words to the Christmas carol 'In the Bleak Midwinter'?

9 What was the name of the character played by Halle Berry in 'The Flintstones' movie?

10 Alan Sillitoe's first novel, made into a film starring Albert Finney, had what title?

ROUND 1 — CHAIN
1 Oops!... I Did It Again
2 New York
3 Kelis (not Katherine Jenkins, who was Octopus)
4 Spanx
5 X Marks the Spot
6 Triage
7 Edgar Degas
8 Sajid Javid
9 Djibouti
10 Io

ROUND 2 — CULTURE CLASH
1 Sparta
2 Ronnie Hazlehurst
3 Henri de Toulouse-Lautrec
4 The Sound of Music
5 The Fates
6 Scaramouche
7 Robert Crumb
8 Dante Gabriel Rossetti (his sister was Christina Rossetti)
9 Sharon Stone
10 Saturday Night and Sunday Morning

ROUND 3 — FOLLOW ON

1 What letter is used for the basic reproduction number of an infection and, in the USA, a rating which means someone under 17 needs to be accompanied by an adult to see a film?

2 What surname links the Israeli author Amos, the Turkish-American physician Mehmet, and the film director and puppeteer Frank?

3 What name did Blackadder's wannabe female servant call herself as she pretended to be a man?

4 What is the palindromic title of the fashion magazine founded in 1945 by Hélène Gordon-Lazareff and her husband, Pierre?

5 What is the title of a 1994 single by The Manic Street Preachers, backwards, and a 2019 album by Taylor Swift, forwards?

6 What fruit is at the centre of the Christmas symbol known as the Christingle?

7 Sean Dyche became manager of which English football club in 2012?

8 Which Greek philosopher was the subject of a number of works by Plato and was given the surname "Johnson" in' Bill and Ted's Excellent Adventure'?

9 On the menu of an Indian restaurant, what specifically would be the name for a leavened, oven-baked flatbread stuffed with mincemeat?

10 Which singer's UK Number 1s include 'Don't Be So Hard on Yourself' and 'I'll Be There'?

ROUND 4 — UP AND DOWN

1 Which of golf's current Major championships was established first, in 1860?

2 Who was UN Secretary-General when Iraq invaded Kuwait in 1990?

3 Which American author and filmmaker wrote the 2001 bestseller 'Stupid White Men'?

4 Which is the only one of the four Gospels in the New Testament that is not classified as synoptic?

5 Stevie Wonder's first UK solo Number 1 also won the Oscar for Best Song. Which song?

6 What name is given to a group of American women's colleges including Mount Holyoke, Vassar and Barnard?

7 11 people died due to a disaster at which British air show in 2015?

8 The registration plates of official state vehicles for which country begin with the letters "SCV"?

9 Which English philosopher's pamphlet titled 'Common Sense' was a large influence on the US Independence movement?

10 Rhythmic gymnasts can be freehand, or use a rope, hoop, ball, clubs or which other piece of apparatus?

ROUND 3 — FOLLOW ON

1 R (R-rate, R-rating)
2 Oz
3 Bob
4 Elle
5 Lover (The Manics single is 'Revol')
6 Orange
7 Burnley
8 Socrates
9 Keema Naan
10 Jess Glynne

ROUND 4 — UP AND DOWN

1 (British) Open Championship
2 Javier Pérez de Cuéllar
3 Michael Moore
4 John (the others are synoptic in that they contain many of the same stories, often in a similar sequence)
5 I Just Called To Say I Love You
6 Seven Sisters
7 Shoreham
8 Vatican City
9 Thomas Paine
10 Ribbon

ROUND 1 — ALPHABET

1 Which M would be the key skill required to succeed in the game of Pelmanism?

2 Which P is the children's character who is the self-proclaimed "strongest girl in the world"?

3 By what S is the Turkish chef and restaurateur Nusret Gökçe better known?

4 In 1993, Rachel Whiteread was the first woman to win which T?

5 Which J is the vegetarian singer who won Series 2 of 'The Masked Singer' in the UK, dressed, ironically, as a sausage?

6 Which H is a ghost town in California, a painting by Hieronymus Bosch and the surname taken by punk frontman Richard Meyers?

7 What B is the English name of what is called Aranciata Rossa in Italy?

8 What A is the annexation of Austria into Nazi Germany on 12 March 1938?

9 What Y is a word that links the likes of Baba Hari Dass to a legend of baseball and one of the most beloved characters of William Hanna and Joseph Barbera?

10 Which Z were added to the title and plot of 'Pride and Prejudice' in a 2009 reworking of Jane Austen's novel by Seth Grahame-Smith?

ROUND 2 — FOLLOW ON

1 What is the long bone in the forearm that runs parallel to the radius?

2 Guy Garvey is the lead singer of which English rock band?

3 There is a Tate gallery in which Cornish town?

4 What mythological name is given to crossings in the UK where special consideration is given to horses and their riders?

5 Meaning "sea to lake", what is the name of Donald Trump's Florida resort?

6 Which quiz show, first broadcast in August 2009, was originally going to be called 'Obviously'?

7 Which member of the Monty Python team died in January 2020?

8 Which beloved character was first seen in the 1928 short animated film 'Steamboat Willie'?

9 "Five years have passed" begins a poem by William Wordsworth called 'Lines Written a Few Miles Above ...' which site in Monmouthshire?

10 Who lost four Wimbledon singles finals, though only one of those was to someone who was not a family member?

ROUND 1 — ALPHABET
1 Memory
2 Pippi Longstocking
3 Salt Bae
4 Turner Prize
5 Joss Stone
6 Hell
7 Blood orange
8 Anschluss
9 Yogi
10 Zombies

ROUND 2 — FOLLOW ON
1 Ulna
2 Elbow
3 St Ives
4 Pegasus
5 Mar-a-Lago
6 Pointless
7 Terry Jones
8 Mickey Mouse
9 Tintern Abbey
10 Venus Williams (three times to sister Serena, once to Garbine Muguruza. She also won five times)

ROUND 3 — MYSTERY YEAR

1 What is the name of the BBC radio station, launched in March of the mystery year, whose DJs have included Guy Garvey, Iggy Pop and Lauren Laverne?

2 Which former mayor of New York was given an honorary knighthood by the Queen on February 13th of the mystery year?

3 Lisa "Left-Eye" Lopes, who was killed in a car crash in the mystery year, was, along with T-Boz and Chilli, a member of which girl group?

4 In the mystery year, what was replaced as the official cash currency of Spain by the Euro?

5 Which Australian tennis player won his only Wimbledon singles title, defeating David Nalbandian in the final, in the mystery year?

6 Which London-based rock band released their debut album 'Up the Bracket' in October of the mystery year?

7 Which country did England lose 2-1 to in the quarter-finals of the men's FIFA World Cup in the mystery year?

8 Which guitarist played 'God Save the Queen' on the roof of Buckingham Palace to mark the Queen's Golden Jubilee in June of the mystery year?

9 In which British city did the Commonwealth Games take place in the mystery year?

10 What is the mystery year?

ROUND 4 — UP AND DOWN

1 Which political party, which would later change its name, did Nigel Farage found in late 2018?

2 Which flower is the symbol of the Japanese Emperor?

3 In which decade did it become compulsory to take a driving test in the UK?

4 The Karolinska Institute is a medical university in which city?

5 In which year was the famous headline, "It's The Sun Wot Won It" printed?

6 Which early police force was founded by the author of 'Tom Jones', Henry Fielding?

7 Who played Jonathan Fraser in the 2020 miniseries 'The Undoing'?

8 How was the Egyptian footballer Ahmed Hossam Hussein Abdelhamid, who played for teams such as Tottenham Hotspur and Middlesbrough, better known?

9 What name was commonly used for the American Party, a political movement in the mid-19th century USA?

10 A famous letter addressed to Mr Lusk (purportedly sent by the serial killer known as Jack the Ripper) had a heading at the top saying it was from where?

ROUND 3 — MYSTERY YEAR
1 BBC 6 Music
2 Rudolph Giuliani
3 TLC
4 Peseta
5 Lleyton Hewitt
6 The Libertines
7 Brazil
8 Brian May (of Queen)
9 Manchester
10 2002

ROUND 4 — UP AND DOWN
1 Brexit Party (It became Reform UK)
2 Chrysanthemum
3 1930s
4 Stockholm
5 1992
6 Bow Street Runners
7 Hugh Grant
8 Mido
9 Know-Nothing Party
10 From Hell

ROUND 1 — CHAIN

1 What is the word that links the names of professional football teams in Bilbao and Wigan?

2 In the sport of rowing, if someone's stroke either misses the water or goes deeply into the water, they are said to catch a ... what?

3 Joel Fearon, who has run the 100 metres in 9.96 seconds, has an Olympic medal in which sport?

4 Kate and Helen Richardson-Walsh both won gold medals in which sport for Great Britain at the 2016 Olympics?

5 What is the unusual name of the football team based in Bern that has won more than ten Swiss championships?

6 What surname links two England footballers who both have over 100 caps?

7 Which former England cricket captain who died in 2021 stood as the Conservative candidate in Cardiff South East in 1964?

8 Which Brazilian was FIFA men's World Player of the Year in 1999?

9 Which goalkeeper, who was on the losing side in the final, won the Golden Ball for Best Player at the 2002 men's FIFA World Cup?

10 Which female tennis player won one Grand Slam singles title in each of 2018, 2019, 2020 and 2021?

ROUND 2 — MYSTERY YEAR

1 Who succeeded Gerald Ford as President of the USA in January of the mystery year?

2 In November of the mystery year, President Anwar Sadat of Egypt became the first Arab leader officially to visit which country?

3 Which British punk band, whose members included Joe Strummer and Mick Jones, released a self-titled debut album in the mystery year?

4 James Earl Ray, who escaped from a Tennessee prison in June of the mystery year, had been convicted years earlier of whose assassination?

5 In which month of the mystery year did Elvis Presley die in Memphis, Tennessee?

6 Who won the Wimbledon Ladies Singles title in the mystery year, defeating Betty Stöve in the final?

7 Members of which Northern Irish rock band, born in the mystery year, named their debut album after that year?

8 Who played his final game of professional football at the Giants Stadium in October of the mystery year?

9 Who was Queen Elizabeth II's first grandchild, born in the mystery year?

10 What is the mystery year?

ROUND 1 — CHAIN
1 Athletic
2 Crab
3 Bobsleigh (part of four-man crew who won bronze at the 2014 Winter Olympics)
4 Hockey (they'd married in 2013)
5 Young Boys
6 Scott (Alex and Jill. Not Smith or Charlton.)
7 Ted Dexter
8 Rivaldo (not Romario, Ronaldo or Ronaldinho)
9 Oliver Kahn
10 Naomi Osaka

ROUND 2 — MYSTERY YEAR
1 Jimmy Carter
2 Israel
3 The Clash
4 Martin Luther King
5 August (16th)
6 Virginia Wade
7 Ash
8 Pelé (Edson Arantes do Nascimento)
9 Peter Phillips
10 1977

ROUND 3 — FOLLOW ON

1. What controversial poem by Tony Harrison shares its name with the Roman numeral for five?

2. Which song from Stevie Wonder's 'Songs in the Key of Life' was covered by George Michael and Mary J Blige in 1999?

3. What is a Rudyard Kipling novel, an Eminem song and the most common surname in Korea?

4. What was the surname of the German engineer generally regarded as the inventor of the gasoline-powered automobile, who was in partnership with his wife Bertha?

5. Which word links a Rubik's game, a game loaded in early Nokia mobile phones, and the protagonist played by Kurt Russell in 'Escape from New York'?

6. In which country is julmust a popular Christmas drink?

7. What is the English name of the city known as Casnewydd in Welsh?

8. Which type of mythical being can also be known as a lycanthrope?

9. In which country is Europos Parkas, a museum claiming to be situated at the geographical centre of a Europe that includes Western Russia?

10. The comedian Doc Brown is the brother of which writer?

ROUND 4 — UP AND DOWN

1. Which African country's national anthem includes words in five different languages?

2. What is the four-letter abbreviated name of the world governing body for aquatic sports such as swimming and diving?

3. Which Nazi minister flew a solo mission to Scotland in 1941 in an attempt to broker peace with the UK?

4. What derogatory nickname was given to the opponents that heavyweight champion Joe Louis defeated in rapid succession in the late 1930s and early 1940s?

5. The Guru Granth Sahib is the holy scripture of which world religion?

6. At the Brit Awards, which band has won the British Single of the Year award a record five times? [up to 2022]

7. What was the name of the British tanker captured by the Iranian navy in June 2019?

8. A monument claiming to be exactly 200 miles from both London and Edinburgh can be found in a suburb of which city?

9. What is the name of the army officer (with a famous namesake) who is believed to have invented the game of snooker?

10. In Christianity, what is the name of the highest order of angels? They are described as having six wings.

ROUND 3 — FOLLOW ON

1. V
2. As
3. Kim
4. Benz
5. Snake (Kurt Russell is Snake Plissken)
6. Sweden
7. Newport
8. Werewolf
9. Lithuania
10. Zadie Smith (his actual name is Ben Bailey-Smith)

ROUND 4 — UP AND DOWN

1. South Africa
2. FINA
3. Rudolf Hess
4. Bum of the Month
5. Sikhism
6. Take That
7. Stena Impero
8. Leeds
9. Neville Chamberlain
10. Seraphim

ROUND 1 — ALPHABET

1 In the tax abbreviation PAYE, what does the E stand for?

2 What B is a word used in the USA for raised, tiered rows of basic seating found at sports arenas?

3 What R is the name by which a Matryoshka is commonly known, as well as being the title of a Netflix series starring Natasha Lyonne?

4 In 'ThunderCats', which M is the main antagonist, an undead sorcerer who calls on the "ancient spirits of evil"?

5 What J is the American author, twice a Pulitzer Prize winner, whose best known works were 'The Witches of Eastwick' and the four-part 'Rabbit' series of novels?

6 What F describes one of the characters in a UK children's show first broadcast in 1977, as well as a marshmallow sweet with the appearance of a twisted helix?

7 Which E was the BBC Sports Personality of the Year in 2021?

8 Which C is the American author who won the 2016 Pulitzer Prize for 'The Underground Railroad'?

9 Which K plays Mare Sheehan in the hit 2021 TV show 'Mare of Easttown'?

10 Tim Paine was forced to resign as which A's test cricket captain in late 2021?

ROUND 2 — FOLLOW ON

1 Which word links a type of apple to the person who steers the boat in the sport of rowing?

2 Which American brand of SUV, founded in 1943, has become, in lowercase, a generic term for an off-road vehicle?

3 Which word goes before d'Abernon, Poges and Mandeville in English place names?

4 Which credit card was described as "Your flexible friend" in a famous advert?

5 What is the largest country in Africa by area but only the ninth largest by population?

6 Which American teen drama starring Zendaya as Rue Bennett shares its name with a song that won Eurovision for Sweden in 2012?

7 Which Irish cyclist-turned-commentator won the Tour de France points classification four times in the 1980s?

8 Which group, led by Shannon Hoon, were best known for their 1993 hit 'No Rain'?

9 Derived from its sweet nectar, what is the best known name of the common shrub Lonicera, which is also sometimes known as woodbine?

10 Who was Poet Laureate of the UK from 1972 to his death in 1984?

ROUND 1 — ALPHABET
1 Earn
2 Bleachers
3 Russian Doll
4 Mumm-Ra
5 John Updike
6 Flump
7 Emma Raducanu
8 Colson Whitehead
9 Kate Winslet
10 Australia

ROUND 2 — FOLLOW ON
1 Cox (apple is, in full, Cox's Pippin, rowing term is, in full, coxswain)
2 Jeep
3 Stoke
4 Access
5 Algeria
6 Euphoria
7 Sean Kelly
8 Blind Melon
9 Honeysuckle
10 John Betjeman

ROUND 3 — MYSTERY YEAR

1 Golda Meir resigned as Prime Minister of which country in April of the mystery year?

2 What BBC public information service went live on September 23rd of the mystery year?

3 The Symbionese Liberation Army demanded food aid in exchange for the release of which heiress in February of the mystery year?

4 What prestigious prize was won by the novelist William Golding, author of 'Lord of the Flies' and 'Rites of Passage', in the mystery year?

5 Albert Finney played Hercule Poirot in 'Murder on the Orient Express' in the mystery year, a film based on which author's novel?

6 Which British supermodel was born in Croydon in January of the mystery year?

7 What is the nickname of the fight in which Muhammed Ali regained his world heavyweight title from George Foreman in the mystery year?

8 Who took over from the disgraced US President Richard Nixon in August of the mystery year?

9 The Netherlands lost their first men's FIFA World Cup Final to which country in the mystery year?

10 What is the mystery year?

ROUND 4 — UP AND DOWN

1 Who is the eldest member of the original five-man Take That line-up?

2 Which P is a word often used in the US to refer to tartan?

3 In the Bible, who is the elder son of Isaac who exchanges his birthright for a bowl of stew?

4 In darts, what score with three darts is nicknamed "bed and breakfast"?

5 What, particularly in the USA, is a term used for an indefinite academic appointment awarded to a member of staff after a period of employment?

6 The largest barrier reef system in the Northern Hemisphere is mainly off the coast of which country?

7 In which year did the building One World Trade Center open?

8 What is the nickname of Northampton Town Football Club?

9 In which historic Wales coastal town is the steepest road in the UK?

10 Which former Labour cabinet minister shares his name with one of the leaders of the Peasants' Revolt of 1381?

ROUND 3 — MYSTERY YEAR
1 Israel
2 Ceefax
3 Patty Hearst
4 Joni Mitchell
5 Agatha Christie
6 Kate Moss
7 The Rumble in the Jungle
8 Gerald Ford
9 West Germany (accept Germany)
10 1974

ROUND 4 — UP AND DOWN
1 Howard Donald
2 Plaid
3 Esau
4 26
5 Tenure
6 Belize
7 2014
8 The Cobblers
9 Harlech
10 Jack Straw

ROUND 1 — CHAIN

1 Which word appears in the names of two independent countries and also in four American states?

2 What was the title of the first episode of Season 1 of 'Game of Thrones', which is also the motto of House Stark in the show?

3 Which 2011 David Walliams book was turned into a TV film with Julia McKenzie in the title role?

4 Which Himalayan mammal was classified by Carl Linnaeus in the 17th century as "Bos grunniens" which means "grunting ox"?

5 Which rapper curated the soundtrack to the 2018 film 'Black Panther'?

6 Singer Paul Robeson was the third African-American student at which New Jersey university, where he would be valedictorian?

7 Situated on the border with Mexico, what is the second largest city in California by population?

8 With its origins in Southern Italy and associated with Mafia organisations, what is the name of the code of conduct which emphasises silence and non-cooperation with authorities?

9 Who, in the Bible, is the first person to die?

10 Which aquatic bird, known as the diver in the UK, also follows "Moon the" in the nickname of a rock'n'roll drummer?

ROUND 2 — MYSTERY YEAR

1 Which singer, who was in a group with her brother Richard, died of complications from anorexia nervosa in February of the mystery year?

2 What was the name of the security company who owned the warehouse near Heathrow Airport from which over £25m worth of gold was stolen in November of the mystery year?

3 Who called the Soviet Union "an evil empire" on March 8th of the mystery year?

4 What prestigious prize was won by the novelist William Golding, author of 'Lord of the Flies' and 'Rites of Passage', in the mystery year?

5 The first World Championships in which sport took place in Helsinki in the mystery year?

6 Which band had an unlikely UK Christmas Number 1 in the mystery year with an a cappella rendition of 'Only You'?

7 Which Scottish club defeated Real Madrid in the European Cup Winners' Cup Final in May of the mystery year?

8 Which 'Star Wars' film, the third to be produced, was first screened in the mystery year?

9 Who was the leader of the Labour Party who led the party to only 27.6% of the overall vote in losing the general election in the mystery year?

10 What is the mystery year?

ROUND 1 — CHAIN
1 New
2 Winter is Coming
3 Gangsta Granny
4 Yak
5 Kendrick Lamar
6 Rutgers
7 San Diego (as opposed to San Francisco or Sacramento)
8 Omerta
9 Abel
10 Loon

ROUND 2 — MYSTERY YEAR
1 Karen Carpenter
2 Brinks Mat
3 Ronald Reagan
4 Nobel Prize for Literature
5 Athletics/Track and field
6 The Flying Pickets
7 Aberdeen
8 Return of the Jedi (Star Wars: Episode VI – Return of the Jedi)
9 Michael Foot
10 1983

ROUND 3 — FOLLOW ON

1 What was the title of the Oliver Stone movie which starred Josh Brolin and featured Thandiwe Newton playing Condoleezza Rice?

2 Which Ford car shares its name with the postcode for the Scottish town of Kilmarnock?

3 Representing individual content creators on the World Wide Web, who was Time Magazine Person of the Year in 2006?

4 Which word links a 1979 album by Fleetwood Mac with a former Polish Prime Minister called Donald?

5 What is the name of the main river that runs through Berlin?

6 At the end of the film '(500) Days of Summer', what is the seasonal name of the woman the lead character Tom meets at a job interview?

7 Which element, with atomic number 48, is named after an ancient Greek king?

8 Which British comedian and actor was the man behind the comic character Dennis Pennis?

9 Which character, originally played by Frank Oz, has a pet poodle called Foo-Foo?

10 In 2021, who broke Kelly Smith's record as the highest goalscorer for the England women's football team?

ROUND 4 — UP AND DOWN

1 Which glitzy US city is served by McCarran International Airport?

2 Which singer had the best selling album in the UK in both 2001 and 2003?

3 In which borough is London's second largest Royal Park?

4 The largest population of people of Lebanese descent is in which South American country?

5 What film from 2000, directed by Ang Lee, won the Oscar for Best Foreign Language Film?

6 Which word describes the splitting up of a word or phrase into two parts?

7 Splatt is a small village next to another one called Pityme - in which English county?

8 Who is the title character in a John Irving novel turned into a 1982 film starring Robin Williams?

9 In 2018, how long, in hours, was the first scheduled direct flight from Australia to the UK?

10 What was the title of former Home Secretary Alan Johnson's second memoir, in reference to his former employment?

ROUND 3 — FOLLOW ON
1 W
2 Ka
3 You
4 Tusk
5 Spree
6 Autumn
7 Cadmium (named after Cadmos)
8 Paul Kaye
9 Miss Piggy
10 Ellen White

ROUND 4 — UP AND DOWN
1 Las Vegas
2 Dido
3 Richmond upon Thames (Bushy Park. The largest is Richmond Park - also in Richmond upon Thames.)
4 Brazil
5 Crouching Tiger, Hidden Dragon
6 Tmesis
7 Cornwall
8 Garp (The World According to)
9 17 hours
10 Please, Mister Postman

ROUND 1 — CHAIN

1 What English word for a catchy piece of music that stays in a person's head is borrowed from the German word "Ohrwurm"?

2 What is the capital city of Belarus?

3 The Japanese author of bestselling books such as 'The Life-Changing Magic of Tidying Up' is Marie ... who?

4 The name of which famous sonnet by Shelley is the Greek name for the Egyptian pharaoh Ramses II?

5 Whose only Grand Slam singles title was the 1976 women's French Open?

6 What is the first name of Ned Stark's eldest son in 'Game of Thrones'?

7 What was the title of the only UK Top 10 hit for American singer Meredith Brooks?

8 What was the surname of the last President of Czechoslovakia, who was also the first President of the Czech Republic?

9 In the 'Star Wars' series, who had Han Solo won the Millennium Falcon from in a card game?

10 What name is given to the main central part of a church?

ROUND 2 — CULTURE CLASH

1 The Oscar-winning song 'City of Stars' is from which 2016 film?

2 The name of which band, led by Mark King, was a reference to 'The Hitchhiker's Guide to the Galaxy'?

3 Which spooky American TV family lives at 1313 Mockingbird Lane?

4 Which acclaimed album by Wilco, with a title containing three words in the NATO alphabet, was rejected by Time Warner subsidiary Reprise, then released by Nonesuch Records, which was also, ironically, a Time Warner subsidiary?

5 Which song from the musical 'Funny Girl' was Barbra Streisand's first Top 40 hit in the USA?

6 Which artist sold the most singles in total in the UK during the 1980s?

7 With which feature film, set in Northern Ireland, did the video artist Steve McQueen make his debut as a director in 2008?

8 What was the highest charting UK single for the all-female duo Shampoo?

9 Which historical figure, who died in 1880, has been played on film by both Mick Jagger and Heath Ledger?

10 Which song by Travis borrows the chords from the Oasis song 'Wonderwall' as well as containing a reference to that song in its lyrics?

ROUND 1 — CHAIN
1 Earworm
2 Minsk
3 Kondo
4 Ozymandias
5 Sue Barker
6 Robb (Robb Stark, played by Richard Madden)
7 Bitch
8 Havel (Vaclav Havel)
9 Lando Calrissian
10 Nave

ROUND 2 — CULTURE CLASH
1 La La Land
2 Level 42
3 The Munsters
4 Yankee Hotel Foxtrot
5 People
6 Shakin' Stevens
7 Hunger
8 Trouble
9 Ned Kelly
10 Writing to Reach You

ROUND 3 — MYSTERY YEAR

1 Sonny Crockett and Rico Tubbs first appeared on our screens in which TV show in the mystery year?

2 The African republic of Burkina Faso changed its name from what in the mystery year?

3 In which country did Walter Mondale lose the presidential election in the mystery year?

4 With major contributions from Gordon Greenidge and Malcolm Marshall, which test cricket team defeated England 5-0 in the mystery year in what was known as the "Blackwash" series?

5 Following nude pictures of her being printed in 'Penthouse' magazine, Vanessa Williams became the first woman to resign from what role in the mystery year?

6 During the filming of a commercial for which drinks company did Michael Jackson seriously burn his scalp in the mystery year?

7 Which film, starring John Hurt as Winston Smith, was released on 10th October of the mystery year?

8 Which country announced that they would boycott that year's Summer Olympics on May 8th of the mystery year?

9 Who sings the very first line of the Band Aid charity single 'Do They Know It's Christmas Time', released in the mystery year?

10 What is the mystery year?

ROUND 4 — MISSING LINK

1 What colour is Jimi Hendrix's 'Haze' and Prince's 'Rain'?

2 In what situation did the actor Gabriel Spenser, the poet Aleksandr Pushkin and the US politician Alexander Hamilton all die?

3 Which 1994 hit single did Jon Bon Jovi originally write for the film 'Romeo is Bleeding', before withdrawing it after he watched the film and didn't like it?

4 Which word links a punch in boxing with a cricket shot hit off the back foot on the leg side?

5 Which football team won the Bundesliga for the 30th time in 2021?

6 In which year of World War II was the German battleship Bismarck sunk in the Atlantic Ocean?

7 Which English city's cathedral is believed to have been the tallest building in the world from around 1311 to 1548?

8 Which James Bond villain's only four words, across two films, are "Well, here's to us!"?

9 Glienicke Bridge in Berlin has what nickname, due to the Cold War practice of exchanging prisoners on it?

10 What is the missing link?

ROUND 3 — MYSTERY YEAR
1 Miami Vice
2 Upper Volta
3 USA (to Ronald Reagan)
4 West Indies
5 Miss America
6 Pepsi
7 Nineteen Eighty-Four
8 Soviet Union / USSR
9 Paul Young ('It's Christmas Time,...')
10 1984

ROUND 4 — MISSING LINK
1 Purple
2 (In a) duel
3 Always
4 Hook
5 Bayern Munich
6 1941
7 Lincoln
8 Jaws (at the end of 'Moonraker')
9 Bridge of Spies
10 Steven Spielberg films

ROUND 1 — CHAIN

1 The two major producers of which sparkling wine are Codorníu and Freixenet?

2 Grace Jones played Mayday in which James Bond film?

3 From the Latin for "wool oil" what is the name of the wax that comes from sheep which has many uses for humans?

4 Who formed the band Chic with Bernard Edwards, as well as playing guitar on the massive Daft Punk hit 'Get Lucky'?

5 What suffix links the professional women's basketball team from Seattle, the professional ice hockey team from Manchester, and a highly successful rugby league team from Melbourne?

6 Which rude abbreviation referring to Stifler's mother in the 'American Pie' films has entered popular parlance?

7 What was David Bowie's first US Number 1 single (it only reached Number 17 in the UK)?

8 Which England footballer, who made his debut in 2015, was born in Cheltenham but grew up in Portugal?

9 Which Japanese form of alternative healing has a name which roughly means "mysterious atmosphere"?

10 In the Old Testament, who is the second son of Abraham and the father of Jacob and Esau?

ROUND 2 — CULTURE CLASH

1 Which of the five original members of Take That never sang lead vocal on a Number 1 single?

2 Who played Eliza Doolittle in the original Broadway production of 'My Fair Lady'?

3 What did the Channel 4 TV show 'Light Lunch' change its name to, when it changed its time-slot from 12.30pm to 6pm in 1998?

4 Who, in 1994, had a book, a film and a TV show he had created simultaneously at the top of the charts in the US?

5 In musical notation, what does a dot after a note mean?

6 Which genre of popular folk dance originated in the mid-19th century in what is now the Czech Republic/Czechia?

7 What historic town in Kent shares its name with a 2008 film about poker?

8 Who was the first person to win an Oscar for both acting and writing (it was for two different films)?

9 'Hellhound on My Trail' and 'Cross Road Blues' were originally written and recorded by which blues singer?

10 Which chat-based radio show was presented by Ned Sherrin from 1986 to 2006?

ROUND 1 — CHAIN
1 Cava
2 A View to a Kill
3 Lanolin
4 Nile Rodgers
5 Storm
6 MILF
7 Fame
8 Eric Dier
9 Reiki
10 Isaac

ROUND 2 — CULTURE CLASH
1 Jason Orange
2 Julie Andrews
3 Late Lunch
4 Michael Crichton
5 Note length increased by half
6 Polka
7 Deal
8 Emma Thompson (acting for 'Howard's End', Best Adapted Screenplay for 'Sense and Sensibility')
9 Robert Johnson
10 Loose Ends

ROUND 3 — MYSTERY YEAR

1 Which film was released in the UK on 11th June in the mystery year with the tagline: "The Fight for the Future Begins"?

2 On December 31st of the mystery year, who stood down as President of Russia?

3 What is the title of Thomas Harris's sequel to 'Silence of the Lambs', published in June of the mystery year?

4 Which band released the album 'Californication' in the mystery year?

5 Which manager exclaimed "Football, bloody hell" after his side Manchester United defeated Bayern Munich in the final of the mystery year's Champions League?

6 In September of the mystery year, in which country was the first ever episode of 'Big Brother' shown?

7 On which date in the mystery year was there a total eclipse of the sun?

8 What was the occupation of Owen Hart, who fell 90 feet to his death before an event in the mystery year?

9 What was the title of Blur's album released in the mystery year, featuring tracks such as '1992', 'Optigan 1', and 'Tender'?

10 What is the mystery year?

ROUND 4 — MISSING LINK

1 Which town in Colorado has hosted the Winter X Games since 2002?

2 Which district in East London, now part of Tower Hamlets, is the setting for the TV series 'Call the Midwife'?

3 Which farmer, played on film by Alan Bates and later by Matthias Schoenaerts, is the main male protagonist of Thomas Hardy's 'Far from the Madding Crowd'?

4 What name is given to the distinctive China-inspired pattern on ceramics that became popular in Britain around the late 18th century?

5 Which morally suspect character is played by Orson Welles in 'The Third Man'?

6 What was the Star Wars-referencing nickname of Canadian dartist John Part?

7 Which series of role-playing video games developed by Bethesda Softworks has instalments called 'Oblivion' and 'Skyrim'?

8 In which 1999 film does William H Macy play "Quiz Kid" Donnie Smith and Tom Cruise play Frank T.J. Mackey?

9 Who plays Captain James T. Kirk in the 2009 film 'Star Trek'?

10 What is the missing link?

ROUND 3 — MYSTERY YEAR
1 The Matrix
2 Boris Yeltsin
3 Hannibal
4 Red Hot Chili Peppers
5 Alex Ferguson
6 The Netherlands
7 August 11th
8 Wrestler (he was making a "dramatic" entrance into the ring)
9 13 (Thirteen)
10 1999

ROUND 4 — MISSING LINK
1 Aspen
2 Poplar
3 Gabriel Oak
4 Willow pattern
5 Harry Lime
6 Darth Maple
7 The Elder Scrolls
8 Magnolia
9 Chris Pine
10 Trees

SUBJECT ROUNDS

There are 2,000 questions in this chapter, all divided up into rounds according to classic quiz topics. This is a good place to come to create your own quizzes, or to test yourself on a particular higher-level subject.

There are several rounds on all the following:

- Arts
- Business & Finance
- Film
- Food & Drink
- Games
- Geography
- History & Politics
- Music
- People
- Science & Nature
- Sport
- TV

GEOGRAPHY 1

1 In which US state would you find the Grand Canyon?

2 In which Italian city is the Rialto Bridge?

3 What is the area which comprises Norfolk, Suffolk and Cambridgeshire called?

4 Which is the smallest and shallowest of the world's five oceans?

5 Which language can be written in Roman letters using a transcription system known as Pinyin?

6 Which is the only country in the world that contains only one vowel in its name and does not also contain the letter Y?

7 In which British county is Keele University?

8 St Peter Port is the only town on which of the Channel Islands?

9 Which Asian country has the only national flag in the world with more than four sides?

10 Which autonomous community is known as Euskadi in its own language?

GEOGRAPHY 2

1 In the harbour of which European capital city stands a statue of the Little Mermaid?

2 Boston is the capital of which American state?

3 In which Middle Eastern country is Damascus?

4 Which ocean lies at the eastern of the two entrances to the Panama Canal?

5 In which African country would you find the continent's highest point, Mount Kilimanjaro?

6 The White Tower, Bloody Tower and Traitors' Gate are all features of which British building?

7 What is the largest island in the Caribbean?

8 Pakistan has two official languages. English is one; what is the other?

9 What is the colour of the cross on the flag of Greece?

10 Which station in Paris contains the Eurostar terminal?

GEOGRAPHY 1
1 Arizona
2 Venice
3 East Anglia
4 Arctic Ocean
5 Chinese
6 Chad
7 Staffordshire
8 Guernsey
9 Nepal (five sides)
10 Basque country

GEOGRAPHY 2
1 Copenhagen
2 Massachusetts
3 Syria
4 Pacific Ocean (counter-intuitively)
5 Tanzania (its peak is at 5895m)
6 The Tower of London
7 Cuba
8 Urdu
9 White
10 Gare du Nord

GEOGRAPHY 3

1 In which English county would you find most of the Peak District?

2 In terms of area, what is the largest country in the Commonwealth?

3 What are the names of the two separate cities from which the one city of Budapest was formed in 1873?

4 What is the highest mountain in the Alps?

5 What five letters follow Woola and Ilfra in the names of North Devon seaside resorts?

6 What is the name of the river that runs through the heart of the city of Chicago?

7 Which city in Normandy, at the mouth of the Seine, runs ferries to Portsmouth and has a name which means 'The Harbour'?

8 What are the first two letters of the postcode for Winchester, in Hampshire?

9 If you were to drill a hole from Auckland in New Zealand directly through the centre of the earth, in which country would you emerge on the other side of the world?

10 In which Kent town is the "Road of Remembrance" a sloped thoroughfare lined with poppies to mark the World War I soldiers walking down to embark for France?

GEOGRAPHY 4

1 Which European river is called "Donau" in German, "Duna" in Hungarian and "Dunaj" in Czech?

2 Which British city is home to Arthur's Seat?

3 Which European country is divided into 54 prefectures including Drama, Arcadia and Magnesia?

4 What is the street address of The White House in Washington DC?

5 Which country in the world is home to more than half of the world's entire population of ducks?

6 Which island is home to the volcano Mount Etna?

7 Which Swiss city gives its name to four treaties and three additional protocols that set the standards for humanitarian treatment of victims of war?

8 What name is given to any Scottish mountain with a height over 3000 feet?

9 Which special administrative region of China was both the first and last European colony in China?

10 What was the currency of the Netherlands before the Euro?

---

1 Derbyshire
2 Canada (the second largest country in the world after Russia)
3 Buda and Pest
4 Mont Blanc
5 combe
6 Chicago river
7 Le Havre
8 SO
9 Spain
10 Folkestone

GEOGRAPHY 4

1 Danube
2 Edinburgh
3 Greece
4 1600 Pennsylvania Avenue (NW, Washington, D.C. 20500)
5 China
6 Sicily
7 Geneva (as in Geneva Conventions)
8 Munro
9 Macau (the other special administrative region of China is Hong Kong)
10 Guilder

GEOGRAPHY 5

1 What is the nearest city to Loch Ness?

2 On which continent is Timbuktu?

3 The fourth largest city in India used to be known as Madras. What is it called now?

4 Which country is home to the volcano Krakatoa?

5 What was the name of the hurricane that caused devastation in New Orleans in 2005?

6 In which country is the holiday resort of Taba Heights?

7 The Bahamas are closest to which American state?

8 What is the largest country in the world, in terms of area, that ends with "stan"?

9 How many of the Ivy League universities are in Massachusetts?

10 What name links an Edinburgh train station, a bus station in Newcastle, and a street in London?

GEOGRAPHY 6

1 How many African countries have names which end with the letters 'bia'?

2 Which US state gets its name from the French for "green mountain"?

3 What is Scotland's third largest city?

4 To which island did Denmark grant home rule in 1979?

5 The capital city of which country contains two gs, two ns and two ys?

6 Which "Cape" contains the northwesternmost point of mainland Britain?

7 In Indian English, what number is a lakh?

8 In Australia, what is the Fremantle Doctor?

9 What is the longest motorway in the United Kingdom?

10 Other than those with which it shares a land border (i.e. Mexico and Canada), which two countries are closest to the USA?

SUBJECT ROUNDS

GEOGRAPHY 5
1 Inverness
2 Africa
3 Chennai
4 Indonesia
5 Katrina
6 Egypt
7 Florida
8 Kazakhstan
9 One (only Harvard)
10 Haymarket

GEOGRAPHY 6
1 Three (Zambia, Gambia, Namibia)
2 Vermont
3 Aberdeen
4 Greenland
5 North Korea (Pyongyang)
6 Cape Wrath
7 100,000 (written as 1,00,000 in India)
8 Wind / Breeze
9 M6
10 Russia, Cuba

GEOGRAPHY 7

1 In which US state is Philadelphia?

2 Which emirate takes up over 80% of the land area of the United Arab Emirates?

3 Which is longer out of the Suez and Panama canals?

4 What is the highest speed limit (in km) for an autoroute in France?

5 Which English city's mainline railway station is called Westgate?

6 In terms of population, what is the second largest city in Spain?

7 What would be found at Leuchars, Northolt, Digby and Cosford?

8 What name is both a city in California and the capital of Costa Rica?

9 Which country contains three of the largest ten (non-continental) islands in the world?

10 Which London borough begins with the letter N?

GEOGRAPHY 8

1 Aston is an area of which English city?

2 What is the second largest city in Sweden?

3 As the crow flies, what is the nearest capital of an independent country to London?

4 What is the largest landlocked country in Africa?

5 Which is the largest country in the world, by area, which does not have a Pacific coastline?

6 The flag of which US state incorporates a Union Flag (commonly known as the Union Jack)?

7 What colour on London tube maps is the Piccadilly Line?

8 Of the ten most populous countries on earth, which one comes first alphabetically?

9 How many countries border Argentina?

10 What is the name of the island, also that of a fictional ship, which is divided into the sovereign states of Haiti and the Dominican Republic?

GEOGRAPHY 7
1 Pennsylvania
2 Abu Dhabi
3 Suez (101 miles vs 48 miles for Panama)
4 130km
5 Wakefield
6 Barcelona
7 RAF bases
8 San José
9 Canada (Baffin, Victoria, Ellesmere)
10 Newham

GEOGRAPHY 8
1 Birmingham
2 Gothenburg
3 Brussels (about 15 miles closer than Paris, with Amsterdam not far behind)
4 Chad
5 Brazil (Russia, China, Canada, USA all do)
6 Hawaii
7 Dark Blue
8 Bangladesh
9 Five (Bolivia, Brazil, Chile, Paraguay, Uruguay)
10 Hispaniola

GEOGRAPHY 9

1 How many American states begin with the word New?

2 The Hammersmith Flyover, in London, is a part of which road?

3 What is the smallest country on mainland Africa?

4 Including islands, the westernmost point of Europe is Monchique Islet, part of which islands group?

5 How many of the 13 stripes on the US flag are white?

6 Which region of Europe is home to the fastest ball game in the world, and a language which bears no concrete relation to any other?

7 Which city in Lancashire is an anagram of the word "Ancestral"?

8 Which European nation has by far the most people per square kilometre in Europe?

9 What is the third largest subdivision of Australia, though it has a population of under 250,000 people?

10 From the summit of a mountain called Snaefell, you can see Scotland, England, Ireland and Wales. Where would you find Snaefell?

GEOGRAPHY 10

1 In which English county are Leeds Castle and Hever Castle?

2 The Apennines form the backbone of which country?

3 The South-Western townships in Johannesburg are better known by what name?

4 What is the full name of the town in Hertfordshire founded in the 1920s by Sir Ebenezer Howard and sometimes referred to as WGC?

5 Lake Maracaibo is within which country?

6 Oxford Street in London is part of which A road?

7 The river Tagus rises about 90 miles east of which city?

8 The capital cities of which two EU countries start with the same two letters and end with the same three letters?

9 There is one UK shipping area which shares its name with a British city – which one? [has to be the full name of an official city]

10 The capital cities Montevideo and Buenos Aires are separated by 200 kilometres across which body of water?

GEOGRAPHY 9
1 Four
2 A4
3 Gambia
4 Azores (belonging to Portugal)
5 Six
6 Basque (the game is Pelota)
7 Lancaster
8 Monaco (16,000 people per square kilometre– it has only 2 square kilometres)
9 Northern Territory
10 On the Isle of Man

GEOGRAPHY 10
1 Kent
2 Italy
3 Soweto
4 Welwyn Garden City
5 Venezuela
6 The A40 – which goes all the way to Fishguard in Wales
7 Madrid
8 Romania and Hungary (Bucharest and Budapest)
9 Plymouth (Dover is not a city)
10 River Plate/Río de la Plata

GEOGRAPHY 11

1 Which is the only borough of New York City to be primarily on the mainland USA?

2 What is the name of the tall spires with onion-shaped crowns seen on many mosques?

3 Lake Nakuru is in which African country?

4 Which river flows from the Burgundy region of France to the English Channel at Le Havre?

5 Which river rises on a mountain called Plynlimon, in Wales?

6 Colombia, Ecuador, Peru and Chile are all South American countries with a coast on which ocean?

7 Sometimes known as the First State, which state of the USA has only three counties, which are called New Castle, Kent and Sussex?

8 How many points are there, in total, on the stars on the flag of Australia?

9 The city of Arkhangelsk in Russia lies on which sea, which is an inlet of the Barents Sea?

10 What is the former name of the South African city officially renamed Gqeberha in 2021?

GEOGRAPHY 12

1 Which English county has a name literally meaning "People of the North"?

2 In which US State is the gambling city of Las Vegas?

3 What confusing name do Italians use for the city of Munich?

4 Cape Horn is at the southern tip of which continent?

5 Nouakchott is the coastal capital city of which country?

6 What is the two-word name of the range that includes Ireland's highest mountain, Carrauntouhill?

7 In which country is the city of Benghazi?

8 Which island was known by the Romans as Vectis?

9 What is the name of the island off the coast of Kenya which is a UNESCO World Heritage Site and the country's oldest continually inhabited town?

10 The largest settlements on which island are Santa Eulalia del Río, San Antonio and a town with the same name as the island itself?

GEOGRAPHY 11
1 The Bronx
2 Minarets
3 Kenya
4 Seine
5 Severn
6 Pacific Ocean
7 Delaware
8 42
9 White Sea
10 Port Elizabeth

GEOGRAPHY 12
1 Norfolk
2 Nevada
3 Monaco (di Baviera)
4 South America
5 Mauritania
6 MacGillicuddy's Reeks
7 Libya
8 Isle of Wight
9 Lamu
10 Ibiza (or Santa Eulària des Riu, and Sant Antoni in the local dialect)

GEOGRAPHY 13

1 In England, what are the Cotswolds and the Quantocks?

2 What huge statue stands on top of Corcovado mountain in Brazil?

3 What, in the United States, is known as "The Cornhusker State"?

4 In which London borough is the Tower of London?

5 How many land borders with other countries does Indonesia have?

6 Islamabad makes up one large metropolitan area with which other large city in Pakistan?

7 Which German city is known in French as Aix-la-Chapelle?

8 In which American state is the city of Roswell, of UFO fame?

9 Which European city has airports called Malpensa and Linate?

10 In which English county is there a road sign which indicates that Ham is ½ a mile away, while Sandwich is 3 miles away?

GEOGRAPHY 14

1 In which country is the city of Ahmedabad?

2 What is the third most populous city in the United States, behind New York and LA and ahead of Houston?

3 After the USA, which country has the second largest Christian population in the world?

4 Founded in 331 BC, what is the largest city, by population, on the Mediterranean?

5 Apart from the City of Westminster, which is the only city of the UK whose name begins with one of the cardinal points?

6 The river Rhine's estuary flows into which sea?

7 The Matterhorn is a mountain on the border between which two countries?

8 John Hanning Speke was the first Briton to document which lake, in 1858, as well as giving it its English name?

9 Which island nation erased a day from their calendar in 2011 when they moved across the international dateline?

10 Which is the only single digit number that is not combined with the letter M to make the name of a motorway in Great Britain?

GEOGRAPHY 13
1 Ranges of hills
2 Christ the Redeemer/Cristo Redentor
3 Nebraska
4 Tower Hamlets
5 Three (with Malaysia, Timor-Leste and Papua New Guinea)
6 Rawalpindi
7 Aachen
8 New Mexico
9 Milan
10 Kent

GEOGRAPHY 14
1 India
2 Chicago
3 Brazil
4 Alexandria (not Athens or Algiers, or Tel Aviv or Tripoli)
5 Southampton
6 North Sea
7 Switzerland and Italy
8 Victoria
9 Samoa
10 M7

GEOGRAPHY 15

1 The Main, Moselle and Neckar are tributaries of which river?

2 The Khutse Game Reserve is in Botswana. It is located in which desert?

3 In which English county is the ancient site of Tintagel Castle?

4 What is the longest river which flows through the USA whose name does not begin with "Miss"?

5 Peberholm is a small artificial island in which strait?

6 In August 2015, a new 22 mile channel of which famous waterway opened?

7 What is the second largest city in Wales?

8 On which line are Nine Elms and Battersea Power Station, new London tube stations which opened in September 2021?

9 On which island would you find the holiday resort of Magaluf?

10 The name of Bedloe's Island was changed in 1956. The new name was taken from an object that had stood on the island since 1886. What is the island now called?

GEOGRAPHY 16

1 The River Tweed empties into which sea?

2 Which city is known as the "Queen of the Adriatic"?

3 The Great Plains are a vast area that stretch down the middle of which continent?

4 Which Somerset town's name contains the Latin phrase for "on sea"?

5 The peninsula known as Asia Minor takes up most of which modern day country?

6 The UNESCO World Heritage Site known as the Darién National Park is in which country?

7 Which island group is separated from the island of Britain by the Pentland Firth?

8 Which architect designed City Hall in London?

9 Beale Street is a significant thoroughfare and major tourist attraction in which southern US city?

10 Which country in the world has the largest Muslim population?

GEOGRAPHY 15
1 Rhine
2 Kalahari
3 Cornwall
4 Yukon (also flows through Canada)
5 Oresund Strait
6 Suez Canal
7 Swansea
8 Northern Line
9 Majorca
10 Liberty Island

GEOGRAPHY 16
1 The North Sea
2 Venice
3 North America
4 Weston-super-Mare (super mare meaning "on sea")
5 Turkey/Türkiye
6 Panama
7 Orkney Islands
8 Norman Foster
9 Memphis
10 Indonesia (ahead of Pakistan, then India)

GEOGRAPHY 17

1 Which is the only vowel that does not appear as the last letter of the name of any US state?

2 Which African state is the only country in the world that lies entirely above 1000 metres altitude?

3 Which town, situated about 12 miles north of Edinburgh, is known as "The Lang Toun"?

4 Western New Guinea is a part of which country?

5 In New York City, what famous building is at the point where Broadway diagonally crosses 5th Avenue?

6 Which country is directly to the north of Namibia on the west coast of Africa?

7 Which city lies at the southern end of the M3 motorway in England?

8 Epping Forest is on the border of London and which county?

9 The body of water that lies between the Italian mainland and the island of Sicily is called the Strait of where?

10 Which town in Kent changed the spelling of its name in the late nineteenth century to avoid confusion with another nearby town?

GEOGRAPHY 18

1 Which river is crossed by the Gateshead Millennium Bridge?

2 The land location which is furthest in the world from open sea is in which country?

3 Which country borders both Greece and Romania?

4 The River Lagan flows through which British city?

5 Which sea lies on the northern shoreline of Poland?

6 On which island is the Phare de Créac'h, the lighthouse considered to stand at the southern entrance to the English Channel?

7 The two closest capital cities in Africa are Brazzaville and which other, just across the Congo River?

8 What is preceded by North in the name of a town in East Lothian, and followed by –upon–Tweed, in the name of a town in Northumberland?

9 Which river forms much of the boundary between Salford and Manchester?

10 How many of the 20 highest mountains in the world (counting height above sea level) are in Europe?

GEOGRAPHY 17
1 U
2 Lesotho
3 Kirkcaldy
4 Indonesia
5 Flatiron Building (the diagonal is the clue – it is famous for its triangular shape)
6 Angola
7 Southampton
8 Essex
9 Messina
10 Tonbridge

GEOGRAPHY 18
1 Tyne
2 China
3 Bulgaria
4 Belfast
5 Baltic
6 Ushant
7 Kinshasa
8 Berwick
9 Irwell
10 None

GEOGRAPHY 19

1 The Colne, Kennet and Wey are major tributaries of which river?

2 How is the Cathedral of St Peter in York more commonly known?

3 Which colour links the national flags of Jamaica, Ukraine and Vietnam?

4 In which country are James Smith and Maria Garcia the most common full names for men and women respectively?

5 Chennai is situated in which Indian state?

6 The Costa del Sol lies on which of Spain's coastlines?

7 The city of Plymouth is located between the mouths of two rivers: the Tamar and which other?

8 Which lake between Switzerland and France is also known as Lake Léman?

9 In which English county is Broadmoor High Security Hospital?

10 Apart from the Waterloo and City line, which is the only line on the London Underground to be entirely underground?

GEOGRAPHY 20

1 What is the official language in the South American country Guyana?

2 The M8 motorway links which two British cities?

3 What name links a city in Gwynedd, Wales and a city in County Down, Northern Ireland?

4 The Eiger and the Jungfrau are part of which mountain range?

5 In 2017, which mountain in Antarctica was found to be the highest in British territory?

6 Meaning "old town", in which capital city is the area called Gamla stan?

7 The Humber Estuary is formed by the coming together of the Trent and which other river?

8 Which is the only Great Lake located entirely inside the United States?

9 Which is Britain's largest town which is not a city, in terms of population?

10 What specifically links the countries Monaco and the Gambia?

GEOGRAPHY 19
1 Thames
2 York Minster
3 Yellow
4 USA
5 Tamil Nadu
6 South
7 Plym
8 Lake Geneva
9 Berkshire
10 Victoria

GEOGRAPHY 20
1 English
2 Edinburgh and Glasgow
3 Bangor
4 Alps
5 Mount Hope
6 Stockholm
7 Ouse
8 Michigan
9 Reading
10 They have a border with only one other country, and the sea

HISTORY AND POLITICS 1

1 Who was the reigning monarch of the United Kingdom at the outbreak of World War II?

2 In which decade did the following take place: the planet Pluto was discovered, Sydney Harbour Bridge was opened and the Jarrow march against unemployment occurred?

3 Who said in 1969: "For years politicians have promised the moon; I am the first one to be able to deliver it"?

4 Which country, which was once known as South-West Africa, gained its independence on March 21st 1990?

5 Which company built the Camel, a World War I fighter plane?

6 Who was the last British Governor of Hong Kong?

7 Which 18th century English navigator captained voyages of discovery on the vessels Endeavour and Resolution?

8 Which British coin, worth one quarter of a penny, ceased to be legal tender in 1960?

9 Tarquin the Proud was the last king of which ancient city?

10 Who was Ronald Reagan's Vice President?

HISTORY AND POLITICS 2

1 In December 2003, Paul Bremer announced "Ladies and Gentleman, we've got him" – who had they got?

2 On which island is Osborne House, where Queen Victoria died?

3 Who was the first Roman Catholic to be elected US President?

4 Who was the American 'Public Enemy Number One' shot and killed by police on July 22nd 1934?

5 In which decade was Labour MP Margaret Bondfield the first woman to be a cabinet minister in the UK?

6 Which very notable year in English history is represented by the seven Roman numerals listed in descending order?

7 Sir Edmond Halley is particularly associated with which science?

8 In what century was King Henry VIII of England born?

9 What links Martin Luther King in 1964, Henry Kissinger in 1973, Yasser Arafat in 1994 and Jimmy Carter in 2002?

10 What famous world landmark was built in 1961 but lasted only 28 years?

HISTORY AND POLITICS 1
1 George VI
2 1930s (Pluto discovered in 1930, Sydney Harbour Bridge opened in 1932, Jarrow march in 1936)
3 Richard Nixon
4 Namibia
5 Sopwith
6 Chris Patten
7 James Cook
8 Farthing
9 Rome
10 George HW Bush

HISTORY AND POLITICS 2
1 Saddam Hussein
2 Isle of Wight
3 John F Kennedy
4 John Dillinger
5 1920s
6 1666 (M=1000, D=500, C=100, L=50, X= 10, V=5, I=1). This was the year of the Great Fire of London
7 Astronomy
8 15th (1491)
9 They won the Nobel Peace Prize in that year
10 Berlin Wall

HISTORY AND POLITICS 3

1 What was prohibited from sale by the 18th Amendment to the US Constitution?

2 Who was elected Deputy Leader of the Labour Party in 2020?

3 In which century did the Black Death, the start of the Hundred Years' War and the Peasants' Revolt all occur?

4 Alongside whom did John Hume win the Nobel Peace Prize in 1998?

5 The "Restoration" period took place during the reign of which English king?

6 The explorer Jacques Cartier claimed Canada for which European country?

7 Who is the most recent Liberal Prime Minister of the UK, from 1916 to 1922?

8 The majority of the fighting in the Thirty Years' War took place in which present day country?

9 In what year did the National Health Service launch, did cricketer Don Bradman play his last test, and was Shakin' Stevens born?

10 Which American hero was born in slavery, probably in 1822, as Araminta Ross?

HISTORY AND POLITICS 4

1 Douglas Hyde was, in 1938, the first President of which country?

2 What did the Idlewild International Airport change its name to in 1963?

3 Which Roman leader removed the senate's power and became dictator in 46 BC?

4 Derek Hatton was Deputy Leader of which English city's council in the 1980s?

5 What was the nickname of King Edward I of England?

6 Which military dictator led Panama from 1983 to 1989?

7 In which month of the year is VE Day celebrated?

8 Carlos Salinas de Gortari was President of which country from 1988 to 1994?

9 Which Russian leader was awarded the Nobel Peace Prize in 1990?

10 What is the better known name of the controversial French nobleman and writer Donatien Alphonse François, who was transferred out of the Bastille Prison on 4th July 1789, 10 days before it was stormed?

HISTORY AND POLITICS 3
1 Alcohol
2 Angela Rayner
3 14th Century (Black Death 1347-51, The Hundred Years' War began in 1337, and the Peasants' Revolt was in 1381)
4 David Trimble
5 Charles II
6 France
7 David Lloyd George
8 Germany
9 1948
10 Harriet Tubman

HISTORY AND POLITICS 4
1 Ireland
2 JFK International Airport
3 Julius Caesar
4 Liverpool
5 Longshanks
6 Manuel Noriega
7 May
8 Mexico
9 Mikhail Gorbachev
10 Marquis de Sade

HISTORY AND POLITICS 5

1 Who was Lord Protector of England, Scotland and Ireland from 1653 to 1658?

2 An 8 foot 4 inch statue of suffragist Millicent Fawcett was unveiled in April 2018 - in which square?

3 In which city was the United States Declaration of Independence signed in 1776?

4 What nine-letter word describes, in British history, the likes of Lambert Simnel, Perkin Warbeck and Charles Edward Stuart? [nine-letter word in the singular]

5 Which controversial figure, who died in 1991, was the Labour MP for Buckingham from 1964 to 1970?

6 The Edmund Pettus Bridge is in which Alabama city?

7 What is the common one-word name used for the founder of the Ayyubid dynasty, who led Muslim forces against European forces during The Third Crusade?

8 Which British politician and one-time President of the European Commission was sometimes referred to by French speakers in Brussels as King John the Fifteenth?

9 In ancient Greece, what were biremes and triremes?

10 Which British Monarch was the first to deliver a Royal Christmas Message?

HISTORY AND POLITICS 6

1 The long Roman road Watling Street crossed which other main highway at Venonis, south of Leicester?

2 What is Joe Biden's middle name?

3 Agamemnon was king of which ancient kingdom?

4 Who was the King of England during the Peasants' Revolt of 1381?

5 Which far-right political party was founded in 1967 by AK Chesterton, a cousin of the author GK Chesterton?

6 Who was the first Prime Minister of the UK to come from the Labour Party?

7 Which dynasty was ruling China whilst the house of Tudor was ruling England?

8 Who succeeded Leo Varadkar as Ireland's Taoiseach in June 2020?

9 The conquistador Francisco Pizarro founded which city, the capital of Peru?

10 Who was the famous maternal grandfather of Charles Darwin, a leading abolitionist who founded a pottery company in 1759 which is still operational?

HISTORY AND POLITICS 5
1 Oliver Cromwell
2 Parliament Square
3 Philadelphia
4 Pretender
5 Robert Maxwell
6 Selma (it is where the 'Bloody Sunday' brutality took place in 1965)
7 Saladin (Salah ad-Din Yusuf)
8 Roy Jenkins (Le Roi Jean Quinze)
9 Ships
10 George V (in 1932)

HISTORY AND POLITICS 6
1 Fosse Way
2 Robinette
3 Mycenae
4 Richard II
5 National Front
6 Ramsay MacDonald
7 Ming (Tudor - 1485 to 1603, Ming 1368-1644)
8 Micheál Martin
9 Lima
10 Josiah Wedgwood (Erasmus Darwin, his paternal grandfather, was also a prominent abolitionist, and a physician)

HISTORY AND POLITICS 7

1 Owain Glyndwr is a hero of which country?

2 In August 1963, a crowd of over 250,000 civil rights protestors marched on which American city?

3 Who was the leader of the Conservative Party directly after John Major?

4 Which New York landmark suffered a terrorist attack which killed seven people in February 1993?

5 In 2009, Ali Bongo Ondimba became President of which African country?

6 A key point on the Silk Road between China and Europe, the ancient city of Samarkand is in which modern-day country?

7 After the death of Bernie Grant in 2000, David Lammy won a by-election to become MP for which constituency?

8 Who is the only US President whose full name begins and ends with the same letter?

9 Reigning from 379 to 395 AD, who was the last Roman emperor to rule over both the Eastern and Western halves of the Roman empire?

10 In 2021, Samia Suluhu Hassan became the first female President of which African country?

HISTORY AND POLITICS 8

1 Which US President said in 1863: "Government of the people, by the people and for the people"?

2 In what year did the Second World War start?

3 Meaning "the die is cast", what phrase is attributed to Julius Caesar when he led his forces across the Rubicon River in 49 BC?

4 What name, of particular significance to England in 1588, is used for the navies of Argentina, Chile, Colombia and Mexico?

5 Which Asian country, whose capital is Thimphu, transitioned from an absolute monarchy to a constitutional monarchy in 2008?

6 In 2017, Sebastian Kurz became the youngest head of government in the world. Of which country was he chancellor?

7 Who became the Supreme Leader of Iran in 1979?

8 Sharing its name with the surname of a British party leader of the late 20th century, in which battle of 871 did King Aethelred and his brother Alfred score an important victory over a Danish Viking army?

9 Victor Jara was a political activist and folk singer who was tortured and killed during the rule of which Chilean dictator?

10 Which prop of political theatre was originally made by Wickwar & Co in 1853 for William Gladstone, used, on and off, for more than 150 years, but has, since 2011, been replaced by a newer version?

HISTORY AND POLITICS 7
1 Wales
2 Washington DC
3 William Hague
4 World Trade Center
5 Gabon
6 Uzbekistan
7 Tottenham
8 Theodore (Teddy) Roosevelt
9 Theodosius the Great
10 Tanzania

HISTORY AND POLITICS 8
1 Abraham Lincoln (in the Gettysburg Address)
2 1939
3 Alea iacta est
4 Armada
5 Bhutan
6 Austria
7 Ayatollah Khomeini
8 Battle of Ashdown
9 Augusto Pinochet
10 Chancellor's red box

HISTORY AND POLITICS 9

1 For how long, in seconds, did the first powered flight last? A) 12 seconds B) 12 minutes C) 12 hours?

2 Who was the first British monarch to be photographed, filmed and shown on stamps?

3 "Operation Desert Storm" was a part of which war?

4 What is the four-word name of the place where the Republican Party organised a press conference, led by Rudy Giuliani, for 7th November 2020?

5 At the age of just 34, Sanna Marin became Prime Minister of which country in late 2019?

6 The warship the Mary Rose saw 33 years of active service during the reign of which English king?

7 The Battle of Naseby was a key event in which conflict?

8 Kings nicknamed Lackland and Longshanks both ruled England in which century?

9 John Diefenbaker, known as "Dief the Chief", was Prime Minister of where?

10 In 2021, Kathy Hochul became the first woman to hold which role?

HISTORY AND POLITICS 10

1 Which word follows War of the Austrian ... and War of the Spanish ... in the names of long-lasting 18th century conflicts?

2 1970s UN Secretary-General Kurt Waldheim later served as President of which country?

3 What is the name given to the series of wars undertaken by Western European nations in the Middle East between 1095 and 1291?

4 What killed about one-fifth of London's population in 1664 and 1665?

5 Which Conservative MP for Tiverton and Honiton was forced to resign because of "tractorgate" in April 2022?

6 In June 1919, Germany signed a peace treaty in the Hall of Mirrors - in which palace?

7 Who was the French Minister of War for three periods between 1922 and 1932, dying several years too early to see his most famous policy fail to work?

8 The 1922 committee is named after the year that which Conservative became Prime Minister?

9 In the First World War, the third Battle of Ypres is also known as ... what?

10 Which leader was defeated by Roman and Visogothic forces in 451 AD at the Battle of the Catalaunian Plains, near Troyes, in France? This was the furthest west his armies ever reached.

HISTORY AND POLITICS 9
1 A) 12 seconds
2 Victoria
3 First Gulf War
4 Four Seasons Total Landscaping
5 Finland
6 Henry VIII
7 English Civil War
8 13th - King John and King Edward I
9 Canada
10 Governor of New York State

HISTORY AND POLITICS 10
1 Succession
2 Austria
3 The Crusades
4 The Great Plague (accept: Plague)
5 Neil Parish
6 Versailles
7 Andre Maginot (he advocated for and oversaw the Maginot Line)
8 Andrew Bonar Law
9 Battle of Passchendaele
10 Attila (the Hun)

HISTORY AND POLITICS 11

1 In 2003, who was the first Russian head of state to make a state visit to the UK since 1874?

2 Botany Bay, where Captain James Cook first landed in Australia, is closest to which modern day city?

3 The Charleston was a dance craze which kicked off in which decade of the 20th century?

4 For where was Tam Dalyell MP in 1977 when he raised the question in parliament of whether Scottish MPs should be able to vote on English matters?

5 Hugo Chávez became President of which South American country in 1999?

6 Which role did Stephanie Grisham hold from July 2019 until April 2020, without ever carrying out the most public responsibility associated with it?

7 Give any year in the life of Galileo Galilei.

8 Who was the Greek leader against the Persian Empire at the Battle of Salamis?

9 Which Liberal economist drafted the 1942 report officially called 'Social Insurance and Allied Services' which was a major influence on the foundation of the Welfare State?

10 Which Republican senator from Arizona did Lyndon B Johnson defeat in the 1964 US presidential election?

HISTORY AND POLITICS 12

1 Which King of England (since 1066) has the shortest name?

2 Successive Labour leaders Jeremy Corbyn and Keir Starmer are both supporters of which London football club?

3 Pioneers from which country founded the American city of New Orleans in 1718?

4 Zewditu, born Askala Maryam, was Empress of which country from 1916 to 1930?

5 Who did Rowan Williams succeed as Archbishop of Canterbury?

6 Toussaint Louverture was an important revolutionary figure in which country?

7 In which Pennsylvania town did Abraham Lincoln deliver a famous 1863 speech?

8 What was the name of the grandfather of King Canute of England, who gave his name to an important technology?

9 Sirimavo Bandaranaike, the world's first female Prime Minister, served three separate terms in Sri Lanka. Who was the President who appointed her, in 1994, for the last term?

10 What surname is shared by two Vice Presidents of the USA, both becoming President on the assassination of the previous incumbent?

HISTORY AND POLITICS 11
1 Vladimir Putin
2 Sydney
3 1920s
4 West Lothian (hence the West Lothian question)
5 Venezuela
6 White House Press Secretary - she never held a briefing
7 1564-1642
8 Themistocles
9 William Beveridge
10 Barry Goldwater

HISTORY AND POLITICS 12
1 John
2 Arsenal
3 France
4 Ethiopia (she was succeeded by Haile Selaissie)
5 George Carey
6 Haiti
7 Gettysburg
8 Harald Bluetooth
9 Her daughter, Chandrika Kumaratunga
10 Johnson (Andrew after Lincoln, Lyndon after Kennedy)

HISTORY AND POLITICS 13

1 Who was England's first Stuart ruler?

2 To whom did the then Duke of York become engaged in January 1923?

3 In which year were the Battle of Midway and the first and second Battle of El Alamein?

4 What is the name of the Director of the FBI fired by Donald Trump in May 2017?

5 Prince Metternich was the "conductor" of which alliance in Europe?

6 Which Somali-American woman became Representative for Minnesota's 5th congressional district in 2019?

7 Idriss Déby, killed by insurgents in April 2021, was President of which central African country?

8 William the Conqueror was crowned in Westminster Abbey on Christmas Day 1066, but who was crowned in St Peter's Basilica exactly 266 years earlier?

9 Which passenger ship docked at the Port of Tilbury, in Essex, on 21 June 1948?

10 What is the name of the character played by the performer Thomas D Rice in the early 1800s who became synonymous, in the USA, with negative views of African-Americans, and who gave his name to the segregation laws which existed from the 1870s to the 1960s?

HISTORY AND POLITICS 14

1 Which Soviet leader died in the same year Queen Elizabeth II was crowned?

2 In 2015, who did Rishi Sunak replace as MP for Richmond in Yorkshire?

3 What is the name of the political party of which Alex Salmond became leader in early 2021?

4 Kevin Brennan, the Labour MP for Cardiff West, became the first sitting MP to do what in October 2021?

5 Who was the first female Secretary of State in the USA?

6 Which nobleman led the baronial revolt against King Henry III of England?

7 Who was the Chancellor of West Germany from 1969 to 1974?

8 In 1941 the important US outpost of Guam was occupied by which nation?

9 Who was the Conservative candidate defeated by Sadiq Khan in the 2016 London mayoral election?

10 What name is given to the agreement regarding the Northern Ireland Peace Process which was signed on 10th April 1998?

HISTORY AND POLITICS 13
1 James I
2 Lady Elizabeth Bowes-Lyon (later Queen consort to George VI and afterwards known as Queen Elizabeth, The Queen Mother)
3 1942
4 James Comey
5 Concert of Europe
6 Ilhan Omar
7 Chad
8 Charlemagne (crownings on Christmas Day seem, historically, quite common)
9 HMT Empire Windrush
10 Jim Crow

HISTORY AND POLITICS 14
1 Josef Stalin
2 William Hague
3 Alba
4 Release an album (it was called 'The Clown and the Cigarette Girl')
5 Madeleine Albright
6 Simon de Montfort
7 Willy Brandt
8 Japan
9 Zac Goldsmith
10 Good Friday Agreement

HISTORY AND POLITICS 15

1 Senegal gained independence from which country in August 1960?

2 Which tribe, originally from Northern Europe, sacked the city of Rome in 455 AD?

3 With whom did Nelson Mandela share the 1993 Nobel Peace Prize?

4 The Council of Clermont in 1095 was the starting point for which historical event?

5 Which former British king was Governor of the Bahamas from 1940 to 1945?

6 Which dictator's remains were exhumed and moved in October 2019?

7 Who, in the 5th century, was the founder of the Merovingian Dynasty, and the first king to unite all the Frankish tribes under one ruler?

8 The President of France is also, along with the Bishop of Urgell, Co-Prince of which independent country?

9 Calotype was an early form of what?

10 The wife of Oscar winner and former US Vice President Al Gore is not usually known by her real name. What is she normally called?

HISTORY AND POLITICS 16

1 Dan Jarvis became Mayor of which English city in 2018?

2 Who was the US Secretary of State from 1973 to 1977?

3 Joko Widodo became President of which large country in 2014?

4 What was the first permanent English settlement in what is now the United States of America?

5 The name of the American polling website FiveThirtyEight, run by Nate Silver, is a reference to what?

6 Vadim Bakatin was the last head of which organisation?

7 Which US presidential candidate's mother died on October 12, 2020, two years after her son died?

8 How many years did Nelson Mandela spend in prison in South Africa?

9 Samora Machel was the first President of which African country?

10 Edwin and Oswald, both venerated as saints, were kings of which Anglo-Saxon kingdom in the 7th century?

SUBJECT ROUNDS

HISTORY AND POLITICS 15
1 France
2 Vandals
3 FW de Klerk
4 First Crusade
5 Edward VIII
6 Francisco Franco
7 Clovis
8 Andorra
9 Photography
10 Tipper (she is Mary Elizabeth Aitcheson Gore)

HISTORY AND POLITICS 16
1 Sheffield
2 Henry Kissinger
3 Indonesia
4 Jamestown
5 Number of electors in US electoral college
6 KGB
7 John McCain/Roberta McCain (she was 108)
8 27
9 Mozambique (His second wife was Graça Machel, who would later marry Mandela)
10 Northumbria

HISTORY AND POLITICS 17

1 Which king came to the English throne in 1509?

2 In August 2021, Ebrahim Raisi became President of which country?

3 British writers George Orwell and Laurie Lee fought in which war?

4 Which British politician, who unsuccessfully faked his own death in 1974, and was later revealed to have been a Czech spy, was the last Postmaster-General of the United Kingdom?

5 When Mayor of Liverpool Joe Anderson was arrested in 2020, he opted not to seek re-election in 2021. What was the name of the woman (no relation to him) who replaced him?

6 Wolfe Tone led a 1798 rebellion against British rule - in which country?

7 Mary II was a joint sovereign of England, Scotland and Ireland. With whom was she joint sovereign?

8 Which US politician was revealed in October 2019 to use the twitter pseudonym Pierre Delecto in order to keep an anonymous eye on political debate?

9 What is the surname of the first father and son to be US President?

10 Portuguese explorer Juan Rodríguez Cabrillo was the first European to explore the California coast - in what century?

HISTORY AND POLITICS 18

1 Yoweri Museveni became head of state in which country in 1986?

2 In 1975 Suriname achieved independence from which colonial power?

3 What was the name of Alexander the Great's father?

4 In 1972, who was the first Black woman to run for one of the two major American party's presidential nomination?

5 Dave Rowntree, who was a Labour councillor in Norfolk from 2017 to 2021, is the drummer in which chart-topping band?

6 25th December is a national holiday in Pakistan - not due to Christmas, but because it is the birthday of the founder of the nation. What was his name?

7 What was the name of Winston Churchill's mother?

8 Which castle in Kent was the childhood home of Anne Boleyn?

9 Born in 1963, Masako took over from Michido, in 2019, as the world's only what (beginning with E)?

10 The name of which small feudal state in Provence, which ceased to exist in 1713, has been taken up by a part of California and of South Africa, as well as in the flag of New York and of the Republic of Ireland?

HISTORY AND POLITICS 17
1 Henry VIII
2 Iran
3 Spanish Civil War
4 John Stonehouse
5 Jo(anne) Anderson
6 Ireland
7 William III
8 Mitt Romney
9 Adams (John Adams and John Quincy Adams)
10 16th

HISTORY AND POLITICS 18
1 Uganda
2 The Netherlands
3 Phillip (of Macedon)
4 Shirley Chisholm (she finished fourth)
5 Blur
6 Muhammad Ali Jinnah
7 Jennie Jerome
8 Hever Castle
9 Empress (Masako is the wife of Naruhito. Michido, the wife of the previous Emperor Akihito, became Jōkōgō, meaning Empress Emerita)
10 Orange

HISTORY AND POLITICS 19

1 Colloquially known as MBS, who became Crown Prince of Saudi Arabia in June 2017?

2 Of which reforming Communist leader did Margaret Thatcher say "we can do business together"?

3 Which African country was in 2008 the first in the world to elect a majority female parliament?

4 Evo Morales was forced to resign as President of which country in 2019?

5 Which former army officer, who shares his name with a famous songwriter, became the MP for Plymouth Moorview in 2015?

6 Margaret Beaufort was the mother of which king of England?

7 In 1961, who was the first American to go into space?

8 From 2001 to 2008, Boris Johnson was the MP for which constituency?

9 In which century did the Battle of Marathon take place?

10 What verb was used to describe the suspension of the UK parliament in Autumn 2019?

HISTORY AND POLITICS 20

1 Which Mediterranean island did Britain annex from Turkey/Türkiye in 1914?

2 Egon Krenz was the last leader of which country?

3 At which battle did Henry V lead the English forces on Saint Crispin's Day in 1415?

4 In which decade of the 20th century were the first British women given the vote for the first time?

5 In which century (after 1066, and not counting the current century) did all the monarchs of England or Britain have a different name from each other?

6 In which city did the "Bonfire of the Vanities" take place in 1497?

7 At which castle was Mary, Queen of Scots, tried and subsequently executed in 1587?

8 The Chilcot Inquiry, in 2016, was into which event?

9 Daniel arap Moi, who died in 2020, was President of which country?

10 What is the meaning of the name of the Roman Emperor Caligula?

HISTORY AND POLITICS 19
1 Mohammed bin Salman
2 Mikhail Gorbachev
3 Rwanda
4 Bolivia
5 Johnny Mercer
6 Henry VII
7 Alan Shepard
8 Henley
9 5th Century BC (490 BC)
10 Proroguing

HISTORY AND POLITICS 20
1 Cyprus
2 East Germany
3 Agincourt
4 1910s (1918)
5 13th century/1200s (John, Henry III, Edward I)
6 Florence
7 Fotheringhay
8 Iraq War
9 Kenya
10 Little Boot

FILM 1

1 Which film features the characters Sally Albright and Harry Burns?

2 What is the first name of Mr Voorhees, the vicious machete-wielding mass murderer and key character in over ten films since 1980?

3 In the films, what is Austin Powers' middle name?

4 In which film does the main character's mother mistakenly call him "Calvin Klein", as that's what's written on his underpants?

5 Brody, Hooper and Quint are three main characters in which 1970s film?

6 What were the names of the three tunnels in the 1963 film 'The Great Escape'?

7 Which singer won the award for Best Actress at the 2000 Cannes Film Festival for her part in 'Dancer in the Dark'?

8 What links the Oscar winners for Best Actor in a Leading Role for 1970 and 1972?

9 Which 1955 film starred James Dean as a disaffected youth and Natalie Wood as his girlfriend?

10 In the 2017 film by Armando Iannucci, the death of which Soviet dictator causes chaos for his associates?

FILM 2

1 How is the film character Henry Jones Junior - son of Dr Henry Jones Sr, a Scottish-born professor of Medieval Literature - better known?

2 Which actor played eight parts in the film 'Kind Hearts and Coronets'?

3 What was the name of Charles Foster Kane's sledge in the film 'Citizen Kane'?

4 In which 1987 film did Patrick Swayze play Johnny Castle?

5 Which actor has been, in three separate films, the husband of Judi Dench, the father of Renée Zellweger, and the employer of Nicole Kidman?

6 In which film from 1971 does Michael Caine say the line "You're a big man, but you're in bad shape"?

7 To what song did the dance troupe Hot Metal perform in the final show in 'The Full Monty'?

8 Who played Clarice Starling in the film 'Hannibal'?

9 According to the Guinness Book of Records, who has won more Oscars than anyone else in the history of the awards?

10 In which 2019 Oscar-nominated drama film do the two lead actors both, separately, sing songs from Stephen Sondheim's musical 'Company'?

FILM 1
1 When Harry Met Sally
2 Jason (from the Friday 13th Films)
3 Danger
4 Back to the Future
5 Jaws
6 Tom, Dick and Harry
7 Björk
8 They declined their awards (George C Scott ('Patton', 1970) and Marlon Brando ('The Godfather', 1972))
9 Rebel Without a Cause
10 Joseph Stalin

FILM 2
1 Indiana Jones
2 Alec Guinness
3 Rosebud
4 Dirty Dancing
5 Jim Broadbent (in 'Iris', 'Bridget Jones' Diary' (and the sequel), and 'Moulin Rouge!')
6 Get Carter
7 You Can Leave Your Hat On (Tom Jones)
8 Julianne Moore (not Jodie Foster)
9 Walt Disney
10 Marriage Story

FILM 3

1. In 1998, which director's Oscar acceptance speech included the line "I'm the king of the world"?

2. Richard Kiel was most famous for playing which menacing character in James Bond films?

3. Which 1997 Danny Boyle film starred Ewan McGregor as Scottish janitor Robert?

4. The movies 'Cobb', 'The Natural' and 'Bull Durham' are all about which sport?

5. The star of movies such as 'Booksmart', which actress is the sister of actor/director Jonah Hill?

6. Which film starring Joaquin Phoenix became the first R-rated film to make $1 billion at the box office?

7. What is the "name" of the lawyer played by Pete Postlethwaite in 'The Usual Suspects'?

8. What 1979 film, starring Burt Lancaster, is about the 1879 Battle of Isandlwana?

9. Thelma Schoonmaker was the wife of the great British movie director Michael Powell in the years before his death. She is the most Oscar-nominated film editor in history, for her work on the movies of which director?

10. Which actress has played the romantic interest of time travellers in films directed by Robert Schwentke, Woody Allen and Richard Curtis?

FILM 4

1. Which actor starred in the films 'Donnie Darko', 'Brokeback Mountain' and 'The Day After Tomorrow'?

2. Which 1997 film starred Julia Roberts as Julianne Potter and Cameron Diaz as Kimberly Wallace?

3. Which Monty Python film closes with the song 'Always Look on the Bright Side of Life'?

4. Whose prime directives were to 'Serve The Public Trust', 'Protect The Innocent' and 'Uphold The Law' as well as a fourth 'Classified' directive?

5. Which actor is reported to have received 4 million dollars for his ten minutes on screen in the 1978 film 'Superman'?

6. What is the name of the angel played by Henry Travers in the film 'It's A Wonderful Life'?

7. Who sang the song 'I Talk to the Trees' in the 1969 film 'Paint Your Wagon'?

8. Who directed the 2018 film 'Ready Player One'?

9. Which actor, who starred in 'Kickboxer', 'Universal Soldier', and 'Cyborg', once described himself as the "Fred Astaire of Karate"?

10. Which actor appeared in the most 'Carry On' films?

SUBJECT ROUNDS

FILM 3
1. James Cameron
2. Jaws
3. A Life Less Ordinary - Trainspotting was in 1996 and he played Mark Renton
4. Baseball
5. Beanie Feldstein
6. Joker
7. Kobayashi (his actual name is uncertain)
8. Zulu Dawn (not 'Zulu')
9. Martin Scorsese
10. Rachel McAdams (in 'The Time Traveler's Wife', 'Midnight in Paris' and 'About Time')

FILM 4
1. Jake Gyllenhaal
2. My Best Friend's Wedding
3. The Life of Brian
4. Robocop
5. Marlon Brando
6. Clarence (Clarence Oddbody)
7. Clint Eastwood
8. Steven Spielberg
9. Jean Claude Van Damme
10. Kenneth Williams (26); Joan Sims (24); Charles Hawtrey (23); Sid James (19)

FILM 5

1. Who played Mary Jane Watson opposite Tobey Maguire in the 'Spider-Man' films?

2. What is the name of the baddie in the film 'Die Hard', played by Alan Rickman?

3. The 2014 film 'Whiplash' is about a prodigy in which musical instrument?

4. In the 1987 film 'Three Men and a Baby', what was the name of the character of the baby girl?

5. Who played Carey Mahoney in the first four 'Police Academy' films?

6. Which British actress has been Oscar-nominated for her roles in 'Blue Jasmine' and 'The Shape of Water'?

7. The 2020 film 'Mank' is about the writing of which legendary film from 1941?

8. Which Bond film shares its name with Bond creator Ian Fleming's Jamaican estate?

9. Which classic 1961 film had the tagline "An impregnable fortress... An invincible army... and the unstoppable commando team"?

10. Which 1978 film was known in Venezuela as 'Vaselina'?

FILM 6

1. For which film did Robin Williams win his only Oscar?

2. Who provided the voice of 'The Corpse Bride' in the Tim Burton movie?

3. Which 2013 film directed by Spike Jonze features Scarlett Johansson as the voice of Samantha?

4. Who played Ebenezer Scrooge in the 2009 Disney movie of 'A Christmas Carol'?

5. In which 1991 film does the title character abdicate the British throne in favour of King Cedric I?

6. Which couple, who married in 2022, play a married couple in the 2021 film 'The Power of the Dog'?

7. Which classic song does Aretha Franklin sing in the 1980 film 'The Blues Brothers'?

8. The early life of a man called Jorge Mario Bergoglio is portrayed in which Oscar-nominated 2019 film?

9. In a 2019 film, Eddie Murphy plays comedian Rudy Ray Moore, who became famous with what foul-mouthed alter ego (which features in the title of the film)?

10. What title connects a 1952 film starring Jennifer Jones and Laurence Olivier with a 1976 film starring Sissy Spacek?

FILM 5
1. Kirsten Dunst
2. Hans Gruber
3. Drums
4. Mary
5. Steve Guttenberg
6. Sally Hawkins
7. Citizen Kane
8. Goldeneye
9. The Guns of Navarone
10. Grease

FILM 6
1. Good Will Hunting (Best Supporting Actor)
2. Helena Bonham-Carter
3. Her
4. Jim Carrey
5. King Ralph
6. Kirsten Dunst and Jesse Plemons
7. Think
8. The Two Popes (he is Pope Francis)
9. Dolemite (Dolemite is My Name)
10. Carrie

FILM 7

1 What kind of animal is Indiana Jones particularly scared of?

2 What 2015 film takes its title from the name given to a left-handed boxer?

3 In which film does Adam Sandler play the part of Robbie Hart?

4 In the film 'Sing 2', which rock star plays the role of singer Clay Calloway?

5 What is the name of the bar in Casablanca where most of the action takes place in the movie of that name?

6 In which movie's climax do an architect and a journalist meet for the first time at the Empire State Building in New York (although the movie's title refers to a different American city)?

7 Which Austrian city is the setting for the denouement of 'The Sound of Music'?

8 Whose first husband is Charles Hamilton, while her third is Rhett Butler?

9 In which 1983 movie did Patrick Swayze star alongside Matt Dillon, Rob Lowe, Ralph Macchio, Emilio Estevez, Tom Cruise and C. Thomas Howell?

10 When describing the movie business, the great screenwriter William Goldman used what three-word phrase, which has passed into common parlance to describe the fact that even the most high profile and lucrative businesses run on luck and ignorance?

FILM 8

1 Which American comic actor sang the Marvin Gaye classic 'Let's Get it On' at the end of the film 'High Fidelity'?

2 Joy, Sadness, Fear, Anger and Disgust are lead characters in which 2015 animated film?

3 How is the character Oswald Cobblepot better known in stories in DC Comics and in a film from 1992?

4 Which 2019 film features Detective Benoit Blanc investigating a suspected murder?

5 Who played Che, the narrator, in the 1996 film version of 'Evita'?

6 What was the nickname of the character played by John Cleese in 1999's 'The World Is Not Enough'? [specifically this film]

7 What was the name of Marilyn Monroe's character in 'Some Like it Hot'?

8 Who played Eliot Ness in the movie version of 'The Untouchables'?

9 Which film from 2000 featured the characters Mickey O'Neil, Turkish, Brick Top, Bullet Tooth Tony and Cousin Avi?

10 Two actresses were Oscar-nominated for playing the same person (at different ages) in which 1997 film?

SUBJECT ROUNDS

FILM 7
1 Snakes
2 Southpaw
3 The Wedding Singer
4 Bono
5 Rick's
6 Sleepless in Seattle
7 Salzburg
8 Scarlett O'Hara (in 'Gone with the Wind')
9 The Outsiders
10 Nobody knows anything

FILM 8
1 Jack Black
2 Inside Out
3 The Penguin (he is in the film 'Batman Returns')
4 Knives Out
5 Antonio Banderas
6 R (Cleese only became Q in 'Die Another Day', after the death of Desmond Llewellyn)
7 Sugar Kane
8 Kevin Costner
9 Snatch
10 Titanic (Rose DeWitt Bukater/Dawson played by Kate Winslet and Gloria Stuart. This happened to Kate Winslet again when she and Judi Dench were nominated for the 2001 film 'Iris'.)

FILM 9

1 What was the first non-English language film to win the Oscar for Best Picture?

2 In the film 'Jumanji', what is Jumanji?

3 Who was the only actor to be part of both the Magnificent Seven and the Dirty Dozen?

4 What was the name of Sean Penn's acting brother who died of a heart attack in early 2006?

5 Who plays Adam Sandler's love interest in both 'The Wedding Singer' and 'Fifty First Dates'?

6 In the film 'Evolution', which brand of shampoo is used to kill off the mutating life-forms?

7 In 'Notting Hill', which publication does Hugh Grant's character claim to work for before his interview with Julia Roberts?

8 In the 'Star Wars' films, the stormtrooper army is originally cloned from which character?

9 Only once has an Oscar-winning actress been played by an actress who won an Oscar for the performance. Who are the two Oscar winning actresses in question?

10 What film role has been played by, amongst others, Robert De Niro, Harvey Keitel, Peter Cook, Al Pacino, Tom Waits and Liz Hurley?

FILM 10

1 The 2020 movie 'The Story of Fire Saga' uses which annual competition as its backdrop?

2 Scott Joplin's classic rag 'The Entertainer' was used as the theme music to which 1973 movie?

3 Tom Hanks, Bruce Willis and Melanie Griffiths starred in a movie called 'Bonfire of the ...' what?

4 In the hit British film 'Pride', what does the name of the activist group LGSM stand for?

5 In which film were the villains called "The Blue Meanies"?

6 Also known as Donostia, which city in the Basque Region has an International Film Festival and was European City of Culture in 2016?

7 Which actor links 'Apocalypse Now', 'The Matrix' and 'Man of Steel'?

8 The title character of which Oscar-nominated 2011 movie lives in the Gare Montparnasse in Paris?

9 Which Anglo-Australian actor had roles in the Best Picture Oscar winners for the years 2009 and 2010?

10 In which James Bond film did Bond first drive the classic Aston Martin DB5?

FILM 9
1 Parasite
2 A (board) game
3 Charles Bronson
4 Chris Penn
5 Drew Barrymore
6 Head and Shoulders (because it contains Selenium)
7 Horse & Hound
8 Jango Fett
9 Katharine Hepburn, who was played by Cate Blanchett (in 'The Aviator')
10 The Devil

FILM 10
1 The Eurovision Song Contest
2 The Sting
3 Vanities
4 Lesbians and Gays Support the Miners
5 Yellow Submarine
6 San Sebastian
7 Laurence Fishburne
8 Hugo (Cabret)
9 Guy Pearce ('The Hurt Locker' and 'The King's Speech')
10 Goldfinger

FILM 11

1 Which film from 1999 starred Will Smith, Kevin Kline, Kenneth Branagh, and Salma Hayek?

2 Which 2020 Adam Sandler film features pop star The Weeknd and basketball star Kevin Garnett as fictionalised versions of themselves?

3 Which 2008 comedy was first thought up by its creator Ben Stiller more than 20 years earlier when he was filming an early role in Steven Spielberg's 'Empire of the Sun'?

4 What first name links the film directors Phillips, Haynes and Solondz?

5 Most films on the IMDB website are given a rating out of 10. What is the only film whose rating goes up to 11?

6 Who plays the part of Nigel Small-Fawcett in the unofficial James Bond film 'Never Say Never Again'?

7 This is the first line of which 2010 film? "Did you know there are more people with genius IQs living in China than there are people of any kind living in the United States?"

8 In which 2004 family film did Tom Hanks provide the voice for five characters?

9 In which 1991 movie did Keanu Reeve play the role of FBI agent Johnny Utah?

10 Richard Bohringer, Michael Gambon, Helen Mirren and Alan Howard play the characters who make up the title of which controversial British film from 1989?

FILM 12

1 Who directed the film 'American Sniper'?

2 What is the job of the dwarves in 'Snow White and the Seven Dwarfs'?

3 Which film features the cash-generating Christmas song, 'Santa's Super Sleigh', which had been written by the main character's father?

4 In which 1980 film were the lead characters Elaine Dickinson and Ted Striker?

5 In the 2022 horror film 'Men', which actor plays all the men in the village?

6 What is the title of the 1966 film starring Michael Caine and featuring Shelley Winters and Jane Asher, remade with Jude Law in the title role?

7 In which Bond film do Mr Kidd and Mr Wint appear?

8 Maria Bakalova gained a Supporting Actress Oscar nomination for her role in which 2020 film?

9 What name (first and surname) links notable cinematic fathers, in a 1964 film played by David Tomlinson and, in a 1991 film, played by Steve Martin?

10 What is the last line of the film 'Gone With the Wind'?

FILM 11

1 Wild Wild West
2 Uncut Gems
3 Tropic Thunder
4 Todd
5 This is Spinal Tap
6 Rowan Atkinson
7 The Social Network
8 The Polar Express (the Conductor, the Hobo, Santa Claus, the unnamed protagonist (as an adult), and the unnamed protagonist's father)
9 Point Break
10 The Cook, The Thief, His Wife and Her Lover

FILM 12

1 Clint Eastwood
2 (Diamond) Miners
3 About a Boy
4 Airplane!
5 Rory Kinnear
6 Alfie
7 Diamonds are Forever
8 Borat Subsequent Moviefilm
9 George Banks ('Mary Poppins' and 'Father of the Bride')
10 "After all, tomorrow is another day!" (spoken by Scarlett O'Hara)

FILM 13

1 In 'Despicable Me' what are Gru's little yellow henchmen called?

2 Who played Private Ryan in 'Saving Private Ryan'?

3 Which 1998 film is about a woman who needs to obtain 100,000 Deutschmarks in 20 minutes in order to save her boyfriend's life?

4 Which pop star provides the voice of Tip Tucci in the movie 'Home'?

5 Who played James Bond directly before Daniel Craig?

6 Which Hollywood actor, born Issur Danielovitch Demsky in 1916, had a son who won the 1987 Academy Award for Best Actor?

7 On which director's films, which are usually referred to as 'joints', do the closing credits always finish with the phrases "By Any Means Necessary", "Ya Dig", and "Sho Nuff"?

8 What was the more common name of the 2019 film titled, in its opening credits, 'I Heard You Paint Houses'?

9 Which 1981 film earned two Academy Awards, one for Best Supporting Actor, won by John Gielgud, and one for Best Song, won by Christopher Cross?

10 Which 1990 British film was called "'Ghost' for grown-ups" by American film critic Roger Ebert?

FILM 14

1 In the film 'Finding Nemo' what is the name of Nemo's father?

2 Fredric March, James Mason and Bradley Cooper all received Best Actor Oscar nominations for the lead male role in films with which name?

3 What number did the car Herbie have painted on his roof?

4 What stage surname links award-winning actors born Diane Hall and Michael Douglas?

5 Who played Sarah Connor in the first 'Terminator' film?

6 Which part of the standard uniform of 'Men in Black' is not black?

7 In which 1987 film did Steve Martin share a bed with John Candy?

8 Actress Christina Hendricks, who played Joan Holloway in 'Mad Men', revealed in 2019 that hers is the hand, though not the stomach, which appears in the iconic poster for which film?

9 Which actor's film roles include Polonius, Hunter S Thompson, Franklin D Roosevelt and Dr Peter Venkman?

10 Which former Oscar winner wrongly announced that 'La-La Land' had won the Oscar for Best Picture at the 2017 ceremony?

FILM 13
1 Minions
2 Matt Damon
3 Run Lola Run ('Lola rennt' in German)
4 Rihanna
5 Pierce Brosnan
6 Kirk Douglas (Michael Douglas won the Oscar for 'Wall Street')
7 Spike Lee
8 The Irishman
9 Arthur
10 Truly, Madly, Deeply

FILM 14
1 Marlin
2 A Star is Born
3 53
4 Keaton (Diane Keaton and Michael Keaton)
5 Linda Hamilton
6 Shirt
7 Planes, Trains and Automobiles
8 American Beauty
9 Bill Murray
10 Faye Dunaway ('Moonlight' actually won. She was with Warren Beatty but she was the one who made the announcement.)

FILM 15

1 Complete the title of this 2022 film, in which Nicolas Cage plays a version of himself; 'The Unbearable Weight of ...' what?

2 In the film '42', actor Chadwick Boseman played which legend of baseball?

3 Richard Linklater directed which innovative film starring Ellar Coltrane from 2014?

4 Which James Bond film has the shortest title?

5 Which actress received six Academy Award nominations between 2006 and 2019 without winning any of them?

6 In the first 'Austin Powers' film, Dr Evil tries to hold the world to ransom for what relatively paltry figure, only to be met by laughter?

7 Which year is the setting for the film sequel to 'Blade Runner'?

8 What is the name of the Semitic language spoken in the Middle East, an ancient form of which was used for the dialogue of Mel Gibson's 'The Passion of the Christ'?

9 Which BAFTA-winning actress announced in 2021 that she would now be using the correct, original spelling of her name, rather than the Anglicised nickname she had, mistakenly, been credited with since she was a teenager?

10 Who was the first woman to win four Best Actress Oscars?

FOOD AND DRINK 1

1 Which vegetable is known as zucchini in the USA?

2 Arabica and robusta are the two chief species of which plant, used to make a popular drink?

3 If you ordered "gambas" in a restaurant, what sort of seafood would you expect to be served?

4 If a frankfurter is a type of sausage as well as a person from Frankfurt, and a hamburger is a lump of meat as well as a person from Hamburg, what is a berliner, other than a person from Berlin?

5 Parmesan cheese is made using the milk of which animal?

6 Which British chef died suddenly in Dubai on 26th November 2019?

7 True or False? Stilton cheese cannot legally be made in the village of Stilton from which the name originates.

8 What is the Turkish word for skewer?

9 Which singer-songwriter makes a bourbon called Heaven's Door?

10 The name of which 12-letter foodstuff has an "a" as every other letter (it's a one-word name, so 'A banana salad', although an inspired guess, would not be acceptable!)?

SUBJECT ROUNDS

FILM 15
1 Massive Talent
2 Jackie Robinson
3 Boyhood
4 Dr. No
5 Amy Adams
6 1 million dollars
7 2049
8 Aramaic
9 Thandiwe Newton (in her debut film, she was credited as Thandie Newton)
10 Katharine Hepburn

FOOD AND DRINK 1
1 Courgette
2 Coffee
3 Prawns/shrimps/giant prawns
4 A (jam) doughnut
5 Cow
6 Gary Rhodes
7 True (the name Stilton can only be given to cheese made in Derbyshire, Leicestershire and Nottinghamshire. The village of Stilton is in Cambridgeshire)
8 Shish (kebab means "grilled meat")
9 Bob Dylan
10 Taramasalata

FOOD AND DRINK 2

1 Venison is meat from which animal?

2 What name is given to a herring which has been split from head to tail, eviscerated, salted and then smoked?

3 If you ordered "grenouilles" in a restaurant, what would you expect to be served?

4 What is the UK name for the vegetable that Americans call eggplant?

5 What is the speciality of the restaurant chain Five Guys?

6 In which English county is the Yeo Valley, where the dairy company is based?

7 What is the English name for the fruit known in France as "ananas"?

8 Which product has a moose called Maynard as its mascot?

9 What, specifically, connects the following brands of beer: Molson Excel, Haake Beck, Nanny State, Special Effects and Kaliber?

10 Which renowned 16th century clergyman is widely credited with first combining strawberries and cream?

FOOD AND DRINK 3

1 Horseradish sauce is usually an accompaniment to which roast meat?

2 What is the "L" element of a BLT sandwich?

3 What is the main colour of a KitKat wrapper?

4 The Ubiquitous Chip is a renowned restaurant that opened in 1971 in which Scottish city?

5 Which manufacturer of bread takes its name from a shortening of the Latin for "strength of man"?

6 Which herb is the basis of a pesto sauce?

7 Which nut is one of the key ingredients of Nutella?

8 Which vegetable is an essential ingredient of moussaka, to go with the mince, tomato and white sauce?

9 Which Mexican food has a name meaning "little donkey"?

10 What was created in a Pittsburgh kitchen by Jim Deligatti, originally called the Aristocrat then the Blue Ribbon Burger, but given its current name by a 21-year advertising secretary named Esther Glickstein Rose?

FOOD AND DRINK 2
1 Deer
2 Kipper
3 Frogs / Frogs' Legs
4 Aubergine
5 Burgers (they also do hot dogs)
6 (North) Somerset
7 Pineapple
8 (Maynard's) Wine gums
9 All are non-alcoholic
10 Cardinal Thomas Wolsey

FOOD AND DRINK 3
1 Roast beef
2 Lettuce
3 Red
4 Glasgow
5 Hovis (Hominis vis)
6 Basil
7 Hazelnut
8 Aubergine (known as Eggplant in America)
9 Burrito
10 Big Mac

FOOD AND DRINK 4

1 Cathedral City is a brand of which type of food?

2 What four letters are at the start of the names of around 25% of the whisky distilleries in Scotland?

3 Which variety of plum is known in France as a Reine Claude?

4 Which German sweets manufacturer was founded by Hans Riegel in Bonn?

5 First introduced in 1997, what is the brand of McDonald's ice cream with flavours including Oreo, Creme Egg and Smarties?

6 What supernatural being gives its name to the hottest chilli pepper in the world (417 times hotter than a bottle of Tabasco sauce)?

7 Tusker and White Cap are beers from which African country?

8 What pasta dish, sometimes known in the USA as "Coal miner's spaghetti" is commonly made with egg, hard cheese, black pepper and lardons of bacon or pancetta?

9 What is the four-letter portmanteau name of the meal replacement brand founded in 2014 by Julian Hearn and James Collier?

10 What is the name of the suburb of Birmingham where you will find Cadbury World?

FOOD AND DRINK 5

1 What is the British name for the salad plant usually called arugula in the USA?

2 Chiquito's is a chain of restaurants serving food of which nationality?

3 Which cheese is one of the main traditional ingredients of a tiramisu?

4 At which London gentlemen's club was Buck's Fizz created in 1921?

5 Who writes the blog 'Cooking on a Bootstrap'?

6 Also known as posho in Uganda, ugali is a staple food in East Africa made from which crop?

7 Kölsch is a type of beer which originated in which city?

8 Which chocolate bar's name is a portmanteau of its co-creator and a type of Italian nougat?

9 Which crisps, once 10p but 30p as of 2022, have a spooky alien countenance on the front and come in flavours such as Spicy, Saucy BBQ, Beef and Pickled Onion?

10 Wilkin & Son manufactures which popular brand of chutneys, jams and other preserves, named after the village in Essex where they are based?

FOOD AND DRINK 4
1 Cheese (Cheddar)
2 Glen
3 Greengage
4 Haribo
5 McFlurry
6 Ghost
7 Kenya
8 Carbonara
9 Huel (Human Fuel)
10 Bournville

FOOD AND DRINK 5
1 Rocket
2 Mexican
3 Mascarpone
4 Buck's Club
5 Jack Monroe
6 Maize
7 Cologne
8 Toblerone (Tobler and torrone)
9 Space Raiders (not Monster Munch)
10 Tiptree

FOOD AND DRINK 6

1 Chianti wine is made in which region of Italy?

2 Which German confectionery company has used the slogan "Quadratisch, praktisch, gut"?

3 Which London restaurant was founded by Rose Gray and Ruth Rogers and has included the likes of Hugh Fearnley-Whittingstall and Jamie Oliver amongst its staff?

4 Which fruit has a name that comes from the medieval Latin for seeded apple?

5 What is the name of a plant of the genus Dioscorea, which is a staple food in much of Africa, as well as being the name given to the sweet potato, a different food, in North America?

6 Who opened his first culinary premises in a wooden hut in Guiseley, Yorkshire in 1928?

7 Which items of fast food, first widely available in 1983, come in four shapes according to their makers - the bell, the bow-tie, the ball and the boot?

8 Which vegetable, a variety of celery, is also called turnip-rooted celery or knob celery?

9 What kind of sandwich is mentioned in the song 'Down Under' by Men at Work?

10 Jonathan Swift is famously quoted as saying "he was a bold man that first ate ..." what?

FOOD AND DRINK 7

1 Which fruit is sometimes known as an alligator pear?

2 Traditionally, what shape is a slice of Lorne sausage in Scotland?

3 If your bag of crisps was seasoned with NaCl and a dash of CH3COOH, what flavour would you be eating?

4 Which brand of confectionery shares its name with a play by the author of 'Peter Pan', JM Barrie?

5 Maracujá is another name for which tropical fruit?

6 In which Cornish town did Rick Stein open The Seafood Restaurant in 1975?

7 What name from the Japanese for "hand pressed" is given to the type of sushi that is an oblong piece of sushi rice, usually topped with fish and served with wasabi?

8 Oyster, portobello and shiitake are all types of which foodstuff?

9 In the book of Exodus, which edible substance is provided from heaven for the Israelites while they're in the desert?

10 Which drink originated in 1927, then had a letter removed from its name two years later and has kept the same name since then?

FOOD AND DRINK 6
1 Tuscany
2 Ritter Sport (Square, practical, good)
3 The River Café
4 Pomegranate
5 Yam
6 Harry Ramsden
7 Chicken McNuggets
8 Celeriac
9 Vegemite sandwich
10 An oyster

FOOD AND DRINK 7
1 Avocado
2 Square
3 Salt and Vinegar
4 Quality Street
5 Passion fruit
6 Padstow
7 Nigiri
8 Mushroom
9 Manna
10 Lucozade (originally Glucozade)

FOOD AND DRINK 8

1 Shepherd Neame is a brewery in which English county?

2 What is the name given to a style of cooking native to Jamaica, in which meat is rubbed with a hot spice mix prior to cooking?

3 Poteen is a strong distilled drink traditionally made in which country?

4 Which sauce is made from butter and egg yolks flavoured with tarragon and shallots, cooked in wine and vinegar?

5 Which British shop claims to have invented the Scotch egg?

6 Simnel cake is traditionally served in the UK at which time of year?

7 What name is given to a Louisiana stew of meat or shellfish, okra, celery, bell peppers, and onions?

8 The dish of omelette containing smoked haddock is named after which English author?

9 Affogato is a dessert traditionally consisting of vanilla ice cream with what poured over it?

10 What drink was certified as kosher in 1935 by Rabbi Tobias Geffen?

FOOD AND DRINK 9

1 The German food stollen is traditionally associated with which time of year?

2 In French cuisine, a poussin is a small ... what?

3 What is the better known name for Patum Peperium, a salty anchovy paste created in 1828?

4 In Thai cuisine, what kind of food is nam pla?

5 Rollmops, which are a snack of rolled fish around a savoury filling, are made of pickled fillets of which fish?

6 'The Silver Spoon' is the English title of a major cookbook associated with the cuisine of which country?

7 In 1959, the Chinese gooseberry's name was changed, in New Zealand, to what?

8 A symbol of what animal is printed on British eggs as a mark of food safety?

9 In 2014 Philip Thorne, a chef from Devon, ate 80 metres of what at the Bottle Inn in Dorset to set a new World Record?

10 Originally described as "energy balls", what sweets were created by Forrest Mars in 1936?

FOOD AND DRINK 8
1 Kent
2 Jerk
3 Ireland
4 Béarnaise
5 Fortnum & Mason
6 Easter
7 Gumbo
8 Arnold Bennett
9 Coffee
10 Coca-Cola

FOOD AND DRINK 9
1 Christmas
2 Chicken
3 Gentleman's Relish
4 Fish sauce
5 Herring
6 Italy
7 Kiwifruit
8 Lion
9 Nettles
10 Maltesers

FOOD AND DRINK 10

1 Dauphinoise, fondant, boulangère and duchess are all ways of cooking or serving what?

2 A lardon is a small cube of meat from which animal?

3 The Reinheitsgebot of 1516 was a law passed in Bavaria, Germany concerning what?

4 In the UK, what colour is the cap on a plastic bottle of skimmed milk?

5 Which foodstuff typically features in a traditional Punch and Judy show?

6 What is the name of the sharp-flavoured green boiled sweets associated with the Scottish town of Galashiels?

7 Which French first name is used to describe a dish of crêpes served with an orange sauce?

8 What kind of food is in muktuk, as eaten by people native to the Arctic?

9 When a Scottish beer is described as "60", "70" or "80", what did that originally refer to?

10 Horseradish sauce was, in 1869, the first product sold by whom?

FOOD AND DRINK 11

1 What colour packet do Walkers Ready Salted crisps come in?

2 What name is given to a common meal in Japanese cuisine, where single portions of various foods are presented in a boxed container?

3 Which drink's English name is derived from an abbreviation of the Dutch for "burnt wine"?

4 Poutine is a Canadian dish consisting of chips with gravy, topped with what?

5 What is the name of the traditional Scottish dessert of oatmeal, whipped cream, whisky, honey and fresh raspberries?

6 What shape, according to its translation, is the pasta orecchiette?

7 What is the name of the city on the border between Uruguay and Argentina which gave its name to a tinned food brand?

8 What type of beans are typically used in a tin of baked beans?

9 Red Baron, Senshyu Yellow and Vidalia are varieties of which vegetable?

10 Which foodstuff did Dr Johnson define in his dictionary as in England being given to horses but in Scotland supporting the people?

FOOD AND DRINK 10
1 Potatoes
2 Pig
3 Purity of beer
4 Red
5 Sausages
6 Soor plooms
7 Suzette
8 Whale blubber
9 Price per barrel in shillings
10 (Henry J) Heinz

FOOD AND DRINK 11
1 Red (they are now a bit reddy-brown)
2 Bento
3 Brandy
4 Cheese
5 Cranachan
6 Ear-shaped
7 Fray Bentos
8 Haricot
9 Onion
10 Oats

FOOD AND DRINK 12

1 Which drink is made from grapes grown near the Spanish town of Jerez?

2 In cookery, what name is given to the process of cooling and heating chocolate to give it a glossy finish?

3 A 9-square mile "triangle" named after which food is located in West Yorkshire?

4 Which pasta dish does the cartoon cat Garfield like to eat?

5 In Sweden, what fruit is "apelsin"?

6 Profiteroles and éclairs are usually made from which type of pastry?

7 The town of Whitstable in Kent has an annual festival celebrating which food item?

8 When translated back into English, how is candy floss known in France?

9 Which liqueur is made exclusively by monks in the Voiron commune of France?

10 Which renowned French chef invented Lobster Thermidor?

ARTS 1

1 Which Dutch artist, who died in 1890, painted a series of pictures called 'Sunflowers'?

2 Heathcliff is the landlord of which property in a famous novel by Emily Brontë?

3 Which bully from 'Tom Brown's Schooldays' became the main character in a series of novels by George MacDonald Fraser?

4 What nationality was the artist Edgar Degas?

5 Who wrote the opera 'Boris Godunov' which premiered in 1874?

6 How many lines does the short poem known as a Clerihew have?

7 Give any year in the life of the composer Giacomo Puccini.

8 Which British sculptor has notable works in Chicago's 'Millennium Park' and in London's Queen Elizabeth Olympic Park (as well as designing the 2018 Brit Award)?

9 In Greek mythology, what name is given to the group of heroes who travelled to Colchis to find the Golden Fleece?

10 The Harry Potter books were published in the UK by which company, which shares its name with an area of London?

FOOD AND DRINK 12
1 Sherry
2 Tempering
3 Rhubarb
4 Lasagne
5 Orange
6 Choux
7 Oyster
8 Dad's beard (Barbe à papa)
9 Chartreuse
10 Auguste Escoffier

ARTS 1
1 Vincent van Gogh
2 Wuthering Heights
3 Flashman
4 French
5 Modest Mussorgsky
6 Four
7 1858-1924
8 Anish Kapoor (Cloud Gate and the ArcelorMittal Orbit)
9 Argonauts (accompanying Jason on the Argo)
10 Bloomsbury

ARTS 2

1 Who wrote novels including 'Jude the Obscure', 'Under the Greenwood Tree' and 'The Return of the Native'?

2 Which commercially successful painter's most famous picture is entitled 'The Singing Butler'?

3 Tamara Rojo succeeded Wayne Eagling as Artistic Director of which institution in 2012?

4 Similarly titled to her acclaimed debut novel, 'Country Girl' is the memoir of which Irish author?

5 The Marlowe Theatre is in which English city?

6 In late 19th century Paris, the 'Galop infernal' from Offenbach's operetta 'Orpheus in the Underworld' came to be associated with which dance?

7 Which Nobel Prize winner's 2021 novel is called 'Klara and the Sun'?

8 The goddess Thetis was the mother of which Greek hero?

9 Winner of the Whitbread Award for a First Novel, which influential semi-autobiographical novel by Jeanette Winterson was published in 1985?

10 Which feature of the festive season originally derives from Greek words meaning, roughly, "imitator of everything"?

ARTS 3

1 The small plastic houses for children which many people have in their garden are, originally, named after a character in which play?

2 In a 1936 novel, who is described as "a visitor from Charleston"?

3 Which Russian composed the '1812 Overture'?

4 Who did the pianist and composer Clara Wieck marry in 1840?

5 What, in October 2019, did 'The Testaments' share with 'Girl, Woman, Other'?

6 Which 1851 painting by the German-American artist Emanuel Leutze commemorates an event that took place on Christmas Day 1776?

7 Which playwright, who had a similar experience to the source material's author JG Ballard as a child in Asia fleeing Japanese occupation during World War II, wrote the screenplay to the 1986 film 'Empire of the Sun'?

8 Give any year in the life of the famous composer Richard Wagner?

9 'Skagboys' is a prequel to which novel?

10 The title of which acclaimed 2006 novel comes from a feature on the flag of the short-lived state of Biafra?

ARTS 2
1 Thomas Hardy
2 Jack Vettriano
3 English National Ballet
4 Edna O'Brien
5 Canterbury
6 Can-can
7 Kazuo Ishiguro
8 Achilles
9 Oranges are Not the Only Fruit
10 Pantomime

ARTS 3
1 Peter Pan (Wendy houses)
2 Rhett Butler (in Gone With the Wind)
3 Pyotr Tchaikovsky
4 Robert Schumann
5 The Booker Prize (novels by Margaret Atwood and Bernardine Evaristo respectively)
6 Washington Crossing the Delaware
7 Tom Stoppard
8 1813–1883
9 Trainspotting
10 Half of a Yellow Sun (by Chimamanda Ngozi Adichie)

ARTS 4

1 Which British artist, who in 2020 won the prestigious Erasmus prize, has an alter ego called Claire and a teddy bear called Alan Measles?

2 What nationality were the artists Paul Gauguin, Claude Monet and Henri Matisse?

3 What English language play was the first to be performed at Copenhagen's new national theatre when it opened in 2008?

4 What ship appears in the title of an operetta by Gilbert and Sullivan?

5 Ford Madox Ford co-wrote three novels with which other great novelist of his era, who famously didn't speak English fluently until his 20s?

6 Sylvie Guillem, Carlos Acosta and Rudolf Nureyev all became famous in which field of the arts?

7 Museums bearing what name (some of which are no longer open) have been designed by the likes of Richard Gluckman, Arata Isozaki, Frank Gehry and Frank Lloyd Wright?

8 Whose plays include 'The Habit of Art', 'Habeas Corpus', 'The Madness of George III' and 'The History Boys'?

9 What is the title of the bestselling debut novel by Candice Carty-Williams, which was shortlisted for Waterstone's Book of the Year in 2019?

10 In 2017, a famous short poem by William Carlos Williams called "This is Just to Say' became a meme on Twitter. The poem is about eating which fruit?

ARTS 5

1 Ebenezer Scrooge is the main character in which book by Charles Dickens?

2 What, in Ancient Greece, was an amphora?

3 Give any year in the life of Robert Louis Stevenson, the author of 'Treasure Island' and 'Dr Jekyll and Mr Hyde'.

4 The Pritzker Prize and the Stirling Prize are awards for excellence in what field?

5 Who is the author of 'Actress', 'The Gathering' and 'The Green Road', who was appointed the inaugural Laureate for Irish Fiction in 2015?

6 What is the name of the character played by Mark Rylance in Jez Butterworth's award-winning 'Jerusalem'?

7 Which American artist became famous for his "drip" paintings, earning him the nickname "Jack the Dripper"?

8 In Greek mythology, which nymph was cursed so that she could only repeat the last words spoken by somebody else?

9 Who was the first Artistic Director of the National Theatre in London?

10 Chortle, galumph and Jabberwock are words coined by which children's author?

ARTS 4
1 Grayson Perry
2 French
3 Hamlet
4 HMS Pinafore
5 Joseph Conrad
6 Ballet
7 Guggenheim (respectively, in Berlin, SoHo New York, Bilbao, New York (original))
8 Alan Bennett
9 Queenie
10 Plums

ARTS 5
1 A Christmas Carol
2 A container (ceramic, usually of wine)
3 1850-1894
4 Architecture
5 Anne Enright
6 Johnny "Rooster" Byron
7 Jackson Pollock
8 Echo
9 Laurence Olivier
10 Lewis Carroll

ARTS 6

1. Whose novels included 'The Black Robe' and 'The Woman in White'?

2. In a popular musical, what is the surname of Liesl, Friedrich, Louisa, Kurt, Brigitta, Marta and Gretl?

3. According to the Shakespeare play, of which city was Pericles a prince?

4. The Turner Contemporary is an art gallery in Margate which celebrates the work of 19th century painter JMW Turner, who was brought up there. The gallery was opened by which other famous artist, also brought up in Margate?

5. In mythology, what famous undertaking was set by King Eurystheus of Tiryns?

6. The Dearlys are the main human characters in which children's classic book?

7. The sacred texts of Hinduism are written primarily in which language?

8. The Baroque artist who painted 'Susanna and her Elders' and 'Judith and her Maidservant' was Artemisia ... who?

9. Odysseus confronts which one-eyed giant in a famous play by Euripides?

10. Which Tom Stoppard play makes several references to the Czech group The Plastic People of the Universe?

ARTS 7

1. In which century did the poet and playwright William Shakespeare die?

2. The Lyceum and the Traverse are theatres in which city?

3. Berthe Morisot was one of the leading figures in which late-19th century artistic movement?

4. Which author, who described his love for confectionery in his memoir, described the 1930s as being to chocolate as the Italian Renaissance was to painting?

5. The best known madrigal by English composer Orlando Gibbons is about which bird "who living had no note"?

6. Which Nobel Prize-winning author was also an editor at Random House publishing company from 1965 to 1983?

7. In Arthurian legend, who is the father of Sir Galahad?

8. In Greek mythology, who is the daughter of King Aeëtes of Colchis, who helps Jason steal the Golden Fleece?

9. Which country is the setting for Ernest Hemingway's novella 'The Old Man and the Sea'?

10. What is the string instrument, of which there are various types, that takes its name from the Latin for sweet and the Greek for song?

SUBJECT ROUNDS

ARTS 6
1. Wilkie Collins
2. Von Trapp (in 'The Sound of Music')
3. Tyre
4. Tracey Emin
5. The Twelve Labours of Heracles
6. The Hundred and One Dalmatians
7. Sanskrit
8. Gentileschi
9. The Cyclops/Polyphemus
10. Rock 'n' Roll

ARTS 7
1. 17th century/1600s (1616)
2. Edinburgh
3. Impressionism
4. Roald Dahl
5. The silver swan (accept: swan)
6. Toni Morrison
7. Lancelot
8. Medea
9. Cuba
10. Dulcimer

ARTS 8

1 Aeschylus, Sophocles and Euripides were the three acknowledged masters of ... what?

2 Who is the author of 'Wolf Hall' and 'Bring up the Bodies'?

3 What nationality was the great composer Béla Bartok?

4 Which Suffolk artist painted 'The Hay Wain'?

5 The John Steinbeck novel 'Of Mice and Men' takes its title from a poem by whom?

6 At the end of Shakespeare's 'Macbeth' who is crowned king of Scotland?

7 Pope Julius II summoned which artist to Rome in 1505 to create his tomb?

8 The Bayreuth Festspielhaus is a German opera house dedicated mainly to performing works by which composer?

9 A clarinet is a woodwind instrument, but what kind of instrument is a clavinet?

10 The Salem Witch Trials of 1692 were the basis for which Arthur Miller play?

ARTS 9

1 Which famous fictional detective first appeared in 'A Study in Scarlet' in 1887?

2 The masterpiece of the artist Pheidias was a statue of which Greek god at Olympia?

3 Which historical novel, published in the 1860s, is known as 'Voyna I Mir' in its own language?

4 Which Jane Austen novel largely takes place at the country estate of the Bertram family?

5 According to Norse mythology, which race lives in the realm of Midgard?

6 Give a year in the life of architect Sir Christopher Wren.

7 In which classic 14th century work of literature do a group of pilgrims travel together from Southwark to the shrine of St Thomas à Becket, telling stories?

8 Who was the titan who supported the heavens in Greek mythology?

9 Who wrote a short story called 'A Child's Christmas in Wales'?

10 In the 'Parade's End' series of novels by Ford Madox Ford, the lead character Christopher Tietjens is described, somewhat prematurely, as "the last ..." what?

SUBJECT ROUNDS

ARTS 8
1 Greek tragedy
2 Hilary Mantel
3 Hungarian
4 John Constable
5 Robert Burns
6 Malcolm
7 Michelangelo
8 Richard Wagner
9 Keyboard
10 The Crucible

ARTS 9
1 Sherlock Holmes
2 Zeus
3 War and Peace
4 Mansfield Park
5 Humans
6 1632–1723
7 Canterbury Tales, by Chaucer
8 Atlas
9 Dylan Thomas
10 Tory

ARTS 10

1 Who always rings twice, according to a novel by James M. Cain?

2 'The Master Builder' is a famous work by which great Norwegian dramatist, who also wrote 'Hedda Gabler', 'A Doll's House' and 'Peer Gynt'?

3 Giorgio Vasari wrote that anyone who had seen which sculpture by Michelangelo had no need to see any other sculpture?

4 In Greek tragedy, Electra was the daughter of which king?

5 What did artists Lawrence Abu Hamdan, Helen Cammock, Tai Shani and Oscar Murillo share in 2019?

6 What was the four-word name of the poem read by 22-year-old Amanda Gorman at Joe Biden's inauguration?

7 What is the name of the 6th century BC Greek lyric poet from the island of Lesbos who was known as the "Tenth Muse"?

8 When Dame Peggy Ashcroft played Desdemona on the London stage in 1930, which American star played Othello?

9 What simple game shares its name with a series of novels by Malorie Blackman, which was adapted to a BBC TV series in 2020?

10 What is the name above the door of the house where Winnie-the-Pooh lives?

ARTS 11

1 Which comedian's novels include 'Stark', 'Inconceivable', 'Dead Famous' and 'Popcorn'?

2 Which songwriter won the 2016 Nobel Prize for Literature?

3 In 2020, Tate Modern had an exhibition of the works of Dora Maar, a French artist also famous for being the subject of many paintings, including 'The Weeping Woman', by whom?

4 What surname links the authors of the acclaimed novels 'Hot Milk' and 'Small Island'?

5 Regularly voted Britain's favourite piece of classical music, a work by Ralph Vaughan Williams based on a George Meredith poem is 'The ...' what?

6 'I Wanna Be Yours', 'Beasley Street' and 'Evidently Chickentown' are works by which British performance poet born in 1949?

7 Baroness Jay, daughter of James Callaghan, is thinly fictionalised as the character Thelma in which 1983 novel by Nora Ephron?

8 In which city did a statue called 'A Surge of Power' depicting a woman called Jen Reid, stand for one day in July 2020?

9 Who, from 1850 to 1892, is the longest standing Poet Laureate of the UK?

10 Which novel by Susanna Clarke won the 2021 Women's Prize for Fiction?

ARTS 10
1 The Postman
2 Henrik Ibsen
3 David
4 Agamemnon
5 The Turner Prize (they asked judges that it be shared)
6 The Hill We Climb
7 Sappho
8 Paul Robeson
9 Noughts & Crosses
10 Mr Sanders (accept just Sanders) (It's the name of a previous resident of Pooh's house)

ARTS 11
1 Ben Elton
2 Bob Dylan
3 Pablo Picasso
4 Levy (Deborah Levy and Andrea Levy)
5 Lark Ascending
6 John Cooper Clarke
7 Heartburn (it is about Jay's affair with Ephron's husband Carl Bernstein)
8 Bristol (it was a statue of protester Jen Reid, in the place where the statue of Edward Colston had been. It was taken down within a day)
9 Alfred, Lord Tennyson
10 Piranesi

ARTS 12

1 Which book has more words - A) Gone With the Wind or B) Lord of the Rings?

2 In ballet, what hyphenated name is given to the position where a dancer bends their knees while keeping their feet turned out and heels on the ground?

3 The Ten Commandments appear in two different books of the Old Testament - Deuteronomy and which other?

4 What should music be doing if the word "Rallentando" is on the score?

5 Who was the author of the allegorical work 'The Pilgrim's Progress'?

6 Who wrote the novel 'Around the World in 80 Days'?

7 Year in the Shared Life: Give any year where the two great French artists Claude Monet and Édouard Manet were both alive?

8 Beethoven, Schubert, Dvorak, Bruckner, Mahler and Vaughan Williams all died shortly after writing which number symphony?

9 Which tragic Greek king has a name that means "swollen foot"?

10 What was, at the time, unique about the 2015 album 'Once Upon a Time in Shaolin' by the hip-hop group the Wu-Tang Clan?

ARTS 13

1 The 16th century Italian Andrea Amati was renowned for making musical instruments from which family of the orchestra?

2 Which artist lived for a time in the French city of Arles, but went into an asylum after slicing off part of his ear?

3 The Shakespeare play 'Troilus and Cressida' is set in and around which ancient city?

4 In between writing 'The Adventures of Tom Sawyer' and 'The Adventures of Huckleberry Finn' what other well known novel, set in England in 1547, did Mark Twain write?

5 Which acclaimed book, and film, takes place at the Marcia Blaine Academy?

6 Which comedy by Aristophanes features a kingdom in the air called Cloud-cuckooland?

7 Which opera by Giuseppe Verdi is about the hunchbacked court jester of the Duke of Mantua?

8 They started building it in 1882 and hope to finish in 2026. Which huge structure is it?

9 Perhaps best known as the illustrator of Roald Dahl books, who was the inaugural British Children's Laureate?

10 Ian Fleming's James Bond holds which rank in the British armed forces?

ARTS 12
1 B) Lord of the Rings (c.480,000 vs c.418,000)
2 Demi-plié
3 Exodus
4 Gradually slowing down
5 John Bunyan
6 Jules Verne
7 1840-1883
8 Ninth
9 Oedipus
10 Only one copy was ever made

ARTS 13
1 Stringed
2 Vincent Van Gogh
3 Troy
4 The Prince and the Pauper
5 The Prime of Miss Jean Brodie
6 The Birds
7 Rigoletto
8 La Sagrada Familia (in Barcelona)
9 Quentin Blake
10 Commander (in the Royal Navy)

ARTS 14

1 In 1815, aged just 18, who began writing 'Frankenstein'?

2 The Starbucks coffee shop chain is named after a character in which novel?

3 The Whitworth Art Gallery is in which English city?

4 Which composer's works include 'An Alpine Symphony' and 'Also sprach Zarathustra'?

5 "Jesus wept" is the shortest verse in the Bible, but whose death prompted Jesus to weep?

6 'I Vow to Thee, My Country', a hymn sung at Margaret Thatcher's funeral, takes its tune from which of the planets in Gustav Holst's 'Planets Suite'?

7 Which knight of the Round Table was the nephew of King Arthur and famous for accepting the challenge of the Green Knight?

8 JK Rowling's birthday is on what day (the same as her most famous character)?

9 The sculpture, 'Maman', by Louise Bourgeois, which was displayed in the Turbine Hall of the Tate Modern, is a huge, bronze ... what?

10 In 1884, which artist completed 'Bathers at Asnières', a painting of working class men sitting by the Seine, which was a precursor to a more famous companion piece, showing people on the other side of the river, which he completed in 1885?

ARTS 15

1 Which children's book by Julia Donaldson was based on a Chinese folktale about a child who tricks a tiger into being scared of her?

2 Which surname links two authors, one whose main character is called Scarpetta, the other whose main character is called Sharpe?

3 In 2019, a street in Brussels was renamed "Ceci n'est pas une rue" in honour of which artist?

4 What does the term "Scherzando" mean on a musical score?

5 How many books is the famous philosopher Socrates known to have written?

6 What is the first book of the Old Testament to take its name from a person?

7 Give any year in the life of Friedrich Nietzsche.

8 Which Thomas Hardy novel's subtitle is 'The Life and Death of a Man of Character'?

9 In 1993, Rachel Whiteread was the first woman to win the Turner Prize. She also was awarded the "Anti-Turner Prize" in the same year, supposedly for the "worst artist in Britain", and awarded by which musical duo?

10 Which novel by John Steinbeck takes its name from the second line in 'Battle Hymn of the Republic'?

SUBJECT ROUNDS

ARTS 14
1 Mary Shelley
2 Moby-Dick
3 Manchester
4 Richard Strauss
5 Lazarus
6 Jupiter
7 Gawain
8 31st July
9 Spider
10 Georges Seurat (the second painting is 'A Sunday Afternoon on the Island of La Grande Jatte')

ARTS 15
1 The Gruffalo
2 Cornwell
3 René Magritte
4 Playfully
5 None (pretty much everything we know about him is via Plato)
6 Joshua
7 1844-1900
8 The Mayor of Casterbridge
9 The KLF/K Foundation (Bill Drummond and Jimmy Cauty)
10 The Grapes of Wrath

ARTS 16

1 The musical 'Oliver!' is based on a novel by whom?

2 What two-word suffix is added to the name of the 18th century British painter Joseph Wright?

3 Who designed the iconic Barack Obama "Hope" poster for the 2008 US election?

4 Edinburgh's main railway station is named after a novel by whom?

5 Which novel by Wilkie Collins featured the first detective hero in English fiction?

6 Which Victorian group of poets and artists included John Everett Millais and William Holman Hunt?

7 Meissen in Germany is best known for the production of items in which material?

8 Which fictional language is described in George Orwell's novel '1984'?

9 The composer sometimes known as the "African Mahler" and named by his mother in honour of a British romantic poet was Samuel ... who?

10 What is the term for painting without lines or borders, created by Leonardo da Vinci, and meaning "to evaporate like smoke"?

ARTS 17

1 Roy Lichtenstein and Robert Indiana were key figures in which art movement?

2 Which 1993 novel by Vikram Seth, adapted into a BBC1 series in 2020, is, at 1,349 pages, one of the longest single-volume novels ever published in English?

3 How many people are portrayed in the Da Vinci painting 'The Last Supper'?

4 Which author wrote romantic novels under the pseudonym Mary Westmacott?

5 Which American street artist, who died in February 1990, created a famous mural in New York City which said "Crack is Wack"?

6 Which book includes the first recorded instance of the word "yahoo"?

7 Which artist, who was inspired by Tahiti and Polynesia, is buried on the Marquesas Islands in the South Pacific?

8 Which figure from history does the adjective Cartesian refer to?

9 In 20th century art, neoplasticism was also known as De Stijl, which means "The Style" in which language?

10 Grey meant world affairs, purple meant essays, red meant drama, yellow - miscellaneous, dark blue - biographies, cerise - travel, green - crime fiction and orange - general fiction. What does this refer to?

ARTS 16
1 Charles Dickens
2 of Derby
3 Shepard Fairey
4 Sir Walter Scott (Waverley)
5 The Moonstone
6 Pre-Raphaelites
7 Porcelain
8 Newspeak
9 Coleridge-Taylor
10 Sfumato

ARTS 17
1 Pop Art
2 A Suitable Boy
3 Thirteen
4 Agatha Christie
5 Keith Haring
6 Gulliver's Travels
7 Paul Gauguin
8 René Descartes (his Latin name being Renatus Cartesius)
9 Dutch
10 The original colour code of Penguin paperbacks (they all had a white stripe in the middle)

ARTS 18

1 The pigs Napoleon and Snowball feature in which George Orwell book?

2 David Cornwell, born in 1931, wrote several bestsellers under what pseudonym?

3 How many lines are there in the Japanese poetic form, the tanka [as in, when written in Roman script]?

4 What is the one-word name of the art movement associated primarily with Georges Braque and Pablo Picasso, that emphasises the flat, two-dimensional surface of the picture plane?

5 Which British ballet star spent 24 hours in a Panamanian jail in 1959 after her politician husband attempted to stage a coup d'état there?

6 Which artist and influential art historian wrote 'Lives of the Most Excellent Painters, Sculptors, and Architects' in the 16th century?

7 Which 2004 novel by Alan Hollinghurst won the Man Booker Prize?

8 What nationality was the author Henry James?

9 What does the S stand for in C.S. Lewis, and is also the name of items that you may find in an office?

10 Which scientist has written books including 'The Selfish Gene', 'The Blind Watchmaker', and 'The Ancestor's Tale'?

ARTS 19

1 Hexameter is poetry with how many metrical feet in each line?

2 Which Greek philosopher's work included 'The Apology', 'The Republic' and 'The Laws'?

3 Which Chinese-American detective was created by Earl Derr Biggers?

4 Who is the author of 'Human Croquet', 'One Good Turn' and 'Behind the Scenes at the Museum'?

5 Which book begins: "It is a truth universally acknowledged, that a single man in possession of a good fortune, must be in want of a wife."?

6 With examples being Dylan Thomas's 'Do Not Go Gentle Into That Good Night' and Sylvia Plath's 'Mad Girl's Love Song', how many lines does a villanelle have?

7 In 1974, which dancer from the Bolshoi ballet defected whilst touring Canada?

8 Who, in June 2020, became the first Black woman to top the British nonfiction chart with her book 'Why I'm No Longer Talking to White People About Race'?

9 In what position did Alice Oswald succeed Simon Armitage in 2019?

10 The poets Keats, Shelley and Byron all died in southern Europe within four years of each other, during which decade?

ARTS 18
1 Animal Farm
2 John le Carré
3 Five (5-7-5-7-7 syllables)
4 Cubism
5 Dame Margot Fonteyn (her husband was Roberto Arias)
6 Giorgio Vasari (He may be the first person to use the word 'renaissance' in print, in this sense)
7 The Line of Beauty
8 American
9 Staples (Clive Staples Lewis)
10 Richard Dawkins

ARTS 19
1 Six
2 Plato
3 Charlie Chan
4 Kate Atkinson
5 Pride and Prejudice (by Jane Austen, published in 1813)
6 19
7 Mikhail Baryshnikov (not Rudolf Nureyev, who was in the Kirov and defected in 1961 in Paris)
8 Reni Eddo-Lodge
9 Oxford Professor of Poetry
10 1820s

ARTS 20

1 Which superstar swore live on TV when presenting the Turner Prize to Martin Creed in 2001?

2 Born of a Native American mother and an Afro-Haitian father, Edmonia Lewis achieved fame in the late 19th century in which field of the arts?

3 In 2015, pictures were published of which author surfing and roller skating in 1911?

4 Which Shakespearean character gives a speech which begins "O, what a noble mind is here o'erthrown!"?

5 In 2012, what was the title of the second book for which Hilary Mantel won the Booker Prize?

6 What name is given to comedies such as 'Man of Mode', 'The Country Wife' and 'The Relapse', written between 1660 and 1710?

7 What was the title of the debut novel by Julian Fellowes, the creator of 'Downton Abbey'?

8 What M is the title of the painting by Roy Lichtenstein which sold for $165 million in January 2017, which shows a woman saying something admiring about her male friend's latest painting?

9 Pearl Buck was the first American woman to win the Nobel Prize in Literature. Who was the second?

10 What is the name of a famous painting by Andrew Wyeth, from 1948, depicting a woman with a disability crawling through a field in Maine?

ARTS 21

1 What type of animal was divided in two and preserved in formaldehyde in Damien Hirst's work 'Mother and Child (Divided)'?

2 Who was the author of the bestselling childhood memoir 'A Child Called It'?

3 Who founded the Johann Strauss Orchestra in 1987?

4 The Wulfhall after which the Hilary Mantel book 'Wolf Hall' is named was the family home of which family?

5 In which children's book is there a deity called Lord Frith?

6 Musicals 'Bugsy Malone' and 'Annie' both contain a song with what title?

7 In a series of books by Frank Richards, which title character is in the Fourth Form of Greyfriars School?

8 Dick Deadeye is a character in which Gilbert and Sullivan musical?

9 What is the name of the theatrical society at Harvard University which gives annual Man and Woman of the Year awards to notable celebrities?

10 What was the name of Antony Gormley's art installation in London in 2007, in which 31 sculpted male figures were placed in prominent places?

SUBJECT ROUNDS

ARTS 20
1 Madonna
2 Sculpture
3 Agatha Christie
4 Ophelia
5 Bring Up the Bodies
6 Restoration comedies (or comedies of manners)
7 Snobs
8 Masterpiece
9 Toni Morrison
10 Christina's World

ARTS 21
1 Cow
2 Dave Pelzer
3 André Rieu
4 Seymour family
5 Watership Down
6 Tomorrow
7 Billy Bunter
8 HMS Pinafore
9 Hasty Pudding
10 Event Horizon

ARTS 22

1 'De Architectura' by the Roman architect Marcus Vitruvius Pollio was the basis for a famous drawing from around 1490 by whom?

2 'La Rêve', painted in 1932, depicted which Spanish painter's mistress Marie-Thérèse Walter?

3 Which Irish author wrote 'The Barrytown Trilogy', all three books of which were made into films?

4 In which classic musical did Paul Robeson, playing the part of Joe, first sing 'Ol' Man River'?

5 In poetry, what name is given to a metrical foot which contains two stressed syllables?

6 Nigel Molesworth is a pupil at which school created by Geoffrey Willans and Ronald Searle?

7 Which art movement, co-founded by Billy Childish, took its name from something said to him by his then-girlfriend Tracey Emin?

8 What title links a play by Ben Jonson and a novel by Paulo Coelho?

9 Which author wrote that a woman wishing to write fiction must have "a room of her own"?

10 In 1982, King Juan Carlos of Spain made which artist the Marquis of Pubol?

ARTS 23

1 Who was the American author of 'I Know Why the Caged Bird Sings'?

2 In 2016, Paul Beatty became the first American to win which award with 'The Sellout'?

3 Dolores Haze, her mother Charlotte, and Clare Quilty are characters in which controversial 20th century novel?

4 Which restaurant, opened in the 1960s by Michel and Albert Roux, was the first in the UK to gain three Michelin stars?

5 In 2013, a three-part painting by Francis Bacon of which other English painter sold for £142 million?

6 What is the title of the 1980 dystopian classic, set in a post-nuclear Kent, written by Russell Hoban?

7 Which small train worked for The Merioneth and Llantisilly Railway Traction Company Limited, and had friends including Jones the Steam and Evans the Song?

8 In 2012 Cecilia Giménez became famous for her work on the fresco 'Ecce Homo', depicting which figure?

9 To whom [two-word answer required] did the composer Ludwig van Beethoven address a famous love letter written in July 1812?

10 Who wrote the 1915 poem 'The Road Not Taken'?

ARTS 22
1 Leonardo da Vinci
2 Pablo Picasso
3 Roddy Doyle
4 Show Boat
5 Spondee
6 St Custard's
7 Stuckism
8 The Alchemist
9 Virginia Woolf
10 Salvador Dalí

ARTS 23
1 Maya Angelou
2 Booker Prize
3 Lolita
4 Le Gavroche
5 Lucian Freud
6 Riddley Walker
7 Ivor the Engine
8 Jesus Christ (she damaged it in a comical way)
9 Immortal Beloved
10 Robert Frost

ARTS 24

1 Which composer wrote 'Music for the Royal Fireworks'?

2 Which hugely successful American author wrote the novels 'The Dream Merchants' and 'The Carpetbaggers'?

3 Who was the first person buried at Poets' Corner in Westminster Abbey?

4 Which opera by Mozart has the subtitle 'The Rake Punished'?

5 In 2016, the location of which London museum moved from Shad Thames in East London to Kensington in West London?

6 Apart from 'King Lear', the title character of which other Shakespeare play is a legendary ancient King of Britain?

7 In 1999, which of Tracey Emin's possessions saw her shortlisted for the Turner Prize?

8 According to legend, the playwright Aeschylus died when an eagle dropped what on his head?

9 The painting 'The Monarch of the Glen' by Sir Edward Landseer depicts ... what?

10 Whose 1943 painting 'Broadway Boogie Woogie' is inspired by the music and street design of New York, where he had recently moved?

ARTS 25

1 Which English poet wrote 'She Walks in Beauty' and 'Don Juan'?

2 On the hill of Montjuïc in Barcelona, there is a museum dedicated to the work of which modern artist?

3 Kazuo Ishiguro's 'An Artist of the Floating World' is set in which country?

4 'Fountain', a porcelain urinal signed R.Mutt, was created by which 20th century artist?

5 Whose wartime experiences are recounted in the book 'Good-Bye to All That'?

6 Which novel by George Eliot is subtitled 'The Weaver of Raveloe'?

7 'The Government Inspector' was written by which playwright?

8 Which sculpture by Auguste Rodin was originally titled 'The Poet'?

9 Who wrote a special poem for a 1936 documentary about the mail train from London to Scotland?

10 In the novel 'Don Quixote', what does the title character fight, thinking they're giants?

ARTS 24

1 George Frideric Handel
2 Harold Robbins
3 Geoffrey Chaucer
4 Don Giovanni
5 Design Museum
6 Cymbeline
7 Bed
8 A tortoise
9 A stag
10 Piet Mondrian

ARTS 25

1 Lord Byron
2 Joan Miró
3 Japan
4 Marcel Duchamp
5 Robert Graves
6 Silas Marner
7 Nikolai Gogol
8 The Thinker
9 WH Auden
10 Windmills

MUSIC 5

1 Who had a h
   Coming Out'

2 What was th
   album relea:

3 Which leade
   band is the r
   band Gorilla:

4 Which Swedi
   greatest hits
   'Don't Bore U

5 What is the s
   name?

6 Which band
   called 'Vanis
   and 'XTRMNT

7 Mark Snow h
   the theme fr

8 How is the G
   musician Ch
   known?

9 Which band
   'The Legend

10 Which cover
   selling single

MUSIC 1

1 What rap duo was made up of Antwan "Big Boi" Patton and Andre "3000" Benjamin?

2 Which word appears in the title of a Police hit in 1981, a Queen hit in 1986 and a Take That hit in 1992?

3 Who is the lead singer of the Arctic Monkeys?

4 Which chart-topping group of the 80s takes their name from a character played by Milo O'Shea in the film 'Barbarella'?

5 Who had a top 20 hit in 1994 with 'Loser'?

6 Which pair wrote the Rolling Stones' first UK Top 20 hit, 'I Wanna Be Your Man', which reached Number 12 in November 1963?

7 The bands The Delgados, Teenage Fanclub and The Sensational Alex Harvey Band were all formed in and around which Scottish city?

8 The actor Robert Downey Jr starred in the video for whose single, called 'I Want Love', in October 2001?

9 What was Billie Piper's first UK number one single, back when she was just known as Billie?

10 What was Pink Floyd's only UK Number 1 single?

MUSIC 2

1 About which other musician did Stevie Wonder write the 1980 song 'Master Blaster (Jammin')'?

2 Bon Scott, who died in 1980, was the original lead singer in what Australian rock band?

3 Which duo represented Russia in the 2003 Eurovision Song Contest after having a Number 1 hit in the UK?

4 What group did Shaun Ryder form in 1995 after the Happy Mondays split up?

5 Jordan, Jonathan, Danny, Donnie and Joe were the founder members of which band?

6 Which rock guitarist, born in 1947, built his guitar (called 'the Red Special') and is an expert in astrophysics?

7 Which Canadian singer was born Eileen Regina Edwards?

8 How did Kate Bush have a Number 5 hit with a "grandmother" in 1980?

9 "The boys of the NYPD choir were singing Galway Bay, and the bells are ringing out for Christmas Day" is part of which city's fairytale?

10 Which band once played on 'Top of the Pops' in front of a huge picture of the darts player Jocky Wilson?

MUSIC 5

1 Diana Ross
2 Please Please M(
3 Damon Albarn (
4 Roxette
5 Steven
6 Primal Scream
7 The X-Files
8 Chance the Rap
9 Dave Dee, Dozy,
10 'I Will Always Lov

MUSIC 1

1 OutKast
2 Magic (Every Little Thing She Does Is Magic, A Kind Of Magic, Could It Be Magic)
3 Alex Turner
4 Duran Duran (the character is called Durand Durand)
5 Beck
6 John Lennon & Paul McCartney
7 Glasgow
8 Elton John
9 Because We Want To
10 Another Brick in the Wall Part II (December 1979)

MUSIC 2

1 Bob Marley
2 AC/DC
3 t.A.T.u.
4 Black Grape
5 New Kids on the Block
6 Brian May (of Queen)
7 Shania Twain
8 Babooshka ('Babooshka' means Grandmother or Old Lady in Russian - and that was the title of her song)
9 New York ('Fairytale of New York' by the Pogues and Kirsty MacColl)
10 Dexys Midnight Runners (the song was called 'Jackie Wilson Said')

SUBJECT ROUNDS

MUSIC 3

1 Which E
stage n
used to

2 Anna M
the late
name?

3 In 1985,
numbe
song?

4 What is
by Lewi
album

5 What w
wonder
which s

6 Which r
degree
had a l
'Savage

7 Who ho
'N' Roll'

8 'Spanis
were tw
by The

9 Who pl
Californ

10 How m
1 single
McCart

MUSIC 7

1 Ginger Baker, Jack Bruce and Eric Clapton made up which 60s rock band?

2 How is the British singer/dancer/actress Tahliah Debrett Barnett, who has released albums including 'LP1' and 'Magdalene', better known?

3 The cover of the 1971 debut album by which singer, who died in 2020, was a picture of him holding his tools on a lunch break in front of the aerospace manufacturer where he was still working?

4 Whose album 'Collapsed in Sunbeams' won the 2021 Mercury Music Prize?

5 What was the name of the legendary BB King's guitar?

6 In which US state does the Burning Man Festival take place?

7 Whose 2013 album is called 'ARTPOP'?

8 The only time the winner of the Grammy Award for Best Rock Song was written by a man called Dylan was in 1998. What is the name of the song?

9 Two different US states are mentioned in Simon and Garfunkel's 'America' - Michigan and which other?

10 What classic 1991 song's title was inspired by a piece of graffiti which made reference to a brand of deodorant?

MUSIC 8

1 Don Henley, Glenn Frey and Joe Walsh have been members of which massively successful American band?

2 Which 1969 rock-opera was about "a deaf, dumb and blind kid who sure played a mean pinball"?

3 1980's 'Boy' was the first album released by which band?

4 Whose album from 2014 was called '1989'?

5 What was Cliff Richard's first UK Number 1, a song that he took to Number 1 again 27 years later in a charity collaboration?

6 Which band released the albums 'Beggars Banquet' and 'Goats Head Soap'?

7 Which enormously successful group of the 70s removed the prefix Ambrose from their name just before becoming famous?

8 Which band, whose hits include 'Run' and Chasing Cars, formed in Dundee (although most of them are from Northern Ireland) and was originally called Polar Bear?

9 Which much-hyped but ultimately unsuccessful 60s rock group took their name from the punchline to the joke "What's big and purple and lives in the ocean?"?

10 Who is the only artist to have charted in the UK and US every year between 1971 and 1999?

MUSIC 3

1 Sting (it w
2 Tina Turne
3 Frankie
4 Grace
5 Telephon
6 Megan Th
7 Joan Jett
8 London C
9 Johnny C
10 None

MUSIC 7

1 Cream
2 FKA twigs
3 Bill Withers
4 Arlo Parks
5 Lucille
6 Nevada
7 Lady Gaga
8 One Headlight (by The Wallflowers, written by Jakob Dylan, Bob Dylan's son)
9 New Jersey (other places mentioned are Saginaw and Pittsburgh)
10 Smells Like Teen Spirit (by Nirvana)

MUSIC 8

1 The Eagles
2 Tommy
3 U2
4 Taylor Swift
5 Living Doll (in 1986, it was with The Young Ones)
6 The Rolling Stones
7 Slade (until the late 60s they were known as Ambrose Slade)
8 Snow Patrol
9 Moby Grape
10 Elton John

MUSIC 5

1 Who had a hit in 1980 with the song 'I'm Coming Out'?

2 What was the name of The Beatles' first album released in the UK?

3 Which leader of a successful British band is the man behind the cartoon band Gorillaz?

4 Which Swedish double act released a greatest hits collection in 1995 called 'Don't Bore Us, Get to the Chorus!'?

5 What is the singer Morrissey's first name?

6 Which band has released albums called 'Vanishing Point', 'Screamadelica' and 'XTRMNTR'?

7 Mark Snow had a hit single in 1996 with the theme from which sci-fi TV series?

8 How is the Grammy-winning Chicago musician Chancelor Bennett better known?

9 Which band had a UK Number 1 with 'The Legend of Xanadu' in 1968?

10 Which cover song was the biggest-selling single in the UK in 1992?

MUSIC 6

1 Which word follows 'Future' in the title of the 2020 album by Dua Lipa?

2 Which band's hits include 'She Will Be Loved' and 'Moves Like Jagger'?

3 Who released the album 'Popped In Souled Out' in 1987?

4 By what nickname is the Manchester musician Bryan Glancy, who died in 2006, immortalised in the title of a 2008 Mercury Prize-winning album?

5 The bassline of which Number 1 single by The Jam is "borrowed" from the single 'I'm Ready for Love' by Martha and the Vandellas?

6 Which former Spice Girl released a solo single called 'Not Such An Innocent Girl' in 2001?

7 What was the Bee Gees' last UK Number 1, released in September 1987?

8 True or False? The lead singers of The Clash, The Jam and The Sex Pistols were all born with the same first name.

9 Which 1970s band have sold almost 23 million copies of their biggest hit, 'In The Summertime', making it one of the highest selling recordings of all time?

10 The second album of which 1990s singer would have been called 'My Sweetheart the Drunk'?

MUSIC 5
1 Diana Ross
2 Please Please Me
3 Damon Albarn (of Blur)
4 Roxette
5 Steven
6 Primal Scream
7 The X-Files
8 Chance the Rapper
9 Dave Dee, Dozy, Beaky, Mick and Tich
10 'I Will Always Love You' by Whitney Houston

MUSIC 6
1 Nostalgia
2 Maroon 5
3 Wet Wet Wet
4 The Seldom Seen Kid (by Elbow)
5 Town Called Malice (it's similar to 'You Can't Hurry Love' but exactly the same as 'I'm Ready for Love')
6 Victoria Beckham
7 You Win Again
8 True: Joe Strummer was born John Graham Mellor, Paul Weller was born John Weller, Johnny Rotten is John Joseph Lydon
9 Mungo Jerry
10 Jeff Buckley (Buckley died in 1997. 'Sketches from My Sweetheart the Drunk' was released in 1998)

MUSIC 7

1. Ginger Baker, Jack Bruce and Eric Clapton made up which 60s rock band?

2. How is the British singer/dancer/actress Tahliah Debrett Barnett, who has released albums including 'LP1' and 'Magdalene', better known?

3. The cover of the 1971 debut album by which singer, who died in 2020, was a picture of him holding his tools on a lunch break in front of the aerospace manufacturer where he was still working?

4. Whose album 'Collapsed in Sunbeams' won the 2021 Mercury Music Prize?

5. What was the name of the legendary BB King's guitar?

6. In which US state does the Burning Man Festival take place?

7. Whose 2013 album is called 'ARTPOP'?

8. The only time the winner of the Grammy Award for Best Rock Song was written by a man called Dylan was in 1998. What is the name of the song?

9. Two different US states are mentioned in Simon and Garfunkel's 'America' - Michigan and which other?

10. What classic 1991 song's title was inspired by a piece of graffiti which made reference to a brand of deodorant?

MUSIC 8

1. Don Henley, Glenn Frey and Joe Walsh have been members of which massively successful American band?

2. Which 1969 rock-opera was about "a deaf, dumb and blind kid who sure played a mean pinball"?

3. 1980's 'Boy' was the first album released by which band?

4. Whose album from 2014 was called '1989'?

5. What was Cliff Richard's first UK Number 1, a song that he took to Number 1 again 27 years later in a charity collaboration?

6. Which band released the albums 'Beggars Banquet' and 'Goats Head Soup'?

7. Which enormously successful group of the 70s removed the prefix Ambrose from their name just before becoming famous?

8. Which band, whose hits include 'Run' and Chasing Cars, formed in Dundee (although most of them are from Northern Ireland) and was originally called Polar Bear?

9. Which much-hyped but ultimately unsuccessful 60s rock group took their name from the punchline to the joke "What's big and purple and lives in the ocean?"?

10. Who is the only artist to have charted in the UK and US every year between 1971 and 1999?

MUSIC 7
1. Cream
2. FKA twigs
3. Bill Withers
4. Arlo Parks
5. Lucille
6. Nevada
7. Lady Gaga
8. One Headlight (by The Wallflowers, written by Jakob Dylan, Bob Dylan's son)
9. New Jersey (other places mentioned are Saginaw and Pittsburgh)
10. Smells Like Teen Spirit (by Nirvana)

MUSIC 8
1. The Eagles
2. Tommy
3. U2
4. Taylor Swift
5. Living Doll (in 1986, it was with The Young Ones)
6. The Rolling Stones
7. Slade (until the late 60s they were known as Ambrose Slade)
8. Snow Patrol
9. Moby Grape
10. Elton John

MUSIC 9

1 'Big Willie Style' in 1997 was the first solo album of which American actor and singer?

2 The Birthday Party, Grinderman and The Bad Seeds are all acts associated with which Australian, who once duetted with Kylie Minogue?

3 Whose singles include 'Good as Hell', 'Truth Hurts' and 'Juice'?

4 Who had a hit in 1990 with the song 'Just Like Jesse James'?

5 Who is Duran Duran's vocalist?

6 'One Last Love Song' was a hit for which British band in 1994?

7 Which British personality guest-starred as the limo-driver in the 2000 video for Madonna's single 'Music'?

8 Richard Fairbrass is the lead singer of the group Right Said Fred. What is the first name of his brother, who is also in the band?

9 What magic word was a working title for the Beatles 1966 album 'Revolver' as well as the name of a 1982 album by The Steve Miller Band'?

10 With which female singer did both Joe Cocker and Bill Medley sing duets which were Oscar-winning songs in the 1980s?

MUSIC 10

1 What song was a Number 1 single in Britain for both Billy Joel and Westlife?

2 Leon Followill is the name of the father of the members of which American rock band?

3 Which Elton John song was taken into the UK charts by Kate Bush in December 1991?

4 Which Scottish band had UK Top 20 singles with songs called 'Turn', 'Sing' and 'Side'?

5 What song begins with this lyric: "I may not always love you, but long as there are stars above you, you never need to doubt it"?

6 Graham McPherson is the frontman of which British band which has lasted from the 70s to the 2020s?

7 Which of the Bee Gees was born first?

8 Which hip-hop artist and producer released 'Compton', his first album in 16 years, in 2015?

9 What K is the band also known as The Timelords and The Justified Ancients of Mu-Mu?

10 Barrowlands and King Tut's Wah Wah Hut are famous music venues in which British city?

MUSIC 9
1 Will Smith
2 Nick Cave
3 Lizzo
4 Cher
5 Simon Le Bon
6 The Beautiful South
7 Sacha Baron Cohen / Ali G
8 Fred (Fairbrass)
9 Abracadabra
10 Jennifer Warnes ('Up Where We Belong' with Joe Cocker (1982) and '(I've Had) The Time of My Life' (1987) with Bill Medley)

MUSIC 10
1 Uptown Girl
2 Kings of Leon
3 Rocket Man
4 Travis
5 God Only Knows
6 Madness (he is Suggs)
7 Barry Gibb (born 1946)
8 Dr Dre
9 KLF
10 Glasgow

MUSIC 11

1 What relation was Karen Carpenter to her bandmate in The Carpenters, Richard?

2 What J is the stage-name of the rapper born Shawn Corey Carter?

3 Which band released the bestselling 1977 album 'Rumours', which contains songs such as 'Dreams', 'Go Your Own Way' and 'The Chain'?

4 Who described himself as 'Mr Loverman' on a Top 10 single in 1993?

5 How is Joscelyn Eve Stoker, born in England in April 1987, better known?

6 Which W is a song by Chip Taylor that was a hit for The Troggs in 1966?

7 'Take Me to Church' was a hit in 2015 for which Irish singer?

8 What sport features in the video for the Robbie Williams song 'She's the One'?

9 Guitarist Bernard Butler collaborated on the 2022 album 'For All Our Days That Tear the Heart' with which actress?

10 What was Meat Loaf's first and only UK Number 1 single?

MUSIC 12

1 What rock 'n' roll alter ego did David Bowie kill off at Hammersmith Apollo in 1973?

2 The Welsh group Space teamed up with Cerys Matthews in March 1998 for a ballad about which other Welsh singer?

3 What was the first track on the Oasis album 'Definitely Maybe'?

4 Fill in the missing lyric from 'Nothing Compares to You' by Sinead O'Connor: "It's been seven hours and ... days since you took your love away".

5 In which General Election year was D:Ream's single 'Things Can Only Get Better' Labour's campaign song?

6 Which band originally included Siobhan Fahey, Sara Dallin, and Keren Woodward when it started in 1981?

7 'The Sun Ain't Gonna Shine Anymore' was a UK Number 1 in 1966 for which so-called brothers?

8 Which item of furniture was the title of a single taken from the debut album by Isle of Wight duo Wet Leg?

9 Robert van Winkle used a sample from Queen to reach Number 1 in the UK in 1990 under what name?

10 Which songwriting pair wrote '(They Long to Be) Close to You', as sung by The Carpenters?

SUBJECT ROUNDS

MUSIC 11
1 Sister
2 Jay-Z
3 Fleetwood Mac
4 Shabba Ranks
5 Joss Stone
6 Wild Thing
7 Hozier
8 Ice Skating
9 Jessie Buckley
10 I'd Do Anything For Love (But I Won't Do That)

MUSIC 12
1 Ziggy Stardust
2 Tom Jones (The Ballad of Tom Jones)
3 Rock 'n' Roll Star
4 Fifteen
5 1997
6 Bananarama
7 The Walker Brothers
8 Chaise Longue
9 Vanilla Ice (the song is 'Ice Ice Baby')
10 Burt Bacharach and Hal David

MUSIC 13

1 Dave Evans and Paul Hewson are, under different names, members of which hugely successful rock band?

2 Who sang lead vocal on Take That's UK Number 1, 'Everything Changes'?

3 Which group had a hit with 'Dancing in the Moonlight' in 2000?

4 How many 'Little Birds' were in the title of a song by Bob Marley in 1980?

5 How is the singer Mark McLoughlin, born in Clydebank in 1965, better known?

6 In 2020, 'Rain on Me' was a duet between Lady Gaga and which other artist?

7 Which boy band's first single, in 1997, was 'Slam Dunk (Da Funk)'?

8 Which American double act released an album called 'Gratuitous Sax and Senseless Violins'?

9 Which non-European country made an appearance in the 2015 Eurovision Song Contest for the first time (to mark 60 years of the contest)?

10 Which band (who had six UK Number 1s) included a song called 'For Your Eyes Only' on their album 'The Hunter', after it had not been chosen as the official Bond theme?

MUSIC 14

1 Which band was Justin Timberlake in before going solo?

2 Which Queen song was UK Christmas Number 1 in 1975 and 1991?

3 What word goes before "the Unstoppable Sex Machine" in the name of a British indie band whose members were called Jim Bob and Fruitbat?

4 Named after his mother, what is the name of Kanye West's 2021 album?

5 The members of hip-hop duo Kris Kross were, in real life, both called Chris. Chris Kelly was known as Mac Daddy, how was Chris Smith known?

6 Which record label was founded in 1983 by Dick Green, Joe Foster and Alan McGee?

7 Which song mentions, in its lyrics, Brazil, the river Tyne, the A45, Selsey Bill, Muswell Hill and Primrose Hill?

8 A statue of which character from a song was created in Liverpool from £1m worth of used banknotes?

9 Which British pop duo had four Number 1 albums in a row from 1988 to 1994, called 'The Innocents', 'Wild', 'Chorus' and 'I Say I Say I Say'?

10 Cascada issued an important health and safety instruction in the title of their 2009 Number 1 hit single - what was it?

SUBJECT ROUNDS

MUSIC 13
1 U2 (they are The Edge and Bono)
2 Robbie Williams
3 Toploader
4 Three
5 Marti Pellow (of Wet Wet Wet)
6 Ariana Grande
7 5ive
8 Sparks
9 Australia
10 Blondie

MUSIC 14
1 *NSYNC
2 Bohemian Rhapsody
3 Carter
4 Donda
5 Daddy Mac
6 Creation Records
7 Driving in My Car (by Madness)
8 Eleanor Rigby (the sculptor is Leonard J Brown)
9 Erasure (not Pet Shop Boys)
10 Evacuate the Dancefloor

MUSIC 15

1 Each year the Reading Festival is paired with a similar event in which city?

2 Who released an album under the name Katy Hudson in 2001, before changing her stage name and achieving global success?

3 Whose 2017 album is called 'Humanz'?

4 Ellie Rowsell is the lead singer of which Mercury-winning British rock band?

5 Which top 20 hit for Mansun in 1996 was inspired by frontman Paul Draper hearing a piece of commentary by John Motson?

6 In the American supergroup of the 60s and 70s, what does the Y stand for in CSNY?

7 Band Aid released 'Do They Know It's Christmas', but what song did USA For Africa release?

8 A play on words based on the title of a famous Harper Lee novel, what is the title of Kendrick Lamar's Number 1 2015 album?

9 How is the 1968 album 'The Beatles' more commonly known?

10 Which band's members were Stacy Ferguson, Alan Pineda Lindo, Jaime Luis Gomez and William James Adams?

MUSIC 16

1 Which music star wrote Sheena Easton's hit 'Sugar Walls', The Bangles' 'Manic Monday' and Sinead O'Connor's 'Nothing Compares 2 U'?

2 Who was the lead singer of The Who?

3 What is the twitter handle of Brit award-winning rapper Dave, a pun on the name of a bank?

4 Reggaeton is a form of music which originated in the 1990s on which island?

5 What was the name of the keyboardist in the band Manfred Mann?

6 In his 1959 high school yearbook page, Bob Dylan stated that his ambition was "to join" which rock'n'roll star, who died in 2020?

7 Which song does this lyric come from: "I've looked at the ocean, tried hard to imagine the way you felt the day you sailed from Wester Ross to Nova Scotia"?

8 Michael Render, a rapper whose powerful speech in Atlanta in the wake of the killing of George Floyd was widely shared, is better known by what moniker?

9 What one-word title links the highest chart entry for both Kasabian in 2009 and The Crazy World of Arthur Brown in 1968?

10 Whose first album, 'Infinite', from 1996, sold around 1000 copies, while his next four albums have sold a combined total of almost 70 million copies?

MUSIC 15
1 Leeds
2 Katy Perry
3 Gorillaz
4 Wolf Alice
5 Wide Open Space (Draper was seeking lyrical inspiration when he heard Motson on MOTD going "He's in a wide open space ...")
6 Young (Neil Young of Crosby, Stills, Nash and Young)
7 We Are The World
8 To Pimp a Butterfly (from 'To Kill a Mockingbird')
9 The White Album
10 Black Eyed Peas (Fergie, apl.de.ap, Taboo, will.i.am)

MUSIC 16
1 Prince
2 Roger Daltrey
3 Santan (Santan Dave)
4 Puerto Rico
5 Manfred Mann
6 Little Richard
7 Letter from America (The Proclaimers)
8 Killer Mike (of Run the Jewels)
9 Fire
10 Eminem

MUSIC 17

1 Who had a UK Number 1 single in 1981 with 'Ghost Town'?

2 Who released the album 'Eivets Rednow' in 1968?

3 What is the name of the island between the Sankey Canal and the estuary of the Mersey that was the site of a famous concert in 1990?

4 How is the British rapper Simbi Ajikawo better known?

5 What is the name of a woman in the title of a Hollies song, who also features in the lyrics of 'Lily the Pink' by The Scaffold?

6 Which Rolling Stones album, recorded primarily in Jamaica, has a title which refers to the cuisine of that country?

7 What was the name of the act whose song 'Spaceman' was used to advertise Levi's in the mid 90s?

8 As well as many solo successes, who has had hits duetting with George Michael, Luciano Pavarotti, LeAnn Rimes, Ironik, Dua Lipa and Kiki Dee?

9 Whose 2022 album was called 'Honestly, Nevermind'?

10 Which song provided Michael Jackson with his only UK Christmas Number 1, doing so in 1995?

MUSIC 18

1 Which word links the professional monikers of DeAndre Cortez Way, Damon Gough and George O'Dowd?

2 Who was the lead singer of The Boomtown Rats?

3 What was the one-word title of The Spice Girls' last UK Number 1 single (as a Double-A side with 'Let Love Lead the Way')?

4 Which band's only UK Number 1 single was 'A Little Time'?

5 Whose debut single in 2011 was 'Swagger Jagger'?

6 Which duo had a massive hit single in 2013 with 'Get Lucky'?

7 Which American band, whose lead singer was Michael Stipe, released a 1994 album called 'Monster'?

8 The Nigerian musician Tony Allen, who died in April 2020, was considered one of the world's greatest exponents of which musical instrument?

9 What is the stage name of Amala Dlamini, the American rapper and online star who had a big hit with 'Say So'?

10 'Old Town Road' by Lil Nas X first achieved viral success on which video-sharing app in early 2019?

MUSIC 17
1 The Specials
2 Stevie Wonder
3 Spike Island (site of a famous Stone Roses concert)
4 Little Simz
5 Jennifer Eccles
6 Goats Head Soup
7 Babylon Zoo
8 Elton John
9 Drake
10 Earth Song

MUSIC 18
1 Boy (Soulja Boy, Badly Drawn Boy and Boy George)
2 Bob Geldof
3 Holler
4 The Beautiful South
5 Cher Lloyd
6 Daft Punk
7 REM
8 Drums/percussion
9 Doja Cat
10 TikTok

SCIENCE AND NATURE 1

1 I is the chemical symbol for which element?

2 Kangaroos and wallabies are two species of macropods. What does the word macropod mean?

3 The word "zorro" is Spanish for which animal?

4 What astrological-sounding name is given to the complex of radiating nerves at the pit of the stomach?

5 The name of which ape is derived from the Malay words for "man of the forest"?

6 What does CPR stand for, as in the emergency first aid procedure?

7 What was the first name of the inventor of the Bunsen Burner?

8 What three letters are usually used to refer to the substance trinitrotoluene?

9 What is the short form for the unit of length used in astronomy which is the parallax of one arc second?

10 What acid is also known as 'Oil of Vitriol' and has the chemical formula H2SO4?

SCIENCE AND NATURE 2

1 Pig-nose, Hawksbill and Leatherback are all species of which animal?

2 What disease takes its name from the medieval Italian for "bad air"?

3 How is the phenomenon aurora australis more commonly known?

4 Which mineral is used as the example of something with a hardness of just 1 on the Mohs Scale?

5 In October 2021, a frosty exchange with climate activist Cameron Ford prompted British radio host Mike Graham to claim that you could "grow" which building material?

6 What planet has many moons including Rhea, Dione, Titon and Tethys?

7 Which violet gemstone takes its name from the Greek for "not intoxicated"?

8 How many limbs do all crabs have?

9 In which decade was a radio signal sent across the Atlantic for the first time?

10 John B Goodenough was, in 2019, the oldest person to receive what?

SCIENCE AND NATURE 1
1 Iodine
2 Long Foot/Big Foot
3 Fox
4 Solar plexus
5 Orangutan
6 Cardiopulmonary resuscitation
7 Robert
8 TNT
9 Parsec
10 Sulphuric Acid

SCIENCE AND NATURE 2
1 Turtle
2 Malaria
3 Southern Lights
4 Talc
5 Concrete
6 Saturn
7 Amethyst
8 Ten
9 1900s (1901)
10 A Nobel Prize (in Chemistry)

SCIENCE AND NATURE 3

1 Which animal has a name literally meaning "earth pig"?

2 In 2014, the Philae lander became the first spacecraft to land and take pictures on a what?

3 'Gorillas in the Mist' told the story of which naturalist's work with mountain gorillas?

4 The SI unit of electric current is named after which scientist?

5 Colony Collapse Disorder is a term used since 2006 to refer to abrupt disappearances of … what ?

6 What name is given in astronomy to a second full moon in a calendar month?

7 Which bird is the emblem of the UK's bird protection society, the RSPB?

8 What colloquial four-word term for the Stop Error in Microsoft Windows is sometimes referred to by its initials BSoD?

9 Asperitas was in 2017 verified as a new formation of which natural feature (the first new formation since 1951)?

10 The longest ever lifespan for which animal was that of Bluey, who died in Australia at 29 years and 5 months?

SCIENCE AND NATURE 4

1 How many arms do starfish typically have?

2 Which animal has species called Grevy's, Chapman's, and Burchell's?

3 The Canary Islands get their name from what type of animal?

4 Which transition metal is used for galvanising iron and steel to prevent rust?

5 There are two species of camel - what are they called?

6 Which significant machines, patented in 1918, were adopted by the German army in 1928?

7 Which American agricultural scientist, who died in 1943, did TIME magazine dub "a black Leonardo"?

8 Scientists use the word "chelonian" to describe what kind of reptiles?

9 Rainbow, brown, flathead, silver and cutthroat are all species of what kind of fish?

10 Which moon was initially, when discovered by Christiaan Huygens, called Luna Saturni, before being given its current name a couple of centuries later by John Herschel?

SCIENCE AND NATURE 3
1 Aardvark
2 Comet
3 Dian Fossey
4 André-Marie Ampère
5 Bees
6 Blue Moon
7 Avocet
8 Blue Screen of Death
9 Cloud
0 Dog (Australian cattle dog)

SCIENCE AND NATURE 4
1 Five
2 Zebra
3 Dogs
4 Zinc
5 Dromedary and Bactrian
6 Enigma
7 George Washington Carver
8 Tortoises and turtles
9 Trout
10 Titan

SCIENCE AND NATURE 5

1 What was the surname of Max, the German physicist who won a Nobel Prize in 1918 for originating Quantum Theory?

2 Where on the body of a rattlesnake is its rattle?

3 Which chemical element is named after a Scottish village?

4 In bees, larvae destined to become Queen Bees are fed on what substance?

5 What is the world's largest reptile?

6 What is the name of the chemical process of extracting metal from its mineral ores?

7 What is the common two-word name of the chemical compound, used in medicine, with the formula KMnO4?

8 Which fish has been recorded as swimming the fastest?

9 Apart from the echidna, what is the only mammal that lays eggs?

10 What type of gazelle is a South African national symbol?

SCIENCE AND NATURE 6

1 Actor Morgan Freeman narrated a famous documentary called 'March of the …' what?

2 Which animal's name comes from the Greek word for "horned nose"?

3 What is the chemical symbol for Lead?

4 What name is given to the study of birds?

5 Where did the small helicopter Ingenuity fly for around a minute on 19th April 2021?

6 If you were suffering from epistaxis, which part of your body would be bleeding?

7 Which planet in the solar system has the highest surface temperature?

8 3,300 kilometres was the distance covered by which scientist's first transatlantic radio signal in 1901?

9 The name "alligator" is derived from the Spanish word for what?

10 In which country is Baikonur, the largest rocket launch site on Earth?

SCIENCE AND NATURE 5
1 Planck
2 Tail
3 Strontium
4 Royal Jelly
5 (Saltwater) crocodile
6 Smelting
7 Potassium Permanganate
8 Sailfish
9 Platypus
10 Springbok

SCIENCE AND NATURE 6
1 Penguins
2 Rhinoceros
3 Pb
4 Ornithology
5 Mars (the first powered, controlled flight by an aircraft on another world)
6 Nose (it is the medical term for nosebleed)
7 Venus (about 300 degrees hotter than Mercury)
8 Guglielmo Marconi
9 Lizard
10 Kazakhstan

SCIENCE AND NATURE 7

1 From the Latin word ferrum, which chemical element has the symbol Fe?

2 Which animal produces a sticky reddish sweat, which led to an old belief that it sweats blood?

3 The cells in the honeycomb of bees are typically what shape?

4 The foul smell that skunks use as a defensive weapon is made by compounds of which element?

5 What rodent is called a "cochon d'Inde" in French?

6 Which breed of cat, which originated in Canada, is known for its lack of hair?

7 Which animal used to be called an "urchin" in old English?

8 What name is given to the process in which insects such as crickets produce noise by rubbing surfaces together?

9 In the late 1960s, where were the minerals armalcolite, tranquillityite and pyroxferroite first discovered?

10 Which species of whale is the titular creature of Herman Melville's novel 'Moby-Dick'?

SCIENCE AND NATURE 8

1 Which carnivorous mammal shares its name with one of the X-Men?

2 Which animal has ossicones sticking out of its head, a bit like horns?

3 In July 2022, which wild animal was released to the British countryside for the first time in 1000s of years?

4 Great, blue, crested, marsh and coal are types of which bird?

5 Which great ape is the largest in size?

6 What two-word term was often used to describe warming of the Earth due to increased emissions of gases such as carbon dioxide and methane into the atmosphere?

7 What is the name given to the larvae of frogs, toads and salamanders?

8 Which medical breakthrough was developed by Wilhelm Röntgen at the end of the 19th century?

9 Which craft orbited Jupiter between 1995 and 2003?

10 Which set of islands, famous for tortoises, did Charles Darwin visit in September 1835?

SUBJECT ROUNDS

SCIENCE AND NATURE 7
1 Iron
2 Hippopotamus
3 Hexagon
4 Sulphur
5 Guinea Pig
6 Sphynx
7 Hedgehog
8 Stridulation
9 The Moon (ARMstrong, ALdrin, COLlins ... small amounts of all have been found on Earth subsequently)
10 Sperm Whale

SCIENCE AND NATURE 8
1 Wolverine
2 Giraffe
3 (European) Bison - in Kent
4 Tit
5 Gorilla
6 Greenhouse Effect
7 Tadpoles
8 X-Ray machines
9 Galileo
10 Galápagos Islands

SCIENCE AND NATURE 9

1 A shortage of which vitamin is the most common cause of rickets?

2 A marabou is a large bird in which family?

3 The hardy plant, with showy flowers, called antirrhinum has what alternative common name?

4 The American engineer Theodore Maiman is credited with inventing the first working example of which piece of technology in 1960?

5 On a horse, what is the common name for the metacarpophalangeal joint?

6 Which scientist invented a thought experiment about a cat to help explain quantum theory?

7 The oldest known individual living trees belong to which species?

8 In 1675 John Flamsteed became the first man to hold which position?

9 What is the collective name for a group of barracuda?

10 What is the name of the largest venomous snake in Africa?

SCIENCE AND NATURE 10

1 What do fish use to breathe underwater?

2 What is a male goose called?

3 On Christmas Day 1758, what did Johann George Palitzsch see, thus confirming a prediction made in 1705?

4 In which European country is the volcano Bardarbunga?

5 What is another name for methanoic acid, the simplest carboxylic acid, that can be found naturally in ants?

6 96% of the planet Saturn is made up of which element?

7 The foothills of what mountain range provide the natural habitat of the red panda?

8 What region of the brain shares its name with the scientific name of the seahorse?

9 What is the name of the hypothesis formulated and developed by James Lovelock and Lynn Margulis, named after the Greek earth goddess, which, roughly, sees the world as one complex synergistic system?

10 Scarabs or dung beetles were sacred to which ancient civilization?

SCIENCE AND NATURE 9

1 D
2 Stork
3 Snapdragon
4 Laser
5 Fetlock
6 Erwin Schrödinger
7 Bristlecone pine
8 Astronomer Royal
9 Battery
10 Black mamba

SCIENCE AND NATURE 10

1 Gills
2 Gander
3 Halley's Comet (it was in 1758 that Edmund Halley's prediction was confirmed and it was named after him)
4 Iceland
5 Formic Acid
6 Hydrogen
7 Himalayas
8 Hippocampus
9 Gaia Hypothesis
10 Egyptians

SCIENCE AND NATURE 11

1 How many legs does an insect have?

2 What sort of bird is a yaffle?

3 What do you get if you divide your mass in kilograms by the square of your height in metres?

4 Ailurophobia is a fear of which domestic animal?

5 Which animal, found in Brazil, is the largest rodent in the world?

6 Whose 1962 book, 'Silent Spring', played an important role in the environmental movement?

7 The kudu is a type of antelope found on which continent?

8 What is the main food of the giant panda?

9 Which scientist wrote 'On The Origin of Species: By Means of Natural Selection', published in 1859?

10 What was the name of the NASA exploratory spacecraft which successfully landed on Mars in August 2012?

SCIENCE AND NATURE 12

1 Eiderdown consists of the feathers of a breed of which animal?

2 A conger is a type of which sea creature?

3 In which part of a cell are the organelles found?

4 Which animal's milk is used to make cheddar cheese?

5 Which part of the human brain is the main controller of hormone production?

6 Which cat is the world's fastest land animal?

7 The presence of which two metals is responsible for "hard" water?

8 Which large flightless bird of New Guinea and Australia has distinctive blue skin on the neck?

9 In computer software, what do the letters EULA stand for?

10 What is the name of the hard skin in which a caterpillar changes into a butterfly?

SCIENCE AND NATURE 11
1 6
2 A woodpecker
3 Body Mass Index (BMI)
4 Cat
5 Capybara
6 Rachel Carson
7 Africa
8 Bamboo
9 Charles Darwin
10 Curiosity

SCIENCE AND NATURE 12
1 Duck
2 Eel
3 Cytoplasm
4 Cows
5 Hypothalamus
6 Cheetah
7 Calcium & magnesium
8 Cassowary
9 End-user License Agreement
10 Chrysalis (allow: pupa or cocoon)

SCIENCE AND NATURE 13

1 Where in your body would you find the bone known as the femur?

2 In the human body, oxygenated blood leaves the heart through which major artery?

3 Which French scientist is credited with naming oxygen and hydrogen?

4 In his famous experiment, the scientist Ivan Pavlov taught a dog to salivate at the sound of ... what?

5 The capercaillie is the largest member of which family of game birds?

6 Adding together the atomic numbers of which two elements makes the number 4?

7 In the field of communications, what does SNR stand for?

8 What is the largest animal in the world which has teeth?

9 Relating to conservation in the UK, in the abbreviation SSSI, what does the third "S" stand for?

10 The first example of which kitchen device was 1947's Radarange?

SCIENCE AND NATURE 14

1 Which chemical element takes its name from the fact it was discovered by analysing the sun?

2 In the southern USA, what kind of creature is sometimes known as a crawdad?

3 Which is the largest bird native to Australia?

4 When Joseph Priestley discovered oxygen gas in 1774, what name did he give it?

5 Hepatology is concerned primarily with the study of which organ?

6 32 Fahrenheit is how many degrees centigrade?

7 What is the more common name for the condition called periorbital haematoma?

8 What is the common name of the hyena-like insectivorous mammal with the Latin name Proteles cristata? Its name starts with two of the same letter.

9 The inner core of planet Earth is thought to be primarily composed of an alloy of iron and which other metal?

10 What colouring does a piebald horse have?

SCIENCE AND NATURE 13
1 Thigh
2 Aorta
3 Antoine Lavoisier
4 A bell
5 Grouse
6 Hydrogen & Lithium
7 Signal To Noise Ratio
8 Sperm Whale
9 Scientific (Site of Special Scientific Interest)
10 Microwave oven

SCIENCE AND NATURE 14
1 Helium (from the Greek word Helios. Helium is the only element not discovered on Earth)
2 Crayfish/Crustacean
3 Emu
4 Dephlogisticated air
5 Liver
6 0
7 Black eye
8 Aardwolf
9 Nickel
10 Black and white

SCIENCE AND NATURE 15

1 Due to the copper that it contains, the blood of a lobster is which colour?

2 What is the name of the biggest species of penguin, which breeds during the Antarctic winter?

3 What name is given to the elements with chemical numbers from 57 to 71, their generic name being taken from the one that has the number 57?

4 Which reptile is unique in having the same scientific name as its common name?

5 Queen Alexandra's Birdwing is the world's largest species of what?

6 The tuatara is a kind of lizard found only in which country?

7 Which breed of dog is traditionally used as a rescue animal in the Swiss Alps?

8 What is the literal meaning of the word gastropod, that describes snails and slugs?

9 What is the name of the part of a cicada that makes their characteristic sound?

10 What name is given to hydrogen that has one proton and two neutrons?

SCIENCE AND NATURE 16

1 Which unit of mass is equivalent to 2.20462 pounds?

2 Moth, slipper and tiger are noted types of which house plant bearing flowers of unusual shapes and showy colours?

3 What is the SI derived unit for pressure or stress?

4 In German, which animal has a name meaning "naked snail"?

5 What does the S in SIM stand for, as in SIM cards used in mobile phones?

6 In terms of animal conservation, which status ranks between Endangered and Near Threatened?

7 Where in your body are your villi?

8 Of all objects in the known universe, the star Kepler 11145123 is considered by scientists to be the ... what?

9 Which national park of the USA takes its name from the large deposits of fossilised wood within it?

10 American inventor Elisha Graves Otis was a crucial figure in the development of which invention?

SCIENCE AND NATURE 15
1 Blue
2 Emperor Penguin
3 Lanthanides (named after Lanthanum)
4 Boa constrictor
5 Butterfly
6 New Zealand
7 Saint Bernard
8 Stomach foot
9 Timbal
10 Tritium

SCIENCE AND NATURE 16
1 Kilogram
2 Orchid
3 Pascal
4 Slug
5 Subscriber
6 Vulnerable
7 Your intestines
8 Roundest
9 Petrified Forest
10 Lifts/Elevators

SCIENCE AND NATURE 17

1 Plantar fasciitis is a term for a disorder affecting which part of the human body?

2 In physics, what is calculated by dividing mass by volume?

3 What does a starfish have at the tip of its arms?

4 Which mosquito-borne disease is also known as Breakbone Fever?

5 Members of which family won the most Nobel Prizes in total?

6 Which island near Edinburgh has the largest community of Northern Gannets in the world?

7 Whose unsuccessful 'E-M@iler' device might have got him fired in 2000?

8 What is the name of the West African monkey with black-grey fur and a distinct white brow, cheeks, beard and front?

9 In physics, what is the name of the elemental particles which are postulated as mediators of the strong force that binds quarks together?

10 An extra copy of chromosome 21 leads to a condition named after which doctor?

SCIENCE AND NATURE 18

1 Which family of small birds gets their common name from the sound made by their rapidly flapping wings?

2 In which branch of science was Charles Francis Richter a specialist?

3 Which bird has sub-species named Golden, Harpy and Bald?

4 Heliciculture is the farming of which animals for human consumption?

5 Jonas Salk developed one of the first vaccines against which disease?

6 Syndactyly, a condition affecting the human feet, results in which unusual bodily feature?

7 In which part of the body is oestrogen produced?

8 What is the common name for large lizards in the genus Varanus?

9 The AK-47 rifle was invented by which Russian designer?

10 The Solar System's main asteroid belt lies between which two planets?

SCIENCE AND NATURE 17
1 Heel/Foot
2 Density
3 Eyes
4 Dengue Fever
5 Curie
6 Bass Rock
7 Alan Sugar
8 Diana Monkey
9 Gluons
10 (John Langdon) Down

SCIENCE AND NATURE 18
1 Hummingbird
2 Seismology
3 Eagle
4 Snails
5 Polio
6 Webbed toes
7 Ovaries
8 Monitor
9 Mikhail Kalashnikov
10 Mars and Jupiter

SCIENCE AND NATURE 19

1 Which scientist's third law of motion states that for every action there is an equal and opposite reaction?

2 Rhinoplasty is the medical name for which cosmetic surgery procedure?

3 In which biological process does a cell divide into two genetically identical cells?

4 A halcyon is another name for what kind of bird?

5 On average, what is the coldest month in New Zealand?

6 A new species of black tarantula found near Folsom Prison, California, was named after which singer in 2016?

7 Synchronous Diaphragmatic Flutter is the medical term for what?

8 Electrum is primarily an alloy of which two metals?

9 The only species of penguin that lives, in the wild, north of the equator is the ... what?

10 A near-complete skeleton of which bird was sold at auction in November 2016 for £280,000?

SCIENCE AND NATURE 20

1 What is the first letter of the alphabet to be the final letter of the name of a chemical element in English?

2 In medicine, if acute pain is short-lasting, what term describes long-lasting pain?

3 Goldeneye and teal are species of which bird?

4 What is the most common domestic use for sodium chlorate?

5 How old was the renowned scientist Stephen Hawking when he died in 2018?

6 What is the preferred food of a silkworm?

7 Which types of fish, of the order Pleuronectiformes, have both eyes on the same side of their heads?

8 From the Latin for "little cavity", alveoli are found in which part of the body?

9 What is the scientific name for "childbed fever", which killed Henry VIII's third wife?

10 In 1967, what did the General Conference of Weights and Measures define as "9,192,631,770 periods of the radiation corresponding to the transition between the two hyperfine levels of the ground state of the caesium 133 atom"?

SCIENCE AND NATURE 19
1 Isaac Newton
2 Nose job
3 Mitosis
4 Kingfisher
5 July
6 Johnny Cash
7 Hiccups
8 Gold and silver
9 Galápagos penguin
10 Dodo

SCIENCE AND NATURE 20
1 C
2 Chronic
3 Duck
4 Weed killer
5 76
6 Mulberry leaves
7 Flatfish
8 Lungs
9 Puerperal fever
10 One second

GAMES 1

1 How many of each numbered card are there in a standard pack of playing cards?

2 Shelley Blond and Keeley Hawes have both provided the voice of which iconic video game character?

3 The original version of the board game Monopoly was set in which American city, which was also the main setting for the TV series 'Boardwalk Empire'?

4 In the online multiplayer game known as PUBG, what does the BG stand for?

5 Which 1991 computer game allowed you to take control of Aztecs and Zulus, amongst others?

6 Kratos is the main protagonist in which video game series?

7 In which year was the Nintendo Wii first released?

8 Which video game character was considered Sega's mascot until the advent of Sonic the Hedgehog?

9 A UK chart hit which was a cover of the 'Tetris' theme was by Doctor Spin – made up of producer Nigel Wright and which composer?

10 On the original iPod, what game would appear if you held down the centre button for several seconds?

GAMES 2

1 In which war is the original game 'Call of Duty' set?

2 In which game might players employ techniques including "ruffing", "finessing", "squeezing" and "dummy reversal"?

3 In which year did the Apple App Store first open?

4 For which video game franchise was the 2021 instalment called 'Rift Apart'?

5 Based on the American figure GI Joe, which toy was introduced in Britain in 1966?

6 Dan Houser, one of the co-founders, resigned from his position in which video game company in March 2020?

7 'Space Duel' and 'Blasteroids' were sequels to which game?

8 Crokinole is a dexterity board game which originated, and has its World Championships, in which country?

9 What words complete this famously poor translation from the game 'Zero Wing', "All your base are ..."?

10 Who gave his name to a 'Decathlon' game released following his gold medal in the 1984 Olympics?

GAMES 1
1 Four
2 Lara Croft
3 Atlantic City
4 Battlegrounds (PlayerUnknown's Battlegrounds)
5 Civilization
6 God of War
7 2006
8 Alex Kidd
9 Andrew Lloyd Webber
10 Brick

GAMES 2
1 World War II
2 Bridge
3 2008
4 Ratchet & Clank
5 Action Man
6 Rockstar Games
7 Asteroids
8 Canada
9 Belong to us
10 Daley Thompson

GAMES 3

1 What colour, primarily, is Sonic the Hedgehog?

2 On the standard London Monopoly board, how much does it cost to buy Mayfair?

3 The modern name for what object is a Filipino word meaning "come-come"? Earlier names for the object include "bandalore", "whirligig" and "quiz".

4 Which strategic board game was invented by the French filmmaker Albert Lamorisse in 1957?

5 Which video game character's enemy is Dr Neo Cortex?

6 Which video game series includes editions named 'Legends Of Rock' and 'World Tour'?

7 Which secret agent has been played in video games by Adam Blackwood and Maxwell Caulfield?

8 Mario's arch enemy Bowser belongs to what race?

9 Who had a global hit single in 2012 with 'Video Games'?

10 Milla Jovovich starred in a 2002 movie based on which video game series?

GAMES 4

1 Who does Mark Hamill voice in 'Batman: Arkham City'?

2 "One for his nob" is a phrase used in the scoring of which card game?

3 What can come after 'Railroad', 'Zoo', 'Transport' and 'RollerCoaster' in video game titles?

4 The best selling boy's toy of 1964 was a toy weapon called Johnny Seven OMA. What does the OMA stand for?

5 How many playable characters were there in the original 'Street Fighter II'?

6 Which company developed the 80s arcade game 'Paperboy'?

7 In Scrabble, what is the tile value of each of the vowels?

8 Which company developed the virtual world 'Second Life'?

9 In 1831, on the Scottish island of Lewis, a group of 12th century pieces from which game were discovered?

10 What drink gives its name to a notorious mini-game in 'Grand Theft Auto: San Andreas'?

GAMES 3
1 Blue
2 £400
3 Yo-Yo
4 Risk (He directed the acclaimed film 'The Red Balloon')
5 Crash Bandicoot
6 Guitar Hero
7 James Bond
8 Koopa
9 Lana Del Rey
10 Resident Evil

GAMES 4
1 The Joker
2 Cribbage
3 Tycoon
4 One Man Army
5 Eight
6 Atari
7 One
8 Linden Lab
9 Chess
10 Hot Coffee

GAMES 5

1 In the 1981 game 'Scramble', what vehicle does the player control?

2 On a standard London Monopoly board, what is the combined value of Leicester Square and Old Kent Road?

3 A parlour game involving two participants blindfolded and trying to hit each other with a rolled up newspaper is called 'Are You There, ...' who?

4 What can go before 'Blitz' and 'Twist' in the name of popular mobile games?

5 In which classic arcade game do you have to direct frogs across a busy road?

6 The 'Dune' games were based on a novel by whom?

7 What character does Ellen McLain voice in 'Portal 2'?

8 In Cluedo, which murder weapon is the first in alphabetical order?

9 In a standard pack of playing cards, what do the Queens hold in their hands?

10 Which early video game featured the character of Evil Otto?

GAMES 6

1 On whose island was 'Super Mario World 2' set?

2 Which video game takes its name from a combination of the Greek word for "four" and the word "tennis"?

3 Who is Fox McCloud's main rival, in the famous Nintendo game, 'Star Fox'?

4 A 2009 expansion pack for 'Grand Theft Auto' is called 'The Ballad of ...' who?

5 How many dice does each player use in a game of Yahtzee?

6 Which popular iPhone app features a candy loving monster called Om Nom?

7 In a game of Rounders, what is the maximum number of players that the fielding team can have on the field at any one time?

8 What instruction do you put into Google to turn the page 360°?

9 In backgammon, how many playing pieces does each player begin with?

10 Which hero battles villains such as Psy-Crow, Queen Slug-for-a-Butt and Evil the Cat?

GAMES 5
1 Aircraft
2 £320
3 Moriarty
4 Bejeweled
5 Frogger
6 Frank Herbert
7 GLaDOS
8 Candlestick
9 Flowers
10 Berzerk

GAMES 6
1 Yoshi's
2 Tetris
3 Wolf O'Donnell
4 Gay Tony
5 Five
6 Cut the Rope
7 Nine
8 Do a barrel roll
9 Fifteen
10 Earthworm Jim

GAMES 7

1 In 1993, what became the first video game character to feature in the Macy's Thanksgiving Day Parade?

2 What is the alliance of aliens in 'Halo' called?

3 What is the name of the online role-playing game set in the world of Norrath?

4 Who referenced the classic game 'Defender' in their 1998 song 'Body Movin''?

5 Which popular pastime has a name derived from a phrase which literally means "the numbers are restricted to single status"?

6 Zangief, Dhalsim and Chun-Li are characters in which video game series?

7 What is the highest number on a standard European roulette wheel?

8 Which Namco game of 1979 was created to compete with 'Space Invaders'?

9 What development studio did Sid Meier create in 1982?

10 'Undercover', 'Hot Pursuit' and 'Carbon' are titles in which series of racing games?

GAMES 8

1 What is the nickname of Markus Persson, the creator of 'Minecraft'?

2 In 2010, Google marked the 30th anniversary of which game with an interactive Google Doodle?

3 Which pairing were responsible for 'Desert Bus', described as "the worst video game of all time"?

4 What regular newspaper teaser first appeared in the 'New York World' in 1913?

5 What was the name of the 1987 video game which bore Mike Tyson's name?

6 What underwater city is the setting for 'BioShock'?

7 What is the name of the protagonist of 'Metroid Prime 3: Corruption'?

8 Which strategy game, originally released in 1989, had the working title of 'Micropolis'?

9 'Knights of the Old Republic' is a set in the universe of which movie franchise?

10 Which square on a London Monopoly board is also an old name for the sport of croquet?

GAMES 7
1 Sonic the Hedgehog
2 The Covenant
3 EverQuest
4 The Beastie Boys
5 Sudoku
6 Street Fighter
7 36
8 Galaxian
9 MicroProse
10 Need For Speed

GAMES 8
1 Notch
2 Pac-Man
3 Penn and Teller
4 Crossword puzzle
5 Punch-Out!!
6 Rapture
7 Samus Aran
8 SimCity
9 Star Wars
10 Pall Mall

GAMES 9

1 What does the EA stand for in EA Sports, the distributors of sport simulation computer games?

2 Complete this quote from a classic early arcade game, "We are the Galaxians / Mission: ..."?

3 Which board game created by Uwe Rosenberg shares its name with a 1st century Roman governor of Britain?

4 'The Legend of Zelda' was named after the wife of which author?

5 In which country is 'Assassin's Creed II' set?

6 Mark Wahlberg's character investigates a drug named Valkyr in a 2008 movie based on which video game?

7 In the world of games, LARP stands for live-action ... what?

8 Johnny Cage, Baraka and Sonya Blade have been characters in which game?

9 Which classic computer game features ghosts nicknamed Blinky, Pinky, Inky and Clyde?

10 In which game are you the sole surviving member of Operation Counterstrike?

GAMES 10

1 Which character plays tennis in a Game & Watch game from 1982?

2 Which sitcom had a 1998 episode about the classic game 'Frogger'?

3 What is the nickname of John MacTavish in 'Call of Duty: Modern Warfare 3'?

4 What fighting series features many of the classic characters from Nintendo games?

5 Which American band produced the song 'Exile Vilify' for 'Portal 2'?

6 What was the subtitle of the 'Animal Crossing' game where online play first became possible?

7 In which game series do you play soldier William Blazkowicz?

8 What is the name of the character controlled in 'Grand Theft Auto: San Andreas'?

9 In the UK board game, how many rooms are there in the Cluedo Mansion?

10 Who is the present day protagonist of 'Assassin's Creed: Revelations'?

GAMES 9

1 Electronic Arts
2 Destroy Aliens
3 Agricola
4 F Scott Fitzgerald
5 Italy
6 Max Payne
7 Role Play
8 Mortal Kombat
9 Pac-Man
10 Quake

GAMES 10

1 Snoopy
2 Seinfeld
3 Soap
4 Super Smash Bros.
5 The National
6 Wild World
7 Wolfenstein
8 CJ
9 Nine (Kitchen, Dining Room, Lounge, Hall, Study, Library, Billiard Room, Conservatory, Ball Room)
10 Desmond Miles

GAMES 11

1 Which character starred in a game with Mario for the first time when they went to the Olympic Games?

2 Raccoon City and the t-Virus outbreak are important features of which game series?

3 The name of which maker of toy vehicles comes from a Sioux word for "big" or "great"?

4 What number accompanies the bingo call "Straight on through"?

5 In 2014, who became the first person to win the European Poker Tour twice?

6 On which 1984 video game would you have found yourself on Easy Street, Middle Road or Hard Way?

7 In which chart-topping free iOS and Android game do you throw crumpled up paper into a rubbish bin?

8 The setting for 'Red Dead Redemption' features two neighbouring countries, the USA and which other?

9 Which Sega handheld console was released in 1990, bundled with a game called 'Columns'?

10 Who had a 'Jet Set' in a 1980s ZX Spectrum game?

GAMES 12

1 In the field of computer games, what does PSP stand for?

2 Which letter in Scrabble is worth 10 points in English but only 1 point in Polish?

3 In the 'Donkey Kong' video game series, what is Donkey Kong?

4 Which video game company developed the 'Street Fighter' series?

5 Which mad scientist is a major character in 'Maniac Mansion' and 'Day of the Tentacle'?

6 Which Duke first went '3D' in 1996 on the PC?

7 In which iOS game is the ultimate goal to defeat the God King?

8 In which game does the player take the role of Lt Jimmy Patterson?

9 Which 'Super Mario' character was in Forbes Wealthiest Fictional People, being worth $1 billion?

10 Which moviemaker created 'Medal of Honor'?

GAMES 11
1 Sonic
2 Resident Evil
3 Tonka
4 82
5 Victoria Coren Mitchell
6 Paperboy
7 Paper Toss
8 Mexico
9 Game Gear
10 Willy

GAMES 12
1 PlayStation Portable
2 Z
3 An ape
4 Capcom
5 Dr Fred Edison
6 Duke Nukem
7 Infinity Blade
8 Medal of Honor
9 Princess Peach
10 Steven Spielberg

BUSINESS AND FINANCE 1

1 Which car manufacturer has had models including the Trafic, the Captur and Clio?

2 Andrew Bailey took up which position on 16th March 2020?

3 Which controversial multinational technology company was founded in 1987 by Ren Zhengfei?

4 Which company's products should you buy because "You're worth it"?

5 The founder of which American brand of personal care products had the first names King Camp?

6 Which Danish company, that specialises in making roof windows, skylights, and ventilation, gets the second part of its name from the Latin word for 'light'?

7 What sports clothing company was registered by Adolf Dassler on 18th August 1949?

8 Which chain of bookshops was founded in 1879 on Broad Street in Oxford?

9 Which chain of French supermarkets has a name meaning "crossroads"?

10 What brand of storage container, named after its creator and now universally used, was founded in Massachusetts in 1946?

BUSINESS AND FINANCE 2

1 What supermarket chain was founded by Karl and Theo Albrecht in 1946?

2 The Tigra, Vectra and Vivaro are all cars made by which company?

3 Which online delivery service was founded in London in 2013 by William Shu and Greg Orlowski?

4 Its logo being a white star on a blue background, what Danish company is the largest container ship and supply vessel operator in the world?

5 What American company was co-founded by Paul Allen in 1975?

6 In which American state is the chocolate-making town of Hershey?

7 Which brand of cigarette, smoked by the likes of John Lennon and Serge Gainsbourg, has a name meaning "Gypsy women"?

8 The logo of the National Trust is the leaves of which tree?

9 Dan and Frank Carney founded which fast food chain?

10 In March 2021, when Peter Foot unexpectedly stood down as the finance boss of Shoezone, what was the surname of the man who succeeded him?

BUSINESS AND FINANCE 1
1 Renault
2 Governor of Bank of England
3 Huawei
4 L'Oréal
5 Gillette (King Camp Gillette)
6 Velux
7 Adidas
8 Blackwell's
9 Carrefour
10 Tupperware

BUSINESS AND FINANCE 2
1 Aldi
2 Vauxhall
3 Deliveroo
4 Maersk
5 Microsoft (with Bill Gates)
6 Pennsylvania
7 Gitanes
8 Oak
9 Pizza Hut
10 (Terry) Boot

BUSINESS AND FINANCE 3

1 Abbey National, Alliance & Leicester and Bradford & Bingley were all taken over by which bank?

2 Which long-running French manufacturer of cars began in 1810 as a steel foundry?

3 In 2006, Daniel Ek co-founded which company?

4 What is the last name of the man who gave his name to his 1949 invention of the whirlpool bath?

5 The founders of which multinational company chose its current name in the 1950s as a combination of the Latin word for "sound" an American slang word for a young boy?

6 Anthelios is a popular brand of which product?

7 What trademark did Reinhold Burger patent in 1904, though the basis of the product was invented by James Dewar 12 years earlier?

8 How many rings are there in the Audi logo?

9 In which decade the first McDonald's in Britain open?

10 Wilbur and Orville Wright, the aviation pioneers, opened a shop in 1892 - what did it primarily sell?

BUSINESS AND FINANCE 4

1 Which web browser is named after the nickname of the red panda?

2 What nationality is the technology company Canon?

3 Which upmarket menswear manufacturer has a name which means "watershield" in Latin?

4 Papa John's is a fast food chain which specialises in what type of food?

5 Which car company is the parent company that makes Lexus cars?

6 What two words appear below the word "Toblerone" on a Toblerone packet?

7 Which former high street fixture, originally a division of an American firm founded in 1879, closed all its 807 UK stores between 27 December 2008 and 6 January 2009?

8 Who was the CEO of Polly Peck who fled to Northern Cyprus in 1993?

9 Which French fashion designer born in 1963 is known for his signature red-soled stilettos?

10 Which family business, founded in Manchester in 1865, is renowned for its positive employment practices, like giving staff their birthdays off, employing ex-offenders, and offering unemployed people a free dry cleaning service before a job interview?

BUSINESS AND FINANCE 3
1 Santander
2 Peugeot
3 Spotify
4 (Candido) Jacuzzi
5 SONY (Sonus and Sonny. Founded by Masaru Ibuka and Akio Morita.)
6 Sun cream (made by La Roche-Posay, Anthelios means loosely 'against the sun')
7 Thermos
8 Four
9 1970s (1974)
10 Bicycles

BUSINESS AND FINANCE 4
1 Firefox
2 Japanese
3 Aquascutum
4 Pizza
5 Toyota
6 of Switzerland
7 Woolworth
8 Asil Nadir
9 Christian Louboutin
10 Timpson's

BUSINESS AND FINANCE 5

1 What day of the week follows "Black" in the nickname for 16th September 1992, when the UK left the European Exchange Rate Mechanism?

2 What, famously, does "exactly what it says on the tin"?

3 What was the name of the short-lived newspaper launched by Eddie Shah in 1986?

4 Which of the world's "supermajor" oil companies has its headquarters in The Hague?

5 Which supermarket opened the first branches of its new "discount" store, called Jack's, in 2018?

6 Which motor manufacturer had models called Spitfire, Dolomite and Herald?

7 What name is given to the decorative rhinestone-covered suits worn by the likes of Elvis Presley and designed by the tailor born Nuta Kotlyarenko?

8 What is the largest motor company in the world, by number of vehicles produced? [2021 figures]

9 Marc Jacobs was the Creative Director of which fashion label from 1997 to 2014?

10 Who was the chief designer of the Volkswagen Beetle?

BUSINESS AND FINANCE 6

1 Which brewery was founded by JC Jacobsen in 1847?

2 Sundar Pichai became CEO of which company in 2015?

3 Which brand of sun lotion takes its name from a mountain in the Alps?

4 What word links a brand of lighter which has been going since 1932 with a popular British circus?

5 In which city did Herbert Austin open a motor car factory at the start of the 20th century?

6 In 1999, which British supermarket became a subsidiary of the American company Walmart?

7 The Sinclair Executive was one of the first you could fit in your pocket - of what?

8 The new £10 notes revealed in September 2017 feature whose face?

9 Which designer from Florence was inspired to launch his fashion brand by his time as a lift boy at the Savoy Hotel in London?

10 What five-word phrase first appeared on Wall's ice cream tricycles in the 1920s?

BUSINESS AND FINANCE 5

1 Wednesday
2 Ronseal
3 Today
4 Royal Dutch Shell
5 Tesco
6 Triumph
7 Nudie suits (Nuta Kotlyarenko known professionally as Nudie Cohn)
8 Toyota
9 Louis Vuitton
10 Ferdinand Porsche

BUSINESS AND FINANCE 6

1 Carlsberg
2 Google
3 Piz Buin
4 Zippo
5 Birmingham
6 ASDA
7 Calculator
8 Jane Austen
9 Guccio Gucci
10 Stop Me and Buy One

BUSINESS AND FINANCE 7

1 Kelvin MacKenzie is the former editor of which newspaper?

2 Which dating app shares its names with pieces of wood or other dry material used to start a fire?

3 What clothing brand, which closed down its UK stores in 2021, was founded in San Francisco in 1969 by Don and Doris Fisher?

4 Giovanni Agnelli founded which car manufacturer in Turin in 1899?

5 Caledonian MacBrayne operates which Scottish transport service?

6 In 2015, Sir Philip Green sold which department store chain for £1?

7 Which country is home to the Sensex stock exchange index?

8 Which digital media company was founded in 2006 by Jonah Peretti and John S Johnson in New York?

9 Which international airline, founded by the American Juan Trippe, declared bankruptcy in January 1991?

10 What began in 1910 as the Shwayder Trunk Manufacturing Company, but changed its name after its best selling product in 1965, which had itself been named after a biblical strongman?

BUSINESS AND FINANCE 8

1 Which bank disappeared from the High Street, only to reappear when it separated from Lloyds in 2013?

2 Vera Wang has gained international fame for designing ... what?

3 Charlie Chaplin was amongst the founders of which film studio in February 1919?

4 Which Secretary-General of the RMT union led a rail strike in the UK in June 2022?

5 Which newspaper was launched in October 1986 by three former journalists from The Daily Telegraph?

6 Which British company was founded by Sidney De Haan to focus on the needs of people over 50?

7 Microsoft acquired which company's mobile phone business in 2014?

8 Which N is the British retailer which was formerly known as Joseph Hepworth & Son before changing to its current name in 1982?

9 In which country were two common banknotes suddenly withdrawn in November 2016 as part of anti-corruption measures?

10 In 2018, which banker, who shares his name with a famous sitcom star, became Chief Executive of the London Stock Exchange?

BUSINESS AND FINANCE 7
1 The Sun
2 Tinder
3 Gap
4 Fiat
5 Ferries
6 BHS (British Home Stores)
7 India
8 BuzzFeed
9 Pan Am
10 Samsonite

BUSINESS AND FINANCE 8
1 TSB
2 Wedding dresses (accept: dresses)
3 United Artists
4 Mick Lynch
5 The Independent
6 Saga
7 Nokia
8 Next
9 India
10 David Schwimmer

TV 1

1 How many questions do you have to answer correctly to win the million in the original version of 'Who Wants to Be A Millionaire', once you are in the main chair?

2 What was the surname of the main family in the 'Darling Buds of May'?

3 What fictional part of London has an E20 postcode?

4 Napoleon Solo was the title character in which TV series?

5 How was the character Templeton Peck commonly known in an '80s TV series?

6 The third series of which TV show had episodes called: 'Dish & Dishonesty', 'Ink & Incapability', 'Nob & Nobility', 'Sense & Senility', 'Amy & Amiability', and 'Dual & Duality'?

7 Lucy Davis, who played Dawn Tinsley in 'The Office', is the daughter of which famous comedian?

8 What is the name of "the building" in the mystery-comedy series 'Only Murders in the Building'?

9 Which character in 'Dad's Army' was played by John Le Mesurier?

10 What acclaimed American crime drama from 2014 starred Woody Harrelson and Matthew McConaughey?

TV 2

1 In the TV show 'Friends', what is the surname of Ross and Monica (before her marriage to Chandler)?

2 Who played club owner Brian Potter in 'Phoenix Nights'?

3 In the children's cartoon, what kind of reptiles were Leonardo, Michelangelo, Donatello and Raphael?

4 What is the name of the ship's computer in the TV show 'Red Dwarf'?

5 What was the name of the detective agency run by Cybill Shepherd and Bruce Willis' characters in the TV show 'Moonlighting'?

6 In which gameshow would you have heard the catchphrase: "There's nothing in this game for two in a bed"?

7 Who played the role of Dermot in Series 1 of 'Men Behaving Badly'?

8 On 'Coronation Street', what colour is the door of the Rovers Return?

9 On what drama did Gary Webster replace Dennis Waterman in the title role in 1991?

10 'Waldorf Salad', 'The Kipper and The Corpse' and 'The Germans' were episodes of which classic sitcom?

TV 1
1 15
2 Larkin
3 Walford (the fictional area in which 'EastEnders' is set)
4 The Man From UNCLE
5 Face (in 'The A-Team', played by Dirk Benedict)
6 Blackadder
7 Jasper Carrott (whose real name is Bob Davis)
8 The Arconia
9 Sergeant (Arthur) Wilson
10 True Detective

TV 2
1 Geller
2 Peter Kay
3 Turtles
4 Holly
5 Blue Moon Investigations
6 Bullseye
7 Harry Enfield
8 Green
9 Minder
10 Fawlty Towers

TV 3

1 Who is the youngest child of Homer and Marge Simpson?

2 How was the character Ernie Pantusso better known in the American comedy 'Cheers'?

3 Which member of a great comic double act, born John Bartholomew, took his stage name from his middle name and the town in which he was born?

4 What was the name of the reality TV show, set on a remote Scottish island, on which Ben Fogle, now a TV presenter, first came into the public view?

5 On children's TV, Everest, Rubble, Chase and Rocky are members of which group?

6 In the hit TV show, 'Vigil', what is Vigil?

7 What was the name of the second family in 'Dynasty', who had a less successful spin-off series which aired from 1985 to 1987 in the US?

8 In which year was 'Big Brother' first shown in the UK?

9 The first edition of which long-running show was broadcast in October 1961 from the Tabernacle Baptist Church in Cardiff?

10 Who was the Master Sergeant in the motor pool at Fort Baxter, Kansas, from 1955 to 1959?

TV 4

1 What is the first name of Hale from the comedy duo Hale and Pace?

2 What is the first name of Pace from the comedy duo Hale and Pace?

3 What is the first name of Rene's wife in "Allo 'Allo'?

4 Who played the title role in 'Doctor Who' between Tom Baker and Colin Baker?

5 On 'The Great British Bake Off' what is the third and final challenge of each show?

6 Who co-presented 'CD:UK' along with Ant and Dec when it started in 1998?

7 Which American actor made his British TV debut as Frank in the 2021 British comedy crime series 'Outlaws'?

8 In which long-running series did Amanda Burton star as Professor Sam Ryan?

9 Which American singer-songwriter is played by actress Sydney Chandler in the 2022 miniseries 'Pistol'?

10 Which long-running television series was set at Glenbogle?

TV 3
1 Maggie
2 Coach (played by Nicholas Colasanto)
3 Eric Morecambe
4 Castaway 2000
5 Paw Patrol
6 A nuclear submarine
7 The Colbys
8 2000
9 Songs of Praise
10 Sergeant Bilko

TV 4
1 Gareth
2 Norman
3 Edith
4 Peter Davison
5 Showstopper
6 Cat Deeley
7 Christopher Walken
8 Silent Witness
9 Chrissie Hynde
10 Monarch of the Glen

TV 5

1 Which TV character lives at 698 Candlewood Lane, Cabot Cove?

2 Who was the original presenter of TV's 'The Crystal Maze'?

3 In 'The League of Gentleman', Pamela Doove is a young woman trying to get work as a ... what?

4 On which island did Father Ted, Father Jack and Father Dougal reside in the 1990s TV series?

5 In which year was the BBC adaptation of 'Pride and Prejudice', starring Colin Firth and Jennifer Ehle, first screened in the UK?

6 What is the name of the manor in the TV series 'To The Manor Born'?

7 Pierce Brosnan was originally offered the role of James Bond in 1986, but he couldn't take the part, due to contractual obligations. What was the name of the series which delayed his ambition?

8 Which TV show featured Matilda, Cassius Chrome, Mr Psycho, Growler, Shunt, and Sir Killalot?

9 In which US television show did one of the main characters, Darrin Stephens, work for the advertising agency McMann and Tate?

10 Who was shot by Kristin Shepard on March 21st 1980?

TV 6

1 In the title of the long-running medical drama, what does ER stand for?

2 What is the name of the holiday camp in 'Hi-De-Hi'?

3 Who played President Josiah Bartlet in The West Wing?

4 The first series of which TV show had the word "Celebrity" in its title, took place in 2005 and was won by presenter Jayne Middlemiss?

5 In the TV series 'Red Dwarf', Dave Lister dreamt of living in which country?

6 Which of the Eggheads, who had the nickname "Tremendous Knowledge", died in 2020?

7 Which 2022 series directed by Ben Stiller and Aoife McArdle is set at Lumon Industries?

8 NCC 1701 was the designation of which spacecraft?

9 What was the name of the project computer in 'Quantum Leap'?

10 In which television series did America Ferrera play a young woman from a struggling Latino family who works as an editorial assistant at MODE fashion magazine?

SUBJECT ROUNDS

TV5
1 Jessica Fletcher (from 'Murder, She Wrote')
2 Richard O'Brien
3 Actress
4 Craggy Island
5 1995
6 Grantleigh Manor
7 Remington Steele
8 Robot Wars (they were some of the house robots)
9 Bewitched
10 John Ross "J.R." Ewing, Jr. (played by Larry Hagman on Dallas)

TV 6
1 Emergency Room
2 Maplins
3 Martin Sheen
4 Love Island
5 Fiji
6 Dave Rainford
7 Severance
8 USS Enterprise (in 'Star Trek')
9 Ziggy
10 Ugly Betty

TV 7

1 How many players are there in each 'University Challenge' team?

2 Vicky McClure plays Detective Sergeant Kate Fleming in which BBC police drama?

3 Arthur Atkinson, Monkfish and Professor Denzil Dexter were all characters on which TV comedy show?

4 In which year was 'EastEnders' first broadcast in the UK?

5 Who played PC "Fancy" Smith in 'Z-Cars'?

6 Who was the presenter of 'Going for Gold' in the 80s and 90s?

7 In 'Arrested Development', Michael Cera's character had what musical name?

8 What, specifically, are Grayling Russell in 'Inspector Morse', George Bullard in 'Midsomer Murders' and Molly Hooper in 'Sherlock'? (and a character played by Jack Klugman in a popular American show)

9 In 'Casualty', what was the name of the male nurse played in the 1990s by Patrick Robinson?

10 What gameshow involved a memory test, an observation round, a flight simulator and an assault course?

TV 8

1 Which fictional TV character wrote an autobiography called 'Bouncing Back'?

2 In 'Doctor Who', what is the name of the scientist from the planet Skaro responsible for the creation of the Daleks?

3 Who directed the acclaimed television play 'Cathy Come Home'?

4 What was the surname of the Goods' neighbours Margot and Jerry in 'The Good Life'?

5 How are the employees of the Charles Townsend Detective Agency better known in the title of a TV series?

6 What was the surname of the main family in 'Bread'?

7 Tanya Turner, Hazel Bailey and Chardonnay Lane-Pascoe were characters in which British TV show?

8 Bill Oddie and Tim Brooke-Taylor were two of 'The Goodies'. Who was the other?

9 Who was the quiz master when Bill McKaig reached the maximum score of 433 in 1999 on a Channel 4 quiz show?

10 Which sitcom character played by Robin Williams had the catchphrase: "Na-Nu Na-Nu"?

TV 7
1 Four
2 Line of Duty
3 The Fast Show
4 1985
5 Brian Blessed
6 Henry Kelly
7 George Michael
8 Pathologists
9 Ash (Martin Ashford)
10 The Krypton Factor

TV 8
1 Alan Partridge
2 Davros
3 Ken Loach
4 Leadbetter
5 Charlie's Angels
6 Boswell
7 Footballers' Wives
8 Graeme Garden
9 William G. Stewart (the show was 'Fifteen to One')
10 Mork (in 'Mork and Mindy')

TV 9

1 What character did Andrew Sachs play in 'Fawlty Towers'?

2 Which TV series has featured the likes of Amber Atherton, Binky Felstead, Olivia Bentley and Jamie Laing?

3 Which of the Chasers has a nickname which is, partially, a pun on their actual surname, in French?

4 Which football team did Warren Mitchell's character Alf Garnett support in 'Til Death Do Us Part' and 'In Sickness and in Health'?

5 In which sitcom does Zooey Deschanel star as Jess Day?

6 Which controversial real-life political figure did Sam Claflin play in Series 5 of 'Peaky Blinders'?

7 What was the name of the 1993 British docusoap which was intended to show six students over the course of a year of shared living in Manchester?

8 Who were the three members of the group of musicians which occasionally featured on the children's show 'Rainbow'?

9 On children's TV, how are Gecko, Owlette and Catboy collectively known?

10 On which Channel 4 TV show did Ian Woodley become the first UK gameshow millionaire in 1999?

TV 10

1 Which sitcom was about the life of the Brockman family?

2 In the TV series 'Game of Thrones', which character, with a limited vocabulary, was originally called Wylis?

3 What kind of establishment was the setting for the TV drama 'Cutting It', which ran from 2002 to 2005?

4 What was the name of Ronnie Barker's character in 'Open All Hours'?

5 If you are watching ITV, and you see a spinning black-and-white ticker in the top corner of the screen, what is about to happen?

6 What is the surname of Martin Freeman's character in 'The Office'?

7 In 'Happy Days', what is the first name of the character The Fonz?

8 Who replaced Arlene Phillips as a judge on 'Strictly Come Dancing', only to leave herself and be replaced by Darcey Bussell?

9 Which TV drama starred Bernard Hill as Yosser Hughes and featured a cameo from Graeme Souness?

10 What is the English name of the hit French show known as 'Dix pour cent' and set at the company ASK? [we want the English name of the French show, not the name of the English language adaptation]

TV 9
1 Manuel
2 Made in Chelsea
3 Mark Labbett/The Beast (La Bête)
4 West Ham
5 New Girl
6 Oswald Mosley
7 The Living Soap
8 Rod, Jane and Freddy
9 PJ Masks
10 TFI Friday

TV 10
1 Outnumbered
2 Hodor (In the book his original name is Walder. All he says is "Hodor")
3 Hairdressing salon
4 Albert Arkwright
5 Adverts
6 (Tim) Canterbury
7 Arthur (Arthur Fonzarelli)
8 Alesha Dixon
9 Boys from the Black Stuff
10 Call My Agent (Agence Samuel Kerr)

TV 11

1 In which popular TV series is AFC Richmond the name of a Premier League football team?

2 Which of the four main characters in 'South Park' has the surname Marsh?

3 What kind of creature is the cartoon character Foghorn Leghorn?

4 Who, in TV episodes, had Honour, Gold, Battle, Revenge, Justice, Waterloo and Rifles, among many others?

5 Which Irish comedian was, along with Phill Jupitus, an original team captain on 'Never Mind the Buzzcocks'?

6 Which comic actor links 'Friday Night Dinner', Chickens' and 'The Inbetweeners'?

7 Which play by James Graham, which first was shown in Chichester in 2017, transferred to TV to great acclaim in April 2020, including a show-stopping turn by Michael Sheen?

8 Who played Dave Tucker and Paddy Garvey in a popular 90s TV show?

9 What character did Alex Kingston play in 'Doctor Who'?

10 What is the name of the criminal defence lawyer played on TV by Raymond Burr between 1957 and 1966?

TV 12

1 Which sitcom created by and starring Larry David began in 2000?

2 Which TV series, in which six main cast members all have first names beginning with the same letter, ran for 20 seasons starting in October 2007?

3 Which actor has had acclaimed roles in 'Mad Men', 'The Crown', 'The Terror' and 'Chernobyl'?

4 Attraction, the shadow dance group who won 'Britain's Got Talent' in 2013, are from which European country?

5 Who was the father of 'EastEnders' characters Janine and Ricky?

6 Murray Hewitt is the put-upon manager of which folk duo?

7 Who was the star of the comedy show 'Trigger Happy TV'?

8 Which TV talent show featured Richard Park as head judge?

9 What was the name of the fictional island resort visited by the lucky couples on the ITV gameshow 'Take Me Out'?

10 Who was the enthusiastic presenter of 90s children's TV show 'Get Your Own Back'?

TV 11
1 Ted Lasso
2 Stan
3 Rooster
4 Sharpe - the episode title always went 'Sharpe's ...'
5 Sean Hughes
6 Simon Bird
7 Quiz
8 Robson Green and Jerome Flynn ('Soldier, Soldier')
9 River Song
10 Perry Mason

TV 12
1 Curb Your Enthusiasm
2 Keeping Up With the Kardashians (Kris, Kendall, Kylie Jenner, Kourtney, Kim, Khloe Kardashian (not to mention Kris Humphries and Kanye West))
3 Jared Harris
4 Hungary
5 Frank Butcher
6 Flight of the Conchords
7 Dom Joly
8 Fame Academy
9 Fernando's
10 Dave Benson Phillips

TV 13

1 Michael "Mickey Bricks" Stone and Albert Stroller were lead characters in which British crime drama series?

2 Which 90s sitcom dealt with the lives of husband and wife Bill and Ben Porter, and their children Jenny and David?

3 What was the surname of the family Will went to stay with in 'The Fresh Prince of Bel-Air'?

4 Who was played by an actor called Neil Burgess, and not actually the world's most enthusiastic Cillit Bang fan?

5 In 'Gavin and Stacey', which politician was a surprise guest at Nessa and Dave's wedding?

6 Which 2014 BBC sitcom starring the likes of Philip Jackson, Alison Steadman and Russ Abbot has a title which is now commonly used as a derogatory term for people of the generation to which those actors belong?

7 Which children's characters had an enemy called Professor Coldheart?

8 Who was the chat show host who insulted the Bee Gees to the point that they stormed off in a huff?

9 Who, in 2006, began as the composer and arranger of the 'Strictly Come Dancing' house band (as announced near the start of each episode)?

10 Which show's episode shown on June 16th 2020 was humorously described as the last of the first series, a series which had lasted 6122 episodes. Which show?

TV 14

1 James Michael Tyler, who died in 2021, became famous for playing, in a popular sitcom, which supporting role?

2 What was the surname of Tom and Pippa, the original foster parents in 'Home & Away'?

3 Who played the minor role of Inspector Japp in a 1985 Agatha Christie film adaptation called 'Thirteen at Dinner'?

4 Which future Oscar winner played Michael "Tealeaf" Fry in the comedy horror series 'Psychoville'?

5 Which fictional youth club was Geoff Keegan in charge of from 1989 to 2000?

6 What was the name of the Channel 4 Teletext quiz game that was discontinued on 15th December 2009?

7 Which comic actor's university nickname was taken by his wife for her starring role in one of Britain's most successful sitcoms?

8 How was Norman Anderson better known as the presenter of 90s youth TV show 'Def II'?

9 "Smoke me a kipper, I'll be back for breakfast" is a catchphrase associated with a guest character in which British sitcom of the 80s and 90s?

10 Ed Howzer-Black, Ray Purchase and Clem Fandango are supporting characters in which TV comedy?

TV 13
1 Hustle
2 2point4 Children
3 Banks
4 Barry Scott (in 'Cillit Bang' adverts)
5 John Prescott
6 Boomers
7 Care Bears
8 Clive Anderson
9 Dave Arch
10 EastEnders (this was the last one recorded before filming was stopped during lockdown)

TV 14
1 Gunther (in 'Friends')
2 Fletcher
3 David Suchet
4 Daniel Kaluuya
5 Byker Grove
6 Bamboozle!
7 Adrian Edmondson (his nickname was Eddie Monsoon – he also played a character called Eddie Monsoon in a 'Comic Strip Presents' episode from the 80s. Edina 'Eddie' Monsoon is the lead character in 'Absolutely Fabulous', played by Jennifer Saunders)
8 Normski
9 Red Dwarf (it's Ace Rimmer, played by Chris Barrie. It's falsely attributed, often, to Flashheart, as played by Rik Mayall in 'Blackadder')
10 Toast of London/Toast of Tinseltown

TV 15

1 Who is the British actor-writer who created and starred in 'Chewing Gum' and 'I May Destroy You'?

2 In 'Friends', Ross and Rachel got married in which city?

3 What is the name of the comic actor behind the characters Keith Lemon and Avid Merrion?

4 Waystar RoyCo is the name of a business in which TV drama?

5 What was the nickname of DC Alfred Lines, a "Bill" character from 1988 to 1998?

6 Which popular BBC mockumentary, which began in 2017, was written by siblings who play cousins in it, while their actual father plays the father of one of them, and their actual uncle plays a character called Len Clifton?

7 How was the 80s comedian and impressionist born Philip Martin better known?

8 Who was the winner of the first UK series of 'The Masked Singer'?

9 Which title character of a children's drama had sisters called Rita and Marilyn, brothers called Humphrey and Albert and a dog called Razzle?

10 Every episode of the anthology TV series 'Inside Number 9', features, at some point, in the background, a silver statue of what animal?

PEOPLE 1

1 What was Cilla Black's original surname?

2 Which supermodel was engaged to illusionist David Copperfield for most of the 1990s?

3 How is Nicolas Coppola, nephew of Francis Ford Coppola, better known?

4 The lead singer of the chart-topping band The 1975 is the son of which actress?

5 Which quiz show host, who once wrote an 'Encyclopaedia of Britain', was played by Mark Gatiss in the film 'Starter for Ten'?

6 The comedian Eddie McGinnis found fame under what name?

7 Beside Mickey Rooney, which other Oscar-winning actor and singer was the film star Ava Gardner married to?

8 Which English actor, who died in 1980, was married to Anne Howe, Britt Ekland, Miranda Quarry, and Lynne Frederick?

9 What was the screen name of Virginia Katherine McMath, who starred opposite Fred Astaire in ten films?

10 Born Vickie Lee Hogan, she married J. Howard Marshall when he was 89 and she was 26. How was she better known?

SUBJECT ROUNDS

TV 15
1 Michaela Coel
2 Las Vegas (there is also an assumption, referred to in passing in the first episode of 'Joey', that they married again after the series ended)
3 Leigh Francis
4 Succession
5 Tosh
6 This Country (written by Daisy May and Charlie Cooper)
7 Phil Cool
8 Nicola Roberts (as Queen Bee)
9 Jonny Briggs
10 Hare

PEOPLE 1
1 White (Priscilla White)
2 Claudia Schiffer
3 Nicolas Cage
4 Denise Welch
5 Bamber Gascoigne (he hosted 'University Challenge')
6 Eddie Large
7 Frank Sinatra (She was also married to clarinettist Artie Shaw)
8 Peter Sellers
9 Ginger Rogers
10 Anna Nicole Smith

PEOPLE 2

1 What was the country of birth of the original 'Mastermind' presenter, Magnus Magnusson?

2 In which century did Florence Nightingale die?

3 For which designer label did the actor Mark Wahlberg model underwear in the early 1990s?

4 In which northern town were the entertainers Bob Mortimer, Roy "Chubby" Brown and Paul Daniels all born?

5 What is the better known name of American actress/comedian/rapper Nora Lum, who has appeared in films such as 'Ocean's 8' and 'The Farewell'?

6 What A was a philosopher who was a student of Plato and a teacher of Alexander the Great?

7 Which of the Bee Gees was married to Lulu for four years from 1969?

8 What were the better known names of the two Americans born Robert LeRoy and Harry Alonzo Longabaugh, both thought to have died in 1908, about whom a film was made in 1969?

9 Which military rank went before the name of Elvis Presley's manager Tom Parker?

10 Which jazz musician had the nickname "Satchmo"?

PEOPLE 3

1 In which country was Che Guevara born?

2 In 2021, who rejected the idea of a statue of them being erected in their home state with the words, "Given all that is going on in the world, I don't think putting me on a pedestal is appropriate at this time"?

3 What word do the initials of the Earl of Wessex spell (not including a surname)?

4 What is the better known name of the singer Claire Boucher, who in May 2020 gave birth to a child whose name attracted great interest?

5 What relation is film star Bridget Fonda to film star Henry Fonda?

6 At one of the Leveson enquiry hearings in late 2011, which actor revealed that one of his middle names was Mungo?

7 Which influential British political figure who died in 1970 was the Nobel Laureate in Literature in 1950?

8 What is the surname of brother and sister, Simon, a former cricketer, and Bettany, a historian?

9 Of the four main cast members of the 'Goon Show', who was a) the first to be born and the last to die, and b) who was the last to be born and the first to die?

10 Who took the West Indies' first wicket in test cricket, then became Trinidad's High Commissioner to the United Kingdom and then the UK's first Black peer?

PEOPLE 2
1 Iceland
2 20th (1910)
3 Calvin Klein
4 Middlesbrough
5 Awkwafina
6 Aristotle
7 Maurice Gibb
8 Butch Cassidy and the Sundance Kid
9 Colonel
10 Louis Armstrong

PEOPLE 3
1 Argentina
2 Dolly Parton
3 EARL, Edward Antony Richard Louis (Prince Edward)
4 Grimes (her child with Elon Musk is X Æ A-12)
5 Granddaughter
6 Hugh Grant
7 Bertrand Russell (Churchill was in 1953, and died in 1965)
8 Hughes
9 a) Spike Milligan b) Peter Sellers (In fact, they were born in the reverse order of which they died)
10 (Baron) Learie Constantine

PEOPLE 4

1 Which Oscar-nominated film director is the comedy partner of Keegan-Michael Key?

2 Which musician married Bianca Pérez-Mora Macías in 1971?

3 Nora Barnacle was the muse and later wife of which great Irish author?

4 Which British Prime Minister was, at university, involved in a romantic relationship with Crown Princess Margarita of Romania?

5 Which Geordie comedian's stand-up tours have had titles including 'Noodlemeister', 'Fizzy Logic' and 'Mindblender'?

6 What name (first and surname) links a retired English comedian, famed for his slapstick style, with the 1968 men's 400m champion who died in 2021?

7 Although she was born in Trinidad, Nicki Minaj grew up, perhaps confusingly, in which neighbourhood of Queen's, New York?

8 Which British political figure's autobiography, published in February 2020, is called 'Unspeakable'?

9 Actress Jodie Comer is a childhood friend of which world champion athlete?

10 Who, in 2021, was the Chief Officer of the Cheshire Association of Local Councils?

PEOPLE 5

1 What place of birth links the Bee Gees to cyclist Mark Cavendish?

2 In August 2020, which former European monarch went into voluntary exile from his home country?

3 As a protest against cease-and-desist letters they'd been sending to small businesses, comedian Joe Lycett briefly changed his name to that of which fashion label in 2020?

4 Which campaigner and host of the 'You, Me and the Big C' podcast died in June 2022?

5 Played by Meg Ryan in the 2004 film 'Against the Ropes', Jackie Kallen is a pioneering manager in which sport?

6 Which author ran the Tokyo jazz club Peter Cat from 1974 to 1981?

7 If James Dougherty was first and Joe DiMaggio was second, which playwright was third?

8 Which legendary comedian and comic actor has played banjo with a bluegrass group called the Steep Canyon Rangers?

9 By what stage name is the rapper Montero Lamar Hill better known?

10 Jerry Springer, Nelson Mandela, Gerard Butler, Bob Mortimer and Rebel Wilson all studied what subject at university?

PEOPLE 4
1 Jordan Peele
2 Mick Jagger
3 James Joyce
4 Gordon Brown
5 Ross Noble
6 Lee Evans
7 Jamaica (strictly, South Jamaica, which is a bit different from main Jamaica, but accept Jamaica)
8 John Bercow
9 Katarina Johnson-Thompson
10 Jackie Weaver

PEOPLE 5
1 Isle of Man (Douglas, specifically)
2 Juan Carlos of Spain
3 Hugo Boss
4 Deborah James
5 Boxing
6 Haruki Murakami
7 Arthur Miller (husbands of Marilyn Monroe)
8 Steve Martin
9 Lil Nas X (His debut album is called 'Montero')
10 Law

PEOPLE 6

1 By what abbreviated name is the actor Lawrence Tureaud, born in 1952, best known?

2 Who is the founder of the multimedia company Syco Entertainment?

3 Which American singer, whose albums include 'Dirty Computer', has appeared in the films 'Moonlight', 'Hidden Figures', 'Harriet' and 'The Glorias'?

4 What position did Dame Sally Davies hold in England from 2010 to 2019?

5 By what three-letter name is Robert Diggs, the leader of the Wu-Tang Clan, best known?

6 Which tenor was discovered while working as a mechanic in Blackpool?

7 What was the nickname of the noted 18th century dandy Richard Nash?

8 Which famous actor conducted the civil partnership ceremony of Judge Robert Rinder in Ibiza in 2013?

9 Which great Swedish tennis player has a name that literally means "Bear Castle"?

10 Which TV presenter is the daughter of the former newspaper editor Eve Pollard?

PEOPLE 7

1 Patrick Kielty married which other TV presenter in 2012?

2 Which NSA operative leaked sensitive documents in 2013?

3 How did the American Paul "Red" Adair make his name?

4 What Apache leader, who lived to be 80, was also known as Goyathlay, which means "one who yawns"?

5 The actor Leonard Nimoy wrote two autobiographies, the first called 'I Am Not Spock'. What was the second one called?

6 Which actor founded the Reclaim party in 2020?

7 What was the name of Frank Sinatra's first wife?

8 Prime Minister William Gladstone is one of only two people whose coffin was transported ... where?

9 Which tennis player left James Bond actor George Lazenby in 2008 after six years of marriage?

10 Bob Crow was the General Secretary of which trade union from 2002 until his death in 2014?

PEOPLE 6
1 Mr T
2 Simon Cowell
3 Janelle Monáe
4 Chief Medical Officer
5 RZA
6 Alfie Boe
7 Beau
8 Benedict Cumberbatch
9 Björn Borg
10 Claudia Winkleman

PEOPLE 7
1 Cat Deeley
2 Edward Snowden
3 Fighting fires
4 Geronimo
5 I Am Spock
6 Laurence Fox
7 Nancy (Barbato)
8 On London Underground
9 Pam Shriver
10 RMT (National Union of Rail, Maritime and Transport Workers)

PEOPLE 8

1 What surname links Paul, an actor, Kevin, a former Australian Prime Minister and Amber, a former British Home Secretary?

2 '50 Shades of Grey' actress Dakota Johnson is the granddaughter of which actress who starred in two Alfred Hitchcock films?

3 In the 1830s, the Englishman Isaac Pitman devised a system, still used to this day, for what?

4 Actor Richard E. Grant was born and raised in which country?

5 By what rhyming nickname was the tabloid journalist Mazher Mahmood best known?

6 As in the name of the celebrity gossip site, what does TMZ stand for?

7 Which of the five Spice Girls has the most children?

8 Tedros Adhanom became Director-General of which organisation in 2020?

9 In 2011, the American basketball player Ron Artest legally changed his name to Metta ... what?

10 Whose last husband was Frédéric Prinz von Anhalt, whom she married in 1986?

PEOPLE 9

1 Which British journalist was the author of 'How to Lose Friends and Alienate People'?

2 What is the name of Jeremy Vine's comedian brother?

3 Prince Charles (as he was then) performed a "cup and ball routine" to enter which organisation?

4 What was the nickname of the 1960s London gangland figure Jack McVitie?

5 Which British singer's "Kitchen Disco" was a popular feature of lockdown in 2020?

6 Which notorious criminal kept four hippos in his private zoo in Colombia?

7 The novelist AS Byatt is the sister of which other renowned British author?

8 Namechecked by Louis Armstrong in the song 'Mack the Knife', who was the songwriter Kurt Weill's wife, who would go on to play Rosa Klebb in 'From Russia With Love'?

9 Which noted British designer's nickname came from a word he'd use to describe the landscaping potential his client's grounds offered?

10 Which dictator's self-bestowed titles included 'Lord of All the Beasts of the Earth and Fishes of the Seas and Conqueror of the British Empire'?

PEOPLE 8
1 Rudd
2 Tippi Hedren
3 Shorthand
4 Swaziland/Eswatini as it is now
5 The Fake Sheikh
6 Thirty Mile Zone
7 Victoria Beckham/Posh
8 World Health Organisation
9 World Peace
10 Zsa Zsa Gabor

PEOPLE 9
1 Toby Young
2 Tim
3 The Magic Circle
4 The Hat
5 Sophie Ellis-Bextor
6 Pablo Escobar
7 Margaret Drabble
8 Lotte Lenya
9 Lancelot Brown (Capability Brown)
10 Idi Amin

PEOPLE 10

1 Who, in 2020, was put in charge of NHS Test and Trace?

2 What profession links the runner Roger Bannister, the politician Liam Fox and the comedian Harry Hill? [looking for a generic answer]

3 Which jazz singer, who died in 1996, was known as the First Lady of Song and recorded three albums with Louis Armstrong?

4 The great magician and escapologist Harry Houdini died of peritonitis after being punched in which part of his body?

5 Who was the last Prime Minister of the UK not to study for an undergraduate degree at university?

6 The brothers who co-founded Methodism had what surname?

7 What valuable job did Steve Buscemi do for several years before achieving success as an actor?

8 Which British woman won a medal in rowing at the 2004 Olympics and at cycling at the 2008 Olympics?

9 How is the British rapper and actor Ben Drew better known?

10 In which American state were Frank Sinatra, Bruce Springsteen and Jon Bon Jovi all born and raised?

SPORT 1

1 Which city will host the 2032 Summer Olympics?

2 What is the name of Spain's equivalent of the FA Cup?

3 Which sports presenter's autobiography was called 'My Animals and Other Family'?

4 The main court at which Grand Slam tennis tournament is the Rod Laver Arena?

5 Which British 400m runner was helped to the finish line by his father after pulling his hamstring in the semi-final at the 1992 Olympics?

6 Andy "The Hammer" Hamilton, Bob "The Limestone Cowboy" Anderson and Darren "Demolition Man" Webster have all made their name in which sport?

7 Who did Jürgen Klopp replace as Liverpool manager?

8 Which great American boxer, who lost to Britain's Joe Calzaghe in 2008, was nicknamed "The Executioner"?

9 The 2003 British movie 'Blackball' starring Paul Kaye, was about Cliff Starkey, a rebellious young star of which sport?

10 Who scored the winning penalty for Czechoslovakia in the shoot-out to win the 1976 European Championship final against Germany?

SUBJECT ROUNDS

PEOPLE 10
1 Dido Harding
2 Doctor
3 Ella Fitzgerald
4 Stomach
5 John Major
6 Wesley
7 Firefighter
8 Rebecca Romero
9 Plan B
10 New Jersey

SPORT 1
1 Brisbane
2 Copa del Rey
3 Clare Balding
4 Australian Open
5 Derek Redmond
6 Darts
7 Brendan Rodgers
8 Bernard Hopkins
9 Bowls
10 Antonin Panenka (He chipped the penalty – a chipped penalty is now called a Panenka)

348

SPORT 2

1 The supporters of which Formula 1 team have a nickname which literally means "those infected by typhoid"?

2 The Kronk is a famous boxing gym in which US city?

3 Who won Great Britain's first gold medal of the 2020 Olympics in Tokyo?

4 How long is a standard indoor athletics track?

5 One of the biggest sporting events in Australia is the State of Origin, a rugby league match between which two states?

6 What former England cricketer was given the nickname "Brigadier Block" for his defensive capabilities?

7 What is the name of the island on which the football player Dwight Yorke was born?

8 In which sport would you score 6 points for a goal, and 1 point for a behind?

9 John Morris and which other cricketer flew a Tiger Moth aeroplane over the ground at an England tour match in Queensland in 1990?

10 Which 1972 Olympic gold medallist's wedding the next year was watched on TV by a global audience of 100 million people?

SPORT 3

1 The Giro d'Italia is a yearly event in which sport?

2 Which men's Olympic 100m champion was a grandfather by the time he lined up to defend his crown four years later?

3 What holy name is given to a pass in American football where the Quarterback throws a long high ball into the EndZone with seconds to go?

4 Who started for Manchester United in central midfield for the first 15 games of the inaugural Premier League season, though played very little more for the club and is better known now as a lower league manager, and for his famous father?

5 What shape is the fighting area for bouts in UFC? (UFC = Ultimate Fighting Championship)

6 Who scored England's try in rugby union's 2003 World Cup Final?

7 What was the nickname of super middleweight boxing champion Carl Froch?

8 How was the Athletics stadium at the 2008 Beijing Olympics widely known?

9 What name is given to holes 11 to 13 of the Augusta National golf course?

10 What two-mile handicap, held at Flemington Racecourse in early November by the Victoria Racing Club, is dubbed "The race that stops a nation"?

SPORT 2
1 Ferrari (The tifosi)
2 Detroit
3 Adam Peaty
4 200 metres
5 New South Wales & Queensland
6 Paul Collingwood
7 Tobago
8 Australian Rules Football
9 David Gower
10 Captain Mark Phillips (not Princess Anne, who did not win an Olympic medal)

SPORT 3
1 Cycling
2 Linford Christie (whose first granddaughter was born in 1995)
3 Hail Mary
4 Darren Ferguson
5 Octagon
6 Jason Robinson
7 The Cobra
8 The Bird's Nest
9 Amen Corner
10 The Melbourne Cup

SPORT 4

1 Which great former swimmer was known as "The Baltimore Bullet"?

2 Who did Frank Bruno face in his last professional fight?

3 In boxing, what does the abbreviation P4P stand for?

4 In tennis, which major championship was never won by John McEnroe, Pete Sampras or Boris Becker?

5 "It's only a game so put up a real good fight" - the theme to which sport-based gameshow?

6 What Olympic sport has 6 outfield players and a goalkeeper per side, and goals 3m wide and only 90 cm high?

7 Which American was Laureus World Sportswoman of the Year in 2017, 2019 and 2020?

8 How many cards are players initially dealt in Texas Hold' em poker?

9 At the 2002 London Marathon, what was Lloyd Scott wearing to cause him to set a record slowest time for the course, of 5 days, 8 hours, 29 mins and 46 seconds?

10 In April 2020, why did former world darts champion Gary Anderson have to withdraw from the inaugural PDC Home Tour?

SPORT 5

1 A flag often seen at Australian sporting events depicts which animal boxing?

2 The Seattle Kraken compete in which sport?

3 Which former Ireland rugby captain, once the World Player of the Year, was nicknamed "The Raging Potato"?

4 Which African team reached the semi-finals of the 2003 men's cricket World Cup?

5 Which word is used for a golf course built near the sea on sandy ground?

6 Which Arsenal footballer scored the winner in the 1993 League Cup final before breaking his arm when he was dropped by Tony Adams while celebrating?

7 How many laps of the athletics track are there in an Olympic 10,000m race?

8 Who became England's first million pound footballer when he signed for Nottingham Forest from Birmingham City in 1979?

9 Which city was due to host the 1944 Olympics, though they were cancelled because of World War II?

10 What nickname links football goalkeeper Peter Bonetti, boxer Carl Thompson and cricketer Phil Tufnell?

SUBJECT ROUNDS

SPORT 4
1 Michael Phelps
2 Mike Tyson
3 Pound for Pound
4 French Open
5 Big Break
6 Water Polo
7 Simone Biles (not Serena Williams, who won the award in 2003, 2006, 2010 and 2018)
8 Two
9 A deep sea diving suit
10 His home wi-fi signal was not strong enough (This was during the first lockdown)

SPORT 5
1 Kangaroo
2 Ice hockey
3 Keith Wood
4 Kenya (The only non-test nation ever to reach the World Cup semi-finals)
5 Links
6 Steve Morrow
7 25
8 Trevor Francis
9 London (it hosted in 1948 instead)
10 The Cat

SPORT 6

1 What was the nickname of renowned wrestler Steve Austin?

2 What was the name given to the dance with which the England cricket team celebrated on the pitch when they won the 2010-11 Ashes?

3 In which acclaimed film do Channing Tatum and Mark Ruffalo play former American Olympic wrestlers Mark and Dave Schultz?

4 In 2015, MTN-Qhubeka was the first professional team from which continent to compete in the Tour de France?

5 In NBA basketball, how many players from each team are there on court at one time?

6 In which sport would a competitor be on either bow side or stroke side?

7 The Chicago Cubs homefield shares its name with what brand of chewing gum?

8 In which year did Duncan Fletcher become the England men's cricket coach?

9 In November 2020, who became the first person to have refereed 100 rugby union test matches?

10 Who, in 2021, was the first woman to win the Ruby Walsh Trophy for leading jockey at the Cheltenham Festival?

SPORT 7

1 Old Tom Morris is regarded as the father of the modern version of which game?

2 Who was the last man to win the Wimbledon Mens' Singles with a wooden racket, doing so in 1981?

3 In rugby union, what number does the scrum half traditionally wear on their shirt?

4 The Silverstone motor racing circuit is actually spread across two counties - which two?

5 Liverpool won the First Division of the English Football League the most times in the eighties. Which team came second the most times in the same decade?

6 Who defeated Steve Davis in the legendary 1985 World Snooker Championship Final?

7 In boxing, what two words are used to instruct the trainers to leave the ring?

8 What American sportsman is mentioned in Madonna's 'Vogue', Simon and Garfunkel's 'Mrs Robinson' and Billy Joel's 'We Didn't Start The Fire'?

9 At what sport was Desmond Douglas 11 times English champion in the 70s and 80s?

10 Which member of the 1966 England FIFA World Cup winning team had a nephew who played in the 2003 England Rugby Union World Cup winning team?

SPORT 6
1 Stone Cold
2 The Sprinkler
3 Foxcatcher
4 Africa
5 Five
6 Rowing
7 Wrigley (Field)
8 1999
9 Nigel Owens
10 Rachael Blackmore

SPORT 7
1 Golf
2 John McEnroe
3 9
4 Northamptonshire and Buckinghamshire
5 Liverpool
6 Dennis Taylor
7 Seconds Out (the trainers are known as the "seconds")
8 Joe DiMaggio
9 Table tennis
10 George Cohen (his nephew is Ben Cohen)

SPORT 8

1 What, in the context of combat sport, does MMA stand for?

2 Chris and Robin were two brothers who played separately for England at cricket in the 1980s - what was their surname?

3 Who was Scotland manager at the 1986 men's FIFA World Cup?

4 How many strikes do you need for a perfect 300 game in tenpin bowling?

5 Which great boxer of the 80s added the word Marvelous to his name by deed poll?

6 Based in Wisconsin and named after the company that first sponsored them $500, what highly successful NFL team is the only non-profit, community-owned major league professional sports team based in the United States?

7 Sharing his name with a former journalist and politician, which British skier finished eighth in the 1988 Olympic men's downhill?

8 In cricket, which nation won the inaugural men's World Test Championship final, held in England in the summer of 2021?

9 In tournament golf, what is the penalty for carrying too many clubs in your bag?

10 Who played former South Africa rugby captain Francois Pienaar in the Clint Eastwood-directed movie 'Invictus'?

SPORT 9

1 How many players are there on an Olympic beach volleyball team?

2 Who was the last British man to be World Formula 1 Champion in the 20th Century?

3 What nickname was given to the boxing match between Muhammad Ali and Joe Frazier on October 1 1975?

4 As celebrated in the film 'Chariots of Fire', who won the men's 400m at the Paris Olympics of 1924?

5 Which Dutch game, based on basketball, is unusual in that it is specifically designed for mixed-sex teams?

6 The winner of the 1968 Olympic high jump title gave his name to which technique, in which the jumper clears the bar head first and backwards?

7 Which racquet sport is believed to have originated at Harrow School and is played on a court about one-third of the size of that used for the sport of rackets, from which it derives?

8 What position did Sylvester Stallone play in the allied football team in 'Escape to Victory'?

9 In the so-called St Valentine's Day massacre on February 14 1951, Sugar Ray Robinson demolished, but failed to put on the canvas, which boxer, known as "The Bronx Bull"?

10 In the Olympic Games, what must have a temperature of between 25-28 Celsius?

SPORT 8
1 Mixed Martial Arts
2 Smith
3 Alex Ferguson
4 12
5 Marvelous Marvin Hagler
6 Green Bay Packers
7 Martin Bell
8 New Zealand
9 Two shots
10 Matt Damon

SPORT 9
1 Two
2 Damon Hill (in 1996)
3 Thrilla in Manila (The Rumble in the Jungle was in October 1974 between Ali and George Foreman)
4 Eric Liddell
5 Korfball
6 Fosbury Flop
7 Squash
8 Goalkeeper
9 Jake LaMotta
10 Swimming Pool

SPORT 10

1 Jason Queally, Victoria Pendleton and Jo Rowsell won Olympic golds for Great Britain in which sport?

2 In rugby union, which number is normally worn by the Hooker?

3 On 6th February 1971, Alan B Shepard hit two golf balls in a place where no one else had ever played before. Where?

4 Which football club was known as Newton Heath until 1902?

5 Which Scot was the 2006 World Snooker Champion?

6 Greco-Roman and freestyle are the two forms of which Olympic sport?

7 What is the standard length, in metres, of all Olympic rowing races?

8 In England, which racecourse in Surrey is the home of the Derby?

9 Writer GK Chesterton described which sport as "an expensive way to play marbles"?

10 In 2017, the Japanese sportsman Kazuyoshi Miura broke a record held by which Englishman for the oldest man to score in professional football?

SPORT 11

1 Lauren Williams, Bianca Walkden, Bradly Sinden, Lutalo Muhammad and Jade Jones have won Olympic medals for Great Britain in which sport?

2 On the way to figures of 8 for 15 in the 4th Ashes test of 2015, which bowler's shocked face at a great catch by Ben Stokes was one of the iconic images of the summer?

3 The great Fred Perry was not only a winner of eight tennis Grand Slams, but also, in 1929, World Champion in which other sport?

4 Which snooker great beat Jimmy White four times in the final of the World Championship?

5 A 2006 film about the Scottish cyclist Graeme Obree shared its title with a famous train service - what was it?

6 The Brave and the Invincibles were the inaugural winners, in 2021, of which much-hyped sporting contest?

7 Retired English boxer Carl Froch was "The Cobra", but what was the animal nickname of the Northern Irish world champion Carl Frampton?

8 Which team competition ended in a draw in 1969 when Jack Nicklaus conceded a missable putt to Tony Jacklin?

9 The cricket documentary 'Fire in Babylon' was about which great test team of the 1970s and 80s?

10 Who won the 2022 men's Australian Open tennis championship?

SUBJECT ROUNDS

SPORT 10
1 Cycling
2 2
3 The Moon
4 Manchester United
5 Graeme Dott
6 Wrestling
7 2000m
8 Epsom Downs
9 Golf
10 Sir Stanley Matthews

SPORT 11
1 Taekwondo
2 Stuart Broad
3 Table tennis
4 Steven Hendry
5 The Flying Scotsman
6 The Hundred (Southern Brave (men) and Oval Invincibles (women))
7 The Jackal
8 Ryder Cup
9 West Indies
10 Rafael Nadal

SPORT 12

1 Which sportsperson's first daughter, born in May 2020 to his partner Kasi Bennett, is called Olympia Lightning?

2 The 2021 Ryder Cup took place at Whistling Straits, in which US state?

3 Which Cameroon striker achieved worldwide fame after dancing with the corner flag when he scored four goals at the 1990 FIFA World Cup?

4 Which huge English stadium, the 5th largest in Europe, is affectionately known as "The Cabbage Patch" (after its original use)?

5 Known as one of the "Four Kings" of 80s boxing, who was the first man to win world titles in five different weight divisions?

6 Elton John is the former chairman of which football club?

7 What, in the world of sport, is WADA?

8 In which state is the Arrowhead Stadium, where the Kansas City Chiefs play their home games?

9 "Filipino Flash" Nonito Donaire's 2019 fight with which Japanese boxer, nicknamed "The Monster", was Ring Magazine's 2019 Fight of the Year?

10 Though more famous for a goal he scored against the Reds, who struck Liverpool's first goal of the 1992 FA Cup Final?

SPORT 13

1 The badge on the Scotland football shirt features the Royal Standard of Scotland, featuring which animal?

2 Which horse won the Cheltenham Gold Cup in 2007 and 2009, as well as winning the King George VI Chase 5 times?

3 Who was the only player making their test debut in the first match of the 2005 Ashes?

4 The 2012 film 'Rush' is about the rivalry between Austrian Formula 1 star Niki Lauda and which British driver, portrayed by Chris Hemsworth in the film?

5 There are fewer than 50 courts in the world dedicated to the sport of real tennis. In which palace close to London is the world's oldest court?

6 What colour ring on the Olympic flag interlocks with the black ring and red ring?

7 Lella Lombardi was the first, and so far only, woman to win points in which sporting competition?

8 In 1882, The Sporting Times published a mock obituary stating that WHAT had died on the 29th August "Deeply lamented by a large circle of sorrowing friends and acquaintances / R.I.P. / N.B. - The body will be cremated and the ashes taken to Australia"?

9 In 2014, who became the first member of the Irish Traveller community to become a boxing world champion?

10 What, uniquely for the Football League, did Brentford's former ground Griffin Park ground have on each corner?

SPORT 12

1 Usain Bolt
2 Wisconsin
3 Roger Milla
4 Twickenham
5 Thomas Hearns
6 Watford
7 World Anti Doping Agency
8 Missouri
9 Naoya Inoue
10 Michael Thomas (scored against Sunderland. Scored title-winning goal for Arsenal vs Liverpool in 1989)

SPORT 13

1 Lion (The Lion Rampant)
2 Kauto Star
3 Kevin Pietersen
4 James Hunt
5 Hampton Court Palace
6 Green
7 Formula 1 World Championship (at 1975 Spanish Grand Prix)
8 English Cricket
9 Andy Lee (at middleweight) (He is Tyson Fury's second cousin)
10 A pub

SPORT 14

1 On what famous Paris thoroughfare does the Tour de France always end?

2 In which two events did Kelly Holmes win Olympic gold medals for Great Britain at the 2004 Olympics?

3 In the 1980s, what linked the football grounds of QPR, Luton Town, Preston North End and Oldham Athletic?

4 If someone endures a "donut" or a "bagel" in a tennis match, what has happened to them?

5 Which former West Indian batter has been on the losing side in more test matches than anyone else in history?

6 Which race course in Britain comes first in alphabetical order?

7 What is the surname of the former boxers nicknamed Dr Steel Hammer and Dr Iron Fist?

8 Complete the line-up of the 1991 GB 4x400m gold-medal winning team – Roger Black, Derek Redmond, John Regis, ... and who else?

9 In cricket, how many inches is it from the outside of the off stump to the outside of the leg stump?

10 In the game of Kabaddi, players are traditionally required to hold their breath during raids. How is an umpire able to tell that a player does not take a breath during a raid?

SPORT 15

1 What colour has the dust jacket of Wisden Cricketers' Almanack been since 1938?

2 Jahangir and Jansher Khan of Pakistan dominated which sport through the 80s and 90s?

3 In an Olympic swimming final, what is the number of the lane in which the fastest qualifier always swims?

4 Which word, used in many countries around the world, originated in England in the 1880s as a shortening of "Association Football"?

5 In which sport might contestants use a jib or a spinnaker?

6 In which year did Linford Christie win the Olympic 100 metres?

7 In which sport did the Swede Oscar Swahn win an Olympic silver medal in 1920 at the record age of 72?

8 What superhero-inspired title is given to the British rugby league player of the season?

9 Which batsman scored the most runs at both the 1996 and 2003 men's cricket World Cups?

10 Known as the Magical Magyars, what was the first foreign football team to beat England at home, doing so 6-3 in 1953?

SPORT 14
1 (Avenue de) Champs-Élysées
2 800m and 1500m
3 They had artificial pitches
4 They've lost a set 6-0. A double bagel is 6-0 6-0
5 Shivnarine Chanderpaul
6 Aintree (not Ascot)
7 Klitschko (Wladimir and Vitali)
8 Kriss Akabusi
9 9 inches
10 The player has to constantly repeat the word Kabaddi out loud

SPORT 15
1 Yellow
2 Squash
3 Lane 4
4 Soccer
5 Sailing
6 1992
7 Shooting (specifically the double shot running deer event. He is the oldest medallist of all time)
8 Man of Steel (now the Steve Prescott Man of Steel)
9 Sachin Tendulkar
10 Hungary

SPORT 16

1 What colour flag do marshals wave in a Formula 1 race to indicate that the safety car has been deployed?

2 The sport of Ultimate is governed by the WFDF. What does WFDF stand for?

3 What is the only stroke in competition swimming that begins in the water?

4 Who scored his 50th goal for England in September 2015?

5 Which English county was Brian Lara playing for when he scored his record 501 not out against Durham in 1994?

6 In what sporting event might you encounter the Col du Tourmalet and the Col du Galibier?

7 What is the name of the 2010 American film, starring Diane Lane and John Malkovich, about the thoroughbred horse which won the 1973 Triple Crown?

8 What name, confusingly, did the great Brazilian striker Ronaldo [Ronaldo Luis Nazario de Lima] have on his shirt in the football tournament at the 1996 Olympics?

9 Traditionally, winners of the Indy 500 in America will drink from a bottle of ... what?

10 Which former England player, whose last test was in 2004, played the record number of test matches, 71, without playing a single One-Day International?

SPORT 17

1 Which is bigger in terms of area - a basketball court or a netball court?

2 Which record-breaking jockey won his only Grand National on Don't Push It in 2010?

3 What three-word name links a monthly football magazine to a 1996 football movie starring Sean Bean?

4 Name either one of the two professional opponents Lennox Lewis lost to?

5 In which year did the great Michael Jordan first win a gold medal for the United States in the Olympic Basketball competition?

6 In football, what do the letters of the organisation LMA stand for?

7 At the 1996 Olympics, who did the Bulgarian Serafim Todorov defeat in the semi-finals of boxing's featherweight competition, a result that, in hindsight, is particularly noteworthy?

8 Don Fardon had a Top 40 hit in 1970 with 'Belfast Boy', a song about which legendary footballer?

9 What is the surname of father Archie and sons Peyton and Eli, who were all successful quarterbacks in the NFL?

10 What was unique about the dismissal of Ed Joyce by Boyd Rankin in a one-day cricket international on September 3rd 2013?

SPORT 16
1 Yellow
2 World Flying Disc Federation
3 Backstroke
4 Wayne Rooney
5 Warwickshire
6 Tour de France (allow "cycling" as there are other events which might take these routes)
7 Secretariat (not Seabiscuit - that film was in 2003, and the horse raced in the 1940s)
8 Ronaldinho (there was an older Ronaldo (Ronaldo Guiaro), so he was Ronaldo. There is, of course, also a later, also great Ronaldinho)
9 Milk
10 Mark Butcher

SPORT 17
1 Netball Court (30.5 x 15.25m) vs 28.65 x 15.24
2 AP McCoy
3 When Saturday Comes
4 Oliver McCall, Hasim Rahman - he also drew with Evander Holyfield
5 1984 (though famed for the 1992 Dream Team, Jordan also played in 1984 as an amateur)
6 League Managers' Association
7 Floyd Mayweather Jr (the last time Mayweather ever lost)
8 George Best
9 Manning
10 Rankin, playing for England, got Joyce out, playing for Ireland. Previously, Rankin, playing for Ireland has got Joyce out, playing for England

SPORT 18

1 In which city is the famous Maracanã stadium?

2 In rugby union, how long does a player spend in the Sin Bin?

3 In 2021, Maheta Molango succeeded Gordon Taylor as Chief Executive of which organisation?

4 What name links sports teams from New Orleans and Northampton?

5 At which 2015 tennis tournament did Flavia Pennetta celebrate winning her first Grand Slam title by immediately announcing her retirement?

6 The Rooney Rule, established by the NFL in 2003 and often suggested for the English Premier League, concerns what?

7 Which batsman hit four sixes off Ben Stokes in the last over of the final of the 2016 World T20, to win the tournament for West Indies?

8 Which European football club, a former Champions League finalist, has a name which is a country, and is based in a country separate from the domestic league it plays in?

9 In September 2019, who, at 20 years of age, became the youngest cricketer to captain a test match side?

10 Who was, in 1960, the only Spanish footballer to win the Ballon d'or (as of 2022)? He shares his name with an even more famous Uruguayan footballer of recent years.

SPORT 19

1 Shuttlecocks for badminton are traditionally made using feathers from which bird?

2 What are the three disciplines of Three-Day Eventing?

3 Where were the 2002 Winter Olympic Games held?

4 In which US city do the National Hockey League's Blackhawks play?

5 Who became, in 1995, the first man to be disqualified from a Wimbledon tournament?

6 Which jockey, who became more famous in another field, was riding Devon Loch in the 1956 Grand National when the horse inexplicably fell on the verge of winning?

7 Which sport featured in the Winter Olympics is also known as "the roaring game"?

8 Who won the men's 800m at the 1980 Olympics?

9 Don Shula, who died in 2020, coached which team to the only perfect season in NFL history in 1972?

10 Who stood down after seven years as England men's white-ball cricket captain in 2022?

SPORT 18
1 Rio De Janeiro
2 Ten minutes
3 PFA (Professional Footballers' Association)
4 Saints (American Football and Rugby)
5 U.S. Open
6 The interviewing and employment of coaches/ managers from minorities (Affirmative Action)
7 Carlos Brathwaite
8 Monaco (AS Monaco)
9 Rashid Khan (of Afghanistan)
10 Luis Suárez

SPORT 19
1 Goose
2 Dressage, Cross-Country, Show jumping
3 Salt Lake City
4 Chicago
5 Tim Henman (he was disqualified from the doubles for hitting a ball into a ballgirl)
6 Dick Francis
7 Curling (after the noise made by the stones)
8 Steve Ovett (Seb Coe was world record holder for 800m but Coe was second in this race)
9 Miami Dolphins
10 Eoin Morgan

SPORT 20

1 What nationality is cycling great Eddy Merckx?

2 In which sport do teams compete for the Stanley Cup?

3 Who was Alex Ferguson's predecessor as manager of Manchester United?

4 In which sport was Katarina Witt a two-time Olympic champion in the 1980s?

5 Which horse won the Grand National in 1992 in the week of a General Election?

6 Diego Maradona died 15 years to the day after which other great of the game?

7 Which action star (made famous by Guy Ritchie films) appeared in the diving competition of the 1990 Commonwealth Games?

8 Who has been involved in the two longest matches in Wimbledon singles history?

9 Which superstar singer played "All the Way" Mae in the 1992 baseball film 'A League of Their Own'?

10 What links the Olympic Games in 1924, 1932 and 1936, and no others? (Clue: this link would not have been possible before 1924, nor after 1992)

SPORT 21

1 How high, in inches, should a table tennis net be?

2 Which Italian football team is sometimes known as 'The Old Lady of Turin'?

3 On which golf course might an unlucky player fall into the Valley of Sin on the 18th hole?

4 Who was the first Briton to win the Formula 1 Drivers' Championship three times?

5 In ten-pin bowling terminology, which bird refers to three strikes in a row?

6 Who is the only British player to be men's European Footballer of the Year more than once?

7 In which US city is Fenway Park, the oldest ballpark still in active use in Major League Baseball?

8 Which feat in darts was first achieved on television in 1984 by John Lowe, with Phil Taylor being the first person to achieve it more than once on television?

9 In which sport did Ballyregan Bob break records in the 80s?

10 In skiing, what name is given to bumps on a course which are used to allow competitors to perform jumps and tricks?

SPORT 20
1 Belgian
2 Ice hockey
3 Ron Atkinson
4 Figure Skating
5 Party Politics
6 George Best (Maradona was 60, Best 59)
7 Jason Statham
8 John Isner (Mahut and Anderson)
9 Madonna
10 The Summer and Winter Olympics were held in the same country (Paris and Chamonix, Los Angeles and Lake Placid, Berlin and Garmisch)

SPORT 21
1 6 inches
2 Juventus
3 St Andrews (The Old Course)
4 Jackie Stewart
5 Turkey
6 Kevin Keegan (in 1978 and 1979)
7 Boston
8 Nine dart finish
9 Greyhound Racing (he won 32 races in a row)
10 Moguls

SPORT 22

1 In a netball team, how many players are allowed to score a goal?

2 In which year did Baron Pierre de Coubertin run his first modern Olympics in Athens?

3 Ingmar Stenmark, Alberto Tomba and Lindsay Vonn are famous names from which sport?

4 When compiling a 147 snooker break, how many times do you have to pot the black ball?

5 Which team sport is divided up into periods of play called a chukka (or chukker) with each chukka normally lasting for seven minutes?

6 How high in feet is the top of the rim from the floor on a regulation basketball net?

7 Which English football team, who play in red and white, are nicknamed "The Black Cats"?

8 How many points is a drop-goal worth in rugby league?

9 Mario Lemieux and Wayne Gretzky are two of the finest players ever in which sport?

10 In athletics, what is the last event of a women's heptathlon?

SPORT 23

1 The Madison and the Keirin are formats used in which sport?

2 In golf's Ryder Cup, four players take part in a foursomes match. How many take part in a singles match?

3 During the opening ceremony of the Olympic Games, which nation's team enters the stadium first?

4 What two words does a squash umpire say if he judges that a rally needs to be replayed?

5 What is the name of the other Major League baseball team in Chicago besides the Cubs?

6 Elise Christie represented Great Britain at which sport in the 2014 and 2018 Winter Olympics?

7 The word "slalom" comes from which Scandinavian language?

8 Although Colin Jackson was never Olympic champion, he was twice world champion, and world record holder - in which event?

9 Which England footballer, who made his debut in 2019, played three games for the Republic of Ireland senior side in 2018?

10 Who was the 1954 European men's 1500m champion?

SPORT 22
1 Two (Goal Attack and Goal Shooter)
2 1896
3 (Alpine) skiing
4 16 (one for each red, and then again at the end)
5 Polo
6 10 feet
7 Sunderland
8 One
9 Ice Hockey
10 800m

SPORT 23
1 (Track) Cycling
2 Two (one against one)
3 Greece
4 Yes let
5 Chicago White Sox
6 (Short track) speed skating
7 Norwegian
8 110m hurdles
9 Declan Rice (not Jack Grealish, who made his England debut in 2020, and though he played for Ireland U21s, never played for their senior side)
10 Roger Bannister (This was the same year he ran the four-minute mile)

SPORT 24

1 Which Englishman won golf's 2022 US Open at Brookline?

2 Which team knocked England's men's team out of both Euro 2004 and the 2006 FIFA World Cup?

3 What nationality is the former sprinter Frankie Fredericks?

4 Which horse died during a race at Exeter racecourse in November 2005 and has his ashes buried at Cheltenham racecourse?

5 Which Scottish team did Sir Alex Ferguson manage before he managed Aberdeen?

6 Which Premiership rugby union team play their home games at The Rec (Recreation Ground)?

7 With whom did John McEnroe win 50 career doubles titles?

8 In which sport did Tracey Neville both play for and coach England?

9 A famous photo emerged in 2005 of Australian star Brett Lee being consoled during the 2005 Ashes by which England all-rounder?

10 Wout van Aert, Biniam Girmay and Tom Pidcock all compete in which sport?

SPORT 25

1 Galacticos is a term associated specifically with which football club in the early 2000s?

2 Who won Great Britain's first gold medal of the 2020 Paralympics, her 15th in total?

3 Lance Armstrong dated which American singer, whose songs include 'Everyday is a Winding Road', 'My Favourite Mistake' and 'Perfect Lie'?

4 Stuart Bingham became World Champion in which sport in 2015?

5 Bafana Bafana is the nickname of which country's national football team?

6 In 1983, which British athlete won the men's 1500m at the first World Athletics Championships?

7 How many times have the modern Summer Olympic Games been cancelled because of war?

8 How many gold medals did Mark Spitz win at the 1972 Olympics?

9 Which Fijian was the leading money-winner on the US PGA Tour in both 2003 and 2004?

10 Assuming they have not pre-qualified, how many frames does a player have to win to become World Snooker Champion?

SPORT 24
1 Matt Fitzpatrick
2 Portugal
3 Namibian
4 Best Mate
5 St Mirren
6 Bath
7 Peter Fleming
8 Netball
9 Andrew Flintoff
10 Cycling

SPORT 25
1 Real Madrid
2 Sarah Storey
3 Sheryl Crow
4 Snooker
5 South Africa
6 Steve Cram
7 Three times (1916, 1940, 1944)
8 Seven
9 Vijay Singh
10 71 (10 + 13 + 13 + 17 + 18)

SPECIALIST SUBJECTS

This is the place to come if you want to test your knowledge in a particular area. This chapter features 150 ten-question quizzes on every topic under the sun, from a specific person to a specific country, animal, or food. There are also questions on words and phrases, and there's a little bit of maths. Hopefully, there's something for everyone.

Here are some of the subjects you'll find:

- Architects
- Board Games
- Cats
- Civil Wars of the World
- Cocktails
- Dolly Parton
- French Films
- Lady Gaga
- Logos
- Mammals
- Nigerian Literature
- Popes
- Reggae
- Scottish Football
- Volcanoes
- West Side Story

UK NUMBER 1s

1 The Clash had their only UK Number 1 single as a result of an advert for which brand?

2 Which superstar produced and sang backing vocals on the UK Number 1 single 'Do the Bartman'?

3 In April 1983, Spandau Ballet had their only UK Number 1 single. What was it?

4 Which keyboard player is co-credited on the Beatles Number 1 single 'Get Back'?

5 In 2001, what was the title of the only UK Number 1 single for So Solid Crew?

6 Which performer, better known as a TV detective, had the shortest title for a UK Number 1 in 1975?

7 Which 1978 UK Number 1 was a tribute to the art work of LS Lowry?

8 'Blinding Lights' by The Weeknd was a UK Number 1 on how many separate occasions in 2020?

9 Which duo's two UK Number 1 singles were 'Boom Boom Boom' and 'Don't Stop (Wiggle Wiggle)'?

10 Diana Vickers had a UK Number 1 single once. What was its title?

MEDITERRANEAN ISLANDS

1 On which island was the 'Colossus' which was one of the Seven Wonders of the Ancient World?

2 Whose childhood memoir, 'My Family and Other Animals', is set on Corfu?

3 Which hero of the Trojan War took many years travelling back to his home island, Ithaca?

4 Along with Cyprus, which other island in the Mediterranean is an independent country?

5 What was Europe's first advanced civilisation, centred on the island of Crete from around 2700 to 1420 BC?

6 On which Mediterranean island was Napoleon Bonaparte born in 1769?

7 Who had a UK Number 1 single in 2016 with 'I Took a Pill in Ibiza'?

8 According to a 1980s Heineken advert, the water "don't taste like what it oughta" on which Mediterranean island?

9 Which small volcanic island north of Sicily takes its name from the Roman god of fire?

10 Who wrote the novel 'Beautiful Losers' while living with Marianne Ihlen on the Greek island of Hydra?

UK NUMBER 1s
1 Levi's (Should I Stay or Should I Go?)
2 Michael Jackson
3 True
4 Billy Preston
5 21 Seconds
6 Telly Savalas (the song was 'If')
7 Matchstalk Men and Matchstalk Cats and Dogs (by Brian and Michael)
8 Three
9 The Outhere Brothers
10 Once

MEDITERRANEAN ISLANDS
1 Rhodes
2 Gerald Durrell
3 Odysseus (accept: Ulysses)
4 Malta
5 Minoan civilisation
6 Corsica
7 Mike Posner
8 Majorca
9 Vulcano
10 Leonard Cohen

TOYS AND GAMES

1 What is the Latin word for peace, used to signify a time out in a children's game of Tag?

2 What name is shared by an Asian board game and a 1999 movie starring Katie Holmes?

3 What is the name of the slot car racing brand originally launched in Harrogate in 1957?

4 In standard chess notation, which letter is used to refer to the Knight?

5 Lego takes its name from the Danish phrase "leg godt", meaning … what?

6 Which sport is the setting for the board game Totopoly?

7 What language do Furbies speak before they begin to learn English?

8 Tamagotchi virtual pets originated in which country?

9 In standard UK Monopoly, based on London streets, which property has a basic rent of £4?

10 What is the name of the gambling game using dice which is central to the plot of 'Guys and Dolls'?

SKYSCRAPERS

1 In which city would you find the Empire State Building?

2 What skyscraper changed its name to the Willis Tower in 2009?

3 In which city is the tallest building in the world, as of 2022?

4 In which Saudi Arabian city is the 120-floor clock tower of the Abraj Al Bait?

5 Which metropolitan area has the most skyscrapers in the world?

6 What does the Q of the 323m Q1 stand for?

7 In which Canadian city is the CN Tower?

8 In Kuala Lumpur, the Petronas Towers are made up of how many towers?

9 For how many years was Taipei 101 officially the world's tallest skyscraper? [allow one year either side]

10 Which Italian architect designed The Shard in London?

TOYS AND GAMES
1 Pax
2 Go
3 Scalextric
4 N
5 Play well
6 Horse racing
7 Furbish
8 Japan
9 Whitechapel Road
10 Craps

SKYSCRAPERS
1 New York
2 Sears Tower
3 Dubai (The Burj Khalifa)
4 Mecca
5 Hong Kong
6 Queensland (it is in Surfers Paradise, Queensland, and is the tallest building in Australia)
7 Toronto
8 Two
9 Five years (2004 to 2009)
10 Renzo Piano

2020 TOKYO OLYMPICS

1 Which tennis player lit the cauldron at the Opening Ceremony for the 2020 Olympics?

2 A new sport at the Tokyo Olympics was basketball played with just one basket and teams of how many people per side?

3 Referring to the pastime he was carrying out throughout the games, diver Tom Daley joked in an interview at Tokyo 2020 that he was proud to represent "Team Great ..." what?

4 Which rock star's daughter won a silver medal for Team USA in the show jumping at the Tokyo Olympics?

5 In which position did the host nation Japan finish in the Olympics 2020 medal table?

6 Sydney McLaughlin and Karsten Warholm both won gold and broke world records in which track event at Tokyo 2020?

7 For which country did Anna Kiesenhofer win an unlikely solo gold medal in the cycling women's road race at Tokyo 2020?

8 The winners of both the men's and women's 400 metres at the Tokyo Olympics represent which small island nation?

9 Simone Biles recovered from "the twisties" to win bronze in which gymnastic event at Tokyo 2020?

10 Which two words complete this question asked by high jumper Mutaz Essa Barshim in a discussion with competitor Gianmarco Tamberi and a rules official at Tokyo 2020: "Can we have ..."?

BOOKER PRIZE WINNERS

1 Hilary Mantel's 'Wolf Hall' is set during the reign of which six-times married English king?

2 Although it would later be renamed as 'Schindler's List', what was the original title of the Booker Prize winner written by Thomas Kenneally?

3 Which 2002 Booker Prize winner would be made into an Oscar-winning film directed by Ang Lee?

4 Who, in 1991, was the first Nigerian to win the Booker Prize with 'The Famished Road'?

5 Pat Barker's 'The Ghost Road', part of the 'Regeneration' trilogy, is set during which war?

6 Which US President is 'in the Bardo' in the title of a Booker Prize winner written by George Saunders?

7 The plot of 'A Brief History of Seven Killings' by Marlon James hinges on the attempted assassination of which singer in 1976?

8 John Banville won the Booker Prize with 'The Sea', but which author won it with 'The Sea, The Sea'?

9 What does the "DBC" stand for in the pen name of the Booker Prize-winning author DBC Pierre?

10 Penelope Fitzgerald's 'Offshore' is set on a collection of houseboats - on which river?

2020 TOKYO OLYMPICS
1 Naomi Osaka
2 Three (3x3 basketball)
3 Knitting
4 Bruce Springsteen (Jessica Springsteen)
5 3rd
6 400 metre hurdles (women's and men's, respectively)
7 Austria
8 Bahamas (Shaunae Miller-Uibo and Steven Gardiner)
9 Balance beam
10 Two golds (Tamberi and Barshim agreed to share gold rather than go to a jump-off)

BOOKER PRIZE WINNERS
1 Henry VIII
2 Schindler's Ark
3 Life of Pi (by Yann Martel)
4 Ben Okri
5 World War I
6 (Abraham) Lincoln
7 Bob Marley
8 Iris Murdoch
9 Dirty but clean
10 Thames

DISNEY FILMS

1 'Tangled' is based on which fairytale?

2 Which 2021 Disney feature stars Stephanie Beatriz as the voice of Mirabel Madrigal?

3 What, in 1937, was the first full-length Walt Disney Animation Studios cinematic release?

4 From which Disney film does the song 'Part of Your World' come?

5 Tod and Copper are the title characters in which Disney film?

6 The vultures in 'The Jungle Book' were loosely modelled on the four members of which band?

7 Which Hollywood star played the Genie in the 2019 remake of 'Aladdin'?

8 In 'Bambi', what kind of animal is Bambi's friend Flower?

9 In 'Wreck-it Ralph' who is the hero of the game in which Ralph is the bad guy?

10 Who provided the voice of Dodger and sang the song 'Why Should I Worry?' in 'Oliver & Company'?

ALL ABOUT AUSTRALIA

1 Australia takes its name from the Latin word "australis". What does "australis" mean?

2 What is the largest city in the Australian state of Victoria?

3 How many stars are there on the Australian flag?

4 What is the name of the ornithorhynchus anatinus, a semi-aquatic mammal native to Australia?

5 What 863m tall rock formation lies 208 miles south west of Alice Springs?

6 In which state is Australia Zoo, made famous by Steve Irwin?

7 What is the name of the train service that runs for 53 hours between Adelaide, Alice Springs and Darwin?

8 Which British captain reached Australia in 1770?

9 What is the name of the longest river in Australia?

10 What was the name of the bush kangaroo, in Waratah National Park, who was a hit on children's television in the 1960s?

DISNEY FILMS
1 Rapunzel
2 Encanto
3 Snow White and the Seven Dwarfs
4 The Little Mermaid
5 The Fox and the Hound (not 'Lady and the Tramp')
6 The Beatles
7 Will Smith
8 Skunk
9 Fix-It Felix Jr.
10 Billy Joel

ALL ABOUT AUSTRALIA
1 Southern
2 Melbourne
3 Six
4 Duck-billed platypus
5 Uluru (Ayers Rock)
6 Queensland
7 The Ghan
8 Captain Cook
9 Murray River
10 Skippy

DUTCH ART

1 Hieronymus Bosch's 'The Garden of Earthly Delights' is housed in which Madrid museum?

2 'The Painter of Sunflowers', by French artist Paul Gauguin, is a portrait of which friend of his at work?

3 Which painting by Carel Fabritius gives its name to a Pulitzer-winning novel by Donna Tartt?

4 What is the Dutch for "The Style", a 20th century movement which gave its name to an album by The White Stripes?

5 'Victory Boogie Woogie' was the last, unfinished, work of which 20th century Dutch artist?

6 Which painting from 1642 is also known as 'The Militia Company of Captain Frans Banning Cocq'?

7 Which band paid tribute to Willem de Kooning on the song 'Interiors', from their 1996 album 'Everything Must Go'?

8 Until 1893, much of the work of the artist Judith Leyster was misattributed to which Dutch golden age painter?

9 In the film 'Night at the Museum: Secret of the Tomb', characters enter the print 'Relativity', by which 20th century Dutch graphic artist?

10 Which Scottish beer company's logo is loosely based on the painting 'The Laughing Cavalier'?

THE FRENCH RESISTANCE

1 Which leader of "Free France" would, in 1959, become the first President of the Fifth Republic?

2 Mathilde Carré, a double agent during World War II, was known as "La chatte" - meaning what?

3 It is estimated 60,000 Republicans from which country's Civil War went north to join the French Resistance?

4 As well as being a symbol used in the UK, which letter, made using two fingers, was also used by the Resistance?

5 Which Irish Nobel Laureate, famed for works such as 'Waiting for Godot', was a courier in the French Resistance?

6 In which town in central France did Marshal Petain's Nazi-affiiliated government have its base?

7 Which American-born singer and dancer, dubbed the "Black Venus", was an agent in the French Resistance?

8 Which cross, with two horizontal bars, was the symbol of the French resistance?

9 Odette Sansom, an agent for the SOE in France, became, in 1946, the first woman to win which British award for bravery?

10 Which British sitcom featured the character Michelle Dubois of the Resistance?

DUTCH ART
1 Museo del Prado
2 Vincent van Gogh
3 The Goldfinch
4 De Stijl
5 Piet Mondrian
6 The Night Watch (by Rembrandt)
7 Manic Street Preachers
8 Frans Hals
9 MC Escher
10 McEwan's

THE FRENCH RESISTANCE
1 Charles de Gaulle
2 The cat
3 Spain
4 V symbol
5 Samuel Beckett
6 Vichy
7 Josephine Baker
8 Cross of Lorraine
9 George Cross (SOE is Special Operations Executive)
10 'Allo 'Allo

90s UK COMEDY

1 Who played the title character Gareth Blackstock in 'Chef!'?

2 Fiona Allen, Doon Mackichan and Sally Phillips were the stars of 'Smack the ...' what?

3 Which sketch show featured 'Ted and Ralph', 'Swiss Toni', and 'Does my bum look big in this?'?

4 In what kind of establishment was the Channel 4 sitcom 'Desmond's' set?

5 Which panel show made use of the catchphrases "Iranu" and "Uvavu"?

6 Who played the neighbour Deborah in 'Men Behaving Badly'?

7 'This Wheel's on Fire', the theme to 'Absolutely Fabulous', was co-written by Rick Danko and which legendary recording artist?

8 In 'The Mary Whitehouse Experience', what is the name of the most sarcastic man in the world, played by Rob Newman?

9 The sketch show 'Goodness Gracious Me' took its name from a song by which comic actor?

10 Which character famously asked Debbie McGee, "So what first attracted you to the millionaire Paul Daniels?"?

THE BRAIN

1 Which half of the body does the left cerebral hemisphere control?

2 The matter of the convoluted outer layer of the cerebrum is associated with which colour?

3 The bottom of the brainstem is attached to which part of the body?

4 What is the occipital lobe primarily responsible for?

5 What is the largest and uppermost part of the human brain?

6 Two major furrows divide each cerebral hemisphere into how many lobes?

7 What part of the forebrain is the main relay centre between the medulla and the cerebrum?

8 Which lobe of the cerebral cortex processes sensory information such as touch, temperature and pain?

9 Which former MP for Havant was known as "Two Brains"?

10 Who starred as Dr. Michael Hfuhruhurr in the 1983 film 'The Man With Two Brains'?

90s UK COMEDY
1 Lenny Henry
2 Pony
3 The Fast Show
4 Barbershop
5 Shooting Stars
6 Lesley Ash
7 Bob Dylan
8 Ray
9 Peter Sellers
10 Mrs Merton (played by Caroline Aherne)

THE BRAIN
1 Right
2 Grey (matter)
3 Spinal Cord
4 Vision
5 Cerebrum
6 Four
7 Thalamus
8 Parietal
9 David Willetts
10 Steve Martin

VOLCANOES

1 The eruption of an underwater volcano in January 2022 caused huge damage in which island nation whose capital is Nuku'alofa?

2 A broad volcano with gently sloping sides that produces swift-flowing basalt lavas is known as a what?

3 On which island of Japan is Mount Fuji?

4 Which Italian island, which contains an active volcano, has the nickname "Lighthouse of the Mediterranean"?

5 In 1492, who witnessed an eruption of the volcano Pico de Teide on Tenerife, while leading an expedition to the New World?

6 An eruption of the volcano Santorini around 1640 BC is thought to have caused the collapse of which civilization?

7 Situated in the Andes, what is the three-word name of the tallest volcano in the world?

8 Mount Fagradalsfjall, which spewed lava for six months in 2021, is in which country?

9 Which volcano is 38 metres higher than its neighbour Mauna Loa and is the highest point in Hawaii?

10 In which year did Mount St Helens erupt, killing 57 people?

FASHION

1 What is the first name of the daughter of Paul and Linda McCartney who is a famous fashion designer?

2 In 1993, Naomi Campbell fell on a catwalk whilst trying to model a ten inch pair of ... what?

3 What name is given to the style of skirt that is fitted at the waist and widens towards the hem?

4 Which fashion house startled the world with the "New Look" in 1947?

5 What nationality was Cristóbal Balenciaga, founder of the fashion house that bears his surname?

6 Virgil Abloh, who died in 2021, founded Pyrex Vision in 2012. What would he rename the company in 2013?

7 With which designer did Malcolm McLaren open a shop in London in 1971?

8 The brand Miu Miu was created in 1992 by which fashion house?

9 The signature bag introduced by Hermes in 1984 is named after which British actress?

10 Adam Driver, Lady Gaga and Jared Leto starred in the 2021 film 'House of ...' what?

VOLCANOES
1 Tonga
2 Shield volcano
3 Honshu
4 Stromboli
5 Christopher Columbus
6 Minoan
7 Ojos del Salado
8 Iceland
9 Mauna Kea
10 1980

FASHION
1 Stella
2 High heels
3 A-Line
4 Dior
5 Spanish
6 Off-White
7 Vivienne Westwood
8 Prada
9 Jane Birkin
10 Gucci

PABLO PICASSO

1 Pablo Picasso was born in 1881 in which southern Spanish city?

2 In 1904, after several years of switching between Spain and France, Picasso moved for good to which French city?

3 Which art movement did Pablo Picasso co-found with Georges Braque?

4 The town of Guernica, famously painted by Picasso, is in which autonomous community of Spain?

5 At which auction house in New York was 'Boy With a Pipe' sold to an anonymous bidder for $104 million?

6 A 1907 painting by Picasso which is said to signal the start of his "African period" is called 'Les Demoiselles d' ...' where?

7 Which acrobats, whose name comes from the Italian for "leap" and "bench", would inspire Picasso and his poet friend Guillaume Apollinaire?

8 What was the first name of Pablo Picasso's daughter with Marie-Thérèse Walter?

9 Picasso painted a portrait of which American writer in 1905-06?

10 Who wrote the song 'Pablo Picasso' for his band the Modern Lovers?

THEATRE

1 42nd Street is a famous thoroughfare associated with theatre - in which city?

2 A play by August Wilson later made into a film is 'Ma Rainey's ...' what?

3 Which playwright's works include 'The Ferryman' and 'Jerusalem'?

4 Which northern English city has a theatre called the Royal Exchange?

5 Which American playwright wrote 'The Iceman Cometh'?

6 Who composed original music for Henrik Ibsen's 'Peer Gynt'?

7 In 2010, which future Oscar winner won the Evening Standard Outstanding Newcomer award for his role in 'Sucker Punch'?

8 What is the Shakespearean theatre company whose three-word name is an ancient expression meaning "in close proximity"?

9 Which "mother of modern theatre" was married to folk singer Ewan MacColl from 1934 to 1950?

10 Which drama by Lucy Kirkwood won the Olivier Award for Best New Play in 2014?

PABLO PICASSO
1 Malaga
2 Paris
3 Cubist
4 Basque country (accept: Biscay)
5 Sotheby's
6 Avignon
7 Saltimbanques
8 Maya
9 Gertrude Stein
10 Jonathan Richman

THEATRE
1 New York City
2 Black Bottom
3 Jez Butterworth
4 Manchester
5 Eugene O'Neill
6 Edvard Grieg
7 Daniel Kaluuya
8 Cheek By Jowl
9 Joan Littlewood
10 Chimerica

MOTOWN

1 Who founded Motown, as Tamla Records, in 1959?

2 Which song by The Marvelettes was Motown's first US Number 1 single?

3 Which Motown star, who fronted the Vandellas, would later serve as an elected councilwoman in Detroit?

4 What is the nickname of the legendary Motown singer, bandleader and songwriter William Robinson?

5 A member of Motown's renowned backing group The Funk Brothers, James Jamerson is primarily associated with which instrument?

6 Which Stevie Wonder studio album contains 'Superstition' and 'You are the Sunshine of My Life'?

7 In 1966, Cindy Birdsong replaced Florence Ballard in which group?

8 Motown moved its operations from Detroit to which city in 1972?

9 For which 1978 album did Marvin Gaye give up half his royalties to his ex-wife Anna?

10 According to Edwin Starr, what is war good for?

ICE CREAM

1 What is the Italian word for ice cream?

2 Neapolitan ice cream contains three flavours - chocolate, vanilla and which other?

3 Ice cream company Baskin-Robbins is famed for advertising how many flavours?

4 Which British band had a 2007 hit with the song 'Ice Cream'?

5 What month was declared National Ice Cream Month in the US by Ronald Reagan?

6 The Ben & Jerry's flavour Cherry Garcia was named after a member of which rock band?

7 Which Joni Mitchell song talks about "ice cream castles in the air"?

8 Which British city endured gangland Ice Cream Wars in its East End in the 1980s?

9 Who, in a Blondie song, was "cold as ice cream but still as sweet"?

10 Which Wall's product was advertised for many years using the tune to the song 'O Sole Mio'?

MOTOWN

1 Berry Gordy
2 Please Mr Postman
3 Martha Reeves
4 Smokey
5 Bass guitar
6 Talking Book
7 The Supremes
8 Los Angeles
9 Here, My Dear
10 Absolutely nothing

ICE CREAM

1 Gelato
2 Strawberry
3 31
4 New Young Pony Club
5 July
6 The Grateful Dead
7 Both Sides, Now
8 Glasgow
9 Sunday Girl
10 Cornetto ("Just one Cornetto")

MARIE CURIE

1 In which city, the capital of modern-day Poland, was Marie Curie born?

2 In what subject did Marie Curie win her second Nobel Prize?

3 In which war did Marie Curie set up France's first military radiology centre?

4 Which yellow flower is the logo of the UK charity named Marie Curie?

5 What was the first name of Marie Curie's eldest daughter, who also won a Nobel Prize in 1935?

6 The Curies shared their first Nobel Prize with which French scientist, who discovered the existence of radioactivity?

7 Named after a British inventor, which "Medal", awarded by the Royal Society of London, did Marie and Pierre Curie win in 1903?

8 Which British actress, Oscar-nominated for 'Gone Girl', played Marie Curie in the 2019 film 'Radioactive'?

9 What is the name of the first element discovered by Marie and Pierre Curie, in 1898?

10 In 2019, a story broke about a cake which had Marie Curie's face on it, instead of that of which similar-sounding singer?

A BIT OF MATHS

1 What is the first prime number over 100?

2 If you add up all the numbers from 1 to 100 and divide the total by 100, what would be the result?

3 If you spell out all the whole numbers in English, from one upwards, which number is the first to contain the letter Y?

4 In the song 'The Twelve Days of Christmas' what do you get if you add the number of swans to the number of French hens?

5 What is the product of 86 and 48?

6 To the nearest whole number, how many weeks are there every 100 years, assuming there is a leap year every four years?

7 In maths, what is one-ninth multiplied by one-ninth?

8 In English, which is the smallest positive whole number whose name contains exactly six letters?

9 How many squares are there in the most common size of sudoku grid, in which each of the numbers 1-9 should be used nine times?

10 What is the missing number in this sequence: 98, 94, ..., 70, 38?

MARIE CURIE
1 Warsaw
2 Chemistry (her first was in Physics)
3 World War I
4 Daffodil
5 Irène (Irène Joliot-Curie)
6 Henri Becquerel
7 Davy Medal
8 Rosamund Pike
9 Polonium
10 Mariah Carey (It turned out the cake, though a true story, was a joke, not a mistake)

A BIT OF MATHS
1 101
2 50.5
3 20
4 10
5 4128
6 5218
7 1/81
8 Eleven
9 81
10 86

THE WIRE

1 In which city is 'The Wire' set?

2 What was the nickname of 'The Wire' character Russell Bell, played by Idris Elba?

3 Which former police reporter, alongside former detective Ed Burns, created 'The Wire'?

4 "Proposition" Joe Stewart was the crimelord in which part of Baltimore?

5 What relation is D'Angelo to Avon Barksdale?

6 "Cheese" Wagstaff was played by which member of the Wu-Tang Clan in 'The Wire'?

7 Which principled and loyal "soldier" was played by Anwan Glover in 'The Wire'?

8 Which actor, who played Omar Little in 'The Wire', died in September 2021?

9 Who is Chris Partlow's partner in crime, played by Felicia Pearson, in 'The Wire'?

10 Who wrote the song that is, in different versions, the theme for every season of 'The Wire'?

FAMOUS BRIDGES

1 The Øresund Bridge links Sweden to which country?

2 The nickname of the Sydney Harbour Bridge is which household item?

3 The Brooklyn Bridge joins Brooklyn to which other borough of New York?

4 What type of bridge is the UNESCO World Heritage Site, the Forth Rail Bridge?

5 Which river does the iconic Ponte Vecchio cross in Florence?

6 The Menai Suspension Bridge was designed by which Scottish engineer, dubbed "The Colossus of Roads"?

7 What is, ironically, the oldest standing bridge over the Seine in Paris?

8 'Misty Morning, Albert Bridge' is a 1989 song by which British-Irish band?

9 The Danyang-Kunshan Grand Bridge is, at 165 km, one of the longest bridges in the world. In which country is it?

10 The Pont Saint-Bénézet is a famous incomplete bridge which inspired a children's song, in which French city?

THE WIRE
1 Baltimore
2 Stringer
3 David Simon
4 East side
5 Nephew
6 Method Man
7 Slim Charles
8 Michael K. Williams
9 Snoop (the full character name is Felicia "Snoop" Pearson, like the actress)
10 Tom Waits (Way Down in the Hole)

FAMOUS BRIDGES
1 Denmark
2 The Coathanger
3 Manhattan
4 Cantilever
5 Arno
6 Thomas Telford
7 Pont Neuf (meaning "new bridge")
8 The Pogues
9 China
10 Avignon (Sur le pont d'Avignon)

MAPPING

1 What is the name of Great Britain's National Mapping Agency?

2 Which lines on a map show the height and shape of land?

3 What C is the name for the study of mapmaking?

4 Which street atlas was first compiled in the 1930s by Phyllis Pearsall?

5 The Carte de Cassini, started in the 1670s and completed in 1793, was the first accurate topographical map of an entire country - which country?

6 Recent calculations have revealed that Britain's tallest mountain is 1 metre higher than previously thought - what is the name of the mountain?

7 In which English cathedral is the largest medieval Mappa Mundi known to exist, which dates from around 1300?

8 Buildings on OS maps are small brown squares outlined with which colour?

9 Who designed the iconic London underground map, first used in 1931?

10 Which band, fronted by Karen O, included the song 'Maps' on their 2003 album 'Fever to Tell'?

BRITISH PRIME MINISTERS

1 In which year did Boris Johnson become UK Prime Minister?

2 At which hotel was Margaret Thatcher staying when she died in 2013?

3 For 14 of the years between 1957 and 1976, the UK Prime Minister had which first name?

4 Who had three separate stints as UK Prime Minister within the 20th century?

5 Which Labour Prime Minister represented a constituency in Wales?

6 David Cameron served as MP for Witney for how many years?

7 William Gladstone and Benjamin Disraeli took turns to be UK Prime Minister in the late 19th century - which party did Disraeli represent?

8 Who is the only British Prime Minister to play first-class cricket (something he did between 1924 and 1927)?

9 Who was both the last Whig and first Liberal Prime Minister of the UK?

10 How old was Tony Blair when he became Prime Minister of the UK?

SPECIALIST SUBJECTS

MAPPING
1 Ordnance Survey
2 Contour Lines
3 Cartography
4 (Geographer's) A-Z
5 France
6 Ben Nevis
7 Hereford Cathedral
8 Black
9 Harry Beck
10 Yeah Yeah Yeahs

BRITISH PRIME MINISTERS
1 2019
2 The Ritz
3 Harold (Macmillan and Wilson)
4 Stanley Baldwin
5 James Callaghan (Cardiff South East)
6 15 years
7 Conservative
8 Alec Douglas-Home
9 Viscount Palmerston
10 43 (he became Prime Minister just before his 44th birthday in May 1997)

AMERICAN NATIONAL PARKS

1 Redwood and Sequoia are National Parks in California named after what kind of living things?

2 The Grand Canyon was carved by which river?

3 Formerly known as Mount McKinley, Denali is in which US state?

4 Which American National Park shares its name with a Terrence Malick film and a Bruce Springsteen song?

5 Which National Park in California is the hottest, lowest and driest place in the USA?

6 The Gateway Arch in St Louis commemorates the start of the expedition of Lewis and ... who?

7 The Carlsbad Caverns are in the Guadalupe Mountains of which US state?

8 Whose 1987 album 'The Joshua Tree' is named after a US National Park?

9 Yosemite Sam, named after a California National Park, is an adversary of which wisecracking rabbit?

10 Yellowstone was the first National Park, signed into law by which US President in 1872?

TOUR DE FRANCE

1 In which month does the Tour de France traditionally finish?

2 Which country has produced the most General Classification winners in the Tour de France?

3 Who was the first British man to win the Tour de France?

4 Who won his first Tour de France in 2020?

5 As well as winning four stages, who won the Green Jersey at the 2021 Tour de France?

6 Unusually, the 1989 Tour de France ended with what type of stage?

7 Cadel Evans was the first winner of the Tour de France from which country?

8 On which island did the 2013 Tour de France begin?

9 Who, in 1957, won the first Tour de France he entered?

10 Which Tour de France cyclist shares his name with the character played by Kiefer Sutherland in the show '24'?

AMERICAN NATIONAL PARKS
1 Trees
2 Colorado River
3 Alaska
4 Badlands
5 Death Valley
6 Clark (Meriwether Lewis and William Clark)
7 New Mexico
8 U2
9 Bugs Bunny
10 Ulysses S Grant

TOUR DE FRANCE
1 July
2 France
3 Bradley Wiggins
4 Tadej Pogacar
5 Mark Cavendish
6 A time trial
7 Australia
8 Corsica
9 Jacques Anquetil
10 Jack Bauer

FAMOUS ONLINE

1 Lil Bub, an internet celebrity who died in 2019, was a ... what?

2 How is the British YouTuber Daniel Middleton better known?

3 Godwin's Law relates to the inevitability of people mentioning what in an online discussion?

4 Amber Lee Ettinger became famous in 2007 as ... who?

5 What is the name of Logan Paul's brother?

6 Online provocateur Milo Yiannopoulos resigned from which news network in February 2017?

7 Which YouTuber, born in 2003, initially came to fame appearing on the TV shows 'Dance Moms'?

8 How is YouTuber Felix Kjellberg better known?

9 YouTuber KSI became famous as a member of which collective (beginning with S)?

10 Which English vlogger wrote 'The Pointless Book'?

SATURN

1 How many planets in the Solar System are larger than Saturn?

2 The atmosphere of Saturn is dominated by helium and which other gas?

3 While NASA contributed the Cassini Spacecraft to explore Saturn, what organisation supplied the Huygens lander?

4 What name is given to Saturn's long-lived storm, which began in 2010, studied by Cassini?

5 Saturn is named after a Roman god – who would be his Greek equivalent?

6 The Roman festival Saturnalia, thought to have influenced Christmas, was held in which month?

7 Titan is Saturn's largest moon – what is its second largest?

8 Allowing one year either side, how long does it take Saturn to orbit the sun?

9 Which moon of Saturn has a plume of water vapour and ice particle jets coming from the fissure across its south pole?

10 'Saturn' was a bonus track on whose classic album 'Songs in the Key of Life'?

SPECIALIST SUBJECTS

FAMOUS ONLINE
1 Cat
2 DanTDM
3 Nazis
4 Obama girl
5 Jake Paul
6 Breitbart
7 JoJo Siwa
8 PewDiePie
9 Sidemen
10 Alfie Deyes

SATURN
1 One (Jupiter)
2 Hydrogen
3 European Space Agency (ESA)
4 Great White Spot
5 Cronos
6 December
7 Rhea
8 29.7 Years (accept: 28.7 to 30.7 years)
9 Enceladus
10 Stevie Wonder

WEST SIDE STORY

1 'West Side Story' is based on which play by William Shakespeare?

2 According to a famous song from 'West Side Story', "everything's free in ..." where?

3 'West Side Story' is set in which borough of New York City?

4 Who directed the 2021 film remake of 'West Side Story'?

5 Who dubbed all of Natalie Wood's songs in the first film version of 'West Side Story'?

6 In 'West Side Story', the Sharks originally come from which island?

7 Who is credited as writing the lyrics for the musical 'West Side Story'?

8 Who plays Tony in the 2021 film version of 'West Side Story'?

9 In an early version of the musical, then named 'East Side Story', what was the nationality of the main male character?

10 The tune of 'Gee, Officer Krupke' was originally composed by Leonard Bernstein for which other musical?

ABBREVIATIONS

1 What is the two-letter abbreviation for a pound, the unit of mass in the imperial system?

2 The word "fax" is an abbreviated form of which word?

3 Meaning "before noon", what does the abbreviation "a.m." literally stand for?

4 What do the letters "FC" after the name of a sports team normally stand for?

5 The name of which country is often abbreviated as UAE?

6 Used in printing, what does the abbreviation "dpi" stand for?

7 What does "p.p." stand for, used for signing a letter on somebody else's behalf?

8 What does the P in the abbreviation PDA stand for?

9 What is the standard airport abbreviation for Los Angeles International Airport?

10 In musical notation, how is the Italian word "fortissimo" abbreviated?

WEST SIDE STORY
1 Romeo And Juliet
2 America
3 Manhattan
4 Steven Spielberg
5 Marni Nixon
6 Puerto Rico
7 Stephen Sondheim
8 Ansel Elgort
9 Italian
10 Candide

ABBREVIATIONS
1 lb
2 Facsimile
3 Ante meridiem
4 Football Club
5 United Arab Emirates
6 Dots per inch
7 Per procurationem
8 Personal
9 LAX
10 ff

ARCHITECTS

1 Which renowned British architect, who designed the Pompidou Centre and the Millennium Dome, died in December 2021?

2 On 'Bridge Over Troubled Water', Simon & Garfunkel said 'Farewell' to which American architect?

3 Which venue did Zaha Hadid design for the 2012 London Olympics?

4 How was the architect Charles-Édouard Jeanneret, who designed the Indian city of Chandigarh, better known?

5 In which century was Sir Christopher Wren born?

6 What was the surname of married couple Charles and Ray, the American designers and architects who died ten years apart, in 1978 and 1988 respectively?

7 Who designed City Hall in London, which was the headquarters of the Greater London Authority from 2002 to 2021?

8 What is the five-letter name of the architecture firm founded by Kazuyo Sejima and Ryue Nishizawa in 1995?

9 Who wrote the 1985 novel 'Hawksmoor', a fictionalised meta-history about a famous London architect?

10 Which American architect of buildings including the Walt Disney Concert Hall voiced himself in a 2005 episode of 'The Simpsons'?

FIFA WORLD CUPS

1 At the 2010 World Cup in South Africa, the same team won the FIFA Fair Play as the actual tournament. Which team?

2 Which Colombian player scored the most goals at the 2014 FIFA World Cup?

3 In which year did both Wales and Northern Ireland reach the quarter-finals of the men's FIFA World Cup?

4 Which football team bleached their hair for their match against England in the 1998 World Cup?

5 Which team famously beat England 1-0 the first time the men's World Cup was held in Brazil, in 1950?

6 In which year was the last men's FIFA World Cup that Scotland qualified for while England failed to qualify?

7 Who scored both a goal and an own goal in the 2018 FIFA World Cup final?

8 For which year's FIFA World Cup was the Russian striker Oleg Salenko the winner of the Golden Boot?

9 What World Cup "first" was provided by France's second goal against Honduras in their group game at the 2014 World Cup?

10 Not including any shoot-outs, how many penalties did Harry Kane score in the 2018 FIFA World Cup?

ARCHITECTS
1 Richard Rogers
2 Frank Lloyd Wright
3 Aquatic Centre
4 Le Corbusier
5 17th century/1600s
6 Eames
7 Norman Foster
8 SANAA
9 Peter Ackroyd
10 Frank Gehry

FIFA WORLD CUPS
1 Spain
2 James Rodriguez (six goals)
3 1958
4 Romania
5 USA
6 1978 in Argentina (in 1994, neither qualified)
7 Mario Mandzukic
8 1994 (he scored five goals in one match vs Cameroon)
9 First World Cup goal given by Goal Line Technology
10 Three

HARRY POTTER

1 At which London railway station is Platform 9¾, from which the Hogwarts Express departs?

2 What, in the world of Harry Potter, is the name of the sport played by wizards and witches on broomsticks?

3 What model of car do Ron and Harry fly to school in 'Harry Potter and the Chamber of Secrets'?

4 What is the first name of Draco Malfoy's mother?

5 Who taught Defence Against the Dark Arts in 'Harry Potter and the Order of the Phoenix'?

6 In 'Harry Potter', Moony, Wormtail, Padfoot and Prongs are referred to by which collective noun?

7 In which village did Harry Potter's parents live at the time of their death?

8 Which Hogwarts house requires the answer to a riddle to enter its dormitory, rather than a password?

9 What do the initials "DA" stand for regarding the secret club founded by students in the fifth book in the 'Harry Potter' series?

10 What, in 'Harry Potter', is the incantation for a Summoning Charm?

JONI MITCHELL

1 A track on Joni Mitchell's 'Ladies of the Canyon' is named after which rock festival of 1969?

2 In which 2003 Richard Curtis film does Emma Thompson's character listen to Joni Mitchell's 'Both Sides Now'?

3 While Joni Mitchell was recording 'Blue' in 1971, Carole King was also recording which other singer-songwriter classic in the same studio?

4 Joni Mitchell's self-portrait on the cover of the album 'Turbulent Indigo' is inspired by which Dutch artist who died in 1890?

5 Joni Mitchell performed the track 'Coyote' at which 1976 concert by The Band, which would be made into a Martin Scorsese film?

6 Joni Mitchell's 1979 album was a collaboration with which jazz great, who died months before its release?

7 'Free Man in Paris' is written about which music executive, who would later co-found Dreamworks SKG?

8 Joni Mitchell grew up in Saskatoon, in which Canadian province?

9 The Joni Mitchell track 'Amelia', on 'Hejira', is inspired by a pioneer in which field?

10 How much would entry cost to the "tree museum" in Joni Mitchell's song 'Big Yellow Taxi'?

HARRY POTTER
1 Kings Cross
2 Quidditch
3 Ford Anglia
4 Narcissa
5 Dolores Umbridge
6 The Marauders
7 Godric's Hollow
8 Ravenclaw
9 Dumbledore's Army
10 Accio

JONI MITCHELL
1 Woodstock
2 Love Actually
3 Tapestry
4 Vincent van Gogh
5 The Last Waltz
6 Charles Mingus (the album is called 'Mingus')
7 David Geffen
8 Saskatchewan
9 Aviation/flight (It is about Amelia Earhart)
10 A dollar and a half

NIGERIAN LITERATURE

1 In 1986, Wole Soyinka was the first Nigerian to win which prestigious global Literature prize, awarded annually in Sweden?

2 Chinua Achebe's 'Things Fall Apart' takes its title from 'The Second Coming', by which Irish poet?

3 Chimamanda Ngozie Adichie appears in the song 'Flawless', on which American superstar's self-titled fifth album from 2013?

4 Which Nigerian author's first two novels, 'The Fishermen' and 'An Orchestra of Minorities', were nominated for the Booker Prize?

5 Ben Okri's 'The Famished Road' inspired the lyrics to the song 'Street Spirit (Fade Out)' by which English rock band?

6 Femi Osofisan's play 'Women of Owu' is a retelling of 'The Trojan Women' by which Greek tragedian?

7 Complete the title of this darkly comic bestselling novel by Oyinkan Braithwaite - 'My Sister, the ...'?

8 Awarded the OBE in 2005, which Nigerian-British author's works include 'Second Class Citizen' and 'The Joys of Motherhood'?

9 Ayobami Adebayo's award-winning 2017 debut novel shares its title with songs by Sam Smith, The Faces and Lorraine Ellison. What is that three-word title?

10 Winning the Hugo Award for Best Novella in 2016, what was the title of the first in a science fiction horror series by Nnedi Okorafor?

BRITISH BEER

1 Which city's 'Brown Ale' is known for its iconic "blue star" logo?

2 Which Faversham company, officially founded in 1698, claims to be "Britain's Oldest Brewer"?

3 What is the name of the strong, dark Theakston beer which has been made since the 1890s?

4 In 2005, which musical superstar described Timothy Taylor's Landlord as the "champagne of ales"?

5 Hells Lager is made by which brewer, named after an area of North London?

6 BrewDog was founded by Martin Dickie and which other Scotsman, who shares his name with a famous scientist?

7 Sharing its name with a famous Noel Coward song, what is the flagship beer of Fuller's?

8 Trooper is an ale which is a collaboration between Robinsons brewery and which band?

9 Which Scottish brewer makes the likes of Caesar Augustus, Joker, and Birds and Bees?

10 In 2005, the Welsh rugby team could not, due to French advertising laws, have the brewer "Brains" on their shirt. Which word did they have instead?

NIGERIAN LITERATURE
1 Nobel Prize in Literature
2 WB Yeats
3 Beyoncé
4 Chigozie Obioma (in 2015 and 2019)
5 Radiohead
6 Euripides
7 Serial Killer
8 Buchi Emecheta
9 Stay With Me
10 Binto

BRITISH BEER
1 Newcastle
2 Shepherd Neame
3 Old Peculier
4 Madonna
5 Camden Town
6 James Watt
7 London Pride
8 Iron Maiden
9 Williams Brothers
10 Brawn

LANGUAGES OF THE WORLD

1 Which Yiddish phrase meaning "good luck" is often used to congratulate people at Jewish weddings?

2 Which word comes from the Japanese meaning "harbour wave"?

3 Spoken by over 10 million people, which Z is the language most widely spoken as a first language in South Africa?

4 Which musical instrument takes its name from the Hawaiian for "jumping flea"?

5 Which religion, once the state religion of Japan, has a name meaning "way of the gods"?

6 Shona is a language which is commonly used in Mozambique and which other African country?

7 Which Hebrew word means, literally, "lord of the flies"?

8 Which term for Britain comes from the Hindi for "far away"?

9 What punctuation mark comes from the Ancient Greek for "turning away"?

10 Which language has the most native speakers in the world?

BRITISH RAPPERS

1 Which British rapper headlined Glastonbury in 2019?

2 Who is Akala's Mercury-winning sister?

3 Slowthai's debut album was called 'Nothing Great About ...' what?

4 With whom did Fredo collaborate on the Number 1 single 'Funky Friday'?

5 What does the BBK in the name of the grime collective stand for?

6 Whose albums include 'Arular', 'Kala', 'Maya' and 'Mathangi'?

7 Rapper Little Simz plays Shelley in which Netflix series?

8 'Dreamy Days' by Roots Manuva samples which classic track written by Jimmy Webb?

9 How is Stephanie Victoria Allen, who had a UK hit with 'Hurtin' Me', better known?

10 With which unlikely duo did Tinchy Stryder collaborate on 'To Me, To You (Bruv)'?

LANGUAGES OF THE WORLD
1 Mazel tov
2 Tsunami
3 Zulu
4 Ukulele
5 Shinto
6 Zimbabwe
7 Beelzebub
8 Blighty
9 Apostrophe
10 Mandarin Chinese

BRITISH RAPPERS
1 Stormzy
2 Miss Dynamite
3 Britain
4 Dave
5 Boy Better Know
6 M.I.A
7 Top Boy
8 MacArthur Park
9 Stefflon Don
10 The Chuckle Brothers

GREEK MYTHS

1 On which island did Theseus slay the Minotaur?

2 Who went to the Underworld to rescue Eurydice, failing at the last moment when he turned back to look at her?

3 In the story of 'Daphnis and Chloe' written by Longus, the protagonists are aided by which goat-like rustic god?

4 Which titan stole fire from the Gods to give it to humans?

5 Who is the daughter of Cepheus and Cassiopeia whom Perseus rescued from a sea monster and then married?

6 What golden objects did the hundred-headed dragon Ladon guard alongside the Hesperides?

7 What is the name of the winged horse that was ridden by Bellerophon?

8 In the second of the 12 Labours of Heracles, which goddess sent a huge crab to assist the Lernaean Hydra against the hero?

9 Pursued by Apollo, Daphne is turned by Peneus into what kind of tree?

10 Who threw the Apple of Discord into the middle of the wedding of Peleus and Thetis?

NATIONAL TRUST PROPERTIES

1 Horsey Windpump, near Great Yarmouth, overlooks which National Park in Norfolk?

2 In which city is 251 Menlove Avenue, the childhood home of John Lennon?

3 Chartwell, in Kent, was the home of which British Prime Minister for over 40 years?

4 Which geological feature in County Antrim is the National Trust's most visited site?

5 Which 16th century castle is on Holy Island, off the coast of Northumberland?

6 In 1961, Cliveden, in Berkshire, was the venue for key events in the scandal that brought down which Secretary of State for War in 1963?

7 What is the name of the island in the Bristol Channel that was "ruled" by Martin Harman in the 1920s?

8 Coleton Fishacre, in Devon, was built for members of which family, famous for hotels and operettas?

9 Knole House, in Sevenoaks, was the home of Vita Sackville-West, renowned for her affair with which author of books including 'Mrs Dalloway' and 'Orlando'?

10 Castle Drogo, in Devon, was designed by which architect who is most famous for designing the city of New Delhi?

SPECIALIST SUBJECTS

GREEK MYTHS
1 Crete
2 Orpheus
3 Pan
4 Prometheus
5 Andromeda
6 Apples
7 Pegasus
8 Hera
9 Laurel tree
10 Eris (Goddess of strife)

NATIONAL TRUST PROPERTIES
1 The Broads (it is a large windmill)
2 Liverpool
3 Winston Churchill
4 Giant's Causeway
5 Lindisfarne Castle
6 John Profumo
7 Lundy
8 D'Oyly Carte
9 Virginia Woolf
10 Edwin Lutyens

COMICS

1 Which star of 'The Dandy' has a beard so tough that he has to shave with a blowtorch?

2 Which Gaulish warrior has been to Corsica, Britain, Belgium and Switzerland in adventures?

3 Who was the "merciless" foe of Flash Gordon?

4 'V for Vendetta' was written by which famous comic book author?

5 In which comic would you have read about Storm Nelson, PC49, Harris Tweed and Dan Dare?

6 What is the surname of Roy in 'Roy of the Rovers'?

7 What does the DC in DC Comics stand for?

8 What is the name of Tintin's dog in the English versions of Tintin?

9 Which superhero appeared on his first cover punching Hitler in the jaw?

10 'When the Wind Blows' is a graphic novel by which artist and author, who also created 'The Snowman'?

AVIATORS

1 What was the nickname of the German ace pilot Manfred von Richthofen?

2 John Alcock and Arthur Brown, in 1919, made the first non-stop crossing of which body of water?

3 What rhyming nickname was given to the Hughes H-4 Hercules, a vast plane built by Howard Hughes?

4 The French aviator Antoine de Saint-Exupéry is best known for which novella, published in 1943?

5 In which US state is Kitty Hawk, where the Wright brothers made the first powered flight?

6 Which Oscar-winning actress played Amelia Earhart in the 2009 film 'Amelia'?

7 At which Grand Slam tennis event is the venue named after an aviator?

8 On which river did Chesley Sullenberger successfully land a US Airways flight in 2009?

9 Who was the first African-American woman to hold a pilot's licence?

10 The English aviator Amy Johnson died in 1941 when she crashed into the estuary of which river?

COMICS
1 Desperate Dan
2 Asterix
3 Ming
4 Alan Moore
5 Eagle
6 Race
7 Detective Comics
8 Snowy
9 Captain America
10 Raymond Briggs

AVIATORS
1 The Red Baron
2 Atlantic Ocean
3 The Spruce Goose
4 The Little Prince (Le Petit Prince)
5 North Carolina
6 Hilary Swank
7 French Open (named after Roland Garros)
8 Hudson River
9 Bessie Coleman
10 Thames

THE OCTOPUS

1 What was the name of the octopus who came to worldwide attention for accurately predicting the results of matches in the 2010 FIFA World Cup?

2 How many hearts does an octopus have?

3 Who wrote and sang the Beatles song 'Octopus's Garden'?

4 What shape are the pupils of an octopus's eyes?

5 What P is the name of the Galician dish of soft-boiled octopus sprinkled with paprika, sea salt, and olive oil?

6 Haemocyanin causes an octopus's blood to be which colour?

7 The word octopus comes from a Greek word meaning ... what?

8 Maud Adams, who played the title character in 'Octopussy', had previously played Andrea Anders in which other Bond film?

9 In 2009, biologists reported veined octopuses using what items as portable shelters?

10 One of the two largest species of octopus, Haliphron atlanticus, is commonly known by what somewhat oxymoronic name?

CHARACTER ACTORS

1 John Cusack has often appeared alongside his sister in movies such as in 'High Fidelity' and 'Grosse Pointe Blank'. What is her name?

2 He started as a character actor, but which Hoffman took the Oscar for 'Capote'?

3 The actress who appeared in 'The Help', 'The Shape of Water', 'Hidden Figures' and 'Snowpiercer' is Octavia ... who?

4 Burt Young played feckless brother-in-law Paulie in which series of boxing movies?

5 'Traffic', 'Carlito's Way', 'Boogie Nights' and 'Magnolia' all feature Latino powerhouse Luis ... who?

6 Irving Rameses Rhames is better known by what name?

7 The distinctive Peter Lorre featured alongside which male star in 'Casablanca' and 'The Maltese Falcon'?

8 Brad Dourif played which slimy character in 'Lord of the Rings'?

9 Whose mother did Jennifer Coolidge play in 'American Pie'?

10 He only appeared in five movies, but all were classics; he was engaged to Meryl Streep. What was his name?

THE OCTOPUS
1 Paul The Octopus
2 Three
3 Ringo Starr
4 Rectangular
5 Pulpo a Feira
6 Blue
7 Having eight feet
8 The Man With the Golden Gun
9 Coconut shells
10 Seven-arm octopus (one of its limbs is coiled up, so it has the appearance of only having seven, though does have eight)

CHARACTER ACTORS
1 Joan Cusack
2 Philip Seymour Hoffman
3 Spencer
4 Rocky
5 Guzman
6 Ving Rhames
7 Humphrey Bogart
8 Grima Wormtongue
9 (Steve) Stifler
10 John Cazale

NORTHUMBERLAND

1 Northumberland takes its name from being the land north of which river?

2 What is the surname of the two great footballers, Jack and Bobby, who were born in Ashington, Northumberland?

3 Which range of hills, including Windy Gyle and Hedgehope Hill, straddles the Northumberland and Scottish border?

4 Which Roman emperor built a wall, around 122 AD, which runs through modern Tyneside, Northumberland and Cumbria?

5 The flag of Northumberland is made up of which two colours?

6 In 1838, which daughter of a lighthouse keeper helped rescue people from the wreck of the Forfarshire, and became a national heroine?

7 Which Irish monk founded the monastery at Lindisfarne in the year 634?

8 Which football team, based in a town in Northumberland, were relegated from Scottish League 2 in 2019?

9 Which castle, where the likes of 'Blackadder' and 'Harry Potter' were filmed, has a famous garden with a huge treehouse and a Poison Garden?

10 What was the nickname of Sir Henry Percy, born in Northumberland in 1364?

TWITTER

1 What name is given to messages posted on Twitter?

2 On Twitter, each single, basic message can have up to how many characters?

3 The co-founder and former CEO of Twitter is Jack ... who?

4 What is the name given to the # symbol on Twitter?

5 Twitter's logo is named after which former Boston Celtics basketball player?

6 Who, as of 2022 and for many years previously, is the most followed person on Twitter?

7 Who, as of 2022, is the most followed sportsperson on Twitter?

8 Justin Halpern achieved fame after starting a Twitter feed repeating things said by ... who?

9 Whose twitter handle is @Pontifex?

10 Taylor Swift's twitter handle is her name and which number?

NORTHUMBERLAND
1 Humber
2 Charlton
3 Cheviot Hills
4 Hadrian
5 Red and yellow
6 Grace Darling
7 Aidan
8 Berwick Rangers
9 Alnwick Castle
10 Hotspur

TWITTER
1 Tweets
2 280
3 Dorsey
4 Hashtag
5 Larry Bird (it's called Larry the Bird)
6 Barack Obama
7 Cristiano Ronaldo
8 His dad
9 The Pope
10 13

CARS

1 The E-type and X-type are both models of ... what?

2 What became compulsory for people in the front seats of British cars from January 1983?

3 Which former 'Top Gear' presenter was involved in a near-fatal dragster crash in 2006?

4 Which Italian car manufacturer's logo features a trident?

5 What was unusual about the 1976 Tyrrell P34 Formula 1 car?

6 Which car company makes the Juke, the Qashqai and the Micra?

7 A UK car number plate with a letter D between two sets of numbers would belong to ... who?

8 Which British-Greek designer was behind the original Mini?

9 Which feature of a car might make use of sodium azide?

10 On which of the Channel Islands are all cars prohibited?

PHOTOGRAPHERS

1 Photographer Linda Eastman married which of the Beatles?

2 Which famous footballer's son, Brooklyn, released a photography book including a notorious picture of an elephant with the caption "so hard to photograph, but incredible to see"?

3 By which shortened name was the 20th century artist and photographer Emmanuel Radnitzky better known?

4 Which German-American photographer died while driving his car in January 2004?

5 From 1965 to 1972, photographer David Bailey was married to which French actress?

6 Which British war photographer was knighted in the 2017 New Years Honours?

7 Mick Rock, fittingly, made his name taking pictures of people in which industry?

8 The Manic Street Preachers had a 1996 hit with a song about which South African photojournalist?

9 The American photographer who took the last professional photo of John Lennon, just a few hours before his death, is Annie ... who?

10 Spencer Tunick is best known for photographing large groups of people in what state of being?

CARS
1 Jaguar
2 Seat belts
3 Richard Hammond
4 Maserati
5 It had six wheels
6 Nissan
7 A diplomat
8 Alec Issigonis
9 Airbags
10 Sark

PHOTOGRAPHERS
1 Paul McCartney
2 David Beckham
3 Man Ray
4 Helmut Newton
5 Catherine Deneuve
6 (Sir) Don McCullin
7 Music industry
8 Kevin Carter
9 Leibovitz
10 Nude

HITCHCOCK FILMS

1 A classic Alfred Hitchcock movie is 'Strangers on a ...' what?

2 A debonair star of many Hitchcock movies was Cary ... who?

3 Which Hitchcock masterpiece is set in only one room?

4 With which Swedish star did Cary Grant star in 'Notorious'?

5 Hitchcock's 'Rebecca' is based on a classic novel by which writer?

6 "Scottie" Ferguson, played by James Stewart, is the main character in which Hitchcock classic?

7 Who plays Marnie's husband in the Hitchcock film of that name?

8 Ray Milland in 'Dial M for Murder' is a former professional at which sport?

9 In which seaside town is 'The Birds' set?

10 'The Man Who Knew Too Much' contains which classic song, sung by Doris Day?

MARATHONS

1 In 1981, the first running of which marathon, founded by Chris Brasher and John Disley, was a tie between Dick Beardsley and Inge Simonsen?

2 Which Brit won the 2012 Olympic wheelchair marathon?

3 In 2003, which former boxer completed the London Marathon in six days?

4 What nationality is the former World Marathon record holder Ingrid Kristiansen?

5 In which park does the New York Marathon finish?

6 In which city was Eliud Kipchoge the first runner to break two hours for a marathon in 2019?

7 Who played Dr Christian Szell in the 1976 film 'Marathon Man'?

8 The official distance of a marathon is 26 miles and how many yards?

9 Which British athlete was the 2005 women's World Marathon champion?

10 Which bestselling Japanese author wrote 'What I Talk About When I Talk About Running' about his experiences running marathons?

HITCHCOCK FILMS
1 Train
2 Grant
3 Rope
4 Ingrid Bergman
5 Daphne du Maurier
6 Vertigo
7 Sean Connery (Marnie is played by Tippi Hedren)
8 Tennis
9 Bodega Bay
10 Que Sera Sera

MARATHONS
1 London Marathon
2 David Weir
3 Michael Watson
4 Norwegian
5 Central Park
6 Vienna
7 Laurence Olivier
8 385 yards
9 Paula Radcliffe
10 Haruki Murakami

WEST INDIES CRICKET

1. What was the nickname of Viv Richards, shared with the title of a Stevie Wonder song about Bob Marley?

2. Whilst captain of the West Indies in 2009, which self-styled "Universe Boss" said that he wouldn't be sad if test cricket came to an end?

3. What was Brian Lara's second highest score in test cricket?

4. Which great 6 ft 8 fast bowler was said to "talk to no man", although he claims he never actually used that specific phrase to refuse interviews?

5. In 1976, England captain Tony Greig made the mistake of saying he intended to make the West Indies team ... do what?

6. In the second test of the 1948 series vs England, at Port of Spain, the West Indies batting positions 3, 4 and 5 were occupied, for the first time, by three men whose surname began with which letter?

7. Which song by former West Indies star Dwayne "DJ" Bravo has over 100 million views on YouTube? (the title is the name of a "Wonder Horse" in an old TV show)

8. Fast bowler Joel Garner shared his nickname with a character voiced for many years by Carroll Spinney - what was it?

9. In 2004, Daren Sammy became the first cricketer from which island nation, whose capital is Castries, to represent the West Indies?

10. After his tragic early death in 1967, Sir Frank Worrell became the first sportsperson honoured by a memorial service in which London venue?

THE GREAT FIRE OF LONDON

1. Who was King of England at the time of the Great Fire of London?

2. The Great Fire of London started on which lane?

3. Many believed 1666 would be a fateful year, due to the number 666 being the number of the Beast, according to which book of the Bible?

4. Who, along with Robert Hooke, designed the Monument that commemorated the Fire of London?

5. Which naval administrator, born in 1633, described the Great Fire in his famous diary?

6. Which war was England fighting during 1666?

7. For future fire safety in the rebuilding of London after the Great Fire, it was proclaimed that eminent streets like Cheapside and Cornhill should be made ... what?

8. Sir Thomas Bludworth, blamed for inadequate leadership during the Fire, held which position in 1666?

9. The weekly list of data about deaths in London during the plague, the year before the Great Fire, were known as the 'Bills of ...' what?

10. Which is nearer in time to the Great Fire of London - the Norman Conquest or England winning the men's FIFA World Cup?

WEST INDIES CRICKET

1. Master Blaster
2. Chris Gayle
3. 375 (his highest was 400 not out)
4. Curtly Ambrose
5. Grovel
6. W (Walcott, Worrell, Weekes)
7. Champion
8. Big Bird
9. St Lucia
10. Westminster Abbey

THE GREAT FIRE OF LONDON

1. Charles II
2. Pudding Lane
3. Book Of Revelation
4. Christopher Wren
5. Samuel Pepys
6. The Second Anglo-Dutch War (accept anything like "Dutch War")
7. Wider
8. Lord Mayor Of London
9. Mortality
10. England winning the World Cup (300 years versus 600 years)

AFRICAN FOOD

1 What kind of food are merguez, commonly eaten in North Africa?

2 Which South African vegetable dish has a name beginning with C and containing four A's?

3 A staple dish in many parts of West Africa is jollof ... what?

4 Which South African submarine sandwich shares its name with the title character of an F. Scott Fitzgerald novel?

5 What kind of food is injera, a staple in Eritrea?

6 Which popular North African stew is named after the pot in which it is cooked?

7 Kelewele is a Ghanaian dish made of which foodstuff, which is sometimes called "cooking banana"?

8 Malva pudding contains what flavour of jam?

9 A popular snack food in East Africa, shaped like a samosa but tasting more like a doughnut, is which M?

10 Garri is a staple food in Nigeria, made from which plant?

THOMAS HARDY

1 Thomas Hardy is buried in Poets' Corner, in which place of worship?

2 Which single name, the same as an Anglo-Saxon kingdom, did Thomas Hardy use for southwest England?

3 A Thomas Hardy novel from 1872 was called 'Under the ...' what?

4 Which Thomas Hardy novel was made into a film starring Julie Christie, Terence Stamp, Alan Bates and Peter Finch?

5 Thomas Hardy wrote the poem 'The Voice' after the death of his first wife. What was her first name?

6 At the end of 'Tess of the d'Urbervilles', Tess is arrested at which ancient landmark in southern England?

7 Eustacia Vye and Clem Yeobright are characters in which Thomas Hardy novel?

8 Which Thomas Hardy novel contains the note "Done because we are too menny"?

9 The title of 'Far From the Madding Crowd' is taken from which poet's 'Elegy Written in a Country Churchyard'?

10 What is the name of the title character in 'The Mayor of Casterbridge'?

AFRICAN FOOD
1 Sausages
2 Chakalaka
3 Rice
4 Gatsby
5 Flatbread (accept: bread)
6 Tagine
7 Plantain
8 Apricot
9 Mandazi
10 Cassava

THOMAS HARDY
1 Westminster Abbey
2 Wessex
3 Greenwood Tree
4 Far from the Madding Crowd
5 Emma (Emma Gifford)
6 Stonehenge
7 The Return of the Native
8 Jude the Obscure
9 Thomas Gray
10 Michael Henchard

BRITISH TREES

1 Conkers are the seeds of which tree?

2 Cricket bats are made from the wood of which tree?

3 In the song, 'The Twelve Days of Christmas', which bird is "in a pear tree"?

4 The Trafalgar Square Christmas tree is a gift to the people of Britain from which country?

5 Which R is another name for the mountain ash?

6 Which tree, associated with Christmas, has the Latin name ilex?

7 Gin comes from the berries of which tree?

8 The Major Oak is a historic tree in which forest, often associated with the legend of Robin Hood?

9 Which town in Kent takes its name from a number of trees growing on a green space called "The Vine"?

10 Which word links a Will Young song to trees which carry their foliage all year round?

CORNWALL

1 The flag of Cornwall is black with what colour cross at its centre?

2 Which tidal island off Cornwall is linked to the town of Marazion by a man-made causeway?

3 Set in Cornwall, who wrote the novel 'Jamaica Inn'?

4 According to its Protected Geographical Indication (PGI) status, a Cornish pasty should be the shape of which capital letter?

5 Which great sculptor died at St Ives in 1975?

6 On 29th July 1588, at Lizard Point, was the first sighting of which military body?

7 What is the name of the Cornish nationalist party founded in 1951?

8 Rough Tor and Brown Willy are high points on which moor in Cornwall?

9 Tresco and St Mary's are islands in which archipelago south of Cornwall?

10 Aidan Turner played which Cornish hero in a TV series based on books by Winston Graham?

BRITISH TREES
1 Horse chestnut
2 Willow
3 Partridge
4 Norway
5 Rowan
6 Holly
7 Juniper
8 Sherwood Forest
9 Sevenoaks
10 Evergreen

CORNWALL
1 White
2 St Michael's Mount
3 Daphne du Maurier
4 D
5 Barbara Hepworth
6 Spanish Armada
7 Mebyon Kernow
8 Bodmin Moor
9 Scilly Isles
10 Poldark

MAGAZINES

1 What do the initials in the former monthly magazine FHM stand for?

2 Which women's magazine was founded in 1937 by Jean Prouvost and Marcelle Auclair?

3 Which magazine was founded by John Bird and Gordon Roddick in 1991?

4 What did the British magazine Dazed and Confused shorten its name to in 2014?

5 Radhika Jones succeeded Graydon Carter as editor-in-chief of which magazine in 2018?

6 Who was editor of the satirical weekly 'Punch' from 1978 to 1987?

7 Which British lifestyle magazine, founded in 1901, is famous for its "Little Black Book"?

8 Wisden is a monthly magazine associated with which sport?

9 The music magazine Q was founded in 1986 by Mark Ellen and which other music journalist?

10 Which magazine for teenage girls, which ran from 1983 to 2004, shares its two-word title with words in the opening line of the song 'I Saw Her Standing There'?

COCKTAILS

1 A gin-based cocktail which shares its name with a type of apple is the Pink ... what?

2 Who stars as Brian Flanagan in the 1988 movie 'Cocktail'?

3 The Mai Tai is a cocktail which takes its name from the Tahitian for which word?

4 Rupert Holmes's biggest chart hit was about which classic cocktail?

5 What is an alcohol-free Bloody Mary commonly called?

6 Vodka, Galliano and Orange Juice is known as a Harvey ...?

7 Which country does the rum-based drink Mojito come from?

8 Which cocktail was invented at the Raffles Hotel between 1910 and 1915?

9 Along with Kahlúa, which spirit is used when making a White Russian?

10 Which cocktail is made with vodka, triple sec, cranberry juice and lime juice?

SPECIALIST SUBJECTS

MAGAZINES
1 For Him Magazine
2 Marie Claire
3 The Big Issue
4 Dazed
5 Vanity Fair
6 Alan Coren
7 Tatler
8 Cricket
9 David Hepworth
10 Just Seventeen

COCKTAILS
1 Lady
2 Tom Cruise
3 Good
4 Piña colada
5 Virgin Mary
6 Wallbanger
7 Cuba
8 Singapore Sling
9 Vodka
10 Cosmopolitan

LADY GAGA

1 Lady Gaga was Oscar-nominated for her role as Ally Maine in which 2018 film?

2 Lady Gaga took her stage name from a song by which band?

3 What is the name of Lady Gaga's debut album, from 2008?

4 Lady Gaga sang the national anthem at which US President's inauguration?

5 Which song did Lady Gaga sing with Lisa Kudrow in the 2021 'Friends' reunion?

6 What two-word phrase, which she had tattooed on herself, does Lady Gaga use to describe her fans?

7 What was the first name of the aunt after whom Lady Gaga named her fifth studio album?

8 Ariana Grande joined Lady Gaga for which 2020 Number 1 hit?

9 Lady Gaga's 2014 album 'Cheek to Cheek' was a collaboration with which renowned singer?

10 The non-profit organisation Lady Gaga launched in 2012 is abbreviated to BTWF - what does that stand for?

FRENCH FILMS

1 By what one-word title is the 2001 film 'Le Fabuleux Destin d'Amélie Poulain' more commonly known?

2 In which 1986 film does Jean-Hugues Anglade star as the writer Zorg and Béatrice Dalle star as the title character?

3 Marion Cotillard won an Oscar for her performance in 'La Vie en Rose', playing which singer?

4 'Manon des Sources' is the sequel to which film?

5 Often known simply as B.B., whose breakout role was in the 1956 film 'And God Created Women'?

6 The real life story of Philippe Pozzo di Borgo and his French-Moroccan caregiver Abdel Sellou inspired which 2011 film?

7 Who directed the 2005 film 'Caché', also known as 'Hidden'?

8 Which British actress starred in the 2008 French film 'I've Loved You So Long'?

9 A 1964 musical film directed by Jacques Demy, starring Catherine Deneuve, is 'The Umbrellas of ...' where?

10 In the 2014 film, 'Girlhood', the four main characters lip-sync in a hotel room to which song by Rihanna?

LADY GAGA
1 A Star is Born
2 Queen (Radio Gaga)
3 The Fame
4 Joe Biden
5 Smelly Cat
6 Little Monsters
7 Joanne
8 Rain on Me
9 Tony Bennett
10 Born This Way Foundation

FRENCH FILMS
1 Amélie
2 Betty Blue (known in France as '37°2 le matin')
3 Edith Piaf
4 Jean de Florette
5 Brigitte Bardot
6 Intouchables/Untouchable
7 Michael Haneke (Haneke is Austrian. The film stars Juliette Binoche and Daniel Auteuil.)
8 Kristin Scott Thomas
9 Cherbourg
10 Diamonds

LOGOS

1 Which computer and electronics manufacturer's logo is an apple?

2 Which sports clothing manufacturer's logo is the "Swoosh"?

3 Which fast food chain's logo is sometimes referred to as the Golden Arches?

4 The logo of which company is a man made of tyres?

5 Which animal is used in the logo of the clothing manufacturer Lacoste?

6 The logo of Mitsubishi comprises how many "diamonds"?

7 Which car manufacturer's logo includes a prancing black horse?

8 What colour is the letter "l" in the standard Google logo?

9 Which US TV station's logo features a coloured peacock's tail?

10 Which film company's logo features a roaring lion?

IN THE BIBLE

1 St Paul's "conversion" happens on the road to which city, now the capital of Syria?

2 In the Bible, who is Adam and Eve's youngest son?

3 Between 1522 and 1536, William Tyndale translated the Bible into which language?

4 In the Feeding Of The 5000 miracle, told in all four gospels, how many loaves of bread did Jesus distribute amongst the crowd?

5 What is the final book of the New Testament?

6 In Protestant Christianity, besides Ruth, what is the only other book of the Bible named after a woman?

7 Which righteous man who lives in the land of Uz gives his name to a book of the Bible?

8 What is the most common letter for a book of the Bible to begin with?

9 According to Luke's Gospel, to what village were two disciples heading when they were joined by a resurrected Jesus?

10 Who was the wife of Ahab in the Old Testament book of Kings, who persuaded him to turn away from the Jewish God to worship Baal?

LOGOS
1 Apple
2 Nike
3 McDonald's
4 Michelin
5 Crocodile
6 Three
7 Ferrari
8 Green
9 NBC
10 MGM

IN THE BIBLE
1 Damascus
2 Seth
3 English
4 Five
5 Book of Revelation
6 Esther
7 Job
8 J
9 Emmaus
10 Jezebel

WILLIAM THE CONQUEROR

1 William the Conqueror, like his father Robert, was Duke of which region of western France?

2 As well as "The Conqueror", due to his father's unmarried status, William was also commonly known as William the ... what?

3 Which English king did William I defeat at the Battle of Hastings?

4 What is the name of the manuscript of the national survey carried out in 1086, which is now at the National Archives in Kew?

5 What astronomical object, which is visible every 76 years and would have been seen in 1066, is depicted on the Bayeux Tapestry?

6 What was the name of William I's half-brother who was Bishop of Bayeux?

7 At which building was William I crowned on Christmas Day in 1066?

8 The rebel Hereward the Wake, active in the early part of William I's reign, had his base on which isle in eastern England?

9 What was the name of William I's wife, who died in 1083?

10 What is the name of the area of woodland in Hampshire (now a National Park) which William I proclaimed a royal forest?

THE FINANCIAL CRISIS

1 Who was the governor of the Bank of England at the time of the 2008 Credit Crunch?

2 What financial term was voted 2007's Word of the Year by linguists of the American Dialect Society?

3 There was a run on which British bank on September 14th 2007?

4 By what two-word name is the Federal National Mortgage Association popularly known in the USA?

5 Which company bought the collapsed American investment bank Bear Stearns in March 2008?

6 Who was the UK's Chancellor of the Exchequer throughout 2008?

7 What P is a kind of pyramid scheme associated with the disgraced financier Bernie Madoff?

8 Landsbanki suffered severely in the 2008 Credit Crunch. In which country was Landsbanki based?

9 Which former Lib Dem leader (and former shadow chancellor) gained prestige in 2008 as "the man who predicted the Credit Crunch"?

10 The financial crisis saw a return to the interventionist ideas of which English economist who lived from 1883 to 1946?

WILLIAM THE CONQUEROR
1 Normandy
2 Bastard
3 Harold (Godwinson)
4 Domesday Book
5 Halley's Comet
6 Odo
7 Westminster Abbey
8 Isle of Ely
9 Matilda
10 The New Forest

THE FINANCIAL CRISIS
1 Mervyn King
2 Subprime
3 Northern Rock
4 Fannie Mae
5 JP Morgan Chase
6 Alistair Darling
7 Ponzi Scheme
8 Iceland
9 Vince Cable
10 John Maynard Keynes

SCOTTISH FOOTBALL

1 Which former England player managed Rangers to the 2020-21 Scottish Premier League?

2 Hampden Park was the home ground of which league club for over a century?

3 Who scored 242 goals in 313 games for Celtic between 1997 and 2004?

4 With an official total of 116 goals, who is the all-time record goalscorer for the Scotland women's team?

5 Which team won the Scottish Premier Division for the first and only time in 1983?

6 Which medical doctor scored 63 league goals for Gretna between 2004 and 2008?

7 Who scored Scotland's only goal of Euro 2020?

8 Raith Rovers FC is based in which Fife town?

9 Complete the famous headline from the Scottish Sun in February 2000; "Super Caley Go Ballistic, ..."?

10 In 2020-21, which club, whose mascot is called Rosco, had players in their squad called Ross Laidlaw, Ross Doohan, Ross Draper, Ross Stewart and Ross Munro?

CHRIS MORRIS

1 With whom did Chris Morris co-write the sitcom 'Nathan Barley'?

2 What colour was Chris Morris' radio 'Jam'?

3 In which sitcom did Chris Morris play the part of Denholm Reynholm?

4 What was the title of Chris Morris' 2010 "terrorist satire" feature film?

5 'The Day Today' emerged out of which radio show?

6 What is the title of the 2019 feature film directed by Chris Morris?

7 What was the name of the "deadly drug" in the 'Drugs' episode of 'Brass Eye'?

8 What is the name of the fictional sitcom in 'The Day Today', wherein something closes (for an hour)?

9 With which comedy icon did Chris Morris collaborate on the radio show 'Why Bother?'?

10 Which incompetent reporter, played by Patrick Marber, did "Chris Morris" humiliate on 'The Day Today'?

SCOTTISH FOOTBALL
1 Steven Gerrard
2 Queen's Park
3 Henrik Larsson
4 Julie Fleeting (now Julie Stewart)
5 Dundee United
6 Kenny Deuchar
7 Callum McGregor
8 Kirkcaldy
9 Celtic are Atrocious
10 Ross County

CHRIS MORRIS
1 Charlie Brooker
2 Blue
3 The IT Crowd
4 Four Lions
5 On The Hour
6 The Day Shall Come
7 Cake
8 The Bureau
9 Peter Cook
10 Peter O'Hanraha-hanrahan

WOMEN'S BOXING

1 Which Brit, in 2012, was the first female boxer to win an Olympic gold medal?

2 With a record of 24 wins and no defeats, what is the surname of Laila, one of the greatest female boxers of all time, who is the daughter of the heavyweight often called "The Greatest"?

3 Sister of heavyweight Daniel, which British Olympian made her professional boxing debut in February 2022?

4 Which Irish boxer is known as "The Bray Bomber"?

5 Boxer Natasha Jonas is the sister of Nikita Parris, who plays which sport for England?

6 Former boxer Ann Wolfe plays Artemis in which 2017 superhero film?

7 In 1998, who was the first officially licensed professional female boxer in Britain?

8 Which American boxer, a multiweight world champion, made her MMA debut on June 10th 2021?

9 Hannah Rankin, the light middleweight world champion from Scotland, also teaches and performs which large woodwind instrument?

10 In 'Million Dollar Baby' what is the nickname Frankie calls Maggie, meaning "my darling"? [spelling doesn't need to be perfect]

AMPHIBIANS AND REPTILES

1 Monocled, Red Spitting, Egyptian and Indian are all types of which snake?

2 Tui Malila, a creature that lived with the Tongan royal family until it was 188 years old, was what kind of reptile?

3 Which reptile's name comes from the Ancient Greek word for "ground lion"?

4 A yellow stripe down its back distinguishes which European toad from the European common toad?

5 What does the diet of the California Giant Salamander usually consist of?

6 What is the world's largest frog species?

7 Using the median lethal dose LD50, what is the most venomous snake in the world?

8 In the 1930s, many cane toads were introduced into which country in an attempt to eradicate a type of beetle?

9 The reptile genus Pogona is usually known as what type of dragon?

10 Which former London mayor was known for keeping newts?

WOMEN'S BOXING
1 Nicola Adams
2 Ali
3 Caroline Dubois
4 Katie Taylor
5 Football
6 Wonder Woman
7 Jane Couch
8 Claressa Shields
9 Bassoon
10 Mo cuishle

AMPHIBIANS AND REPTILES
1 Cobra
2 Tortoise
3 Chameleon
4 Natterjack toad
5 Earthworms
6 Goliath Frog
7 Inland taipan
8 Australia
9 Bearded
10 Ken Livingstone

D-DAY

1 On D-Day, Allied troops landed in which region in the north of France?

2 On which date in 1944 were the D-Day Landings?

3 The D-Day assault was led by which American general, who would later go on to be President of the USA?

4 The two main landing beaches assaulted by American forces on D-Day were Omaha and which other?

5 The key objective for D-Day was the capture of which city south of the British assault area?

6 Neptune was the codename for the naval operation on D-Day, but what was the name of the subsequent ground campaign?

7 By what name did the canal bridge at Bénouville become known, after the winged horse emblem worn by the liberators?

8 What was the easternmost of the five designated invasion beaches on D-Day?

9 On D-Day, the Allies used hundreds of DD Sherman tanks in their beach assaults. What does "DD" stand for in this context?

10 For many hours, German leaders believed the D-Day invasions were just a diversion prior to the main Allied attack - where did they imagine it would be?

STEPHEN SONDHEIM

1 The composer Stephen Sondheim died in November of which year?

2 "Isn't it rich? Are we a pair?" begins which Sondheim song?

3 With which actor, most famous for playing Norman Bates in 'Psycho', did Stephen Sondheim co-write the film 'The Last of Sheila'?

4 In the 2014 film version of 'Into the Woods', who played Cinderella?

5 Which song, associated with Zero Mostel, begins 'A Funny Thing Happened on the Way to the Forum'?

6 Sondheim's 1974 musical 'The Frogs' was adapted from a comic play by which ancient Greek author?

7 In a 1979 musical by Sondheim, Sweeney Todd is the Demon Barber of ... where?

8 Sondheim composed music for which 1990 Warren Beatty film based on a comic book detective?

9 Who played Stephen Sondheim in the 2021 film 'Tick, Tick... Boom!'?

10 Which song from 'Gypsy' shares its title with a 1998 hit for Robbie Williams?

D-DAY
1 Normandy
2 6th June
3 Dwight Eisenhower
4 Utah
5 Caen
6 Overlord
7 Pegasus
8 Sword
9 Duplex Drive (they were also sometimes nicknamed "Donald Duck", so accept that)
10 Pas De Calais (accept: Calais, further north)

STEPHEN SONDHEIM
1 2021
2 Send in the Clowns
3 Anthony Perkins
4 Anna Kendrick
5 A Comedy Tonight
6 Aristophanes
7 Fleet Street
8 Dick Tracy
9 Bradley Whitford
10 Let Me Entertain You (accept: May We Entertain You, as the song appears with both titles in 'Gypsy')

HALOGENS

1 The names of all the halogens end in which three letters?

2 Which of the halogens, widely used in swimming pools, has the chemical symbol Cl?

3 Which of the halogens, with the chemical symbol F, takes its name from the Latin for "to flow"?

4 Sometimes considered a halogen, the recently discovered synthetic element with atomic number 117 is named after which US state?

5 The word "halogen" derives from the Greek name of which substance?

6 Which of the halogens is the only element beside mercury which is liquid at room temperature?

7 Which of the halogens is so named because it is "violet-coloured"?

8 By what common two-word name is an aqueous solution of HCl known?

9 In a halogen lamp, which metal is the filament made from?

10 Which of the halogens is the rarest naturally occurring element in the earth's crust?

DAVID BOWIE

1 What was the title of David Bowie's last studio album, released two days before his death in 2016?

2 In which modern-day country was David Bowie's second wife Iman born?

3 Which David Bowie studio album contains 'Changes' and 'Life on Mars?'?

4 Taken from a line in the song 'Let's Dance', what was the name of David Bowie's 1983 worldwide tour?

5 Who directed 'The Last Temptation of Christ' in which David Bowie played Pontius Pilate?

6 With which city are the David Bowie albums 'Low', 'Heroes' and 'Lodger' commonly associated?

7 As a "disguise" so that people did not approach him, David Bowie used to carry a newspaper in which language around New York?

8 In which year, fittingly, was the song 'Space Oddity' first released?

9 David Bowie was a member of which rock band from 1988 to 1992?

10 When, in 2016, Angie Bowie was on 'Celebrity Big Brother' and announced "David's dead", which other "David" did fellow housemates think she was referring to?

HALOGENS

1 ine
2 Chlorine
3 Fluorine
4 Tennessee (it is Tennessine)
5 Salt
6 Bromine
7 Iodine
8 Hydrochloric acid
9 Tungsten
10 Astatine

DAVID BOWIE

1 Blackstar
2 Somalia
3 Hunky Dory
4 The Serious Moonlight tour
5 Martin Scorsese
6 Berlin
7 Greek
8 1969
9 Tin Machine
10 David Gest (Gest would die later in 2016)

CONSERVATIVES

1 Who was the first Conservative Prime Minister of the 21st century?

2 What is the actual name of the newspaper sometimes known as "The Torygraph"?

3 In 2019, which Brexiter used the phrase "perfidious Albion on speed" in a threat to the EU?

4 Who was Secretary of State for Education from 2016 to 2018, before resigning as an MP in 2019?

5 Owen Paterson is the former MP for which constituency - the answer is a cardinal direction followed by an English county?

6 Who became chairperson of the Conservative Party's 1922 Committee in 2010?

7 Which Conservative MP for Lichfield appeared on 'Celebrity First Dates' in November 2017?

8 What is the surname of the MP for Worcester from 1961 from 1992 and then again from 2010 onwards?

9 Which former MP for Dover was handed a two-year prison sentence in July 2020?

10 In 2020, Conservative MP Gary Sambrook took offence at a piece of graffiti saying he did what? [it is a specific three-word answer]

MARTIN LUTHER KING JR

1 On October 14, 1964, Martin Luther King Jr won which prestigious award?

2 In 1963, Martin Luther King Jr delivered a speech in Washington which has been given which four-word title?

3 In order to understand the appeal of communism, Martin Luther King read 'The Communist Manifesto' in 1949 - by which author?

4 Which U2 song is about the assassination of Martin Luther King Jr?

5 What, in the context of Martin Luther King, do the initials SCLC stand for?

6 What two-word alliterative name is given to the geological region of the USA which was, during slavery, the epicentre of the plantation-style agricultural system?

7 Which British actor played Dr King in the 2014 film 'Selma'?

8 Who was the Governor of Alabama at the time of the Selma marches?

9 At which bridge was the civil rights leader John Lewis repeatedly struck on the march from Selma to Montgomery?

10 What was the first name of Martin Luther King's wife, who he married in 1953?

CONSERVATIVES

1 David Cameron
2 The Daily Telegraph
3 Mark Francois
4 Justine Greening
5 North Shropshire
6 Graham Brady
7 Michael Fabricant
8 Walker (Peter Walker then his son Robin Walker)
9 Charlie Elphicke
10 Eats Big Dinners

MARTIN LUTHER KING JR

1 Nobel Peace Prize
2 I have a dream
3 Karl Marx
4 Pride (In the Name of Love)
5 Southern Christian Leadership Conference
6 Black Belt
7 David Oyelowo
8 George Wallace
9 Edward Pettus Bridge
10 Coretta (Coretta Scott King)

UNDERWATER CREATURES

1 Which L is the common name of the family of fish which makes up a large proportion of deep-sea fish and makes significant use of bioluminescence?

2 Which sort of sea creatures are Anguilliformes?

3 What name is given to the main fin at the top of a fish's back?

4 Caviar is the roe of which fish?

5 What is the name of the whisker-like features that give catfish their name?

6 What kind of large, fast fish does the "old man" catch in Hemingway's 'The Old Man and the Sea'?

7 Which kind of fish has a luminescent light dangling in front of its face to lure prey?

8 The sharp-shooting archerfish are in what taxonomic genus of creatures?

9 What is the common name of the small and popular member of the carp family Carassius auratus auratus?

10 Which fish has fins that are used as wings allowing it to glide above the water's surface?

SWALLOWS AND AMAZONS SERIES

1 Who wrote the 'Swallows and Amazons' series?

2 Which boy is the oldest of the Walker children in 'Swallows and Amazons'?

3 In which English county were the books 'The Big Six' and 'Coot Club' set?

4 Which imaginary friend becomes the main title character in the third book in the 'Swallows and Amazons' series?

5 What is the name, in various of the books, of Dick Callum's sister?

6 In 'Swallows and Amazons', what name is given to the island where the Walkers camp?

7 What is the name of Tom Dudgeon's boat in 'Coot Club'?

8 In 'We Didn't Mean to Go to Sea', the Walkers find themselves reaching which mainland European country?

9 What piratical name, in 'Swallows and Amazons', is used for the Blackett sisters' Uncle Jim?

10 What Himalayan name is given by the Walker children to the mountain The Old Man of Coniston?

UNDERWATER CREATURES
1 Lanternfish
2 Eels
3 Dorsal fin
4 Sturgeon
5 Barbels
6 Marlin
7 Anglerfish
8 Toxotes
9 Goldfish
10 Flying fish

SWALLOWS AND AMAZONS SERIES
1 Arthur Ransome
2 John
3 Norfolk
4 Peter Duck
5 Dorothea
6 Wild Cat Island
7 Titmouse
8 The Netherlands
9 Captain Flint
10 Kanchenjunga

BIRDS OF PREY

1 Which bird of prey shares its name with a shape and a type of flying toy?

2 The plumage of the snowy owl is largely which colour?

3 The Andean condor, the largest bird of prey, lives on which continent?

4 What is the main diet of the bald eagle? [the answer we're looking for does not have to be too specific]

5 Which bird is the fastest member of the animal kingdom?

6 Sharing its name with a wizard, which bird of prey is sometimes known as the pigeon hawk?

7 Which S is the small bird of prey which belongs to the genus accipiter?

8 Lappet-faced, griffon and white-rumped are species of which bird of prey?

9 Who wrote the book 'A Kestrel for a Knave', on which the film 'Kes' is based?

10 The eagle Gwaihir appears in the epic works of which author?

JOHN HUGHES FILMS

1 In a 1984 John Hughes film, which birthday does Sam Baker celebrate?

2 What relation is Macauley Culkin to John Candy in 'Uncle Buck'?

3 A song by which group gave the title to a 1986 Molly Ringwald movie?

4 Who is Steve Martin's unlikely bedfellow in 'Planes, Trains and Automobiles'?

5 In 'The Breakfast Club', who is the "criminal", played by Judd Nelson?

6 In which fictional town in Illinois are John Hughes movies often set?

7 Who plays the "perfect woman" in 'Weird Science'?

8 John Hughes wrote and produced 'Home Alone' but didn't actually direct it. Who did?

9 Who was John Hughes' leading man in 'She's Having A Baby'?

10 "Class ... Class ... Anyone? ... Anyone?" - a classic line from which John Hughes movie?

BIRDS OF PREY
1 Kite
2 White
3 South America
4 Fish
5 Peregrine falcon
6 Merlin
7 Sparrowhawk (or sparhawk)
8 Vulture
9 Barry Hines
10 JRR Tolkien (Lord of the Rings)

JOHN HUGHES FILMS
1 16th (Sixteen Candles)
2 Nephew
3 The Psychedelic Furs (Pretty in Pink)
4 John Candy
5 John Bender
6 Shermer
7 Kelly LeBrock
8 Chris Columbus
9 Kevin Bacon
10 Ferris Bueller's Day Off

CIVIL WARS OF THE WORLD

1 Which king was deposed and executed as a result of the English Civil War?

2 The Russian Civil War pitted the Red Army against the ... what?

3 The Rhodesian Bush War took place in which modern day country?

4 The Spanish Civil War ended in the year that which larger conflict began?

5 In which decade was the Rwandan Civil War?

6 In which country's civil war was the Republic of Biafra briefly established?

7 A leader of the pro-treaty forces in the Irish Civil War, played by Liam Neeson in a 1996 film, was Michael ... who?

8 Charles Taylor became President of which country as a result of its first Civil War?

9 The Selangor Civil War, from 1867 to 1874, is also known as which K?

10 Who wrote the famous 'Bellum Civile' about the Roman civil war fought between Caesar and Pompey?

90s US COMEDY

1 'Frasier' is set primarily in which US city?

2 Jada Pinkett Smith played Lena James in the final season of which sitcom that was a spin-off from 'The Cosby Show'?

3 In 'South Park', soul singer Isaac Hayes provided the voice of which character?

4 In 'Friends', which of the main six characters has the longest surname?

5 Carla Tortelli and Woody Boyd are staff at which Boston bar?

6 On which show did Rip Torn play the TV producer Artie?

7 In 'The Fresh Prince of Bel-Air', Will was born and raised in the west of which city?

8 Within which show does Tim Taylor present the DIY show 'Tool Time'?

9 Who composed the theme music to 'The Simpsons'?

10 What is the name of the teacher played by William Daniels in 'Boy Meets World'?

CIVIL WARS OF THE WORLD
1 Charles I
2 White Army
3 Zimbabwe
4 World War II
5 1990s
6 Nigeria
7 Collins
8 Liberia
9 Klang War
10 Lucan

90s US COMEDY
1 Seattle
2 A Different World
3 Chef
4 Joey (Tribbiani)
5 Cheers
6 The Larry Sanders Show
7 Philadelphia
8 Home Improvement
9 Danny Elfman
10 Mr (George) Feeny

DETECTIVE NOVELS

1 Who used the pseudonym Robert Galbraith to write 'The Cuckoo's Calling'?

2 In which country does Alexander McCall Smith's Precious Ramotswe live and work?

3 The Continental Op and Sam Spade are characters created by which detective fiction writer?

4 The reformed master criminal Flambeau assists which detective?

5 'Miss Pym Disposes', from 1946, was written by which author, whose actual name was Elizabeth MacKintosh?

6 Which Agatha Christie novel, the last to feature Miss Marple, is named after the Greek goddess of revenge?

7 Frederic Dannay and Manfred Bennington Lee used which pseudonym to write together - also the name of their lead character, a mystery writer/ detective?

8 The crime-solving partner of Andrew Dalziel, created by Reginald Hill, is Peter ... who?

9 In the books by Ruth Rendell, what is the first name of Inspector Wexford's wife?

10 The first 'Inspector Morse' novel was 'Last Bus to ...' which Oxfordshire town?

WORDS AND MEANINGS

1 What, in early 20th century Britain, was a charabanc?

2 What surname links a crime novelist, a former England cricket captain and the Latin for "right"?

3 On a suit of armour, which part of the body would have been covered by a gauntlet?

4 What five-letter word can mean both a beaver's home and a Masonic meeting place?

5 What term did Alfred Hitchcock use to describe something that triggers the main plot in a film, but is never properly explained?

6 A character in the play 'The Rivals' gives its name to what example of incorrect speech?

7 What is the name of the idea that your personality can be "read" from your skull?

8 Which word, derived from the Greek for "skilled in many arts" describes a type of educational institution phased out in the UK in 1992?

9 In the original meaning of the acronym "quango", what do the letters "Q" and "A" stand for?

10 What is the Italian word for "German"?

DETECTIVE NOVELS
1 J K Rowling
2 Botswana
3 Dashiell Hammett
4 Father Brown
5 Josephine Tey
6 Nemesis
7 Ellery Queen
8 Pascoe
9 Dora
10 Woodstock

WORDS AND MEANINGS
1 A bus
2 Dexter
3 Hand
4 Lodge
5 MacGuffin
6 Malapropism
7 Phrenology
8 Polytechnic
9 Quasi-autonomous
10 Tedesco

CHAMPAGNE ETC

1 Which musical instrument shares its name with a type of champagne glass?

2 Three Graces is a sparkling wine made by which English winemaker based near Tenterden in Kent?

3 Named after a 17th century monk, what is the prestige champagne of Moët & Chandon?

4 Which former Arsenal and Celtic footballer, born in 1961, was nicknamed "Champagne Charlie"?

5 Searcy's is a champagne bar in which London railway station, from which passengers catch the Eurostar?

6 Sharing its name with an Italian operatic composer, what is a cocktail of prosecco and peach puree called?

7 'Champagne Problems' is a track on whose 2020 album 'evermore'?

8 Which French fashion designer, born in 1883, is quoted as saying, "I only drink champagne on two occasions, when I am in love and when I am not"?

9 Which reunited Irish girl group released an EP called 'Champagne or Guinness' in 2014?

10 L'Avenue de Champagne is a famous street in which town in the Grand Est region of France?

PETER JACKSON

1 Peter Jackson's 'Lord of the Rings' trilogy was based on books by which author?

2 In which country was the director Peter Jackson born?

3 Who does Sean Astin play in the 'Lord of the Rings' trilogy?

4 The 2021 documentary series 'Get Back' is about the making of an album by which band?

5 What is the name of the 2018 documentary made by Peter Jackson with original footage, colourized, from World War I?

6 Peter Jackson's 'The Lovely Bones' is based on a novel by which author?

7 Who plays Ann Darrow in Peter Jackson's 'King Kong'?

8 What was the 1987 "splatter" movie directed by Peter Jackson?

9 Which actress played the part of Juliet Hulme in Peter Jackson's 1994 movie 'Heavenly Creatures'?

10 What is the name of the pub in Bree, in 'Lord of the Rings'?

CHAMPAGNE ETC
1 Flute
2 Chapel Down
3 Dom Pérignon
4 Charlie Nicholas
5 St Pancras
6 Bellini
7 Taylor Swift
8 Coco Chanel
9 B*Witched
10 Épernay

PETER JACKSON
1 JRR Tolkien
2 New Zealand
3 Sam Gamgee
4 The Beatles
5 They Shall Not Grow Old
6 Alice Sebold
7 Naomi Watts
8 Bad Taste
9 Kate Winslet
10 The Prancing Pony

MARTIAL ARTS

1 In a 1974 hit for Carl Douglas, what kind of fighting was everyone doing?

2 In which then-British territory was the action star Jackie Chan born?

3 What is the surname of the Texas Ranger played by Chuck Norris in the TV show of that name?

4 Bruce Lee's son Brandon was accidentally shot dead during the making of which movie in 1993?

5 Meaning "place of the Way", what four-letter word is used for a venue for martial arts?

6 In what sport was martial arts star Cynthia Rothrock world champion from 1981 to 1985?

7 Which singer starred with Jean-Claude Van Damme in the 1994 movie 'Street Fighter'?

8 Capoeira is a martial art which has its origins in which country?

9 Which British taekwondo athlete missed out in a gold medal at the 2016 Olympics at the last second, losing out to Ivorian competitor Cheick Sallah Cissé?

10 "Ecky thump" is a Lancashire martial art in which comedy show?

ASTERIX

1 What is the name of Asterix's best friend, a menhir delivery man?

2 Armorica, the region where Asterix and his friends live, is equivalent to which region of modern France?

3 What is the character known in French as Panoramix called in the English 'Asterix' books?

4 In 'Asterix and the Roman Agent', what colour are the speech bubbles caused by the troublemaking Convolvulus?

5 Which modern city had the name of Lutetia in the 'Asterix' books?

6 In 'Asterix and Son', which couple does the baby turn out to be the son of?

7 Which real-life Gaulish warrior is the "chieftain" in question in the title of 'Asterix and the Chieftain's Shield'?

8 Which was the first of the 'Asterix' books designed and written by Albert Uderzo alone, following the death of René Goscinny?

9 Which volume, published in the UK in 1973, was the first whose English title did not contain Asterix's name?

10 In 1959, 'Asterix' was first serialised in which French magazine?

MARTIAL ARTS
1 Kung Fu Fighting (Those cats were fast as lightning)
2 Hong Kong
3 Walker
4 The Crow
5 Dojo
6 Karate
7 Kylie Minogue
8 Brazil
9 Lutalo Muhammad
10 The Goodies

ASTERIX
1 Obelix
2 Brittany
3 Getafix
4 Green
5 Paris
6 Julius Caesar and Cleopatra
7 Vercingetorix
8 Asterix and the Great Divide
9 The Mansion of the Gods
10 Pilote

GIACOMO PUCCINI

1 The title of which famous aria from 'Turandot' means "Let no one sleep" in English?

2 Which musical set in Vietnam was based on the Puccini opera 'Madama Butterfly'?

3 Watching a performance of whose opera 'Aida' in 1876 convinced Puccini that opera was his vocation?

4 Rodolfo and Mimi are major roles in which opera by Giacomo Puccini?

5 In 1903, Giacomo Puccini was seriously injured in what kind of incident?

6 Which Puccini opera contains the aria 'Vissi d'arte'?

7 What was the first name of the woman Giacomo Puccini married in 1904?

8 Complete the first line of a famous aria from the 1918 musical, ' Gianni Schicchi' – "O mio babbino ..." what?

9 Puccini's opera 'Manon Lescaut' was based on an 18th century novel by which French author?

10 Puccini died in 1924, after complications from treatment in which Belgian city?

TV QUIZ SHOWS

1 A hit show on BBC2 is 'Richard Osman's House of ...' what?

2 The film 'Starter for Ten' sees the main character Brian Jackson appear on which TV quiz show?

3 In 2021, Clive Myrie was announced as the host of which long-running quiz show?

4 In the USA, who was the host of 'Jeopardy' from 1984 until his death in 2020?

5 What daytime quiz show did Warwick Davis begin presenting in 2016?

6 Amitabh Bachchan has presented almost every series of 'Kaun Banega Crorepati', the version of 'Who Wants to Be a Millionaire' filmed in which country?

7 What is the name of the man who created the gameshows 'Tipping Point', 'Impossible' and 'Decimate'?

8 In 2019, which journalist won the 'Celebrity Mastermind' 'Champion of Champions'?

9 Once achieved by Bill McKaig, what is the highest possible score on 'Fifteen-to-One'?

10 Which former 'Only Connect' champion was one of the "Trappers", alongside Bobby Seagull, on Channel 4's 'The Answer Trap'?

SPECIALIST SUBJECTS

GIACOMO PUCCINI
1 Nessun dorma
2 Miss Saigon
3 Giuseppe Verdi
4 La bohème
5 Car crash
6 Tosca
7 Elvira
8 Caro
9 Abbé Prévost
10 Brussels

TV QUIZ SHOWS
1 Games
2 University Challenge
3 Mastermind
4 Alex Trebek
5 Tenable
6 India
7 Hugh Rycroft
8 Samira Ahmed
9 433
10 Frank Paul

JANELLE MONÁE

1 Janelle Monáe played Teresa in which Oscar-winning film from 2016?

2 What was the title of Monáe's acclaimed 2010 debut album?

3 Which British actress played Harriet Tubman in the 2019 film 'Harriet' in which Janelle Monáe also appeared?

4 With which soon-to-be star did Monáe co-headline the 2011 tour 'Hooligans in Wondaland'?

5 Monáe was a guest vocalist on which chart-topping single by Fun?

6 Monáe appeared on which 2006 album by OutKast (which shares its title with the former name of a New York airport)?

7 On January 10th 2020, what hashtag did Monáe tweet?

8 'Django Jane' and 'Make Me Feel' are from which Janelle Monáe studio album?

9 In 'Hidden Figures', Monáe played Mary Jackson, who in 1958 became the first female engineer in which organisation?

10 What is the title of the 2020 horror film starring Janelle Monáe as Veronica Henley (the title being a term used for a period in American history)?

BOARD GAMES

1 In the game chess, the knight normally takes the form of which animal?

2 What colour is the entertainment triangle in the Genus edition of 'Trivial Pursuit'?

3 What commonly accompany snakes to make the name of a popular board game?

4 The board game created by Klaus Teuber in 1995 was 'Settlers of ...' where?

5 In the game 'Risk', which continent contains the most territories?

6 In which battery-operated game, created by John Spinello, do players have to remove organs from a human body?

7 How many squares on a 'Monopoly' board require the player landing on it to pay a tax?

8 What is the highest rank to appear in the game 'Stratego'?

9 Which railway-themed board game created by Alan R Moon shares its name with a Beatles hit?

10 In which G might a player ask the question "Do you have a moustache?"?

JANELLE MONÁE
1 Moonlight
2 The ArchAndroid
3 Cynthia Erivo
4 Bruno Mars
5 We Are Young
6 Idlewild
7 #IAmNonbinary
8 Dirty Computer
9 NASA
10 Antebellum

BOARD GAMES
1 A horse
2 Pink
3 Ladders
4 Catan (It is now just called Catan)
5 Asia
6 Operation
7 Two
8 Marshal
9 Ticket to Ride
10 Guess Who?

THE BLAIR YEARS

1 Which incumbent Conservative leader did Tony Blair defeat to become Prime Minister?

2 What is the first name of the youngest child of Cherie and Tony Blair, born in 2000?

3 Tony Blair supported which US President in the so-called "War on Terror"?

4 Who was Secretary of State for Northern Ireland from 1997 to 1999?

5 Which term links Charlie Whelan and Alastair Campbell to the band which had a UK hit with 'Two Princes'?

6 Peter Mandelson famously said "I am a fighter not a quitter" when he regained which parliamentary seat in 2001?

7 How many General Elections did Tony Blair win as Labour leader?

8 The UK made an intervention in which African country's civil war in 2000?

9 Who resigned as Leader of the House of Commons in 2003 as a protest against the invasion of Iraq?

10 What was banned in British pubs and restaurants in the same week that Tony Blair stood down as Prime Minister?

EUROPEAN LANGUAGES

1 Found in many names, what is the Dutch word for "of"?

2 In the south of which country might you hear the Occitan language being spoken?

3 From which European language do the words gauntlet and ombudsman come?

4 Which country of the UK is known as "Le pays de Galles" in French?

5 Which EU language is, along with Hungarian and Finnish, part of the Finno-Ugric language group?

6 What is the German name for the Polish city Gdansk?

7 What is the Gaelic name used for the Irish police force?

8 What is the Italian name for the city Florence?

9 Which German word meaning "look-alike" is also the name of an enemy of Spiderman in Marvel Comics?

10 Which word comes from the Czech for "forced labour" or "drudgery"?

THE BLAIR YEARS
1 John Major
2 Leo
3 George W Bush
4 Mo Mowlam
5 Spin Doctors
6 Hartlepool
7 Three (1997, 2001 and 2005)
8 Sierra Leone
9 Robin Cook
10 Smoking

EUROPEAN LANGUAGES
1 Van
2 France
3 Swedish
4 Wales
5 Estonian
6 Danzig
7 Garda
8 Firenze
9 Doppelganger
10 Robot

GOING VIRAL

1 A video watched on YouTube over 4 billion times is 'Baby ... WHAT ... Dance'?

2 In a famous YouTube video from 2007, 'Charlie Bit My ...' what?

3 Whose 2011 song 'Friday' went viral and was acclaimed as the "worst song ever"?

4 In early 2022, an online furore developed about the dating habits of "West Elm ..." who?

5 In December 2017, Kristen Roupenian wrote a controversial story for the 'New Yorker' called what?

6 Carter Wilkerson got over 3 million retweets while trying to get WHAT for free from Wendy's?

7 What was the first video to reach 1 billion views on YouTube?

8 What does Christopher Walken's Bruce Dickinson demand in a famous viral 'SNL' sketch?

9 "30-50" of which animals went viral in 2019, after a reply to a tweet by musician Jason Isbell?

10 Who was behind the viral YouTube video 'Chocolate Rain'?

INTERNATIONAL FOOTBALLERS

1 Former Arsenal player Alexis Sanchez represented which country?

2 Which Spanish goalkeeper retired from football in August 2020, more than 20 years after he first won the Champions League?

3 Which country did former Sheffield Wednesday striker Gilles de Bilde represent at international football?

4 Who was sent off two minutes after coming on as a substitute on his international debut in a match against Hungary on 17th August 2005 (that has not stopped him from winning over 100 caps for his country)?

5 Which Norwegian was the first man to win the English Premier League playing for two different clubs?

6 Which Dutch striker, who played for Celtic then Hull City, had the longest surname in Premier League history?

7 Who scored the winning goal in the final of the 2008 European Championships?

8 What did the French footballer Lucien Laurent achieve on 13th July 1930?

9 What was the name of the referee Paolo di Canio pushed over on 26th September 1998?

10 The Ivorian footballer Gervinho played for which Premier League team from 2011 to 2013?

GOING VIRAL
1 Shark
2 Finger
3 Rebecca Black
4 Caleb
5 Cat Person
6 Chicken nuggets
7 Gangnam Style
8 More cowbell
9 Feral hogs
10 Tay Zonday

INTERNATIONAL FOOTBALLERS
1 Chile
2 Iker Casillas
3 Belgium
4 Lionel Messi
5 Henning Berg (Blackburn Rovers and Manchester United)
6 Jan Vennegoor of Hesselink
7 Fernando Torres (Spain beat Germany 1-0)
8 He scored the first goal in the World Cup Finals
9 Paul Alcock
10 Arsenal

TOM STOPPARD

1 Tom Stoppard's award-winning 'Rock'n'Roll' is set in Cambridge and which Czech city?

2 For which film script, set in Elizabethan London, did Tom Stoppard win an Academy Award?

3 Minor characters in 'Hamlet', 'Rosencrantz and Guildenstern' are what, according to the title of a Tom Stoppard play?

4 An affair with which actress led to the end of Tom Stoppard's marriage to Miriam Stoppard?

5 Tom Stoppard's 'The Real Inspector Hound' mirrors which Agatha Christie play closely?

6 In which decade was Tom Stoppard born in Czechoslovakia?

7 Set in the Jewish community of early 20th century Vienna, which Tom Stoppard play debuted in 2020?

8 With which conductor did Tom Stoppard collaborate on 'Every Good Boy Deserves Favour'?

9 Which 2002 Tom Stoppard work is a trilogy of plays called 'Voyage', 'Shipwreck', and Salvage'?

10 'The Invention of Love' by Tom Stoppard focuses on the life of which writer of 'A Shropshire Lad'?

BIRDS IN GENERAL

1 What colour, primarily, is the underpart of the blue tit?

2 The rhea is a large flightless bird native to which continent?

3 Rockhopper, Macaroni and Adelie are all species of which birds?

4 Which long-legged African bird of prey gets its name from its crest which looks like a quill pen stuck behind the ear?

5 Which bird has an elaborate blue-green plumage with markings known as "eyes" for attracting mates?

6 Which bird of prey is sometimes known as the sea hawk or fish eagle?

7 The Siamese fireback is a species of what type of bird?

8 Puck, who, at 1728 words, had the largest vocabulary of any bird, was of which species?

9 What is the European name for the bird known as the snow chicken or partridge in the US?

10 Which birds of the family Otididae were reintroduced to Britain in around 2009, having been common on Salisbury Plain until the early 1800s? [careful how you say it]

TOM STOPPARD
1 Prague
2 Shakespeare in Love
3 Dead
4 Felicity Kendal
5 The Mousetrap
6 1930s (1937)
7 Leopoldstadt
8 Andre Previn
9 The Coast of Utopia
10 AE Housman

BIRDS IN GENERAL
1 Yellow
2 South America
3 Penguin
4 Secretary Bird
5 Peacock
6 Osprey
7 Pheasant
8 Budgerigar/common parakeet
9 Ptarmigan
10 Bustards

WACKY RACES

1 In which decade did the 'Wacky Races' first start broadcasting in the USA?

2 In 'Wacky Races' what was the Ant Hill Mob's way of utilising "getaway" power?

3 What was the company that produced 'Wacky Races'?

4 Which of the wacky racers never won a race?

5 What was the collective name of the two cavemen who drove the Boulder Mobile in 'Wacky Races'?

6 What colour does Penelope Pitstop wear in 'Wacky Races'?

7 Who accompanied Lazy Luke in the Arkansas Chuggabug?

8 What adjective describes the "Twosome" who drove the Creepy Coupe?

9 Who drove the Convert-a-Car in 'Wacky Races'?

10 What 1965 movie is 'Wacky Races' based on?

US CIVIL WAR

1 The Emancipation Proclamation of 1862 sought to bring an end to what (the issue that was the main cause of the Civil War)?

2 Who was the President of the USA from 1861 to 1865?

3 What does CSA stand for, when describing the southern states that seceded from the United States in 1861?

4 By what nickname was General Thomas Jonathan Jackson, who died in 1863, better known?

5 Which abolitionist led the raid on Harper's Ferry in 1859 which is seen as the trigger for the US Civil War?

6 Which fort in South Carolina was attacked by southern troops in April 1861?

7 Which battle, in July 1863, saw the largest number of casualties in the whole US Civil War and is seen as one of the decisive events?

8 What is the only novel by Margaret Mitchell, set during the US Civil War?

9 By what metallic nickname were anti-war Democrats known during the Civil War?

10 Mary Edwards Walker's actions during the Civil War led to her being the only woman ever to win America's most prestigious military decoration - what is it called?

WACKY RACES
1 1960s
2 Running
3 Hanna-Barbera
4 Dick Dastardly (and Muttley)
5 The Slag Brothers
6 Pink
7 The Blubber Bear
8 Gruesome
9 Pat Pending
10 The Great Race

US CIVIL WAR
1 Slavery
2 Abraham Lincoln
3 Confederate States of America
4 Stonewall
5 John Brown
6 Fort Sumter
7 Battle of Gettysburg
8 Gone With the Wind
9 Copperheads
10 Medal of Honor

STAR TREK

1 Leonard Nimoy played which character in the original series of 'Star Trek'?

2 What is the name of the creator of 'Star Trek'?

3 Who directed the 2009 movie 'Star Trek'?

4 What so-called grammatical error is in the statement "to boldly go where no man has gone before"?

5 In the movie 'Star Trek: First Contact', Picard's crew go back in time to defeat which enemy?

6 The inhabitants of which planet salute each other with the words "Live long and prosper"?

7 What was the title of the 'Star Trek' episode in which Kirk and Uhura kissed?

8 Who played Captain Benjamin Sisko, commander of Deep Space Nine space-station?

9 Which word means "Klingon" in the Klingon language?

10 What is the title held by the head of state of the Ferengi?

GILBERT & SULLIVAN

1 Out of Gilbert and Sullivan, which one wrote the music?

2 Which theatre was built by Richard D'Oyly Carte for the express purpose of putting on the works of Gilbert and Sullivan?

3 From which musical is the song "I am the very model of a modern Major-General' taken?

4 Which 1881 Gilbert and Sullivan operetta shares its name with a genre of card games?

5 In which country is 'The Mikado' set?

6 True or False? WS Gilbert died whilst trying to save a young woman he was giving a swimming lesson to.

7 In which film is the lead character Harold Abrahams an enthusiast for Gilbert and Sullivan?

8 In which city does the action of the Gilbert and Sullivan opera 'The Gondoliers' open?

9 'Princess Ida' was based on the poem 'The Princess: A Medley' by whom?

10 Which award-winning British actor played WS Gilbert in the 1999 film 'Topsy-Turvy'?

STAR TREK
1 Mr Spock
2 Gene Roddenberry
3 JJ Abrams
4 Split infinitive
5 The Borg
6 Vulcan
7 Plato's Stepchildren
8 Avery Brooks
9 TlhIngan
10 Grand Nagus

GILBERT & SULLIVAN
1 Arthur Sullivan
2 The Savoy Theatre
3 The Pirates of Penzance
4 Patience
5 Japan
6 True (in London)
7 Chariots of Fire
8 Venice
9 Alfred, Lord Tennyson
10 Jim Broadbent

MORE WORDS

1 A tonsure is a religious practice involving what?

2 A man described as uxorious would be particularly attached to whom?

3 The Tam o'Shanter is what type of traditional Scottish garment?

4 Someone described as a costermonger traditionally sold what?

5 What name is given to a prolonged speech which is used as a delaying tactic to prevent progress in a political debate?

6 Once the name of a school of Greek philosophy, what is the original meaning of the word "cynic"?

7 In which European country is "hygge" a word that means something along the lines of cosiness?

8 If a road tilts in a way that might cause a high-sided vehicle to overturn when going round a bend, it is said to have what sort of camber?

9 At sea, what is a "Mae West"?

10 If you were a stegophilist, what would be the height of fun for you?

SMALL CREATURES

1 Russian Blue, Persian and Siamese are all breeds of which animal?

2 In which continent do piranhas live in the wild?

3 Although they strike fear into many of us, how many species of tarantula actually possess bites which are fatal to humans?

4 What name links the smallest breed of dog to the largest state in Mexico?

5 The weta is an insect found in which country?

6 What type of animal has at least 250 fewer legs than its name suggests?

7 One of very few mammals defined as eusocial, which East African burrowing rodent, known for its unusual appearance and characteristics, is also known as the sand puppy?

8 Which class of molluscs have a name which literally means "head-feet"?

9 All pet hamsters are descended from animals from which country?

10 Which breed of shrew is the smallest living mammal?

SPECIALIST SUBJECTS

MORE WORDS
1 Head shaving
2 His wife
3 Hat
4 Fruit & vegetables
5 Filibuster
6 Dog-like
7 Denmark
8 Adverse
9 A life jacket
10 Climbing onto rooftops

SMALL CREATURES
1 Cat
2 South America
3 None
4 Chihuahua
5 New Zealand
6 Millipede
7 Naked mole-rat
8 Cephalopods
9 Syria
10 Etruscan shrew

PAUL ROBESON

1 Which actor, who has twice voiced the character Mufasa in films, played Robeson in a 1978 one-man play?

2 In 1960, Robeson sang on the construction site of which later-to-be-iconic venue in the most populous city in Australia?

3 What was Paul Robeson's middle name, the same as that of the actor Samuel L. Jackson?

4 Which Welsh band had a Top 20 UK hit in 2001 with 'Let Robeson Sing'?

5 In 1922, Paul Robeson graduated from Columbia University in which subject, and thereafter briefly practised it professionally?

6 Robeson played for the Akron Pros, then the Milwaukee Badgers, in the early seasons of which American sporting league?

7 Which Oscar-winning director of 'Widows' and '12 Years a Slave' created the art installation 'End Credits' about the political persecution of Robeson?

8 In 1938, Paul Robeson travelled to Spain to support the cause of the International Brigades against Fascist forces led by which General?

9 Apart from the Mississippi, which other river is mentioned in the lyrics of Robeson's signature tune 'Ol' Man River'?

10 Paul Robeson died in 1976, in which city in Pennsylvania?

NON-BRITISH BEER

1 What is the country of origin of Stella Artois?

2 What is the Spanish word for beer?

3 What is the favourite beer of Homer Simpson?

4 Which beer takes its name from the river running through Amsterdam?

5 Although many thought its sales would fall significantly, which Mexican beer was crowned the world's most valuable beer brand in 2020?

6 Samuel Adams is a famous beer from which American city?

7 VB is a very popular beer from Australia - VB stands for what?

8 Lager takes its name from the German for ... what?

9 What sequence of letters goes after Castlemaine to make a famous beer brand?

10 What does "Nastro Azzurro" mean in English?

PAUL ROBESON
1 James Earl Jones
2 Sydney Opera House (he was the first ever performer there)
3 Leroy
4 Manic Street Preachers
5 Law
6 NFL
7 Steve McQueen
8 Francisco Franco
9 Jordan
10 Philadelphia

NON-BRITISH BEER
1 Belgium
2 Cerveza
3 Duff
4 Amstel
5 Corona
6 Boston
7 Victoria Bitter
8 Store
9 XXXX
10 Blue Ribbon (as in Peroni)

OLIVIA COLMAN

1 On which Netflix TV show did Olivia Colman play Queen Elizabeth II?

2 Who played Margaret Thatcher in 'The Iron Lady', in which Olivia Colman played Carol Thatcher?

3 Olivia Colman attended which university, where she met future co-stars David Mitchell and Robert Webb?

4 On which TV comedy did Olivia Colman play Alexandra Smallbone?

5 Olivia Colman won the Best Actress Oscar in 'The Favourite' for playing which queen?

6 Who directed Olivia Colman in 'Tyrannosaur'?

7 'The Lost Daughter' is based on a book by which author?

8 As what G is Olivia Colman credited in 'Fleabag'?

9 What is Olivia Colman's actual first name?

10 On 'The Graham Norton Show' in 2021, Olivia Colman gently mocked which comedian's American accent?

BRITPOP

1 Jarvis Cocker was the lead singer of which band whose album 'Different Class' won the Mercury Prize?

2 Sonya Aurora Madan was the lead singer of which band, whose hits included 'Great Things'?

3 What UK chart position was reached by Supergrass's 'Alright' and The Bluetones's 'Slight Return'?

4 At which football stadium did Oasis play headlining shows on 27th and 28th April 1996?

5 Which Britpop frontwoman went on to write novels called 'Goodnight Steve McQueen' and 'The Half Life of Stars'?

6 The band Kenickie was founded in which city near the mouth of the River Wear?

7 What was the name of the lead guitarist in The Longpigs, who went on to have a successful solo career?

8 Which 1996 hit for Lush shares its name (almost) with a 1955 black comedy from Ealing Studios?

9 April of which year saw the death of Kurt Cobain and the release of the Blur album 'Parklife'?

10 Crispian Mills was the lead singer of a Britpop band with Indian influences whose first album was simply the first letter of the name of the band. What was the album's name?

OLIVIA COLMAN
1 The Crown
2 Meryl Streep
3 Cambridge University
4 Rev.
5 Queen Anne
6 Paddy Considine
7 Elena Ferrante
8 Godmother
9 Sarah
10 Jack Whitehall

BRITPOP
1 Pulp
2 Echobelly
3 Number 2
4 Maine Road
5 Louise Wener (of Sleeper)
6 Sunderland
7 Richard Hawley
8 Ladykillers (the film was 'The Ladykillers')
9 1994
10 K (Kula Shaker)

BALLET

1 Which word links an item of ballet wear with an Archbishop and campaigner who died in 2021?

2 'Dance of the Knights' comes from which ballet by Sergei Prokofiev?

3 Who became principal dancer of the Royal Ballet in 1989?

4 What nationality is the retired ballerina Sylvie Guillem?

5 In which 1948 film did Moira Shearer play Victoria Page?

6 Which great ballet dancer's name was given to a horse which won the English Triple Crown in 1970?

7 Which ballet composed by Léo Delibes tells the story of a young man who falls in love with a mechanical doll?

8 Which great ballet dancer was born Edris Stannus in Ireland in 1898?

9 Who served as the Director of the Paris Opera ballet from 1983 to 1989?

10 In 2015, who became the first African-American to be principal dancer for the American Ballet Theatre?

HORATIO NELSON

1 Which "little corporal" was France's military and political leader during the early 19th century?

2 In which English county was Horatio Nelson born in 1758?

3 In which year was the Battle of Trafalgar?

4 Which former actress and wife of the British Ambassador to Naples did Nelson have an affair with?

5 How is the Battle of Aboukir Bay, in August 1798, better known?

6 Nelson partially lost sight in one eye during the capture of which Mediterranean island in 1794?

7 In which city was "Nelson's Pillar" severely damaged by explosives in 1966?

8 Sharing his name with a famous author, who was the captain of HMS Victory when Nelson died?

9 At which battle of April 1801 did Admiral Nelson ignore Sir Hyde Parker's signal to withdraw, saying "I have a right to be blind sometimes"?

10 HMS Victory is on display at which English city?

BALLET
1 Tutu
2 Romeo and Juliet
3 Darcey Bussell
4 French
5 The Red Shoes
6 (Vassily) Nijinksy
7 Coppelia
8 Dame Ninette de Valois
9 Rudolf Nureyev
10 Misty Copeland

HORATIO NELSON
1 Napoleon Bonaparte
2 Norfolk (Burnham Thorpe)
3 1805
4 Emma Hamilton
5 Battle of the Nile
6 Corsica
7 Dublin
8 Thomas Hardy
9 Battle of Copenhagen
10 Portsmouth

RIOTS AND STRIKES

1 Which famous musical, based on a Victor Hugo book, is set around the 1832 June Rebellion in Paris?

2 What animal gives its name to the kind of unofficial strikes that took place across France in May 1968?

3 Which film, and musical, is based on a 1968 strike of Ford workers looking for equal pay for women?

4 The Battle of Orgreave was a pivotal event in which UK strike of the 1980s?

5 The police raided which New York bar on 28th June 1969, prompting a riot?

6 Broadwater Farm, the scene of a notorious riot in 1985, is in which area of North London?

7 Which Stone Roses song, from their self-titled debut album, is about the 1968 Paris riots?

8 Whose beating by an LA policeman in 1991 sparked the 1992 Los Angeles riots?

9 In which African country did "Bread Riots" take place in January 1977?

10 Which band's fifth album, from 1971, was called 'There's a Riot Goin' On'?

THE X FACTOR

1 Who was the female judge on the first UK series of 'The X Factor'?

2 Who was Shayne Ward's mentor when he won 'The X Factor'?

3 Whom did Dermot O'Leary follow as 'X Factor' host?

4 What was the first single of the first 'X Factor' winner Steve Brookstein?

5 Rowetta, from 'X Factor' Series 1, was the longtime backing singer for which band?

6 On 'The X Factor', what were Little Mix originally called before they had to change their name?

7 What job was Andy Abraham doing before entering 'The X Factor'?

8 Who wrote the first single released by Alexandra Burke, winner of 'X Factor' Series 5?

9 Who won Series 15, the last main series of 'The X Factor' in the UK?

10 Matt Cardle was first. Rebecca Ferguson was second. Who came third?

RIOTS AND STRIKES
1 Les Misérables
2 Wildcat (strikes)
3 Made in Dagenham
4 Miners' Strike
5 Stonewall Inn
6 Tottenham
7 Bye Bye Badman
8 Rodney King
9 Egypt
10 Sly and the Family Stone

THE X FACTOR
1 Sharon Osbourne
2 Louis Walsh
3 Kate Thornton
4 Against All Odds
5 The Happy Mondays
6 Rhythmix
7 Binman
8 Leonard Cohen (It was 'Hallelujah')
9 Dalton Harris
10 One Direction (in 2010)

SHAKESPEARE

1 In the work of Shakespeare, who was the Prince of Denmark?

2 What is Juliet's surname in William Shakespeare's 'Romeo and Juliet'?

3 In Shakespeare's 'The Taming of the Shrew', what is the first name of the so-called "shrew"?

4 Which Shakespearean king says: "A horse! A horse! My kingdom for a horse!"?

5 Which Shakespearean king has daughters called Cordelia, Regan, and Goneril?

6 What do "rough winds shake", according to Shakespeare's Sonnet XVIII?

7 In the Shakespeare play, what is the first name of the Merchant of Venice?

8 Which character appears in both 'Henry IV Part I' and 'The Merry Wives of Windsor'?

9 Which Shakespeare play is often thought to have had its first performance on 6th January 1602?

10 Which character has the most number of lines in total in Shakespeare plays?

DINOSAURS

1 The word "dinosaur" means "terrible ..." what?

2 The Cretaceous-Paleogene extinction event which is thought to have wiped out the dinosaurs took place how many million years ago? [allow to within 5 million]

3 Who played John Hammond in 'Jurassic Park'?

4 Was a triceratops a carnivore or a herbivore?

5 Which small dinosaur (about the size of a chicken) has a name derived from the Greek for "elegant jaw"?

6 What word is given to someone who studies dinosaurs and other fossils?

7 Diplodocus fossils were first discovered by SW Williston, in 1877, in which continent?

8 Which creatures in 'Lord of the Rings' did JRR Tolkien describe as pterodactylic?

9 If a triceratops had three horns on its face, how many did a pentaceratops have?

10 Which cartoon family had a pet dinosaur called Dino?

SHAKESPEARE
1 Hamlet
2 Capulet
3 Katherine
4 Richard III
5 Lear
6 The darling buds of May
7 Antonio
8 Sir John Falstaff
9 Twelfth Night
10 Henry V

DINOSAURS
1 Lizard
2 66 million
3 Richard Attenborough
4 Herbivore
5 Compsognathus
6 Palaeontologist
7 North America
8 Nazgûl/Black riders/Ringwraiths
9 Five
10 The Flintstones

ENGLISH AROUND THE WORLD

1 In the US, it is called a "sidewalk". What is it called in Britain?

2 The phrase "fair dinkum" is associated with English speakers in which country?

3 English is the official language of which mainland Central American country?

4 English speakers in which country would typically use the word "lekker"?

5 The southern New Zealand accent with a Scottish twang is commonly known as what S?

6 What do the English call what in the US is usually called a "cookie"?

7 The word "fall" is used by Americans to refer to which season of the year?

8 In Australia, it's a "barbie" - what B is it in South Africa?

9 Which T is the word used in American English to refer to a gearbox?

10 What is the official language of Kenya along with English?

BLACK HOLES

1 Which physicist, played by Eddie Redmayne in 'The Theory of Everything', suggested that there may be, as well as stellar and galactic black holes, mini black holes?

2 What name is commonly given to the bridges, or tubes, in black holes, that connect one part of space to another?

3 The first black hole to be called a black hole was Cygnus X-1 - what does Cygnus mean in Latin?

4 Describing the largest types of black hole, what does the SM in SMBH stand for?

5 What do physicists call the point beyond which photons cannot escape from a black hole?

6 A black hole called Gargantua features in the plot of which 2014 Christopher Nolan film?

7 Which American physicist coined the term black hole in the 1960s?

8 What is the name of the American scientist who led the team which, in 2019, developed the first image of a black hole?

9 What two-word term is used to describe the fact that information about objects that fall into a black hole is not recovered by Hawking radiation?

10 'Black Holes and Revelations' was the fourth album by which British rock band?

ENGLISH AROUND THE WORLD
1 Pavement
2 Australia
3 Belize
4 South Africa
5 Southland burr
6 Biscuit
7 Autumn
8 Braai
9 Transmission
10 Swahili

BLACK HOLES
1 Stephen Hawking
2 Wormholes
3 Swan
4 Supermassive
5 Horizon/Event Horizon
6 Interstellar
7 John Archibald Wheeler
8 Katie Bouman
9 Information Paradox
10 Muse

NETFLIX SHOWS

1 'Cobra Kai' is a TV show spun off from which film franchise?

2 The mystery thriller 'Lupin', starring Omar Sy, is primarily in which language?

3 'Bridgerton' is set in the Regency Era, which took place in which century?

4 The Netflix reality show 'Selling Sunset' is concerned with what line of business?

5 In Season 1 of 'You', Joe Goldberg is manager of Mooney's - what kind of shop is Mooney's?

6 In which Netflix show does Henry Cavill play Geralt of Rivia?

7 In 'After Life', what is the name of the newspaper Tony Johnson, played by Ricky Gervais, works for?

8 Who plays Marty Byrde in 'Ozark'?

9 Nicknamed "The Worm", which controversial basketball star who once appeared on 'Celebrity Big Brother' is one of the stars of Netflix documentary 'The Last Dance'?

10 What is the name of the first game in, and first episode of, 'Squid Game' Season 1?

GIRAFFES

1 On which continent do giraffes live in the wild?

2 What is the word used for a male giraffe?

3 To which other species, which is also part of the giraffidae family, is the giraffe closely related?

4 Which part of a giraffe can be up to 20 inches long and is a blue-black colour to ensure it doesn't burn in the sun?

5 What can't giraffes do, according to a popular children's book by Giles Andreae?

6 Which surrealist artist depicted giraffes with burning manes in his paintings, considering the image to be a "masculine cosmic apocalyptic monster"?

7 In the 19th century, the French naturalist Jean Baptiste Lamarck used the giraffe's long neck as an example of his alternative theory of ... what?

8 Which species of giraffe has the taxonomic name Giraffa giraffa?

9 In months, what is a female giraffe's gestation period? [allow one month either way]

10 Which Ottoman viceroy of Egypt, who shares his name with a famous boxer, dispatched three diplomatic giraffes to Europe in the early 19th century?

NETFLIX SHOWS
1 The Karate Kid
2 French
3 19th century/1800s
4 Real estate/Estate agents
5 Book shop
6 The Witcher
7 Tambury Gazette
8 Jason Bateman
9 Dennis Rodman
10 Red Light, Green Light

GIRAFFES
1 Africa
2 Bull
3 Okapi
4 Tongue
5 Dance (Giraffes Can't Dance)
6 Salvador Dalí
7 Evolution
8 Southern Giraffe
9 15 Months
10 Muhammad Ali

AUSTRALIAN MUSIC

1 In 1997, what was Natalie Imbruglia's debut UK hit?

2 With only one word different from the title of an Amy Winehouse album, which album by AC/DC has sold over 50 million copies worldwide?

3 Which Australian singer had a worldwide hit in 2014 with 'Chandelier'?

4 Which Australian actress did the country singer Keith Urban marry in 2006?

5 Stefan Dennis, who had a UK hit with 'Don't It Make You Feel Good', played which archvillain in 'Neighbours'?

6 In the song 'Down Under' by Men at Work, the narrator is "buying bread from a man" in which European city?

7 Which Australian represented the United Kingdom in the 1974 Eurovision Song Contest?

8 'Lonerism' and 'Currents' are albums by which Australian band fronted by Kevin Parker?

9 In 2019, 'Dance Monkey' by Tones and I was Number 1 in the UK for how many weeks in total? [we will allow one wrong either side]

10 Which Kylie Minogue song did Nick Cave describe as being "a message to God that cries out into the yawning void, in anguish and self-loathing, for deliverance"?

THEME PARKS AND FUNFAIRS

1 What was the original name, when it opened in 1992, of the amusement park now called Disneyland Paris?

2 Which common funfair ride's name would also mean someone doing a dance in 3/4 time?

3 In which US state is the EPCOT theme park located?

4 In which English theme park would you find the Duplo Valley?

5 What is the name of the rollercoaster at Lightwater Valley in Yorkshire which was the longest in the world from 1991 to 2000?

6 The Thrill-O-Matic, which opened at Blackpool in 2013, is themed around which TV and film characters?

7 In which country is Formula Rossa, the world's fastest rollercoaster when it opened, which travels at 149mph?

8 Just outside Paris is a theme park containing attractions such as Tonnerre 2 Zeus and Menhir Express. The park is based on which comic book character?

9 Which future Oscar-winning actress starred opposite Gary Busey and Robbie Robertson in the 1980 film 'Carny'?

10 Who had a UK Number 1 in 2000 with 'Life is a Rollercoaster'?

SPECIALIST SUBJECTS

AUSTRALIAN MUSIC
1 Torn
2 Back in Black (The Amy Winehouse album is 'Back to Black')
3 Sia
4 Nicole Kidman
5 Paul Robinson
6 Brussels
7 Olivia Newton-John
8 Tame Impala
9 11 (so 10, 11 or 12 allowed)
10 Better the Devil You Know

THEME PARKS AND FUNFAIRS
1 Euro Disney
2 Waltzer
3 Florida
4 Legoland (Windsor)
5 The Ultimate
6 Wallace and Gromit
7 United Arab Emirates (it's at Ferrari World in Abu Dhabi)
8 Asterix (Parc Astérix)
9 Jodie Foster
10 Ronan Keating

BRONTË SISTERS

1 What was the name of Emily Brontë's only published novel?

2 Which of the Brontë sisters wrote the novel 'Agnes Grey'?

3 Charlotte Brontë used the pseudonym Currer Bell, Anne Brontë was Acton Bell. What was Emily Brontë?

4 The clergyman Patrick Brontë received a post in which remote Yorkshire town in 1820?

5 Who had a Number 1 UK single with 'Wuthering Heights'?

6 Which acclaimed novel by Jean Rhys is a "prequel" to 'Jane Eyre'?

7 The rejection of Charlotte Brontë's poetry by which Poet Laureate caused her and her sisters to publish their work under male pseudonyms?

8 In which decade was 'The Professor' by Charlotte Brontë posthumously published?

9 "At the end we are steeped through and through with the genius, the vehemence, the indignation of Charlotte Brontë" - a quote from which 20th century author?

10 Which author and friend published 'The Life of Charlotte Brontë' shortly after Brontë's death?

REGGAE

1 Reggae music first developed in which country?

2 Which religious movement, in which Haile Selassie has key importance, is closely linked to reggae music?

3 What was the nickname of Lee Perry, the renowned reggae producer who died in 2021?

4 What was the name of Bob Marley's backing group?

5 In the traditional form of reggae music, how many beats are there in a bar?

6 Which legendary leader of the Maytals died in September 2020?

7 Which British reggae act's 1978 debut album was called 'Handsworth Revolution'?

8 Singer Jimmy Cliff starred in which 1972 film which popularised reggae around the world?

9 Which "lovers rock" track written by Dennis Bovell was a UK Number 2 hit for Janet Kay in 1979?

10 Which Bob Marley song, released shortly before his death, has been covered by the likes of Stevie Wonder, Joe Strummer and Johnny Cash?

BRONTË SISTERS
1 Wuthering Heights
2 Anne Brontë
3 Ellis Bell
4 Haworth
5 Kate Bush
6 Wide Sargasso Sea
7 Robert Southey
8 1850s (1857)
9 Virginia Woolf
10 Elizabeth Gaskell

REGGAE
1 Jamaica
2 Rastafari
3 Scratch
4 The Wailers
5 Four
6 Toots Hibbert (accept: Toots)
7 Steel Pulse
8 The Harder they Come
9 Silly Games
10 Redemption Song

JOHN MAJOR

1 What is the first name of John Major's wife, who he married in 1970?

2 Who did John Major directly follow as Prime Minister of the UK?

3 Throughout his time in parliament, John Major was MP for which constituency?

4 From 1999 to 2003, John Major's son James was married to which gameshow hostess?

5 In 2007, John Major wrote an award-winning book called 'More than a Game' about the early years of which sport?

6 In May 2018, John Major was the only current or former Prime Minister at whose marriage to Meghan Markle?

7 From July to October 1989, which was the first of the "Great Offices of State" John Major held?

8 Which Eurosceptic challenged John Major for the Tory leadership in 1995?

9 In which city in the Netherlands did John Major co-sign a famous treaty on 7th February 1992?

10 Which publication satirised John Major with the column 'The Secret Diary of John Major, age 47¾'?

FOX NEWS

1 Fox News originally used the slogan 'Fair and …' what?

2 What was the name of the show Bill O'Reilly hosted on Fox News until 2017?

3 Which Australian media mogul founded Fox News?

4 Who criticised Fox News in his book 'Lies and the Lying Liars Who Tell Them'?

5 Which punk frontman, born Jeffrey Hyman, released a song called 'Maria Bartiromo' about a Fox News host?

6 Who hosted 'On The Record' on Fox News from 2002 to 2016?

7 Which 2019 film was about the women at the centre of a sexual harassment scandal at Fox News?

8 Which Fox News host published the 2021 book 'The Long Slide'?

9 Fox News host Steve Hilton is a former Director of Strategy for which British Prime Minister?

10 In March 2009 Fox News host Greg Gutfeld called for an invasion of which "ridiculous country"?

JOHN MAJOR
1 Norma
2 Margaret Thatcher
3 Huntingdon (known as Huntingdonshire until 1983)
4 Emma Noble
5 Cricket
6 Prince Harry/Duke of Sussex
7 Foreign Secretary
8 John Redwood
9 Maastricht
10 Private Eye

FOX NEWS
1 Balanced
2 The O'Reilly Factor
3 Rupert Murdoch
4 Al Franken
5 Joey Ramone
6 Greta Van Susteren
7 Bombshell
8 Tucker Carlson
9 David Cameron
10 Canada

THE MILITARY

1 In the British Army, which rank is directly above Captain?

2 What is the three-word motto of the SAS?

3 True or False? The Queen's Company of the Grenadier Guards are traditionally used as pallbearers for monarch's funerals, because all members of the company are over 6 ft tall.

4 The Battle of Goose Green was an engagement in which war?

5 What is the name of the Royal Military Academy that crosses the border of Berkshire and Surrey?

6 Sometimes abbreviated to ACM, what is the most senior rank in the Royal Air Force?

7 Which king formally founded the Royal Navy in 1546?

8 What is the surname of "Tommy", as in the slang term for a common soldier in the British Army?

9 What does the W stand for in WAAF, who served in the Second World War?

10 Which singer wrote the song 'No Bravery' about his time serving as a soldier in Kosovo?

MODERN ROM-COMS

1 The director behind hit films such as 'Knocked Up' and 'Trainwreck' is Judd ...?

2 How many 'Days of Summer' did Joseph Gordon-Levitt have with Zooey Deschanel?

3 Which 'Scrubs' star wrote and starred in 'Garden State'?

4 Kristen Stewart starred in indie drama 'Adventureland', and played Bella Swan in which film series?

5 In 'Palm Springs', who plays Sarah Wilder, who gets stuck in a time loop?

6 Which movie, naturally enough, went after 'Before Sunrise' and before 'Before Midnight'?

7 In the movie, with whom did Nick share an 'Infinite Playlist'?

8 In what kind of shop does Rob work in 'High Fidelity'?

9 Charlize Theron's character, Charlotte Field, holds which significant position in the 2019 film 'Long Shot'?

10 In 'Sideways' which alcoholic drink is Miles' great love?

THE MILITARY
1 Major
2 Who Dares Wins
3 True
4 Falklands War
5 RMA Sandhurst
6 Air Chief Marshal
7 Henry VIII
8 Atkins
9 Women's (Women's Auxiliary Air Force)
10 James Blunt

MODERN ROM-COMS
1 Apatow
2 500 (in (500) Days of Summer)
3 Zach Braff
4 Twilight
5 Cristiana Milioti
6 Before Sunrise
7 Norah
8 A music store
9 US Secretary of State
10 Wine (specifically, a 1961 Château Cheval Blanc)

US VICE PRESIDENTS

1 Which President of the USA chose Joe Biden to be their Vice President?

2 Hannibal Hamlin served as US Vice President during all but the last month of which war?

3 Former Vice President Al Gore was the subject of which Oscar-winning 2006 documentary about climate change?

4 Played by Leslie Odom Jr in a famous musical, who was the first Vice President of the USA who did not themselves become President?

5 Before becoming Vice President, Kamala Harris was previously Attorney-General, and then a senator, for which US state?

6 What was the title of the 2018 film in which Christian Bale portrayed former Vice President Dick Cheney?

7 What was the name of the fourth Vice President of the USA, which is also the name of a prominent funk musician?

8 What is the name of the fictional Vice President played by Julia Louis-Dreyfus in 'Veep'?

9 A member of which famous business dynasty was Vice President of the USA from 1974 to 1977?

10 Who became Vice President of the USA following the resignation of the elected Vice President, and then became President following the resignation of the elected President?

MEANINGS AND WORDS

1 Coracle, skiff and cutter are all words for types of what?

2 What is the proper name for a prong on a fork?

3 What would someone be afraid of if they were gymnophobic?

4 If you suffered from narcolepsy, what might you do at inappropriate times?

5 If you were travelling by Shanks' Pony, what would you be doing?

6 What is an iatrophobe afraid of?

7 Which animal was once called the camelopard?

8 Which word literally means to remove one in every ten of a group?

9 Adam's Ale is a term which is used for which liquid?

10 Which word, often used to refer to "useless information", comes from the Latin for "three ways"?

SPECIALIST SUBJECTS

US VICE PRESIDENTS
1 Barack Obama
2 US Civil War
3 An Inconvenient Truth
4 Aaron Burr
5 California
6 VICE
7 George Clinton
8 Selina Meyer
9 Rockefeller (it was Nelson Rockefeller)
10 Gerald Ford

MEANINGS AND WORDS
1 Boat
2 Tine
3 Nudity
4 Fall asleep
5 Walking
6 Doctors
7 Giraffe
8 Decimate
9 Water
10 Trivia

SPOOKY TV

1 Which spin-off from 'Buffy the Vampire Slayer' starred David Boreanaz as the title character?

2 What horror anthology, which initially ran from 1959 to 1964, was created by Rod Serling?

3 Telling the story of the Krampus, 'The Devil at Christmas' was the first episode of Series 3 of which TV show?

4 Which British medium, known for 'Most Haunted', died in January 2020?

5 Which pseudo-documentary starring Michael Parkinson, Sarah Greene and Mike Smith terrified Britain on Halloween 1992?

6 In 2015, Timothy Spall and Juliet Stevenson starred in a series about a 'Haunting' in which London suburb?

7 Which Scottish band composed the music for the French TV series 'The Returned'?

8 What is Millie Bobby Brown's numerical nickname in 'Stranger Things'?

9 Jeffrey Dean Morgan played which frightening character in 'The Walking Dead'?

10 Which acclaimed film director 'Presents' a thrilling anthology series between 1955 and 1965?

POPES

1 In the Roman Catholic church, the Pope is the bishop of which city?

2 Pope John Paul II died in the same month that which son of Queen Elizabeth II married for the second time?

3 Pope Francis once worked as a club bouncer in which city?

4 If a new pope has been elected, what colour is the smoke that comes out of the chimney on top of the Sistine Chapel?

5 From 1309 to 1376, seven successive popes resided in which French city?

6 Augustine, sent by Pope Gregory I as a missionary to England, became the first Archbishop of which city in Kent?

7 Who played Pope Benedict XVI in the film 'The Two Popes'?

8 Pope Adrian IV, born Nicholas Breakspear, is the only pope to have come from which country?

9 In which year of the 20th century were there three popes?

10 Pope Callixtus III and Pope Alexander VI belonged to which notorious family?

SPOOKY TV
1 Angel
2 The Twilight Zone
3 Inside Number 9
4 Derek Acorah
5 Ghostwatch
6 Enfield (The Enfield Haunting)
7 Mogwai
8 Eleven
9 Negan
10 Alfred Hitchcock

POPES
1 Rome
2 Charles
3 Buenos Aires
4 White (the smoke is black if a pope has not been chosen)
5 Avignon
6 Canterbury
7 Anthony Hopkins
8 England (accept: Britain)
9 1978
10 Borgia

TOP GUN

1 The classic 80s movie 'Top Gun' is about young men who are training to do what?

2 Who played Tom "Iceman" Kazansky in 'Top Gun'?

3 In which year was 'Top Gun' released to the cinema?

4 What is Maverick's actual name in 'Top Gun'?

5 In 'Top Gun', Iceman told Maverick he could be his ... what, "anytime"?

6 Who directed the film 'Top Gun'?

7 Who plays Goose's wife in 'Top Gun'?

8 Who, in the movie, drops out so that Maverick can go to 'Top Gun'?

9 Who sang the songs from 'Top Gun' called 'Danger Zone' and 'Playing with the Boys'?

10 Who plays Bradley "Rooster" Bradshaw in the 2022 sequel 'Top Gun: Maverick'?

SHOPS

1 How is the firm founded as Associated Dairies in 1949 now more commonly known?

2 What is the Swiss company Rolex mainly famous for making?

3 Which chain is known as Penneys in the Republic of Ireland, where it was founded?

4 Which supermarket bought Bejam Freezer Centre, its significantly larger rival, in 1989?

5 In which country was the first IKEA store opened in 1958?

6 The first Westfield shopping centre was opened in which area of West London in 2008?

7 "Omnia Omnibus Ubique" is the motto of which London department store?

8 What do the letters "B" and "Q" stand for in the store name B&Q?

9 Which auction house conducted its first sale in December 1766?

10 In which US state is the Mall of America?

TOP GUN
1 Fly planes
2 Val Kilmer
3 1986
4 Pete Mitchell
5 Wingman
6 Tony Scott
7 Meg Ryan
8 Cougar
9 Kenny Loggins
10 Miles Teller

SHOPS
1 Asda
2 Watches
3 Primark
4 Iceland
5 Sweden
6 Shepherd's Bush
7 Harrods
8 Block and Quayle
9 Christie's
10 Minnesota

THE PLANETS

1 If it was named after its Greek equivalent, what would the planet Venus be called?

2 The four largest moons of which planet are called the Galilean moons?

3 What is the name of the largest volcano on Mars?

4 In the comic strip 'Dan Dare', the Treens come from which planet?

5 Which helicopter completed a powered controlled flight on Mars in April 2021?

6 Which dwarf planet is named after the creator god of the Rapa Nui people?

7 The Cassini-Huygens space mission was launched in 1997 to investigate which planet?

8 Named after a Dutch astronomer, which "belt" lies beyond the orbit of the planet Neptune?

9 How many of the main planets of the Solar System are smaller than Ganymede and Titan, the two largest moons?

10 In the original 1968 film 'Planet of the Apes', the titular planet turns out to be which planet of the Solar System?

HOLLYOAKS

1 'Hollyoaks' is set in a fictional suburb of which town?

2 What was the surname of a family in 'Hollyoaks' containing Hannah, Rhys, Josh and Neville ?

3 The name of the long-running pub in 'Hollyoaks' was The Dog in the ... what?

4 Which TV guru, also responsible for 'Brookside' and 'Grange Hill' devised 'Hollyoaks' in 1995?

5 Who played the part of Jambo in early episodes of 'Hollyoaks'?

6 On which channel was 'Hollyoaks' first broadcast in the UK?

7 Who is the long-running restaurateur and entrepreneur played by Nick Pickard on 'Hollyoaks'?

8 Who played Lisa Hunter in 'Hollyoaks'?

9 Joanna Taylor, who played Geri in 'Hollyoaks', went on to marry which England footballer?

10 Which former member of Eternal plays Martine Deveraux in 'Hollyoaks'?

THE PLANETS
1 Aphrodite
2 Jupiter
3 Olympus Mons
4 Venus
5 Ingenuity
6 Makemake
7 Saturn
8 Kuiper Belt
9 One (just Mercury)
10 Earth

HOLLYOAKS
1 Chester
2 Ashworth
3 Pond
4 Phil Redmond
5 Will Mellor
6 Channel 4
7 Tony Hutchinson
8 Gemma Atkinson
9 Danny Murphy
10 Kelle Bryan

THE CRIMEAN WAR

1 Crimea is a peninsula on the northern coast of which sea?

2 In which decade did the Crimean War take place?

3 The Charge of the Light Brigade took place during which battle of the Crimean War?

4 Which young author wrote up his experiences in the Crimean War in a series of pen pictures called 'Sketches from Sebastopol'?

5 Which nurse who treated the wounded during the Crimean War was, in 2004, voted the Greatest Black Briton?

6 One officer who took part in the Charge of the Light Brigade blamed it on the rivalry between the British cavalry and which group of Russian soldiers?

7 In the Crimean War, what famous nickname (shared with a Terrence Malick film) is given to the actions of the 93rd Highlanders in resisting a Russian cavalry charge?

8 The Crimean War was officially brought to an end by The Peace of ... which city?

9 Who immortalised the Light Brigade with the contemporary poem which read, "Into the valley of death/ rode the Six Hundred"?

10 The siege of Sevastopol lasted for how many months? [we'll allow two either side]

AVOCADOS

1 In which modern-day country is the avocado believed to have originated?

2 Which H is the avocado that makes up the majority of those which are commercially available today?

3 Which popular dip has a name that literally means "avocado sauce"?

4 In 2015, which moustachioed actor was accused of stealing water for his California avocado farm?

5 A typical avocado contains 975 grams of which chemical element?

6 What part of the avocado is also known as the exocarp?

7 Which actress popularised avocado toast with her book 'It's All Good'?

8 After it changed colour in the sun, what did Spanish conquistadors use the liquid from the avocado seed for?

9 What is the English meaning of the Aztec word for avocado, "ahuacatl"?

10 In 2017, Australian property mogul Tim Gurner told millennials that they would need to stop buying avocado toast if they wanted to do what?

THE CRIMEAN WAR
1 Black Sea
2 1850s
3 The Battle Of Balaclava
4 Leo Tolstoy
5 Mary Seacole
6 Cossacks
7 The Thin Red Line
8 Paris
9 Alfred, Lord Tennyson
10 11 months

AVOCADOS
1 Mexico
2 Hass Avocado
3 Guacamole
4 Tom Selleck
5 Potassium
6 Skin
7 Gwyneth Paltrow
8 Ink
9 Testicle
10 Buy a house

FAMOUS MURDERS

1 Lee Harvey Oswald was arrested for the murder of ... who?

2 Andrew Cunanan murdered which famous fashion designer?

3 Who was the victim in TS Eliot's 'Murder In The Cathedral'?

4 Who killed Abraham Lincoln?

5 Who was the partner in crime of William Burke?

6 'The Suspicions of Mr Whicher' is a book about a 19th century murder in which English county?

7 Which rock star was arrested for the murder of his girlfriend Nancy Spungen?

8 In which year was serial killer Ted Bundy executed?

9 Which famous TV show, created by David Lynch, asked the question "Who killed Laura Palmer?"

10 In which city did Gavrilo Princip assassinate Archduke Franz Ferdinand in 1914?

MAMMALS

1 What is the name of a female sheep?

2 In North America, it's a moose. What is it called in Europe?

3 Serengeti National Park in Tanzania is famous (among other things) for the annual migration of over 1 million of what animal?

4 What does the word "hippopotamus" mean?

5 What can tigers and lions do which cheetahs and cougars cannot?

6 Which Australian mammal has a name that is the Latin for "I am able"?

7 Gombe Stream National Park is located just north of Kigoma, Tanzania. What animals did Jane Goodall study there?

8 What South American relative of the camel did the Incas use as a pack animal?

9 Which archipelago off the coast of Alaska gives its name to a species of bear?

10 There are two families of sloth - how are they described?

FAMOUS MURDERS
1 John F Kennedy
2 Gianni Versace
3 Thomas Becket
4 John Wilkes Booth
5 William Hare
6 Wiltshire
7 Sid Vicious
8 1989
9 Twin Peaks
10 Sarajevo

MAMMALS
1 Ewe
2 Elk
3 Wildebeest/gnu
4 River horse
5 Roar
6 Possum
7 Chimpanzees
8 Llama
9 Kodiak
10 Two-toed and Three-toed

CHARLES DICKENS

1 The title of which book by Charles Dickens makes reference to London and Paris?

2 Which specifically does Oliver Twist want more of in the Charles Dickens novel? (and indeed in the musical 'Oliver!')

3 Give any year in the life of Charles Dickens.

4 Who is the final Ghost that Ebenezer Scrooge encounters in Charles Dickens' 'A Christmas Carol'?

5 Which character did Tuppence Middleton play in the 2015 series 'Dickensian'?

6 What was the first novel by Charles Dickens?

7 Which Danish author, who stayed with Charles Dickens for several weeks, was described by Dickens' daughter as "a bony bore, who stayed on and on"?

8 Which Charles Dickens novel centres on the legal case Jarndyce versus Jarndyce?

9 In 'Oliver Twist' by Charles Dickens, what is the name of Bill Sikes' dog?

10 Which actor played Charles Dickens in the 2005 'Doctor Who' episode 'The Unquiet Dead'?

GENERAL FOOTBALL

1 Due to the team he represented and his standing up for player's rights, which former England footballer with 85 caps was nicknamed "Red Nev"?

2 Which team won the last FA Cup held at the old Wembley Stadium in 2000?

3 Which Liverpool striker tried to stop the referee awarding a penalty when he fell over in the box in a 1997 match against Arsenal?

4 Which England midfielder, born in 1980, has the distinction of making his first four England appearances while at four different clubs?

5 In which UK city did TGI Fridays need to change their uniform due to negative reactions from locals? (This also happened in Madrid)

6 Where did Denis Law leave Manchester United for in 1973?

7 In which decade did Liverpool win their first FA Cup Final?

8 In the early to mid 80s, Sharon Phillips was the long-term girlfriend of which footballer?

9 Which teenage Manchester United left-winger was PFA Young Player of the Season for 1990-91?

10 What are the three English football clubs which were managed by Sir Bobby Robson?

SPECIALIST SUBJECTS

CHARLES DICKENS
1 A Tale Of Two Cities
2 Gruel
3 1812-1870
4 Ghost of Christmas Yet To Come
5 Miss Havisham
6 The Pickwick Papers
7 Hans Christian Andersen
8 Bleak House
9 Bull's Eye
10 Simon Callow

GENERAL FOOTBALL
1 Gary Neville
2 Chelsea
3 Robbie Fowler
4 Scott Parker - the clubs were Charlton, Chelsea, Newcastle, West Ham
5 Newcastle - the red and white striped uniform looks like a Sunderland strip (also Atlético Madrid)
6 Manchester City
7 1960s (1965)
8 Ian Wright (She's the mother of Shaun and Bradley Wright-Phillips (Ian adopted Shaun three years after he was born))
9 Lee Sharpe (not Ryan Giggs, who won it the next two years)
10 Fulham, Ipswich Town, Newcastle United

GLEE

1 In the TV series 'Glee', which activity do the members of the Glee Club participate in?

2 In 'Glee', what is the name of the Glee Club directed by Mr Schuester?

3 In 'Glee', what is the name of the cheerleading coach played by Jane Lynch?

4 The school in 'Glee' is named after which US President?

5 In which US state is 'Glee' set?

6 Which of the 'Glee' girls is revealed to be pregnant in the first series?

7 'Don't Stop Believing' was sung at the end of the first episode of 'Glee', but who originally performed it?

8 Which rapper and singer played the principal of rival school The Jane Addams Academy?

9 What is the name of the character played by guest 'Glee' star Kristen Chenoweth?

10 Which song does Kurt have played as he kicks the winning football goal in the 'Glee' episode 'Preggers'?

19TH CENTURY NOVELS

1 'Captains Courageous' is a novel by which author, most famous for 'The Jungle Book'?

2 Which Nathaniel Hawthorne novel inspired the Emma Stone film 'Easy A'?

3 The last novel by Fyodor Dostoevsky was 'The Brothers ...' what?

4 In Gustave Flaubert's 'Madame Bovary', what is the title character's first name?

5 Leopold von Sacher-Masoch's 1870 novella 'Venus in Furs' gave its title to a song on which band's debut album?

6 Who was the author of the 1898 work 'The Turn of the Screw'?

7 Fanny Price is the heroine of which Jane Austen novel?

8 Which French author wrote 'The Count of Monte Cristo'?

9 The titular mill in George Eliot's 'Mill on the Floss' is in which English county?

10 What was the title of the 1871 novel by Louisa May Alcott which had the subtitle 'Life at Plumfield with Jo's Boys'?

GLEE
1 Singing/Dancing
2 New Directions
3 Sue Sylvester
4 William McKinley
5 Ohio
6 Quinn
7 Journey
8 Eve
9 April Rhodes
10 Single Ladies (Put a Ring on It)

19TH CENTURY NOVELS
1 Rudyard Kipling
2 The Scarlet Letter
3 Karamazov
4 Emma
5 The Velvet Underground (and Nico)
6 Henry James
7 Mansfield Park
8 Alexandre Dumas
9 Lincolnshire
10 Little Men

ISAMBARD KINGDOM BRUNEL

1 The famous Clifton Suspension Bridge spans which river?

2 Isambard Kingdom Brunel and Charles Dickens were born in the same city a few years apart - in which city?

3 Who played Brunel in the Opening Ceremony of the 2012 Olympics?

4 The original "Thames Tunnel", constructed between 1825 and 1843, still runs between Wapping, north of the Thames, and which R, south of the Thames?

5 The Wharncliffe Viaduct was the first major project of which railway line constructed by Brunel, abbreviated to GWR?

6 The last project completed by Brunel was the "Three Bridges" in West London, in which the canal was below the road, and what was below the canal?

7 Brunel designed the prefabricated Renkioi Hospital for use during which war?

8 Taken by Robert Howlett in 1857, the most famous photo of Brunel is entitled 'Isambard Kingdom Brunel Standing Before the Launching Chains of the ...' what?

9 Brunel's SS Great Britain is now a museum ship in which city?

10 In 1843, what did Brunel get stuck in his throat while performing a conjuring trick?

THE GOLDEN GIRLS

1 The theme music for 'The Golden Girls' goes "Thank you for being a ... " what?

2 The Golden Girls live in which city in Florida?

3 Who created the sitcom 'The Golden Girls'?

4 Which of the four actresses who played the Golden Girls was born last?

5 Which young actress, who'd go on to front the indie rock band Rilo Kiley, made an appearance in the opening episode of Season 3 of 'The Golden Girls'?

6 What was the name of the short-lived British sitcom starring Sheila Hancock which was based on 'The Golden Girls'?

7 In Season 3 of 'The Golden Girls', representatives from which world leader get in touch about Rose's letter pleading for nuclear disarmament?

8 In which American state was 'The Golden Girls' character Rose Nylund born?

9 At the end of 'The Golden Girls', Dorothy marries Lucas - played by which comic legend?

10 What was the spin-off of 'The Golden Girls' (without Dorothy) called?

SPECIALIST SUBJECTS

ISAMBARD KINGDOM BRUNEL
1 Avon (Avon Gorge)
2 Portsmouth
3 Kenneth Branagh
4 Rotherhithe
5 Great Western Railway
6 Railway
7 Crimean War
8 Great Eastern
9 Bristol
10 Coin (half-sovereign)

THE GOLDEN GIRLS
1 Friend
2 Miami
3 Susan Harris
4 Rue McClanahan (who played Blanche) (Order of birth: White, Arthur, Getty, McClanahan)
5 Jenny Lewis
6 The Brighton Belles
7 Mikhail Gorbachev
8 Minnesota
9 Leslie Nielsen
10 The Golden Palace

WORDS AGAIN

1 What name is given to the supports, traditionally made of wood, that railway tracks rest on?

2 The sackbut is an early medieval version of which musical instrument?

3 "Without this there is nothing" is a translation of which Latin phrase?

4 Which German word used in English means "pleasure taken from someone else's misfortune"?

5 Which land feature has a name that means "almost an island" in Latin?

6 Designed as a military training discipline, what P is the name given to the activity of getting from one point to another in the fastest and most efficient way possible?

7 Where on the body would you wear an Anthony Eden?

8 On which part of a horse's body would you find its poll?

9 Arithmomania is the obsessive desire to do what?

10 What, in English history, was a cat o' nine tails?

BARACK OBAMA

1 Which political party did Barack Obama represent?

2 What is Michelle Obama's maiden name?

3 Who sang the US national anthem at Obama's 2009 inauguration?

4 Who was the Republican candidate Barack Obama defeated to become US President in 2008?

5 For which state was Barack Obama Junior Senator from 2005 to 2008?

6 Whom did Barack Obama defeat for the Democratic party nomination in 2008?

7 With which musician has Barack Obama done the podcast 'Renegades'?

8 In which city was Barack Obama born in 1961?

9 Sharing his name with a Hollywood actor, who was made Obama's Director of Speechwriting in 2009?

10 Which slogan links Barack Obama to 'Bob the Builder'?

SPECIALIST SUBJECTS

WORDS AGAIN
1 Sleepers
2 Trombone
3 Sine qua non
4 Schadenfreude
5 Peninsula
6 Parkour
7 On your head
8 Head (it is between the ears)
9 Count things
10 A whip

BARACK OBAMA
1 Democrats
2 Robinson
3 Aretha Franklin
4 John McCain
5 Illinois
6 Hillary Clinton
7 Bruce Springsteen
8 Honolulu
9 Jon Favreau
10 Yes We Can!

MONEY

1 What preceded the Euro as the currency of France?

2 In Scotland, notes are issued by RBS, Bank of Scotland and ... which other institution?

3 Pre-decimalisation, how many shillings were there in the British Pound?

4 What currency would you use if shopping in Egypt?

5 The letters ZAR represent the currency of which country?

6 What is the currency used in the Vatican City?

7 The appearance of which motto on all US currency was made mandatory in 1955?

8 Which country uses a currency called the colón?

9 Which country reported an inflation rate of 9,030,000% in June 2008?

10 On British banknotes, if £10 are orange, £20 are purple, what colour are £50 notes?

SEINFELD

1 Who co-created 'Seinfeld' with Jerry Seinfeld?

2 In 'Seinfeld', what is Jerry's job?

3 Who played Elaine Benes in 'Seinfeld'?

4 According to Jerry Seinfeld, the idea first arose after the Season 3 episode 'The Pitch' that 'Seinfeld' was a show about ... what?

5 In 'Seinfeld', what is the name of Jerry and Kramer's vengeful neighbour who works as a postal carrier?

6 In a Season 8 episode of 'Seinfeld', what phrase does George's girlfriend use to gloss over parts of her stories?

7 In 'Seinfeld', what is Jerry's apartment number within 129 West 81st Street?

8 Appearing in 101 of the 180 episodes of 'Seinfeld', what is the name of the cashier at Monk's Café?

9 What character did Jason Alexander play in 'Seinfeld'?

10 What four-word phrase was used by the 'Seinfeld' creators to sum up the idea that the show must avoid sentimentality and moral lessons?

MONEY
1 Franc
2 Clydesdale Bank
3 20
4 Pound
5 South Africa
6 The Euro
7 In God We Trust
8 Costa Rica
9 Zimbabwe
10 Red

SEINFELD
1 Larry David
2 Stand-up comedian
3 Julia Louis-Dreyfus
4 Nothing
5 Newman
6 Yada Yada Yada
7 5A
8 Ruthie Cohen
9 George Costanza
10 No Hugging, No Learning

CLASSICAL AUTHORS

1 At the start of the 'Aeneid', the title character flees from which fallen city?

2 Plato's 'Apology' recounts the self-defence of which philosopher, charged with corruption and impiety?

3 The poet Sappho was from which island, Greece's third largest?

4 In which BBC comedy series did Willie Rushton play the comic playwright Plautus?

5 The mascot of which company is called Bibendum - a name taken from the line from a Horatian ode; "nunc est bibendum"?

6 'Eumenides' is the third play in which tragedian's trilogy, the 'Oresteia'?

7 The 'Satyricon' of Petronius contains a famous passage recounting which freedman's extravagant "Dinner"?

8 Which daughter of King Alcinous does Odysseus encounter in Book 6 of 'The Odyssey'?

9 Which Roman poet's surviving works include 'Epistulae Ex Ponto'?

10 Which great statesman and orator was ridiculed for the line of poetry; "O fortunatam natam me consule Romam"?

FLAGS

1 If a flag is a tricolore, how many coloured stripes does it have?

2 Which nation's flag contains a blue "Star of David" on a white background?

3 What colour is the Q-flag, or Quarantine flag?

4 What name, shared with a TV show, is given to a signal flag for the letter P, which is flown by a vessel about to leave port?

5 What is the name of a diagonal cross stretching from corner to corner of a flag?

6 The flag of Isle of Man has a red background and, at its centre, a figure with how many legs?

7 What does the dark blue background of the flag of Micronesia represent?

8 The flag of Puerto Rico resembles that of which other Caribbean island, but with the colours reversed?

9 Which country's flag has a Masai shield and two crossed spears at its centre?

10 Which country held a series of referendums on changing its flag in 2015 and 2016, before sticking with what it already had?

CLASSICAL AUTHORS
1 Troy
2 Socrates
3 Lesbos
4 Up Pompeii!
5 Michelin
6 Aeschylus
7 Trimalchio
8 Nausicaa
9 Ovid (It means "letters from the sea" and was written when he was in exile)
10 Cicero

FLAGS
1 Three
2 Israel
3 Yellow
4 Blue Peter
5 Saltire
6 Three
7 The Pacific Ocean (accept: ocean/sea)
8 Cuba
9 Kenya
10 New Zealand

DOLLY PARTON

1 What is the name of Dolly Parton's theme park in Tennessee which, disappointingly, is not open from nine to five?

2 Which Dolly Parton classic is about a red-headed bank clerk who flirted with the singer's husband?

3 In which 1989 drama, also starring Sally Field, Julia Roberts and Shirley MacLaine, did Dolly Parton play Truvy Jones?

4 In 1987, Dolly Parton released the album 'Trio', a collaboration with Emmylou Harris and which other singer?

5 What was the title of Dolly Parton's 1967 debut studio album? It is the same as the title of a well-known musical except with the word "I'm" in the middle.

6 Dolly Parton donated $1 million to research on which Covid-19 vaccine?

7 In 1983, Dolly Parton received a Golden Globe Best Actress nomination for her role in 'The Best Little Whorehouse in ..." where?

8 Which song written by Dolly Parton was a Number 1 for Whitney Houston in 1992?

9 At which UK festival did Dolly Parton play the "Legends Slot" in June 2014?

10 Clare Torry sang a Dolly Parton song as the theme for which British sitcom starring Wendy Craig and Nicholas Lyndhurst?

DECEMBER

1 In the chorus of the carol 'The First Nowell' how many times is the word "Noel" sung?

2 The Decembrist Uprising took place in December 1825 in which country?

3 On what number street was there a Miracle in December, according to the 1947 and 1994 movies?

4 Which saint's day is celebrated on 26th December in western Christianity?

5 December 1st is the date of an annual event dedicated to raising awareness of which health condition?

6 In 'The OC', what was the name for the Cohen family's joint Christian and Jewish December celebration?

7 Why was December 7th 1941 "a date which will live in infamy", according to Franklin D Roosevelt?

8 In which Leonard Cohen song is it "four in the morning, the end of December"?

9 On December 16 1965 what became the first song broadcast from space to Earth?

10 On 15th December 2020, Boris Johnson was pictured participating in, specifically, what kind of event at Downing Street?

SPECIALIST SUBJECTS

DOLLY PARTON
1 Dollywood
2 Jolene
3 Steel Magnolias
4 Linda Ronstadt
5 Hello I'm Dolly
6 Moderna
7 Texas
8 I Will Always Love You
9 Glastonbury
10 Butterflies (the song was 'Love is Like a Butterfly')

DECEMBER
1 Four (it's usually "Nowell" in the title and "Noel" in the lyrics)
2 Russia
3 34th Street
4 St Stephen
5 AIDS
6 Chrismukkah
7 Japan attacked Pearl Harbor
8 Famous Blue Raincoat
9 Jingle Bells
10 (Zoom) Quiz

SOMETHING ELSE

This is where we've let our hair down a little. Like the Specialist Subjects section, but just a little off-kilter, this is where you'll find round titles we hope you won't have seen anywhere else. Where the round requires special instructions, we'll give them.

Here are some of the rounds you'll find:

- Bad Ideas
- Classic British Chocolate Biscuits
- Doctors Doing Other Jobs
- Essex
- Famous Eggs
- Ladies & Tramps
- New Parenting
- People Being Unexpectedly Struck By Things
- Pirates
- Quite Good Footballers
- Songs About Jumping
- The Seaside
- Things That Get Smaller
- Trousers
- Wales & Whales
- Well-Known Bears

HAPPY DAYS

1 Stevie Wonder's 1981 track 'Happy Birthday' was written as a tribute to which civil rights leader?

2 Which spin-off from 'Happy Days' starred Robin Williams as an extraterrestrial?

3 Who is the lead singer and founder of the Happy Mondays?

4 Australian golfer Jason Day's first Major triumph was in 2015 - at which of the four Majors?

5 In the gospel song 'Oh Happy Day!' who, specifically, "washed my sins away"?

6 In what kind of institution is the 1950 British comedy film 'The Happiest Days of Our Lives' set?

7 "Happy days!" is a catchphrase often used by which former England left-arm spinner turned commentator and cricket media personality?

8 The International Day of Happiness is celebrated throughout the world on the 20th of which month?

9 In the 1977 'Happy Days' episode, 'Hollywood, Pt 3', what did the Fonz do after ascending a ramp while water skiing?

10 In which 1950 film, based on the musical 'No, No, Nanette', does Doris Day sing 'I Want to be Happy'?

LADIES AND TRAMPS

1 In films like 'City Lights' and 'Modern Times', which silent film star is best known for his "tramp" persona?

2 A painted lady is a colourful example of which type of insect?

3 In 'Lady and the Tramp', what breed of dog is Lady?

4 Claudia, aka Lady Bird, was the wife of which President of the USA?

5 In which novel does the tramp Magwitch encounter the boy Pip in a graveyard?

6 In the film 'Pal Joey' who plays Joey Evans and sings 'The Lady is a Tramp' to Vera Simpson, played by Rita Hayworth?

7 In which soap opera did Abi Branning find a dog called Tramp, which mated with another dog called Lady Di?

8 Lady Dimitrescu is a villainous character in which 2021 video game?

9 It was revealed in 2020 that Bob Dylan had written the song 'Lay Lady Lay' for which actress-singer?

10 Who wrote a book called 'The Lady in the Van' which was turned into a film?

HAPPY DAYS
1 Martin Luther King
2 Mork & Mindy
3 Shaun Ryder
4 (US) PGA Championship
5 Jesus
6 A school
7 Phil Tufnell
8 March
9 Jumped the shark (The phrase became synonymous with the moment a TV show started going downhill)
10 Tea for Two

LADIES AND TRAMPS
1 Charlie Chaplin
2 Butterfly
3 Cocker spaniel
4 Lyndon B Johnson
5 Great Expectations
6 Frank Sinatra
7 EastEnders
8 Resident Evil Village
9 Barbra Streisand
10 Alan Bennett

ANAGRAMS

In this round, there are five pairs of answers which are anagrams of each other.

1 Which actress has starred opposite Tom Hanks in four films, including 'Sleepless in Seattle' and 'You've Got Mail'?

2 Which day of the week was 'Blue' for New Order and 'Manic' for the Bangles?

3 Which city hosted the Summer Olympics in 1900 and 1924?

4 From the Greek for "power", which word was coined by Michael Faraday in 1831 for a type of electrical generator?

5 Which band, fronted by Jimmy Somerville, had a 1984 hit with 'Smalltown Boy'?

6 What is the most populous member state of the European Union?

7 The order Psittaciformes is made up of which birds?

8 Which card game is also known as "Concentration" or "Pelmanism"?

9 What is the name of Toronto's NBA team?

10 Which actress, sister of Ted, mother of Emily Atack and cousin of Paul McCartney, wrote the original theme to the TV show 'Surprise, Surprise'?

POP DUOS

1 Sonny Bono was in a pop duo with his future wife. Who is she?

2 Which rap duo split their album between each member with 'Speakerboxx/The Love Below'?

3 What name goes, in different duos, with Ansel Collins, Sam and Chas?

4 Which rock duo was a formerly married couple called Jack and Meg?

5 In which song did Paul Simon use an old nickname for Art Garfunkel to sing "Tom, get your plane ride on time"?

6 'Hippy Chick' was a hit for which duo, named after an area in central London (and in New York)?

7 Glenn and Chris had a 1987 hit with 'Diamond Lights'. What were their rhyming surnames?

8 What was the first name of Kim Appleby's sister, who died in 1990?

9 Vince Clarke found Andy Bell, his partner in Erasure, by putting an ad in which music publication?

10 Which future comedy star was in the 80s new wave duo Seona Dancing?

ANAGRAMS
1 Meg Ryan
2 Monday
3 Paris
4 Dynamo
5 Bronski Beat
6 Germany
7 Parrots
8 Pairs
9 Raptors
10 Kate Robbins

POP DUOS
1 Cher
2 OutKast
3 Dave
4 The White Stripes
5 The Only Living Boy in New York
6 Soho
7 Hoddle and Waddle
8 Mel
9 Melody Maker
10 Ricky Gervais

QUITE GOOD FOOTBALLERS

1 What was the first name of French footballer Joel Cantona's much more successful older brother?

2 Which presenter of 'The Chase' and 'Cash Trapped' was a professional at Brentford FC, though he never played for the first team?

3 Gordon Ramsay was, as a teenager, a trialist with which major Glasgow football club?

4 In 1996, a Senegalese footballer managed to play once for Southampton by convincing manager Graeme Souness that he was the cousin of which Liberian footballing superstar?

5 One Direction's Louis Tomlinson played for which Yorkshire club's reserve team in February 2014?

6 Which English cricketing legend played 11 professional football matches for Scunthorpe United in the 70s and 80s?

7 Who played around 100 games in Portuguese lower league football before taking his first managerial role at Benfica in 2000?

8 After retiring from athletics, Usain Bolt played some friendlies for Central Coast Mariners, a football team in which country?

9 Daley Thompson, who played reserve team football for Mansfield Town, was twice Olympic champion at which athletics event?

10 What name links a defender who played 45 times for England and a TV personality who played twice for Crawley Town? [we want first name and surname]

NO VOWELS

None of the answers contain the vowels a,e,i,o,u.

1 Which word in a title links songs by George Gershwin, Janet Jackson, Snap!, Jason Donovan and Rod Stewart?

2 What is the surname of the pizza delivery boy who is the main character in the TV series 'Futurama'?

3 Which single reached Number 2 in the UK charts for Crash Test Dummies in late 1993?

4 What was the short, questioning title of the board game which was based on the TV series 'Alfred Hitchcock Presents'?

5 In the New Testament, which incense did the Magi present to the infant Christ, along with Frankincense and Gold?

6 Which role in the James Bond films links Desmond Llewellyn and Ben Whishaw?

7 What links a UK snack maker with the nickname of an England cricketer who made his debut in the 2005 Ashes?

8 Ted Turner founded which new channel in 1980?

9 Which medium-sized big cat has a Eurasian, Canada and Iberian species?

10 By what three-letter initialism was the US President from 1933 from 1945 commonly known?

QUITE GOOD FOOTBALLERS
1 Eric
2 Bradley Walsh
3 Rangers
4 George Weah (the player was called Ali Dia)
5 Doncaster Rovers
6 Ian Botham
7 José Mourinho
8 Australia
9 Decathlon
10 Mark Wright

NO VOWELS
1 Rhythm
2 Fry
3 Mmm Mmm Mmm Mmm
4 Why
5 Myrrh
6 Q
7 KP
8 CNN
9 Lynx
10 FDR (Franklin D Roosevelt)

THE SEASIDE

1 What does she sell by the seashore, according to the tongue twister?

2 Which chain has holiday resorts at Minehead, Bognor Regis and Skegness, amongst other places?

3 Coney Island is a seaside resort within which New York borough?

4 What is The Big One, which opened in Blackpool in 1994?

5 In the UK, a flag indicating an area is overseen by lifeguards is made up of which two colours?

6 Who played CJ Parker in 'Baywatch'?

7 'Faded Seaside Glamour', containing the singles 'Nearer than Heaven' and 'Long Time Coming', was the debut album by which British band?

8 Which birds will be over the White Cliffs of Dover, in the famous song?

9 'Surf's Up', 'Surfer Girl' and 'Surfin' USA' are songs by which band?

10 What is the name of the beach town which is the setting for 'Jaws'?

TROUSERS

1 In the UK, they call them trousers. In the US, they are more usually called … what?

2 'The Wrong Trousers' was a 1993 animation, created by Nick Park, featuring Wallace and his dog. What is the dog's name?

3 What style of trouser, popular in the 1950s, got their name because they were originally worn by cyclists?

4 'Baggy Trousers' was a massive hit for which London band?

5 What C is the type of smart casual trousers that take their name from the Italian cloth from which they are made?

6 Which fictional street's No 30 was for several years known as the House of Trouser?

7 Which band was famous in the 1970s for their ankle-length tartan trousers?

8 In which French town was the material of blue jeans invented?

9 The word "dungarees" has come into the English language from its original use in which country?

10 Plus Fours are distinctive trousers associated with which sport?

THE SEASIDE
1 Seashells
2 Butlin's
3 Brooklyn
4 A rollercoaster
5 Red and yellow
6 Pamela Anderson
7 Delays
8 Bluebirds
9 Beach Boys
10 Amity Island

TROUSERS
1 Pants
2 Gromit
3 Pedal Pushers
4 Madness
5 Chinos
6 Ramsay Street (in 'Neighbours')
7 Bay City Rollers
8 Nîmes (De Nîmes)
9 India
10 Golf

TALL SUPPORTING CHARACTERS

1 In which comedy did Stephen Merchant play "the Oggmonster"?

2 Which comic actress, who had her own extremely successful sitcom, played Barbara in 'Not Going Out'?

3 In 'Creed 2', Dolph Lundgren returned to the role he played in 'Rocky IV' – what was the name of his character?

4 Jaws appears in two James Bond films – 'The Spy Who Loved Me' and which other?

5 Ken Cosgrove is an account executive for Sterling Cooper in which American TV series?

6 In 'Game of Thrones', Brienne, played by Gwendoline Christie, is from which island?

7 Who played Nearly Headless Nick in 'Harry Potter and the Philosopher's Stone'?

8 In 'Parks and Recreation', what is the first name of Jean-Ralphio Saperstein's sister, played by Jenny Slate?

9 In which 'Star Wars' spin-off film does Phoebe Waller-Bridge play the android L3-37?

10 Who does Slim Charles shoot in the final episode of 'The Wire?

ALL RHYMES

All the answers rhyme with each other.

1 Which part of the body contains the larynx and the pharynx?

2 Duster, Chesterfield and Trench are types of which item of clothing?

3 In the witch trials of the 17th century, when a woman was dunked in water, if she were truly a witch, it was thought that she would ... what?

4 In the 1975 film 'Jaws', Chief Martin Brody famously says "You're gonna need a bigger ..." what?

5 What is the common name for the animal also known as an ermine?

6 Which British bookmaker, with its headquarters in Wigan, is known in rhyming slang as "the nanny"?

7 In France, "chèvre" refers to cheese that comes from which animal?

8 What was the supermini hatchback produced by Nissan which ceased UK production in 2017?

9 What was the name of the now-defunct English coin which was worth four pence?

10 What was the title of a 1993 single by Chaka Demus and Pliers which took its name from a detective series starring Angela Lansbury?

TALL SUPPORTING CHARACTERS
1 The Office
2 Miranda Hart
3 Ivan Drago
4 Moonraker
5 Mad Men
6 Tarth
7 John Cleese
8 Mona-Lisa
9 Solo: A Star Wars Story
10 Cheese (Wagstaff)

ALL RHYMES
1 Throat
2 Coat
3 Float
4 Boat
5 Stoat
6 The Tote (nanny goat = Tote)
7 Goat
8 Note
9 Groat
10 Murder She Wrote

CLASSIC BRITISH CHOCOLATE BISCUITS

1 Complete the following phrase : "If you like a lot of chocolate on your biscuit, ..."?

2 Which chocolate biscuit made by Fox's shared its name with a boxing film franchise starring Sylvester Stallone?

3 What was a "chocolatey biscuit with a toffee taste too"?

4 What biscuit, produced by Asda, was accused by McVitie's of cashing in on the 'Penguin' brand?

5 "You can't sing. You can't play. You look awful ... You'll go a long way." An 80s ad for ...?

6 How many layers of caramel are there in a Tunnock's Caramel wafer?

7 The chocolate version of which oaty classic became available in the UK in 1987?

8 What was a Twix called in France through the 1980s?

9 A Taxi contained chocolate cream, caramel and which other key element, all covered in chocolate?

10 Which writer called the chocolate digestive a "British masterpiece" in 'Notes From a Small Island'?

DRESSES

1 What does LBD stand for, as in the name of an iconic dress designed by Coco Chanel?

2 The dress Björk wore to the 2001 Oscars was made to look like which bird?

3 By whom is the children's novel 'The Boy in the Dress'?

4 Who wore a Union Jack minidress onstage at the 1997 Brit Awards?

5 Kleinfeld Bridal in New York is the site for the original version of which TV series?

6 Which film star wore an iconic halter dress in 'The Seven-Year Itch'?

7 Which fashion company made the black dress, held together by safety pins, that Elizabeth Hurley wore to the 'Four Weddings and a Funeral' premiere?

8 In 2015, a viral phenomenon made online viewers unsure whether a certain dress was black and blue, or ... what other pair of colours?

9 Sarah Burton designed whose wedding dress for 29th April 2011?

10 'White Dress' was the opening track on whose 2021 album 'Chemtrails Over the Country Club'?

CLASSIC BRITISH CHOCOLATE BISCUITS
1 Join our Club
2 Rocky
3 Trio
4 Puffin
5 KitKat
6 Four
7 Hobnob
8 Raider
9 Wafer
10 Bill Bryson

DRESSES
1 Little Black Dress
2 Swan
3 David Walliams
4 Geri Halliwell/Horner (Ginger Spice)
5 Say Yes to the Dress
6 Marilyn Monroe
7 Versace
8 White and gold
9 Kate Middleton/Duchess of Cambridge
10 Lana Del Rey

ORANGES, LEMONS, BELLS, SAINTS, CLEMENTS

1 Adam Brody, Rachel Bilson and Mischa Barton were among the stars of which TV show set in Orange County, California?

2 Jason Orange is a former member of which successful band?

3 Liz Lemon, played by Tina Fey, was a character in which American comedy series?

4 "Difficult difficult lemon difficult" is a phrase used in which film, a spin-off of the TV series 'The Thick of It'?

5 Scientist Alexander Graham Bell was born in which city in 1847?

6 The Liberty Bell is located in which American city?

7 Former footballer Ian St John and his TV partner Jimmy Greaves both died in which year?

8 In which city is the NFL team named after the song 'When the Saints Go Marching In' based?

9 Clement Attlee was leader of the UK Labour Party for how many decades?

10 As well as being one-half of 'Flight of the Conchords', Jemaine Clement voiced the giant crab Tamatoa in which Disney film?

SLEEP

1 Derived from Middle English, what L is a soothing song designed to get a child to sleep?

2 In which musical was Wayne Sleep the first person to play Mr Mistofelees?

3 In the UK, a speed bump is colloquially known as a sleeping ... what?

4 In the names of the "Seven Dwarfs", only one comes after Sleepy in the alphabet. Which one?

5 The "Night Riviera" is a sleeper service that runs from Paddington to which station in Cornwall?

6 Who had a UK hit in 1978 with 'Talking in Your Sleep'?

7 Oneirology is the scientific study of which aspect of sleep?

8 What are the opening six words of the Shakespeare soliloquy that contains the phrase "to sleep, perchance to dream"?

9 Which Frenchman directed the 2006 film 'The Science of Sleep'?

10 By what S is somnambulism better known?

ORANGES, LEMONS, BELLS, SAINTS, CLEMENTS
1 The OC
2 Take That
3 30 Rock
4 In the Loop
5 Edinburgh
6 Philadelphia
7 2021
8 New Orleans
9 Two (for twenty years)
10 Moana

SLEEP
1 Lullaby
2 Cats
3 Policeman
4 Sneezy
5 Penzance
6 Crystal Gayle
7 Dreams
8 To be or not to be
9 Michel Gondry
10 Sleepwalking

SUFFRAGETTE CITY

1 In which British city was the suffragette leader Emmeline Pankhurst born in 1858?

2 The song 'Suffragette City' originally appears on which David Bowie album?

3 Emily Davison died jumping in front of the king's horse Anmer, during which horse race?

4 Emmeline Pankhurst was imprisoned in 1913 after an explosive device went off in an unoccupied house being built for which politician?

5 In 1893, what became the first self-governing country in the world to give all women the right to vote in parliamentary elections?

6 In which musical does Winifred Banks sing 'Sister Suffragette'?

7 Founded by Catherine Mayer and Sandi Toksvig, what does WEP stand for, in the name of a modern political party?

8 Who stars as Maud Watts in the 2015 film 'Suffragette'?

9 Which British suffragette leader was nicknamed "The General"?

10 Which British newspaper first used the term "suffragettes" rather than "suffragists" to describe Emmeline Pankhurst's group?

THINGS THAT GET SMALLER

1 The European Union shrunk for the first time when which country withdrew its membership on 31st January 2020?

2 Between 2016 and 2018, which Swiss chocolate bar outraged consumers by increasing the space between its triangles to make it smaller, before reverting to its original shape?

3 Which iconic 2300km long ecosystem off the coast of Australia has been shrinking for several years due to the effects of climate change?

4 In a famous children's book, who shrinks when she drinks from a bottle labelled "Drink me"?

5 In feet, how much less wide is a tennis singles court than a doubles court?

6 Which 2017 Matt Damon comedy takes its name from a term used in business for reducing a workforce?

7 "Deflategate" was a major NFL controversy involving which New England Patriots quarterback?

8 Which Trinidadian-British author's novel 'In a Free State' was republished in 2011 with only its central narrative, not its framing short stories?

9 The 1984 cinematic release of which gangster epic was cut down by US distributors to 139 minutes, a full hour and a half shorter than the version desired by director Sergio Leone?

10 Boxer Billy Joe Saunders had to accept a smaller ring than he wanted for his May 2021 fight with which Mexican pound-for-pound great?

SUFFRAGETTE CITY
1 Manchester
2 The Rise and Fall of Ziggy Stardust and the Spiders from Mars
3 Epsom Derby
4 David Lloyd George
5 New Zealand
6 Mary Poppins
7 Women's Equality Party
8 Carey Mulligan
9 Flora Drummond
10 The Daily Mail

THINGS THAT GET SMALLER
1 United Kingdom
2 Toblerone
3 Great Barrier Reef
4 Alice (in Wonderland)
5 9 feet (each tramline is 4.5 feet wide)
6 Downsizing
7 Tom Brady
8 VS Naipaul
9 Once Upon a Time in America
10 Saul "Canelo" Alvarez

TWINS

1 In which band did twins Matt and Luke Goss come to fame in the late 80s?

2 Who, in Roman myth, was the brother of Romulus?

3 Of the three sporting Neville siblings, one is not a twin. Which?

4 What is the Latin word for twins?

5 What M is the scientific term for siblings who are commonly called "identical" twins?

6 Which Shakespeare play features the twins Viola and Sebastian?

7 What is the name of the 'twin city' in Minnesota that is not Minneapolis?

8 Which fictional character has a pair of sisters called Patty and Selma?

9 Which diminutive actor starred opposite Arnold Schwarzenegger in the comedy film 'Twins'?

10 In which sport have twins Bob and Mike Bryan enjoyed enormous success together?

TWO-LETTER ANSWERS

Each answer is just two letters.

1 Which title links a Lindsay Anderson film, a Bluetones song, and a Rudyard Kipling poem?

2 What was the first Pixar film to receive an Oscar nomination for Best Picture?

3 What is the ISO country code for Switzerland, based on its formal Latin name?

4 What is the short catchphrase of the housemates in Russell T. Davies's TV drama 'It's a Sin'?

5 What is the word for "and" in Latin and in French?

6 Which Peter Gabriel album contains 'Sledgehammer', 'Don't Give Up' and 'Big Time'?

7 Which "Day" in 1945 is celebrated on 15th August each year?

8 Which dessert-making company, noted for its glass ramekins, was founded in 2003 by James Averdieck?

9 What is the title of a 2014 book by David Nicholls and a 2019 horror film directed by Jordan Peele?

10 What is the chemical symbol for Manganese?

TWINS

1 Bros
2 Remus
3 Gary (Tracey and Phil are twins)
4 Gemini
5 Monozygotic
6 Twelfth Night
7 Saint Paul
8 Marge Simpson
9 Danny DeVito
10 Tennis (One plays left-handed, one plays right-handed)

TWO-LETTER ANSWERS

1 If
2 Up
3 CH (Confoederatio Helvetica)
4 La
5 Et
6 So
7 V–J (Day) (Victory in Japan)
8 Gü
9 Us
10 Mn (Magnesium is Mg)

BAD IDEAS

1 On which show have businesspeople like Deborah Meaden, Tej Lalvani and Peter Jones famously responded to bad ideas by saying "I'm out"?

2 Which British jeweller disastrously described his own merchandise as "crap" in 1991?

3 Baldrick was famous for his cunning plans - who was his slightly more cunning boss?

4 What was the name of the Sinclair battery electric vehicle which bombed on its 1985 UK release?

5 Who included the song 'Bad Idea' on her 2019 album 'Thank U, Next'?

6 Which musical by Robert Lopez, Jeff Marx and Jeff Whitty features puppet characters called the Bad Idea Bears?

7 How many shots did Jean Van de Velde take on the 18th hole at Carnoustie in the 1999 British Open?

8 Which amateur sailor died during his disastrous attempt at the 1968-9 Golden Globe Race?

9 In which month of 2007 did Gordon Brown issue a statement ruling out a snap general election?

10 Which member of the British royal family sat down for an interview with the BBC's Emily Maitlis on 16th November 2019?

CHEESE OF THE WORLD

1 Mozzarella and parmesan are cheeses from which country?

2 Gouda cheese comes from the milk of which animal?

3 Which cheese is an ingredient in a traditional Greek salad?

4 What colour wax is the Babybel packaging famous for?

5 What F is the Italian for cheese?

6 Complete the 90s advertising slogan: 'Du pain, du vin, ...'?

7 "Saag paneer" is a common Indian dish which combines paneer cheese with which foodstuff?

8 Which country does Havarti cheese come from?

9 Pantysgawn and Caerphilly are cheeses from which country of the UK?

10 Which cheese, produced in the town of Hawes, can be Blue, Smoked, Mature or Real Yorkshire?

BAD IDEAS
1 Dragon's Den
2 Gerald Ratner
3 Blackadder
4 C5
5 Ariana Grande
6 Avenue Q
7 Seven
8 Donald Crowhurst
9 October
10 Prince Andrew

CHEESE OF THE WORLD
1 Italy
2 Cow
3 Feta
4 Red
5 Formaggio
6 Du Boursin
7 Spinach
8 Denmark
9 Wales
10 Wensleydale

ACROSTIC 1

In this round, if you take the first letter of each answer, it will spell out something relevant to getting them all right.

1 What name, according to legend, did Saul of Tarsus take after his conversion on the road to Damascus?

2 Which university in Devon was attended by the likes of Sajid Javid, Thom Yorke and JK Rowling?

3 Which American fashion designer, whose birth surname was Lifshitz, had a cameo as himself in 'Friends'? [give full name]

4 What is the word for a strawberry in Italian?

5 What physical features of the colossal squid are, at 27cm in diameter, believed to be the largest of any living creature?

6 What is the name of the album released by Drake in September 2021?

7 Which word links a coastal village in northern Scotland with a muscle of the human body attached at only one end?

8 What common expression in Arabic means "God willing"? [any spelling allowed]

9 What, specifically, was the profession of Stephen Ward, who was heavily involved in 1963's Profumo Affair?

10 Which TV chef's pronunciation of the word "Microwave" sent Twitter into a spin in 2020?

MINISTERIAL RESIGNATIONS

1 Gordon Brown took over as British Prime Minister on whose resignation?

2 Who resigned as the UK's International Development Secretary in 2017 following a scandal over meetings with Israeli ministers, though she would later be appointed Home Secretary?

3 The cabinet minister John Profumo resigned after having an affair with whom?

4 Which Cabinet position was held by Geoffrey Howe when he resigned in 1990?

5 When a British minister resigns they are said to apply for stewardship of what?

6 Which health secretary resigned in 2021 after revelations about his affair with a colleague?

7 Which parliamentary scandal caused several British cabinet ministers to resign in 2009?

8 Which Labour minister resigned twice from the UK government between 1998 and 2001?

9 From which British ministerial position did Geoff Hoon resign on 5 June 2009?

10 Who resigned as Education Secretary in 2002 because she did not feel she was up to the job?

ACROSTIC 1

1 Paul (In fact it is more likely he used both names all along)
2 Exeter
3 Ralph Lauren
4 Fragola
5 Eyes
6 Certified Lover Boy
7 Tongue
8 In sha'Allah/Inshallah
9 Osteopath
10 Nigella Lawson (Mee-crow-wah-vay)

MINISTERIAL RESIGNATIONS

1 Tony Blair
2 Priti Patel
3 Christine Keeler
4 Deputy Prime Minister (ALSO Lord President of the Council, and Leader of the House of Commons)
5 Chiltern Hundreds (OR Manor of Northstead)
6 Matt Hancock
7 Expense claims
8 Peter Mandelson
9 Transport Secretary
10 Estelle Morris

RHYME TIME

There are five pairs of answers - distributed haphazardly throughout the round - that (loosely or exactly) rhyme.

1 Which word from Yiddish, which is now a loanword in (particularly American) English means "a person of honour and integrity"?

2 East Thrace is the European part of which country?

3 Which NFL team, which plays at the MetLife Stadium, won their only Super Bowl in 1969?

4 Which Major League Baseball team played their home games at Shea Stadium from 1964 to 2008?

5 Which fish has the Latin name Tinca tinca and is also known as the doctor fish?

6 Which word goes before "Books" in the name of Stormzy's publishing imprint?

7 Which six-time married American author wrote 'The Executioner's Song' and 'The Fight'?

8 What sporting item would you usually find precisely 7 ft 9 ¼ inches from a wall?

9 What nickname links real-life boxers named Fielding, Graziano and Marciano?

10 What are the next two words of a nursery rhyme that starts "Tinker Tailor"?

HERBS AND SPICES

1 Saffron is derived from which flower?

2 Which spice shares its name with a move in football where you collect the ball after putting it through an opponent's legs?

3 Which duo's third studio album was called 'Parsley, Sage, Rosemary and Thyme'?

4 In the USA it is known as cilantro - how is it known in the UK?

5 Which spicy green paste, commonly used in Japanese cuisine, is also known as Japanese horseradish?

6 Which of the Spice Girls never had a UK Number 1 single outside the group?

7 Which brass instrument did the American bandleader Herb Albert primarily play?

8 Which nationality goes after "Fenu" in the name of a fragrant herb?

9 Often eaten at Christmas, what B is the sauce made with milk, onions, crumbs, butter, nutmeg and cloves?

10 The official twitter account for which brand only follows 11 other accounts on twitter, namely the five original members of The Spice Girls, and six gentlemen all named Herb?

RHYME TIME
1 Mensch
2 Turkey (now officially "The Republic of Türkiye")
3 New York Jets
4 New York Mets
5 Tench
6 Merky
7 Norman Mailer
8 Oche
9 Rocky
10 Soldier Sailor

HERBS AND SPICES
1 Crocus (commonly known as the saffron crocus)
2 Nutmeg
3 Simon and Garfunkel
4 Coriander
5 Wasabi
6 Victoria Beckham (her highest chart entry was Number 2)
7 Trumpet
8 Greek (Fenugreek)
9 Bread sauce
10 KFC (11 Herbs and Spices)

RICH PEOPLE

1 Floyd Mayweather Jr, nicknamed "Money", was the best paid sportsperson in the world between 2010 and 2019. In which sport did he make his name?

2 What was the first name of the man who founded the Ford Motor Company?

3 Which king of Lydia, who reigned for around 40 years in the 6th century BC, is renowned for his great wealth?

4 Which child star played the world's richest boy, Richie Rich, in a 1994 film?

5 In the gospel of Matthew, Jesus says that it is easier for WHAT to go through the eye of a needle than for a rich person to enter the kingdom of heaven?

6 Liliane Bettencourt, one of the richest women to have ever lived, was the principal shareholder in which French cosmetics company?

7 Which comedian created the character "Loadsamoney"?

8 What did the D in John D Rockefeller (considered the richest person in modern history) stand for?

9 In which US state did Jeff Bezos found Amazon in 1994?

10 Which rapper who released the album 'Get Rich Or Die Tryin'' declared bankruptcy in 2015?

FAMOUS EGGS

1 A hard-boiled egg wrapped in sausage meat and coated in breadcrumbs is known as what S?

2 A question often posed is "Which came first, the WHAT or the egg"?

3 Who included the unfortunate egg Humpty-Dumpty in their book 'Through the Looking-Glass'?

4 What was the surname of the Russian jeweller Peter Carl, who lived from 1846 to 1920, famous for his ornate eggs?

5 At what time of year do people traditionally roll eggs down Arthur's Seat in Edinburgh?

6 Egg, played by Andrew Lincoln, was a lead character in which iconic 90s drama?

7 Which Beatles classic started life in Paul McCartney's head as 'Scrambled Eggs'?

8 Which 'Egghead', born in Winchester in 1959 and considered one of the greatest quizzers of all time, won 'Mastermind' in 1995?

9 What was the first name of the famous Victorian artist, born in 1816, Mr Egg?

10 Which sauce tops up the dish Eggs Benedict?

RICH PEOPLE
1 Boxing
2 Henry (Ford)
3 Croesus
4 Macauley Culkin
5 Camel
6 L'Oréal
7 Harry Enfield
8 Davison
9 Washington
10 50 Cent

FAMOUS EGGS
1 Scotch Egg
2 Chicken
3 Lewis Carroll
4 Fabergé
5 Easter
6 This Life
7 Yesterday
8 Kevin Ashman
9 Augustus
10 Hollandaise

THE ANSWER'S A QUESTION?

Each answer is a question, isn't it?

1 What is Bugs Bunny's catchphrase and a 1972 film directed by Peter Bogdanovich?

2 Martin Handford created which hugely successful series of puzzle books featuring a character wearing red and white, who has a slightly different name in the USA?

3 The standard "appeal" in cricket is an abbreviated question. As what six-letter word is it usually expressed?

4 The KLF had a 1991 Number 1 single with '3 a.m. Eternal'. What was the name of their previous single?

5 What title links Top 10 hits for Annie Lennox, Carly Simon and Anthony Newley?

6 Which 1962 film starred Bette Davis and Joan Crawford as Jane and Blanche Hudson?

7 Which song, a 1968 hit for Dionne Warwick, was inspired by the place Hal David was stationed when he was in the US Navy?

8 In 'Dirty Harry', Harry Callahan says "You've got to ask yourself one question ...". What are the next four words?

9 Also known as 'In the Pines', Nirvana covered which blues track by Leadbelly on their 'MTV Unplugged in New York' album?

10 In 'The Fast Show' what is, along with "How queer!", the catchphrase of old school comedian Arthur Atkinson?

WELSH CASTLES

1 Whose investiture took place at Caernarfon Castle on 1st July 1969?

2 In 2020, the 20th series of which UK TV series was held at Gwrych Castle near Abergele?

3 Which renowned patriotic song was written about a seven-year siege during the Wars of the Roses at a castle in northwest Wales?

4 In which town, also famous for cheese, is the largest castle in Wales?

5 Chepstow Castle overlooks which river?

6 Considered one of the most perfect 13th century examples of symmetrical design, Beaumaris Castle is on which island?

7 The first National Eisteddfod of Wales is thought to have been held by the Lord Rhys at which castle overlooking the River Teifi in 1176?

8 In the 13th century, which English king instigated the "Iron Ring" of castles in northwest Wales? [name and regnal number required]

9 John Crichton-Stuart, who oversaw extensive renovations to Cardiff Castle in the 19th century, was the 3rd Marquess of ... where?

10 In 1189, King Richard I gifted Pembroke Castle to which Anglo-Norman soldier and statesman?

THE ANSWER'S A QUESTION?
1 What's Up Doc?
2 Where's Wally?/Where's Waldo?
3 Howzat (short for "How is that?")
4 What Time is Love?
5 Why?
6 Whatever Happened to Baby Jane?
7 Do You Know the Way to San Jose?
8 Do I feel lucky? (then "Well, do you, punk?")
9 Where Did You Sleep Last Night?
10 Where's me washboard?

WELSH CASTLES
1 Prince Charles/Prince of Wales
2 I'm a Celebrity... Get Me Out of Here
3 Men of Harlech
4 Caerphilly
5 Wye
6 Anglesey
7 Cardigan Castle
8 Edward I
9 Bute
10 William Marshal (accept: Earl of Pembroke)

A OR B

You've got a 50/50 choice on each of these questions.

1 Which day of the week has more letters in French – A) Thursday or B) Friday?

2 Which continent has the most independent countries – A) Asia or B) Africa?

3 True or False? The all-time top goalscorer for the Papua New Guinea national women's football team is named Margaret Thatcher.

4 Which has been an official royal residence longer – A) Buckingham Palace or B) Windsor Castle?

5 True or False? The letters in the chemical formula for sodium citrate, the secret ingredient that gives nacho cheese its smooth, creaminess, spells out NACHO.

6 Which newspaper did Lord Salisbury describe as written "by office boys for office boys" – A) the Daily Express or B) the Daily Mail?

7 Who has had more UK Number 1 singles – A) Michael Jackson or B) Prince?

8 Who scored more goals for Brazil – A) Ronaldo or B) Ronaldinho?

9 Are there more episodes of A) Cheers or B) Frasier?

10 True or False? The battleship USS Phoenix, which survived Pearl Harbor undamaged, was later sold by the USA to Argentina and ended up as the General Belgrano, famously sunk in the Falklands War.

APPLES

1 A person will describe someone they love as the "apple of my …" what?

2 Which type of apple shares its name with a cocktail and with the likes of Rizzo and Frenchy in 'Grease'?

3 Along with Steve Wozniak and Ronald Wayne, who founded Apple Inc. in 1976?

4 In which 1998 film does the title character, played by Matt Damon, ask a love rival "Do you like apples?"?

5 Apple bobbing is an activity particularly associated with which October celebration?

6 What is the title of the acclaimed 2020 album released by Fiona Apple?

7 Which "apple" is also known as the laryngeal prominence?

8 In Cockney rhyming slang, "apples and pears" mean what?

9 The apple tree which is said to have inspired Sir Isaac Newton to formulate his law of universal gravitation is near Grantham, in which English county?

10 'Cider with Rosie' is a novel by which Gloucestershire author?

A OR B

1 B) Friday (Vendredi vs Jeudi)
2 B) Africa (has 54, Asia has 48)
3 False
4 B) Windsor Castle (by a long way)
5 True (Na3C6H5O7)
6 B) Daily Mail
7 A) Michael Jackson
8 A) Ronaldo (62 to 33)
9 A) Cheers (270 to 264)
10 True

APPLES

1 Eye
2 Pink Lady
3 Steve Jobs
4 Good Will Hunting
5 Halloween
6 Fetch the Bolt Cutters
7 Adam's Apple
8 Stairs
9 Lincolnshire
10 Laurie Lee

CHEEKS AND CHEEKIES

1 Which restaurant chain, founded in South Africa, is particularly associated with the adjective "cheeky"?

2 Which British rapper's 2009 album, which included the hit song 'Bonkers', was called 'Tongue n' Cheek'?

3 Cheeky Girl Gabriela Irimia was once engaged to which former Liberal Democrat MP?

4 According to Jesus in 'The Sermon on the Mount', what should you do if someone strikes you on the cheek?

5 What is the first word in the lyrics of the classic Irving Berlin song 'Cheek to Cheek'?

6 Which London club did footballer Ruben Loftus-Cheek play for, on loan, in the 2020-21 Premier League season?

7 A cocktail combining Blue WKD and ruby port is known as a Cheeky ... what?

8 Cheek by Jowl is a theatre company founded in 1981 by which director (whose name is similar to a member of a famous double act)?

9 The American actress Molly Cheek played Jim Levenstein's mother in which series of comedy films?

10 Txiki Begiristain became Director of Football at which club in 2012?

INTERESTING WORDS

1 What S is a word that describes the right-hand side of a boat?

2 What is the main area of expertise of a sommelier?

3 What was the short-lived name of the rebranded Post Office from 2000 until 2002?

4 Which word is used for the jail on a naval ship and is also a type of two-masted boat?

5 At American universities, what name is given to the female equivalent of a fraternity?

6 The words banshee and smithereens originate from which European language?

7 What is a "sgian-dubh", a ceremonial item that is tucked inside a Scotsman's sock?

8 What would you spend a lot of time doing if you were a rhinotillexomaniac?

9 Aibohphobia is a term coined to describe an irrational fear of what type of word play?

10 "Hippopotomonstrosesquipedalio-phobia" has been suggested as the name for a fear of what?

CHEEKS AND CHEEKIES
1 Nando's
2 Dizzee Rascal
3 Lembit Öpik
4 Turn to him the other also (accept: Turn the other cheek)
5 Heaven (Heaven, I'm in heaven ...)
6 Fulham
7 Vimto
8 Declan Donnellan
9 American Pie
10 Manchester City

INTERESTING WORDS
1 Starboard
2 Wine
3 Consignia
4 Brig
5 Sorority
6 Irish (accept: Gaelic)
7 A knife
8 Picking your nose
9 Palindromes (The word itself is a palindrome)
10 Long words

ESSEX

1 What short word did the narrator of 'The Only Way is Essex' add to her name when she was a teenager?

2 'Essex Dogs' was a track on the eponymous 1997 album by which band, whose frontman grew up in Colchester?

3 What was the surname of the Essex cricketer who captained England from 1989 to 1993?

4 The flag of Essex has three of what on it?

5 Which Essex-born footballer and manager received an A* in GCSE Latin at Brentwood school?

6 In which Essex city is the longest pleasure pier in the world, stretching over 2 km?

7 Which star of 'The Only Way is Essex' released a single (which didn't chart) called 'Reem' in 2011?

8 On the Central Line, between Hainault and Chigwell, is which tube station, sharing its name with a famous fictional school?

9 Which island on the east coast of Essex derives its name from words meaning "bird headland"?

10 Which son of Essex, born David Cook, played Che in the original West End production of 'Evita'?

LONELINESS

1 Which US state is known as the Lone Star State?

2 What word links a Bond girl played by Jane Seymour and "the only game in town", according to Neil Sedaka?

3 In a famous poem, when William Wordsworth "wandered lonely as a cloud", which flowers did he see?

4 Lonesome George, who died in 2012, was the last known individual of a species of which animal? [you don't need to be too specific]

5 Point Nemo, the location on Earth furthest from land, is in which ocean?

6 Who designed the cover of the Beatles album 'Sgt Pepper's Lonely Hearts Club Band'?

7 In the 5th century AD, Symeon the Stylite spent 37 years in which solitary location?

8 Which composer's 'Ode to Joy' was the most common choice for castaways in the first 60 years of 'Desert Island Discs'?

9 'The Lonely Londoners' is an influential 1956 novel by which Trinidad-born writer?

10 In which 1976 film does Travis Bickle describe himself as "God's lonely man"?

ESSEX
1 Van (she was originally Denise Outen)
2 Blur
3 Gooch (not Cook or Hussain)
4 Cutlasses/seaxes/swords
5 Frank Lampard
6 Southend-on-Sea
7 Joey Essex
8 Grange Hill
9 Foulness
10 David Essex

LONELINESS
1 Texas
2 Solitaire
3 Daffodils (A crowd/a host, of golden daffodils)
4 Tortoise (he was the last known Pinta Island tortoise)
5 (South) Pacific
6 Peter Blake
7 On top of a pillar
8 Ludwig van Beethoven
9 Sam Selvon
10 Taxi Driver

QUOTE UNQUOTE

1 In which European city did John F Kennedy proclaim "Ich bin ein Berliner"?

2 While stinging "like a bee", Muhammad Ali also floated "like a ..." what?

3 Which of The Beatles controversially said "We're more popular than Jesus now"?

4 Which British Prime Minister famously said "You turn if you want to. The lady's not for turning."?

5 Calvin Coolidge proclaimed that "the chief business of the American people is ..." what?

6 Which rapper said in 2019, "I'm unquestionably, undoubtedly, the greatest human artist of all time"?

7 How did René Descartes express the thought "I think therefore I am" in Latin?

8 Who, on stage at the Winterland, San Francisco, in 1978, asked "Ever get the feeling you've been cheated?"?

9 Talking to 'US Weekly', which Antipodean actor claimed "There's nothing like sitting back and talking to your cows"?

10 Which American author wrote that "Truth uncompromisingly told will always have its ragged edges"?

PAPS, PEPS, PIPS, POPS AND PUPS

1 Philip Pirrip, nicknamed Pip, is the main character in which Charles Dickens novel?

2 Pep Guardiola played the majority of his club career for which Spanish club?

3 Pep&Co is the discount clothing line associated with which British bargain retailer?

4 Michael Clarke, known as "Pup", is a former captain of which national cricket team?

5 Who was the producer on the Iggy Pop album 'The Idiot'?

6 The Pup, a biplane used by Britain in World War I, was made by which aviation company?

7 Which singer had a 2009 Top 10 hit with the song 'Paparazzi'?

8 The word "Paparazzi" comes from the character Paparazzo, in which Federico Fellini film?

9 Which American pop artist, whose surname is almost the same as that of a European country, painted 'Masterpiece', 'Drowning Girl' and 'Whaam!'?

10 'Thou Shalt Always Kill', by Dan Le Sac vs Scroobius Pip, was "Single of the Week" in which publication, despite containing the lyric "Thou shalt not read ..." said publication?

QUOTE UNQUOTE
1 Berlin
2 Butterfly
3 John Lennon
4 Margaret Thatcher
5 Business
6 Kanye West
7 Cogito ergo sum
8 Johnny Rotten/John Lydon
9 Russell Crowe
10 Herman Melville

PAPS, PEPS, PIPS, POPS AND PUPS
1 Great Expectations
2 Barcelona
3 Poundland
4 Australia
5 David Bowie
6 Sopwith
7 Lady Gaga
8 La Dolce Vita (accept: "The Sweet Life" or "The Good Life")
9 Roy Lichtenstein
10 NME (New Musical Express)

NEW PARENTING

1 In the USA, what do they call what are known as nappies in the UK?

2 What product do Aptamil, SMA and Cow & Gate make?

3 What is the soft spot on a newborn baby's skull called?

4 In the medical specialism that deals with childbirth sometimes shortened to OB/GYN, what is the OB short for?

5 Which word for a specific type of birth companion comes from the ancient Greek for "servant woman"?

6 Founded by Paul Lindley in 2006, whose "Kitchen" is one of the UK's leading suppliers of baby and toddler food?

7 By what alliterative names are the crusty or oily patches on a baby's scalp known?

8 What M is the name of the green-brown first stool of a human infant?

9 What does NCT stand for, when referring to groups that expectant parents go to in the UK?

10 The title of which 1995 film starring Hugh Grant and Julianne Moore refers to the gestation period of a human?

ROCK STAR OFFSPRING

1 Who married Elvis Presley's daughter Lisa-Marie in the 1990s?

2 The son of which rock star directed films such as 'Moon' and 'Source Code'?

3 The son of which Beatle spent some years drumming for Oasis?

4 Who wrote the song 'Little Green' about her adopted daughter?

5 Singer Ben Taylor is the son of James Taylor and who?

6 Which rock singer wrote the song 'Little James' about his stepson?

7 Rocco and Lourdes are children of which superstar?

8 Actress Zoë Kravitz is the daughter of Lennie Kravitz and which actress?

9 Model Daisy Lowe is the daughter of Pearl Lowe and which singer, the frontman of Bush?

10 Rufus Wainwright is the son of Loudon Wainwright and which singer who died in 2010?

NEW PARENTING
1 Diapers
2 Baby milk/formula
3 Fontanelle
4 Obstetrics
5 Doula
6 Ella's Kitchen
7 Cradle cap
8 Meconium
9 National Childbirth Trust
10 Nine Months

ROCK STAR OFFSPRING
1 Michael Jackson
2 David Bowie (Duncan Jones)
3 Ringo Starr (Zak Starkey)
4 Joni Mitchell
5 Carly Simon
6 Liam Gallagher
7 Madonna
8 Lisa Bonet
9 Gavin Rossdale
10 Kate McGarrigle

FIZZY DRINKS

1 Which citrus-flavoured soft drink gave its name to the first of a documentary series made by Michael Apted?

2 Which singer's father wrote and sung the song 'Secret Lemonade Drinker' in adverts for R White's Lemonade?

3 Inca Kola is one of the most popular fizzy drinks in which country?

4 Which fizzy drink brand has a name which is the Latin for "I touch" and also a Latin American dance?

5 Which "clear" cola did Coca-Cola introduce to the UK in early 1993, though it was quickly discontinued?

6 In the 1990s, which British fizzy drink used the poems of Purple Ronnie in its adverts?

7 Which red-coloured soft drink was originally made by Fred and Tom Pickup of Pudsey, then made by AG Barr and has a name which is a shortening of a longer word?

8 Which unique soft drink was created in the 1880s by Charles Alderton in Waco, Texas?

9 Which British maker of "posh" soft drinks including Dandelion & Burdock and Victorian Lemonade is based in Hexham, Northumberland?

10 Which fizzy drink does the brand Old Jamaica specialise in?

WIND

1 Which part of a sailing boat captures the blow of the wind to propel the boat?

2 Which city in Illinois is known as the "Windy City"?

3 The Hornsea Wind Farm, which began construction in 2018, is located in which sea?

4 Which German band sang about the 'Wind of Change' in a 1991 hit single?

5 If a wind is described as "northerly", in which direction does it blow?

6 Who was the god of the wind in Greek mythology?

7 Which bird is traditionally featured in the design of a weather vane?

8 Windy Miller was a character in which classic children's TV show?

9 Which B is the scale used to measure the speed of the wind?

10 The "libeccio" is a south-westerly wind predominant on which Mediterranean island?

FIZZY DRINKS
1 7 Up
2 Elvis Costello (Elvis Costello was born Declan McManus, and his father was Ross McManus)
3 Peru
4 Tango
5 Tab Clear
6 Vimto
7 Tizer (short for Appetizer)
8 Dr Pepper
9 Fentimans
10 Ginger beer

WIND
1 Sail
2 Chicago
3 North Sea
4 The Scorpions
5 South
6 Aeolus
7 Cockerel
8 Camberwick Green
9 Beaufort scale
10 Corsica

ALIENS AND MONSTERS

1 If they exist, what planet do Martians come from?

2 Don't feed it after midnight. Don't get it wet ... what is it?

3 Which X is a word that comes from the Ancient Greek for "fear of an alien"?

4 Which singer was, in 1985, 'Loving the Alien'?

5 "Nice planet. We'll take it!" was the tagline of which 1996 film featuring aliens?

6 In which TV comedy does Alan Tudyk play Dr Harry Vanderspeigle?

7 Which 90s alien-related show was created by Chris Carter?

8 The Mysterons are the principal enemy of which TV title character?

9 What planet do Daleks come from?

10 What kind of creature is Dan Dare's adversary The Mekon?

ANSWERS RHYME WITH US PRESIDENTS

1 According to a Van Halen hit, you might as well ... do what?

2 In 1348, King Edward III created a prestigious order of chivalry called The Order of the ... what?

3 If you were experiencing ennui, you would be profoundly ... what?

4 What surname links the man who wrote the music for 'How the West Was Won' with his nephew, who wrote the music for 'Toy Story'?

5 Premiered in 1924, the most famous comic opera by Leos Janacek is 'The Cunning Little ...' what?

6 What was the surname of the manager of Liverpool FC between 1983 and 1985?

7 Though some events took place in the resort of Whistler, the 2010 Winter Olympics were mainly based in which city in western Canada?

8 The actor, with underworld connections of his own, who played gangster "Spats" Colombo in 'Some Like It Hot' was George ... who?

9 In which prison in Northern Ireland did Bobby Sands conduct a hunger strike which led to his death in 1981?

10 The alternative title of Gilbert and Sullivan's 'HMS Pinafore' was 'The lass that loved a ...' what?

ALIENS AND MONSTERS
1 Mars
2 A mogwai/gremlin
3 Xenophobia
4 David Bowie
5 Mars Attacks!
6 Resident Alien
7 The X-Files
8 Captain Scarlet
9 Skaro
10 Treen

ANSWERS RHYME WITH US PRESIDENTS
1 Jump (Trump)
2 Garter (Carter)
3 Bored (Ford)
4 Newman (Alfred and Randy. Truman)
5 Vixen (Nixon)
6 Fagan (Joe Fagan. Reagan)
7 Vancouver (Hoover)
8 Raft (Taft)
9 Maze (Hayes)
10 Sailor (Taylor)

COLOUR

1 Blue is the colour of the British Conservative Party. What is the colour of the USA's Republican Party?

2 What colour between red and blue was named after a battle in Italy in 1859?

3 How many different colours of snooker ball are on the table at the start of the frame?

4 The experience of seeing colours when one experiences another sensory pathway has what name?

5 What colour do you get when you remove red from white light?

6 What C are the colour receptor cells in the human eye also known as?

7 "Look at the stars, see how they shine for you" – what colour?

8 Who directed the 1986 film 'The Color of Money' which starred Tom Cruise and Paul Newman?

9 Which French artist's 1957 exhibition featured 11 identical blue canvases?

10 In which city is the NFL team known as the Browns based?

CROSSED FILMS

There are TWO films in these (apart from when we indicate there are THREE) and you need all the films for the point. EXAMPLE: Which Daniel Day-Lewis film, based on the book 'Oil!', is set during the Sierra Leone Civil War? EXAMPLE ANSWER: There Will Be Blood Diamond

1 Which Stanley Kubrick film starring Peter Sellers shows ten different romantic stories, mainly based around London?

2 Which film features Robert De Niro playing mob boss Paul Vitti, terrorizing his stepson played by Leonardo DiCaprio?

3 Which 2005 Disney comedy about a bird who is scared of the sky falling tells the story of an offbeat family travelling to a children's beauty pageant?

4 Which star-studded 90s action film about a released prisoner returning to his family is a spoof of disaster films of the 70s?

5 Starring Sylvester Stallone as John Spartan, which film tells the story of Andy Kaufman?

6 Which 2002 drama about a 50s housewife starring Julianne Moore is an update of the 1941 film 'Here Comes Mr Jordan'?

7 Which classic film noir starring Bogart and Bacall is directed by Tim Burton and features the character Ichabod Crane?

8 Which martial arts homage starring Uma Thurman, split into Volume 1 and Volume 2, starred Tom Courtenay as a fantasist?

9 Which comedy about an unlikely couple having a baby together stars George Clooney as a travelling corporate downsizer?

10 THREE FILMS: Which first official James Bond film is the 25th official James Bond film, which is the 20th official James Bond film?

COLOUR
1 Red
2 Magenta
3 Eight (including white)
4 Synaesthesia
5 Cyan
6 Cones
7 Yellow (in the song by Coldplay)
8 Martin Scorsese
9 Yves Klein
10 Cleveland

CROSSED FILMS
1 Doctor Strangelove Actually
2 Analyze This Boy's Life
3 Chicken Little Miss Sunshine
4 Con Airplane!
5 Demolition Man on the Moon
6 Far From Heaven Can Wait
7 The Big Sleepy Hollow
8 Kill Billy Liar
9 Knocked Up in the Air
10 Dr No Time to Die Another Day

FUNNY NORTHERNERS

1. What was the name of Liza Tarbuck's famous father, who was a schoolmate of John Lennon?

2. Who provided a memorable cameo as Ray the Fishmonger in 'Peter Kay's Car Share'?

3. One of the best loved comedy songs by Victoria Wood was 'The Ballad of Barry and ...' who?

4. With her stand-up shows including 'Chatterbox' and 'Bobby Dazzler', who married fellow comedian Gary Delaney in 2014?

5. Which comedy legend, part of a double act, was born in Ulverston, Lancashire in June 1890?

6. Julian Barratt and Daniel Rigby were among the stars of which offbeat comedy from 2016 written by Will Sharpe?

7. In which town was Eric Morecambe born in 1926?

8. Johnny Vegas is a lifelong fan of which rugby league team?

9. Which funny man's characters include "Train guy", who talks to Col about THE Geoff Linton and says "Have a campachoochoo on me"?

10. What was the house band for the first two series of 'The Mrs Merton Show'?

LONG WORDS

1. Which musical made famous the word "supercalifragilisticexpialidocious"?

2. The village whose 48-letter name begins 'Llanfairpwll ...' is on which island?

3. How many letters are there in the word "counterrevolutionaries"?

4. Dermatoglyphics is the joint-longest English word without any ... what?

5. Honorificabilitudinitatibus is notable for being the longest word in whose body of work?

6. Which British Prime Minister was said to have coined the term antidisestablishmentarianism?

7. According to a study, what U is the longest word in everyday popular use?

8. What's the longest word made up of only musical notes?

9. What's the longest word in the English dictionary containing none of the five vowels?

10. Rupturewort is the longest word formed only of letters from ... where?

FUNNY NORTHERNERS
1. Jimmy Tarbuck
2. Reece Shearsmith
3. Freda
4. Sarah Millican
5. Stan Laurel
6. Flowers
7. Morecambe
8. St Helens
9. Bob Mortimer
10. Hooky and the Boys (featuring Caroline Aherne's then-husband Peter Hook)

LONG WORDS
1. Mary Poppins
2. Anglesey/Ynys Môn
3. 22
4. Repeated letters
5. William Shakespeare
6. William Gladstone (he probably didn't coin it, but is one of the earliest documented users of it)
7. Uncharacteristically
8. Cabbaged
9. Rhythms
10. Top row of keyboard

EALING, QUEEN OF THE SUBURBS

1 Mick Jagger and Keith Richards first saw Charlie Watts play drums at Ealing Jazz Club - which band would they form together with Brian Jones, Bill Wyman and Ian Stewart?

2 Which Oscar-winning director named his production company, Lammas Park Productions, after a park in Ealing?

3 Which MP for Ealing Central and Acton is the sister of a former 'Blue Peter' presenter?

4 A classic comedy made at Ealing Studios was 'Kind Hearts and ...' what?

5 Northfields and South Ealing are tube stations on which line?

6 Which singer of classics such as 'You Don't Have to Say You Love Me' and 'Son of a Preacher Man' grew up in Ealing?

7 Which S is the area of Ealing which is home to one of the largest Punjabi communities in the world outside India?

8 Which tennis player, winner of eight Grand Slam singles titles, grew up in Brentham Garden Suburb, in Ealing?

9 Under what name would Farrokh Bulsara, who went to Ealing Art College, become a superstar?

10 Which "gyratory" in the north of Ealing was named in 2007 as Britain's scariest junction?

FILM TAGLINES

1 Which film had the tagline: "In space no one can hear you scream"?

2 Which 1986 film had the tagline: "Be afraid. Be very afraid"?

3 The first 'Star Wars' film had the tagline: "A long time ago in a ..." what? [four-word answer]

4 Which boxing film had the tagline: "His whole life was a million-to-one shot"?

5 Which film had the tagline: "Who you gonna call?"?

6 The tagline to which film was: "Houston, we have a problem"?

7 Which 2009 film had the tagline: "Enter the world"?

8 The tagline to which 2005 remake was: "The eighth wonder of the world"?

9 Which film had the tagline: "An adventure 65 million years in the making"?

10 Which film had the tagline: "In love, there are no boundaries"?

EALING, QUEEN OF THE SUBURBS
1 The Rolling Stones
2 Steve McQueen
3 Rupa Huq
4 Coronets
5 Piccadilly Line
6 Dusty Springfield
7 Southall
8 Fred Perry
9 Freddie Mercury
10 Hanger Lane Gyratory

FILM TAGLINES
1 Alien
2 The Fly
3 Galaxy far, far away
4 Rocky
5 Ghostbusters
6 Apollo 13
7 Avatar
8 King Kong
9 Jurassic Park
10 The English Patient

SOMETHING ELSE

MEMES

1 The "Rickrolling" phenomenon involves which singer?

2 Which gorilla at Cincinnati Zoo became a huge meme in 2016?

3 One of the most popular memes of the last few years is of which singer saying "I don't know her"?

4 Which actor features in the "Condescending Wonka" meme?

5 A clip of which 'Star Trek' actor asking bizarre questions has been a very popular meme in recent times?

6 Spoof 'Downfall' videos, a popular internet meme, feature which leader ranting about mundane topics?

7 A popular meme based on three people in stock photography is "Distracted ..." what?

8 What is British actor Kayode Ewumi pointing at in a popular meme?

9 Constantine, part of a hugely popular meme, is an "evil" version of which frog?

10 A popular meme shows actor Jason Momoa sneaking up on which other actor on a red carpet?

MULTIPLES OF 3

1 How many holes are there on a professional golf course?

2 What do you call a vanilla ice cream cone with a chocolate flake in it?

3 In the USA, what is the Minimum Legal Drinking Age (MLDA)?

4 How many steps are there in the title of the first of John Buchan's novels featuring Richard Hannay?

5 In Greek mythology, how many Graces, or Charites, are there?

6 Which 1998 comic book series by Frank Miller inspired a film starring Gerard Butler and Lena Headey?

7 How many goals did Gary Lineker score for England?

8 In which year was the sealing of Magna Carta?

9 What is the name of the musical film starring Daniel Day-Lewis which is based on Federico Fellini's '8½'?

10 The former French international footballer who managed Togo from 2011 to 2014 was Didier ... who?

MEMES
1 Rick Astley
2 Harambe
3 Mariah Carey
4 Gene Wilder
5 Jonathan Frakes
6 Adolf Hitler (played by Bruno Ganz)
7 Boyfriend
8 His head
9 Kermit
10 Henry Cavill

MULTIPLES OF 3
1 18
2 99
3 21
4 39
5 Three
6 300
7 48
8 1215
9 9
10 Six

NON-CAPITAL CITIES

1 Lagos is the largest city, but not the capital, of which country?

2 Istanbul is the largest city, but not the capital, of which country?

3 New York City is neither the capital of the USA - Washington DC is - nor of New York state. What is in fact the capital of New York state?

4 What is the largest non-capital city in the EU by population?

5 It's not Zurich, it's not Geneva - what is Switzerland's capital?

6 What is the city with the largest population in Brazil?

7 What is Pakistan's largest city, albeit not its capital?

8 How many cities are there in Australia which are larger by population than its capital?

9 What is the former name of the huge Indian city of Kolkata?

10 Though not the capital of Spain, Barcelona is the capital of which "autonomous community"?

PEOPLE BEING UNEXPECTEDLY STRUCK

1 On 25 January 1995 Matthew Simmons, a fan of Crystal Palace soccer club, was unexpectedly struck by whose foot?

2 A popular story claims that an apple falling onto his head inspired which scientist to formulate his theories of gravity?

3 At which British politician did Craig Evans throw an egg in 2001, causing the politician in turn to throw a punch at him?

4 British comedian Simon Brodkin threw money at which former president of FIFA in 2015?

5 Belgian Noel Godin flung pies at a number of figures he viewed as pompous - what E was the nickname he earned from this?

6 What colour were the flour bombs which unexpectedly hit British Prime Minister Tony Blair in the House of Commons in 2004?

7 At which British music festival were pop duo Daphne and Celeste hit with bottles of urine thrown by rock fans?

8 Jonnie Marbles tweeted "It is a far better thing that I do now than I have ever done before #splat" just before attacking which newspaper tycoon in 2011?

9 Which Chelsea footballer was applauded for the solid shoulder barge she applied to a pitch invader in December 2021?

10 Tom Cruise was hit by a squirt from a water pistol disguised as a microphone at the London premiere of which 2005 movie?

SOMETHING ELSE

NON-CAPITAL CITIES
1 Nigeria
2 Turkey/Türkiye
3 Albany
4 Hamburg
5 Bern
6 São Paulo
7 Karachi
8 Seven
9 Calcutta
10 Catalonia

PEOPLE BEING UNEXPECTEDLY STRUCK
1 Eric Cantona
2 Isaac Newton
3 John Prescott
4 Sepp Blatter
5 Entarteur
6 Purple
7 Reading
8 Rupert Murdoch
9 Sam Kerr
10 War Of The Worlds

HALLOWEEN

1 In the Western Christian calendar, what A is the name given to the day after Halloween?

2 What was Bobby "Boris" Pickett's smash hit novelty song of 1962?

3 According to the Guinness Book of Records in 2021, the largest WHAT ever recorded weighs 1226 kg?

4 Which actor appeared in 1958's 'Dracula', 1959's 'The Hound of the Baskervilles', 1964's 'The Evil of Frankenstein' and 1977's 'Star Wars'?

5 What is the modern descendant of the Halloween activity which was originally known in 19th century Scotland as "guising"?

6 In which 1990 thrill-fest is the town of Canaima terrorised by a collection of deadly hybrid spiders?

7 What Halloween-related feat did New Yorker Ashrita Furman achieve 33 times in one minute to break a world record in 2008?

8 Which scary film is an anagram of NO THEME?

9 Which comic series has had Halloween seasonal specials called 'Pinkeye', 'Spookyfish' and 'Korn's Groovy Pirate Ghost Mystery'?

10 In which James Bond film did the voodoo character Baron Samedi come back to life?

THE GOLDEN AGE OF NEIGHBOURS

1 In 1986, who replaced Darius Perkins in the role of Scott Robinson on 'Neighbours'?

2 In 'Neighbours', what profession linked Clive Gibbons and Karl Kennedy?

3 In 'Neighbours', what breed of dog was Bouncer?

4 Complete the nickname given to the character played by Annie Jones in 'Neighbours' - "Plain Jane ..."?

5 The final episode of 'Neighbours' was filmed in 2022 - how many years since the first?

6 What was the nickname of the 'Neighbours' character Jarrod Rebecchi?

7 What was the first name of the iconic 'Neighbours' villain Mrs Mangel?

8 What was the name of the priest who married Scott Robinson and Charlene Mitchell in 1987?

9 Kerry Bishop, daughter of Harold, was shot and killed while protesting against what?

10 Which Japanese businessman, played by Lawrence Mah, had regular dealings with Paul Robinson in 'Neighbours'?

HALLOWEEN
1 All Saints' Day OR All Hallows' Day
2 Monster Mash
3 Pumpkin
4 Peter Cushing
5 Trick-or-treating
6 Arachnophobia
7 She bobbed for 33 apples in one minute
8 The Omen
9 South Park
10 Live and Let Die

THE GOLDEN AGE OF NEIGHBOURS
1 Jason Donovan
2 Doctor
3 Labrador Retriever
4 Superbrain
5 37 years (since 1985)
6 Toadfish
7 Nell (Eleanor)
8 Reverend Sampson
9 A duck hunt
10 Mr (Toshiro) Udagawa

TOAST

1 French toast is a dish which involves sliced bread, fried after being soaked in what?

2 The "Toast to the Laddies" follows the "Address to the Lassies" in which 'Supper' on the 25th January?

3 In the UK and Commonwealth countries, to whom do people make the "loyal toast"?

4 In 'Toast of London' who is the sound engineer to whom Steven Toast often angrily says "Yes, I can hear you ..."? [first name and surname needed]

5 Musician Ranking Roger employed the vocal style known as "toasting" as a member of which two-tone band?

6 Which word, meaning "health", is a common toast in Irish?

7 On which 2010 track does Kanye West sing "Let's have a toast for the douchebags"?

8 What do you call a croque monsieur with a fried egg on top?

9 'Tea and Toast' was a single released in 2013 by which singer who'd been a contestant on 'The X Factor' in 2012?

10 'Toast' is the title of a memoir by which British chef and food writer?

ENIGMAS

1 In DC Comics, what is Edward Nigma's villainous alter ego?

2 What was the name of the site near Milton Keynes where scientists such as Alan Turing broke the code of the Enigma cipher?

3 The sphinx was an ancient creature famous for its riddle - in which modern day country is the Great Sphinx of Giza?

4 In 1993, the German band Enigma had a UK hit with 'Return to ...' what?

5 Which politician, in 1939, described Russia as "a riddle, wrapped in a mystery, inside an enigma"?

6 Who, in 1918, patented the original Enigma machine?

7 Edward Elgar's 'Enigma Variation IX' is named after which mighty hunter?

8 Which enigmatic actress famously said "I want to be alone" in the film 'Grand Hotel'?

9 The 1974 film 'The Enigma of Kaspar Hauser' was directed by which German auteur?

10 Which enigmatic and idiosyncratic singer also has acted in films such as 'Rumblefish', 'Short Cuts' and 'Licorice Pizza'?

TOAST
1 (Beaten) egg
2 Burns Supper
3 The Queen/Monarch
4 Clem Fandango
5 The Beat
6 Sláinte
7 Runaway
8 Croque madame
9 Lucy Spraggan
10 Nigel Slater

ENIGMAS
1 The Riddler
2 Bletchley Park
3 Egypt
4 Innocence
5 Winston Churchill
6 Arthur Scherbius
7 Nimrod
8 Greta Garbo
9 Werner Herzog
10 Tom Waits

GAY ICONS

1 Which Australian pop star has a sister, who was also a pop star, called Dannii?

2 Which country artist, despite her initial protests, was elevated to the Rock and Roll Hall of Fame in 2022?

3 In a 1995 interview with Martin Bashir, how many people did Princess Diana say were in her marriage?

4 In which US city is the Liberace Museum, dedicated to the outrageous pianist?

5 Cher won an Oscar for Best Actress for her role in which movie?

6 Which singer and actress is also known by her informal stage name "The Divine Miss M"?

7 In Thomas Mann's short-story, in which city does Aschenbach fall in love with Tadzio?

8 A Michelangelo sculpture of which biblical man was made for the Palazzo della Signoria in Florence?

9 Which movie star died in London only a week before the Stonewall Riots in 1969?

10 Which 3rd century saint, usually depicted as a young man pierced by arrows, became a gay icon (as well as giving his name to a city in Spain)?

HILLS AND DALES

1 Which fictional village was known as Beckindale until 1994?

2 In 'Pretty Woman', which famous street in Beverly Hills does Vivian, played by Julia Roberts, have a shopping spree on?

3 Whernside is the highest peak in which English National Park?

4 How many times, combined, did Graham and Damon Hill win the Formula 1 World Championship?

5 Edale, in Derbyshire, is the southernmost point of which hiking trail?

6 In the Gospels, on which hill outside Jerusalem, with a name meaning "place of skulls", was Jesus crucified?

7 Which famous comedy "Hill" would the medical doctor Matthew Hall become?

8 Which show, presented by Dale Winton from 1993 to 2007, returned with Rylan Clark-Neal presenting in 2019?

9 "King of the surf guitar" Dick Dale's track 'Misirlou' was prominently used in which cult 1994 film?

10 In September 1961, what did the New Hampshire couple Barney and Betty Hill claim had happened to them?

GAY ICONS
1 Kylie Minogue
2 Dolly Parton
3 Three
4 Las Vegas
5 Moonstruck
6 Bette Midler
7 Venice (Death in Venice)
8 David
9 Judy Garland
10 Saint Sebastian (the city is San Sebastián)

HILLS AND DALES
1 Emmerdale (the show was 'Emmerdale Farm' until 1989, then it became 'Emmerdale', then in 1994 the place itself became Emmerdale)
2 Rodeo Drive
3 Yorkshire Dales
4 Three (two for Graham, one for Damon)
5 Pennine Way
6 Golgotha (accept: Calvary)
7 Harry Hill
8 Supermarket Sweep (Winton died in 2018)
9 Pulp Fiction
10 Abducted by aliens

CHILDREN OF FOOTBALLERS

1 In what role was Suzanne Charlton, daughter of Bobby Charlton, a regular on British TV?

2 Eidur Gudjohnsen made his international debut as a sub for his father Arnor Gudjohnsen - they were playing for which country?

3 What is the numerical middle name of Harper, the youngest child of the Beckhams?

4 Which son of a great footballer called George won Series 2 of 'Celebrity Love Island' in 2006?

5 Which national football team did Sergei, the father of British tennis player Elena Baltacha, represent in the 1980s?

6 Cesare, Paolo and Daniel - all of whom played for AC Milan - are from three generations of which family?

7 Which singer of 'The Revolution Will Not Be Televised' was the son of the first Black man to play for Celtic?

8 Which Grand Slam singles tournament did tennis player Kim Clijsters, daughter of a former Belgian international footballer, win three times?

9 Who was commentating when his son Charlie made his first-team debut for Manchester United in December 2021?

10 Which cycling presenter wrote the award-winning book 'My Father and Other Working Class Football Heroes'?

AT THE CURRY HOUSE

1 Which hot curry gave its name to a 1998 English football anthem recorded by Fat Les?

2 Which bird gives its name to the largest-selling beer brand in India?

3 With its name coming from Sanskrit, which G is the clarified butter commonly used in Indian cuisine?

4 In which century did the UK's first Indian restaurant, the Hindoostane Coffee House, open in London?

5 Which film star's 2012 visit to the Veer Dhara restaurant in St Albans was made into a short film?

6 Which hot curry takes its name from the former name of the city which is now called Chennai?

7 In 2011, extremist groups in which East African country banned samosas for being "too western"?

8 A dopiaza has a name meaning two of which vegetable?

9 Which 2003 novel by Monica Ali is named after a thoroughfare in East London famed for its many curry houses?

10 The 1991 romantic film 'Mississippi Masala' starred Sarita Choudhury and which Oscar-winning American actor?

CHILDREN OF FOOTBALLERS
1 Weather forecaster
2 Iceland
3 Seven
4 Calum Best
5 USSR
6 Maldini
7 Gil Scott-Heron
8 US Open
9 Robbie Savage
10 Gary Imlach (about his father Stuart)

AT THE CURRY HOUSE
1 Vindaloo
2 Kingfisher
3 Ghee
4 19th century (it opened in 1810)
5 Tom Cruise
6 Madras
7 Somalia
8 Onions
9 Brick Lane
10 Denzel Washington

SOMETHING ELSE

PETS, SHOPS AND BOYS

1 In a famous children's book, what type of dogs are Mr and Mrs Dearly's pets, Pongo and Missis?

2 Shakespeare & Company is a famous bookshop on the Rive Gauche of which river?

3 Which "Boy" performed the soundtrack to the film 'About a Boy'?

4 What is the name of the Jack Russell cross adopted by Boris Johnson and Carrie Symonds in 2019?

5 What was the first name of Karl Albrecht's brother, with whom he founded Aldi?

6 The Game Boy was a handheld console developed by which games company?

7 Kari and Oke were, for many years, the pet cats on which children's TV programme?

8 The 1940 film 'The Shop Around the Corner' was remade in 1998, starring Tom Hanks and Meg Ryan. What was the title of the remake?

9 What is the name of the dog in the painting 'His Master's Voice', who in turn featured in the logo for the retailer HMV?

10 All the Pet Shop Boys studio albums have exactly how many words in their title? [up to 2022]

RHYME TIME

There are five pairs of answers - distributed haphazardly throughout the round - that (loosely or exactly) rhyme.

1 Who captained England's men's rugby team to back-to-back Grand Slams in the 1991 and 1992 Five Nations?

2 In which BBC comedy did Jack Dee play the part of Rick Spleen?

3 The classic 1956 French film following a boy around Paris, which is the only short film to win the Oscar for Best Original Screenplay, is 'The ...' what?

4 What name links the mother of Tony Soprano to the wife of Augustus Caesar?

5 Which adjective goes before "Boy" in the title of a 1955 blues standard by Muddy Waters?

6 In a love song from the album 'The Times They Are a Changin'', Bob Dylan sings about boots of what nationality of leather?

7 Who is the only English footballer apart from Geoff Hurst to score in a FIFA World Cup Final? [Up to end of 2021]

8 Which singer-songwriter released her seventh solo album, 'Song for Our Daughter' to great acclaim in April 2020?

9 Which German toiletries company's name is an anagram of a French mineral water brand?

10 What are known as "parcmètres" in France?

PETS, SHOPS AND BOYS
1 Dalmatians ('The Hundred and One Dalmatians' by Dodie Smith)
2 Seine
3 Badly Drawn Boy
4 Dilyn
5 Theo
6 Nintendo
7 Blue Peter
8 You've Got Mail
9 Nipper
10 One (Please, Actually, Very etc.)

RHYME TIME
1 Will Carling
2 Lead Balloon
3 Red Balloon
4 Livia
5 Mannish
6 Spanish
7 Martin Peters
8 Laura Marling
9 Nivea (Evian)
10 Parking meters

TEACHERS

1 Albus Dumbledore is the headmaster of which fictional school?

2 In the Roald Dahl book, who is Matilda's favourite teacher?

3 Which student does Dean Edward R. Rooney spend a day trying to catch, in a 1986 John Hughes movie?

4 Comedian Romesh Ranganathan is a former teacher of which subject?

5 What James Hilton novel describes the life of an inspirational teacher called Mr Chipping?

6 Which long-running TV series stars Bryan Cranston as a chemistry teacher who turns to producing crystal meth?

7 Who was made Lucasian Professor of Mathematics at England's Cambridge University in 1669?

8 Which TV series featured Mr Belding, the principal of Bayside High School?

9 Who sang the theme tune to the 1967 school movie 'To Sir, With Love'?

10 Which head teacher at 'Grange Hill' was played by Gwyneth Powell?

WELL KNOWN BEARS

1 Which well known bear was best friends with Boo Boo?

2 What colour is Rupert Bear's normal jumper?

3 Aloysius is the teddy bear of Lord Sebastian Flyte in which Evelyn Waugh novel?

4 An armoured bear named Iorek Byrnison is a character in a series of books by which author?

5 A famous number sung by Baloo the Bear is the 'Bare ...' what?

6 Which public school did the adventurer Bear Grylls attend?

7 What name is the Swedish word meaning "bear"?

8 Which fairytale character had a bit of trouble with Three Bears?

9 Which character in 'Family Guy' has a teddy bear called Rupert?

10 "Exit, pursued by a bear" is a stage direction in which Shakespeare play?

TEACHERS
1 Hogwarts
2 Miss Honey
3 Ferris Bueller
4 Mathematics
5 Goodbye, Mr. Chips
6 Breaking Bad
7 Isaac Newton
8 Saved by the Bell
9 Lulu
10 Mrs McClusky

WELL KNOWN BEARS
1 Yogi Bear
2 Red
3 Brideshead Revisited
4 Philip Pullman (His Dark Materials)
5 Necessities
6 Eton College
7 Björn
8 Goldilocks
9 Stewie
10 The Winter's Tale

A OR B

You've got a 50/50 choice on each of these questions.

1 Is Morocco in the A) Northern Hemisphere or B) Southern Hemisphere?

2 What is the meaning of the word Fleech: is it A) to coax or flatter or B) a sharp bit of toenail?

3 True or False? Before creating 'Wallace and Gromit', Nick Park worked at a factory making tennis racquets, where he was responsible for the bits of plastic at the top of racquets, called grommets.

4 Who was US President first out of A) Theodore Roosevelt and B) Franklin D Roosevelt?

5 Which of these board games has sold more copies in total, worldwide, than the other - A) Scrabble or B) Monopoly?

6 True or False? Captain/Colonel Tom Moore (of walking up and down the garden raising money for the NHS fame) was a contestant on a 1983 Christmas edition of 'Blankety Blank'.

7 Which National Park is more westerly out of A) the North York Moors and B) the Yorkshire Dales?

8 Who was born first out of A) Gary Numan or B) Gary Oldman?

9 True or False? For the first hour of its life, a baby giraffe uses its head and long neck as a "fifth leg" to stop if falling over as it learns to control its gangly limbs.

10 True or False? The operations headquarters for South Yorkshire police is on Letsby Avenue.

KEVIN BACON

1 For which film did Kevin Bacon prepare by going undercover as a high school student?

2 In which film does Bacon star alongside Tom Cruise, Demi Moore and Jack Nicholson?

3 In which American city was Kevin Bacon born and raised?

4 In which 1982 film, considered a turning point in Bacon's career, did he play the self-destructive rich boy Fenwick?

5 What is the name of Kevin Bacon's actress wife?

6 In which cult Bacon movie from 1990 is a small desert town attacked by giant worm-like creatures?

7 Who directed Kevin Bacon in 'Apollo 13'?

8 What is the name of the band Kevin Bacon formed with his brother Michael?

9 In 2010, which artist created a piece of art called 'Bacon Kevin Bacon', made from "bacon bits" glued to a Styrofoam representation of the actor's head?

10 How many degrees of Kevin Bacon are there in the title of a popular game about connectivity?

A OR B
1 A) Northern
2 b) to coax or flatter
3 False
4 A) Theodore Roosevelt (1901 vs 1933)
5 B) Monopoly
6 True
7 B) The Yorkshire Dales
8 A) Gary Numan is, ironically, two weeks older
9 False
10 True

KEVIN BACON
1 Footloose
2 A Few Good Men
3 Philadelphia
4 Diner
5 Kyra Sedgwick
6 Tremors
7 Ron Howard
8 The Bacon Brothers
9 Mike Lahue
10 Six Degrees of Kevin Bacon

ACROSTIC 2

In this round, if you take the first letter of each answer, it will spell out something relevant to getting them all right.

1 Shortly before Thanksgiving, what kind of bird is ritually "pardoned" at the White House by the US President?

2 Which TV series starred Jonny Lee Miller as Sherlock Holmes and Lucy Liu as Dr Joan Watson?

3 Trent Bridge is the international cricket ground in which English city?

4 As in the name of the Kenyan President Uhuru Kenyatta, what does the Swahili word "uhuru" mean?

5 Arborio and basmati are types of which food?

6 Named after a German physicist, what is the SI derived unit of electrical resistance?

7 Born around 1280 and thought to have been one of the wealthiest figures in world history, who was the ninth leader of the Mali Empire?

8 Which TV series which ran from 1979 to 1988 was based, initially, on short stories by the author Roald Dahl?

9 Which opera by Pyotr Tchaikovsky, first performed in 1879, is based on the verse novel of the same name by Alexander Pushkin?

10 What is the name of the novel on which the film 'Die Hard' is based, as well as being the title of a 1997 hit song for Echo and the Bunnymen?

BLACK PANTHERS

1 Which actor, who played T'Challa in the 2018 film 'Black Panther', died in 2020?

2 Afeni, a member of the Black Panther Party, was the mother of which rapper-actor who was murdered in 1996?

3 Darcus Howe and Barbara Beese, members of the British Black Panther party, were members of which "Nine" as portrayed in a film in Steve McQueen's 'Small Axe' series?

4 In 1969, which FBI Director described the Black Panther Party as "the greatest threat to the internal security of the [USA]"?

5 The character of Black Panther was created in 1966 by Jack Kirby and which comics legend, who died in 2019?

6 Which artist, whose real name is Annie Clark, included the song 'Huey Newton' on her self-titled 2014 album?

7 Bagheera is a black panther who mentors Mowgli in which book by Rudyard Kipling?

8 The works of which Black Panther-affiliate author and activist include 'Women, Race and Class' and 'Are Prisons Obsolete?'?

9 Kwame Ture, who died in 1998, was a Black Panther leader formerly known as Stokely ... what?

10 Which member of the British Black Panther Party was the first Black poet published in the Penguin Modern Classics series?

ACROSTIC 2
1 Turkey
2 Elementary
3 Nottingham
4 Freedom
5 Rice
6 Ohm
7 Mansa Musa (accept: Musa)
8 Tales of the Unexpected
9 Eugene Onegin
10 Nothing Lasts Forever

BLACK PANTHERS
1 Chadwick Boseman
2 Tupac Shakur/2Pac
3 Mangrove Nine
4 J. Edgar Hoover
5 Stan Lee
6 St Vincent (Huey Newton was a co-founder of the Black Panther Party)
7 The Jungle Book
8 Angela Davis
9 Carmichael
10 Linton Kwesi Johnson

DOCTORS DOING OTHER JOBS

1 What is former doctor Paul Sinha's Chaser name?

2 Licensed physician Ken Jeong has been a panellist on the US and UK versions of which singing contest?

3 Which great footballer and practising doctor, who died in 2011, captained Brazil at the 1982 FIFA World Cup?

4 What show, which took a look at the week's television, did Harry Hill host on ITV from 2001 to 2012?

5 Which writer, comedian and former doctor wrote the bestseller 'This Is Going to Hurt'?

6 Which hospital doctor used the pseudonym John MacUre to write his first TV drama 'Cardiac Arrest'?

7 Which great Russian playwright of works such as 'Three Sisters' and 'Uncle Vanya' said "Medicine is my lawful wife"?

8 Jill Stein was which party's presidential candidate at the 2012 and 2016 US presidential elections?

9 Qualified doctor Jamie Roberts represented which country at rugby union for many years?

10 In which event did doctor Steph Cook win gold for Great Britain at the 2000 Olympics?

EXTINCTION

1 In 'Alice's Adventures in Wonderland', which extinct bird is a caricature of the author, Lewis Carroll?

2 The city of Edinburgh contains two extinct volcanoes - Castle Rock, and which other landmark?

3 An amphibian that may have been extinct in the wild since around 2007 is the Panamanian golden ... what?

4 The Cretaceous-Paleogene extinction event which took place around 66 million years ago is widely thought to have been caused by the impact of what?

5 In 2012, Bobby Hogg, the last native speaker of the Cromarty dialect, died at the age of 92 - in which country of the UK?

6 Russia's Wrangel Island is thought to have been the last location to support which now-extinct species (until about 2000 BC)?

7 Which dinosaur has a name meaning "swift seizer"?

8 The Christmas Island pipistrelle, which went extinct in 2009, was a species of which animal?

9 The logo of activist group Extinction Rebellion is a circle containing which symbol of time running out?

10 Which flightless bird which became extinct in the 19th century was the only modern species in the genus Pinguinus? [two-word answer required]

DOCTORS DOING OTHER JOBS
1 Sinnerman
2 The Masked Singer
3 Socrates
4 TV Burp
5 Adam Kay
6 Jed Mercurio
7 Anton Chekhov
8 Green Party
9 Wales
10 Modern Pentathlon

EXTINCTION
1 Dodo
2 Arthur's Seat
3 Frog
4 Asteroid (It is thought the Chicxulub crater in Mexico is where the asteroid struck)
5 Scotland
6 Woolly mammoth
7 Velociraptor
8 Bat
9 Egg timer
10 Great auk

FRIENDS CAMEOS

1 Which character, in 'Friends', does Brad Pitt's character Will hate?

2 Noah Wyle and George Clooney, who had cameos in 'Friends' as doctors, were starring in which hospital drama at the time?

3 Which businessman turned up in a "London" episode of 'Friends' as a street vendor?

4 Which supermodel plays Joey's flatmate Janine in 'Friends'?

5 In 'Friends' who played Paul Stevens, the father of a student Ross dates?

6 Billy Crystal's 'Friends' cameo was opposite which other comic star?

7 Kyle Gass, who plays a mugger and old friend of Phoebe's in 'Friends', is famous as a member of which comedy band?

8 Rebecca Romijn plays what kind of "girl" in 'Friends', giving the title of the episode?

9 What does Joey use in Charlton Heston's dressing room in 'Friends'?

10 Which actor does Rachel sit next to on her flight to London in 'Friends'?

KRISS AKABUSI

1 Kriss Akabusi's parents were from which African country?

2 As well as being a professional sportsperson, Kriss Akabusi was in which branch of the armed forces?

3 What long-running children's BBC show did Akabusi present in the early 90s?

4 Which American did Akabusi hold off to win 4x400m relay gold for Britain at the 1991 World Championships?

5 In which year did Kriss Akabusi win an individual Olympic bronze?

6 Whose British 400m hurdles record did Kriss Akabusi break in 1990?

7 Akabusi appeared in 'Last of the Summer Wine' in 1997 - playing someone of which profession?

8 Akabusi said in a 2008 interview that people still stop him on the street wanting to hear him do what?

9 In which city on the Adriatic did Kriss Akabusi win 400m hurdles gold at the European Championships in 1990?

10 On which 90s entertainment show did Kriss Akabusi receive a "Gotcha Oscar"?

FRIENDS CAMEOS
1 Rachel (played by Jennifer Aniston, his then-wife)
2 ER
3 Richard Branson
4 Elle Macpherson
5 Bruce Willis
6 Robin Williams
7 Tenacious D
8 Dirty girl
9 His shower
10 Hugh Laurie

KRISS AKABUSI
1 Nigeria
2 Army
3 Record Breakers
4 Antonio Pettigrew
5 1992
6 David Hemery
7 Milkman
8 Laugh
9 Split
10 Noel's House Party

PHOEBES

1 Phoebe Snow was guest vocalist on 'Gone at Last', a track from which singer's album 'Still Crazy After All These Years'?

2 In Phoebe Waller-Bridge's 'Fleabag', what is the name of the sister of the title character?

3 In the New Testament, who mentions a deacon called Phoebe in his letter to the Romans?

4 Phoebe Nicholls played Cordelia Flyte in a TV adaptation of which Evelyn Waugh novel?

5 Actress Phoebe Cates played Kate Beringer in which 1984 comedy horror film and its sequel?

6 On which TV series did Alyssa Milano play Phoebe Halliwell?

7 Phoebe Caulfield is the sister of the title character of which American novel?

8 Discovered in 1899, Phoebe is a moon of which planet?

9 Phoebe Philo was creative director of which French luxury goods brand from 2008 to 2018?

10 What is the 'Big Lebowski'-referencing title of singer Phoebe Bridgers' debut album, from 2017?

POET ANAGRAMS

The answers are all anagrams of the surnames of poets - or in one case the single name by which the poet is usually known.

1 In their first US Number 1 single, from 1986, Simply Red were 'Holding Back the ...' what?

2 Which word links Charles Dickens' 'House' and Christina Rossetti's 'Midwinter'?

3 By what three-letter name is Erythropoietin, often used in sports doping, better known?

4 Which word links a cartilaginous fish with a sporting item that can be "ice" or "roller"?

5 What is the first name that links the rock guitarist Allman to the surf guitarist Eddy?

6 Which band fronted by Mark Mothersbaugh had a hit with 'Whip It!'?

7 Which portmanteau word is used for members of the male subculture of fans of the show 'My Little Pony: Friendship Is Magic'?

8 A famous book about mountaineering by Joe Simpson is 'Touching the ...' what?

9 A word often seen on estate agent signs, what was the name of the 1987 debut solo album by Boy George?

10 In the phrase BYOB used by some restaurants, what do the first B and the O stand for?

PHOEBES
1 Paul Simon
2 Claire
3 St Paul
4 Brideshead Revisited
5 Gremlins
6 Charmed
7 The Catcher in the Rye
8 Saturn
9 Celine
10 Stranger in the Alps

POET ANAGRAMS
1 Years (Ayres [Pam])
2 Bleak (Blake [William])
3 EPO (Poe [Edgar Allan])
4 Skate (Keats [John])
5 Duane (Auden [WH])
6 Devo (Dove [Rita])
7 Brony (Byron [Lord])
8 Void (Ovid)
9 Sold (Olds [Sharon])
10 Bring Own (Browning [Robert])

PUZZLING

1 What is the 13th letter of the English alphabet?

2 Using a code of A = Z, B = Y, C = X and so on, what would be correct encoding for the letter Q?

3 How many vowels are there in the word ABRACADABRA?

4 If A = 1, B = 2, C = 3 etc, what is the value of Q + U + I + Z?

5 Which US State is this: SSSSSSSSSSE ?

6 How many vowels are there in this question?

7 How many vowels are there in this somewhat self-referential question?

8 If A = 2, B = 4, C = 6 etc, what is the value of Z?

9 What comes next in this sequence: O,T,T,F,F,S,S,?

10 Who is the author of these famous words, with all the vowels and spaces removed: TBRNTTBTHTSTHQSTN?

PARLEZ-VOUS FRANCAIS?

1 What does "Au revoir" mean in French?

2 If a French person began a sentence "Je m'appelle", what are they going to tell you?

3 If Pierre said to you "Fermez la fenêtre", what would you do?

4 If Marie invited you over for "le petit déjeuner", at what time of day would you arrive at her house?

5 Sebastien asks you for "un chapeau" from his wardrobe - what do you give him?

6 You invite Jacques for dinner and he says he doesn't eat "les poissons": what shouldn't you cook?

7 "Pardonnez-moi, oú est La Joconde, s'il vous plaît?"

8 If you answered "Oui" to the question "Voulez-vous coucher avec moi, ce soir?" which room of the house would you most likely be going to?

9 Which B would you go to in France to borrow a book?

10 Franglais is a bastardised version of French et quel autre langue?

PUZZLING
1 M
2 J
3 Five (or one, if you interpret the question as "different vowels")
4 73
5 Tennessee
6 14
7 23
8 52
9 E
10 William Shakespeare

PARLEZ-VOUS FRANCAIS?
1 Goodbye
2 Their name (Leur nom)
3 Close the window
4 The morning (Le matin)
5 A hat
6 Fish
7 Le Louvre (La Joconde is the Mona Lisa)
8 Bedroom (La chambre)
9 La bibliothèque
10 Anglais/English

THE LIFE AND TIMES OF MICKEY ROURKE

1 In which film did Mickey Rourke play Randy "The Ram" Robinson?

2 Who starred opposite Mickey Rourke as Louis Cyphre in 'Angel Heart'?

3 In 2020, Mickey Rourke appeared as "Gremlin" in which singing contest?

4 Which villain did Mickey Rourke play in 'Iron Man 2'?

5 Which Enrique Iglesias video did Mickey Rourke star in?

6 Which boxing trainer did Mickey Rourke help with buying a gym?

7 In 'Barfly', Mickey Rourke played Henry Chinaski, the alter ego of which famous writer?

8 To whom did Mickey Rourke lose out for the Best Actor Oscar for 2008?

9 How many of his eight professional boxing bouts did Mickey Rourke lose?

10 What was the name of Mickey Rourke's dog he carried everywhere while publicising 'The Wrestler'?

STICKS AND STONES, BREAKS AND BONES

1 What is the actual first name of "Bones" McCoy in 'Star Trek'?

2 The Blarney Stone is situated at Blarney Castle, which is in which Irish county?

3 In March 2019, which snooker player became the first to 1000 century breaks in competition?

4 Which children's laureate wrote the children's book 'Stick Man'?

5 Sharon Stone received a Best Actress Oscar nomination for her role in which Martin Scorsese film?

6 In which game, inspired by an AA Milne book, are sticks dropped from a bridge into water?

7 Which precious gemstone, a variety of corundum, was used in 2017 to describe the 65th anniversary of the reign of Queen Elizabeth II?

8 Which director, later an Oscar winner, directed the cult 1991 film 'Point Break'?

9 In the human body, what is the medical name of the tailbone?

10 'The Breaks' is an early hip-hop classic by which rapper, who would later be ordained as a minister?

THE LIFE AND TIMES OF MICKEY ROURKE
1 The Wrestler
2 Robert De Niro
3 The Masked Singer
4 Whiplash/Ivan Vanko
5 Hero
6 Freddie Roach
7 Charles Bukowski
8 Sean Penn
9 None
10 Loki

STICKS AND STONES, BREAKS AND BONES
1 Leonard
2 Cork
3 Ronnie O'Sullivan
4 Julia Donaldson (with Axel Scheffler's illustrations)
5 Casino
6 Poohsticks
7 Sapphire (it was called the Sapphire Jubilee, though a Sapphire Anniversary usually describes a 45th wedding anniversary)
8 Kathryn Bigelow
9 Coccyx
10 Kurtis Blow

ACCLAIMED ALBUMS

1 A much acclaimed 70s album by Pink Floyd is 'The Dark Side of the ...'?

2 Which British singer went 'Back to Black' to vast acclaim in 2006?

3 What was the title of Oasis's initially acclaimed third studio album?

4 Whose "magnum opus" is 'What's Going On' from 1971?

5 Which former Byrd released the "great lost album" 'No Other'?

6 Which Kanye West album includes the songs 'New Slaves', 'Blood on the Leaves' and 'I am a God'?

7 Whose 1995 album 'It's Great When You're Straight ... Yeah!' received an amazing 10/10 from NME?

8 Which American rock band's acclaimed albums include 'Alligator' and 'Boxer'?

9 How many tracks are there on the classic Van Morrison album 'Astral Weeks'?

10 Which 2016 album by Frank Ocean was judged by Pitchfork to be the Best Album of the 2010s?

CONDIMENTS

1 In a chip shop in Scotland, you may be asked, "Red sauce or brown sauce?". What is the red sauce?

2 Which star of films such as 'Hud' and 'Cool Hand Luke' founded his own not-for-profit food company in 1982?

3 Sriracha is a hot sauce which has its origins on which continent?

4 What P is the name Nando's gives its flame-grilled chicken and accompanying sauces?

5 In which film does Gunnery Sergeant Foley call the lead character Zack Mayo "Mayonnaise"?

6 What colour is the playing piece for Colonel Mustard in the game Cluedo?

7 In a curry house, which P is the flat deep fried starter that is served with the likes of mango chutney, chopped onion and chillies?

8 Which brand of hot sauce is made by the McIlhenny Company of Avery Island, Louisiana?

9 What was the title of the massive 2002 global hit for the group Las Ketchup?

10 What is the literal meaning of the Mexican salsa "pico de gallo"?

ACCLAIMED ALBUMS
1 Moon
2 Amy Winehouse
3 Be Here Now
4 Marvin Gaye
5 Gene Clark
6 Yeezus
7 Black Grape
8 The National
9 Eight
10 Blonde

CONDIMENTS
1 Tomato ketchup
2 Paul Newman
3 Asia
4 Peri-peri
5 An Officer and a Gentleman
6 Yellow
7 Papadam
8 Tabasco
9 The Ketchup Song (Aserejé)
10 Rooster's beak (accept anything like "chicken's beak")

ROSS OR DANNY

Are these TV factual shows or videos that starred Ross Kemp or Danny Dyer? (the two blank space represent either the name Ross Kemp or Danny Dyer)

1 _____ _____'s Deadliest Men

2 _____ _____ on Gangs

3 The Millennium Dome Heist with _____ _____

4 _____ _____'s Right Royal Family

5 _____ _____ in Search of Pirates

6 _____ _____'s Funniest Football Foul-Ups

7 _____ _____ & the Armed Police

8 _____ _____: Extreme World

9 _____ _____'s Alternative Christmas Message

10 _____ _____ in Afghanistan

FAMOUS HATS

1 At a wedding, a gentleman in formal wear is said to be in "top hat and …" what?

2 What two letters go before Z and Dora to make two types of hat?

3 At which fictional school, created by J.K. Rowling, are pupils assigned their house by the "sorting hat"?

4 Besides white, what colour is the hat of Dr Seuss's 'Cat in the Hat'?

5 Which S is the surname of the man who founded a Missouri hat firm, which specialised in wide brimmed felt hats, in the 19th century?

6 Which Conservative leader was widely mocked for wearing a baseball cap in the late 1990s?

7 Which K is a famous brand of beret associated with everyone from Field Marshal Bernard Montgomery to Samuel L Jackson?

8 Which British singer-songwriter whose real name is Damon Gough is rarely seen without his beanie hat?

9 In early westerns, what colour hat did the villain of the movie traditionally wear?

10 Who stars as Jerry Travers, opposite Ginger Rogers, in the movie 'Top Hat'?

ROSS OR DANNY
1 Danny Dyer
2 Ross Kemp
3 Ross Kemp
4 Danny Dyer
5 Ross Kemp
6 Danny Dyer
7 Ross Kemp
8 Ross Kemp
9 Danny Dyer
10 Ross Kemp

FAMOUS HATS
1 Tails
2 Fe
3 Hogwarts
4 Red
5 (John B) Stetson
6 William Hague
7 Kangol
8 Badly Drawn Boy
9 Black
10 Fred Astaire

FIFTH BEATLES

1. Who was the Beatles' producer, very often called "the Fifth Beatle", who died in 2016?

2. Which Northern Irish football legend was sometimes called "The Fifth Beatle" or "El Beatle" in the 1960s?

3. Klaus Voormann, a long-time friend of the Beatles who they met in Hamburg, designed the cover of which of the band's albums, released in 1966?

4. A childhood friend of Paul and George, Neil Aspinall went on to be CEO of which company founded by the Beatles?

5. In which year did the Beatles' manager Brian Epstein die?

6. Played by Stephen Dorff in the film 'Backbeat', which former member of the Beatles died in 1962?

7. On which 1968 Beatles track, written by George Harrison, did Eric Clapton play guitar?

8. Who was the Beatles' road manager from 1963 to their split in 1970?

9. "Fifth Beatle" Billy Preston had a hit duet in 1979 with Syreeta - what was the title of the song?

10. Sharing its title with an Alan Partridge quote, what was the name of the 1965 album opportunistically released by the band's former drummer Pete Best?

FUNNY PLACE NAMES

1. Which town in Ontario, Canada would Matt Lucas and David Walliams feel very at home in?

2. A small hamlet in Yorkshire, which might be a good place for a sleep, is Land of ... what?

3. Innaloo is a suburb of which Western Australian city?

4. Ganja is the third largest city in which country, whose capital is Baku?

5. Bell End, Lickey and Lickey End are within the Bromsgrove district of which English country?

6. Middelfart is a town in which European country?

7. Bitter End is a small community in which US state?

8. In Colorado, there is a road sign which has No Name on it. What is the name of the small town it is directing you towards?

9. Shitterton is a hamlet in which English county?

10. What I is the unfortunate name of the town in Pennsylvania which used to be called Cross Keys?

FIFTH BEATLES
1. George Martin
2. George Best
3. Revolver
4. Apple Corps
5. 1967
6. Stuart Sutcliffe
7. While My Guitar Gently Weeps
8. Mal Evans
9. With You I'm Born Again
10. Best of the Beatles

FUNNY PLACE NAMES
1. Little Britain
2. Nod
3. Perth
4. Azerbaijan
5. Worcestershire
6. Denmark
7. Tennessee
8. No Name
9. Dorset
10. Intercourse

PEOPLE CALLED TAYLOR

1 The American director Taylor Hackford, whose films include 'Ray', married which Oscar-winning British actress in 1997?

2 Katie Taylor, as well as her stellar boxing career, also played which sport for Ireland?

3 Taylor Hanson is the lead singer of which band of brothers?

4 In which sport have Taylor Dent and Taylor Fritz been successful American participants?

5 Who sang 'Tell It to My Heart' in 1987?

6 Taylor Hicks won Series 5 of which US talent show?

7 Which British pop band had three members called Taylor - Andy, Roger and John?

8 The lead singer of which rock band has the name Courtney Taylor-Taylor?

9 Taylor Swift's 'Love Story' is a reworking of which classic tale?

10 The author of 'Mrs Palfrey at the Claremont' shared her name with which Anglo-American acting legend?

PLAYING WITH WORDS

1 What completes the palindrome: A man; a plan; a canal ... ?

2 Which letter of the alphabet is not in the following "sentence": Cwm fjord bank glyph vext quiz?

3 "The quick brown fox jumps over a lazy dog" is an example of what P?

4 Which tube station on the London Underground contains none of the letters of the word MACKEREL?

5 What three words complete this palindrome: May a root atop a moor groom a potato ...?

6 The English names of how many independent countries in the world begin with an A but do not end with an A?

7 What is the only whole number under one hundred that has its letters in alphabetical order?

8 What letter of the alphabet appears in every single odd number?

9 Which number under one hundred comes last in alphabetical order if you spell them all out?

10 What is the answer to the classic crossword clue: HIJKLMNO (5)?

PEOPLE CALLED TAYLOR
1 Helen Mirren
2 Football/Soccer
3 Hanson
4 Tennis
5 Taylor Dayne
6 American Idol
7 Duran Duran
8 The Dandy Warhols
9 Romeo & Juliet
10 Elizabeth Taylor

PLAYING WITH WORDS
1 Panama
2 S
3 Pangram (contains every letter of the alphabet)
4 St John's Wood
5 or a yam
6 Two (Afghanistan and Azerbaijan)
7 Forty
8 E
9 Two
10 Water (H to O)

SALTY SNACKS OF THE WORLD

1 What brand of crisp's basic flavour is called 'Cool Original'?

2 What company is responsible for Skips?

3 What is the predominant colour on packets of Walkers Cheese and Onion crisps?

4 What flavour are Frazzles?

5 What is the correct name of a snack which traditionally has the shape of a three-looped knot?

6 What is a form of dried meat that gets its name from Dutch words meaning "rump" and "strip"?

7 Which frontman of Slade was used to advertise Nobby's Nuts in Great Britain?

8 What numerical name is commonly given in the UK to a mid-morning snack?

9 What N is the adjective which was in the original name of Pringles in the USA?

10 What snack is the American company Orville Redenbacher's famous for making?

SONGS ABOUT JUMPING

1 Which Rolling Stones song begins "I was born in a crossfire hurricane"?

2 'Jump' by Girls Aloud was a cover of a track by which sisters?

3 Who was the lead singer of Van Halen when they had a massive hit with 'Jump'?

4 According to Destiny's Child, at what time is the club 'Jumpin', Jumpin"?

5 Which group's second UK Number 1, after 'In the Summertime', was 'Baby Jump'?

6 Two different versions of the song 'Keep on Jumpin" were Top 10 hits in the UK in 1996 - one for Todd Terry, the other for which act?

7 What three-word instruction begins 'Jump Around' by House of Pain?

8 The man who wrote and produced 'Jump Jump' by Kris Kross was Jermaine ... who?

9 Whose 1993 single 'Jump They Say' was said to be written about his half-brother Terry, who committed suicide in 1985?

10 'One Jump Ahead' is a song from which 1992 Disney film?

SALTY SNACKS OF THE WORLD
1 Doritos
2 KP
3 Blue
4 Bacon
5 Pretzel
6 Biltong
7 Noddy Holder
8 Elevenses
9 Newfangled
10 Popcorn

SONGS ABOUT JUMPING
1 Jumpin' Jack Flash
2 The Pointer Sisters
3 David Lee Roth
4 11:30 (in the evening, we presume)
5 Mungo Jerry
6 The Lisa Marie Experience
7 Pack it up (Pack it up, pack it in, let me begin)
8 Dupri
9 David Bowie
10 Aladdin

INITIALLY

Each word of the question will just be represented by its first letter. But, to give you more of a chance, numbers will be represented in full. Your answer can also just be first letters of words. Good luck!

1 W N H A V O, R, 22/7?

2 W H T W 100m R W A T O 9.59s?

3 W Q O E D I 1603?

4 W C T 383 W A S 5200 R I T M F E?

5 W C E H A A N O 1?

6 M U T 100 F, A W U T 200 T, W I T L A O E?

7 W D A H A H W '(I G B) 500 M '?

8 W I 1000 D B 5?

9 W I T A O 'F 451'?

10 W T C T W C O W T D A A?

CHEESE OR WHEEZE?

Are these real or made up cheeses? Your answer should be either Cheese or Wheeze accordingly.

1 Stinking Bishop

2 Red Devil

3 Wychwood Blue Tickler

4 Barry's Bruised Wobbler

5 Dungbuster

6 Blue Monday

7 Menace of the Mountains

8 Lord of the Hundreds

9 Coxon's Whiffer

10 Rochester Rumbler

INITIALLY
1 P (Pi)
2 U B (Usain Bolt)
3 E I (Elizabeth I)
4 I B (Ian Botham)
5 H (Hydrogen)
6 B W (Blue Whale)
7 T P (The Proclaimers)
8 200
9 R B (Ray Bradbury)
10 S (Shaft!)

CHEESE OR WHEEZE?
1 CHEESE
2 CHEESE
3 WHEEZE
4 WHEEZE
5 WHEEZE
6 CHEESE
7 WHEEZE
8 CHEESE
9 WHEEZE
10 WHEEZE

DADDIES

1 Boney M had a massive hit singing about 'Daddy ...' what?

2 What famous prayer begins "Our Father, who art in Heaven"?

3 Who played Charlie Sheen's character's father in 'Wall Street'?

4 What P is the correct word for the murder of one's father?

5 Who did Kid Creole & the Coconuts have to tell 'I'm Not Your Daddy' in a 1982 hit?

6 Who is the father of Viscount Severn?

7 The "Big Daddy" of British wrestling was a man whose actual name was ... what? [first and surname please]

8 Which American author, born in 1932, wrote a poem called 'Daddy' which was published posthumously?

9 In which brutal British movie did Ray Winstone ask "Who's the Daddy?"?

10 Bob's your uncle. Jack's your son. Tom's Bob's brother. Sam's Bob's father. Who's your daddy?

BLOND'N'BLONDE

1 Whose 1990 concert tour was called 'Blond Ambition'?

2 Which chemical element with atomic number 78 goes before "blonde" to make a silvery-white hair colour?

3 Mr Blonde is one of the characters in which 1992 film, which was Quentin Tarantino's directorial debut?

4 In 1966, whose first ever single on the US Country charts was called 'Dumb Blonde'?

5 Which Law School does Elle Woods attend in 'Legally Blonde'?

6 What was the oxymoronic title of the influential 2010 book by Phillip Blond subtitled 'How Left and Right Have Broken Britain and How We Can Fix It'?

7 Whose 1989 solo album was called 'Def, Dumb and Blonde'?

8 Whose 2000 novel based on the life of Marilyn Monroe was called 'Blonde'?

9 Which actress, later Oscar-nominated, starred at the Royal Court Theatre in the 2003 production 'Hitchcock Blonde'?

10 If you were to put one copy of the 2016 Frank Ocean album on top of another copy of the 2016 Frank Ocean album, what 1966 Bob Dylan album would you get?

DADDIES
1 Cool
2 The Lord's Prayer
3 Martin Sheen/his father
4 Patricide
5 Annie
6 Prince Edward (James, his son, born in 2007)
7 Shirley Crabtree
8 Sylvia Plath
9 Scum
10 Tom

BLOND'N'BLONDE
1 Madonna
2 Platinum
3 Reservoir Dogs
4 Dolly Parton
5 Harvard Law School
6 Red Tory
7 Deborah Harry
8 Joyce Carol Oates
9 Rosamund Pike
10 Blonde on Blonde (Frank Ocean's album was 'Blonde')

FILM QUOTES

1 What does Rod Tidwell demand that Jerry Maguire show him?

2 Where does nobody put Baby?

3 What, in 'Love Story' does love mean never having to say you are?

4 Which director's mother said "I'll have what she's having" in 'When Harry Met Sally'?

5 In 'The Godfather', with what does Luca Brasi sleep?

6 Which 90s cult film starring Gabriel Byrne, amongst others, took its name from a line in 'Casablanca'?

7 In 'White Heat', Cody Jarrett's final line is "Made it, ma! Top of the World!" Who played him?

8 Which two words does the phlegmatic Osgood Fielding say at the end of 'Some Like It Hot'?

9 Complete the quote from 'Four Weddings and a Funeral': "Is it raining? ..."

10 In which movie did Robert De Niro's character replicate Marlon Brando's "I coulda had class" speech?

GORILLAS

1 There are two species of gorilla, the western and the ... what?

2 Which cricketer was known as "Guy the Gorilla" though his nickname later became "Beefy"?

3 While dominant male gorillas are called silverbacks, what are gorillas between eight and twelve years old known as?

4 Who wrote the 1980 novel 'Congo', in which scientists encounter killer gorillas?

5 What is the name of the "drummer" in the cartoon band Gorillaz?

6 In which video game franchise, adapted into a film in 2018, is George a giant monster gorilla?

7 Which gorilla, who lived in California from 1971 to 2018, adopted a kitten called All Ball and was also known as Hanabiko?

8 Which English darts player was nicknamed "Silverback"?

9 What is the name of the anthropomorphic gorilla in 'The Mighty Boosh'?

10 What is the three-word taxonomic name of the western lowland gorilla?

FILM QUOTES
1 The money
2 In the corner (from 'Dirty Dancing')
3 Sorry
4 Rob Reiner
5 The fishes
6 The Usual Suspects
7 James Cagney
8 Nobody's perfect
9 I hadn't noticed
10 Raging Bull (The original is from 'On the Waterfront')

GORILLAS
1 Eastern
2 Ian Botham
3 Blackbacks
4 Michael Crichton
5 Russel Hobbs
6 Rampage
7 Koko
8 Tony O'Shea
9 Bollo
10 Gorilla gorilla gorilla

NUMBERS GAME

1 What repetitive name describes a children's game which combines elements of It and Hide-and-Seek?

2 'The Twilight Barking' was the sequel to which much loved children's book?

3 King James I of England was what number King James of Scotland?

4 The 1992 U2 single 'One' originally was on which album?

5 The friendly robot Number 5, or "Johnny 5" is the main character in which 1986 comedy film?

6 In which medical TV series did Olivia Wilde play Dr Remy "Thirteen" Hadley?

7 Which neighbourhood of Manhattan, traditionally associated with the Black Community, has 110th Street as its southern border?

8 'Away from the Numbers' was a track on which band's 1977 debut album 'In the City'?

9 The Hundred was, in 2021, a new competition in which sport?

10 Named after a great German physicist, which element has the chemical number 99?

PFAMOUS KNAMES

1 Which TV handyman released the 2017 album 'Every Kind of People'?

2 Johnny Knoxville was the co-creator of which stunt show, first shown in 2000?

3 In 'The Fabulous Baker Boys', Michelle Pfeiffer starred opposite which two acting brothers?

4 Charles F. Erhart founded a medicine business with his cousin in 1849 - what was his cousin's surname (much in the news in recent times)?

5 Which Motown singer's backing band was called the Pips?

6 The great England wicketkeeper Alan Knott played his whole career for which county?

7 Jean-Marie Pfaff played 64 times as a goalkeeper - for which country?

8 'The Whistle Song' was a 1991 hit for which pioneer of house music?

9 In 1989, English businessman Michael Knighton attempted to buy (and did keepy-uppies on the pitch of) which football club?

10 Wally Pfister has been nominated for the Best Cinematography Oscar several times (the first time in 2006) for his work on films directed by which British director?

NUMBERS GAME
1 Forty Forty
2 The Hundred and One Dalmatians
3 VI (Six)
4 Achtung Baby
5 Short Circuit
6 House
7 Harlem
8 The Jam
9 Cricket
10 Einsteinium

PFAMOUS KNAMES
1 Nick Knowles
2 Jackass
3 (Jeff and Beau) Bridges
4 Pfizer (Charles Pfizer)
5 Gladys Knight
6 Kent
7 Belgium
8 Frankie Knuckles
9 Manchester United
10 Christopher Nolan

DOWN THE PUB

1 What two-word phrase is the word "pub" short for?

2 What is the term for a pub not owned by the brewery that supplies it?

3 Aioli is a favourite condiment of the gastropub. What is the main flavour of aioli?

4 What sauce, often supplied in sachets in pubs, takes its name from an ethnic group in Russia?

5 In July of which year was smoking banned in English pubs and bars?

6 In which pub do the heroes of 'Shaun of the Dead' make a stand?

7 The Woolpack is a pub in which soap opera?

8 Black Bush is a drink often found in a pub - what type of drink is it?

9 Many Wetherspoon pubs are called The Moon Under Water because of an essay by which writer?

10 Who is, according to his stage persona, 'The Pub Landlord'?

RAIN

1 Which continent has the lowest average annual rainfall?

2 What is the French word for rain?

3 What rained down at the climax of the movie 'Magnolia'?

4 What is the name usually given to rain with a pH under 5.6?

5 According to a famous nursery rhyme, who went to Gloucester in a shower of rain?

6 Who had a Number 14 hit on the Billboard 100 in 1993 with her single 'Rain'?

7 Michelle Rodriguez played Rain Ocampo in which video game-based movie?

8 According to the musical 'My Fair Lady', where in Spain does the rain mainly fall?

9 Pop singer, model and actor Rain, who appeared in the films 'Speed Racer' and 'Ninja Assassin', hails from which country?

10 Which Beatles song begins with the words "Words are flowing out like endless rain into a paper cup"?

DOWN THE PUB
1 Public House
2 Free House
3 Garlic
4 Tartare
5 2007
6 The Winchester
7 Emmerdale
8 (Irish) Whiskey
9 George Orwell
10 Al Murray

RAIN
1 Antarctica
2 La pluie
3 Frogs
4 Acid Rain
5 Doctor Foster
6 Madonna
7 Resident Evil
8 On the plain
9 South Korea
10 Across the Universe

SCARY MONSTERS AND SUPER CREEPS

1 Which hero of Old English literature kills the monster Grendel and then Grendel's mother?

2 Who included the track 'Meet Ze Monsta' on her 1995 album 'To Bring You My Love'?

3 Who released the 1980 album 'Scary Monsters (And Super Creeps)'?

4 Which monster has "jaws that bite, and claws that catch" according to Lewis Carroll?

5 Who is famous for the stop-motion monsters he created for the 1963 movie 'Jason And The Argonauts'?

6 In the 1970s, the "Committee to Re-elect the President", known as "CREEP", wanted to get which US President re-elected?

7 What mythological creature had the body of a horse but the torso, head and arms of a man?

8 Which band released the single 'Creep' in 1992?

9 A monster who takes the creepy form of Pennywise the Clown first appears in which Stephen King book?

10 Who directed the 1982 horror-comedy movie 'Creepshow'?

ACRONYMS

1 What acronym, standing for the National Aeronautics and Space Administration, gives the name of the US space agency?

2 The acronym "NIMBY" stands for "not in my ..." what?

3 What does the "a" of the acronym "scuba" stand for?

4 Which legendary Swedish pop band's name is an acronym formed from the names of the band members?

5 What does the last "r" of the acronym "radar" stand for?

6 What do both "W"s stand for in the computer acronym "WYSIWYG"?

7 What does the acronym AWOL stand for, when referring to army desertion?

8 The acronym SWAT stands for "Special Weapons and ..." what?

9 The army corps called ANZAC was formed during which war?

10 In a common internet acronym, what does FTW stand for?

SCARY MONSTERS AND SUPER CREEPS
1 Beowulf
2 PJ Harvey
3 David Bowie
4 The Jabberwock
5 Ray Harryhausen
6 Richard Nixon
7 Centaur
8 Radiohead
9 It
10 George A. Romero

ACRONYMS
1 NASA
2 Back yard
3 Apparatus (Self-Contained Underwater Breathing Apparatus)
4 ABBA
5 Ranging (radio detection and ranging)
6 What (What You See Is What You Get)
7 Absent Without Leave
8 Tactics
9 First World War (Australian and New Zealand Army Corps)
10 For the Win

BIG FEET

1 Who went with Bigfoot to create the UK Number 1 single 'Sweet Like Chocolate' in 1999?

2 Who was the tallest man in history, whose feet by the time he was 18 were over 18 inches long?

3 The big-footed myotis is a species of which creature?

4 In the movie 'Bigfoot And The Hendersons', what was the Sasquatch Bigfoot's more human name?

5 Former basketball star Shaquille O'Neal's shoe size is 23. How tall is he? [within an inch either side]

6 On children's TV, which big-footed creature first appeared in 1969, voiced by Carroll Spinney?

7 Coulrophobia is the word for the fear of which big-shoed beings?

8 A man who has size 14 shoes in Britain will have what size shoes in the USA?

9 Where was the great chief Big Foot killed by US troops in 1890?

10 'Big Foot' is a 1982 episode of which popular comedy show whose stars were Graeme Garden, Bill Oddie and Tim Brooke-Taylor?

BUTCH AND BUTCHERS

1 A common phrase in English is "as fit as a butcher's ..." what?

2 Butch Vig, as well as producing 'Nevermind' by Nirvana, is a member of which band fronted by Shirley Manson?

3 In which film did Bruce Willis play the boxer Butch Coolidge?

4 Which of the members of 'Dad's Army' is a butcher?

5 Which former Chelsea and England midfielder, who died in 2018, was nicknamed Butch?

6 'Butch Queen' was the 10th studio album by which singer and drag queen?

7 Bill "The Butcher" Cutting is the main antagonist in which Martin Scorsese film?

8 Which author of 'Horrible Histories' was a butcher's boy in his father's shop as a young man?

9 Which F contrasts with "Butch" when describing two archetypes in lesbian culture?

10 Fred Elliott, played by John Savident, was a butcher character in which soap opera? I say, Fred Elliott, played by John Savident, was a butcher character in which soap opera?

BIG FEET
1 Shanks
2 Robert Wadlow
3 Bat
4 Harry
5 7 foot 1 inch (around 216 cm)
6 Big Bird
7 Clowns
8 15
9 Wounded Knee
10 The Goodies

BUTCH AND BUTCHERS
1 Dog
2 Garbage
3 Pulp Fiction
4 Lance Corporal Jones
5 Ray Wilkins
6 RuPaul
7 Gangs of New York
8 Terry Deary
9 Femme
10 Coronation Street

THE HOFF

1 In the original run of 'Baywatch', David Hasselhoff's Mitch Buchannon patrolled the beaches of which US state?

2 Which Brit was a judge with David Hasselhoff on Season 1 of 'America's Got Talent'?

3 What was the name of David Hasselhoff's 2006 UK Top 10 single?

4 David Hasselhoff played the coach of which nation's 'Dodgeball' team in the 2004 movie?

5 How many people drowned in the history of 'Baywatch'?

6 Who provided the voice of KITT in 'Knight Rider'?

7 In which city in Maryland was David Hasselhoff born?

8 What was the title of the critically acclaimed mockumentary about David Hasselhoff screened in 2015 and 2016?

9 In which production did Hasselhoff make his Broadway debut in 2000?

10 What was the unlikely name [first and surname] of the man David Hasselhoff's first wife Catherine Hickland married (in 1992) after she divorced Hasselhoff?

CROSSED MEDIA

The answer will blend two titles which are either books, films, or songs (in some order). EXAMPLE: In 1985, the biggest hit for King, which novel by Jane Austen is about Elizabeth Bennet and Fitzwilliam Darcy?" EXAMPLE ANSWER: Love and Pride and Prejudice

1 Which Thomas Hardy novel about Michael Henchard was a massive hit by Simon and Garfunkel?

2 The second James Bond film to star Timothy Dalton, which classic novel by Harper Lee features Atticus Finch?

3 Which huge hit for Bobby Darin, based on French song 'La Mer', won Iris Murdoch the Booker Prize?

4 What Joseph Conrad book, on which 'Apocalypse Now' is based, is the title track from a 1978 album by Bruce Springsteen?

5 Which UK Number 1 for Terry Jacks tells the story of faded film star Norma Desmond?

6 Which teen musical comedy starring Anna Kendrick is a Lou Reed song used in the film 'Trainspotting'?

7 Which classic adventure novel by Jack London was a 1984 hit for Duran Duran?

8 What is Herman Melville's novel about a whale which starred Warren Beatty as a comic book detective?

9 Which 1927 novel by Virginia Woolf about a family's visits to the Isle of Skye provided Madness with their only UK Number 1?

10 Which extremely long novel by James Joyce was a Britpop-era hit for the Boo Radleys?

THE HOFF
1 California
2 Piers Morgan
3 Jump in My Car
4 Germany
5 None
6 William Daniels
7 Baltimore
8 Hoff the Record
9 Jekyll and Hyde
10 Michael Knight (Michael Knight is Hasselhoff's character in 'Knight Rider')

CROSSED MEDIA
1 The Mayor of Casterbridge over Troubled Water
2 Licence to Kill a Mockingbird
3 Beyond The Sea, The Sea
4 Heart of Darkness on the Edge of Town
5 Seasons in the Sunset Boulevard
6 Pitch Perfect Day
7 The Call of the Wild Boys
8 Moby-Dick Tracy
9 To the Lighthouse of Fun
10 Finnegans Wake Up Boo

CHIMPS

1. On which continent are chimpanzees found in the wild?

2. Where did Ham the Chimp go on January 31st 1961?

3. Which chimp is forever associated with the classic 'Tarzan' movies of the 1930s and 40s?

4. Nim Chimpsky, used for linguistic experiments in the 20th century, was named after which American linguist and philosopher?

5. The British anthropologist noted for her work with chimpanzees is Dame Jane ... who?

6. The chimpanzee belongs to which genus (which shares its name with a Greek god)?

7. What is the usual name for the animal sometimes called the pygmy chimpanzee?

8. Chimps were used for many years in Britain to advertise which brand of tea?

9. Which American music legend owned a pet chimpanzee called Scatter?

10. Which actor portrayed the chimp Dr Cornelius in the original 'Planet of the Apes' film?

SEQUELS

1. What was the first sequel to 'Meet the Parents' called?

2. Which sequel was, apparently, 'Full Throttle'?

3. Which 2021 sequel had the subtitle 'Let There Be Carnage'?

4. 'The Klumps' was the subtitle of the sequel to which Eddie Murphy comedy?

5. Who directed 'The Godfather Part III' (then recut it for release in 2020)?

6. Jake Gittes is the lead character in 'Chinatown' - what is its sequel called?

7. Which sequel to a film based on a beloved children's story features David Oyelowo as publisher Nigel Basil Jones?

8. Which football star appears in the opening scene of 'Basic Instinct 2'?

9. What was the sequel to the film 'Get Shorty' called?

10. Which Australian singer-songwriter wrote an unused script for a sequel to 'Gladiator'?

CHIMPS
1. Africa
2. Space (he was the first great ape launched into space. His flight lasted 16 minutes, he survived and lived many more years)
3. Cheeta
4. Noam Chomsky
5. Goodall
6. Pan
7. Bonobo
8. PG Tips
9. Elvis Presley
10. Roddy McDowall

SEQUELS
1. Meet the Fockers
2. Charlie's Angels
3. Venom
4. The Nutty Professor
5. Francis Ford Coppola
6. The Two Jakes
7. Peter Rabbit 2
8. Stan Collymore
9. Be Cool
10. Nick Cave

THE FEMALE OF THE SPECIES

1 Mrs Dickinson and Miss Sawyer are the first names of which partners in crime in a 1991 film?

2 What is the name of Meryl Streep's character in 'The Devil Wears Prada'?

3 What is "latrodectus mactans", a spider whose female has been known to eat the male after mating?

4 Who plays the alien Sil in 'Species' and 'Species II'?

5 Who was the last woman to receive the death penalty in the UK?

6 Who played the serial killer Aileen Wuornos in the movie 'Monster'?

7 Which British crime author's middle name was Leigh?

8 Who was the mother of Queen Mary I of England, known as "Bloody Mary"?

9 Which great leader and companion of Marcus Antonius committed suicide in 30 BC?

10 Which Liverpool band had a 1996 hit single with 'Female of the Species'?

RHYME TIME

There are five pairs of answers – distributed haphazardly throughout the round – that (loosely or exactly) rhyme.

1 What is the lowest-pitched musical instrument in the brass family?

2 What was the name of the final Hercule Poirot novel?

3 The great Olympic boxers Mario Kindelán, Félix Savón and Teófilo Stevenson are all from which Caribbean country?

4 In an animated TV series, Denver was the last of which type of creature?

5 Who directed films such as 'Alien', 'Thelma and Louise' and 'Gladiator'?

6 Which creature is the son of Pasiphaë and a bull?

7 Which compound term for "nothing" originates in an American slang term for excrement?

8 Which London borough is home to the All England Club, where the Wimbledon Championships take place?

9 Which chain of "natural fast food" restaurants was founded in 2004 by John Vincent, Henry Dimbleby and Allegra McEvedy?

10 Which noble gas, with the atomic number 10, takes its name from the Greek for "new"?

THE FEMALE OF THE SPECIES
1 Thelma & Louise
2 Miranda Priestly
3 Black Widow
4 Natasha Henstridge
5 Ruth Ellis
6 Charlize Theron
7 Dorothy L Sayers
8 Catherine of Aragon
9 Cleopatra
10 Space

RHYME TIME
1 Tuba
2 Curtain
3 Cuba
4 Dinosaur
5 Ridley Scott
6 Minotaur
7 Diddly Squat
8 Merton
9 Leon
10 Neon

COUNTRIES THAT DON'T EXIST

1 In which author's book do children enter the land of Narnia through a wardrobe?

2 Which comic Evelyn Waugh novel takes place in the fictional African republic of Ishmaelia?

3 What is the name of the Prince of Eternia?

4 By the sea, in the land of Honah Lee, lived Puff the Magic Dragon and which little boy?

5 In which US drama would you have come across Prince Michael of the fictional European kingdom of Moldavia?

6 In the 1949 Ealing comedy film, which area of London claims independence from British law?

7 Which English county, which has long sought independence, has its administrative centre at Truro?

8 What was the actual name of the man who wrote 'Alice's Adventures In Wonderland'?

9 In 'The Wizard Of Oz', Dorothy Gale is "not in ..." which US state anymore?

10 Where, reasonably enough, is the movie 'Yellow Submarine' set?

FAMOUS SECONDS

1 What is the second month of the year in the Gregorian calendar used in the UK?

2 In the Christian faith, what is the second book of the Old Testament?

3 Who was the second man on the moon?

4 What term in the USA describes someone in their second year of study?

5 Which Australian cricketer with 128 test caps has been described as the "second best player in his family"?

6 Who was the second President of the USA?

7 Which magic man was the host of the TV show 'Every Second Counts'?

8 Which Namibian sprinter won seven Olympic and World silver medals in the 1990s but only one gold?

9 In which century did Henry II reign as King of England?

10 Which band's second studio album, from 1994, was called 'The Second Coming'?

COUNTRIES THAT DON'T EXIST
1 CS Lewis (The Lion, The Witch and the Wardrobe)
2 Scoop
3 Adam (who becomes He-Man)
4 Little Jackie Paper
5 Dynasty
6 Pimlico (Passport to Pimlico)
7 Cornwall
8 Charles Dodgson (the real name of Lewis Carroll)
9 Kansas
10 Pepperland

FAMOUS SECONDS
1 February
2 Exodus
3 Buzz Aldrin (Edwin "Buzz" Aldrin)
4 Sophomore
5 Mark Waugh
6 John Adams
7 Paul Daniels
8 Frankie Fredericks
9 12th/1100s (1154 to 1189)
10 The Stone Roses

MEAT LOAF

1 Meat Loaf's first UK Number 1 single was 'I'd Do Anything For Love (…)' – but what five words in brackets complete the title?

2 When, in the lyrics of a famous song, will Meat Loaf be gone "like a bat out of hell"?

3 What was Meat Loaf's real name?

4 Who was Meat Loaf's great songwriter-collaborator, who died in 2021?

5 With whom did Meat Loaf duet on the Top 5 single 'Dead Ringer for Love'?

6 In which cult 'Picture Show' did Meat Loaf play the part of Eddie?

7 Which rock wizard produced Meat Loaf's 'Bat Out of Hell'?

8 In which 1997 movie did Meat Loaf portray a bus driver?

9 Meat Loaf died, aged 74, in January of which year?

10 In 'South Park', what did Meat Loaf claim he started his career calling himself?

NAME CHAIN

The second part of each name is the first part of the next name. (In this case, the surname of the 10th answer doesn't overlap to the first name of the 1st.)

1 Which singer-songwriter's albums include 'Blood on the Tracks' and 'Highway 61 Revisited'?

2 Which Welsh poet wrote the poem 'Do Not Go Gentle Into That Good Night'?

3 Which American inventor, who invented the phonograph, was known as the 'Wizard of Menlo Park"?

4 Which Colombian boxer was knocked out by Tony Bellew in the ninth round of their fight in September 2012?

5 Which Australian actress played the part of Eowyn in Peter Jackson's 'Lord of the Rings' films?

6 Which businessman was the father of the girl whose 'Diary of a Young Girl' is one of the most famous documents of World War II?

7 Who was the older brother of the outlaw Jesse James?

8 Which English batter captained the Southern Brave to the inaugural men's Hundred in 2021?

9 Who was the lead vocalist of the metal band Mötley Crüe?

10 Which American singer-songwriter's songs include 'Cracklin' Rosie' and 'Sweet Caroline'?

MEAT LOAF
1 But I Won't Do That
2 When the morning comes
3 Michael Lee Aday. He was actually born Marvin Lee Aday but became Michael Lee Aday, so either is fine
4 Jim Steinman
5 Cher
6 Rocky Horror
7 Todd Rundgren
8 Spice World
9 2022
10 Couscous

NAME CHAIN
1 Bob Dylan
2 Dylan Thomas
3 Thomas Edison
4 Edison Miranda
5 Miranda Otto
6 Otto Frank
7 Frank James
8 James Vince
9 Vince Neil
10 Neil Diamond

PIRATES

1 A famous flag associated with 18th century piracy is the Jolly ... who?

2 Which letter, traditionally, marks the spot where pirates bury their treasure?

3 In which English county is the operetta 'The Pirates of Penzance' set?

4 By what nickname was the pirate Edward Teach better known?

5 Which US city has a Major League Baseball team called the Pirates?

6 Who played Captain Jack Sparrow's father in the 'Pirates of the Caribbean' film franchise?

7 Where did Peter Pan's nemesis, Captain Hook, go to school?

8 Which character is the narrator of the great pirate novel 'Treasure Island'?

9 The US ship briefly captured by pirates off Somalia in April 2009 had what name?

10 What date is "International Talk Like A Pirate Day"?

SPELLING TEST

1 How many letters are there in the name of Scotland's capital city?

2 Which word can mean a sweet perfume used in religious ceremonies, or to enrage?

3 Which day of the week comes first in alphabetical order in French?

4 How many letters of the alphabet are not used in the names of any of the months of the year?

5 What is the second letter in the surname of the man who played Elwood in 'The Blues Brothers' and Raymond in 'Ghostbusters'?

6 Which is the only letter not to appear in the name of a US state?

7 Advise is to advice as counsel is to ...?

8 Complete this mnemonic to help with spelling: "i" before "e" except after ... what?

9 Spell the first name of the man who became UK Labour leader in 2020.

10 How many times does the letter "s" appear in the name of the US state whose capital is Jackson?

PIRATES
1 Roger
2 X
3 Cornwall
4 Blackbeard
5 Pittsburgh
6 Keith Richards
7 Eton
8 Jim Hawkins
9 Maersk Alabama (Depicted in the Tom Hanks film 'Captain Phillips')
10 September 19

SPELLING TEST
1 Nine (Edinburgh)
2 Incense
3 Sunday (Dimanche)
4 Six (F, K, Q, W, X, Z)
5 Y (Dan Aykroyd)
6 Q
7 Counsel
8 c
9 Keir (not Kier)
10 Four (Mississippi)

TRADITIONAL SWEETS

1 Which French word for a sweet takes its name from a duplication of the word "good"?

2 Black, liquorice-flavoured lozenges are named after which two branches of the armed forces?

3 What type of boiled sweet shares its name with an expression of irritation used by Scrooge in Dickens' 'A Christmas Carol'?

4 Which popular black and white mint shares its name with a football club on Merseyside?

5 The name of which red and yellow sweets was taken (with a slight misspelling) by a children's TV series narrated by Richard Briers?

6 Who wrote the 1938 novel 'Brighton Rock', named after a traditional seaside confectionery?

7 The green boiled sweets soor plooms are associated with which town in the Scottish borders, sometimes shortened to Gala?

8 A children's TV series of the 70s and 80s shares its name with which helix-shaped marshmallow sweets?

9 Which aniseed-flavoured chewy sweet has the same name as the star of 'School of Rock', except with the words reversed?

10 The first "flying saucers" were made by a Belgian company which had, up to then, specialised in which more sacred items?

SONGS THAT WEREN'T HIT SINGLES

1 Whose track 'Stairway to Heaven', on their fourth album, is often voted one of the greatest songs of all time though it has never been a UK hit single?

2 'A Day in the Life' is the last track on which Beatles studio album?

3 Whose track 'Highway to Hell', released in 1979, was not a Top 40 hit?

4 Which Elton John song, which didn't make the UK Top 40 on release, features in a scene on a bus in the film 'Almost Famous'?

5 Never released as a single in the UK, what is the closing track on the Oasis album '(What's the Story) Morning Glory'?

6 'A Certain Romance' is the closing track on which English band's debut album?

7 Which Welsh band had 18 Top 40 singles without having one Top 10 single?

8 Which band's track, 'The Rat', was one of the most acclaimed rock songs of the 2000s but not a hit single?

9 Whose song, 'That's Entertainment', only reached the UK singles charts in 1982 as an import single?

10 Who only reached Number 47 in the UK in 1980 with the song '9 to 5'?

TRADITIONAL SWEETS
1 Bonbon
2 Army and Navy
3 Humbug
4 Everton Mints
5 Rhubarb and Custard (the show was 'Roobarb & Custard')
6 Graham Greene
7 Galashiels
8 (The) Flumps
9 Black Jack
10 Communion wafers

SONGS THAT WEREN'T HIT SINGLES
1 Led Zeppelin
2 Sgt Pepper's Lonely Hearts Club Band
3 AC/DC
4 Tiny Dancer
5 Champagne Supernova
6 Arctic Monkeys
7 Super Furry Animals
8 The Walkmen
9 The Jam
10 Dolly Parton

VROOM

1 What type of car is driven by Mr Bean?

2 What make of car is "borrowed" by Ferris Bueller during his 'Day Off'?

3 What type of van is driven by the Trotters in 'Only Fools and Horses'?

4 David Essex stars in which 1980 movie about a revolutionary prototype motorcycle?

5 Which movie sees Burt Reynolds being chased around Georgia in a black Pontiac Trans Am?

6 In the 1980s, who bought a car with the registration plate MAGIC?

7 In 'Die Another Day', what make of car is James Bond able to make invisible?

8 What type of car is the movie character 'Herbie'?

9 Which make of sports car shares its name with a former England rugby union player?

10 Which car had the number plate GEN 11?

BEARDIES

1 Which bearded entrepreneur is the man behind the Virgin brand?

2 Fidel Castro ruled which country for most of the second half of the 20th century?

3 In which city did Karl Marx die in 1883?

4 What does the L stand for in the beard-based organisation the BLF?

5 Which bearded man stood against John Major for the Referendum Party in the 1997 General Election?

6 Who is the only non-bearded Beatle on the cover of 'Abbey Road'?

7 What was the name of the bearded American scientist played by John Thompson in 'The Fast Show'?

8 Bill Oddie sang lead vocals on the Goodies first UK Top 5 hit in 1975 - what was its name?

9 Cricketer Moeen Ali started playing for which English county in 2007?

10 Labour candidate Frank Dobson was reportedly advised to shave off his beard for the London mayoral election in which year?

VROOM
1 Mini (yellow)
2 Ferrari (1961 Ferrari GT)
3 Reliant Regal (not Reliant Robin)
4 Silver Dream Racer
5 Smokey And The Bandit
6 Paul Daniels
7 Aston Martin
8 VW Beetle
9 Austin Healey
10 Chitty Chitty Bang Bang

BEARDIES
1 Richard Branson
2 Cuba
3 London
4 Liberation (Beard Liberation Front)
5 David Bellamy
6 Paul McCartney
7 Denzil Dexter
8 Funky Gibbon
9 Worcestershire
10 2000

BORN ON THE 23RD OF MARCH

1 Roger Bannister, who was born on 23rd March 1929, was, in 1954, the first person to run which distance in under four minutes?

2 Born on 23rd March 1953, which American "Queen of Funk" had hits with 'I Feel for You', 'Ain't Nobody' and 'I'm Every Woman'?

3 Which Japanese film director, whose works include 'Ran', 'Yojimbo' and 'Seven Samurai', was born on March 23rd, 1910?

4 What position did Rex Tillerson, who was born on March 23 1952, hold from February 2017 to March 2018?

5 In 'Pulp Fiction', where Tim Roth played "Pumpkin", who did Amanda Plummer (born on 23rd March 1957) play?

6 Born on 23rd March 1921, Donald Campbell died while attempting a speed record on which lake in January 1967?

7 Born on 23rd March 1983, Mo Farah won two Olympic gold medals at both the 5000 metres and which other event?

8 23rd March in 1968 is the shared birthday of both singer Damon Albarn and which England cricket captain?

9 Joe Calzaghe, who was born on 23rd March 1972, won his final professional fight against which American great?

10 Track cyclists Chris Hoy and Jason Kenny were both born on 23rd March. How many years apart?

FICTIONAL US PRESIDENTS

1 In which TV show did David Palmer become the first Black President of the USA?

2 Who plays the American President opposite Hugh Grant's British Prime Minister in the movie 'Love Actually'?

3 Tony Goldwyn plays President Fitzgerald "Fitz" Thomas Grant III in which TV series starring Kerry Washington?

4 In which movie did Jack Nicholson play President James Dale?

5 Who played the role of President William Harrison Mitchell and the presidential decoy Dave Kovic in the movie 'Dave'?

6 Who becomes President in 2030 after Donald Trump, Chastity Bono and Ted Kennedy in 'The Simpsons' episode 'Bart To The Future'?

7 Who called George W Bush a "fictitious president" at the 2002 Academy Awards?

8 In which movie did Morgan Freeman play President Tom Beck?

9 Lancelot R Gilligrass is US President in 'Charlie And The Great Glass Elevator', a book by which author?

10 Which fruits provide the name of a 1996 Top 10 UK hit by Presidents Of The United States Of America?

BORN ON THE 23RD OF MARCH

1 Mile
2 Chaka Khan
3 Akira Kurosawa
4 US Secretary of State
5 Honey Bunny (Her character's actual name is Yolanda)
6 Coniston Water
7 10,000 metres
8 Michael Atherton
9 Roy Jones Jr
10 12 (1976 and 1988)

FICTIONAL US PRESIDENTS

1 24
2 Billy Bob Thornton
3 Scandal
4 Mars Attacks!
5 Kevin Kline
6 Lisa Simpson
7 Michael Moore
8 Deep Impact
9 Roald Dahl
10 Peaches

FUNNY NAMES

1 The European shag and the brown booby are what kind of animals? [generic answer is fine]

2 By trade, what was the great Victorian, Thomas Crapper?

3 Which actress claims that she gained her stage name from her flatulent habits as a young actress?

4 What four-letter word links an Italian brand of home appliances with a curse word regularly used by Dave Lister in 'Red Dwarf'?

5 As revealed by former 'Doctor Who' actress Jodie Whittaker on 'The Graham Norton Show', what is the slightly unfortunate nickname of her home village of Skelmanthorpe in West Yorkshire?

6 Tokyo Sexwale was a leading figure in which country's anti-apartheid movement?

7 'The Adventures of Totor, Chief Scout of the Cockchafers' was the first comic strip by which Belgian cartoonist?

8 An agra cadabra is what kind of insect?

9 The seventh child of which member of a successful family pop group is called Jermajesty?

10 Which C was the renowned Welsh baptist preacher born on 25th December 1766 - it might help you to answer if you know that his surname is the fourth most common in Wales, and his first name reflects his birthday?

KAZAKHSTAN

1 In 1991, Kazakhstan became the last republic to declare independence from which Union?

2 What is the largest religion in Kazakhstan?

3 The flag of Kazakhstan has a gold sun on what colour background?

4 The land of Kazakhstan was subjugated in the 13th century by which Mongol leader?

5 In 2019, the name of the capital of Kazakhstan was changed from Astana to what?

6 Kazakhstan is the world's largest landlocked country - what is the second largest?

7 Kazakhstan literally means "Land of the ..." what? [the answer begins with W]

8 Known as "Triple G", Gennady Golovkin is a famous Kazakh name in which sport?

9 Though not the capital, what is the largest city of Kazakhstan?

10 In October 2020, what two-word term from a comedy film did Kazakh Tourism reveal as its slogan?

FUNNY NAMES
1 Birds
2 Plumber
3 Whoopi Goldberg
4 Smeg
5 Shat
6 South Africa
7 Hergé (real name Georges Prosper Remi)
8 Beetle (Coleoptera)
9 Jermaine Jackson
10 Christmas Evans

KAZAKHSTAN
1 Soviet Union (10 days before Soviet Union ceased to exist)
2 Islam (around 70%)
3 Blue
4 Genghis Khan
5 Nur-Sultan (although it was announced in 2022 that it was changing back)
6 Mongolia
7 Wanderers
8 Boxing (Middleweight)
9 Almaty
10 Very nice

MUPPETS

1 In 'Sesame Street', where does Oscar the Grouch live?

2 Animal is the drummer in the Muppet band called Dr Teeth and the ... what?

3 Which number from 'The Muppet Movie' won the Oscar for Best Song in 1979?

4 Which "Muppeteer" originally performed the character of Miss Piggy?

5 Which Muppet has the catchphrase "Wocka Wocka Wocka!"?

6 Michael Caine played which famous miser in 'The Muppet Christmas Carol'?

7 What nationality was the chef who had an occasional cooking segment on 'The Muppet Show'?

8 The Muppets appeared in the music video for 'Keep Fishin'' - a song by which band?

9 What are the names of the two old men who sit in a box at the Muppet Theatre complaining?

10 Which veteran film actor/director starred as Lew Lord in 'The Muppet Movie'?

RHYME TIME

There are five pairs of answers - distributed throughout the round - that (loosely or exactly) rhyme.

1 Which actor played the same role, the King of Siam, 4625 times on stage?

2 What is the second name of the main protagonist in 'The Nightmare Before Christmas'?

3 What facet of British life did Jamie Oliver address in a four-part documentary series first broadcast in early 2005?

4 What is the world's southernmost national capital city?

5 Which Canadian-American band's members were Garth Hudson, Richard Manuel, Levon Helm, Rick Danko and Robbie Robertson?

6 Which epic post-apocalyptic novel by Stephen King, first published in 1978, has spawned two miniseries, one in 1994, one in 2020?

7 What name links a police show starring Gillian Anderson with a band fronted by Mark E Smith?

8 What was the nickname of the obdurate Indian batsman Rahul Dravid?

9 What three-letter word was the Oxford English Dictionary's Word of the Year for 2021?

10 In the sport of rugby union, each team has eight forwards, and seven ... what?

MUPPETS
1 In a dustbin
2 Electric Mayhem
3 Rainbow Connection
4 Frank Oz
5 Fozzie Bear
6 Ebenezer Scrooge
7 Swedish
8 Weezer
9 Statler and Waldorf
10 Orson Welles

RHYME TIME
1 Yul Brynner
2 Skellington (Jack Skellington)
3 School Dinner(s)
4 Wellington (capital of New Zealand)
5 The Band
6 The Stand
7 The Fall
8 The Wall
9 Vax
10 Backs

THE CAST OF 'SKINS'

1 Dev Patel, Anwar in 'Skins', played Jamal Malik in which Oscar-winning film directed by Danny Boyle?

2 Hannah Murray and Joe Dempsie, both in Series 1 of 'Skins', played Gilly and Gendry, respectively, in which epic TV drama?

3 Nicholas Hoult played Marcus in the film 'About a Boy', based on a book by which author?

4 Kaya Scodelario played Carina Smyth in 'Dead Men Tell No Tales', the fifth film in which swashbuckling film series?

5 Olly Alexander is the frontman for which pop band, who had a UK Number 1 with 'King'?

6 Which 'Doctor Who' actor plays Sid's father in 'Skins'?

7 In Series 3 and 4 of 'Skins', Lily Loveless played a character who shared her name with which British supermodel?

8 Daniel Kaluuya won an Oscar for 'Judas and the Black Messiah', playing which Black Panther?

9 Which character did Luke Pasqualino play in the BBC series 'The Musketeers'?

10 'Skins' actress Freya Mavor played Liz Henshaw in the film musical 'Sunshine on Leith', based on the songs of which band?

WALES & WHALES

1 Which species of whale is the largest mammal on earth?

2 Welsh politician Nye Bevan oversaw the creation of which organisation in 1948?

3 Who was the author of 'Moby-Dick'?

4 Dolphins are commonly seen in summer in which large bay which stretches from Bardsey Island in the north to Strumble Head, Pembrokeshire, in the south?

5 What book of the bible tells the story of Jonah and the "whale"?

6 Ryan Reynolds and Rob McIlhenney became owners of which Welsh football club in 2021?

7 What was the name of the whale who starred in the 'Free Willy' films?

8 Which King of England, who lived from 1457 to 1509, was born in Pembroke Castle, Wales?

9 What was the name of the 1977 horror film, starring Richard Harris, about a killer whale?

10 Which Welsh singing star had Number 1 hits with 'This Ole House' and 'Green Door'?

THE CAST OF 'SKINS'
1 Slumdog Millionaire
2 Game of Thrones
3 Nick Hornby
4 Pirates of the Caribbean
5 Years and Years
6 Peter Capaldi
7 Naomi Campbell
8 Fred Hampton
9 D'Artagnan
10 The Proclaimers

WALES & WHALES
1 Blue whale
2 NHS
3 Herman Melville
4 Cardigan Bay (Ceredigion)
5 Jonah (It's a big fish)
6 Wrexham
7 Keiko
8 Henry VII
9 Orca
10 Shakin' Stevens

PLAYED BY ANDY SERKIS

1 Andy Serkis plays the villainous Ulysses Klaue in which cinematic universe?

2 What is the actual name of Gollum, as played by Andy Serkis in 'Lord of the Rings'?

3 Which unconventional rock star did Andy Serkis play in the 2010 film 'Sex & Drugs & Rock & Roll'?

4 What is the name of the evolved ape Andy Serkis plays in the 'Planet of the Apes' films?

5 In which film directed by Michael Winterbottom did Andy Serkis play the producer Martin Hannett?

6 Which notorious killer did Andy Serkis play in the 2006 film 'Longford'?

7 Which Captain did Andy Serkis play in the 2011 film 'The Adventures of Tintin'?

8 Who played William Burke opposite Andy Serkis's William Hare in the 2010 film 'Burke & Hare'?

9 In which 1999 TV adaptation did Andy Serkis play the criminal Bill Sikes?

10 Who directed the 2018 film 'Mowgli: Legend of the Jungle' in which Andy Serkis played Baloo?

BUBBLES

1 'I'm Forever Blowing Bubbles' is particularly associated with which football club?

2 'The Boy in the Bubble' is a song from which 1986 album by Paul Simon?

3 Specifically, what type of creature was Bubbles, the friend of Michael Jackson?

4 In which TV show did Jane Horrocks play a PA called Bubble?

5 Bubbles is a regular snitch for the Baltimore cops in which acclaimed TV show?

6 Bubbles is traditionally the nickname for which French beverage?

7 What goes with Bubble to make a traditional English dish of fried-up leftovers?

8 In which country was Bubble Wrap invented in the 1950s?

9 'Bubbles' is a famous painting, used in a soap advert, by which Pre-Raphaelite artist?

10 The Bubble Eye is a fancy breed of which common pet?

PLAYED BY ANDY SERKIS
1 Marvel
2 Smeagol
3 Ian Dury
4 Caesar
5 24 Hour Party People
6 Ian Brady
7 Captain (Archibald) Haddock
8 Simon Pegg
9 Oliver Twist
10 Andy Serkis

BUBBLES
1 West Ham United
2 Graceland
3 Chimpanzee
4 Absolutely Fabulous
5 The Wire
6 Champagne
7 Squeak
8 USA
9 John Everett Millais (used in an advert for Pears soap)
10 Goldfish

HOTELS

1 Which 1960 film is set at the Bates Motel?

2 The original Raffles Hotel is in which city?

3 Which band sued a Mexican hotel in 2017 for implying it was associated with one of their songs?

4 Who bought the Cromlix Hotel in Dunblane, Scotland, in 2013?

5 Born in 1945 and one of Britain's most famous hoteliers, what is the surname of Rocco, the son of Charles?

6 Devon hotelier Donald Sinclair was the inspiration for which renowned comedy character?

7 About whom did Leonard Cohen sing "I remember you well at the Chelsea Hotel"?

8 The Chateau Marmont is a hotel on which Los Angeles thoroughfare?

9 Who was the manager of London's Savoy Hotel from 1889 to 1897, before going on to found his own hotels?

10 Monsieur Gustave H is the concierge of which hotel in the fictional republic of Zubrowka?

A OR B

You've got a 50/50 choice on each of these questions.

1 Who was born first of the famous artists – A) Michelangelo or B) Vincent Van Gogh?

2 At their highest capacity in the days of Ancient Rome, which held more people – A) The Colosseum or B) the Circus Maximus?

3 Which lived longer – A) the oldest elephant or B) the oldest human?

4 True or False? 'EastEnders' star Sid Owen revealed in his 2021 autobiography, 'Rags to Ricky', that Hollywood legend Al Pacino had considered adopting him when they played father and son in the film 'Revolution'.

5 Which is higher above sea level – A) the Sugarloaf mountain in Rio de Janeiro or B) the Rock of Gibraltar?

6 True or False? Harry Corbett, the puppeteer who created Sooty, was the nephew of fish and chips pioneer Harry Ramsden.

7 England's highest mountain is in which National Park – A) the Peak District or B) the Lake District?

8 True or False? In the 1000th episode of Countdown, the conundrum was the word "Millenium", spelt MILLENIUM, which is not the correct spelling of millennium.

9 Who has won more Grand Slam singles tournaments – A) Venus Williams or B) Serena Williams?

10 Which of these was published first – A) Encyclopaedia Britannica or B) Oxford English Dictionary?

HOTELS
1 Psycho
2 Singapore
3 The Eagles (Hotel California)
4 Andy Murray
5 Forte
6 Basil Fawlty (Fawlty Towers)
7 Janis Joplin
8 Sunset Boulevard
9 César Ritz
10 The Grand Budapest Hotel (in the 2014 film of that name)

A OR B
1 A) Michelangelo (born in 1475)
2 B) Circus Maximus (150,000+ vs 80,000ish max)
3 B) The oldest human (Oldest human 122 (Jeanne Calment), oldest elephant something like 88)
4 True
5 B) The Rock of Gibraltar (426m to 396m)
6 True
7 B) the Lake District (Scafell Pike)
8 True
9 B) Serena Williams ((as at end of 2021) 23 for Serena vs seven for Venus)
10 A) Encyclopaedia Britannica (1768 vs 1884)

KEITH CHEGWIN

1 According to the classic 80s children's show, 'Cheggers Plays ...'?

2 Who was Keith Chegwin's DJ sister, who died in late 2021?

3 Keith Chegwin's autobiography was called 'Shaken But Not ...'?

4 What was the name of the UK's first naked gameshow, which Keith Chegwin presented naked?

5 On which Ricky Gervais comedy did Cheggers have a close-to-the-bone cameo in 2006?

6 On which show did Cheggers present the 'Down Your Doorstep' outside broadcast segment?

7 Who did Keith Chegwin marry in 1982?

8 Keith Chegwin had a brief role in which director's 1971 movie of 'Macbeth'?

9 On which channel did Cheggers present the revived 'It's a Knockout' in 1999?

10 Keith Chegwin died in December of which year?

LATIN PHRASES

1 Which statesman used the phrase "veni, vidi, vici" in a letter to the Roman senate in 47 BC?

2 Also known as an autopsy, what does PM stand for when referring to the examination of a body?

3 What two-word Latin term does the abbreviation i.e. stand for?

4 The word "communiter" was added to the Olympic motto "Citius, altius, fortius" in 2021 - what does "communiter" mean?

5 Which Latin phrase means "buyer beware"?

6 "Carpe diem" is a phrase associated with which Peter Weir-directed Robin Williams film from 1989?

7 Which year did Queen Elizabeth II describe as her "annus horribilis"?

8 The phrase "panem et circenses" meaning "bread and circuses", originated with which Roman satirist?

9 Wilfred Owen borrowed the phrase "Dulce et decorum est pro patria mori" from Horace for a poem written during which war?

10 Which Premier League club has the Latin motto "Nil satis nisi optimum"?

KEITH CHEGWIN
1 Pop
2 Janice Long
3 Stirred
4 Naked Jungle
5 Extras
6 The Big Breakfast
7 Maggie Philbin
8 Roman Polanski
9 Channel 5
10 2017

LATIN PHRASES
1 Julius Caesar (The phrase means "I came, I saw, I conquered")
2 Post mortem (meaning "after death")
3 Id est (meaning "that is")
4 Together (The whole motto means "Faster, Higher, Stronger, Together")
5 Caveat emptor
6 Dead Poets Society (meaning "seize the day". Williams was also in a 1986 film called 'Seize the Day')
7 1992
8 Juvenal
9 World War I (The phrase means "It is sweet and fitting to die for one's country")
10 Everton (The motto means "Nothing but the best is good enough")

TALL TALES OF SUPER FURRY ANIMALS

1 Which Beatle chewed carrots and celery as the rhythm track to the Super Furry Animals song 'Receptacle for the Respectable'?

2 What is the name of the lead singer of Super Furry Animals, who learnt to play a left-handed guitar upside down?

3 Which former drug smuggler, known as "Mr Nice", were Super Furry Animals 'Hangin' Out With ...' in a track on their debut album?

4 What kind of vehicle did the SFA turn into a portable techno sound system in the late 1990s?

5 Brian Harvey of East 17 was SFA's first choice to sing which single, the first to be released from 'Rings Around the World'?

6 In 2000, which Super Furry Animals album was mentioned in the British Parliament for being the best selling Welsh-language album of all time?

7 Which Welsh actor, known for his roles on the likes of 'Notting Hill' and 'Enduring Love', was the singer in an early line-up of the Super Furry Animals?

8 The title of the Super Furry Animals track 'Hermann Loves Pauline' refers to the parents of which scientist?

9 Which flamboyant former Reading footballer features on the cover of SFA's single 'The Man Don't Give a F***'?

10 A possible early album title for the 'Rings Around the World' album was 'Text Messaging is Destroying the ...' what? [six word answer]

BARBADOS

1 Which city is the capital of Barbados?

2 What kind of alcoholic drink is Mount Gay, made in Barbados?

3 The flag of Barbados has two blue stripes and a central golden stripe, which has what symbol on it?

4 Who was Gordon Greenidge's fellow Bajan record-breaking opening partner for the West Indies?

5 What was the title of Rihanna's debut album, from 2005?

6 In Barbados, which sport does the historic Garrison Savannah host?

7 Which act had a UK Number 1 in 1975 with the song 'Barbados'?

8 The island group that Barbados is a part of is the Lesser ... what?

9 Which great Barbadian fast bowler, who took 376 test wickets, died in 1999 aged only 41?

10 Which Barbadian group (with a cricket-related name), had a UK Number 1 with the song 'Twilight'?

TALL TALES OF SUPER FURRY ANIMALS
1 Paul McCartney
2 Gruff Rhys
3 Howard Marx
4 Tank
5 Juxtapozed With U
6 Mwng
7 Rhys Ifans
8 Albert Einstein
9 Robin Friday
10 Pub Quiz As We Know It

BARBADOS
1 Bridgetown
2 Rum
3 Trident
4 Desmond Haynes
5 Music of the Sun
6 Horse racing
7 Typically Tropical
8 Antilles
9 Malcolm Marshall
10 Cover Drive

WITCHES & WIZARDS

1 In which city does 'The Wizard of Oz' live?

2 Which Shakespeare play begins with the title character's encounter with three witches?

3 The NBA franchise The Wizards are based in which city?

4 Who, besides Michelle Pfeiffer and Susan Sarandon, played one of the 'Witches of Eastwick' opposite Jack Nicholson?

5 At what particular game was Tommy a "wizard", according to The Who?

6 The real life Salem witch trials of 1692 took place in which American state?

7 Which witch was a common adversary for Rod Hull and Emu?

8 Which Stoke City and Blackpool footballer, who died in 2000, was known as "The Wizard of Dribble"?

9 Who was the author of 'A Wizard of Earthsea'?

10 Who was the singer and leader of the band Wizzard?

ANNOYING ADVERTS

1 Which actor, who starred in films such as 'Footloose', has been the face of EE for many years?

2 In the 2000s, which chocolate bar was advertised with the slogans "It's not for girls" and "Not available in pink"?

3 Henry Cooper, Paul Gascoigne and Vinnie Jones have all advertised which deodorant?

4 Howard Brown came to fame as the face of which bank?

5 Opera singer Wynne Evans has helped advertise which insurance company for more than a decade?

6 In an advert for moneysupermarket. com, who provided the voiceover as "Dave" danced to the Pussycat Dolls, saying "Now he feels epic"?

7 Which film director advertised esure with the catchphrase "Calm down, dear"?

8 The man who voiced Alexander the Meerkat also played Michael the hotel porter and friend of which comedy chat show host?

9 Which frontman for The Streets starred in an advert for BT Sport in 2021 with the tagline 'We Belong Together'?

10 In 2017, an advert for which product, which saw model Kendall Jenner at a protest march, caused controversy?

WITCHES & WIZARDS
1 The Emerald City
2 Macbeth
3 Washington
4 Cher
5 Pinball
6 Massachusetts
7 Grotbags
8 Stanley Matthews
9 Ursula Le Guin
10 Roy Wood

ANNOYING ADVERTS
1 Kevin Bacon
2 Yorkie
3 Brut
4 Halifax
5 GoCompare
6 Sharon Osbourne
7 Michael Winner
8 Alan Partridge (Simon Greenall, in 'I'm Alan Partridge')
9 Mike Skinner
10 Pepsi

THE KEEGAN YEARS

1 Kevin Keegan managed which national team at Euro 2000?

2 "I will love it if we beat them! Love it!" Which team is the "them" Kevin Keegan referring to?

3 Which club did Kevin Keegan leave in a helicopter after his final playing appearance?

4 On which TV show did Kevin Keegan crash his bike and suffer severe cuts and grazes?

5 In which make of 4x4 car was Kevin Keegan sleeping when he was attacked in Surrey in 1991?

6 A haircut associated with Kevin Keegan in the 70s was the poodle ... what?

7 How many times was Kevin Keegan European Footballer of the Year?

8 Kevin Keegan was sent off in the 1974 Charity Shield for a scuffle with which other alliterative player?

9 Who is the author of the parody novel 'Galactic Keegan'?

10 What was the title of Kevin Keegan's 1971 UK Number 31 single?

CROSSED LYRICS

In each case, the answer is two "crossed" songs. The clues are lyrics from the two songs crossed over. EXAMPLE: "Though I never knew you at all you had the magic of the moment on a glory night." EXAMPLE ANSWER: Candle in the Wind of Change

1 The night we met I knew I needed you so and if I'm hooked and I can't stop staring.

2 Beyond the Palace, hemi-powered drones scream down but you're the one that always turns me on, you keep me comin' 'round.

3 Where trouble melts like lemon drops, away above the chimney tops, that's where you'll find me, who said that every wish would be heard and answered when wished on the morning star.

4 Old pirates yes they rob I need you, pleased to meet you.

5 A few questions that I need to know, how you make me feel I'm dirt and I'm hurt.

6 I still don't understand just how your love can do, you know I love you, I always will, my mind's made up by the way that I feel.

7 Ignite the light and let it and reverse it, Ti esrever dna ti pilf nwod gnaht ym tup i.

8 People, people we are the same, No we're not forsake 'cause I'm your lady and you are my man, whenever you reach for me I'll do all that I can.

9 Hope that God exists, I hope, I pray, drawn by the undertow, my life, and thought about my wife 'cause they took the keys, and she'll think it's me.

10 Why leave me standing here, let me know where we're going but we don't know where we've been.

THE KEEGAN YEARS
1 England
2 Manchester United
3 Newcastle United
4 Superstars
5 Range Rover
6 Perm
7 Two (1978 and 1979)
8 Billy Bremner
9 Scott Innes
10 Head Over Heels in Love

CROSSED LYRICS
1 Be My Baby Got Back
2 Born to Run to You
3 Over the Rainbow Connection
4 Redemption Song 2
5 Never Ever Fallen in Love
6 Crazy In Love Is All Around
7 Firework it
8 Fight the Power of Love
9 Sit Down in the Tube Station at Midnight
10 The Long and Winding Road to Nowhere

MORE ANAGRAMS

1 Which nine-letter anagram of CARTHORSE can go after Electric Light in the name of a band?

2 Which anagram of the word RABIES is the name of a country?

3 Which anagram of ANGERED is a word with a similar meaning?

4 The TV show 'Torchwood' is a spin-off and anagram of which other show?

5 What C is the name given to the nine-letter anagram puzzle at the end of the TV show 'Countdown'?

6 Which specialist in anagrams and palindromes has poetry collections called 'Slate Petals' and 'Stray Arts'?

7 The name of which former US President (indeed two former US Presidents) is an anagram of HE BUGS GORE?

8 Which word is both an anagram of DEDUCTIONS and a word with a (roughly) related meaning?

9 SEAGROUND is an anagram of which word (also the title of a Michael Jackson album)?

10 Which 'Harry Potter' character's name is an anagram revealing his true identity?

THE BIG LEBOWSKI

1 What is The Dude's actual first name in 'The Big Lebowski'?

2 Which movie-making brothers were behind 'The Big Lebowski'?

3 Who plays The Dude in 'The Big Lebowski'?

4 In which US state is 'The Big Lebowski' set?

5 In 'The Big Lebowski', what is the first name of Quintana, he of the purple jumpsuit?

6 In 'The Big Lebowski' what Kahlúa-based cocktail is The Dude's favourite drink?

7 On what day of the week does Walter Sobchak definitely not bowl in 'The Big Lebowski'?

8 'The Big Lebowski' is set at the time of which war?

9 Which rock bassist plays a nihilist in 'The Big Lebowski'?

10 Which future Oscar-winner plays the sycophant Brandt in 'The Big Lebowski'?

MORE ANAGRAMS

1 Orchestra
2 Serbia
3 ENRAGED
4 Doctor Who
5 Conundrum
6 Anthony Etherin
7 George Bush
8 DISCOUNTED
9 DANGEROUS
10 Tom Marvolo Riddle (an anagram of "I am Lord Voldemort")

THE BIG LEBOWSKI

1 Jeffrey
2 The Coen Brothers
3 Jeff Bridges
4 California
5 Jesus
6 White Russian
7 Saturday (Shabbos, the Jewish day of rest)
8 The Gulf War
9 Flea
10 Phillip Seymour Hoffman

ACROSTIC 3

The first letters of each answer will spell out something relevant to getting all the answers right.

1 Chandler Bing, Francisco Scaramanga and Krusty the Clown all have three of which body part?

2 What is the branch of medicine that deals with cancer?

3 Which dance hit, a Number 1 all over the world, was the biggest hit for the Spanish duo Los Del Rio?

4 In 'Lord of the Rings', what is the name of the fortress, containing the tower Orthanc, ruled by the wizard Saruman?

5 The first major published collection by which poet, who died in 2013, was 'Death of a Naturalist'? [first name and surname]

6 What is the Latin name for the human chest, and the name of one of three main divisions of an insect's body?

7 One of the largest cities in Africa, what is the capital of Côte d'Ivoire?

8 Which track on Kendrick Lamar's 'To Pimp a Butterfly' references the lead character in Alex Haley's novel 'Roots'? [we need track name, not just name of character]

9 In French cuisine, seeing which word on the menu will alert you to the fact that you could order snails?

10 "Taste the Difference" is a brand associated with which supermarket?

ELEMENTAL MUSIC

1 According to Sia, "You shoot me down, but I won't fall, I am ..." which element?

2 'Elemental' was a 1993 album for which duo, made up of Kurt Smith and Roland Orzabal?

3 Which month provided a huge hit for Earth, Wind and Fire in 1978?

4 Which East London boy band had a hit with 'Gold' in 1992?

5 Rapping, deejaying, graffiti and breakdancing are seen as the four elements of which art form?

6 Which essential element links JJ72 in 2000 with Willy Mason in 2004?

7 A tin whistle is a wind instrument which commonly has how many finger holes?

8 On which Kendrick Lamar studio album is the song 'Element'?

9 Neon Neon was a collaborative project between producer Boom Bip and which Welsh frontperson?

10 The name of which German act, who had a massive hit in 1983, can be made with the chemical symbols for Elements 10 and 11 in the periodic table?

ACROSTIC 3
1 Nipples
2 Oncology
3 Macarena
4 Isengard
5 Seamus Heaney
6 Thorax
7 Abidjan
8 King Kunta
9 Escargots
10 Sainsbury's

ELEMENTAL MUSIC
1 Titanium
2 Tears for Fears
3 September
4 East 17
5 Hip-hop
6 Oxygen
7 Six
8 Damn.
9 Gruff Rhys
10 Nena (Neon is 10 (Ne), Sodium is 11 (Na))

KEVINS

1 In which movie series does Macauley Culkin play Kevin McCallister?

2 Which country does Kevin De Bruyne represent at football?

3 'We Need to Talk About Kevin' is a 2003 novel by which author?

4 Which mercurial British band contained Kevins Archer and Rowland?

5 Which former England cricket star is known as "KP"?

6 In which movie does Kevin Pollak play criminal Todd Hockney?

7 Kevin Rudd became Prime Minister of which country in 2007?

8 Kevin Durant was NBA champion in 2017 and 2018 with which California team?

9 Which band had a "perfect cousin" called Kevin?

10 Kevin Federline was married to which singer from 2004 to 2007?

BANKERS

1 Which large American banking firm, founded in 1847, went bankrupt in September 2008?

2 What C do the British call the bank employee known in the US as a bank teller?

3 Who formed a banking firm in 1869 with Marcus Goldman? [surname only required]

4 Who was Governor of the Bank of England from 2013 to 2020?

5 Who was the "rogue trader" who caused Barings Bank to collapse?

6 'The Blind Banker' was the title of the second ever episode of which TV drama starring Benedict Cumberbatch and Martin Freeman?

7 Which classic board game, derived from 'The Landlord's Game' created by Lizzie Magie, requires one player to act as a banker?

8 Which banking family produces red wines under the French Château Lafite label?

9 Which gameshow involved host Noel Edmonds having several tense phone conversations with "The Banker"?

10 Who was the first governor of the Bank of England and has featured on £50 notes?

SOMETHING ELSE

PINK

1 Which other cartoon pig goes with 'Pinky'?

2 The shop Thomas Pink is known for making and selling what specific items of clothing?

3 Which wading birds get their pink colour from nutrients in their food?

4 In 20th century America, a "pinko" would be sympathetic to which ideology?

5 What is singer Pink's real name? [first and surname]

6 Whose influential album was 'Music From Big Pink'?

7 Pink and turquoise were removed from the original design of which flag designed by Gilbert Baker in 1978?

8 In the USA, if you're getting your "pink slip", what are you getting?

9 Who were the male counterparts to the Pink Ladies in the movie 'Grease'?

10 Who wrote the classic theme to the 'Pink Panther"?

FILM PSYCHOS

1 What is the name of the psycho in 'Psycho'?

2 With which 'Street' would you associate Freddy Krueger?

3 Ben Kingsley went from playing Gandhi to which terrifying character in 'Sexy Beast'?

4 "Funny like what?" Which actor utters these frightening lines in 'GoodFellas'?

5 Two great actors played Max Cady in the movies – Robert De Niro and …?

6 Which writer created Hannibal Lecter?

7 Who starts off as Castor Troy in 'Face/Off' before he is taken over by John Travolta?

8 In 'The Shining', at which hotel does Jack Torrance live and work?

9 "Stellaaaa!" Who is the Marlon Brando character who utters that immortal line?

10 In which film does Sean Penn play the brutal soldier Tony Meserve?

PINK
1 Perky
2 Shirts
3 Flamingos
4 Communism
5 Alecia Moore
6 The Band
7 Rainbow flag (LGBT)
8 The sack
9 The T-Birds
10 Henry Mancini

FILM PSYCHOS
1 Norman Bates
2 Elm Street
3 Don Logan
4 Joe Pesci
5 Robert Mitchum (in two different versions of 'Cape Fear')
6 Thomas Harris
7 Nicolas Cage
8 The Overlook Hotel
9 Stanley Kowalski
10 Casualties of War

POETRY

1 The word "poetry" comes from the Ancient Greek "poiein", meaning what?

2 Which poet plays Jeremiah Jesus in 'Peaky Blinders'?

3 'Therefore, send not to know For whom the bell tolls, ...' – what four words come next?

4 Where were the plums that were so delicious and so cold and which you were probably saving for breakfast?

5 This question is a line of which "IP"? [by which I mean, what is it, metrically?]

6 If you add the number of lines in a sonnet to the number of lines in a limerick, you get the number of lines in which V?

7 "Shall I compare thee to a summer's day?" What seven words come next, as the comparison gets underway?

8 How many syllables are there, as standard, in each verse of common metre?

9 How might you describe/this pattern of syllables/(beginning with H)?

10 Now here comes a question like this/ Whose purpose is easy to miss./It contained Simmons, Gene/Which band do I mean/...?

JOKES

1 On which date are April Fool's jokes traditionally played?

2 When telling jokes, what is the usual response to "Knock, knock"?

3 What does Ronnie Barker try to buy from a hardware shop owned by Ronnie Corbett at the start of a famous sketch?

4 According to Monty Python, what does nobody expect?

5 For which part was Dudley Moore auditioning in Peter Cook's 'One Leg Too Few' sketch?

6 What was the name of the infamously rude joke around which a 2005 documentary film was made?

7 In 1958, 'Panorama' managed to convince some viewers that which foodstuff grew on trees?

8 Where did Napoleon keep his armies?

9 Why didn't the skeleton go to the ball?

10 When is a door not a door?

POETRY
1 Make/do
2 Benjamin Zephaniah
3 It tolls for thee (in the poem by John Donne)
4 The icebox
5 Iambic Pentameter
6 Villanelle (14+5=19)
7 Thou art more lovely and more temperate
8 28 (8 + 6 + 8 + 6)
9 Haiku
10 The answer you're needing is Kiss (accept any attempt to complete the limerick, ending with the word Kiss)

JOKES
1 April 1st
2 Who's there?
3 Fork handles
4 The Spanish Inquisition
5 Tarzan
6 The Aristocrats
7 Spaghetti
8 Up his sleevies
9 He had no body to go with
10 When it's ajar

TOMORROW

1 Complete the line from the song in the movie Annie: "Tomorrow, tomorrow, I love you tomorrow, ..."?

2 What is the French word for "tomorrow"?

3 Who played the character Sam Hall in 'The Day After Tomorrow'?

4 The UK music festival All Tomorrow's Parties took its name from a song by which rock band?

5 "Tomorrow and tomorrow and tomorrow" is a line spoken by which Shakespearean title character?

6 What was the alternative three-word title for the 2014 Tom Cruise film 'Edge of Tomorrow'?

7 On which Beatles album did 'Tomorrow Never Knows' first appear?

8 Who played the part of Paris Carver in the James Bond movie 'Tomorrow Never Dies'?

9 In which film with a long title did Gwyneth Paltrow play the part of Polly Perkins?

10 If today is Sunday, what is the day after the day after the day after the day after the day after tomorrow?

ANSWERS ARE CATEGORIES

Every answer in this round is a category title from this section of the book.

1 Cameo, Fuji and Golden Delicious are all which fruit?

2 Dedham Vale AONB straddles the border of Suffolk and which other English county?

3 In which comedy drama did Andrew Lincoln play Simon Casey, who worked at Summerdown Comprehensive?

4 What was the predominant colour of the kit originally worn by the Italian football team Juventus, before they started wearing black and white?

5 In which field are Warsan Shire, Hollie McNish and Raymond Antrobus famous names?

6 Which film franchise, which began in 1978 and has continued into the 2020s, was created by John Carpenter and Debra Hill?

7 In which country is the test cricket ground called the Kensington Oval?

8 Alexander Vinoukorov, the winner of the 2012 Olympic men's cycling road race, was from which country?

9 In which 1998 film does David Huddleston, who died in 2016, play the title character, although another character with the same surname is the main character?

10 In 2003, the BBC claimed that which rock star was seeking a home in Hartlepool and was a fan of Hartlepool United FC?

TOMORROW
1 You're always a day away
2 Demain
3 Jake Gyllenhaal
4 The Velvet Underground
5 Macbeth
6 Live Die Repeat
7 Revolver
8 Teri Hatcher
9 Sky Captain And The World Of Tomorrow
10 Saturday

ANSWERS ARE CATEGORIES
1 Apples
2 Essex
3 Teachers
4 Pink
5 Poetry
6 Halloween
7 Barbados
8 Kazakhstan
9 The Big Lebowski
10 Meat Loaf (the story turned out not to be true)